Guidelines for Guidance
READINGS IN THE PHILOSOPHY OF GUIDANCE

BROWN

EDUCATION SERIES

Edited by

Lowry W. Harding, Ph.D.
The Ohio State University
Columbus, Ohio

Guidelines for Guidance
READINGS IN THE PHILOSOPHY OF GUIDANCE

Carlton E. Beck, Ph.D.
Associate Professor of Education
University of Wisconsin-Milwaukee

WM. C. BROWN COMPANY PUBLISHERS
DUBUQUE, IOWA

Copyright © 1966
by
Carlton E. Beck

Manufactured by WM. C. BROWN CO., INC., Dubuque, Iowa
Printed in U. S. A.

To my father and mother,
Mr. and Mrs. S. C. Beck

Acknowledgments

As is obvious in any collection of readings, the major contribution has been the permission and cooperation of the many journals and authors to allow the reprinting of their materials. Sincere gratitude, also, is in order to those men who created new materials especially for this book, in order that important gaps might be filled in places where the literature had been silent to date.

I am sure I speak for all members of our writing team when I say that we all owe far more to our students than we can ever express as they listen, respond, and suggest alternatives in our lectures and seminars, with so much patience and forbearance.

I am grateful to the many readers of my *Philosophical Foundations of Guidance* who took time to write and encourage me in producing the present volume. Their kind words and suggestions cannot be repaid by me, but I hope that the book itself makes partial repayment for their time and efforts.

Thanks, too, is in order to the cooperative staff of the Wm. C. Brown Company Publishers and to Mrs. Yvonne Anderson Ader and Mrs. Shirley Kersey, my graduate assistants, whose efficiency contributed greatly to production of the manuscript.

C. E. B.

Foreword

The field of guidance and counseling is undergoing a critical degree of expansion. It is critical in that it represents both special opportunities and special dangers. The expansion can be seen especially in the United States, but there are also interesting auguries from abroad. In England, which has been slow to recognize the necessity for special training in this field, there have now been instituted courses for school counselors at Keele and Reading Universities and at Edgehill Training College.

It is especially at such a time of critical expansion that there is a need for careful, rigorous, and fundamental examination of the directions and assumptions that prevail in the field. There is a dangerous temptation for workers in an expanding field to concentrate upon satisfying exigent, practical needs and to neglect the less immediately rewarding and more difficult and demanding tasks of philosophical clarification. Moreover, it is in exactly such a developing field that rigorous philosophical investigation will bear greatest fruit, for careful thinking now will produce multiplied benefits in the expanded conditions of the future.

The present volume therefore is particularly timely. There are signs that the prevailing momentum of the field is less frequently being regarded as self-justifying. An increasing number of thoughtful scholars and practitioners are engaging in a healthy process of self-examination and self-criticism.

This tendency is to be welcomed wholeheartedly, but there arises the antithetical danger that immoderate or unbalanced self-criticism may produce discouragement or despair, especially among the young and inexperienced. There is an acute need, therefore, for a well balanced and selective presentation of some of the more thoughtful and seminal contributions to this process of critical self-appraisal.

The editor has collected here the thinking of some of the key writers who have given consideration to this issue. The volume should provide invaluable material for critical discussion among those entering the field of guidance and those more experienced workers who are preparing counselors, as well as those for whom long familiarity with practical problems may have dulled the habit of questioning basic assumptions.

It is not too much to claim that the person who masters the material in this volume will have gained an epitomized view of what the major scholars in the field consider to be the principal philosophical issues that deserve our attention in the coming decades. There is little doubt that the intellectual sophistication attendant upon familiarity with this material would contribute significantly to raising the critical standards of those entering the field of guidance and counseling at this crucial time.

In particular, it draws attention to the excellent treatment of the relationship between existentialism and counseling. One could argue that American philosophical thinking, which has been much influenced by pragmatism and more recently by linguistic analysis, stands in need of correction by the particular emphases and concerns brought by the existential philosopher. However this may be, the present volume is strengthened significantly by its inclusion of some of the most profound and searching recent contributions to the examination of the implications of existentialism for counseling.

Paul Nash
Boston University

Preface

Seneca once said, "God divided man into men that they might help one another." This book is addressed to all those who are involved, or are soon to be involved, in helping relationships: in schools and colleges, in pastoral offices, in hospitals, in private offices, in community service agencies, or wherever else man finds his existential journey too much to bear alone. It focuses on the conditions under which the helping relationship takes place, the views and trends of those who are engaged in such work, and the nature of both persons who meet together in the universe-of-two familiar to us.

Since writing *Philosophical Foundations of Guidance* (Prentice-Hall, 1963), I have been watching the journals in counseling and related areas to see whether the leaders in the field would respond with greater emphasis on the philosophical aspects of the helping relationship. One need make only a cursory sweep through the journals to see that a great stirring is evident. It is sincere, thoughtful, and searching. It is addressed to the human condition, to life-as-lived. We may begin seeing developments which can truly revolutionize our fields. Not all the voices, however, are those of the established leaders in counseling. There are strong new voices. One of my most rewarding experiences at a recent APGA convention was the flurry of questions coming from the younger members. They sincerely want to make contact with Man; they are restless with old formulae; they are interested in the human condition far more than in pat answers; they are willing to risk "life in an incomplete world view."

This book, then, is an attempt to bring together some of the most thoughtful essays of a "directional" nature, or of a more directly philosophical sort, so that the "new voices" can readily examine what has been said by these thoughtful men and women. Some of the essays are to be found only in relatively inaccessible small journals which rarely find a wide readership among counselors. It is the "new voices" who will continue "adding chapters" to this book. It is they, I hope, who will pay particular attention to the discussion questions at the end of each chapter and who will raise others.

Many of the articles herein will raise hackles and eyebrows as well as questions. This, too, has been deliberately built into the book. No one is expected to accept all that is written here, for the whole idea behind the

ix

book is a searching, questioning exploration of the helping relationship in all its richness, its frustrations, and its rewards. I can assume no responsibility for the *views* the writers express, nor can I assume credit for them. I do assume gladly the responsibility for choosing the articles and presenting the thinking to the wider readership which I feel they deserve.

One will note by skimming the table of contents that there are no articles at all by Carl Rogers, although several essays by some of his staunchest followers do appear. This does not indicate a lack of respect for his work, because, as I have said elsewhere, Rogers' work has been perhaps the most important change of direction in counseling since its inception. The point is that Rogers' articles have been reprinted so often, and his views so much discussed (pro and con) in classes that I feel that would serve little purpose to include a few of his many articles here. Instead, I would encourage the reader to read Rogers' complete books, not bits and pieces here and there. I would recommend the same for the works of C. Gilbert Wrenn, E. G. Williamson, Edward Shoben and others whose works are often quoted in the literature.

Much favorable comment has been made about the work of those trying to apply concepts from existential philosophy to the counseling. The major criticisms have centered around vagueness, poetic language, subjectivity, lack of theoretical framework, not enough case illustrations, and lack of uniqueness in method. Only the future holds the answers to these criticisms.

Throughout the present book there appears a common thread: concern for man as he seeks meaning in his life. The thinking of these writers can provide guidelines to those who are aiding in the search for meaning.

C. E. B.
Milwaukee, Wisconsin

Contents

CHAPTER 1
Important Issues

CHAPTER 2
Changing Views

CHAPTER 3
The School Counselor Today

CHAPTER 4
Ethical and Moral Outlooks

CHAPTER 5
New Directions

Chapter

1

Important Issues

It has been said that "*Issues* never change; only our *views* of them change." Whether we choose to agree with this or not, it is apparent that views on issues — like all views — can be narrow or wide, nearsighted or clearly discerned. It is and must be the task of the sincere counselor candidate to wipe the steam from his lenses, examine his vision periodically, and keep his eyes open. His continued effectiveness as a counselor depends upon his vision.

The issues dealt within this chapter are recurring ones in the fields of guidance, counseling, and related helping relationships. They focus on scope, utilization of available resources, value problems related to practice, and common assumptions which have recently been called to question. Some of the central questions running through the whole chapter are those which call upon the reader to ask himself, "Within what limits shall I operate? In what phase of helping relationships have I the most to offer to my fellow man? How well do I really understand the social context in which counseling and guidance takes place? What old ways of viewing issues must I re-examine immediately? What issues must be studied at length, and over an extended period of time?"

The essays in this chapter, of course, are not all-inclusive. They raise *some* of the vital issues in counseling and guidance. As our views of issues become clearer, other issues will come into focus. Issues emerge to our view as research is forthcoming, as men think through the assumptions under which they have been operating, and as life in the larger society changes because of far-reaching technological and human development. The counselor must never fall victim to what I have termed elsewhere "completism" (the feeling that "Now at last I am a counselor, certified and educated, once and for all")! To do so would be tantamount to stating that people and societies are static, not dynamic. A counselor must attune to the nuances of the total society in which he functions and must think of himself as always "in process" of becoming an effective counselor. His commitments, hopefully, will grow with him and aid him in seeing the commitments and meanings of others.

1

ISSUES IN COUNSELING: ELUSIVE AND ILLUSIONAL

Donald H. Blocher
University of Minnesota

An examination of the questions which continue to command attention in most discussions of counseling theory, practice, and research seems to reveal an interesting dichotomy. The first set of these questions comprises a group that are frequently discussed, often elicit considerable emotion, and are generally quite unproductive in terms of the consequences which they generate. These questions can well be called illusions in counseling. The second set of issues are frequently avoided in discussions; they are extremely difficult to frame clearly but have very important consequences. They are indeed elusive in character.

ILLUSIONS IN COUNSELING

It is perhaps easier to begin by demolishing illusions than by attempting to trap the elusive. One of the foremost illusions in counseling concerns the old question of should counseling be "directive" or "non-directive." This is one of the oldest, most decrepit, and least productive arguments in the field of counseling. Part of its feebleness is drawn from the fact that as an issue it is not even clear in meaning. Two kinds of questions are involved. The first concerns whether or not the counselor influences his client. The answer to this question is really no longer at issue. Writers as different in orientation as Williamson (16) and Patterson (10) agree that counselors do, should, and cannot avoid influencing clients. The relevant questions which survive around this part of the issue concern only directions and degrees of influence.

The second aspect of this sterile controversy over "directive vs. non-directive counseling" concerns the distribution of responsibility for the content of the interview or the nature of the counseling process as apart from its outcomes. Research by Robinson (13) and others of the so-called "communications" school of counseling has indicated rather clearly that division of responsibility for the content of the counseling interview is one and only one of a number of relevant dimensions in the counseling process. This research suggests that virtually all counselors vary their behavior along this continuum from client to client or from one point to another in the counseling process. No counselors completely abdicate responsibility for the nature of the interview. For example, many so-called non-directive counselors use formal structuring techniques at the beginning of counseling which are quite "directive" in one sense. Decisions to respond to affect or content, to clarify, to accept, all require some degree of responsibility on the part of the counselor.

Reprinted by permission of the Author and the *Personnel and Guidance Journal*, Vol. XLIII, April 1965, 796-800.

Again, the relevant questions which survive in this issue are merely how much and in what directions should counselor responsibility be exerted.

A second rather moribund question is whether or not counselors should diagnose. This is illusion number two. The term diagnosis has been an emotionally loaded word in the counseling vocabulary for some years. Two basic reasons seem to account for this fact. First, the term diagnosis was largely borrowed from medicine, and to many counselors it carries a strong flavor of telling clients what is wrong with them. This connation does violence to values which many counselors hold concerning building on the assets of clients, distinguishing between counseling and psychotherapy, and so forth.

A second reason for this emotional reaction is the connection which many counselors see between diagnosis and the use of tests. Many counselors apparently feel that if they do not use tests, they also do not diagnose.

Most of the thinking surrounding both of these reactions to diagnose is fallacious. The only philosophical assumption which really affects the question of diagnostic activity is whether or not the counselor views one of his tasks in the counseling process as that of understanding the counselee. Diagnostic activities are merely those activities which have as one of their purposes helping the counselor understand his client. Research on the nature of this kind of activity by Koester (5), McArthur (7), and Parker (9) has indicated that for many counselors this activity resembles a hypothesis-testing process. The Pepinskys (11) have called attention to the counselor as a scientist-practicioner and have described the process of observation and inference by which the counselor builds a hypothetical model through which to understand his client.

The question again is not whether or not to diagnose. All counselors who attempt to understand their clients are engaged in diagnosis. The degree to which a particular counselor is committed to differential treatment for different clients may influence the nature and extent of his diagnostic activities. The counselor with a strong client-centered approach may not vary treatment processes from one client to another to as great a degree as one who considers himself eclectic. The difference in diagnostic activity between the two refers to differential diagnosis rather than to the process of diagnosis itself, however.

Diagnosis also has nothing to do with the use of tests. Tests are merely samples of behavior from which other behavior is inferred. The moment that the counselor makes inferences about behavior from any source, he is diagnosing.

From what we know about diagnostic processes now, we must conclude that all counselors do diagnose but that diagnostic activities contribute most when they are *continuous, tentative,* and *testable.* Diagnosis in this sense is a continuous process which is integrated into the total counseling. It is always tentative and subject to revision as further behavior samples become available. Finally, it is testable in the sense that diagnostic constructs or hypotheses are rooted in behavior and are operationally defined so that they may be confirmed or rejected through prediction.

A third illusion revolves around the question of whether counseling is personal-emotional or informational-didactic in nature. This question is another which has generated more heat than light in recent years. When either side of this issue is explored thoroughly, it can be reduced to a set of patent absurdities.

First, examine the didactic-informational side. The logical extensions of this position are:

1. Counseling is impersonal.
2. Counseling is teaching occupational information to a class of one.
3. Only sick people have emotions.
4. The affective and intellectual functions of human beings can be separated and treated as self-contained entities.

These are obvious absurdities. A look at the opposite side of the coin, however, reveals some equally indefensible propositions.

1. Human behavior is not mediated by rational-intellectual problem-solving processes. (How did the client get to the counselor in the first place?)
2. The counseling interview is characterized by primarily verbal communication processes, but it is still an entirely emotional rather than an intellectual exchange.
3. All problems arise out of emotional conflicts rather than vice versa.
4. Personal problem-solving is not an important matter for counseling. People can solve all personal problems readily once their deep-seated emotional conflicts are removed.

These propositions seem equally absurd. If counseling is a process which helps whole human beings cope with total life situations, it seems clear that both affective and intellectual aspects of life will have to be considered.

Three illusions in counseling which have commanded research time and energy from counselors have been discussed and hopefully disposed of.

ELUSIVE ISSUES

The second set of issues which are dubbed elusive in character are naturally more difficult to discuss than those mentioned previously. These issues are important, have vital consequences, and are exceedingly difficult to resolve. The first of these is set up in terms of the following question, "Is counseling developmental-educative-preventive, or is it remediating-adjustive-therapeutic?"

It seems better to deal with this issue in terms of goals rather than in terms of methodologies. Efforts to distinguish between counseling and psychotherapy have dealt largely with methodologies and their applications. The intensity of the process, its level of impact upon the client or patient, the setting in which it is done all have been used as distinguishing criteria. Writers such as Perry (12) and Brammer and Shostrom (4) have characterized human personality in terms of a sort of onionskin analogy, with the counselor busy peeling away the outer layers of skin while the therapist penetrates to the inner and apparently more pungent layers of the onion core. Presumably, every counselor should stop at whatever point his eyes begin to water.

None of these kinds of distinctions seem particularly useful. Counseling and psychotherapy are processes which are aimed at changing human behavior. If any real differences exist between the two processes, they must involve the kinds of outcomes which are specified for each, and possibly with the underlying assumptions which translate such outcomes into goals.

It seems to this writer that when the usual outcomes for counseling and psychotherapy are pooled and an impromptu factor analysis performed, two rather dominant clusters of goals appear. These can be characterized as (1) developmental-educative-preventive goals, and (2) remediating-adjustive-therapeutic outcomes.

It may be worthwhile examining these two clusters for a moment. One part of the first cluster deals with developmental goals. An underlying assumption here is that human personality grows or unfolds in terms of a largely healthy interaction between the growing organism itself and the culture or environment. From this point of view, development is seen as a reasonably ordered and patterned process of change moving in directions which are typically desirable for both the individual and society. The function of counseling in such a framework is to facilitate normal development. The outcomes may be stated in terms of mastering developmental tasks or moving from one stage of development to another.

The whole concept of development is closely tied to education, obviously. As part of this cluster, one may then include understanding of self, understanding of environment (world of work, for example), development of problem-solving skills, etc. Also associated with this cluster are preventive mental hygiene outcomes such as preventing too great frustrations, anxieties, or stresses; avoiding unhealthy relationships or experiences; etc.

The second cluster of outcomes can be described by labels much as remediative, adjustive, and therapeutic. These outcomes are generally characterized by goals that involve breaking down and replacing defenses; learning new adjustments to particular situations which may be family, institutional, or societal; and removing conflicts in personality organization. These goals cluster around concepts of removing pathological components, adjusting people to environmental demands, and restoring mental health.

When the processes which are familiarly called counseling and psychotherapy are examined in the light of these two presumed clusters of outcomes, reasons for confusion in terms become apparent. Much of what is attempted in the name of counseling has been as remediative and adjustive in purpose as anything attempted in the name of psychotherapy. Counselors have attempted to "adjust" youngsters to the demands of schools and teachers. They have attempted to remediate and remove presumed pathological elements, for example, "laziness," "negativism," "aggression," and so forth.

One important issue facing counseling is whether distinctions on the basis of the kinds of clustering which have been described will be strengthened or whether they will be further broken down and no valid differences will exist between counseling and therapy. Perhaps, of course, writers such as Rogers (14) and Arbuckle (2) believe this has already happened.

A second elusive issue which faces counseling today is not unrelated to the first. It can be stated in its strongest terms in this question: Is counseling liberating or conditioning in nature? Modern psychology has generally tended to look upon man, as Allport (1) says, as a reactive being or at best a reactive being in depth. Personality or learning theories based upon such a view tend to search for a set of uniform variables to which all behavior is subject. In a sense, such a system is closed. It tends to produce models based upon homeostatic principles and to view the human being functioning in a mechanistic-deterministic environment. Changing behavior in terms of this model, whether in counseling, therapy, or whatever, involves primarily identifying and controlling these variables.

The philosophical background from which counseling and guidance has emerged is not one in which formulations of this kind are comfortable. Instead, as Beck (3) points out, these philosophical antecedents place great emphasis upon terms like individualism, responsibility, independence, personal freedom, etc. The philosophical frame of reference and American behavioristic *Zeitgeist* have now collided. This collision has become disturbingly clear in the controversies between those who term themselves existential psychologists such as May (6), Rogers (14), Maslow (6), and Allport (1), and the radical behaviorists best exemplified by Skinner (15) and represented in the guidance literature by writers such as Michael and Meyerson (8).

Two rather distinctly alternative directions seem to open before counseling. The existentialist position seem a philosophically attractive but scientifically unclear path. The Skinnerian-behavioristic road is scientifically rigorous, but philosophically frightening. Can or should counselors specify the outcomes of counseling in rigorous behavioral terms and proceed to shape them by conditioning processes? Do they instead deal in such quasi-behavioral commodities as self-awareness, immediate experience, and self-actualization? If counseling takes the latter course, what is its eventual relationship to a behaviorist psychology? If counseling takes the path of conditioning, what becomes its commitment in a philosophical sense?

These issues are elusive but vital in terms of their consequences. Counselors above all need to spend less time and energy tilting at the illusional windmills of the past and more time in resolving the elusive but inescapable issues which will shape the future.

BIBLIOGRAPHY

1. Allport, G. W. Psychological models for guidance. *Harvard educ. Rev.*, 1962, 32, 4, 373-381.
2. Arbuckle, D. S. *Counseling: an introduction.* Boston: Allyn and Bacon, 1961.
3. Beck, C. *Philosophical foundations of guidance.* Englewood Cliffs, New Jersey: Prentice-Hall, 1963.
4. Brammer, L. & Shostrom, E. *Therapeutic psychology: fundamentals of counseling and psychotherapy.* Englewood Cliffs, New Jersey: Prentice-Hall, 1960.
5. Koester, G. A. A study of the diagnostic process. *Educ. psychol. Measmt.*, 1954, 14, 473-486.
6. May, R. (ed.) *Existential psychology.* New York: Random House, 1961.
7. McArthur, C. Analyzing the clinical process. *J. counsel. Psychol.*, 1954, 1, 203-208.
8. Michael, J. & Meyerson, L. A behavioral approach to counseling and guidance. *Harvard educ. Rev.*, 1962, 32, 4, 382-401.
9. Parker, C. As a clinician thinks. *J. counsel. Psychol.*, 1958, 5, 4, 253-262.
10. Patterson, C. H. The place of values in counseling and psychotherapy. *J. counsel. Psychol.*, 1958, 5, 216-233.
11. Pepinsky & Pepinsky. *Counseling: theory and practice.* New York: Ronald Press, 1954.
12. Perry, W. G. On the relation of psychotherapy and counseling. *Annals of the New York Academy of Sciences*, 1955, 63, 396-407.

13. Robinson, F. P. *Principles and procedures in student counseling.* New York: Harper and Brothers, 1950.
14. Rogers, C. R. *Client-centered therapy.* Boston: Houghton-Mifflin Co., 1957.
15. Skinner, B. F. *Verbal behavior.* New York: Appleton-Century-Crofts, 1957.
16. Williamson, E. G. Value orientation in counseling. *Personnel guid. J.,* 1958, 36, 520-528.

2

ON THE PHILOSOPHICAL NEUTRALITY OF COUNSELORS

Robert L. Browning
Methodist Theological School, Ohio (Delaware)

Herman J. Peters
The Ohio State University, Columbus, Ohio

THERE APPEARS TO BE AN URGENT DEMAND AMONG GUIDANCE COUNSELORS FOR A CLARIFICATION OF THE RELATIONSHIP BETWEEN THE COUNSELOR'S BASIC PHILOSOPHY AND HIS COUNSELING PROCEDURES. *Can* a counselor remain philosophically neutral, on the one hand, and *should* the counselor do so, on the other hand. Is Vordenberg's dictum true that "Regardless of the *kind* of personal philosophy evolved by the counselor, it must surely affect the techniques he uses and the evaluation of the effectiveness of his work"? (16:440)

I. DEMANDS FOR THE CONSIDERATION OF THE INFLUENCE OF PHILOSOPHY OF COUNSELING

After giving a survey of the inadequacies of the current attempts to develop a philosophical foundation and direction for guidance, Donald Walker and Herbert Peiffer issue a call to action. They say, ". . . we would urge close and careful attention to the problems of the goals of counseling, both at the general theoretical level and as they affect the progress of the individual counseling case. . . . We are handicapped by the fact that in psychotherapy we are, to some extent, the victims of our disease orientation, our bias against value judgments and our contradictory cultural goals." (17:209) Mathewson says that the old myth of economic man is inadequate. He says, "A new myth may be forming; we cannot tell what it may be and perhaps we cannot hasten its formation, or even consciously affect its form. But unless we wish to take a completely passive position in the determination of our national destiny, it seems necessary to think about and to choose between alternative sets of social and moral values, especially in the education and guidance of our youth." (9:26)

Arbuckle compares the counselor and the surgeon, saying that the philosophy of the surgeon may have very little effect on the recovery or death of a

Reprinted by permission of the Authors and *Educational Theory*, Vol. X, April 1960, 142-147.

patient. "The attitude and the philosophy of the counselor, however, are all important and in any research it is difficult to keep such an inconsistent factor consistent." (2) In Arbuckle's thinking the personnel point of view must include a consideration of every aspect in the development of the student — ". . . his intellect, his emotions, his physical being, his moral values, his skills and aptitudes, his means of recreation, his esthetic and religious values, his social adjustment, and his environmental situation. (3:3) This is a big order! The fulfillment of such a goal in guidance is greatly complicated by the fact that the counselor, in dealing with the counselee's development along such broad lines, is confused about whether or not his own loyalties, his own philosophy of life, should be shared, or whether, in fact, he can keep himself from sharing it!

> Counseling involves the interaction of two personalities through the medium of speech and other symbolic behavior. It is reasonable to suppose, therefore, that the structure of each of these personalities will have a marked influence on the interaction. It may be hypothesized further that the ways in which the personality structure of each of the counseling participants is symbolized in the speech of the interview will also have a marked effect upon the interaction.
>
> If it is true that the counselor's personality influences the direction, course, and outcome of the counseling interaction, it might be profitable to speculate about the kinds of counselor personality traits which are likely to facilitate counseling and those which are not.

Strang states,

> The counselor should be himself but not impose himself. He should be genuine and sincere. He is likely to fail if he tries to play a role that is not natural for him. If a person cannot risk being himself in the counseling relationship, he should not try to be a counselor. Moreover, he is consciously or unconsciously influenced by his theory of counseling; his attitude toward school policies, his outlook on life, his attitude toward people. In short, his counseling is an expression of his personality, not merely a technic applied at will. (14:   )

Pepinsky and Pepinsky, writing in 1954, state,

> There is no denying that the counselor's behavior, also, is subject to change as a function of his experience in working with clients." (11:173)

A little later under this same topic, "The Primary Function of Interaction," they go on to say,

> Indeed, the more closely we examine the counselor's motives, the more they become suspect! It appears to be, at best, nonsense and, at worst, a delusion to try to maintain that the counselor does or ought to leave his own needs parked outside the door while he interviews a client. We can state only that the explicit function of the counseling relationship — to help the client to change — should not be interfered with or destroyed. (11:174)

Perhaps the greatest single influence on counselors to be philosophically neutral has come from the work of Carl Rogers. His non-directive theory of psychotherapy was built on the belief that man could be trusted to work his way through to insights and new orientation if he could have a genuinely permissive relationship with the counselor in which he could open his inner life to himself and the helping person. Early research by Rogers led him to state that, "One can read through a complete recorded case or listen to it, without finding more than a half dozen instances in which the therapist's views on any point are evident. . . . One could not determine his diagnostic views, his standards of behavior, his social class." (12:358) Rogers did not, at that time, comment on the effect of the half dozen times and the absolute inevitability of such sharing of values. More recently, but only after a number of years of general confusion about the issue, has he addressed himself more directly to this pressing concern. In 1957, he said, in answer to certain articles challenging his position, that, "One cannot engage in psychotherapy without giving operational evidence of an underlying value orientation and view of human nature. It is definitely preferable, in my opinion, that such underlying views may be open and explicit, rather than covert and implicit." (13:199) Rogers' insistence upon as much neutrality as possible has been a helpful technique and allowed him and his associates to see deeply into the inner dynamics of the self. From his research there is ample evidence that the self, when free from threat or attack, is able to consider "hitherto rejected perceptions, to make new differentiations and to reintegrate the self in such a way as to include them." (12:365) Rogers' method seems honestly to help the person change. ". . . as changes occur in the perception of self and in the perception of reality, changes occur in the behavior." (12:363) The fact that persons often integrate their lives on levels that are not ultimately satisfactory but which only give the illusion of well-being must now be faced by Rogers and others.

II. ATTEMPTS TO CLARIFY THE RELATIONSHIP OF BASIC PHILOSOPHY TO COUNSELING

One of the most powerful attempts to do away with philosophical relativism has been made by the humanistic psychotherapist and author, Erich Fromm, in his several writings, especially in *The Sane Society*. Fromm seeks to establish a solid foundation for the development of mental health for all men in whatever society. He observes that man has not only physiological and anatomical commonalities but that he is governed universally by certain basic psychic factors as well. His system of right and wrong is therefore built squarely upon whether or not man as man, in his essential being, is having his basic human needs fulfilled.

Fromm's inclusion in his list of basic needs the necessity for a "frame of orientation and devotion" has led him to be most sympathetic toward the insights of the great religions and philosophies of the past and present. He is sensitive also to the moral standards propagated in our varying societies, because he believes that whole culture can become full of *defects* which can and do tend to make men mentally ill. Societal arrangements, therefore, often must be changed before man's needs can be met. This observation forces counselors to be concerned with social, political, and religious philosophies which have created and are sustaining, often, such unhealthy social structures.

Fromm's theory is an attempt to build on what man's needs are *objectively* and not on what man *feels* his needs to be. This concept challenges in many ways the goal of non-directive counseling which tends to center on the process of man's expression of his inner feelings of need without reference to the fact that such needs are often a result of cultural defects which will not and cannot bring ultimate health to the client. This is true because of the very nature of his human condition, and the breadth of his needs which are in the area of ultimate loyalties and basic, undergirding frames of orientation, about which most counselors feel insecure and from which discussions they tend to steer clear!

A similar trend to that of Fromm's can be seen in the writings of Kurt Lewin. He stated as far back as 1935 that, "The individual psychical experiences, the actions and emotions, purposes, wishes and hopes, are rather embedded in quite definite psychical structures, spheres of the personality, and whole process." (8:54)

Also to be found in Fromm and Lewin thought is an emphasis on man's freedom and the necessity to broaden the range of that freedom in psychotherapy as well as in intelligent political action. Lewin observed that often the individual area of freedom is very small due to the vectors and forces in his field of psychic experience, built on past identifications, inhibitions and loyalties. Yet, this freedom existed. Man as man had qualities beyond the realm of the animal. Therapy should help man use his freedom to find the paths to growth, and to overcome the psychic barriers.

One of the most dramatic and controversial attempts to deal with the question of philosophy in psychotherapy has been made by Dr. Viktor E. Frankl, the Director of the Neurological Polyclinic in Vienna and a Professor of Psychiatry at the University of Vienna. Frankl's point of view grows out of the emphasis in existentialist philosophy on man's actual conditions of existence. Man in his essence is endowed with certain capacities for freedom, for decision making, for determining his destiny. Man is a responsible being with the power to transcend his own situation and to prophesy the results of his decisions. His intellectual powers and his psychic powers are qualitatively different than other animals. Frankl joins Fromm, at this point, in that he is seeking to analyze man's basic need for a value system on which he will increase his freedom and his meaning.

He recognizes the significance of both individual psychology, stemming from Adler, and psychoanalysis, stemming from Freud. He maintains, however, that psychotherapy will be incomplete until man has a "psychotherapy of the mind" which deals with philosophical issues. Differing with Freud and others, he says, "The individual's philosophical attitude is part and parcel of his psychological one and emerges in every case." (6:34) He also believes, against the stream of thought in psychotherapy, that, "In no case should the intellectual problems of a person be written off as a 'symptom.'" (6:33)

Frankl honestly discusses the many profound problems related to his point of view, and pushes ahead, along with Fromm, to establish certain fundamental values inherent in man's situation. And yet, he maintains that existential analysis must not interfere with the ranking of values. ". . . what values he elects is and remains the patient's own affair. Existential analysis must not be concerned with what the patient decides for, what goals he sets himself, but only that he decides at all. . . The physician should never be allowed to take over the patient's responsibility; he must never permit that responsibility to be shifted to himself; he must never anticipate decisions or impose them upon the patient. His job is to make it possible for the patient to reach decisions; he must endow the patient with the capacity for deciding." (6:270)

Such a view has been given great impetus by the philosophical writings of Martin Buber. Buber's philosophy urges man to relationships of trust with other men — very much like that between the counselor and the client in a permissive setting; and yet, he believes that real trust must allow and encourage honest *dialogue* between both parties. When there is a real meeting of persons (Buber describes this meeting in terms of an I — Thou relationship — very similar to Schweitzer's "reverence for life" concept) each person is bringing his full self to the dialogue. He must "be willing . . . to say what is really in his mind about the subject of conversation. And that means further that on each occasion he makes the contribution of his spirit without reduction and without shifting ground." (4:112)

Dialogue on a philosophical level, on the level of the quest for ultimate meaning is a basic need for every human being. The counselor must be sensitive, nevertheless, to the existential situation in which the client finds himself at any given time.

Gordon Allport emphasizes the profundity of this renewed interest in studying the basic conditions of man's existence. He says, "Existentialism calls for a doctrine of an active intellect, for more emphasis upon propriate functions, including self-objectification and oriented becoming. In particular it calls for a wider and fresher view of anxiety, of courage, and of freedom. (1:80) Allport stresses the fact that Freud and his followers have dealt mostly with the anxiety in man aroused by feelings of guilt and fear of punishment and not at all the anxiety which comes from a fear of *nonbeing* (death — either actual or psychological, in the Buber sense of being not in relation; not affirmed and confirmed by others).

Allport believes that the consideration of philosophical matters has been greatly de-emphasized in counseling, to the detriment of our whole concept of personality structure. Philosophic and religious decisions have to do with what he terms *Intentional Characteristics* which become a part of the personality. He believes that, "Intentional characteristics represent above all else the individual's primary modes of addressing himself to the future. As such they select stimuli, guide inhibitions and choices, and have much to do with the process of adult becoming. Relatively few theories of personality recognize the pre-emptive importance of intentional characteristics." (1:89)

So, we are seeing a powerful movement within the guidance field, psychotherapy, philosophy, theology, and psychology for a deeper view of man's problems of existence, his wide and deep needs, his essential freedom of being, and his finite situation which forces him to go beyond knowledge to an ultimate devotion — built on faith (not an irrational faith, but faith, nonetheless).

Buber, in his William Alanson White Lectures given at the Washington School of Psychiatry, says that the counselor or educator "cannot wish to impose himself, for he believes in the effect of the actualizing forces. . . . The propagandist who imposes himself, does not really believe even in his own cause, for he does not trust it to attain the effect of its own power, without his special methods." (4:111) While Buber believes so strongly in the power of honest meeting between persons in an I — Thou relationship of mutual trust and confirmation, even with differences of loyalties, he is very *cautious about the right of the psychotherapist* to embark upon a 'treatment of the essential in man.' He agrees with the late Viktor von Weizsaecker who said that it is not the privilege of the therapist or counselor to deal with the final destiny of man.

Returning to the area of guidance and student personnel services, it is becoming equally well established that basic educational philosophy does inevitably influence the procedures of the guidance counselor. If he is thoroughly pragmatic in his orientation he will probably be inclined to play down or ignore the importance of religious or metaphysical beliefs that the student brings to the counseling situation. He may feel that value judgments must be left out of the considerations. Of course, with this Pragmatic Philosophy which seems on the surface to be a neutral position, goes a basic commitment just as much so as the student may have, with his religious commitment. It seems to us that considerations of ultimate values cannot be avoided by the counselor as a person, and that he must operate from some philosophical point of view — some form of Idealism, Realism (Christian or otherwise), Pragmatism, Naturalism, or Existentialism (again religious or otherwise).

It seems imperative that guidance counselors and educators must join other leaders in education, psychology, psychotherapy, philosophy and religion in doing basic research in this field.

In this spirit of scientific inquiry (even with its obvious limitations in the area of ultimate values) and also in the spirit of dialogue (with free discussion of important questions related to man's basic needs and his basic conditions of existence) we should proceed to clarify and come to decisions about the foundation and goals of counseling.

Recently, Williamson has stated that, "I have further argued for making explicit our own value orientations as individual counselors, not in order that we may adopt a counselor's orthodox creed, but rather that we may responsibly give societal and moral direction to our individual work in terms of the explicitly desired goals chosen by our student clients." (19:528)

When guidance counselors, psychotherapists, or religious counselors admit that they are not philosophically neutral, then we will be able to study more systematically the effect of our philosophical loyalties upon our counseling.

BIBLIOGRAPHY

1. Allport, Gordon W. *Becoming: Basic Considerations For a Psychology of Personality.* Yale University Press, 1955.
2. Arbuckle, Dugald S. *Student Personnel Services in Higher Education.* McGraw-Hill. N.Y. 1953.
3. Arbuckle, Dugald S. *Teacher Counseling.* Addison-Wesley Press. Cambridge, Mass.
4. Buber, Martin. "William Alanson White Memorial Lectures." *Psychiatry* No. 20, No. 2, May 1957.
5. Buber, Martin. "The Teacher and Teaching" — compiled by Dr. Ross Snyder, Univ. of Chicago. Unpublished form.
6. Frankl, Viktor E. *The Doctor and the Soul.* Alfred Knopf. N.Y. 1955.
7. Fromm, Erich. *The Sane Society.* Rinehart & Co. N.Y. 1955.

8. Lewin, Kurt. *A Dynamic Theory of Personality.* McGraw-Hill Co. New York. 1935.
9. Mathewson, Robert H. *Guidance Policy and Practice.* Harper and Bros. New York. 1955.
10. Oates, Wayne E. *The Religious Dimensions of Personality.* Assoc. Press. N.Y. 1957.
11. Pepinsky, Harold B. and Pepinsky, Pauline N. *Counseling: Theory and Practice.* New York: The Ronald Press Company. 1954.
12. Rogers, Carl. "Some Observations on the Organization of Personality." *The American Psychologist.* Vol. 2. 1947.
13. Rogers, Carl. "A Note on the Nature of Man." *Journal of Counseling Psychology.* Vol. 4. No. 3. 1957.
14. Strang, Ruth. *The Role of the Teacher in Personnel Work.* 4th ed. 1953.
15. Tillich, Paul. *Systematic Theology.* Vol. 1. University of Chicago Press. 1952.
16. Vordenberg, Wesley. "The Impact of Personal Philosophies on Counseling." *The Personnel and Guidance Journal.* XXXI. April 1953.
17. Walker, Donald and Peiffer, Herbert. "The Goals of Counseling." *Journal of Counseling Psychology.* Vol. 4. No. 3. 1957.
18. Weitz, Henry. "Counseling as a Function of the Counselor's Personality." *The Personnel and Guidance Journal.* Vol. XXXV. No. 5 January 1957.
19. Williamson, Edmond G. "Value Orientation in Counseling." *The Personnel and Guidance Journal.* XXXVI. April 1958.

(3)

FIVE PHILOSOPHICAL ISSUES IN COUNSELING[1]

Dugald S. Arbuckle

Boston University

Philosophy should probably be discussed in philosophical terms, but many of the philosophical issues in counseling are of a realistic and down-to-earth nature. This paper is an attempt to look realistically at some of these issues.

THE SELF CONCEPT

1. The first issue has to do with the relationship between the self concept, the goals and objectives of the counselor, and the techniques and methods that he may use to achieve these objectives. What the counselor does during the counseling process is not only a measure of his techniques and methods, but it is also a measure of his self concept, which in turn, is surely related to his goals and objectives as a counselor. Goals and purposes may be thought of as having a philosophical orientation, but the more pragmatic techniques and methods are merely the tools which are used to implement these objectives and to achieve these goals.

Reprinted by permission of the Author and *Journal of Counseling Psychology,* Vol. V, No. 3, 1958, 211-215.
[1]A paper presented at the Fall meeting of the New England Personnel and Guidance Conference, at Hartford, Connecticut.

The counselor's techniques, for example, are reflections of his attitude that the client must be directed, since he does not have the capacity for growth; that the client needs little or no direction, since he is capable of self determination; that the client must be told what is good and what is bad for him, since he is incapable of determining right from wrong; that respect for the integrity of the individual implies respect for the right of the individual to make his own decisions as to what might be good and what might be bad for him; that the client cannot be trusted to take positive action; the client can be trusted to take action that is generally socially acceptable. These counselor attitudes are reflected in the counselor's counseling, and they tend to be a portrait of the individual's concept of his self.

The discrepancy then, between what the counselor verbalizes he *should* do, what he actually *feels* that he should do, and what he actually *does* in an operational situation would appear to be a measure of the individual's total personality, rather than something that he has learned in his professional preparation at Chicago, or Boston, or New York. A study of Arbuckle and Wicas (2) tends to indicate that counselors receiving their doctorate education from one institution appear to differ in their attitudes and their techniques of counseling in just as many ways as those receiving their professional preparation in different institutions. One does not become a "Rogerian" by attending Chicago, or, more recently, Wisconsin, nor does one become a "Superian" or "Williamsonian" by attending Columbia or Minnesota. There would seem to be some evidence to indicate that the counselor, as he actually works, is giving a display of his philosophy of life rather than showing how well he has learned certain techniques and procedures in a graduate school.

Thus a real problem for the counselor is that ancient and honorable, although by now, well-worn phrase, "Know Thyself." As one listens to counselors describe first their concept of their role, and then what they do, he is struck by the discrepancy between their concept and their operation, and also by the frequency with which he hears the statement, "I know I shouldn't do this, and I don't particularly like what I am doing, but you know how it is . . . I just have to do it . . ." Such a statement is surely a rather unhappy expression of the counselor's real concept of his role, and of the counselor himself. He would sometimes appear to see himself as the echoer of his superior officer, as one who has no responsibility other than to do as he is told, and one who recognizes no professional responsibility whatsoever. Again, here, the counselor would appear to be expressing his personal concept of himself, and his attitudes toward his fellow man.

An article by Walker and Peiffer (6), while aimed at raising serious questions as to the validity of some of the goals of counseling, also tends to imply that the counselor, in what he does, is primarily displaying his self concept and his value system.

RELIGION

2. Another somewhat allied problem, very much related to the counselor's self concept, is his religious orientation, or lack of it. A case in point on this item is a fairly recent publication called "The Catholic Counselor"; another is the fact that the author of this present article, in writing a paper for a

religious group, was criticized gently because his paper described the "secular" counselor, rather than the "Christian" counselor. Some counselors would feel that anything that is of importance to the Catholic counselor, *as a professional counselor*, is of equal importance to every other counselor, and vice versa; some would also feel that one cannot talk about the "Christian way" of counseling any more than one can talk about the Christian way of removing one's appendix, the Jewish way of teaching reading, and the Moslem way of solving a problem in mathematics.

To what extent, then, does one's religious philosophy, orientation or bias act as a controlling agent, and affect the counselor's relationship with the client? Does the fact that the readers of this article represent a number of different religious denominations mean that they function in a different manner, as counselors, because of this religious difference? If we assume that there is such a thing as a "Catholic counselor," or a "Methodist counselor," or a "Baptist counselor," then this would also seem to assume that there must be something different about a Catholic counselor when compared with a Seventh Day Adventist counselor or a Southern Baptist counselor. Is this so? If it is, it would seem necessary to readjust our concepts of the goals and the objectives of the counseling process, since they would apparently vary according to the religious concepts of the counselor.

This also tends to imply that one's professional preparation can be effective only to a point, but from that point on there can be no change or growth. Does the Mormon counselor operate in a different manner with a Mormon client who talks about his heavy drinking than he would with a similar client who was a Methodist? Is there any difference in the relationship between an Orthodox Jewish counselor and a Jewish client who describes his feelings about the foolishness of the acceptance of the use of Kosher foods, and the relationship between a similar client and a Presbyterian counselor? One may say, offhand, that there will be no difference in the *actions* of the counselors toward the clients although there will be differences in the *attitudes* of the counselors toward the clients. And yet, if this is so, is it possible to operate in the same way with a client, regardless of one's attitudes? Can counseling be a professional task, then, if the goals as well as the methods to be used by the counselor are to be affected by his religious orientation, first, and secondly, by his professional preparation!

THE NATURE OF MAN

3. Related to the counselor's religious concepts will be his concept of the nature of man. This again raises some interesting questions. The *Journal of Counseling Psychology* carried an article by Walker (5) on this subject. In later issues there were several "letters" on this article, and more recently Rogers (3) has written on this subject. The counselor's philosophical concept of the nature of man is, probably, more than anything else, an indication of the extent to which he holds to a client-centered concept of counseling. It is difficult to see how one can accept the Freudian view of man as being basically hostile and carnal and still describe himself as a client-centered counselor. If one is oriented to a client-centered philosophy he has a more Rousseau-ian and optimistic picture of man as being basically a perfect creature who may

have been corrupted and injured by numerous pressures. Rogers raises the
intriguing question as to how the counselor can have a deep feeling of caring
for the client if his own basic and innate tendency is to destroy! He also postulates the theory that the fact that Freud in his self-analysis was denied a
warmly acceptant relationship may have meant that although he came to
know the denied and hidden aspects of himself, he could never really come
to accept them as a part of himself. One's concept of the nature of man, then,
must surely affect his operation as a counselor since it means that the counselor must see both himself and the client in a different light. A basic measure of the extent to which one is Freudian or client-centered would appear to
be related to his concept of the nature of man. Is he Freudian and pessimistic
à la Karl Menninger, or is he client-centered and optimistic a la Carl Rogers?

COUNSELOR RESPONSIBILITY

4. Another somewhat obvious problem is the counselor's concept of his
role in his society, and the question of the confidentiality of the information
the client may receive. Does the counselor think of his sole responsibility as
being the client and will he therefore never divulge information of a confidential nature? We can then push this to an extreme case and say if the client,
in talking about his hatred for society and particularly for those who are the
rulers, describes in some detail his elaborate plot to assassinate the President
of the United States, would the counselor maintain the client's confidence?
We might ask the same question of the Catholic Priest who hears the same
thing in the confessional, or we might ask the same question of the defense
lawyer who has just heard his client describe in detail the manner in which
he raped and murdered a little girl. Does the counselor, does the priest, does
the defense lawyer remain silent? There is much argument for saying that
surely they would not remain silent, and yet, once one enters into the realm
of the relative, one becomes the judge (even the Rogerian) who determines
when the price that society may have to pay for counselor silence is too great.
It would also be safe to say that there are very few school counselors who
err on the side of maintaining confidence too much, and there are many who
maintain confidences practically not at all.

The author recently read a paper on personnel work and counseling before
a group of top administrators of teacher preparation institutions in Massachusetts. It was interesting to note that a significant number of them apparently felt that a counselor should be expected to reveal any information that
he might have on a student to a dean or other administrative officer. This
question is also related to the first one, since if the counselor himself does
not have any concept of his role he will probably see no reason why he should
not tell the principal about Mary's plans to run away, about Bobby's sexual
deviations, about John's cheating in class. It is likely also, of course, that the
number of his clients will rapidly decline and all those who do come in will
be extremely wary and come forth with safe and innocuous statements.

This also raises the question of the counselor as a source of references.
It is unfortunate that counselors are used for references since even a statement to the effect that one has a policy of not giving references on students
who have been clients implies that the student in question was a client, and

to some employers this can mean only something bad. A client recently commented to the author that a neutral statement by a former employer or teacher was almost always interpreted as being a negative statement.

COUNSELOR EDUCATION

5. Finally, these philosophical issues raise questions on the whole problem of counselor education. Can we educate counselor-trainees regarding the use of certain techniques or methods? How does one educate a counselor-trainee to be acceptant (inside as well as outside) of hostility as expressed by the client? How does one educate a counselor-trainee to be unaffected and acceptant as the client describes some extremely deviate behavior? How does one educate the counselor-trainee to see his own hostility, to realize that his narrowness of procedure might be because of his own insecurity? How does one educate the counselor-trainee so that he may develop a self-understanding of who he is and what he is trying to achieve as a counselor, and as a result, possibly leave counseling and go into another occupation where he will be less dangerous to himself and to others. How does the formal education of the counselor-trainee help him to perform the tasks described by Tooker (4), Wrenn (7), and a host of others. How, indeed, can we "educate" the counselor-trainee to be the sort of person described in an earlier article by this author (1).

Certainly it would seem that the education of the counselor cannot be at a remote academic and intellectual level. One must become involved in hostility before one can come to see where he stands on the acceptance of hostility; one must hear highly risqué stories from the lips of a handsome woman before he knows how he will react to such stories when he hears them from such a source; one must, indeed, become accustomed to the psychological equivalent of the bloody and gory wound before one can even come close to understanding the degree of his capacity to accept, let alone to understand. In this last comparison, however, there is one important difference. The surgeon can become accustomed to the gory wound, but he can also become a relatively unfeeling individual, intrigued by physical wounds and defects. In fact, he might even be a somewhat sadistic individual, and still win high regard for his capacities as a surgeon. The counselor, however, cannot accept the deviation of behavior as described by the client if he does not accept the client. The education of the counselor-trainee must change him, it would seem, rather than increase his store of knowledge. The more basic question for the counselor-educator is not what does the student know, but rather what can he do with what he knows?

Thus counselor education should probably be primarily centered on self-evaluation, self-measurement, and, might we dare to say, self-analysis. It might well be that the counselor-educator should be more of a counselor than an educator.

EXPERIENCE NEEDED

A final problem on this question has to do with the need for and the extent of the counseling experience that the counselor should have, as a client.

The American Academy of Psychotherapists requires personal counseling for admittance to the Academy so that "there may be an evaluation of the applicant by his personal therapist." If a counselor-trainee feels no particular pressures, issues or problems, however, what sort of client will he be when the purpose of the counseling would then appear to become an evaluation of him by the counselor? This is a particular problem in client-centered counseling. If the student gives every appearance of being a sound person, in class work, in practicum, in small group sessions, in the regard he appears to have for himself and for others, must the counselor-educator say, in effect, "You must come in to us as a client, even though you feel that you have no particular pressures and have no evidence that you have any problems that you cannot work out effectively yourself."? This would appear to place the client-centered counselor-educator in a rather contradictory and even Freudian position!

REFERENCES

1. Arbuckle, D. S. Client perception of counselor personality. *J. counsel. Psychol.*, 1956, 3, 93-96.
2. Arbkucle, D. S. & Wicas, E. The development of a counseling perception instrument. *J. counsel. Psychol.*, 1957, 4, 304-312.
3. Rogers, C. R. A note on the nature of man. *J. counsel. Psychol.*, 1957, 4, 199-204.
4. Tooker, E. D. Counselor role: counselor training. *Personnel guid. J.*, 1957, 36, 263-268.
5. Walker, D. E. Carl Rogers and the nature of man. *J. counsel. Psychol.*, 1956, 3, 89-92.
6. Walker, D. E. & Peiffer, H. C., Jr. The goals of counseling. *J. counsel. Psychol.*, 1957, 4, 204-210.
7. Wrenn, C. G. Status and role of the school counselor. *Personnel guid. J.*, 1957, 36, 175-184.

$$4$$

THE UTILIZATION OF CREATIVE POTENTIAL IN OUR SOCIETY

Walter Gruen

VA Hospital, Canandaigua, N.Y.

The title of this paper was also the title of a symposium at the 1960 APA Convention in Chicago. My purpose here is to examine the reasons for scheduling such a discussion in the first place, and to report some of the conclusions emanating from the meeting.

The question is raised with increasing insistence whether everyone in our society is living up to his own maximum potentials, and one is apt to ask quickly: "Why not?" if one encounters people who are somehow found wanting. We even have ready-made and sometimes quasi-scientific labels for such people. The terms "underachievers" in the schools and "beatniks" and "non-

Reprinted by permission of the Author and the *Journal of Counseling Psychology*, Vol. 9, No. 1, 1962, 79-83.

conformists" in the adult world attest to the increasing tendency to spotlight the offender and to advertise our concern with keeping everyone at top effficiency.

There are three reasons why the concern is so much greater and more acute today.

1. We are engaged in a critical examination and reaffirmation of the basic democratic ideal, the worth of the individual. The Bill of Rights has been interpreted as proclaiming the right of the individual to develop himself to the full extent of his capacity. Not only should he be free from adverse pressures and from countercoercive forces, but he should be encouraged at every step to fulfill this destiny.

2. The second reason rests with the soul-searching into the mental health of the individual in our increasingly complex society. This concern has been partially influenced by the social problems of our time, such as delinquency, mental illness, alcoholism, including changes in social organization brought about by urbanization, mechanization, increase in leisure time, the growing influence of the mass media of entertainment, and others. The concern has also been partially fanned by some of our social scientists and by the "social prophets" of our time. The latter especially have warned us of the handwriting on the wall, by depicting the "organization man," the "marketing personality," the "suburban conformist," the "apathy of the voter," as setbacks in the development and in the progress of western man.

3. The final reason is tied up with our not-so-peaceful rivalry with Russia. We are suddenly awakened to the possibility that Russian society and Russian education may utilize the existing talents of their population more effectively, while we may keep talent dormant or siphon it off into other less socially creative channels. I need not remind anyone that the philosophical and practical issues as to where we should go as a society of humans is involved in the third reason but also in the other two.

Hence the concern with utilization of the creative potential rests on ethical considerations, on developmental theories about man, and on national objectives in a world where rival social systems compete strenuously for attention and for hegemony over the globe.

A DEFINITION OF CREATIVITY

The very moment that anyone, including the writer, takes up an examination of creativity and its socio-cultural underpinnings, it becomes necessary to define and limit the terms. Hence a creative act designates the making of something new or different out of existing objects, the reorganization or reorientation of given elements, or the utilization of existing objects and ideas in a different way. The use of a round wooden block as a wheel, the combination of wood and wire for a mouse trap, the discovery of a new principle for the organization of colors into a pattern pleasing to a number of others, are all examples. However, the creative act need not be defined by popular acclaim, nor by the label of greatness tagged on by a large number of people. The person with limited abilities and below average intelligence is "creative," if he utilizes his native and acquired skills to bring about a reorganization of words and symbols. The creative act is thereby distinguished from the habitual reaction to given elements and objects; and the latter reaction is usually known as adaptation or adjustment.

The creative act may further be a discovery of a relationship that is already known to others, but new to the individual. The discoveries of children and of culturally or socially more isolated individuals are often expressed by an idea which is new in the life space of the person, even if it is already known to adults or to other cultural groups.

Of course, the dividing line between creativity and habitual behavior is not easy to make. When is the constantly changing pattern of words in ordinary speech just adaptation and when does it become a poem or an essay? While disclaiming above the judgment of many others about the creative value of an act in the popular sense, we have to bring a consensus of some people back into play at this point. Just as some philosophers remind us that statements about truth must be statements of probability depending on some consensus of relevant individuals, the judgment of creative behavior must in the final analysis rest with a consensus or with a judgment.

The creative act can be defined by a consensus of experts or by a jury of trained peers. While we must reject the acclaim by even a majority as a criterion, we are not taking refuge into scientific double-talk when we propose the reliable judgment of more than one person as a measuring device. The experts would look into the antecedents in a given person's training and experience and judge an act as creative on the basis of past accomplishments and its different use of given elements of experience.

The Person and the State

Most of us make the implicit assumption that everyone in a democracy *should* be able to utilize all of his potentials for creative purposes for his own and society's good. This assumption is a value judgment and is one of the very cornerstones of our western choice of social organization. We do not pay only lip service to it, but we make many provisions for it and encourage it with many different institutions. Scholarships, endowments, grants-in-aid, self-development courses and workshops, are all relevant examples.

When we introduce national concern for creativity and also remember our third reason for concern, namely world competition of social systems for the attention of man, we are talking about a different meaning of the term. It is then defined as the development of talent for the production of new ventures in the fields of art and science for the advancement of society, and changes are hopefully evaluated as progress. It is worthwhile to distinguish clearly between the two meanings of creativity, because our first and primary focus here is taken to be a stage in the development of a person and may not necessarily be related to the greatness of a society. We should therefore distinguish the concern for developing "inner" creativity as a target of the ethical principles of a democracy which wants man to develop to his fullest measure from the concern for developing "popular" creativity for the sake of social progress and world competition. Of course a good case can and has been made that the full development of inner creative potential is the necessary prerequisite of a rich harvest of useful ideas for the advance of society.

THE FOUR PAPERS

Pepinsky and Productive Nonconformity

The contributions of the four papers in the symposium perhaps shed some new light on the development of creativity. Pepinsky (1960) is concerned with it by contrasting nonconformity with conformity. She examines some of the conditions under which creativity emerges in contrast to those conditions where it is inhibited. She attempts a definition of nonconformity involving both statistical and psychological criteria by distinguishing a creative from a habitual act. She distinguishes productive nonconformity as behavior contributing to task accomplishment of a group or of a society or of an individual, and shows how it differs from mere conformity to another set of values. She accomplishes this by contrasting it clearly with nonproductive nonconformity of — for instance — the persistent rebel. Her points are illustrated by finding different antecedents for each type of nonconformity in three different settings, where she carefully studied the people and the environment. The antecedents are not merely concerned with personality attributes, but also with social conditions which allow productive nonconformity as behavior to emerge.

She asks an important question which she wisely does not answer, and which we can pass on to the reader to ponder. She mentioned that we have studied people in extreme social disorganization and trained them to cope with it from what we have learned. However we do not train people to cope with the extreme social organization which she found to be a pre-disposing social milieu factor for conformity and which also has been found to be prevalent in many urbanized and highly routinized sections of our western world. The question arises here whether we can train people to cope with such conditions without killing their potential for productive nonconformity and their desire to change the social conditions toward a more fertile climate. One of the important issues implied in her paper concerns the nature and locale of such a training program.

Another very important point of issue concerns our and Pepinsky's implication that productive nonconformity is an important prerequisite for the health and progress for human society. If we equate productive nonconformity with certain aspects of Maslow's self-actualization and Erikson's generativity, we find that in such theories creative behavior becomes an important criterion of the mental health of the individual and constitutes the apex of human development. Fromm and others have felt that the accumulation of healthy individuals in these terms insures a healthy society. The fact that the questions have been answered in the affirmative by certain thinkers and scientists still does not put an end to speculation. The answer, as Smith (1961) and others have pointed out, may well depend in the final analysis on one's own goals and values so that we are faced with the need for a consensus, which we raised in the process of justifying a definition.

Fiedler and the Group Climate

Fiedler (1960) investigates some of the social conditions under which members of a discussion group become more creative. While antecedents in both inner man and in his social organization with others were investigated by Pepinsky, Fiedler concentrated on structural antecedents of group productivity under carefully measured conditions. He concentrated on the variables of formality of leadership, homogeneity of group composition, and psychological distance of leaders from members. Starting from the same definition of creativity as we have used, he devised a task for group creative action of very high reliability. His findings suggest that creative group action may require different group structure than those found beneficial in task-oriented groups. His paper represents a contribution to our knowledge of group structure and group practices, especially in the light of some of the wild claims for greater group creativity that are made by the inventors of new gimmicks in group discussion techniques.

It also suggests strongly that a group climate that is task and efficiency oriented may breed social conditions which inhibit creative behavior. We can see all kinds of implications here for work groups, research teams and even educational settings, where choices about individual creativity versus getting something accomplished are involved. Since two of the papers have studied and identified some of the antecedents for creativity, we can ask whether we now have a recipe for unfolding the creative behavior in a large number of individuals. A catalogue of these findings suggests creativity and the unfolding of potentials in an individual if we provide a family structure which contains independence-training and lack of conflict between members, the experience of unpopularity with the social leaders and with the majority of teachers while the child is in school, securing a sponsor for him outside his family and circle of friends. We must allow for diversity of expression in the groups he will enter as an adolescent and as an adult, but the groups themselves should be homogeneous in composition. I suspect that the problem is less simple, especially in view of the discussion by Bronfenbrenner (1960), who investigated the effects of parental discipline, social class, sex of child, dominance of father or mother, and social setting of father's job on initiative and independence in the child. Nevertheless the recipe coming from the symposium sounds like an intriguing hypothesis for a future action research study.

The prescriptions suggested by our research studies are too simple precisely because they leave out a consideration of the values already encountered in trying to arrive at a definition. What is a good society for human beings and what is a productive and creative individual are two important value questions which must be decided before we can answer on more empirical grounds which of several training methods are more effective.

Gruen and Attitudes toward Creativity

Gruen's (1960) study addressed itself to values by probing for attitudes toward creativity as defined here. It was found that preferences for unfolding of potentials and for creative activity are gratifyingly very wide-spread in a sample of upper-middle class adults. The findings here tie in with Riesman's (1960) observation that there are a good many private Utopias among contemporary Americans but no public movement or program for a better world. That is, people have visions among themselves and within their family and friendship circles, but on the national and public scene there seems to be a void. Similarly, Gruen's adults professed both private feelings of inspiration and application on one questionnaire but adhered on another to publicly proclaimed values of upward mobility for higher status, of emotional control and of devitalization in some areas of living.

One wonders how such findings contrast with some of the conclusions drawn by Gurin, Veroff, & Feld in *Americans View Their Mental Health* (1960). In this recent study many respondents seemed to function with little zest and joy, but stressed effortlessness and comfort as goals.

Drews on Creativity in the Schools

Drews' (1960) study showed that intellectual and creative activity is de-emphasized in the public schools. The alternate preference for status and popularity has often been identified as components of the accepted official "American core culture," which the second of Gruen's questionnaires attempted to measure. It has also been mentioned by some as a possible inhibitor of the creativity we are investigating here. The question therefore arises whether the social atmosphere in the schools described by Drews is correlated with lack of creativity later on in the lives of the children as adults. Since we find both informally and by our researches a good number of creative adults in our society, we may wonder if they went through the same schooling and social climate so eloquently described by Drews and emerged despite it, or whether their schooling was different in the past. There is encouraging evidence that dormant intellectual ability can be encouraged in adult years. I am thinking here of the Bell Telephone Middle Management Program in which executives are placed into a humanistic university program for one year. It has been amazing to competent observers how much stimulation this program produces and how much unfolding goes on in the "students" as they read and study various ideas and sources.

CONCLUSIONS

Evident in the four papers is our tendency to study the emergence and the nature of creative behavior in so-called elite groups. In these groups our findings are somewhat encouraging of favorable results but we still have not investigated creativity in lower class groups. I suspect that our concentration "above the belt" represents an implicit acceptance of the doctrine of natural selection. It does not answer the question whether or not the development and use of creativity in lower class groups is also a criterion for a healthy society, or for a healthy climate in which man can develop. Just as Terman's gifted children did not all become creative adults, it may be just as reasonable to assume that the ungifted or the unprivileged children will not always remain unproductive. However, someone should find out if this is so.

Obviously we need to know a lot more. We have not decided whether creativity is the ultimate pinnacle of development of all men, as postulated by some of our cross-cultural theories of personality, or is a typical American ideal and not exportable as a goal for man in other societies. Undoubtedly we are committed to a search for the factors that will facilitate or impede our western type of creativity. We have also become detectives searching for the forces in our society that will guarantee the use of all the human and psychic resources contained therein. This issue was not raised fifty years ago. A complex society and the peculiar requirements of increased interdependence in the urbanized life of today and in the One World of the future have molded this issue into a new frontier. We are increasingly examining our values, our institutions, our training and personality shaping techniques for this purpose. We also compare ourselves with other contemporary cultures to see how they may have solved the common human problems. Whatever our findings, we are now convinced that it is later than we think.

REFERENCES

Bronfenbrenner, U. The changing American child — a speculative analysis. Paper read at American Psychol. Assn., Chicago, September, 1960.

Drews, Elizabeth. Aspirations and achievement motives in gifted adolescents. Paper read at American Psychol. Assn., Chicago, September, 1960.

Fiedler, F. E. Leadership, group composition, and group creativity. Paper read at American Psychol. Assn., Chicago, September, 1960.

Gruen, W. So-called core culture attitudes and the belief in one's own creative potential. Paper read at American Psychol. Assn., Chicago, September, 1960.

Gurin, G., Veroff, J., & Feld, Sheila. *Americans view their mental health.* New York: Basic Books, 1960.

Pepinsky, Pauline N. The social dialectic of productive non-conformity. Paper read at American Psychol. Assn., Chicago, September, 1960.

Riesman, D. The search for challenge. *New university thought.* Spring, 1960, 3-15.

Smith, M. B. Mental health reconsidered: A special case of the problem of values in psychology. *Amer. Psychol.,* 1961, 16, 299-306.

COUNSELING: PHILOSOPHY OR SCIENCE[1]

Dugald S. Arbuckle
Boston University

Psychology and medicine have long regarded themselves as sciences, and those individuals involved in psychology or medicine have generally been considered as being of the empirical scientific mind, using the products of science, if not actively involved as scientists. When Freud first presented psychotherapy to the world, it was presented as a science; and religion, which probably felt itself as the world's custodian of philosophy, bristled, and the battle that had been joined for centuries between science and religion was joined between psychotherapy and religion. There has been much in the way of rapprochement, although it is somewhat uneasy, and while magazines are quick to print articles by scientists on topics which indicate the closeness of religion and science, they are not so eager to print a similar number of articles on the more threatening and, therefore, more unpopular topics which might indicate why science and religion must remain apart. In recent years, however,

Reprinted by permission of the Author and the *Personnel and Guidance Journal,* Sept. 1960, 11-14.

[1]Presidential Address delivered on April 12, 1960, during the APGA Convention, Bellevue-Stratford Hotel, Philadelphia, Pennsylvania.

the question of the relationship of psychotherapy to science and/or philosophy has put a somewhat different light on this issue, since psychotherapy viewed as a science will not be seen to have quite the same relationship with religion as if it is viewed as being heavily weighted on the philosophical side. Let us look at this question or counseling as a science, or a philosophy, or both.

CAPACITY AND SKILL

As long as counseling was thought of as an integral part of medicine it was thought of, rightly or wrongly, as an empirical science. The younger field of psychology was probably pushed even more in the scientific direction by its fierce desire to be as good as, or to excel and in some way surpass, its more well established brother, medicine. Thus, psychology took on the jargon of medicine. While psychologists do not think of themselves as medical personnel, medicine, with some ignorance of psychology, considers psychology to be a slightly wayward son, but still, without question, a member of the family to be controlled and directed by the older head of the household! Psychologists, not without cause, became proud of themselves as scientists, and it is likely that the psychologist of old, being somewhat less of a service individual than the family doctor, became more scientific, and possibly more unapproachable, than the family doctor. Involvement in research was, and is, as important to medical doctors as it is to psychologists, despite the fact that both of these individuals, when they are involved in service relationships with their fellow humans, make use primarily of learned skills and of their capacity to develop a warm relationship with another person. The medical doctor, working more *on* the physical body of a patient, possibly has more need of overt skills, whereas the psychotherapist, working *with* the individual as a person of feelings and emotions, has more need of the capacity (surely not a skill) to establish a close and warm relationship with another person. They can use the research findings of others, but they themselves are not researchers.

Psychiatrists and psychologists whose fulltime job was a service relationship have not generally functioned as scientists, but until the advent of Rogers, psychotherapy was generally accepted, professionally, as an almost completely scientific pursuit. Rogers' careful elaboration through the years of client-centered psychotherpay, however, brought to the fore this question of the relationship of counseling to philosophy. For many of the more empirical psychologists, philosophy was, and is, a dirty word, and this writer has more than once heard Rogers described somewhat scornfully as "nothing but a philosopher." The psychologist as a scientist is by no means all wrong, of course, in being somewhat suspicious of the philosopher, who may sometimes be too prone to accept on "faith." History does tend to present a rather dismal picture of what happens when people do not insist on asking "why" and do not require some evidence before they accept something as the truth to be followed blindly. They do not want the faith that makes one say "I know that I can see a new body in the heavens, but my faith says it cannot be there so it cannot be there." This is the sort of faith that has made religion the enemy of science.

THE LOSS OF THE PERSON

In discussing the counselor's responsibility in rehabilitation, Patterson [2] effectively describes what is all too often thought of as the scientific method in counseling:

> He *determines* the eligibility of clients as clients and the feasibility of their rehabilitation; he *appraises* the client's vocational potential and the probability of his success; he *evaluates* the suitability of various jobs; he *interviews* the client *toward realistic* (as defined by himself) goals; he *develops* a vocational rehabilitation plan with all its parts; he *carries out* the plan, implementing and administering its various aspects; he *makes referrals* to related services. One might ask: What is the client doing all this time? Too often he is literally doing nothing, except what he is told to do by the counselor.

And might we add that the possible reason that the client is doing nothing is because he is viewed as an object, a piece of material, to be manipulated, after all, by the counselor who has the knowledge and the know-how not possessed by the client. Patterson wrote this as a protest against the all too prevalent concept of vocational counseling, but surely it describes, frighteningly, what happens when the client becomes lost as a person, as a human being, as one who is not to be accepted and understood as he is, but rather as something which must be manipulated and modified so that he can become another faceless creature in a one man Big Brother Society.

Thus it would seem to me that the scientific method with objects and things is fine, and while we cannot suggest that we should toss the scientific method out of the window when we deal closely and intimately with people as we do in counseling, we might at least look with some caution at certain aspects of counseling which might be associated with the more scientific approach:

1. The function of science is to determine what is, and, as a result of this determination, predict what might be, but the scientific prognosis is based on evidence and facts. It is not concerned with values, with what ought to be, and this has not generally been a problem for the medical doctor, since man's physical body is not concerned with what ought to be either. A leg is smashed; there are certain proven techniques which have shown themselves to be superior over others in the mending of the broken leg. The leg does not ask, "Why should I mend?" or "What difference will it make if my leg does mend?" or "How did I come to get into this situation which resulted in a broken leg?" Thus as long as the medical doctor functioned as a surgeon, he could well be scientific, but as soon as he began to work with the owner of the leg, a human being who had a mind, his organic scientific knowledge began to fail him. This probably posed no problem for the earlier medical doctor, who actually knew very little other than how to use his few skills and dispense his medicines, but if he was an intelligent individual, concerned with human values, then he probably functioned very much as a philosopher and a counselor. When Freud appeared on the scene with the first studied presentation of psychotherapy it was offered as a science, although Freud was probably thinking of the dangers of the "too scientific" approach when he said, "Cases which are thus destined at the start to scientific purposes and treated accordingly suffer in consequence; while the most suc-

cessful cases are those in which one proceeds, as it were, aimlessly, and allows oneself to be overtaken by any surprises, always presenting to them an open mind, free from any expectations" [1, p. 326-327]. Freud was no doubt influenced by his medical background; and with his generally anti-religious point of view, it is little wonder that there was not too much in the way of a philosophical approach to psychotherapy. It should be noted too that, then as now, philosophy tends to be related to religion, and while this is obviously true, it is not correct to assume, as some theologians do, that in order to be a philosopher, one must be allied with a denominational religion. Some of the greatest current and past minds in philosophy have been, and are, looked at with some suspicion by the more orthodox of their theological brethren.

Thus, in a way, man moved into the study of the psychological and philosophical nature of man, with very little in the way of knowledge about the former and a general bias toward the latter. To some degree this skill holds today, with the psychologist, as the new comer in the field, taking on many of the characteristics of the medical profession even while he strives with might and main to prove that he is different, as obviously he is!

SCIENCE AND VALUES

The theologian has not generally been considered to be very scientific, being, rather, a man of faith. As he moves into the therapeutic arena, however, will he tend to become more scientific, and if he does, what will this do to his faith? While one might agree with Walters [3] that "existential anxiety is properly the object of priestly concern, while pathologic anxiety is the concern of the psychotherapist," this author could not accept the implication that existential anxiety is not the concern of the psychotherapist. This very example might be an excellent indication of the difference between the psychotherapist as a scientist, and the psychotherapist as a philosopher. If the therapist is concerned only with the pathological, and this is often thought of as the logical concern of the medical doctor and the clinical psychologist, then he can probably remain as the empirical scientist. Once, however, he becomes concerned with the more "existential" aspects of anxiety (and how could one be a psychotherapist without having this concern) then he has entered the realm of philosophy. Certainly it is not man's acts that cause him stress and strain so much as it is the guilts, the anxieties, the fears, the frustrations that have come to be associated with these acts. An individual is not disturbed by the physical act of masturbation until he learns that it is bad for him to masturbate, and something dreadful will happen to him if he does; one is not distressed about hating a miserable parent unless one has learned that one is always supposed to love one's parents; one is not too concerned about killing one's fellows as long as we know they are our enemy and must be killed, and that we will be rewarded for the act. These are surely matters of values that bring in questions about who we are, what we are around for, what is right and what is wrong, and these are questions for which it is difficult to pose a clear-cut empirical answer. One might be scientific in his attempts to evaluate what happens as a result of his counseling, what might happen if he does this instead of that, what happens if a certain variable (difficult to isolate in the social sciences) is introduced, and so on, but how scientific can he be in his actual relationship with the client, which after all is what counseling is.

Certainly the organic aspects of psychotherapy can be scientific. Neither the patient nor the medical doctor is in the realm of philosophy when both are involved in a brain lobotomy or an electro-shock or in the injection of various drugs. Here one can be somewhat pragmatic and, on the basis of statistical evidence, say that we will use thus and so procedure on this helpless patient, with no involvement on his part, and we know the statistical odds that this, instead of that, will happen.

2. The traditional case study approach, revered by social workers, might also be considered to be somewhat scientific, since it tends to be an investigation of what is, without the personal involvement of the client and without the personal involvement and intrusion of the values and ideas and thoughts and feelings of the counselor, other than those which are based on evidence. Again, however, when the social worker becomes a counselor, she is no longer working *on* a case, but *with* a human being, and again the question arises. How scientific can one be in the actual close personal relationship between client and counselor or does the very "scientificness" of one's approach render him less effective?

3. Many of the techniques and methods of counseling might logically be described as being scientific. Thus, diagnosis is an empirical means of assessment of an individual or his problems. The whole process of analysis and interpretation can really be defended only on the basis of a scientific validation of their use. Thus, it would probably be correct to say that psychotherapy, as it is allied with, or the son or relative of medicine and/or psychology, will tend to have a strongly scientific tinge, and certainly many counselors, in their descriptions of psychotherapy, would refer to it as "the science of . . . ." Surely one could agree with the counselor who states that if psychotherapy and counseling are to have the status of a profession, then its practitioners cannot say that they operate on faith and intuition, and that they don't need any evidence as to whether the client is any better or any worse because of their ministrations. This is surely the road to quackery, and counselors unfortunately already have more than their share of quacks! On the other hand, if one thinks of counseling in more Rogerian terms, with the stress on the relationship between the client and the counselor, rather than on the things that the counselor does with or to the client during the relationship, then one enters the realm of the more subjective, the realm of feelings, and, one might even say, possibly the realm of intuition, at last educated intuition! This does not mean, however, that there is not a great need for empirical evidence on the counseling process, but it does raise the question as to whether or not the counselor can be the empiricist who does the research.

The actual counseling, of course, is simply a reflection of the counselor himself, and the general low level of counselor competence is, I fear, due not so much to the lack of training, as it is to the lack of education. In fact, it might well be that a real education has an inhibiting effect on one's training. We train technicians who ask the more empirical question "how," but only the educated man can ask the more philosophical question "why." If counseling is concerned with human dignity, and freedom, and integrity, then surely the "why" of our counseling takes precedence over the "how." We need more counselors, possibly, who know how to do things, but we need in vastly greater numbers those who know why they do what they do. When this happens we may have hope that counselors, as individuals who have found for themselves that wonderful deep sense of their own worth and dignity and integrity, will then be able to help children to slowly gather this strength in themselves. Then they too can stand, alone, if need be, unshatterable and unafraid. These are the people we need desperately in our present day society, where individual acquiescence to the group is considered to be democracy, and where individualism would almost seem to be akin to treason.

REFERENCES

1. Freud, Sigmund. Recommendations for physicians on the psychoanalytic method of treatment. In *Collected Papers,* Vol. II London: Hogath Press, 1925.
2. Patterson, C. H. The counselor's responsibility in rehabilitation. *J. Rehabilit.,* January-February, 1958, 24, 7-11.
3. Walters, Orville S. Metaphysics, religion and psychotherapy. *J. Counsel. Psychol.,* Winter, 1958, 5, 243-252.

COUNSELING IN THE PUBLIC SCHOOLS — SOME LEGAL CONSIDERATIONS

Henry E. Butler, Jr.
University of Rochester

This essay is concerned with some of the more obvious legal considerations that should be kept in mind by guidance counselors in the public schools. It is general in nature, and in large measure nontechnical. For the most part, it is exploratory and speculative rather than expository, and it is selective rather than comprehensive in its approach.[1] Attention is focused more on problems involving the exercise of judgment than on questions that are resolved by judicial or legislative mandate, because it seems to the writer that such an emphasis is more likely to provoke fruitful discussion than a more "cut and dried" presentation. Finally, this essay reflects the writer's point of view on a number of matters about which there is, admittedly, a legitimate difference of opinion. At the outset, the setting in which guidance activities take place needs to be defined as clearly as possible.

THE SETTING

Guidance counselors in the public schools are, legally, specialized teachers, whose function is performed for the most part outside the classroom. They are employees of a public agency, and as such are charged primarily with a public, not a private, responsibility. They share with classroom teachers, administrators, and other specialists, including noncertified employees, respon-

An original article for this book.
[1]For a detailed treatment of the topic see Martha L. Ware (Editor), *Law of Guidance and Counseling* (Cincinnati: The W. H. Anderson Company, 1964).

sibility for providing and maintaining an educational program that is as effective as it can be for each pupil enrolled in the public schools.

It should be noted that the guidance counselor performs his specialized functions in a system that is controlled externally by relevant provisions of the United States Constitution and by the constitutions, statutes, and administrative regulations of the respective states. Furthermore, and perhaps equally important here, his activities take place in an organizational structure that is still characterized predominantly by line-staff relationships. While it is frequently difficult to identify a function that is purely "line" or purely "staff," it seems evident that insofar as internal controls are concerned the guidance counselor, as the teacher, occupies a subordinate position and is subject to policies legally adopted by a local board of education and to administrative rules, and decisions which implement these policies, whether made arbitrarily or on a consultative basis.

Many guidance activities concern individual pupils, unemancipated minors, whose parents have a substantial legal right to control the education of their children, and who themselves have legal rights that will be protected by the courts if suit is instituted by the parents. Inasmuch as it is doubtful that such minor pupils can waive any of these rights without the agreement of the parents, the guidance counselor, in dealing with individual pupils, needs to be aware of the legal presence of the parent in the background.

The setting in which the guidance counselor conducts his activities involves the relationship between ethical and legal standards. A code of ethics, rooted in "professional" consensus but lacking legal acceptance or sanction, may have little relevance to the outcome of litigation.[2]

Finally, the role and function of the guidance counselor in the public educational system have not been clearly defined. As specialists, guidance counselors are expected to provide educational and vocational guidance and counseling of an informative nature. In some school systems they are assigned disciplinary functions. Increasingly, it appears, guidance counselors are undertaking, and are being permitted to undertake, a conscious therapeutic function in relation to individual students. If a more favorable student-counselors ratio results as greater numbers of guidance counselors are trained and placed in the public schools, this trend can be expected to accelerate in response to the need of young people "for someone to talk to."

Acceptance of the concept of psychotherapy and recognition of the widespread need for therapeutic services leave unanswered two questions: (1) Are guidance counselors appropriately trained to provide such services? and (2) Should such services be provided by guidance counselors in the public schools? Whatever answer one may give to these questions, as of this writing guidance counselors have the general legal status of teachers, not of psychologists or psychiatrists. The point is, of course, that in the absence of a clear legal definition of his specialized role and function, the guidance counselor faces uncertainty insofar as his legal rights and responsibilities are concerned. This uncertainty increases the farther he departs from the specialized teaching role and undertakes a consciously therapeutic function.

---

[2]The Board of Trustees of the Lassen Union High School District v. Jack Owens, 23 Cal. Rptr. 710 (1962).

POTENTIAL AREAS OF LEGAL INVOLVEMENT

As guidance counselors engage in their daily routine, some of their activities hold a potential for legal involvement that warrant identification here.

Cumulative records for individual students are frequently maintained by the guidance counseling department of a school district. These records may be transferred from one school district to another as students change their residence, and are an important source of information for members of the school staff whose function relates to the instruction of individual students. They may contain derogatory data or information which, if disclosed without the protection of qualified privilege would indefensibly embarrass the student concerned and could lead to legal complications for the individual who disseminated the information improperly. The parents of a particular student have a right, in the absence of a controlling statute or state regulation, to consult the school records that pertain to their children.[3] Similarly, those members of a school staff who work directly with a particular student may properly have access to his records. Beyond this, great care should be exercised in general not to release information contained in a student's records without parental permission or a parental request in writing. In situations where the authorization of a parent or guardian cannot be obtained because his whereabouts are unknown, the written authorization of the student concerned should be obtained.

In this regard, it is highly desirable that administrative rules implementing locally adopted school board policy be formulated to protect the privacy of such records and to enjoin silence with respect to the data included in them on members of the clerical and secretarial staff who may assist in posting information in individual students records. Unless such measures are taken and enforced, a violation of the security of information by a member of the secretarial staff might be legally imputed to the professional member of the staff charged with responsibility for maintaining the records or to the school district itself.

Information obtained from a student during an interview should be treated in a similar fashion. The problem here is likely to arise when a student reveals information about himself or other students that makes it impossible to base a decision on whether to report the information (orally or in writing) to the building principal or other responsible administrator or to the parents of a student, solely on a consideration of the "confidential relationship" with the student who provided the information. If a guidance counselor receives information which implies harm or danger to the counselee or others, his failure to report this information, even at the risk of revealing the identity of the counselee supplying the information, could constitute the basis for a successful negligence action. Under some conditions, it is conceivable that it might also expose the guidance counselor to a criminal prosecution. For example, if a counselee reveals to a guidance counselor an intention to participate in a criminal act, this information should be reported to the responsible superior in the school system or to the parent in such a way that the guidance counselor has a record of the fact that the report has been made. Failure to make such a report would leave the counselor in the position of possibly being

---

[3]Van Allen v. McCleary, 211 N.Y.S. 2d 501 (1961).

involved legally in any criminal act committed in fulfillment of the expressed intention, or of being unable to establish the fact that he had made an appropriate report.

Tests and questionnaires that seek directly or indirectly to elicit information of an intimate nature relating to conditions in the homes of student-respondents and their feelings about themselves in the home environment present another source of potential conflict. It may well be that the relevance of such tests and questionnaires to educational and vocational decisions affecting a particular student make it desirable to use them. The fact remains, however, that the administration of such instruments may, in effect, invade the privacy of the home through the participation of a minor child. If such tests are administered without parental permission as part of a testing program approved by a local board of education, presumably the board of education, not the guidance counselor, would be answerable to complaining parents. On the other hand, if a guidance counselor administers such tests without parental permission that are not part of the approved district testing program or have not otherwise been approved by the governing board of the district, he would be answerable as an individual to complaining parents.

BASIC GUIDELINES

The sparsity of cases involving guidance counselors suggests that statistically the specialized activities of guidance counselors involve but slight exposure to legal liability.[4] This exposure can be minimized if the guidance counselor exercises sound judgment based on an understanding of the legal principles that apply to his activities. These principles have been discussed comprehensively elsewhere and are not repeated here. It does seem appropriate, however, to suggest a number of operational guidelines calculated to help guidance counselors avoid potential legal pitfalls.

1. Guidance counselors should seek a definition in writing of the functions they are expected to perform consistent with the policies of the specific school district that employs them. Particular attention should be given to the procedures to be followed in maintaining the security of information contained in student records, and in releasing such information to parents and to others in the school system and to prospective employers and institutions of further education upon request. In addition, the administrator to whom guidance counselors should report information which implies harm or danger to a counselor or to others should be identified, and the procedure for making referrals for diagnosis and possible therapeutic treatment should be clearly defined, consistent with parental rights in such matters.
2. Guidance counselors should make as clear as possible to counselees that while they have an obligation to exercise good faith toward the counselee and generally to maintain in confidence information provided by a coun-

---

[4]For a significant, related discussion see Reynolds C. Seitz, "The Law of Privileged Communications As It Affects The Work and Responsibility Of The Principal" in *Law and the School Principal* (Reynolds C. Seitz, Editor, Cincinnati: The W. H. Anderson Company, 1961).

selee, they also have an obligation to a counselee's parents, other students, and to the employing school system, and under some circumstances might have to divulge to others information which the counselee would prefer not to have reported. Unless a forthright position is taken in this matter, a guidance counselor may readily find himself torn between what he perceives to be his ethical obligation to a counselee and his legal responsibility as a professional employee of a school district.

3. Guidance counselors should limit their activities to their specialized area of competence and should not become involved with the diagnosis and alleviation of emotional problems. If doubtful as to whether such problems exist, the guidance counselor should resolve such doubt by a referral in accordance with approved procedures.

4. Guidance counselors should conduct their activities in a manner consistent with the substantial right of parents to control the education of their children. Providing opportunities for parent-student conferences and parent participation in reaching decisions growing out of educational and vocational guidance activities appears to be the most effective way to make allowance for the legitimate interest of parents in educational decisions affecting their children.

Guidance counselors have an assured future in the public schools. They cannot capitalize on this future if they walk in fear and trembling. Neither can they realize their potential if they plunge ahead blindly without regard to the possible legal consequences of their actions. They are likely to function best if they educate themselves carefully concerning their legal responsibilities, and exercise educational discretion in the light of this knowledge.

$$7$$

PROJECT CAUSE, THE FEDERAL ANTI-POVERTY PROGRAM, AND SOME IMPLICATIONS OF SUBPROFESSIONAL TRAINING

Jesse E. Gordon
University of Michigan

The Federal Anti-Poverty Program has brought home an awareness of a developing problem in our national life, that of youth unemployment. The magnitude of the problem can be sensed from the following statistics. The rate of unemployment for those in the age range of 16 to 21 years is approximately 15%, three times the national average of 5.7%. There were 1.2 million jobless youth in 1963, not counting those who were in school. This unemployment is not evenly distributed over all youth; it is heaviest among nonwhites. Twenty-seven percent of nonwhite youths within the 16- to 21-year age range are jobless. This is double the rate of unemployment for white youth. Further, the unemployment rate for nonwhites is rising twice as fast as the rate for whites, a trend which has existed at least since 1955. That these differences

Reprinted by permission of the Author and *The American Psychologist*, Vol. 20, No. 5, May 1965, 334-343.

between whites and nonwhites in unemployment are not only a product of differences in educational attainment is indicated by the fact that when education is comparable (i.e., comparing nonwhites with high school diplomas with high school graduated whites), the unemployment rate for the nonwhites is still twice that of the whites.

These problems will further multiply in the immediate future. Between 1964 and the end of this decade, 17 million youth will reach labor market age. Current estimates indicate that 7 million will have quit school before the twelfth grade. These 7 million are very likely to include the 3.5 million young people growing up in poverty families (i.e., families earning less than $3,000 a year) containing five or more children to be supported by this inadequate income.

We know what tends to happen to out-of-work and out-of-school youth. They concentrate in slums where they can find "something" to do — as reflected in crime statistics. Eighty-eight percent of all car thefts are committed by people under 25 years of age. For crimes of homicide, rape, robbery, burglary, aggravated assault, larceny, and auto theft, 46% of all arrests are of young people 18 years or younger.

To make matters worse, the national trends are for an increasing loss of entry level jobs. While there are increasing needs for older, skilled technical personnel, farm employment which has functioned as an introduction to the world of work for young people has declined. Automation tends to displace the least skilled, the least trained, the least educated, the youngest workers.

The evolution of societies and cultures is highly coordinated with the kinds of economic situations within which the societies and cultures exist. Linton and Kardiner (1952) showed us how the culture of Tanala-Betsileo changed in response to the change from dry to wet rice cultivation. It is no less true that the subculture of America in which unemployment has been most chronic, and indeed, has become hereditary, has made its adaptations. Where work has traditionally not existed, there is little achievement motivation. Where opportunity does not exist, there is disbelief in the rewards for work. We thus have a growing group of young people who do not value work, who do not believe in the rewards of work, and who therefore have no skills appropriate to the labor market. Even if they would, they do not know how to apply for a job, they do not know how to behave in the social role of an employee, and thus they do not know how to keep a job. As this group grows in size, it will constitute an ever-increasing danger to the larger society; the irony of it is that the subculture of chronically unemployed youth has evolved to the point at which even the availability of work is insufficient by itself to end the unemployment. Making jobs available to people who have little interest in work, little belief in its rewards, and no skills, produces the paradox of continued unemployment together with labor shortage. We are thus in the unfortunate position of sitting on a powder keg and not knowing how to defuse it.

If the availability of jobs is no longer sufficient to solve the problem, then perhaps job availability plus vocational counseling, guidance, and employability development is what is needed. Indeed, it seems to be the only possible solution and it is the one which forms the organizing principle for several aspects of the Federal Economic Opportunity Program. But in many ways this may seem to be a most unpromising solution. The very existence of masses of chronically unemployed and unemployable youth testifies to the continued failure of counseling and guidance as professions and as a body of social institutions to meet the need. And this failure is as deeply rooted and structural as is the problem of chronic unemployment. I would like to discuss quite briefly some of the dynamics which have prevented counseling and guidance, psychology, and social work from dealing effectively with this problem in the past. Much of what follows may be generalized from the field of vocational counseling to other aspects of the helping professions which may be involved in the several antipoverty programs, such as teaching, casework and group work, family counseling, child guidance, programs for the aging, etc.

PROFESSIONAL UNPREPAREDNESS

1. Lack of Techniques

The counseling process and its array of associated techniques as represented in the standard textbooks and educational curricula is one which has been evolved through decades of practical experience and research with middle-class clients and subjects, most in both categories being students. The techniques which have been developed are therefore specifically appropriate to well-motivated applicant-clients who are verbally expressive and quite accepting of middle-class values relative to work and achievement. They are accustomed to accepting the kind of role assigned to a student-client vis-à-vis a counselor, social worker, or psychologist, and to working within that role.

While some experimental and demonstration agencies in recent years have tried various new procedures for making contact with disadvantaged youth, for motivating them, counseling them, and training them, these techniques have not yet been collected into a coherent body of principles and methods, they have not been adequately communicated to the profession, and they have not found their ways into university programs of counselor preparation, into textbooks, and into the repertories of counseling agencies by and large. Some idea of the inappropriateness of the standard techniques can be gathered from the difficulties faced by the Selective Service Rehabilitant Program. The program was started last February 17 to help disadvantaged youth, mostly school dropouts and unemployed, to find employment and a place in society. The program hoped to do this by guiding draft rejectees into state employment offices for interviews, counseling, and job placement, in the traditional model of vocational counseling.

Underemployed and unemployed rejectees were invited by letter to visit employment service counselors in their offices to talk about jobs and career planning. Of the 234,000 rejectees so invited, of whom 78,000 were unemployed, only 42,000 showed up for interviews, and of these 32,000 were unemployed or underemployed. Thus the majority of the unemployed and underemployed who received letters — 46,000 — failed to respond. And of the 42,000 who did respond, fewer than 13,000 were referred to jobs; fewer than 7,000 of these hired, and some for only a few days. One-third of these invited Selective Service rejectees had less than an elementary education; 80% were school dropouts. It is apparent from this experience that arranging for an office appointment for counseling services is an unsuccessful way of making counsel-

ing services available to these youth, and that the services available for those
who do respond are inappropriate and relatively nonproductive. The United
States Employment Service recognizes this now, and has begun a program of
stationing Employment Service personnel in the induction centers themselves;
they are going to where the clients are instead of waiting for these unemployed
to come to them.

2. Class Bias in Recruitment and Training of Professionals

Where it is cause or effect of the middle class orientation of counseling
techniques and procedures, it is true that counselor education, and even more
so, clinical psychology, devotes almost all its resources to the preparation of
counselors and psychologists for middle-class secondary schools, middle-class
agencies, and for universities, thus missing entirely the body of needy, out-of-
school non-middle-class people. The result has been that almost 90% of the
graduates of counseling and guidance training programs find employment in
schools and universities. The figures for psychology are comparable in indicating an overwhelming orientation toward serving the educational and counseling needs of the middle class. A number of factors contribute to this state
of affairs:

a. Students of counseling and guidance, psychology, and social work
typically come from marginal middle-class backgrounds. Their need to confirm and enhance their social status leads them to a preference for the ac-
coutrements of a professional identity, such as office work, the use of verbal
and conceptual skills, connection with solidly respectable social institutions
such as schools, job security, and a public identity which, if not outright
prestigeful, is at least considered respectable. They prefer to work with
people who will enhance their identities, and they tend to feel threatened by
association with the millieu from which the marginal middle class is so anxious
to separate itself. Thus social psychological factors within the personnel available for the helping professions incline them towards school counseling with
college-bound youth.

b. When such candidates for training find themselves in a professional
training program, their inclinations are reinforced. The prestigeful role models
most available to them are their professors, the conditions of whose employment (teaching and research, publish or perish) result in staff selection factors
which emphasize research, theorizing, scholarship, verbal-conceptual skills,
and the enjoyment of theoretical and academic discussion with peers. These
available role models thus omit reference to actual counseling, to actual contact and involvement with disadvantaged youth, to familiarity with the culture
of poverty, and with lower-class orientations and values. Within such a faculty,
processes take place which maximize the rewards of grades, honors, and
scholarships for those students who most completely incorporate the characteristics of their models. These are the students who are most highly recommended for the most prestigeful job placements upon completion of training.
These organizational factors within the university thus operate to further move
students away from work with disadvantaged youth. The university community thus tends to further attract students whose interests and attitudes are
consonant with the university ethos and which are therefore inappropriate
for work with disadvantaged youth, and to repel the action oriented who thus

do not gain access to the profession. While these action oriented may possess some of the skills and characteristics necessary for counseling with disadvantaged youth, they may not possess the skills and characteristics most frequently rewarded in training programs ostensibly designed to prepare them for service work. This is a reflection of a situation in which the skills required for successful completion of training are different from, and perhaps even negatively correlated with, the skills needed for successful performance on the job.

It is worth noting here that those professionals who rise to the top of their professions are often those who best exemplify some of the factors described above. These are the people who constitute the professional leadership and who help to define the profession for the public and for potential recruits to it.

3. Inappropriateness of the Model for Personal Help

Another related factor which has rendered the helping professions inappropriate for meeting the problems of current youth unemployment is in the nature of the professional model for helping work which has been developed and amplified through the course of the class-restricted history of the helping professions. This model is one in which a fully qualified professional person takes all responsibility for the counseling. He carries out personally all aspects of the process, including public information, motivating of clients, intake, testing and diagnosis, interviewing, referral, and follow-up and evaluation. A fully qualified professional practices in all areas. As new knowledge has been created concerning each of these functions, there is a press to increase the length of training and preparation to acquire more and more information about all of these aspects, and no more may be graduated with a professional degree who has not mastered all of them. This lengthening of the training process further restricts and limits the supply of professional counseling personnel, and so further intensifies the self-selection of lower middle-class students and increases the time in which conformity pressures within the training institution can operate.

This model of the professional as the "compleat clinician" and the implied model of the helping process are based on implicit acceptance of the transference hypothesis which sees personal counseling as evolving and moving forward only in the context of a continued personal and intimate relationship between client and counselor. It is assumed that the intimate concerns and life activities of a client can only be exposed where there is an intimate personal relationship. I would like to suggest the possibility that this assumption is valid for the middle class, but may not be valid in lower-class culture. Middle-class children are raised within an ethic of modesty. They are taught that there are spheres of their own activities, mostly those involving biological functions of toileting, eating, and sexuality, which may not be shared or made public to anyone outside of the immediate family, and may even be entirely private within the family. The possibilities for such privacy hardly exist in crowded tenements in which several families live together and share inadequate facilities. I suspect that one of the results of these living conditions is a reduction in the demand for intimacy as a precondition for "exposing" personal matters. Furthermore, the dynamic bases for transference are attenuated in lower-class culture in which children are brought up by a variety of other people, a shifting group of adults, neighbors, temporary parents-consorts, and whatever siblings happen to be around at the moment. There is thus less investment of affect in a single reliable person, and there may also, therefore, be a greater readiness to relate to the *roles* of others rather than to the individual characteristics of the individuals filling those roles. For these reasons I suggest that there is less need for a transference relationship as a precondition of counseling, less readiness to develop transference attitudes, and a smaller demand for intimacy with a particular counselor, in lower-class culture. Thus the professional model of counseling as a one-to-one relationship may not be necessary or even desirable for working with disadvantaged youth.

One consequence of the primacy of this "transference model" of counseling is that it makes no room for subprofessionals, and it therefore makes no demand for professionals to be skilled in supervision of subprofessional roles or in training people for subprofessional roles. I shall return to this point in another section of this paper.

4. Shortage of Professionals

Even without these social and psychological dynamics, the helping professionals are ill fit to cope with the problems of youth unemployment by the severe shortage of trained professional workers. The current demand for psychologists, social workers, and counselors far exceeds the supply, and the demand is growing at a much greater rate than the student bodies in these professions. For years we have been telling ourselves that we were not turning out enough qualified professionals to meet the social needs, and some of the leading universities have even abdicated from any attempt to meet the needs by concentrating their efforts on turning out theoreticians and researchers and leaving others to turn out practitioners. The others, of course, attempt to emulate the leaders, and in the scramble for academic prestige few concern themselves with whether anybody has picked up the responsibilities of which the leaders have divested themselves.

TWO SOLUTIONS

Two solutions to the problem of providing services to the disadvantaged have been offered. The first is akin to the phenomenon studied by Festinger (1956) in his *When Prophecy Fails*. If the existing structuring of the professions is failing to meet the need, then increase the dosage. Thus pleas are made for more Federal aid for faculty and for student support so that more professionals can be trained. But of course, if the middle-class orientation are left undisturbed, there is no reason to think that an increased supply of professionals would result in more effective counseling with the disadvantaged, or a greater quantity of such counseling, particularly as middle-class affluence grows and makes it increasingly capable of absorbing more of the services of the trained professionals being produced. This is, then, a solution which does not solve anything except the problem of enhancing and protecting the traditional identities of the professions which have evolved, by a total preservation of the models on which their activities are based.

Until recently, this was the only solution offered by the helping professions, and as the problems of youth unemployment grew, it remained for the Federal Government to step in and take political action. The Department of Labor's Project CAUSE was one of the actions taken. In the summer of 1964, Project CAUSE recruited almost 1,900 people for intensive 8- to 10-week training courses conducted by 27 universities around the country, designed to prepare these recruits for subprofessional roles in Youth Opportunity Centers, conceived of as specialized branches of existing employment services.

Despite intensive intraprofessional discussions about subprofessional training in the recent past, the major thrusts have been away from terminal MA training in psychology, from a 1-year MA to a 2-year MA in counseling and guidance, and to the 2-year MSW as a minimum requirement in social work. Thus none of the helping professions have made room for subprofessional roles of the kind for which Project CAUSE recruits were to be trained. This led inevitably to ambiguity and uncertainty regarding the roles for which they were being trained. Nevertheless, the character of the training made it clear that the successful trainees, designated as Counselor Aides and Youth Advisors to discriminate them from the fully qualified professionals, would be some kind of a cross between social workers and vocational counselors, and would work under the supervision of qualified professionals. Thus the solution to the problem of the shortage of professional personnel who can deal with disadvantaged youth posed by Project CAUSE is one in which a new subprofession has been created by Federal action. The recruitment, selection, and training, as dedescribed by Kranz (1964), were intended to create a subprofession which would be particularly appropirate for the needs of disadvantaged youth. Project CAUSE, while the largest, is just one of many programs designed to produce subprofessionals, such as pilot projects in training retirees to supervise sheltered workshops, training of tutors for literacy training projects, psychiatric aide training, job retraining counselors, and many others.

The helping professions are thus faced with a fait accompli, and they are unprepared for it. In the absence of any other viable solution to the shortage of counselors for disadvantaged youth, the professions must either adapt to this new subprofession and include it within their structures, or leave the field of counseling with the disadvantaged to an entirely independent and potentially rivalrous subprofession.[1]

I believe that subprofessional training can be a most appropriate and effective solution to the problems described above, and that Project CAUSE presages a new and exciting day of development and revision in the helping professions which will add considerable vitality to them. It poses some chal-

---

[1]Many of the projects with vocational orientations which have excited the most interest, because of their inventiveness and willingness to break out of traditional molds — projects such as Mobilization for Youth, JOIN, JOBS, Haryouth-Act, the Los Angeles Youth Opportunity Board — are heavily staffed by social workers, with almost minimal participation by professionals in vocational counseling and guidance. These agencies make extensive use of personnel with varieties of academic and special training, but without specific professional identities (in the sense of having the usual degrees); they are "home grown" to meet the specific needs of the projects, have developed exceptional competence, and have made some of the most original contributions to the field.

lenges which, if met, will involve exciting growth and development in the helping professions which have had so much success in meeting other challenges in the past. The consequences of not meeting the challenges include the further restriction of psychology, counseling, and social work to more and more limited ranges of activities, to increasing concentration on minutia and esoterica, and to an early senescence.[2]

IMPLICATIONS FOR THE PROFESSIONS

I see the challenges posed by Project CAUSE as falling into five general areas:

1. How can the counseling process be subdivided into roles which can be filled by subprofessionals operating in a team under the direction of a qualified professional?

2. How are subprofessionals to be supervised, and how can students in professional training programs be trained for supervision?

3. If some part of subprofessional training is to take place in service agencies, how can the professional staffs of these agencies develop skills in training methods and techniques?

4. If much of the service work is done by subprofessionals, shall they be administered by a professional person who does not provide direct service to clients, or should agencies be administered only by those who are intimately and experientially familiar with the services to be provided by the agency?

5. Given the already overburdened staffs of university departments, where is subprofessional training to be located and by whom conducted?

I would like to make some brief comments about each of these challenges in the remainder of this paper.

1. Job Specifications and the Counseling Team

The most important challenge faced by the helping professions today is that of attempting to break down the professional role into subprofessional classifications or subroles, each of which may be filled by people with less than complete professional training and whose training is specific to the roles. I must admit that I cannot think of how this might be done; however, I have no doubt that it can be done. I can conceive of a team, operating under the direction of a professional, in which each member of the team bears a responsibility for one part of the total helping process. Thus one might be an outreach person whose job it is to make contact with the youths to be served. A second might specialize in dealing with other commuity agencies. A third might play a "big brother" role in such matters as teaching a young man how to fill out an application, or going with him to his first job interview. Still another member of the team might be the one who specializes in home visits, and yet another might be the test administrator. Intensive psychological interviewing can probably only be done by a professional person, but intake work

---

[2]In one leading graduate department, almost all the students in clinical psychology receive the bulk of their training in agencies serving moderately disturbed out-patient middle-class adults. Few of the students are interested in hospitalized people; none are interested in lower-class youth.

could well be done by a subprofessional, which in many agencies would be an improvement over the secretary-receptionist who fulfills this function.

Thus far, such a breakdown into subroles has not been developed, except in medicine, which makes use of practical nurses, nurses aides, nurses, laboratory technicians, and medical technologists, all of whom can be trained at less than the BA level. It was the absence of such a breakdown which produced the ambiguity and confusion concerning the job specifications for Counselor Aides and Youth Advisors in Project CAUSE, and may pose similar difficulties for the VISTA volunteers and the staffs of Job Corps Centers and Camps, Neighborhood Youth Corps, and other such eleemosynary programs. Without such job specifications which can fit the subprofessional into a structure for providing appropirate and high quality services, and which can make the training of the subprofessionals specific to their roles, the training programs must opt for a generalized introduction to the professional field, thus turning out junior professionals who know a little bit about everything the professional knows a lot about, and who therefore can be expected to do a little bit of everything the professional does. With the continued shortage of personnel, it is no wonder that agencies rapidly come to use their subprofessionals as if they were fully qualified, thus producing lowering of professional standards. But the fault for such a development lies not with the concept of subprofessional training, or with the Governmental agencies which are specifically responsible for taking action in the interests of the public welfare; the fault lies with the professions which, lacking a clear mechanism which requires responsiveness to the needs of the public, have done little to meet the needs, and have not prepared themselves to use and incorporate subprofessionals in their structures. It is no use to demand that subprofessionals trained by the Government must be supervised, and must not simply be ill-trained junior professionals, if the professions take no steps to develop valid subprofessional roles, and to train their members for using and supervising those who fill the roles adequately and appropriately. In brief, the lowering of standards which the professions fear so much as a consequence of subprofessional training is more likely to occur as a result of the professions' unpreparedness than it is a necessary consequence of the use of subprofessionals. And each restrictive step taken by the professions to protect and enhance standards increases the pressures which lead to Government action in creating subprofessionals who must then operate without clearly defined roles and without appropriate supervision, thus ultimately further threatening the professional standards. We recognize such self-defeating defensive reactions to perceived threat as neurotic in clients. The cure lies in making adaptations of the needs, skills, and goals of the professions to the realities; such an adaptation can be much more enhancing than blind resistance, defense, and denial.

There are some attractive advantages to a team model. The specialized training for each of the roles can probably be done in short intensive training programs which could probably recruit from indigenous personnel and from other groups such as the early retired, married women, etc., for whom long-term academic work is either inappropriate, unavailable, or unwanted. Thus the helping professions can tap a much larger pool of potential workers who can be trained fairly rapidly and with much less expense than is required for full professionals. The fully qualified professional can probably lead up two or more such teams, since he would be spending much less time in activities which can be handled by the subprofessionals. Thus each professional person could service a greater number of clients, effecting a needed economy in the use of scarce professional resources.

For example, the problems of the Selective Service Rehabilitant Program, described above, indicate that counseling with disadvantaged youth requires that steps be taken actively to contact clients, rather than waiting for the clients to come to the agency. Counseling personnel cannot sit in an office and wait; they must go out to where the clients are. Further, counseling with such clients poses some additional problems which require that counseling personnel work directly in the living environment of the clients. Relatively nonverbal, nonexpressive, and educationally disadvantaged clients, unlike the middle-class patients in psychotherapy which forms the model for counseling services, cannot reproduce verbally within an interview all of the factors and events which exist in their life spaces. Nor can they carry back to their home environments the processes and events which took place during the interviewing and counseling and translate them into actions in their homes and neighborhoods by converting the verbal dialogue into appropriate specific actions. In dealing with this population, the professional must go to the client's home and talk to him there; he must meet him at work; he must hold family conferences in the client's home; he may have to meet with the client and his peers in the neighborhood gathering places. He may have to visit the client's school, his employer, the police, and other social agencies. Such visits outside the agency office are essential, but they are also incredibly costly of time and money. Considering the present and future shortage of fully qualified professionals, I do not see how they can justify the time and money which will be eaten up in city traffic jams, in public transportation systems; a counselor with a 2-year master's degree who spends 2 or more hours a day between here and there is far too expensive. Out-of-office work may be essential, but much of it can be done by subprofessionals who may even be stationed in the communities and neighborhoods being served.

A second major advantage of the helping team is that it may include workers from the same milieu as the clients served by the team, and these workers could well be much more successful than the fully qualified professional in making contact with potential clients, in motivating them, and in interpreting the agency to the client. Where they have been well trained and well supervised, indigenous leaders have made important contributions which cannot be made by anyone else. There are dimensions of expression, voice inflection, gesture, body language, which are almost instantly recognizable as signs of class and ethnic origin. The indigenous leader can communicate instantly to the suspicious and distrustful client, avoiding *noblesse oblige,* in a way that many middle-class professionals cannot do when dealing with disaffected, hostile, anomic youths who see the middle-class agency worker as part of the system against which he is fighting. In the long run, disparities between the class castes of counselor and client might make no difference in the outcome of the counseling, if the long run is long enough and the counseling approaches psychotherapy in its depth and intensiveness. But the kind of work which will be most common in the various phases of the Anti-Poverty Program is not likely to use the long run, and, in brief contacts, first impressions can be all important in determining whether the client will be relaxed and receptive, or on his guard and defensive. Indigenous personnel who "speak the client's language" can form an extremely effective bridge between the milieu of agency; they can make important contributions to the counseling team in contacting the clients to be served, in maintaining them through their agency contacts, and may be particularly effective in follow-up work with the clients in their home, community, and on the job. A client is more likely to be able to report continuing difficulties, after his counseling contacts, to an indigenous worker, than he is to the professional interviewer toward whom the ethic of mutual cooperation and courtesy requires that he affirm the success of the counseling and deny continued problems.

2. Supervision

If we are going into subprofessional training, perhaps using a team concept such as that suggested above, then the second challenge to the helping professions involves training for supervision. In the current model of counseling, the worker "on the line" requires no skills in supervision, since there is no one present to supervise. In graduate training programs it is generally assumed that as the recent graduate acquires more and more experience, he will begin to move up in the organizational hierarchy. He will gradually take on supervisory responsibilities and will develop his skills in supervision by emulating those who supervise him. Even with the current model of counseling, this assumption is false. Many graduates find that their very first job is that of head of an agency or a service. They are immediately expected to supervise, with no prior training in supervision. Typically, they fall back on the kinds of supervision they experienced as graduate students. But this kind of supervision is specifically appropriate to highly verbal, academic, intelligent, professionally trained personnel. It is not appropriate for subprofessionals. But if a counseling team is going to work effectively, much will depend on the quality and competence of the supervision it receives, supervision which is designed for subprofessional roles. Recognition of this important function in professional training is long overdue, and the renewed recognition of the importance of supervision which was stimulated by Project CAUSE and similar programs may be listed as among the achievements of these programs. It is of no use for the professions to seek guarantees that subprofessionals will be given adequate supervision if the professions do not produce people who are trained to provide it.

3. Training Skills

A third challenge posed by subprofessional training is concerned with training methods. While subprofessionals might be trained for varying periods of time in academic settings, it seems likely that such training will serve best as a prologue or introduction to the professional field, while the major portion of the skill training for the specific roles to be filled by the subprofessionals can best be handled by representative agencies in which the subprofessionals will be employed. The local community agency is likely to be the best place in which to train indigenous leaders, but the task of providing such in-house training for subprofessionals is a large one, and is one for which most agencies are ill equipped. When the notion of using indigenous personnel was first developed in the lower East Side of New York, the very first problem which had to be faced was that of providing suitable training within the agency, and with the only available models of training being those derived from academic education, the burden for innovation and creativity fell on the training agencies. When asked to do training, many agencies automatically fall back on the patterns established by their own professional training, and so they institute workshops, lectures, and seminars. Such procedures, as imitations of university education, can just as well be done at a university which is experienced with them. They fail to capitalize on the distinctive contributions which can be made by an operating social agency. It is the agency's work setting which must be involved if the agency is to do the kind of training for which it is best suited.

Training of residents and interns has been a standard part of the tasks of many agencies for years. However, there is a certain amount of arrogance implied by the fact that despite this traditional role, little or no training in methods of education is given to the students in the profession who man these training agencies. Is our level of insight into human behavior so complete and deep that we have nothing to learn from the specific studies and skills of educators? Thus I suggest that increased demand for agencies to do role-specific training implies a recognition of training functions as part of the role of a fully qualified professional person. This recognition further implies the building into professional training of courses in training methods and procedures.

4. Who Shall Administer?

The picture which emerges from the above discussion is that of a fully qualified professional person more highly trained in supervision and in training methods than in the past; he heads a team or teams of subprofessionals, trains people for the team, and supervises the activities of the team members. In brief, the professional person functions as an administrator. But where is he to learn agency administration? If he is a social worker, he may have learned it in the course of his graduate training. If he is a vocational counselor or a clinical psychologist, he will have learned it only by imitation of university professors who operate captive agencies which function very differently from those serving the disadvantaged poor. This indicates still another implication of subprofessional training.

I think it worth noting that there are some psychological factors which impinge on supervision and administration in the helping professions. It seems to me as if people in the helping professions as a group are reluctant to supervise and administer. They seem to dislike being in superior-subordinate relationships. This may be connected with the antiauthoritarianism which is so characteristic of those in the helping professions, or it may come from a variety of other sources about which one could speculate. The point is simply that there does seem to be an avoidance or reluctance, which must be overcome if supervision and administration are to be institutionalized as part of the professional's function and as elements in his training.

One problem in connection with administration should be mentioned. The age-old question involved here is of whether an agency ought to be run by people specifically trained in supervision, or whether it should be run by professionals who are completely experienced in the function being administered. If the fully qualified member of the team devotes himself to administration, supervision, and training, there is the danger that he will become so far removed from the realities of actual work with the clients as performed by the subprofessionals that his supervision and administration may become unrealistic. This problem has not been solved in the schools, in the universities, in business, or in Government; it is unlikely to find its completely adequate solution in the helping professions. Nevertheless, it is a problem which needs to be recognized, and it is part of the challenge posed by the broadening of counseling to include subprofessionals.

5. Who Shall Train?

The last problem I would like to discuss here concerns the locus of subprofessional recruitment and training. In Project CAUSE, the training was located in universities and was denominated by academic instruction. As indicated earlier, the success of such instruction rests heavily on the academic skills and the verbal-conceptual orientation of the trainees. It was also suggested earlier that these skills may be different from those which are required for successful performance in subprofessional roles. One is not likely to find many indigenous leaders, for example, who will be able to fit themselves into the academic mold even for brief, intensive training. Furthermore, the very concept of an indigenous leader is destroyed when one thinks of sending such a person to a university distant from his neighborhood, and away from his milieu. On the other hand, there are no other institutions which can marshal the intellectual and professional resources for providing such training. It is possible that local community colleges and junior colleges may be able to play a role in subprofessional training, especially if they are able to make use of personnel from higher institutions and community agencies.

Such training will demand an interdisciplinary approach, if it is specifically designed for workers with the disadvantaged. Skill and technique instruction will have to come from experienced clinicians, workers, and/or counselors, but the limitations in their experience to middle-class populations will require supplementation from sociologists, economists, criminologists, housing authorities, community action specialists, jurists, and others who have devoted their attentions to problems of the poor. It was the experience of many of the universities which participated in Project CAUSE training that contact with these other fields proved to be a source of renewed excitement and stimulation to the members of the counseling and guidance departments. Continued interaction of this sort can do much to invigorate counseling and guidance both as a profession and as a field of scholarship.

To capitulate: There are overwhelming social needs requiring increased professional attention. There is a shortage of professional personnel, and the models which underlie the structures of the professions as presently constituted are inappropriate for meeting the social needs. One solution to these problems lies in subprofessional training, to implement a team concept which may provide services more appropriate to the population needing them and which can compensate for the shortage of fully qualified professionals. The establishment of subprofessional training requires attention to ways in which helping work can be subdivided into subprofessional roles which are effective and economical, the development of techniques for supervision, the training of professionals in supervision, attention to methods of in-service training and the development of training skills in professional personnel, the use of the fully qualified professional person as an administrator of services, and attention to the location and institutionalization of subprofessional training. The helping professions must attend to these problems if they are to remain responsive to the changing nature of the social needs, and if they are to continue to make the kind of contributions to society for which they are the most appropriate social institutions currently available. Failure to meet these challenges through a rigid clinging to methods no longer appropriate to the needs could render these professions so inappropriate that new ones may have to arise to fill the gap.

PROFESSIONAL   STANDARDS   AND   RESISTANCE   TO   CHANGE

I would like to make a final comment about professional standards. As I see it, the development of subprofessional roles involves both a lowering and a raising of traditional standards. The establishment of specific subprofessional roles affords an economy of training which many will see as a lowering of professional standards (Odgers, 1964). On the other hand, the inclusion of these roles within the professional structures, as suggested above, requires that the fully qualified professional develop new and more advanced skills than those which are currently included in his repertoire. In this sense, we have a call for higher standards. There are those who criticize Project CAUSE and other similar programs as an attack on professional standards. I believe this to be a short-sighted view which implies a refusal on the part of the professions to adapt to the current needs, with the standards-enhancing implication of such an adaptation. The appeal to standards is traditionally the socially accepted defense against disturbance of the established status quo. Segregation in the neighborhoods has been defended by reference to standards of neighborhood care and upkeep; the exclusiveness and hegemony of medieval guilds was defended by reference to craftsmanship standards; the segregation of school children has similarly been justified. I see little use for high and restrictive standards for professional treatment if, because of those standards, treatment is completely denied to those needing it. And the data clearly indicate that effective and appropriate treatment is being denied to the disadvantaged youth of today. While such denial may not be willful or intended, its reality testifies that opposition to an expansion of appropriate services in the service of a defense of standards is in the interests of maintenance of the Establishment rather than in the interests of those needing help.

REFERENCES

Festinger, L. *When prophecy fails.* Minneapolis: Univer. Minnesota Press, 1956.
Kranz, H. A crash program to aid disadvantaged youth. *Guidepost,* 1964, 6, 3-6.
Linton, R., & Kardiner, A. The change from dry to wet rice cultivation in Tanala-Betsileo. In G. E. Swanson, T. M. Newcomb, & E. L. Hartley (Eds.), *Readings in social psychology.* New York: Holt, 1952. Pp. 222-230.
Odgers, J. Cause for concern. *Counselor Education and Supervision,* 1964, 6, 17-20.

(8)

GUIDING THE EDUCATIONALLY DISADVANTAGED

Martin Haberman
University of Wisconsin—Milwaukee

By using data from the 1960 decennial census, one can calculate the dropout rate for the United States as a whole; these data show that approximately 60 percent of twenty-year old youths were high school graduates in 1960, and therefore the dropout rate for the country was 40 percent before 1960.[1] But those who argue that the dropout is a major national educational problem are neglecting the question of absolute numbers; that is, although the high school population expanded by 500 percent between 1920 and 1960 and will probably increase by another 400 percent between 1960 and 1975, the number of high school dropouts has remained relatively constant. From 1900 to 1930 there were about 500 thousand dropouts annually; from 1930 to 1950 this number increased to 600 thousand; and since 1950 there have been about 650 thousand dropouts annually.[2] Whereas the large number of former dropouts could be absorbed by an economy in need of unskilled labor, the present group are just added to the ranks of the unemployed. Whether the absolute number of dropouts has actually increased therefore is a less important concern than what kind of life opportunities await those unprepared for work in a technical society.

The popular conclusion that if there were enough guidance counselors to work with these youngsters then the dropout problem could be ameliorated is not borne out by the research evidence. A six-year study has found that individual counseling of potentially delinquent high school girls is ineffective in improving their school behavior or in reducing the number of dropouts.[3] The investigators concluded that persons suffering from poverty, discrimination or a disorganized family life could not be expected to respond to individual therapy with any major character change.

The study, involving 400 fourteen-year-old high school girls who entered a Manhattan central vocational high school eight years ago, is the first long term experimental study of its kind to be made. The girls were identified as potentially delinquent on the basis of their junior high school records and divided into two groups of 200 each. One group received individual attention and group therapy while the control group received no special attention. The experimental group included 54 percent Negroes and 18 percent Puerto Ricans.

An original article for this book.

[1] R. J. Havighurst. *The Public Schools of Chicago.* The Board of Education of the City of Chicago. Chicago, 1964. p. 274.

[2] R. A. Dentler. "Dropouts, Automation and the Cities." A paper delivered to Third Work Conference on Curriculum and Teaching in Depressed Urban Areas. Teachers College, Columbia University. June 22-July 3, 1964.

[3] E. F. Borgatta, H. J. Meyer and W. C. Jones. Interim Report of a Study sponsored by the Russell Sage Foundation and presented to the Eastern Regional Conference of the Child Welfare League of America. (Reported by the New York Times News Service, Sunday, February 21, 1965.)

At the completion of the study it was found that the same number of girls in each group graduated from high school and that there were no statistical differences in their grades, truancy, tardiness, school service, pregnancy or performance of psychological tests. Although many of the girls who received therapy felt they had been helped in their general attitudes, there was no real effect on any form of their measurable behavior. The researchers recommend that an attack on changing the whole community would be more effective than counseling which attempts to solve individual emotional problems.

But the number of physical dropouts is easy to calculate in comparison to the number of intellectual and emotional dropouts. How many of the 60 percent who complete high school by age twenty are never really affected in any important ways by the process of schooling? How many youngsters merely live through their school experiences without any real intellectual and emotional involvement? The development of more effective guidance principles will invariably improve the services offered to emotional dropouts who continue to attend, as well as those who remove themselves physically.

The discussion which follows will attempt to (1) describe the approaches used to define the disadvantaged; (2) suggest the characteristics of the disadvantaged which are most relevant to the process of schooling; (3) draw implications from these characteristics relevant to the work of the school guidance counselor; and (4) recommend fruitful areas of future study and development.

WHO ARE THE EDUCATIONALLY DISADVANTAGED?

Researchers and writers define the disadvantaged using a variety of conceptual schemes. Sociologists concerned with group behavior and interaction tend to use concepts related to the process of alienation. The means by which selected individuals become detached from their primary groups and the processes by which subgroups become disaffected and move into conflict with the majority group are a major emphasis of those who study alienation. Psychologists and others whose major unit of study is the individual rather than the group are more likely to utilize the concept of dependency than alienation in delimiting the disadvantaged. Educators, forced to focus on symptoms rather than causes, will more likely use a term like "nonachieving."

But the matter of delimiting the disadvantaged has become more complex than merely designating those who are alienated, dependent and nonachieving as disadvantaged. Figure 1 is a brief attempt to indicate how various realms of knowledge are led to concentrate on different human processes, analyze different orders of behavior and arrive at different terminology of symptoms by which to identify the disadvantaged.

The one generalization that can be made about all of these approaches is that the disadvantaged are conceived of as individuals who lack, miss or never develop attributes and characteristics considered to be necessary and positive. Very few social scientists stress the positive qualities and strengths among those designated as culturally deprived, since to recognize strengths among the disadvantaged would require rejecting many of the norms which structure middle-class society. Frank Riessman is an outstanding spokesman for those who, seeing more personal congruence in the lives of lower-class individuals than among members of the middle-class, stress the term culturally different rather than culturally deprived.[4]

In response to the naive term "cultural deprivation" which was popular a few years ago, scholars raise the simple objection that no one can lack culture any more than he can lack personality and that what was really needed was a specification of cultural differences rather than a definition of deprivation. It was not long, however, before the question was raised, "Different from whom?" and the term difference took on a value connotation which clearly implied that those who were different were missing elements of culture they should have. In most conceptualizations, whether they are termed deprivations or differences, it is crucial to recognize three facts: (1) that some individual with a particular frame of reference is deciding who is deprived; (2) that with some notable exceptions these definitions will focus on elements of personality or culture which are considered to be underdeveloped or missing; and (3) that there is an assumption that these gaps or inadequacies *should* be made up or rectified.

But who will decide when a cultural difference is no longer a disadvantage? What criteria will be used to make this determination? Does the middle class furnish so adequate a milieu for the development of individual potential that non-middle-class views must be eliminated?

There is no way to resolve the issue of whether the middle-class or the lower-class person is more mentally healthy, more congruent in his responses to life, or more satisfied in meeting his basic needs. The lives of members of the lower class are generally more open to inspection than the lives of middle-class individuals. Welfare workers, social workers, doctors, nurses, building inspectors, landloards, school representatives, policemen and even salesmen gain entry into the homes of poor people more frequently than they visit middle-class individuals' homes. Lower-class homes are more open to inspection and as a result social scientists have a greater amount of data about the poor and their life styles than they have about others. Middle-class problems frequently tend to be smoothed over and confined to the immediate family and the physical limits of the home. This basic difference in available data is one reason that individuals of various class groups cannot be adequately compared.

Although lower-class life is more public and middle-class life more private, the lower-class person is no longer a complete outsider to the affluent society. Through mass media — particularly television — he is vulnerable to all the lures and attractions of the good life. Whereas he formerly was ignorant of a middle-class orientation, he must now suffer the dilemma of having his expectations raised while he is kept from acquiring the means for realizing them. Riessman may be right about the strengths in the lives of lower-class individuals which are overlooked in designating them as deprived or disadvantaged. At the same time conditions of poverty, ignorance and disease in a society of plenty must be regarded as absolute disadvantages. In response to a psychologist's presentation which emphasized the more emotionally stable life led by members of the lower-classes in comparison to the striving and straining of middle-class persons, a well-known educator was heard to remark,

---

[4]F. Riessman. *The Culturally Deprived Child.* New York: Harpers, 1962.

Discipline	Major Area of Study	Examples of Behaviors and Responses Analyzed	Terminology
Linguistics[1]	Communication	–The process of learning to speak –Verbal interaction with mother –Speech patterns –Responses and interpretations to language –Linguistic interactions	1. Nonverbal 2. Illiterate 3. Nonfunctional reader 4. Inarticulate 5. Uncommunicative
Psychology[2]	Perception	–Self-concept –Identification with significant others –Motivation –Habits, responses, behavior patterns –Stages of conceptual development	1. Unmotivated 2. Unaspiring 3. Experience-poor 4. Perceptually-blocked 5. Dependency-prone
Sociology[3]	Values	–Child-rearing practices –Ethnic influences in socialization process –Status, role in early family life –Race, religion, class influences on child's values –Migration	1. In-migrant 2. Mobile 3. Lower class member 4. Member of minority ethnic groups 5. Alienated
Psychiatry[4]	Needs and Drives	–Sexual role definitions –Masculine-feminine learning –Corporal punishment –The role of love in the home –Physiological need satisfaction	1. Prone to seek out immediate gratification 2. Physically oriented 3. Lacking successful adult models 4. Unloved 5. Unattended
Education[5]	Knowledge	–Interest in school –Ability to learn school behaviors –Achievement –I.Q. –Academic motivation	1. Educationally disadvantaged 2. Remedial reader 3. Underachiever 4. Hard-to-reach 5. Difficult-to-serve 6. Disaffected
Economics[6]	Resources	–Consumption –Distribution –Production –Money and banking –Employment	1. Underdeveloped 2. Unskilled 3. Nonproductive 4. Unemployed 5. Consumer

Figure 1

Conceptual Schemes for Studying the Nature of Culturally Different Children and Youth

Social Work[7]	Human Welfare	-Family breakdown -Delinquency -Individual adjustment to social conditions -Providing for basic human needs	1. Antisocial 2. Maladjusted 3. Neglected 4. Unprovided for 5. Poor

[1]B. Bernstein. "Some Sociological Determinants of Perception: An Inquiry into Sub-Cultural Differences." The British Journal of Sociology. June, 1958.

[2]M. Deutsch. "The Disadvantaged Child and the Learning Process." An unpublished paper. New York Medical College, July, 1962.

[3]A. Davis and R. J. Havighurst. "Social Class and Color Differences in Child Rearing." American Sociological Review, April, 1953.

[4]D. R. Miller and G. E. Swanson. Inner Conflict and Defense. New York, 1960.

[5]H. H. Davidson, (et al.). "Characteristics of Successful School Achievers from a Severely Deprived Environment." Unpublished Report. Department of Education, The City University of New York. October, 1962.

[6]O. Hamlin. The Uprooted, Boston: Little, Brown and Co., 1951.

—————, The Newcomers: Negroes and Puerto Ricans in Changing Metropolis. Garden City, New York, 1962.

[7]S. and E. Glueck. Family Environment and Delinquency. Boston: Houghton Mifflin Co., 1962.

Figure 1 (continued)

"Anytime you want to give up your place in the middle class, just say so. I know a couple of people who would be happy to take your place."

It is no longer useful for educators to pursue the academic discussions related to terminology alone. It is necessary only to admit that because of the nature of the *forces* controlling the schools, there are large populations of youngsters who are not being offered equal opportunity to develop their potentialities. The term educationally disadvantaged is used not only to indicate lacks or failures in the personalities or backgrounds of the youngsters, but also to recognize that the perceptions of the middle-class persons who run our schools are a self-fulfilling prophecy: those whom they perceive as educationally disadvantaged become so.

Contrary to popular notions, lower-class people place a high value on education, but lack the confidence and know-how to realize their goal.[5] Even the process of schooling — which is a negative experience for many of them — still does not undermine their belief in the value of education.

Recent research is placing more and more emphasis on the actual learning disadvantages suffered by the non-middle-class children because of differences in their home environments. Benjamin Bloom lists four specific factors which handicap children in a deprived environment compared with what he calls children in an "abundant environment."[6]

1. Poor speech habits and language patterns in the home discourage language development and restrict the number and variety of words which

[5]F. Riessman. "Workers' Attitudes Towards Participation and Leadership." Unpublished Ph.D. dissertation, Columbia University, 1955.

[6]B. S. Bloom. *Stability and Change in Human Characteristics*, (New York: John Wiley and Sons, Inc. 1964), p. 77.

the child recognizes; this contributes to lower scores on I.Q. tests and lower school achievement, especially in reading.

2. Families have less time, opportunity, or know-how to take their children on expeditions to the zoo, museums, stores, or different neighborhoods; the children also have fewer indirect experiences with the world around them through books, pictures, films, etc. Such experiences not only increase verbal facility but help in making distinctions, comparing objects, ideas, etc. — all important not only for I.Q. tests but for learning itself.

3. Children in these disadvantaged homes have fewer opportunities for solving problems or for thinking about a variety of issues, as compared with children in more abundant environments. The former's parents do not have the habit of encouraging children to ask questions or to think things out for themselves.

4. There is less interaction between adults and children. Discipline tends to be authoritarian and the "good" child is quiet and out of the way. This, too, limits the background of experience and language which the child brings to school.

The term "disadvantaged" is useful to educators because it can be used to designate the populations of youngsters who are not making the desired responses to the process of schooling. Rather than seeking out the conceptualization of various social scientists trying to define deprivation or cultural differences, educators can begin by focusing on the real problem presented by the large number of physical and emotional dropouts who do not achieve according to their capabilities. From this orientation of underachievement, the condition of educational disadvantagement can be considered as being fed by four basic sources: (1) the innate disabilities which can prevent an individual from achieving in school situations; (2) the preschool family conditions which would socialize a youngster in such a manner that he is not predisposed to realize his potentialities in subsequent school situations; (3) the process of schooling itself (particularly the teachers under whose aegis the youngster is placed) which may be of a debilitating rather than an enhancing nature; and (4) the self-concept or educational aspirations which a youngster develops by the later stages of his elementary school experience that may have a negative or deprecating effect.[7]

These four kinds of elements must be viewed as interrelated; for example, a child's preschool and family life experiences can affect the development of his innate abilities, and the quality of his school experiences will markedly influence the self-concept and aspirations which he develops.

Through consideration of the factors of inheritance, the conditions of preschool family living, early school experiences and the self-concept, youngsters can be accurately designated as educationally disadvantaged; that is, they will not experience equal educational opportunities in our schools as these institutions are presently constituted. Before drawing implications for the role of the guidance worker, it would be useful to consider the behavioral characteristics of youngsters who are educationally disadvantaged.

---

[7]R. J. Havighurst. *op. cit.* p. 33.

CHARACTERISTICS OF THE EDUCATIONALLY DISADVANTGED

In order to provide clues that may help to explain differences in school performance, one group of researchers conducted a pilot study of disadvantaged pupils in a New York City elementary school. In comparing good achievers, these researchers came up with the following hypotheses:[8]

1. Good achievers are more controlled, cautious and constructed than poor achievers.
2. Good achievers exhibit a greater "need to know" and more of them show a "need for achievement"; they are also more work oriented and less concerned with immediate gratification than poor achievers.
3. Good achievers have a more positive attitude toward authority figures than poor achievers and see the world as less threatening.
4. Good achievers are more accepting of adult standards and expectations than poor achievers.
5. Good achievers have a more positive self-image and greater self-confidence.
6. Good achievers are less anxious and fearful than poor achievers.
7. Good achievers show greater ability to view themselves and the world about them objectively, accurately and critically.
8. Good achievers are superior to poor achievers in general verbal behavior; they do not excel, however, in divergent production.
9. Good achievers are superior to poor achievers in memory and attention.
10. Good achievers show better analyzing, organizing, elaborating and generalizing abilities than poor achievers.

There did not seem to be any consistent differences between good and poor achievers with respect to such factors as willingness to cooperate and eagerness to do well. From the findings of this study, the hypothetical good achiever from an underprivileged environment emerges as:

. . . . . a child who is relatively controlled and cautious, often stereotyped and constricted, but who still retains a degree of originality and creativity. He seems more willing than his less successful classmates to conform to adult demands, has a more positive view of authority figures and greater self-confidence. In cognitive functioning he excels chiefly in tasks requiring memory, attention and verbal abilities. He is also superior in analytical and organizational abilities and generally in processes that require convergent thinking.

In contrast, the composite picture of the poor achiever is that of a child burdened by anxiety, fearful of the world and authority figures and lacking in self-confidence. He is more apt to be impulsive and labile with relatively poor controlling mechanisms. His defenses against anxiety and feelings of inadequacy may be expressed in excessive talking and in uncritically favorable surface attitudes toward self and others. Nevertheless the poor achiever still seems to have sufficient potential for adaptive behavior which the school could build upon. His cognitive activities are often quite similar in content

[8]H. H. Davidson, J. W. Greenberg, J. M. Garver. "Characteristics of Successful School Achievers from a Severely Deprived Environment." School of Education, The City University of New York, Mimeograph, October, 1962. (Reported at the American Educational Research Association, Chicago, February, 1963.)

approach and process to those of a good achiever and in fact, he demonstrates greater facility in divergent production. Many of his reactions give evidence of creative capacity which might be directed and controlled. From this behavior in the testing situations and in tasks requiring social comprehension, the poor achiever seems to possess substantial understanding of the world around him although he seems less able to act upon this understanding than the good achiever.

It must be remembered in considering results like these that the "good achievers" would be just average in terms of national norms. Yet it seems clear that disadvantaged youngsters who are most successful are most like middle-class youngsters.

There are indications from recent research that the disadvantaged youngster needs a structured classroom environment and much help in order to learn to control his impulses and to cope with a freer learning situation.[9] In addition, he seems to need help in developing the cognitive bases for improving his memory and attention levels, as well as his listening, speaking and verbal abilities. In response to the frequently cited need to raise self-confidence and expectations, it must be emphasized that continued success is not enough; youngsters don't need easy success but do need learning activities that stimulate and challenge them. Classrooms and teaching must be deliberately organized to provide initial and continued success in worthwhile and challenging activities.

Thus far there has been a deliberate attempt to avoid a discussion of the social class and ethnic differences between lower-class and middle-class individuals and to focus on the differences which appear in the process of schooling. As educators it is important that we develop means for dealing with factors which block learning and do not become embroiled in the fruitless debate over lower-class characteristics vis-à-vis middle-class characteristics. It may very well be that in spite of the monumental accumulation of sociological literature on the subject of social class differences, such differences are merely after-the-fact descriptions and not the designation of characteristics or values which would allow us to predict how an individual will behave in subsequent situations. Perhaps the catalog of differences which have been attributed to social class and ethnic differences are merely the differences in response to different life situations, and changes in the conditions of existence will lead to changes in behavior which we have heretofore regarded as the reflection of deep-seated, permanent value systems. The implication of this assumption that changing conditions will change behavior offers educators the basis for believing that changes in curriculum teachers, procedures and materials will effect changes among the disadvantaged. But what characteristics of the disadvantaged should guidance workers seek to change? And what can they do to effect these changes?

[9]J. H. Jackson. "The Relationship Between Psychological Climate and the Quality of Learning Outcomes Among Lower Status Pupils." Unpublished Ph.D. thesis. University of Chicago, 1957.

THE GUIDANCE FUNCTION IN SCHOOLS SERVING
THE EDUCATIONALLY DISADVANTAGED

The nature of a youngster's inheritance and his early family experiences are the two most critical factors for predicting the degree of his educational disadvantages. The power of environmental factors to compensate for inherited deficiencies is greatest in the early years. Bloom summarizes the research which indicates the degree to which early family life can compensate for inheritance and states:

> A conservative estimate of the effect of extreme environments on intelligence is about 20 I.Q. points. This could mean the difference between a life in an institution for the feeble-minded or a productive life in society. It could mean the difference between a professional career and an occupation which is at the semi-skilled or unskilled level. . . . . The implications for public education and social policy are fairly clear. Where significantly lower intelligence can be attributed to the effects of environmental deprivations, steps must be taken to ameliorate these conditions as early in the individual's development as education and other social forces can be utilized.[10]

It is necessary to recognize, therefore, that the most powerful factors for determining those who will be educationally disadvantaged are in large measure beyond the aegis of the school and the guidance counselor. Somewhat less powerful but nevertheless important contributing factors for determining who will be disadvantaged are events which occur in later stages of childhood; the nature of school experiences and the self-image and aspirations which these experiences engender have the most far-reaching influence. The guidance worker has some possibility for professional service in these areas but even here his influence is often indirect and minimal in comparison to the impact of the teachers, the curriculum and the total school setting.

The guidance counselor faced with the challenge of service to a disadvantaged population can maximize his effectiveness by utilizing principles which take account of the nature of the youngsters and the nature of the process of schooling, that is, operational principles which have as their goal the equalization of educational opportunities and the unblocking of human potentialities. Four principles which can give such direction relate to the need for affecting parents and community wherever possible, directing choices for those who lack the experiences on which to make them, building aspirations and counseling with teachers.

1. *Effective school guidance programs for the disadvantaged include goals of parent education and community change.* As children move from elementary to secondary schools, contact with parents is usually diminished. Unfortunately the number of important educational choices which must be made increase as a youngster advances. In essence, we have a system which fosters greatest parental involvement at a time when their advice about educational choices is least useful.

Civil rights groups, community associations, religious organizations and special governmental crash programs are all attempting to influence parents

---

[10]B. Bloom. *op. cit.,* p. 89.

and the community regarding the equalization of educational opportunities. This is particularly true in large urban areas. It is important that professional guidance people also reach parents. While parental attitudes are a powerful influence on their children's choice of program, the currently aroused community interest in educational programs will be an even greater pressure on schools in the future.

One critical example of the need for guidance programs in schools serving the disadvantaged to affect change in parents and community attitudes is in the area of school integration. Many well-meaning but uninformed civil rights and community leaders are creating the impression that all efforts at compensatory education and guidance are attempts to prevent integration or preserve inequities. In such situations any effort to give added services or courses — even on a temporary basis — is rejected. Equal educational opportunity becomes defined as the *same* educational opportunity. It is the role of guidance workers serving the disadvantaged youngsters to help them, their parents and the community understand that while good education has the same long-term purposes for all, there are different means for reaching them. In a slum high school where youngsters may be an average of two years behind in reading and study skills and where there is a poor general science program, it is just as dangerous for a local civil rights leader to demand an advanced placement physics class as it is for the school principal to dismiss such a demand as ridiculous. By procedures of special help, special materials and special effort such a goal may be realized. But this means treating some youngsters differently for temporary periods. It is a major responsibility of all guidance workers to help teachers, youngsters, parents and the community to understand that truly equal educational opportunity is individualized and that there is a significant educational distinction between differentiation of instruction based on need and that on planned segregation.

In addition to seeking to inform and work directly with parents, the guidance program can be most effective by working indirectly through teachers, principals, nurses, school secretaries, janitors, attendance officers and the other personnel with whom parents come into contact. As experts in the way people relate to one another, the guidance counselors in schools serving the educationally disadvantaged should have time built into their work loads which will enable them to help to improve any contacts parents have with school personnel. Disadvantaged parents may understandably regard any person employed by the school as representative of the "school's opinion." Since it is well known that a callous school secretary or a bigoted custodian can be detrimental to school-community relations and the educational program, there should be planned, organized effort by guidance personnel to work with all those who are part of the school setting.

A third way of affecting parents and community is to serve as a clearing house for information which can upgrade the parents themselves. There must be better coordination and greater effectiveness in informing parents of opportunities related to literacy programs, adult education, vocational training, consumer education and health services. Improving these efforts will not only upgrade the quality of parental influence on youngsters now in school but may make parents better models for their preschool youngsters on whom their influences are currently even greater.

This description of responsibilities of guidance personnel is not an attempt to make them individually responsible for affecting marked changes in parents and communities. It is instead a recognition that parents are the greatest environmental determinant of who will be educationally disadvantaged and that early, minimal efforts with parents will have an intense and pervasive effect on the youngsters.

2. *Disadvantaged children and youth should be directed to make decisions which will give them the widest choices in future.* The outstanding characteristics of the American educational system are threefold: it is universal, diverse and lifelong. The system intends that everyone have the opportunity to develop in the direction of his abilities and interests and that his opportunity for extended and adult education always be kept open. These basic beliefs should guide school counselors into helping youngsters make choices which will not channel them into specializations at an early age. The longer youngsters can be kept in general studies the greater the possibility for mature choice-making on their part. This means that rather than taking a nondirective or laissez-faire role the guidance counselor serving disadvantaged youngsters must often be quite directive. His experience enables him to predict that if he can keep a youngster from limiting himself to some narrow specialization too early the youngster's future choices will be broader.

It is comomn to hear the rationalization that the need for a job and skills which are marketable should take precedence over programs of general studies; "If he had a job and some pocket money, he wouldn't have any problem" But the purposes of American education are not to "get a job and stay out of jail" — even for the disadvantaged. The real goals involve participation as a citizen and the individual fulfillment which can come only through participation in a wide sampling of the fields of human knowledge and endeavor.

Narrow specialization begun too early inevitably fails youngsters in two basic ways: it does not provide the general education required by most postsecondary education programs nor does it develop the level of skills needed for securing technical employment. Such specializations are effective preparation for personal disaster.

It is unfortunate for the guidance counselor serving a disadvantaged population if his preparation has led him to believe that nondirective methods are always "good" and directive ones always "bad," since he must not hesitate to authoritatively make those decisions which he knows will provide youngsters with the greatest number of alternative courses of action at some future time.

3. *The major goal of counseling disadvantaged children and youth is the development of a positive self-image and high educational and life aspirations.* Poverty, parental neglect and related social conditions impose certain stresses on youngsters which frequently cause negative perceptions of self. Unfortunately, effective school learning can take place only if children view themselves as important and valuable people. The normal universal need of all children for feelings of self-esteem becomes accentuated in disadvantaged youngsters who more frequently face unsuccessful experiences in the process of schooling. Beginning with experiential handicaps, the school program itself is often the cause of developing strong negative self-images among disadvantaged populations. Some experts place the age at which these negative

self-perceptions are conceptualized at age 10.[11] It is very likely, however, that the process of schooling has reinforced enough unsuccessful attempts at learning so many youngsters are educationally disadvantaged by age 7. It is often possible to predict who will drop out or be generally unsuccessful in subsequent school situations by the completion of third grade. We have this ability to predict not because youngsters will not change but because most school situations do not adapt to fit the students; more frequently students are expected to adjust to rigid, unchanging conditions of mass education.

Disadvantaged youngsters often overcompensate for these feelings of inadequacy by assuming superficially high aspirations. It is not uncommon to hear nonreaders in eighth and ninth grade respond to questions regarding their future occupational goals with choices such as "brain surgeon," "astronaut," or "banker." It is not the role of guidance counselors to discourage even apparently unrealistic aspirations. This recommendation is in direct conflict with more usual guidance positions.

> One might well imagine a present-day counselor exhorting Columbus to give up this mad confusion of sailing westward to find the East and to settle down quietly in a pleasant villa on the outskirts of Genoa. This advice would not be completely foolish; on the contrary, it would be sound practical counseling from the advisor's point of view, because while he could not help the adventurer at all on his proposed journey, he could be of great assistance in helping him choose a pleasant villa. . . . .[12]

Such an approach, although popular, would be disastrous in guiding the disadvantaged. There are no villas along the Mediterranean or anywhere else for one who is educationally disadvantaged. His best chance for an existence which will enable him to realize his potentialities is to break from the stereotyped but safe ideas of his ghetto, his family or his ethnic group. In the absence of a villa, his choice is to be Columbus or no one.

But high aspirations are not merely the fostering of day dreams. The implications for guidance personnel are clear: they must encourage youngsters to develop, keep and expand all their aspirations, and at the same time help to affect the changes in curriculum and teaching which will afford youngsters real success experiences on which to grow. Healthy aspirations derive from some form of success experience in the real world. In addition to working directly with youngsters, guidance personnel who wish to affect the education of the disadvantaged therefore must become involved in curriculum development and in-service teacher education.

4. *The most effective means of implementing the school guidance program for disadvantaged children and youth requires direct work with teachers and principals.* There will never be enough guidance personnel to work with the school age youngsters who could use their services. Evidence cited earlier indicates that even if there were sufficient personnel, such services would have minimal effect in the absence of simultaneous changes in the community and in school programs. Given the present limited supply of guidance counselors and the fact that others (e.g. teachers, principals, nonprofessional staff,

---

[11]R. J. Havighurst. *op. cit.* p. 34.
[12]R. Mammarella and J. Crescimbeni. *"Guidance Problems: Cultural or Cosmic?"* *Saturday Review,* Nov. 21, 1964, p. 76.

etc.) have more consistent influence on youngsters' self-concepts, guidance personnel in all schools should spend more time working directly with teachers and principals than with children or youth. This is not to imply that teachers and principals are emotionally disturbed to a greater degree than any other group in the general population, but to recognize the need for extending the influence of guidance personnel as broadly as possible. By affecting change in teachers' self-concepts, attitudes and values, it is likely that almost all disadvantaged children and youth can be influenced to some degree.

One teacher who believes "these children can't be expected to learn" may influence from 30 to 150 youngsters on a daily basis. Consider how much more effective it would be to work with Miss Jones rather than the large number of pupils she regularly sends out of class as behavior problems. In some instances the guidance counselor may just serve as a nonjudgmental, nonthreatening listener with whom teachers would be free to share their complaints and problems.

Organizational procedures should be created which would open regular channels of communication between counselors and teachers. It is necessary to recognize that even the most successful teacher working with disadvantaged youth is engaged in a physically taxing, emotionally stressful situation. Such a teacher needs to be recognized as having the professional right to have his problems and concerns listened to and receiving the counsel of an experienced guide in working out ways of handling his own and his youngsters' problems. Principals and supervisors have similar needs. It is unrealistic to believe that individuals with great professional responsibility, engaged in human relations which are often tense and highly emotional for long periods of time, should not be helped by accepted procedures of guidance and counseling. Given the tremendous influence of teachers' attitudes on youngsters' self-concepts, it seems sensible that limited guidance resources be devoted to helping professional personnel.

RECOMMENDATIONS FOR FUTURE STUDY

What kinds of information are needed to implement the suggestions implied in the preceding discussion? Rather than await well-controlled research it is necessary to begin on the action level utilizing the most efficient means of evaluation available. Following are some of the questions which, when answered, will help establish more effective guidance programs for serving the disadvantaged.

1. How should guidance personnel be selected? (Can we assume that successful classroom teaching or college course work are the only appropriate bases, or are there other criteria of selection?)

2. How should guidance personnel be supervised? (Can we assume that these individuals can function best in complete professional isolation, or do they need closer association with colleagues performing comparable roles?)

3. What criteria should be used to evaluate guidance personnel? (Can we assume that the work is so complex and long-term that it is beyond evaluation, or that observable, behavioral objectives can be specified?)

4. What are some effective ways of reaching parents and effecting changes in the community? (Can we assume a narrow role for the school, or is the school serving the disadvantaged a community school?)

5. What are the results of follow-up studies which compare disadvantaged youth given directive guidance with those given indirect counseling? (Can we assume that nondirective methods are best for everyone in all situations, or does effective guidance involve the selection of various procedures for realizing different purposes?)

6. What are some effective means of working directly with youngsters to build their self-concepts and aspirations? (Can we assume that only pre-school and early elementary children are susceptible to emotional growth, or are there procedures which are equally effective with adolescents?)

7. What methods have been used to work with teachers, principals and nonprofessional staff? (Can we assume that guidance counselors will be most effective working only with youngsters, or that they would be most useful working predominantly with teachers?)

8. What means have guidance counselors used for effecting curriculum change? (Can we assume that the basic purpose of the counselor is pupil — or even teacher — adjustment, or that he has a concommitant responsibility for trying to induce change in the system?)

Before summing up, it would be useful to note the numerous items which have been omitted from this discussion. Nothing has been said about the physical facilities in which the counselor operates or the clerical help he is provided. Neither has there been an emphasis on issues such as the purposes of elementary guidance as opposed to secondary guidance, or whether the functions of vocational, educational and emotional guidance should be performed by separate individuals or the same person. Nothing has been said about the problems of testing and those measures which can most effectively assess disadvantaged children and youth. All of these, as well as other items, are important concerns for describing the work of the counselor. In order to limit this discussion, however, the issues and problems selected for analysis are those considered to be the most crucial for guiding the disadvantaged.

SUMMARY

There are a variety of approaches used for studying the problems of the educationally disadvantaged. It is suggested that studying the nature of children's inheritance, early family life and school experiences, with particular reference to the self-concept engendered by these experiences, is the most fruitful approach. Selected characteristics of the educationally disadvantaged are presented which indicate the nature of the difference between high and low school achievers. On the basis of these characteristics four action principles are presented for guidance counselors serving disadvantaged youngsters. These guidelines emphasize working with parents, community, curriculum and teachers, in addition to working directly with youngsters. Recommendations are made which attempt to outline the basic questions about which more information is needed before the work of the guidance counselor serving the educationally disadvantaged can be specified in further detail.

BIBLIOGRAPHY

Bloom, B. S. *Stability and Change in Human Characteristics,* (New York: John Wiley and Sons, Inc., 1964).

Borgatta, E. F., Meyer, J. H., and Jones, W. C. Interim Report of a study sponsored by the Russell Sage Foundation and presented to the Eastern Regional Conference of the Child Welfare League of America. (Reported by the New York Times News Service, Sunday, February 21, 1965.)

Davidson, H. H., Greenberg, J. W., and Garver, J. M. "Characteristics of Successful School Achievers from a Severely Deprived Environment." School of Education, The City University of New York, Mimeograph, October, 1962. (Reported at the American Educational Research Association, Chicago, February, 1963.)

Dentler, R. A. "Dropouts, Automation and the Cities." A paper delivered to Third Work Conference on Curriculum and Teaching in Depressed Urban Areas. Teachers College, Columbia University. June 22-July 3, 1964.

Havighurst, R. J. The Public Schools of Chicago. The Board of Education of the City of Chicago. Chicago, 1964.

Jackson, J. H. "The Relationship Between Psychological Climate and the Quality of Learning Outcomes Among Lower Status Pupils." Unpublished Ph.D. thesis. University of Chicago, 1957.

Mammarella, R., and Crescimbeni, J. "Guidance Problems: Cultural or Cosmic?" Saturday Review, Nov. 21, 1964, p. 76.

Riessman, F. The Culturally Deprived Child. New York: Harpers, 1962.

Riessman, F. "Workers' Attitudes Towards Participation and Leadership." Unpublished Ph.D. dissertation, Columbia University, 1955.

(9)

WHERE DO ALL THE PROBLEMS GO?

Donald L. Frye

North Carolina Wesleyan College

Today nearly every college and university provides living accommodations for its students. Although student personnel work has expanded to include such services as financial aid, student activities, the health service, job placement, and many other elements of the total campus organization, there is still a strong emphasis on its early general interpretation: the service of advising and counseling.[1]

Much of this advising and counseling is done within the framework of residence hall counseling programs. As an extension of the office of the dean of students, the residence hall counselor has become an important part of the student personnel program. In many small liberal arts colleges the residence hall counselors are upper-class undergraduates. It is expected that students functioning in this capacity will contribute to the development of the students in their charge. As individuals and members of a group the students will likely be influenced by the counselors. There are two fundamental reasons why the counselor in the residence hall becomes the first person to be consulted when a student is confronted by a problem. First, he is the experienced person who is closest at hand, and second, he is a peer. His being a peer plays a part far more important than might be suspected at first.

In all probability residence hall counselors will increase in importance in the future. As the campus population expands the residence hall counselor

_____

An original article for this book.

may be increasingly consulted as the most "close-to-home" source of aid when problems arise. We, as student personnel workers, will need to know much more about counseling in residence halls. We will need to remind ourselves of the extent to which the residence hall becomes the student's home during his years at college. Ruth Strang points out that in residence halls "a cooperative, responsible, family-like group cán be developed — an intimate kind of association in which each student learns the art of living with others."[2] No one who has been in student personnel work for very long need be reminded, however, that it can be sorrowfully unlike this. Often students, while living in the midst of many, are unable to communicate and become lonely, disappointed, and isolated.

The residence hall counselor is called upon to be many things to many students. Is he adequately trained to cope with the kinds of situations that are thrust upon him? Do personnel administrators have a real understanding of the breadth and depth of the problems their residence hall counselors are being asked to help solve?

The philosophy of residence hall counseling in any college, while perhaps formulated by a highly trained student personnel administrator is, for the most part, implemented by the residence hall counselors. To a great degree it is they who determine the success or failure of the residence hall counseling program. Are they equal to the task? Can they be trained to be equal to the task in the year or two they spend as full time students and part time counselors?

Seeking an answer to these questions, the writer chose to investigate the matter of where students voluntarily take their problems as his doctoral research. First, the investigation sought to determine if the residents of men's dormitories take a greater number of their problems more commonly to the residence hall counselors or to the dean of men. Second, the study investigated the difference in the number of each type of problem to discover if there is a significant difference in the frequency with which each type is taken to the dean of men and to the counselors. In addition to these two basic questions, the study also sought to investigate which problems the counselors "refer" and which problems they tend to handle on their own without referral.

Most small liberal arts colleges use experienced upperclassmen as counselors in residence halls. These young men usually have been chosen because they have demonstrated the completeness of their own judgment to adult freedom and because they have a good working knowledge of the campus organization and the academic program. It is expected that they will be able to help their fellow students with many of their problems simply because they have themselves worked out intelligent, acceptable, and workable solutions to these problems. Because they lack the proper training, there will occasionally be more serious problems they will not be expected to help the students solve. These are the problems they are expected to refer to the dean of men or to some other more highly trained person on the college staff.

It was the writer's hope that the findings of the study could be of help to deans of men as they attempt to improve the orientation and in-service training programs for their counselors. It was felt that any study that points out the depth, breadth, and frequency of the problems brought to the counselors in small liberal arts colleges could be of help in giving deans of men some positive pointers in planning training programs for the counselors.

The study did not attempt to go into the psychological reasons why a student would take one kind of problem more commonly to a counselor than to the dean and another to the dean more commonly than to a counselor. Since the study was completed, however, the writer has sought some answers to that aspect of the problem, and they will be brought out toward the close of the present article. The study also did not attempt to investigate the effectiveness of the counseling done by either the counselors or the deans.

The method of investigation was as follows: Ten liberal arts colleges and universities were included in the study; these were in the five-state area of Michigan, Indiana, Illinois, Wisconsin, and Minnesota. Each campus was visited and the writer explained the project fully to each of the deans and to all of his counselors. At that time worksheets, known as the *Problem Check List,* were given to the deans and the counselors. The check list had been tested for its problem coverage in a pilot study conducted at Northwestern University. The problem categories were the same on both types of worksheets. Only the instructions at the top of the worksheets, which concerned the direction of referrals, were different for the deans and the counselors. *The Problem Check Lists* were kept for a period of a month by the ten deans and all of their residence hall counselors. A *Problem Check List (worksheet)* for the counselors is illustrated. For the deans' worksheet the instructions read as follows:

Make a check like this ✔ each time for each problem.

Put *ONE* line through the check if the problem was referred to you by a residence hall counselor ⩗.

Put *TWO* lines through the check if the problem was referred to you by anyone other than a counselor ⩊.

NO line through the check if the problem had not been referred but the student came directly to you ✔.

A dittoed sheet of instructions for using the *Problem Check List* was given to each of the deans and each of the counselors.

The counselors were asked not to count the problems that were discussed by a student who had been *requested* to come for an interview; the research involved only those problems that were brought voluntarily by the students. It was also important to make clear to the deans that they were to count only those problems that were brought voluntarily to them by students who lived in dormitories staffed with counselors; the problems of students who lived off campus, at home, in fraternities, or in residence halls not staffed with counselors were not to be counted by the deans. For the purpose of the statistical analysis of the data it was important that the number of students available to the dean and to the counselors for counseling in each college be the same. In other words, the total number of counselors must have had the same number of potential counselees as the dean in any one school.

One more point of method should be made; this involves the timing of the study. The study was conducted during the months of February and

March in the academic year of 1960-61. These months seemed ideal for several reasons. They were months that included some of the gloom of Winter and some of the promise of Spring. Early February would reflect the start

PROBLEM CHECK LIST (WORKSHEET)
COUNSELORS

Make a check like this √ each time for each problem.
Put ONE line through the check if the problem was referred by you to the Dean of Men ⩗.
Put TWO lines through the check if the problem was referred by you to anyone other than the Dean ⩘.
No line through the check if the problem was not referred √.

The Problem Categories

1. University Rules and Dorm Information
2. Academic Information (Courses, Sequences, Probation, Requirements, etc.)
3. Questions and Discussions of Morals and Ethics (Of a transitory nature stemming from recent experiences such as sex relations on dates, cheating, plagiarism, etc.)
4. Theological and Religious Problems (Such as conflicts between old beliefs and new learning)
5. Interpersonal Adjustment Problems in the House or on the Floor
6. City and State Laws or Legal Problems
7. Vocational Selection Problems
8. Financial Problems (including part-time employment problems)
9. Family Relations Problems
10. Aid in Homework and Study Problems
11. Physical Health Problems
12. General Questions about Social Poise and Etiquette (Dating, getting dates, where to go)
13. Intrapersonal Conflicts (The more long-standing and serious problems)
    a. Depression
    b. Inferiority
    c. Homosexuality
    d. Hostility
    e. Guilt
    f. Others (Explain)
14. Others (Explain)

64

of a new semester on several of the campuses and yet avoid the great confusion that is present in September in the minds of new students. In some cases, the early February dates and the mid-March dates reflected the students' concern with final exams or midterm exams. Several of the schools used a delayed rush fraternity system which could raise potential problems for students at the beginning of the second semester. Also, this same period was the activation time for schools with fraternity systems that used Fall rushing. Last, but not least, February and March seemed ideal simply because they are midterm months for college, on a large scale reflecting neither the joy, hope, and confusion of the beginning of the school year nor the excitement or despair that can come at the end of the school year. In summary, during February and March the students are involved in academic and extracurricular activities at a typical pace.

The collected data showed that the male dormitory residents of the ten colleges voluntarily brought to their residence hall counselors a total of 3,786 problems, while they brought only 857 problems to the deans of men, as shown in Tables I and II. More than four times as many problems were taken by the students to their counselors as to the deans. Of the total number of problems brought to the counselors, 280 or only 7 per cent were referred to anyone; 69 of the 280 (1 per cent) were referred to the deans, and 211 of the 280 (6 per cent) referred to someone other than the deans, as shown in Tables III and IV. On the other hand, of the 857 problems taken to the deans, 180 of them had been referred. Those 180 referred problems constituted 21 per cent of the total problems brought to the deans, 15 per cent, or 132 problems, having been referred by someone other than a counselor and only 6 per cent, or 48 problems, having been referred to the deans by the counselors. Thus, nearly three times as many problems that were referred to the deans came from sources other than the counselors as came from the counselors. At the same time, slightly more than three times as many problems as were referred to the deans were referred by the counselors to someone other than the deans. Forty-eight of the problems brought to the deans were referred by counselors, according to the deans' count, while according to the counselors' count, 69 had been referred by them to the deans. It thus would appear that not every student who was *advised* by a counselor to take his problem to the dean of men followed the counselor's referral suggestion. Fewer than the scant *one per cent* of the problems passed on to the deans by the counselors actually reached the deans' offices.

The problem type brought to the counselors in the greatest number was "Aid in homework or study problems" (problem category #10), while the problem type brought to the deans of men in the largest number was "academic information" (problem category #2), as shown in Tables I and II. There is nothing unusual or unexpected about this. Problems concerning "University rules and dorm information" (category #1) were brought to the counselors and to the deans with the second greatest frequency. A look at Tables 1 and II also shows that this type of problem was referred by the counselors to the deans with the highest percentage of any referred problem, and that the deans also show this type as having been referred by the counselors with the highest percentage. In other words, of the 69 problems the counselors saw fit to refer to the deans, 39.13 per cent were problems concerning "University rules and dorm information"; and of the 48 problems

TABLE I

Summary of the Number of Problems Voluntarily Brought to the Counselors

The Problem Categories	Problems not referred to anyone (treated only by a counselor)		Problems referred to the deans		Problems referred to someone other than the deans		Total problems brought	
	Number of 3,506	Percent	Number	Percent of 69	Number of 211	Percent	Number of 3,786	Percent
1. University rules and dorm information	606	17.28	27	39.13	40	18.96	673	17.78
2. Academic information	438	12.49	15	21.74	38	18.01	491	13.00
3. Questions and discussions about morals and ethics	155	4.42	2	2.90	4	1.90	161	4.25
4. Theological and religious problems	152	4.33	0	0	11	5.21	163	4.31
5. Interpersonal adjustment	185	5.28	5	7.25	12	5.69	202	5.34
6. City and state laws or legal problems	83	2.37	6	8.70	6	2.84	95	2.51
7. Vocational selection	100	2.85	1	1.45	14	6.64	115	3.04
8. Financial problems	95	2.71	4	5.80	5	2.37	104	2.75
9. Family relations	86	2.45	3	4.35	3	1.42	92	2.43
10. Aid in homework and study problems	912	26.01	2	2.90	32	15.17	946	24.99
11. Physical health problems	98	2.80	0	0	30	14.22	128	3.41
12. Social poise and etiquette	368	10.50	0	0	5	2.37	373	9.85
13. Intrapersonal conflicts	87	2.48	2	2.90	3	1.42	92	2.43
a. Depression	(37) (1.06)		(2) (2.90)		(1) (.47)		(40) (1.06)	
b. Inferiority	(17) (.48)		(0) 0		(0) 0		(17) (.45)	
c. Homosexuality	(7) (.20)		(0) 0		(0) 0		(7) (.18)	
d. Hostility	(11) (.31)		(0) 0		(2) (.95)		(13) (.34)	
e. Guilt	(14) (.40)		(0) 0		(0) 0		(14) (.37)	
f. Others (explain)	(1) (.03)		(0) 0		(0) 0		(1) (.03)	
14. Others (explain)	141	4.02	2	2.90	8	3.79	151	3.99
a. Fraternity	(92) (2.62)		(1) (1.45)		(2) (.95)		(95) (2.51)	
b. Extracurricular	(30) (.86)		(1) (1.45)		(6) (2.84)		(37) (.98)	
c. Becoming a counselor	(9) (.26)		(0) 0		(0) 0		(9) (.24)	
d. Miscellaneous	(10) (.29)		(0) 0		(0) 0		(10) (.26)	
Total	3,506		69		211		Grand Total 3,786	100.00

66

TABLE II

Summary of the Number of Problems Voluntarily Brought to the Ten Deans

The Problem Categories	Problems voluntarily brought to the deans		Problems referred by a counselor		Problems referred by someone other than a counselor		Total problems voluntarily brought to the deans	
	Number	Percent of 677	Number	Percent of 48	Number	Percent of 132	Number	Percent of 857
1. University rules and dorm information	118	17.43	19	39.58	20	15.15	157	18.32
2. Academic information	136	20.09	10	20.83	46	34.85	192	22.40
3. Questions and discussions about morals and ethics	26	3.84	0	0	2	1.52	28	3.27
4. Theological and religious problems	9	1.33	2	4.17	3	2.27	14	1.63
5. Interpersonal adjustment	38	5.61	1	2.08	1	.76	40	4.67
6. City and state laws or legal problems	4	.59	1	2.08	1	.76	6	.70
7. Vocational selection problems	66	9.75	0	0	5	3.79	71	8.28
8. Financial problems	85	12.56	1	2.08	5	3.79	91	10.62
9. Family relations	17	2.51	1	2.08	0	0	18	2.10
10. Aid in homework and study problems	68	10.04	7	14.58	26	19.70	101	11.79
11. Physical health problems	20	2.95	1	2.08	13	9.85	34	3.97
12. Social poise and etiquette problems	2	.30	0	0	0	0	2	.23
13. Intrapersonal conflicts	23	3.40	4	8.32	6	4.55	33	3.85
a. Depression	(9)	(1.33)	(1)	(2.08)	(4)	(3.03)	(14)	(1.63)
b. Inferiority	(2)	(.30)	(1)	(2.08)	(1)	(.76)	(4)	(.47)
c. Homosexuality	(1)	(.15)	(0)	(0)	(1)	(.76)	(2)	(.23)
d. Hostility	(5)	(.74)	(1)	(2.08)	(0)	(0)	(6)	(.70)
e. Guilt	(3)	(.44)	(0)	(0)	(0)	(0)	(3)	(.35)
f. Others (explain)	(3)	(.44)	(1)	(2.08)	(0)	(0)	(4)	(.47)
14. Others (explain)	65	9.60	1	2.08	4	3.03	70	8.17
a. Fraternity	(11)	(1.62)	(0)	(0)	(0)	(0)	(11)	(1.28)
b. Extracurricular	(6)	(.89)	(0)	(0)	(0)	(0)	(6)	(.70)
c. Selective Service	(35)	(5.17)	(1)	(2.08)	(1)	(.76)	(37)	(4.31)
d. Miscellaneous	(13)	(1.92)	(0)	(0)	(3)	(2.27)	(16)	(1.88)
	Total 677		Total 48		Total 132		Grand total 857	100.00

TABLE III

The Percentage of Total Problems and of Each Problem Type Referred and Not Referred by the Counselors

Problem type	Total problems brought to counselors	Problems brought to counselors which were not referred (treated only by a counselor)		Problems brought to counselors which were referred to the dean of men		Problems brought to counselor which were referred to someone other than the dean		Problems brought to counselors which were referred	
		No.	Per cent	No.	Per cent	No.	Per cent	No.	Per cent
1.	673	(606)	90	(27)	4	(40)	6	(67)	10
2.	491	(438)	89	(15)	3	(38)	8	(53)	11
3.	161	(155)	96	(2)	1	(4)	3	(6)	4
4.	163	(152)	93	(0)	0	(11)	7	(11)	7
5.	202	(185)	92	(5)	2	(12)	6	(17)	8
6.	95	(83)	88	(6)	6	(6)	6	(12)	12
7.	115	(100)	87	(1)	1	(14)	12	(15)	13
8.	104	(95)	91	(4)	4	(5)	5	(9)	9
9.	92	(86)	94	(3)	3	(3)	3	(6)	6
10.	946	(912)	96	(2)	.5	(32)	3.5	(34)	4
11.	128	(98)	77	(0)	0	(30)	23	(30)	23
12.	373	(368)	99	(0)	0	(5)	1	(5)	1
13.	92	(87)	95	(2)	2	(3)	3	(5)	5
14.	151	(141)	94	(2)	1	(8)	5	(10)	6
All problems	3,786	(3,506)	93	(69)	1	(211)	6	(280)	7

TABLE IV

The Percentage of Total Problems and of Each Problem Type Brought Initially to the Deans and Those That Were Referred to Them

Problem type	Total problems brought to the deans	Problems brought initially to the deans (not taken elsewhere first)		Problems brought to the deans which were referred by the counselors		Problems brought to the deans which were referred by someone other than counselors		Problems brought to the deans which were referred to them	
		No.	Per cent	No.	Per cent	No.	Per cent	No.	Per cent
1.	157	(118)	75	(19)	12	(20)	13	(39)	25
2.	192	(136)	71	(10)	5	(46)	24	(56)	29
3.	28	(26)	93	(0)	0	(2)	7	(2)	7
4.	14	(9)	64	(2)	14	(3)	22	(5)	36
5.	40	(38)	95	(1)	2.5	(1)	2.5	(2)	5
6.	6	(4)	67	(1)	16.5	(1)	16.5	(2)	33
7.	71	(66)	93	(0)	0	(5)	7	(5)	7
8.	91	(85)	93	(1)	1	(5)	6	(6)	7
9.	18	(17)	94	(1)	6	(0)	0	(1)	6
10.	101	(68)	67	(7)	7	(26)	26	(33)	33
11.	34	(20)	59	(1)	3	(13)	38	(14)	41
12.	2	(2)	100	(0)	0	(0)	0	(0)	0
13.	33	(23)	70	(4)	12	(6)	18	(10)	30
14.	70	(65)	93	(1)	1	(4)	6	(5)	7
All problems	857	(677)	79	(48)	6	(132)	15	(180)	21

the deans recorded as having been referred by the counselors, 39.58 per cent were problems of this type. No other problem category had a higher percentage of referral. When Tables III and IV are consulted, however, it is clear that this type of problem was not referred with the highest frequency from the grand total of 3,786 problems handled by the counselors. When the total number of problems is considered, "Physical health problems" (category #11) were referred by the counselors with the greatest frequency (23 per cent). This is not unusual, nor is it unusual that these problems were not referred to the deans but rather to someone other than the deans, very likely the school nurse or school physician. Interestingly enough, this same problem type was referred to the deans with the greatest frequency when the 857 total number of problems they handled was considered (38 per cent), and these problems were not referred by the counselors but rather by someone other than the counselors.

Again, it is interesting to note that when the grand total of problems is considered in Tables III and IV, the third column in each table shows that problem category #6, "City and state laws or legal problems," was referred to the deans by the counselors with the highest percentage and was received by the deans from the counselors with the highest percentage. That percentage is not very high from the counselors, however, when it is seen to be only 6 per cent.

The problem types voluntarily brought to the counselors with the smallest frequency were "Family relations" and "Intrapersonal conflicts" (categories #9 and #13 respectively). The writer considers that these two problem types are probably the most serious problems on the check list. They are strongly charged with emotion and require a high degree of professional skill in counseling. It might be considered fortunate that these two problem types were brought the least frequently to the counselors, since they are not highly trained. Of the total number of problems the counselors treated, categories #9 and #13 each represented only 2.43 per cent of the total, as shown in Table I. Table III, however, presents figures that should cause a feeling of concern, for here it is shown that only 3 per cent of the "Family relations" problems and only 2 per cent of the "Intrapersonal conflicts" problems were referred to the deans by counselors. Only 6 per cent and 5 per cent respectively of these two problem types were referred to anyone, including the deans, by the counselors. And it is startling to realize that when all of the problems are considered together, only 7 per cent of the 3,786 problems treated by the counselors were referred to anyone, with only 1 per cent being referred to the deans and 6 per cent being referred to someone other than the deans.

When analyzed statistically the findings appeared as follows: The chi-square test showed that there was a significant difference in the total number of problems brought to the undergraduate residence hall counselors and to the student personnel deans. Students who lived in dormitories voluntarily took more of their problems to the counselors than to the deans of men. Of the total number of problems brought to both the deans and the counselors in the ten colleges studied, 81 per cent were brought to the counselors while only 19 per cent were brought to the deans. The counselors obviously served in an important counseling capacity for the students living in residence halls, since they took the bulk of their problems to the counselors. The dormitory residents more commonly took every type of problem to the counselors than to the deans except for "Financial problems" (category #8). There was no significant difference in the frequency with which students brought financial problems to the counselors and to the deans.

Some implications of the study must be considered now. An examination of the findings should give insight to student personnel deans who are charged with the responsibility of the residence hall counseling programs for men in small liberal arts colleges. It is to be hoped that the findings may lead to improvement of these counseling programs.

1. In view of the fact that male students voluntarily brought a significantly large number of their problems to their undergraduate dormitory counselors than to the student personnel deans, serious consideration should be given to making these counselors capable of rendering better service.

2. The in-service training program and the selection procedure should be given very special attention when plans for improving the service of the residence counseling programs are being considered. In many schools the present counselors are asked to recommend fellow students for counseling positions. These counselors should be educated to the value of conscientiously recommending only those whom they know to be the most capable.

3. The study showed that the counselors were called upon to treat a great variety of problems, some of them in areas which included problems of a serious nature. It seems unlikely that these student-counselors could be trained to be completely effective in their counseling roles in view of the limitations of age, time, and status. Much more could, however, be done to teach them to be more effective referral agents. The study showed that the counselors referred only 7 per cent of the problems that were brought to them. It seems safe to say that the percentage should have been higher. In-service training programs could more readily teach the counselors to refer than they could prepare them capably to counsel students with every kind of problem.

4. Since the residence hall counselors were called upon to counsel students the most frequently in the areas of "Aid in homework and study problems" and "Academic information," these areas should be given special attention in the counselors' training program.

5. The "Intrapersonal conflicts" problems were defined in the study as "the more long-standing and serious problems," and the "family relations" problems were considered to be of a possible serious nature too; and yet, only 5 per cent of the former and 6 per cent of the latter types of serious problems were referred by the counselors to any other source of aid. This would again suggest that the counselors need more training in recognizing serious problems that need to be referred. The 5 per cent and 6 per cent figures also imply that the counselors tended to "bite off more than they could chew" when it came to counseling. Regarding problems concerning physical health, however, apparently the deans or the school physician or the counselor's own apprehension about giving counsel in this area made clear the importance of referral, for that problem category had the largest percentage of problems referred by the counselors.

6. The counselors apparently were not taught, or otherwise convinced, that they should think of the dean of men as a counselor to whom they should refer difficult problems, since they sent to the deans only 1 per cent of the

problems brought to them. The dean of men should be a capable counselor and should be known to his staff as such.

7. The study implied that "Financial problems" held a unique position in the minds of students, since it was the only problem type not brought to the counselors in a significantly greater number than to the deans.

One cannot read the foregoing without asking some questions, questions that press for answers: Why is it that when well-trained deans of men are available to the students, they take their problems to undergraduate dormitory counselors who are not highly trained? Why is it that the counselors, who take part in in-service training programs that constantly remind them of the importance of referring serious problems, treat 93 per cent of the problems themselves? Of the low percentage of problems they *do* refer, why do the counselors refer only 1 per cent of them to the deans of men? Future researchers might profitably address themselves to these questions.

The following possible explanations, among others, might be considered: (a) after being counseled by the resident hall counselor, the student feels no need to seek further counseling; (b) the student is dissatisfied with the counseling he receives from the dormitory counselor and therefore does not feel inclined to seek more of what he thinks might be the same from a further source; (c) the counselors are unable to accept the fact that further counseling is necessary, because to do so would forcefully remind them that people their own age can have problems so serious that only an adult can properly help, and they do not want to be reminded of this because it would increase their anxiety about the seriousness of their own problems; (d) the students honestly believe that their peers know more about their type of problems than does any adult including the dean of men, (e) to the students the dean of men represents values that they are not willing to trust or accept; (f) the students do not agree with the general standards that the college represents and which to them the dean seems to epitomize; (g) although going to anyone for help with a problem is to some extent a denial of the independence students hold so dear, going to a fellow-student dormitory counselor does not reach the same degree of denying independence as does going to the dean of men with a problem. The last four explanations may be seen as a reflection of the "problem of generations," popularly known today as the US/THEM issue.

The writer has himself been interested in some of these questions and has included some of the more extreme explanations because they have been emphasized many times in the answers he has received to questions repeatedly posed to students concerning why they take their problems where they do. Oddly enough, however, the answer he received most often is a rather simple one. As a matter of fact, it is almost a technical one, although possibly a difficult one to remedy. There appears below a composite statement that represents the most frequently stated reason for the student's taking his problem to his undergraduate residence hall counselor instead of the dean of men:

> My reason for going to the dorm counselor with my problems is simple. When I have a problem and I am asking for help, I want to structure the situation; I want to pace the conversation. The dean may be a real nice guy, but he's a busy man. I go in to see him, I sit down across his desk from him, he looks at me, smiles, and very pleasantly says: "What can I do for you?" Well, heck, I have to get on with it right away then. I have to come out with

it all in a lump. There is always the possibility that he might not be in the mood to deal with my particular kind of problem. There is even a very real chance that he might not know anything about my type of problem. I can't insult the dean by saying: "Well, I can sense that you are in no mood to talk about this," and I certainly can't say, "I guess you don't know anything about this," and walk out. You see, these things aren't a problem in the dorm. I can wander down the hall to the counselor's room when the mood is right for me. I can go in and shoot the breeze with him for maybe even an hour while I feel him out and see if he is in the mood to talk about it, or get him in the mood. If I decide he doesn't want to talk or doesn't know anything about it, I can simply say: "See ya," and walk out. You can't do that with the dean. And anyway, you always worry if the dean thinks your problem is stupid; you even wonder if he ever had such problems; if he was ever nineteen; and if he ever was, does he remember it.

That is a rather clear and simple statement of the problem in the student's own words, and this statement raises some further questions for future research. (a) Is this a simple but insoluble US/THEM problem? (b) Do the students simply refuse to think of the dean of men as a counselor? (c) And do the residence hall counselors, because they are first students, tend not to think of the dean as a counselor themselves, and so do not communicate to the troubled student that he is the man to consult? (d) Can it be that the best possible way for the dean of men to work on this problem is to conduct himself in such a way as to communicate unmistakably to his counselors (the students he knows best and is closest to) that he is their counselor (much as a bishop is a pastor's pastor)? If he gets this idea across to his counselors will they in turn communicate to their fellow-students that the dean of men is a well-equipped and understanding and wise counselor? This, of course, begs the question: Is a particular dean indeed this kind of person? What if he is not? The problem is traced back until ultimately basic issues of personnel selection within the college are concerned, back further to issues of student selection for graduate training programs in college personnel work; and thus personality assessment questions must be faced. Is there a dean of men type? Maybe not. Are there at least certain personality traits a man must possess in order to communicate to students what must be communicated, in order that he can be a valuable and helpful person in their lives? Maybe so. What are these traits? As a man who is a dean of men gets older, can these characteristics be counted on to stay with him? Perhaps they will improve. Perhaps they will fade. Finally the ever-recurring question: Can colleges expect to find "deaning" and counseling abilities in the same person and will students permit the same person to perform both functions? The questions multiply and become more pithy. Seeking out the answers is a tremendous research task, and student personnel workers eagerly await those answers.

Chapter 1: Questions for Discussion

1. What are the major difficulties generated by what Blocher terms "elusive issues" in counseling? What ethical issues arise from each of them?

---

[1]C. Gilbert Wrenn, *Student Personnel Work in College* (New York: The Ronald Press Company, 1951), p. iii.

[2]Ruth Strang, "Housing and Dining Facilities," in Wrenn, *op. cit.*, p. 294.

2. What are some of the advantages and disadvantages of "trying to remain as philosophically neutral" as possible in counseling? To you, do the advantages outweigh the disadvantages, or vice versa? Why?

3. Consider the five philosophical issues raised by Arbuckle. Might you add a sixth category which you feel is of equal importance? Which of Arbuckle's five issues interests you most? What pertinent comments have you read about that issue in the literature?

4. What recent developments in our schools and in the larger society have hindered effective use of creative potential? What recent developments have furthered it? Which of Gruen's points seems most meaningful on college campuses today?

5. What evidences do you see in our society of what Arbuckle terms the "loss of the person"? Do you see any recent developments in the literature of counseling and guidance which seem to offer hope in dealing with this "loss"?

6. What sorts of preventive measures can a counselor take to minimize his chances of falling into legal difficulties in the performance of his duties?

7. Gordon raises the question of using "subprofessionals" in guidance work. What disturbs you about his proposed use of such persons? What advantages might the use of subprofessionals have?

8. Haberman presents a number of recommendations for working with the "educationally disadvantaged." What are the largest obstacles which interfere with counselor effectiveness in dealing with the sorts of youngsters he describes?

9. Frye discusses a little-studied aspect of counseling: residence counseling. If his major findings are correct, what actions then seem appropriate for the college officials in charge of counseling centers and programs?

Chapter

2

Changing Views

This chapter presents some significant changes and trends in the field of guidance and counseling, and calls to question some long-held beliefs about the goals, operations, and responsibilities of the counselor. As Lord Tennyson once put it, "Our little systems have their day; they have their day, and cease to be. . ." While the poet was not speaking about counseling, the message is clear. "The old order changeth, and giveth place the new" — but only reluctantly. The weight of tradition is heavy in any field of endeavor, and many assumptions often go unexamined all too long. Bold thinking, insightful syntheses, and serious philosophical critiques are at a premium. The articles in this chapter present interesting ways of viewing the important trends and problems in the field.

The concept of self and the ultimate objectives of counseling, guidance and therapy are the central focus of these essays. There emerges from the aggregate of these ideas a far different picture of man from that which our textbooks presented at earlier stages in the developmental of the fields.

Of significance to the counselor is the ever-present self-question, "What ways of viewing my client and my position as counselor will raise the probabilities of my being able to help him?" Subsidiary, yet vital, considerations are "What alternative ways of viewing society and social problems will aid me in understanding my clients and their meaning-structures?" "What unanswered questions from older theories now demand intensive attention?" "What trends are visible in my field, as research and theory add to our store of knowledge?"

The counselor must be alert constantly to "related" articles, i.e., articles about therapy, when the reader deals almost exclusively with the so-called "normal range" of students in school; he must decide what he can sift and winnow from these before they can be applied in his daily work. He must not dismiss them because they are "not in my field." This has been a fundamental weakness, fully as much as applying "borrowed" concerts blindly. This form of "professional myopia" must be avoided in all human helping relationships.

THE BEHAVIORAL GOALS OF GUIDANCE

Edward C. Glanz

Provost, Southampton College, New York

The free and responsible person strives to solve problems of life as they are encountered; he also is able to reflect upon himself and his life. He uses his total capacity to know and to understand himself as he seeks to integrate education with his concept of self to create a life.

He chooses among available alternatives. He recognizes that his freedom is limited by his nature as a person and the culture that gives meaning to his life. He learns to be free and responsible, progressively building upon past experience to face the present and future.

He recognizes that he is cumulatively a product of his physical, emotional and psychological nature as he learns from experiences. The values he learns and accredits are determining forces in the establishment of life objectives and life purposes.

He understands that freedom is the opportunity to solve problems with the total capacity present within himself. He views his freedom to create his own life as his most precious possession. He knows he is constantly in the process of becoming.

He defends and attempts to extend the freedom of others to live their lives with a dignity and integrity that are extensions of his respect for his own dignity and integrity as a person. He respects and is responsible to his own free, open society and culture as a surrounding and supporting force that permits him to be free to choose and to value.

The free person accepts the responsibility for his decisions. He is free to seek aid and counsel from others in resolving any issue, but accepts the implications and consequences of his actions.

He accepts youthful dependence while striving for mature independence. He attempts to understand the irrational and the rational in life. He seeks security, acceptance, and self-esteem in psychologically healthful ways. He is capable of loving and being loved.

He values education as an opportunity to learn creatively about life while preparing himself to live a fuller life. Educational decisions become related to step-by-step formulations of career concepts. He views work and career development as expressions of his own relations to the world.

The free and responsible person views life as an opportunity to realize his own potential as an individual while demonstrating by each act of life that he knows self-realization is at the same time social self-realization.

SOME SOCIAL IDEAS OF PIONEERS IN THE GUIDANCE MOVEMENT

Perry J. Rockwell, Jr.
Indiana University

John W. M. Rothney
University of Wisconsin, Madison

The guidance movement was born in the welter and confusion of protest, reform, utopian idealism, and defenses of the *status quo* which were rampant in the late nineteenth and early twentieth centuries. Those who have written about the beginnings of the guidance movement have tended to touch very lightly on the many social factors which led to the development of guidance services. The social ideas which inspired pioneers to initiate organized guidance services have not been given enough consideration. In the study described below an attempt was made to do this by examining the writings of five of the pioneers in guidance during its organizational period (1900-1916). The criteria of selection of the individuals were their activity in organizing guidance services, the extent to which they published the results of their efforts, the availability of their publications for study, and the geographical area in which they did their work. Using the methodology of historical research and analysis, the published writings of Frank Parsons, Jessie B. Davis, Anna Y. Reed, Eli W. Weaver, and Davis S. Hill were examined for evidence about their views of society. The ideas are noted below under the heading of social reform, the social gospel, social Darwinism, and the new science.

SOCIAL REFORM

The writings of Frank Parsons, a utopian social reformer, ranged from a lengthy tome about the history and political development of New Zealand to brief paragraphs of comment about incidents of the day which seemed to him to be of some social significance. He expressed his ideas about society often and at length. The culmination of his career of concern for the welfare of mankind was reached in the organization of the Vocation Bureau in Boston in 1908 [12].

His study of history and economics had led him to formulate what he called his philosophy of mutualism, a kind of gradual socialism. This idea was the frame of reference for all his thinking and writing. He believed in the

Reprinted by permission of the Authors and the *Personnel and Guidance Journal* December 1961, 349-354.

Perry J. Rockwell is Assistant Professor of Education at Indiana University, Bloomington. John W. M. Rothney is Professor of Education at the University of Wisconsin, Madison.

This article is part of a doctoral dissertation by Dr. Rockwell. The thesis entitled "Social Concepts in the Published Writings of Some Pioneers in Guidance, 1900–1916" is on file at the University of Wisconsin.

perfectability of mankind and in the movement of society toward that perfection on earth.

Parsons was against private ownership by monopolies and what he considered the evils of competition. He believed that government should play a major role in causing changes in society by legislating hours of work, prohibiting child labor, and controlling the growth of industry. Parsons studied and wrote about successful government ownership experiments in Switzerland, Northern Europe, and in New Zealand [10, 11]. He wanted to develop in the American system the democratic methods which had brought about the success of these experiments.

Many of the reforms for which he fought have been realized. Our senators are chosen by the direct vote of the people, and the initiative, referendum, and direct primaries are part of our state political systems. Women have achieved the right to vote and the progressive income tax has become a large source of support of our government. Monopolies have grown to undreamed-of proportions but so have the regulations which encompass their movements, and government seems to have more control of business practices today than at any other time in our history. Guidance has become an accepted part of the school system in all states of the union and has been recognized by federal legislation.

A fundamental concept in Parson's counseling was the belief that counselee had the power to analyze himself and to make wise decisions on the basis of that analysis. The forms developed by Parsons for use with the Vocation Bureau were aimed at helping the individual make as complete an analysis of himself as was possible [13]. A person would be asked such questions as "Are you honest?" In the context of social reform it seemed logical that a counselor should ask such questions since one of the basic tenets of the reform group was faith in man's ability to control his evolution to higher stages through conscious purposeful actions.

Another characteristic of Parson's counseling was his prescriptive advice to counselees. If he noted a peculiarity about a client which he felt would hinder him in achieving his goal, Parsons would inform the client and tell him that the characteristic should be modified or eliminated. Otherwise, he indicated, failure would surely result. Parsons also recommended certain books to be read to improve the client's mind or stimulate his interest in civic affairs.

The peculiarities noted by Parsons were those which might make life as a member of a closely knit cooperative society a bit difficult. The books recommended for reading included much of the reform and exposé literature published by the social reform group and critics of the power class. Henry D. Lloyd and Ida Tarbell's accounts of the Standard Oil Company's rise to power, the economics of John R. Commons and Richard T. Ely, the sociology of Lester F. Ward and E. A. Ross and many of his own works about needed social improvements were prominent on his recommended reading lists.

Activities such as those noted above indictated that Parsons wanted counselors to work toward social goals as well as the development of the individual client. It suggests that Parsons' guidance could have been used as a means toward the achievement of the mutualistic society which he sought.

THE SOCIAL GOSPEL

While attending Cornell University Jessie B. Davis worked through his uncertainty of career choice by self-analysis, occupational study, and an examination of self in relation to his chosen occupation. As soon as he could he introduced the study of self and occupation to his classes in Detroit and later in Grand Rapids. His description of counseling [1] suggests that he preached to students about the moral value of hard work, ambition, honesty, and the development of good character as assets to any person who planned to enter the business world.

As principal of a school in Grand Rapids he launched his program in English classes because they reached every pupil in the school and because composition work in English classes lent itself to his technique of occupational study. In order to help students to think about careers he had them write themes on such topics as "The Kind of Man (or Woman) I should Like to Be," "What I Will Do When I Grow Up," "A Call to Service," and "To What Extent Am I Indebted to the Social Interest of Others?" [1]

Examination of his published writings reveals that Davis was an advocate of what social historians have called the social gospel. This was essentially an attempt to bring the church closer to the mass of the people. The practice of the Golden Rule was looked upon as a panacea for the ills of society. It was most popular in urban centers where the evils of an industrialized society seemed to be most prominent. Adherents to the social gospel were concerned equally with the effects upon the individual of the excesses of corporate wealth and the formation of a socialistic state as advocated by the naturalists of the social reform movement. The social gospel was developed as a compromise between unrestrained competition on the one hand and socialism on the other.

Since the social gospel was concerned with social problems, its adherents often supported many of the same reforms as the social utopians. Theirs, too, was a campaign to alter current society until it recognized the goodness of each individual. There is no suggestion in Davis' writings of the achievement of a socialistic state but there is recognition and discussion of some of the evils existing in society. He referred frequently to the need for making morally sound decisions.

Davis' position within the social gospel philosophy was enhanced by his use of the "call" concept of the ministry in relation to the way one should choose a vocation. When an individual was "called" to a vocation he would approach it with the noblest and highest ideals which would serve society best by uplifting humanity.

The significance for guidance of the social gospel approach lies in the accent placed upon the development of the individual in accord with the particular moral code of the Christian concept of brotherly love. Individuals who made choices not consistent with this ideal needed to be guided toward the correct path. The social gospel of Jessie Davis brought to guidance a touch of a supernatural force. The moral code would be the standard by which the excellence of decisions by counselors and counselees alike could be judged.

SOCIAL DARWINISM

The ideas of Anna Y. Reed and Eli W. Weaver were both identified with the concept of social Darwinism although they did their work in areas geographically a continent apart. Eli Weaver worked with the High School Teachers' Association in New York City to establish a vocational guidance service while Anna Reed established her service in the schools of Seattle. Of the two, Anna Reed was the most fluent and prolific in the presentation of her ideas.

Working with Seattle school leaders and their employers, Reed accepted the prevailing concepts of business and business ethics in a free enterprise system. She seemed to equate morality and business ethics. She was much concerned that any course of action on a social question be taken on the basis of social research, economy, and how it would be accepted by the business world.

The system rather than persons seemed most important to Reed. She urged that schools use the example of business and keep the dollar sign before children since it was something every pupil understood. [14]. She advocated stiff competition for grades in school and suggested that only 100 per cent success was good enough in school as it was in industry. Whenever she advocated curriculum changes such as the addition of commercial courses, she justified them by reference to complaints she had received from business men about employees they hired directly from schools. Business standards and moral principles seemed synonymous in her lexicon, and she urged educators to be thoroughly imbued with them so that they might better serve their pupils [16]. She believed that by adding guidance services to a school system she would help prevent much of the "waste" of the educational product. Her guidance services were organized and operated with business methods [15]. She believed that the social service attitude did not have a place in a guidance organization because quick decisions associated with successful business methods were required.

Her admiration of business philosophy and methods resulted in criticism of all programs of guidance which placed the welfare of the individual above the needs of industry. In the guidance services which she developed an individual's worth was judged by his acceptability to employers. Other guidance programs, she said, "savored too much of a philanthropic or social service proposition and too little of a practical commercial venture."[17]

Anna Reed looked upon life in American society as a competitive struggle. The success which an individual achieved in the struggle depended upon his adjustment to the demands of business which dominated society. She accepted the dominance of business philosophy and methods as positives and did not join in Davis' and Parsons' criticisms of the activities of business.

Eli Weaver, on the other hand, gained the respect of Davis, Reed, and other pioneers in guidance by his quiet, capable and persistent work with students in New York City. He did not write much about his work but reported to the First National Conference on Vocational Guidance in 1910 that every high school in the city of New York had a committee of teachers who were actively attempting to aid boys and girls to discover what they could do best and how to secure a job in which their abilities could be used to the fullest advantage of both employer and employee. [18]

He did not comment about the organization of society as a whole in his writing. He did, however, advise young persons to develop character as the best means of securing and holding a job. He seemed content to work within the framework of society as it existed and to look upon guidance as a means of keeping the wheels of the social machinery well oiled. Employers, he felt, should set up standards which they wished workers to have and publicize them through the schools so that students would know what was expected of them and be able to prepare themselves more effectively.

The ideas of Reed and Weaver seem to be an integral part of the social Darwinist doctrine so popular as a defense for some of the business practices of the day. The supporters of social Darwinist doctrine maintained, as Darwin had in biology, that man and his social forms had evolved from lower to higher forms through a competitive process of natural selection which allowed only the strongest and best to survive.

The wealthy businessman of the day was identified as the strongest and best in the evolutionary concept and was believed to be highest on the social evolutionary scale. Competition was the means by which he had evolved and by which newer forms would be developed. The possession of money was the measure of his success.

Social Darwinists believed that education should mirror and prepare students for entry into the competitive world by teaching self-dependence, adjustment to the existing system, and for fighting for survival. The implication of this view is that guidance of an individual should be toward conformity with whatever social mores had come to be respected within the society. It suggests that the training which an individual needs is that training which will enable him to be most like the current power group. If an individual adjusted to whatever demands an employer made and maintained his loyalty to that employer he might advance to higher and higher positions within his employer's company and, if his competitive spirit and strength among his peers was of a high enough order, he might take over the company and become an employer.

Acceptance of the Social Darwinist evolutionary concept in guidance would lead a counselor to the position of guiding individuals toward conformity with the expectancies of superiors while urging them to fight their co-workers for advanced status. In a school, the authorities would determine what "outward" social mores should be. A system of rewards and punishments for those who succeeded or failed within its framework would be established. Simultaneously the peer culture would determine what "inward" school social mores would be and develop a system of rewards and punishments based largely upon the idea of social acceptance. Since these systems of the school and of the group might clash, the social Darwinist counselor would call the attention of a counselee to the points of conflict and the possible results of choosing one course over another. When this had been done and the individual had made a decision he would be "on his own" to survive or fail according to his capacity to succeed in the course he had chosen.

THE NEW SCIENCE

Perhaps the most significant of all the approaches to the development of guidance services was the scientific approach used by David S. Hill, Director of the Educational Research Bureau in New Orleans. His concern for guidance did not grow out of a conscious desire to direct the reform of society toward a specific social or economic goal. It grew out of his belief that any decisions which would affect the educational system, and this society, should be based upon sound scientific research.

Hill used more complete methods to study individuals than any of his contemporaries. He utilized the techniques of medical science to examine the physical fitness of boys and girls who were referred to his research bureau, used the newest psychological tests including the Binet individual intelligence test, and he sent a trained social investigator into homes to learn about the environments of children.

Society, according to Hill, was constantly evolving, and it was necessary for an individual to adapt himself to the changing conditions within the society in order to survive. It was the obligation of all to study scientifically the changes that were occurring and to guide youth toward a more perfect society. [2] He did not strike out at specific abuses of wealth nor formulate definite plans to alleviate poverty. His recognition of them as problems on the social scene was couched in general terms and usually as a prelude to the statistical study in which he was currently engaged. [4, 6-8] He mentioned the need for a scientific approach to education to eliminate political influence and corruption in government, labor-capital strife, spread of poverty, and the waste of natural resources.

Most of the forces active in bringing about changes in society were beyond the control of man, but Hill believed that man had the ability to work toward a goal and to make choices of behavior which would help him to achieve the goal. The school was society's tool for changing boys and girls into men and women who, by their choices toward what was beautiful, good, and true, would improve society.

His research revealed the great diversity of aims and objectives of those for whom American education was designed. He concluded that vocational guidance and diversified curricula were necessary for the fullest development of the individual student and the transmission to the future of the convictions, aspirations, and faith of the American people in the democratic process.

Hill's scientific approach to social problems was based on the assumption that answers to social problems could be discovered through research on specific problems. If the immediate situation were resolved perhaps the solution to the problem could be applied to other problems and society would be improved. Through the methods of science man could learn about the forces which caused social evolution, and by controlling his environment man could control the direction of evolution.

Scientific methodology so permeated the thinking of early twentieth century society that none of the pioneers in guidance was unaffected by it. Anna Reed used many techniques of social science research in her studies of state institutions, children in Seattle, and newsboys. Jessie Davis used the technique of personal visitation, interview, and discussion in his attempts to get more accurate information about occupations. Parsons used research continuously in his approach to social problems and in his discussion of techniques for use with counselees.

An approach to guidance problems through scientific research implies that answers to a problem can be obtained through a study of the problem itself.

A scientific frame of reference required that techniques for studying individuals and their environments be developed. It meant that guidance would be a continuous process of helping persons solve their problems until they became skillful in doing so.

SUMMARY

Regardless of their approach to social problems each of the guidance pioneers discussed above indicated that there was a need for guidance services and each looked to education as the proper instrument for implementing such services. Each was affected by several streams of thought which flowed through society in the late nineteenth and early twentieth centuries. Their acceptance or rejection of these broad streams of thought affected the conception of guidance which each developed.

Despite the diversity of social ideas among the pioneers in guidance they had many ideas in common. Each of them viewed society as a progressive development. Each believed that man had the power to change his weaknesses to strength or to fortify his areas of strength if he were aware of them. If the desires of the masses of the people could be changed through the increase of political reforms, the application of Christian ethics to everyday living, the increased acceptance of business methods or the application of scientific procedures, society could be changed.

All of the guidance activities organized by these early workers were designed to make the individual fit closer to a mold that would include all the values which these workers thought would result in successful living. To achieve this would require that guidance counselors know what was best for society and that they guide their counselees to fit the best mold. Current comments in the press and statements by guidance workers about the use of guidance services to "straighten out" individuals and to recruit certain kinds of workers for selected occupations indicate that the issue has not been completely resolved. Toward what kind of a society are guidance workers dedicated today? How much real change has occurred during the first 50 years of guidance movement?

REFERENCES

1. Davis, J. B. *Moral and vocational guidance*. New York: Ginn and Co., 1914.
2. Hill, D. S. The education and problems of the protestant ministry. *Amer. J. Rel. Psychol.*, 1907, 2, 204-256 & 1908, 3, 29-70.
3. Hill, D. S. *An experimental study of delinquent and destitute boys in New Orleans and notes concerning preventive and ameliorative measures in the United States*. New Orleans: Commission Council, 1914.
4. Hill, D. S. *Facts about the public schools of New Orleans in relation to vocation*. New Orleans: Commission Council, 1914.
5. Hill, D. S. Problems of vocational guidance in the South. *Sch. & Soc.*, 1915, 1, 257-263.
6. Hill, D. S. Significant problems of education in New Orleans. *Sch. & Soc.*, 1916, 4, 197-203.
7. Hill, D. S. *Educational research in public schools*. New Orleans: Div. of Educ. Res., 1915.

8. Hill, D. S. *A study of manufacturing establishments of New Orleans and mechanical occupations of boys and men with reference to education*. New Orleans: Commission Council, 1916.
9. Parsons, F. The philosophy of mutualism. *The arena*, 1894, *10*, 783-815.
10. Parsons, F. *The story of New Zealand*. Philadelphia: C. F. Taylor, 1904.
11. Parsons, F. Nationalization of railways in Switzerland. *The arena*, 1906, *36*, 557-658.
12. Parsons, F. The Vocation Bureau. *The arena*, 1908, *40*, 3-19, 171-183.
13. Parsons, F. *Choosing a vocation*. Boston: Houghton Mifflin Co., 1909.
14. Reed, Anna Y. *Vocational guidance report 1913-1916*. Seattle: Board of School Directors, 1916.
15. Reed, Anna Y. Vocational guidance — problem of organization and administration. *N.E.A. Proc.*, 1917, 443-449.
16. Reed, Anna Y. *Newsboy service*. Yonkers-on-Hudson: World Book, 1917.
17. Reed, Anna Y. *Junior wage earners*. New York: Macmillan, 1920.
18. Rockwell, P. J. Social concepts in the published writing of some pioneers in guidance, 1900-1916. Unpublished Ph.D. dissertation. University of Wisconsin, 1958.
19. U. S. Bureau of Education. *Papers presented at the organization meeting of the Vocational Guidance Association, Grand Rapids, October, 1913*. Bull. 14, 5-94. Washington, D. C., GPO, 1914.

(12)

EMERGING CONCEPTS AND PATTERNS OF GUIDANCE IN AMERICAN EDUCATION

Edward C. Glanz

Provost, Southampton College, New York

Guidance, counseling, and personnel work have recently been cast into a significant new role in American education. Congressional action has helped to focus attention upon this area of America's educational program. The increased concern for guidance by accrediting agencies, the changing patterns of teacher training, the spurt in post World War II training in guidance, these factors, among many other similar forces, have provided a background against which national legislation served as a catalytic agent to bring about the heightened concern for guidance in American education.

Public school administrators on all educational levels, college presidents, deans, faculty members and parents, as well as guidance personnel themselves, now need to face an increased responsibility for providing effective and adequate guidance for America's youth. Guidance, as an emerging force in education, has largely been accepted as a valuable and required factor in the total educational process. The major question which must now be faced by all concerned with education is: *"How and in what patterns may guidance best be integrated into the total educational process?"*

The patterns of "Topsy-like" growth in guidance services and programs need now to be changed into mature conceptual designs or constructs for

Reprinted by permission of the Author and the *Personnel and Guidance Journal*, November 1961, 259-265.

educators to utilize in educational institutions. A brief examination of the
historical perspectives within the guidance field and a review of present
structures may provide a basis for the projection of emerging concepts and
patterns of guidance for the future.

PERSPECTIVE

Counseling, guidance, and an increased concern for the individual student
and his welfare is largely a development of the early twentieth century in
American education. The vocational guidance movement, child guidance
clinics, and the mental health emphasis in clinics and hospitals, as well as
early personnel services for women on the college campuses were all early
signals of the significant change to occur in the American educational pattern
in the years to follow. The American Personnel and Guidance Association now
has approximately fourteen thousand members in six divisions. Thousands
more devote part time to counseling, guidance, and related efforts. New training institutes, financed by the federal government, are supplying thousands
of new guidance personnel for American schools.

The counseling and guidance movement in the first part of the century
was spurred on by an identification with reform and revolt. Education had
to be "humanized"; the individual student needed to be recognized and aided;
individual differences and intelligence variables needed to be identified;
different counseling methods were developed; these and many more approaches were re-emphasized or brought into American education by counselors, guidance workers, and other school personnel.

The zeal arising out of the reform spirit and the "revolt character" of the
personnel and guidance movement led to a patch-work pattern of organization and chance-determined character in schools and colleges. The recent
past and the present have, however, begun to cast definite shadows for the
future.

THE RECENT PAST AND THE PRESENT

Lloyd-Jones [45], described general education programs in education as
being divided into three major patterns: classical, neo-classical, and instrumental. A similar characterization can conveniently be utilized with education
as a whole and to the development of guidance in personnel services and
counseling in education. Counseling and guidance, or its absence, were related and patterned after the basic structure of the schools or colleges serving
as models. The classical or traditional point of view in education generally has
refused to recognize counseling and guidance as a professional specialty.
These institutions have preferred to assign any or all of these so-called
"personnel duties" to academic faculty members. The neo-classical or more
modern institutions, usually with varied curricula, have generally accepted
counseling and guidance. Varied patterns of organization have emerged as
philosophy and/or budget have dictated or allowed. Instrumental (or progressive?) institutions have not only accepted counseling and guidance, but
have provided the environment for experimental and highly individualized
programs.

Patterns of guidance and counseling in all types of institutions have continued to develop within the presently recognized twofold pattern of "specialist" and "generalist" as characterized by Lloyd-Jones [45], and Barry and Wolf [42]. Highly organized patterns of bureaus, centers, and clinically oriented specialists have compartmentalized personnel services into smaller and more compact units. At the same time, guidance personnel have begun to recognize the essential weakness of a specialized approach and an interest in the guidance efforts of the teacher or faculty member has grown stronger. The defenders of the classroom teacher or professor as the primary guidance agent have in turn recognized the contributions of the specialist and have moved toward a position reflecting the combined efforts of both. Also, new approaches paralleling the older "specialist-generalist" dichotomy are now appearing as guidance continues to grow and develop.

Guidance is a virile force and is now becoming an entrenched feature of American education. The integration of guidance into education as a mature professional discipline as described by Wrenn [47, 48] is a direct concern of administrators, budget makers, taxpayers, parents, and ultimately students. Prediction is always dangerous but virtually 50 years are now in the past of counseling and guidance. It is time to seek generalizations, constructs, and patterns which will serve to make problem-solving in counseling, guidance, and personnel work an easier task tomorrow than it is today.

MODELS FROM THE PRESENT AND FOR THE FUTURE

The practices of the past are becoming channeled into major trends and it appears that at least four basic structural or organizational patterns are emerging. Other emphases are present but appear to be below the surface of widespread present attention. Four major models of counseling and guidance seem to be:

1. Centralized Specialism
2. Decentralized Generalism
3. Curricular Counseling and Guidance (Group Guidance)
4. Human Relations and Group Work (Mental Health)

These four trends may be labelled differently or be recognizable in other ways; however, they seem to be basic to the many present approaches to the guidance problem in schools and colleges.

1. Centralized Specialism

The skilled techniques of clinical counselors, reading consultants, test administrators, school social workers, and many other specialists offer highly qualified aid to students of all ages and in all types of school programs. Coordination and administration needs in such programs have demanded a strong administrator or coordinator. The classroom teacher or faculty member, in the beginning, was usually encouraged to "leave it to the specialists"; in recent years, the significant contribution which can be made by faculty members as cooperating partners in guidance has been recognized. Somewhat reluctantly the teacher and non-specialist have been urged to consider a small contribution to the program.

Strengths. Many strengths are inherent in this view of guidance, personnel services and counseling. These strengths include:

1. *highly qualified personnel* in specific positions to solve difficult problems;
2. *coordinated services* through centralized control and administration;
3. *referral resources.*

Weaknesses. Certain problems or weaknesses are basic to this construct of guidance. These weaknesses include:

1. *cost and supply* — specially trained personnel are expensive and often difficult to find;
2. *centrifugal tendencies,* bureaus, clinics, and even individual specialists often tend to seek independence and separation. Such action sometimes strengthens individual units, but weakens the total program.
3. *de-emphasis of teachers'* role, classroom personnel often feel to be unimportant and unneeded in personnel and guidance work;
4. *compartmentalization of students,* particular problems of students are often treated and the *whole* student is forgtten or ignored.

Examples. College programs are usually coordinated by deans of students (student personnel, personnel services) or even vice-presidents. Public school programs are administered by directors of pupil personnel or assistant superintendents. *Services* is an important word and concept in this approach. Areas of action usually include: psychological counseling, reading clinics, school social workers, testing specialists, speech and/or hearing centers, and activities or student life. Discipline is usually handled by administrative deans (of men, boys, girls, women). Large city school systems, many elementary schools, state universities, and urban universities are frequent examples of this model of a guidance system in action.

Variations. Certain programs of this type have developed from one clinic or bureau within the system. Chronologically, this approach may be recognized by an examination of how services have been added and where the control is (or will be). Services are often "tacked on" and variations of this approach are as widespread as are new ideas, services, equality in an administrative view, and the *presence* or *need* for a purely administrative control center.

2. Decentralized Generalism

The importance of a guidance or personnel point of view in all areas of education has led to a movement designed to involve all educative personnel in the guidance or counseling process. All areas and levels of education have been affected by this view. Single coordinators or directors have attempted to involve faculty members, administrators, students, and others in the guidance program. Specialists were avoided at an early time, but have been sought in recent years to serve in a buttressing or supportive role. "Every teacher a better counselor" has often been the watchword of adherents to this view of the program.

Strengths. A concern for the total learning atmosphere and the apprecia-tion of the contributions of every person within an educational program has been a major pillar in the approach of this group. Other strengths include:

1. support for the contributions of the classroom teacher;
2. a concern for the process and climate for learning and growth;
3. identification with classroom learning experiences.

Weaknesses. The broadness of this approach has bred inherent weakness which must be faced when it is adopted or implemented. Among these weak-nesses are:

1. poorly trained practitioners in some problem areas of guidance (testing, clinical services, etc.);
2. vitiated efforts because of trying to do (and to be) all things to all people;
3. a depreciation of the value or merit of guidance through the belief that everyone should get into "the act";
4. poor practices in areas where standards should be tenaciously upheld.

Examples. A broad philosophical view of guidance and education is basic to those who profess to support this approach to guidance. Single units (schools, colleges) of city systems or universities; small public school systems; small and medium sized colleges; and junior colleges offer examples of pro-grams adopting this position.

High schools and colleges with a restricted budget and the services only of a single guidance person often have adopted this approach toward a particular view of guidance and education. Similar kinds of institutions have expanded funds to hire guidance leaders and to develop and train faculty members in order to implement a freely selected concept of guidance. The latter examples are more truly representative of a conceived and chosen po-sition rather than an imposed or financially dictated position.

Variations. Recent innovations in "generalist" programs have included the integration of specialized or service units within the total program; clinics, clinicians, and even psychiatrists have been added and used to strengthen a given concept of guidance, counseling, and personnel work. The essential feature, recognizable within any variation of this approach, is a stress upon philosophy, program, and *integration of effort* rather than upon the "services concept." Specially trained guidance or personnel workers may not even be on the staff or a school or college in certain variations of this pattern. The *rationale or perspective* or the faculty, administration, and even staff are the key factors to seek in recognizing variations.

3. Curricular Counseling and Guidance

The integration of guidance and counseling into the academic curriculum of the schools and colleges was a flirtatious affair for many years. Educators, counselors, and guidance workers hoped for this pattern but were unable to evolve a model capable of successful implementation. Experimentation in group guidance, vocations courses, life adjustment courses, as well as social planning and orientation courses were the forerunners of this third major pattern in guidance. The general education movement [46] with its roots in the past and its forward view of the educational process frequently provided a sensitive and nurturing environment for the growth of such programs on the college level. Foundation support for experimental programs has, at the same time, made it possible for such patterns to be constructed on the junior high and senior high school levels.

Curricular approaches have been characterized by the offering of guidance and counseling preparation within a classroom setting through a course in psychology or life adjustment. The early lack of meaningful subject matter for such courses was a deterring factor in its growth. Group Guidance became almost a "dirty word" in high schools. Content study areas of self-concept study, self-analysis, vocational and educational planning, values, and the increasingly varied aspects of individually psychology have overcome this problem for classroom activity.

Strengths.
1. parallel structure with other academic courses in high schools and colleges;
2. use of psychological content to aid in individual counseling and guidance;
3. placement of counselors, guidance workers, etc., within the framework of academic teacher rather than in the role of administrators and coordinators;
4. realistic emphasis of guidance as a continuing process rather than a "one shot cure."

Weaknesses.
1. group guidance offered as a shallow, superficial, and meaningless time-filler;
2. pressure for dual qualifications as effective classroom teacher *and* counselor;
3. inflexibility demanded by classroom contact and scheduling;
4. need for a larger number of well-qualified personnel to implement the goals of program;
5. high cost (compared to 1-300/500-counselor-student ratio).

Examples. College and high school programs have predominated thus far in the implementation of this approach. Occupation courses, [24] and curricular approaches to guidance [18, 19] have often provided the subject-matter foundation for these courses. Private and public junior colleges have also experimented in this area. Junior high schools and senior high schools across the country have been involved through foundation support and the efforts of the Educational Testing Service [25]. Recent developments in the program of text materials spurred this pattern of guidance [20, 26].

Variations. Curricular patterns are a recent product of earlier experimentation in the previously cited areas of group guidance, occupations, orientation, and life adjustment courses. These programs pre-date the curricular pattern but are still technically variations on a theme.

The significant factor in this guidance concept is the *classroom contact with meaningful subject matter content.* Elements of the first two major patterns of centralized specialism and decentralized generalism can be seen in variations of the curricular pattern, but the broad concept of guidance and counseling necessary for successful teaching and counseling activities has tended to bring the generalist view rather than the specialist view into the curriculum and the classroom.

4. Human Relations and Group Work

A fourth pattern of guidance has recently emerged as a method of providing guidance for youth. Human relations centers, mental health programs, group work activities, and related inter-personal approaches have crystallized into programs designed to promote student growth. These programs have not been narrowly focused on such topics as vocational and educational counseling or psychological testing but have tended to strive for the broad general outcomes of adjustment, mature thinking, effective inter-personal skills, and mental health.

The "group dynamicists" and "human relations" specialists, with the help of Naval research funds, began a national training laboratory program at Bethel, Maine, shortly after World War II. Since the beginning of the training concept, this group has published a tremendous number of skill manuals and integrative, cross-disciplinary approaches to education and guidance. Guidance workers have often viewed with suspicion the emergence of this force within a school or college. Somewhat belatedly many guidance workers have realized that the goals of this human relations-group work approach were almost identical to those of guidance.

Specialized programs for maladjusted children, school-wide programs of mental health, and developmental programs on skill training have all demonstrated the techniques of this varied approach and its application.

Strengths.

1. a broad concept of guidance and education which stresses adjustment and maturity;
2. a special tool of group work — highly developed and utilizable by all workers in guidance;
3. a desire to cooperate (and to effect better total programs) with any existing program of guidance;
4. a cross-disciplinary approach with strong roots in the social sciences;
5. a stress on the importance of all personnel (teachers, *et al.*) in working for common goals.

Weaknesses.

1. the lack of specificity in the major tools of guidance, viz. counseling, testing, occupational techniques, etc.;
2. the need for recognition as a "guidance pattern" since many guidance personnel are provincial and often chauvinistic in their own techniques and tools;
3. the tendency for some workers trained in human relations and group work to lack thorough or even minimal training in one of the major disciplines upon which guidance rests — (psychology, sociology, education.)

Examples. Human relations and group work specialists have entered high school and college programs as catalysts in aiding others. Such personnel aid in the development of a focus on helping students and faculty alike in identifying common goals in education, guidance, and personal growth. Such programs were then allied with specialized or clinical programs, curricular, generalists or faculty-advisor programs. As catalysts, these personnel tend to lose their own identity occasionally and to serve as strengthening units in existing programs. As such, this pattern may be denied as a pure model, and yet it has been an increasingly effective and practical method of reaching guidance goals. Samler and others [40] have described several variations on this basic theme.

SUMMARY AND CONCLUSION

Guidance has become a significant force in American education in the recent past. Guidance traces its roots to the early part of this century but has thus far been unable to identify basic patterns or constructs for its functioning. Because of the need to strengthen the entire guidance movement in view of the focus of national, regional, and local scrutiny, four patterns or models of guidance organizational structures have been offered. The four patterns were identified as:

1. Centralized Specialism
2. Decentralized Generalism
3. Curricular Counseling and Guidance
4. Human Relations and Group Work

Many strengths can accrue to a coordinated and clear concept of guidance programming on any educational level. Inconsistent organizational patterns can vitiate the inherent strengths of any single approach. Educational standards of policy and practice demand excellence in any guidance pattern. Future research designs will need to test the relative effectiveness of each approach. Beginning research designs [43-44] show only indications rather than clearly demonstrable results.

The future basic questions which must be answered by administrators on all school and college levels as well as guidance personnel, are three:

1. Do different patterns of guidance actually exist?
2. What is the relative effectiveness of each pattern?
3. Can and should American education accept a pluralistic philosophy of guidance?

ILLUSTRATIVE REFERENCES[1]

[1]Listings are more detailed in patterns III and IV, since these aproaches are less well known than patterns I and II.

I. *Centralized Specialism*
1. Arbuckle, Dugald S. *Student personnel services in higher education.* New York: McGraw-Hill, 1953.
2. Blum, Milton I., & Balinsky, Benjamin. *Counseling and psychology.* New York: Prentice-Hall, 1951.
3. Callis, Robert, Polmantier, Paul C., & Roeber, Edward C. *A casebook of counseling.* New York: Appleton-Century-Crofts, 1955.

4. Froehlich, Clifford P. *Guidance services in schools.* (2nd. ed.) New York: McGraw-Hill, 1958.
5. Hahn, Milton E., & MacLeon, M. S. *Counseling psychology.* New York: McGraw-Hill, 1955.
6. Hatch, Raymond H., & Stefflre, Buford. *Administration of guidance services.* Englewood Cliffs, N. J.: Prentice-Hall, 1958.
7. Traxler, Arthur E. *Techniques of guidance.* (Rev. Ed.) New York: Harper & Bros., 1957.

II. *Decentralized Generalism*

8. Arbuckle, Dugald S. *Counseling and guidance in the classroom.* Boston: Allyn and Bacon, 1957.
9. Arbuckle, Dugald S. *Teacher counseling.* Cambridge, Mass.: Addison, Wesley, 1950.
10. Cantor, Nathaniel. *The teaching-learning process.* New York: The Dryden Press, 1951.
11. Gordon, Ira. *The teacher as a guidance worker.* New York: Harper & Bros., 1956.
12. Gordon, Ira. The class as a group: the teacher as a leader — some comments and questions. *Educ. Admin. Superv.,* 1951, 37, 108-118.
13. Johnston, Edgar G., Peters, Mildred, & Evraiff, William. *The role of the teacher in guidance.* Englewod Cliffs, N. J.: Prentice-Hall, 1959.
14. Lloyd-Jones, Esther, & Smith, Margaret Ruth (eds.) *Student personnel work as deeper teaching.* New York: Harper & Bros., 1954.
15. Strang, Ruth. *The role of the teacher in personnel work* (4th ed.) New York: Bureau of Publications, Teachers College, Columbia University, 1953.

III. *Curricular Counseling and Guidance*

16. Anthony, V. A., *et al.* The team approach to general education. *Junior Coll. J.* 1956, *26,* Part I, 319-327, Part II, 405-410.
17. Bernard, Harold W. *Toward better personal adjustment.* New York: McGraw-Hill, 1951.
18. Borow, Henry. Curricular approaches to personal development: some problems of research. *J. counsel. Psychol.,* 1958, *5,* 63-69.
19. Borow, Henry, & Lindsey, Robert V. *Vocational planning for college students.* Englewood Cliffs, N. J.: Prentice Hall, 1959.
20. Glanz, Edward C., & Walston, E. B. *An introduction to personnel adjustment.* Boston: Allyn and Bacon, 1958.
21. Glanz, Edward C. Personnel and guidance work in a new era. *Junior coll. J.,* 1958, *24,* 141-145.
22. Glanz, Edward C. *Groups in guidance.* Boston: Allyn and Bacon, 1962.
23. Glanz, Edward C. The faculty team in general education. *J. Higher Educ.,* 1956, *26,* 389-392.
24. Hoppock, Robert. Group guidance. New York: McGraw-Hill, 1949.
25. Katz, Martin. *You: today and tomorrow.* (3rd. ed.) Princeton, N. J.: Educational Testing Service, 1959.
26. Mahoney, Harold, & Engle, R. *Points for decision.* (Rev.). Yonkers-on-Hudson, New York: World Book Co., 1961.
27. Richardson, Harold, & Borow, Henry. Evaluation of a technique of group orientation for vocational counseling. *Educ. psychol. Measmt.,* 1952, *12,* 587-597.
28. Warters, Jane. *Guidance in groups.* New York: McGraw-Hill, 1959.

IV. *Group Work and Human Relations*

29. American Council on Education. *Helping teachers understand children.* Washington, D. C.: American Council on Education, 1945.

30. Association for Supervision and Curriculum Development. *Fostering mental health in our schools*. Washington, D. C.: National Education Association, 1950.
31. Association for Supervision and Curriculum Development. *Guidance in the curriculum*. Washington, D. C.: National Education Association, 1955.
32. Benne, K., & Muntyan, N. *Human relations in curriculum change*. New York: The Dryden Press, 1951.
33. Cartwright, Darwin, & Zander, Alvin. (eds.) *Group dynamics: research and theory*. Evanston, Ill.: Row Peterson & Company, 1953.
34. Founce, Roland C., & Bossing, Nelson L. *Developing the core curriculum*. Englewood Cliffs, N. J.: Prentice-Hall, 1952.
35. Kolinsky, Ruth, & Witmer, Helen I. *Community programs for mental health*. Cambridge, Mass.: Harvard University Press, 1955.
36. National Society for the Study of Education. *Mental health in modern education*, Fifty-fourth Yearbook. Chicago: University of Chicago Press, 1955, part 2.
37. Hymes, James L., Jr. *A child development point of view*. Englewood Cliffs, N. J.: Prentice-Hall, 1955.
38. Prescott, Daniel A. *The child in the educative process*. New York: McGraw-Hill, 1957.
39. Redl, Fritz, & Wattenberg, William W. *Mental hygiene in teaching*. (Rev. ed.) New York: Harcourt Brace and Company, 1959.
40. Samler, Joseph, *et al*. *Basic approaches to mental health in the schools*. Washington, D. C.: American Personnel and Guidance Association, 1959. (Reprint series of seven articles from the *Personnel and Guidance Journal*, 1958-1959.)
41. Thelen, Herbert A. *Dynamics of groups at work*. Chicago: University of Chicago Press, 1954.

V. *General Sources*

42. Barry, Ruth, & Wolf, Beverly. *Modern issues in guidance-personnel work*. New York: Bureau of Publications, Teachers College, Columbia University, 1957.
43. Glanz, Edward C., & Penney, James F. Developing a cooperative research design for curriculum validation. *J. Higher Educ.*, 39, 39-44.
44. Ivy, Allan F. A study of two types of guidance staff organizations and their relationship to student perception and use of college guidance services. Unpublished Ed.D. dissertation, Harvard University, 1959.
45. Lloyd-Jones, Esther M. Personnel work and general education, in National Society for the Study of Education, *General education*, Fifty-first Yearbook. Chicago: University of Chicago Press, 1952. Part I, 214-229.
46. National Society for the Study of Education. *General education*, Fifty-first Yearbook. Chicago: University of Chicago Press, 1952.
47. Wrenn, C. Gilbert. Professions and professional membership. *Occupations*, 1951, *30*, 24-29.
48. Wrenn, C. Gilbert. Status and role of the school counselor. *Personnel guid. J.*, 1957, *36*, 175-183.

THE SELF IN RECENT ROGERIAN THEORY[1]

C. H. Patterson
University of Illinois

The objective of this paper is to sketch the place of the self in the current client-centered approach to personality. While the self is today becoming of central importance in all theories of personality, it constitutes the core of the Rogerian approach which has, in fact, been designated by some writers (e. g., 9, 15) as "self-theory." Perhaps this is because client-centered theory is based upon the observations of individual clients in therapy.

ROGERS' FORMULATIONS

1947. Rogers' earliest formulation was presented in 1947 (17): "The self is a basic factor in the formation of personality and in the determination of behavior." As the perception of self changes, behavior changes. The person's feeling of adequacy is basic to psychological adjustment. The absence of threat is important for the development of an adequate self-concept and is a condition for changes in the self-concept. The self-concept is, by definition, a phenomenological concept: it is the self as seen by the experiencing person.

1951. In 1951 Rogers (18) amplified and extended his discussion of the self in nineteen propositions. The point of view remained perceptual and phenomenological; there is no reality for the individual other than that given by his perceptions. The self is the central concept of personality and behavior. While the basic drive of the organism is the maintenance and enhancement of the organism, the psychological self may take precedence over the physiological organism.

Once the self has developed, experiences are perceived and evaluated in terms of their relevance and significance to the self. Behavior is normally consistent with the self-concept, even at the expense of the organism. However, organic experiences or needs which are unsymbolized (because they are unacceptable) may at times lead to behavior inconsistent with the self-concept ("I was not myself"), or to psychological tension and maladjustment. Experiences which are inconsistent with the self-concept may be as threatening, and may be rejected, denied, or distorted; the self-concept is defended.

Psychological adjustment or integration, on the other hand, exists when the self-concept is congruent with all the experiences of the organism. Under conditions of absence of threat to the self, all experiences — including the organismic — may be examined and assimilated into the self-concept, leading to changes in the self-concept. This occurs in therapy.

Reprinted by permission of the Author and *Journal of Individual Psychology,* Vol. 17, May 1961, 5-11.

[1]Paper read at the symposium on "Phenomenological Conceptions of Personality" at the annual meeting of the American Psychological Association, Chicago, Illinois, September 2, 1960.

1959. The most recent and most detailed of Rogers' theoretical discussions, a more systematic and extended formulation of earlier expressions, appeared in mimeographed form in 1955 and in print in 1959 (19). Self-actualization becomes an important aspect of a general actualizing tendency.

The self-concept is defined as "the organized, consistent conceptual Gestalt composed of characteristics of the 'I' or 'me' and the perceptions of the relationships of the 'I' or 'me' to others and to various aspects of life, together with the value attached to these perceptions" (19, p. 200). The ideal self is introduced into the theory and is defined as "the self-concept which the individual would most like to possess, upon which he places the highest value for himself" (19, p. 200).

Several concepts having to do with regard are included. Rogers postulates a basic, though secondary or learned, need for positive regard from others — that is for warmth, liking, respect, sympathy, and acceptance — and a need for positive self-regard, which is related to or dependent upon positive regard from others.

Unconditional self-regard is a state of general positive self-regard, irrespective of conditions. Positive self-regard may be conditional, however, when the individual "values an experience positively or negatively solely because of . . . conditions of worth which he has taken over from others, not because the experience enhances or fails to enhance his organism" (19, p. 209). In this case the individual is vulnerable to threat and anxiety.

The central ideas in Rogers' theory of the self may be stated as follows:

1. The theory of the self, as part of the general personality theory, is phenomenological. The essence of phenomenology is that "man lives essentially in his own personal and subjective world" (19, p. 191).

2. The self becomes differentiated as part of the actualizing tendency, from the environment, through transactions with the environment — particularly the social environment. The process by which this occurs is not detailed by Rogers, but is presumably along the lines described by the sociologists Cooley (8) and Mead (13).[2]

3. The self-concept is the organization of the perceptions of the self. It is the self-concept, rather than any "real" self, which is of significance in personality and behavior. As Combs and Snygg note, the eixstence of a "real" self is a philosophical question, since it cannot be observed directly (6, p. 123).

4. The self-concept becomes the most significant determinant of response to the environment. It governs the perceptions or meanings attributed to the environment.

5. Whether learned or inherent, a need for positive regard from others develops or emerges with the self-concept. While Rogers leans toward attributing this need to learning, I would include it as an element of the self-actualizing tendency.

---

[2]Sociology, I think, anticipated psychology in reacting against behaviorism and recognizing the importance of the self. In the middle thirties, as an undergraduate in sociology at the University of Chicago, I was exposed to the writings of Cooley (8) and Mead (13) on the self. This was where I took on the phenomenology logical approach. Not until several years later were the self and phenomenology introduced, or rather reintroduced, into psychology. I say reintroduced because James (12) had recognized the importance of the self, and was a phenomenologist as well.

6. A need for positive self-regard, or self-esteem, according to Rogers, likewise is learned through internalization or introjection. of experiences of positive regard by others. But, alternatively, it may be an aspect of the self-actualizing tendency.

7. When positive self-regard depends on evaluations by others, discrepancies may develop between the needs of the organism and the needs of the self-concept for positive self-regard. There is this incongruence between the self and experience, or psychological maladjustment is the result of attempting to preserve the existing self-concept from the threat of experiences which are inconsistent with it, leading to selective perception and distortion or denial of experience.

This highly condensed summary does not include the vicissitudes of the self through the processes of disorganization, or the processes of reorganization which take place in therapy.

While a number of persons have contributed to the theory, including Raimy (16), Snygg and Combs (21), and many others who have been associated with Rogers, there has been no other comparable exposition of the theory nor are there any adequately stated alternatives or variations of it. Rogers' terminology differs in some respects from that used by other client-centered writers, but the basic concepts are similar if not identical. For example, some theorists, including myself (14), have used the term self-esteem to refer to what Rogers designates as positive self-regard.

COMPARISON WITH OUR FORMULATIONS

"Me" Versus "I"

Several theorists (2, 4, 13, 22) have emphasized two aspects of the self, essentially distinguishing between the *self as object,* the "me," and the *self as subject,* the "I." The first is often referred to as the *self-concept,* the second as the *ego,* although, as Hall and Lindzey (9, p. 468) point out, there is no general agreement upon terms. James called the "me" the empirical self and the "I" the pure ego — the sense of personal identity or the judging thought. This personal identity, he suggested, may not exist as a fact, "but it would exist as a *feeling* all the same; the consciousness of it would be there, and the psychologist would still have to analyze that" (12, p. 333). The ego would appear to be self-consciousness. Mead's conceptions of the "I" and the "me" appear to be similar, although his discussion is difficult to follow. The "I" appears to be the awareness of the self as of the moment of action (13, pp. 173-178, 192).

These concepts, while preferable to the idea of the "I" as an executive, which lends itself to reification, are vague and difficult to pin down. At least I am not able to differentiate actually, practically, or operationally between the executive aspects of the self, and the self as an object to the self. The self of Snygg and Combs is both an object and doer. Others, including Allport (1) and Sherif and Cantril (20), also appear to adopt this view. Hilgard (10) suggests that the concept of the self as a doer is an error into which psychologists have been led by the common-sense or lay view that behavior seems to be self-determined.

In Rogers' theory the self-concept, although an important determiner of behavior, is not an executive or doer. There is no need for positing such an executive. The organism is by nature continually active, seeking its goal of actualization, and the self as part of the organism is also seeking actualization through its constant activity. The self-concept thus influences the direction of activity, rather than initiating it and directing it entirely. Thus Rogers avoids the problem of reification and the ambiguousness of the concept of the "I" or the ego as an executive. James' sense of personal identity might be considered a part of the self-concept, and the ego or "I" as the awareness of the self-concept. However, I am not sure that this solution is entirely satisfactory.

Ideal Self

In his recent formulation of the concept of the ideal self Rogers indicates that the perception of the ideal self becomes more realistic, and the self becomes more congruent with the ideal self, as an outcome of therapy. This suggests that personality disturbance is characterized by an unrealistic self-ideal, and/or incongruence between the self-concept and the self-ideal. This formulation has been the basis of some research by the client-centered school (e. g., 3). But it is not incorporated in Rogers' statement of the theory. The theory apparently does not recognize conflict between the self-concept and the self-ideal as a source of disturbance, but emphasizes the conflict between the self-concept and organismic experiences as its source. This is in contrast to some other theories in which the self-ideal is a central concept and an important factor in psychological adjustment or maladjustment, e. g., Horney (11).

The Self

The notion of the self, or the self-structure, is broader than the self-concept. It includes the self-concept and the ideal self. What else it includes, is not clear. Combs and Snygg speak of the phenomenal self, defined as the "organization of all the ways as an individual has of seeing himself" (6, p. 126). The self-concept includes "only those perceptions about self which seem most vital or important to the individual himself" (6, p. 127). How these are to be differentiated is not indicated. Rogers considers the self-concept to be in the person's awareness, whereas the self may include aspects not in awareness.

PROBLEMS OF OPERATIONAL DEFINITION

Rogers made an effort to keep his constructs and concepts so that they can be operationally defined. The phenomenological approach, it seems to me, fosters this effort. One is not concerned about the "real" self, the "real" environment, etc., but with the perceptions of particular individuals. The self-concept and the self-ideal are perceptions which can be studied and objectified by instruments such as the Q-sort, or by tests of the "Who am I" variety. The latter, though ideally suited for use with client-centered theory, have not, however, to my knowledge, been used in connection with this theory.

Rogers points out the problem of operationally defining the organismic experiences which, it is assumed, conflict with the self-concept. The aspects of the self other than the self-concept and the self-ideal, are also not operationally defined. Maybe we do not need these concepts. I see no need for unconscious elements of the self, for example. Aspects of the self which are not in awareness but which can be brought into awareness, can be tapped by instructions such as "Sort these statements in terms of your concept of yourself as a father." The self, insofar as it is behaviorally effective, may consist only of the various self-perceptions — thus resolving the problem posed above about the area of the self apart from the self-concept and the self-ideal. The organismic experiences, on the other hand, as an essential aspect of the theory, must be brought within the realm of measurement. The approach of Chodorkoff (5), using Q-sorts of self-referent items by clinicians as an "objective description" of the total experience of the individual, though operational, may be questioned as to its validity.

There is also the problem, pointed out by Combs and Soper (7), that although the self-concept may be operationally defined as the individual's statements about himself, these statements do not necessarily correspond to his perception of himself. His statements may be inaccurate for a number of reasons, including inability or unwillingness to give an accurate report. Yet there is no other approach to determining the self-concept, since by definition it is the perception of the self by the individual, and no one else can report upon it or describe it.

In general, what is needed is a more formal theoretical statement which would lead to testable hypotheses for research, not only with clients in therapy, but in many other situations, with many other kinds of subjects.

SUMMARY

The aspects of Rogers' theory which relate to his central formulation of the self-concept have been summarized. A comparison with the thinking of others regarding the self attempted to clarify some differences and showed other differences in need of resolution. Some problems of operational definition were briefly discussed.

REFERENCES

1. Allport, G. W. The ego in contemporary psychology. *Psychol. Rev.* 1943, 50, 451-468. Also in *Personality and social encounter: selected essays.* Boston: Beacon Press, 1960. Pp. 71-93.
2. Bertocci, P. A. The psychological self, the ego and personality. *Psychol. Rev.,* 1945, 52, 91-99.
3. Butler, J. M., & Haigh, G. V. Changes in the relation between self-concepts and ideal concepts consequent upon client-centered counseling. In C. R. Rogers & R. F. Dymond (Eds.), *Psychotherapy and personality change.* Chicago: Univer. Chicago Press, 1954. Pp. 55-76.
4. Chein, I. The awareness of the self and the structure of the ego. *Psychol. Rev.,* 1944, 51, 504-514.

5. Chodorkoff, B. Self-perception, perceptual defense, and adjustment. *J. abnorm. soc. Psychol.*, 1954, 49, 508-512.
6. Combs, A. W., & Snygg, D. *Individual behavior. Rev. ed.* New York: Harper, 1959.
7. Combs, A. W., & Soper, D. W. The self, its derivative terms, and research. *J. Indiv. Psychol,* 1957, 13, 134-145. Also in A. E. Kuenzli (Ed.), *The phenomenological problem.* New York: Harper, 1959. Pp. 31-48.
8. Cooley, C. H. *Human nature and the social order.* New York: Scribner's, 1902.
9. Hall, C. S., & Lindzey, G. *Theories of personality.* New York: Wiley, 1957.
10. Hilgard, E. R. Human motives and the concept of the self. *Amer. Psychologist,* 1949, 4, 374-382. Also in H. Brand (Ed.), *The study of personality.* New York: Wiley, 1954. Pp. 347-361.
11. Horney, K. *Neurosis and human growth.* New York: Norton, 1950.
12. James, W. *The principles of psychology.* Vol. 1. New York: Holt, 1890.
13. Mead, G. H. *Mind, self and society.* Chicago: Univer. Chicago Press, 1934.
14. Patterson, C. H. *Counseling and psychotherapy: theory and practice.* New York: Harper, 1959.
15. Pepinsky, H. B., & Pepinsky, P. N. *Counseling: theory and practice.* New York: Ronald, 1954.
16. Raimy, V. C. Self-reference in counseling interviews. *J. consult. Psychol.,* 1948, 12, 153-163. Also in A. E. Kuenzli (Ed.), *The phenomenological problem.* New York: Harper, 1959. Pp. 76-95.
17. Rogers, C. R. Some observations on the organization of personality. *Amer. Psychologist,* 1947, 2, 358-368. Also in A. E. Kuenzli (Ed.), *The phenomenological problem.* New York: Harper, 1959. Pp. 49-75.
18. Rogers, C. R., *Client-centered therapy.* Boston: Houghton Mifflin, 1951.
19. Rogers, C. R. A theory of therapy, personality, and interpersonal relationships, as developed in the client-centered framework. In S. Koch (Ed.), *Psychology: a study of science.* Vol. 3. New York: McGraw-Hill, 1959. Pp. 184-256.
20. Sherif, M., & Cantril, H. *The psychology of ego-involvements.* New York: Wiley, 1947.
21. Snygg, D., & Combs, A. W. *Individual behavior.* New York: Harper, 1949.
22. Symonds, P. M. *The ego and the self.* New York: Appleton-Century-Crofts, 1951.

(14)

SELF-PERCEPTION: A STUDY OF DELINQUENT BOYS

Edward H. Selden

Wisconsin State University—River Falls

Examination of the extensive literature on delinquency indicates a continuing concern with efforts to understand the delinquent and the "why" of his behavior. These efforts often involve the use of psychological measures (personality inventories, projective methods) and/or observations of behavior recorded in case histories.

In the context of a more extensive study (Selden, 1960) an attempt was made to approach this problem through examination of the delinquent's self-perceptions. Of course, it was recognized that the factor of social desirability

---

An original article for this book.

enters into responses on a self-evaluation measure as it does into responses on personality inventories (Edwards, 1957) and that this would provide some distortion of the "true" self-perception.

The term "self" as used in this discussion is similar in definition to prior definitions by Raimy (1943) and Symonds (1951). That is, it refers to those aspects of the individual that are perceived as objects in his environment. "The self concept is the more or less organized perceptual object resulting from present and past observations. The self concept is the map which each person consults in order to understand himself, especially during moments of crisis, or choice" (Raimy, 1943). This self-as-object is to be distinguished from the ego-processes of thinking, perceiving, remembering, doing. The interaction between the self and the ego-processes has been described by writers who have stated that when the ego-processes are coping effectively with inner demands and outer reality the person tends to think well of himself (Symonds, 1951; Hall and Lindzey, 1957).

In most discussions of the self we are referring to a construct which is inferred from certain observable behavior of the individual. One method from which such inferences may be drawn regarding the self would seem to depend on the use of "I – sentences" or the checking or rating of descriptive adjectives. Another approach to self-structure that has been employed by various investigators is the use of a level of aspiration task (Hoppe, 1931; Frank, 1935; Rotter, 1942; Lewin, 1944).

The present study used two approaches to self-perception: a method of rating descriptive adjectives and a level of aspiration task. Each approach had been used in prior research on delinquent or criminal samples but no attempt had been made to examine the interrelationships of these two approaches to self-perception on the same delinquent or criminal sample (Cassel and Van Vorst, 1954; Balester, 1956; Rotter, 1943).

Several workers have conjectured regarding a relationship between self-esteem and aspiration behavior. Lepine and Chodorkoff felt that the individual who was lacking in self-esteem was more likely to be "situation-dominated," more dependent on a changing performance score, and would be more likely to obtain a lower goal-discrepancy score (1955). Holt has contended that the level of aspiration should be interpreted in terms of the defense of the individual's self-esteem (1942). Merrill, using a level of aspiration based on vocational goals, emphasizes the many blows to self-esteem that the delinquent suffers in his failures of ego-functioning and finds that his choice of vocational goals is lower than for nondelinquents (1947).

Although there had been several suggestive studies of self-evaluation, none of the studies came to grips with the problem of interrelationship between goal-setting behavior on a level of aspiration task and several aspects of self structure and in particular the application of such measures to a delinquent sample.

Some general assumptions underlying the present study are (1) that measurement of an individual's self-evaluations are possible and that these will differ for diverse categories of individuals; (2) that these evaluations are consistent and interrelated and related to an individual's level of aspiration; (3) that because of lower self-esteem the delinquent will tend to set lower goals in an effort to avoid failure and to protect his threatened self-esteem; (4) that as a result of previous failure experiences the delinquent will have a lower self-evaluation, lower self-esteem, a lower valued self (self-ideal) and will tend to be more critical of others than will the nondelinquent individual.

METHOD

Subjects

The subjects were a sample of 50 delinquent boys between the ages of 15 to 18 selected from a population of delinquents committed to a home school for delinquent boys. A further restriction was imposed on the population from which the sample was drawn by limiting selection to those individuals in the range from one standard deviation above to one standard deviation below the mean in measured intelligence (approximately IQ 84 to IQ 116).

A control sample of 50 nondelinquent boys, comparable in measured intelligence and in age, was selected from a population of nondelinquent boys in the same schools and from the same neighborhoods that had provided the great majority of the delinquent sample. It was felt that to some extent such selection would control the effect of the socioeconomic variables on the variables under study.

Procedure

Both the delinquent and nondelinquent samples were administered the Renzaglia modification of the *Index of Adjustment and Values* developed by Bills, Vance, and McLean (Bills et al, 1951; Renzaglia, 1952). The *Index* had been shown in several earlier studies to be a valid and reliable measure of such variables as self-concept, self-acceptance, self-ideal, and a concept of others. This instrument used a Likert-type five step scale for rating the individual's response to forty-nine adjectives or trait words ranging from *acceptable, alert, annoying*, through *responsible, sarcastic, sincere*, and *worthy*. For example, to obtain a measurement of the subject's present self-evaluation (self-concept) he would be asked to rate himself on the five-point scale as follows for each of the trait-words:

(1)   if it is *seldom* like you
(2)   if it is *occasionally* like you
(3)   if it is like you *about half* the time
(4)   if it is like you a *good deal* of the time, or
(5)   if it is like you *most* of the time

A similar five point rating provides a measurement of self-acceptance, the self-ideal, and the concept of others.

The level of aspiration task administered to both groups was the Group Level of Aspiration Test developed by Cassel (1952). This paper and pencil motor task requires the subject to draw small circles above and below a row of x's, as many as possible in a 30-second interval. On each of the twelve trials he writes down the number that he intends to complete. Thus, a measurement of performance is obtained for each trial and a statement of goal as well. A measure of the goal discrepancy (the traditional D-score) is obtained by using the difference between the goal and the prior performance. Another variable, not usually measured, investigated was the total amount of shift in goals.

With both samples the instruments were administered in a small group situation with the subjects separated by enough distance to prevent discussing ratings or goals with their neighbor.

A rough determination of the reading level of the list of trait-words was provided by checking the 49 trait-words or adjectives against the Thorndike word-frequency lists (1932, 1944). With one exception, the trait-words were found to be in the category referred to as the "Juvenile count" (most common words in grades 3 through 8). As a further precaution against misunderstanding of the trait-words a list of synonyms was prepared for each of them.

The scoring of both instruments followed the procedure recommended by the authors (Bills, 1951; Cassel, 1952).

RESULTS

Table I presents normative scores reported by Bills in the manual accompanying the *Index*. Inspection of the mean scores obtained by Bills and those obtained on the delinquent sample in this study (Table II) indicate lower scores for the delinquent group on all three variables on which comparison is possible (self-concept, self-acceptance, self-ideal). On the self-concept and self-ideal variables the control group in this study obtains a lower score than the normative group. The normative group, however, is a random sampling of high school seniors and the control group was, as indicated, selected from a lower socioeconomic population in a high delinquency area of Minneapolis.

The comparison of the mean scores (Table II) obtained on the self-structure variables finds the delinquent group scoring below the control group on all three self-scales. On the scale designed to measure the self-ideal ("I would like to be a(n) .... person") the delinquent sample mean score is significantly lower than the mean score of the control sample. The importance of this finding is discussed later in this article.

Table III portrays what would be anticipated in a study of self-structure, that a positive relationship exists between the several aspects of such a self-esteem and that the coefficients of correlation differ significantly from zero. It should be noted that the relationship between the individual's self-concept and his concept of others is slightly closer than the relationship between his self-concept and his self-ideal. This might be interpreted as indicating that the average subject in the delinquent sample perceives himself as more similar to others than to his own ideal.

Table IV presents the mean scores for both the delinquent and control samples on the level of aspiration variables. The delinquent sample scores significantly below the control on all the variables investigated. The average goal set up by the delinquent group was not only lower but closer to previous performance as shown by the lower discrepancy score (D-score). This would seem to indicate a desire to avoid failure experiences by keeping the goal close to the performance level.

TABLE I

Mean Scores On Index Of Adjustment And Values: Normative Group of 1,599 High School Seniors (Bills, Manual).

Variable	H. S. Seniors	
	Mean	S. D.
Self–Concept	188.01	21.58
Self–Acceptance	177.68	26.19
Self–Ideal	219.49	21.80

TABLE II

Comparison Of Mean Scores Obtained On The Index Of Adjustment And Values: Delinquent And Control Samples.

Variable	Delinquent (N=50)		Control (N=50)		Diff.	t
	Mean	S. D.	Mean	S. D.		
Self–Concept	175.78	19.614	183.58	20.029	7.80	1.947
Self–Acceptance	174.66	27.262	179.62	18.727	4.96	1.050
Self–Ideal	198.72	23.149	210.72	19.945	12.00	2.781**
Other–Concept	175.32	17.797	175.08	22.385	.24	.059

** = .01 level of confidence.

The amount of shift of goals, with the delinquents again significantly below control group, would indicate that the nondelinquent is more flexible in a goal-setting situation and is less situation-dominated. This is shown by not only a greater amount of shift but by greater variability.

The data presented in Table IV is similar to data previously reported by Rotter in a study of level of aspiration behavior in a criminal population (Rotter, 1942). This similarity takes on greater significance when we note that the tasks used as a measure of goal-setting behavior are considerably different in the two studies.

The findings of this study support most of the assumptions made regarding the self-evaluation and goal-setting behavior of delinquent boys. An ex-

TABLE III

Intercorrelation Of Self-Structure Variables (Index Of Adjustment And Values): Delinquent Sample (N = 50).

Variable	S-A	S-I	O-C
Self-Concept (S-C)	.649**	.576**	.684**
Self-Acceptance (S-A)		.458**	.468**
Self-Ideal (S-I)			.409**
Other Concept (O-C)			

** = .01 level of confidence.

TABLE IV

Comparison Of Mean Scores On Level Of Aspiration Variables, From The Group Level Of Aspiration Test: Delinquent And Control Samples.

Variable	Delinquent		Control		Diff.	t
	Mean	S.D.	Mean	S.D.		
Average Goal	31.78	4.710	35.90	5.634	4.118	3.926**
Perfect Score	31.50	5.645	34.47	6.391	2.974	2.442*
D—Score	1.30	.550	1.73	1.139	.436	2.409*
Amount of Shift	19.76	9.873	29.94	16.504	10.18	3.695**

* = .05 level of confidence or less.
** = .01 level of confidence or less.

ception is the evaluation of others which had been assumed would be lower than for the control group. The general assumption was that an individual would tend to evaluate others lower when his own self-esteem is lower.

DISCUSSION

The results of the present study would suggest that the delinquent boy, in this instance, tends to have a lower evaluation of self than a comparable group of boys who are not categorized as delinquent. This lower evaluation is most marked in the perception of the valued self (self-ideal).

Allport has stressed the value of the ideal-self image in the ongoing development and growth of the individual toward greater integration and adequacy in his book *Becoming* (Allport, 1955). In discussing the self-image Allport says,

> "The image has two aspects: the way the patient regards his present abilities, status, and roles; and what he would like to become, his aspirations for himself . . the ideal-self image is the imaginative aspect of the proprium, and whether accurate or distorted, attainable or unattainable, it plots a course by which much propriate movement is guided" (1955, p. 47).

This propriate movement or "propriate striving" he considers important in the understanding of motivation in humans as contrasted to understanding motivation in lower forms of life. He later states that "guilt . . . is a sense of violated value, a disgust at falling short of the ideal-self image" (Allport, 1955, p. 73). Lynd in her book *On Shame and the Search for Identity* (1958) approaches the function of the ideal-self image somewhat differently. She has said that,

> the question of the meaning and role of the ideal-self image is at the core of . . . distinction between guilt and shame —that guilt is the transgression of a prescribed boundary or taboo, shame a falling short of one's own ideal, which may or may not occur in the presence of others. The role of the self-ideal goes to the heart of the search for identity (Lynd, 1958, p. 169).

It is obvious that both Allport and Lynd recognize the importance of the individual's self-ideal in the control of his behavior, through the operation of either a sense of guilt or shame. In the case of the delinquent this sense of shame would seem to be lessened by a significantly lower self-ideal. Thus, in choice situations involving delinquent behavior he might be less likely to reject the delinquent choice because such behavior is not as inconsistent with his ideal-self as it would be in the case of an individual with more favorable perception of his ideal or valued self.

If the ideal-self reflects the social or cultural standards of a group it may be conjectured that the delinquent has not formed as adequate an identification with society as has the nondelinquent individual. If the ideal-self is an outgrowth of identification with parents or other meaningful adults, it would appear, again, that the delinquent has not achieved the level of identification of the nondelinquent. This might be supported by the subjective observation that in the large majority of delinquent cases there was a lack of affection and understanding on the part of parents, and the process of identification was thwarted.

The delinquent appears to show a greater need to avoid failure than does the nondelinquent individual as evidenced by a lower level of aspiration and a smaller goal-discrepancy score. The nondelinquent has often had more experiences of successful ego-functioning and was less threatened by a goal-setting situation than the delinquent. The delinquent was more situation-dominated, i.e., his responses were keyed more closely to the immediately preceding situation and he was more sensitive to environmental factors.

For the individual working with adolescent youth this study would seem to suggest that continued failure experiences are associated with less favorable self-perception and a tendency toward a lower level of aspiration with a greater need to avoid failure and to defend a weakened self-esteem. The individual must be provided with success experiences to enable him to gain greater self-esteem and self-acceptance and to reduce his dependence on the immediate situation and thus increase his time perspective.

This does not imply, however, that assisting the individual toward a more adequate self-structure will per se eliminate the likelihood of delinquent behavior, but it should improve his chances of making a nondelinquent choice at the choice-point.

REFERENCES

Allport, G. W. *Becoming: basic considerations for a psychology of personality.* New Haven: Yale University Press, 1955.

Balester, R. J. The self-concept and juvenile delinquency. *Dissertation Abstract.* 1956, 16, 1169-1170.

Bills, R. E., Vance, E. L., & McLean, O. S. An Index of Adjustment and Values *J. Consult. Psychol.,* 1951, 15, 257-261.

Cassel, R. N. *Manual: The Cassel group level of aspiration test.* Beverly Hills, Calif,: Western Psychol. Serv., 1952.

Cassell, R. N., & Van Vorst, R. B. Level of aspiration as a means for discerning between "in-prison" and "out-of-prison" groups of individuals. *J. Soc. Psychol.,* 1954, 40, 121-135.

Edward, A. L. *The social desirability variable in personality assessment and research.* New York: Dryden, 1957.

Frank, J. D. Some psychological determinants of the level of aspiration. *Amer. J. Psychol.,* 1935, 47, 285-293.

Hall, C. S., & Lindzey, G. *Theories of personality.* New York: Wiley, 1957.

Holt, R. R. Levels of aspiration: ambition or defense? *J. Exper. Psychol.,* 1946, 36, 398-416.

Hoppe, F. Erfolg und misserfolg. *Psychol. Forsch.,* 1931, 14, 1-62.

Lepine, L. T., & Chodorkoff, B. Goal setting behavior, expressed feelings of adequacy and the correspondence between the perceived and ideal self. *J. Clin. Psychol.,* 1955, 11, 395-397.

Lewin, K., Dembo, Tamara, Festinger, L., & Sears, Pauline S. Level of aspiration. In J. McV. Hunt (Ed.) *Personality and the behavior disorders.* Vol. I. New York: Ronald, 1944. pp. 333-378.

Lynd, Helen M. *On shame and the search for identity.* New York: Harcourt-Brace, 1958.

Merrill, Maud A. *Problems of child delinquency.* New York: Houghton-Mifflin, 1947.

Raimy, V. C. The self concept as a factor in counseling and personality organization. Unpublished doctoral dissertation, Ohio State Univ., 1943.

Renzaglia, G. A. Some correlates of the self-structure are measured by an index of adjustment and values. Unpublished doctoral dissertation, Univ. of Minnesota, 1952.

Rotter, J. B. Level of aspiration as a method of studying personality: I. a critical review of methodology. *Psychol. Rev.,* 1942, 49, 463-474.

Rotter, J. B. Level of aspiration as a method of studying personality: III. group validity studies. *Charct. & Pers.,* 1943, 11, 255-274.

Selden, E. H. A study of self structure and level of aspiration in delinquent and non-delinquent boys. Unpublished doctoral dissertation, Univ. of Minnesota, 1960.

Symonds, P. M. *The ego and the self.* New York: Appleton-Century, 1951.

Thorndike, E. L. *A teacher's word book of the twenty thousand words most commonly used.* Teach. Coll. Columbia Univ., 1932.

Thorndike, E. L., & Lorge, I. *The teacher's word book of 30,000 words.* Teach. Coll. Columbia Univ., 1944.

THE CONCEPT OF SIN AND GUILT IN PSYCHOTHERAPY

Charles A. Curran

Loyola University

You are all familiar with the perceptual figures used in psychology, especially to illustrate Gestalt concepts. One in particular you recall, is, either an attractive young girl or, an extremely ugly old hag, depending on which perceptual clues you are focused. If, by chance, you see the old hag first, it is sometimes extremely difficult to see the young girl. Alternately, if one has pleasantly focused on the young girl, one finds great difficulty in appreciating how others are reacting to the ugliness of the old hag.

This seems to fit something of the problem of guilt and sin. Understandably in psychotherapy we usually see the effects of these concepts in very ugly forms in the ways they have affected the lives of disturbed people. And from this focus, it is often difficult to see that these same concepts might have, for others, a positive and constructive value. Alternately, when one sees sin and guilt in a positive psychological or theological context as the absence of desirable goodness for which one is striving and the stimulation and urging oneself on to greater efforts to acquire that goodness, one is apt to have difficulty understanding the horror and ugliness these same things can produce in many people's lives.

SIN IS A FAILURE TO LOVE

I would like, therefore, to consider both aspects of this question. Aquinas defined vice or evil as turning completely to oneself and away from others, whereas virtue, as he saw it, was the consistent capacity to turn to others, not as rejecting or opposing oneself but as giving oneself in an act of love to others. Christ summed up all the Commandments positively when He said, "Love God above all and your neighbor as yourself." That is to say, this is a balanced integration between our own rights and duties to ourselves and our own self-meaning and the rights others have and their meaning as persons and our duty and love towards them.

Looked at in another way, sin is always a failure to love. "The sinner," said Aquinas, "does not love himself enough." In not loving and respecting himself adequately, he cannot really give himself as something worthwhile to others in love or to God and he does evil to himself in place of good.

Reprinted by permission of the Author and the *Journal of Counseling Psychology,* Vol. 7, 1960, 192-197.

SIN IS NOT WORTHLESSNESS

It would, therefore, be a patient or client distortion to make a state of individual sin synonymous with worthlessness. On the contrary, David in the Jewish tradition and Paul and Augustine in the Christian tradition could be held up as classic examples of people who admitted having committed very grave sins and yet as sinners recognized their own worth in God's forgiveness and redemption. Christ said, "He that is without sin cast the first stone" to the crowd around the adulterous woman and no one dared and the crowd sheepishly and shamefully dispersed. Of Mary Magdalen he said only, "because she has loved much, much is forgiven her." In fact, the classic figure of Judas does not really involve his sin as such — Peter's was probably as great — but his horrible and violent self-condemnation and his despair. This is the final temptation of sin, to refuse the possibility of being made whole again and of being a decent person in one's own eyes who is worthy of others' love and the love of God. In the light of this, what sins a patient or client has committed are not the issue, but his willingness to love again and to let himself be forgiven and to forgive himself.

The positive notion of love — not sin — is the real basis of the central Judaeo-Christian theological tradition.

MEETING THE SITUATION

Intellectual Insight Not Enough

We certainly must come to grips with the questions Mowrer has raised —the basic inadequacy of either psychology or psychiatry to resolve the essential fear of loss that is behind every human achievement or purpose. We must face too, that while there is not an intrinsic tendency towards evil in man, there is a tendency towards disorder, a lack of expected integration between what man knows and is convinced he should do and what he actually does. Paul stated it thus, "The good I would I do not, and the evil I would not, that I do." That is, insight alone is certainly not enough as Mowrer has emphasized. Rank, we know, soon saw this and insisted, contrary to Freud, that when people changed, they changed not because someone gave them insights but because they acquired a whole new view of themselves in the therapeutic experience of feeling and willing. This awareness has had very significant results not only in psychoanalysis itself, but in social work practice and especially in the increasing psychotherapeutic research and skill, particularly under the title of client-centered therapy.

Such concepts would definitely relate to a value scheme of very ancient Judaeo-Greek-Christian origin. This is quite a different view of morality and values, than the Kantian categorical imperatives and Rousseauian simple insights and goodness, with which our most recent ethical concepts have been so heavily influenced.

Exaggerated Self-Condemnation

But we must meet too, Ellis' equally cogent points, particularly his stress on the horrible self-condemnation that sin and guilt so often produce as we witness them in their distortions in the psychotherapeutic interview. If sin is not really the issue — we are in fact all sinners in some form or other — but this violent self-condemnation and rejection, under the guise of a distorted notion of sin and guilt, something must be done to help change this.

Exchange of Viewpoints

Certainly, as Mowrer suggests, more intelligent cooperation and mutual understanding and respect must develop between the clergy and the psychological and psychiatric professions. Serious thought must be given too, to those factors which cause this distorted view of sin and guilt to be prevalent and the degree to which this gravely affects mental illness.

At a recent conference in which I had the opportunity to participate, a group of representative people gathered and discussed the place of religious education in the training of psychiatrists. There was much agreement on the idea that some basic religious awareness were necessary for the psychiatrist so that he could distinguish between his patient's religious distortions and confusions, and the actual theological doctrines which the patient's religion really teaches. This would, I believe, apply equally to the psychologist, social worker, etc. A number of the people in the group — among them psychiatrists and psychologists — maintained that the clergy as a whole probably knew more about what the psychiatrist and psychologist were doing than these professions understood of the religious backgrounds of their patients or clients.

Be that as it may, we surely need much more mature religious and theological presentation particularly on a university and professional training level. We must bring together adequately prepared people in psychology, psychiatry and theology to examine, as we are doing here, some of the complex problems which these interrelationships inevitably involve. Finally, perhaps, this kind of mature and informed interchange must become a consistent part of all our professional training — clergy, psychology, and psychiatry.

THE PARALLEL BETWEEN PAIN AND GUILT

There is another way, however, of considering this question. We are all familiar with the child who is, by a strange and rare exception of nature, born without any reaction to pain. We know that he is tragically handicapped because he has no capacity to feel the warnings of pain and thus to avoid or recoil from, or at least to face, situations that are physically very dangerous or injurious to him.

In somewhat the same way sin and guilt can be perceived in a positive light even if they are not the main point of the Judaeo-Christian theological tradition. They warn us of the dangers to ourselves, they alert us to the issues that we must face at the time when we wish to avoid facing them. We would be seriously handicapped without some warning and alerting signals in our psychical, spiritual life. This does not mean that we seek guilt and sin any more than we seek to increase pain. Yet we have only done ultimate harm to a patient if by drugs or neurosurgery we have removed his feeling of pain without in any way removing the causes of this pain. He is all the more gravely handicapped and his cure can be all the more difficult for him because he has been led to think that feeling no pain, he is actually well.

FREEDOM AND RESPONSIBILITY

Consequently, in the light of this function of the feeling of sin and guilt as alerting man psychologically and spiritually, I wonder if anything would be accomplished by changing names. "A rose — and sin — by any other name" would both come out to be the same thing after all. They are intrinsically bound up with both man's freedom and his responsibility. Rank pointed this out, in the following quotation:

> Free will belongs to the idea of guilt or sin as inevitably as day to night and even if there were none of the numerous proofs for the inner freedom of the conscious will, the fact of human consciousness of guilt alone would be sufficient to prove the freedom of the will as we understand it psychologically beyond a doubt. We say a man reacts *as if* he were guilty, but if he reacts so it is because he is guilty psychologically but feels himself *responsible,* consequently no psychoanalysis can relieve him of this guilt feeling by any reference to complexes however archaic (1936, p. 62).

Looked at in this way, it would seem that, however desirable it might or might not be, we cannot separate feelings of guilt and sin from the whole psychological process of personal and social reasoned responsibility. To do otherwise would only weaken the person psychologically.

The Therapeutic Conscience

In the last century or so, as a result of what seems to me to have been a Cartesian, Rousseauian and especially Kantian philosophical influence, we have tried to separate moral responsibility from reasoned self-understanding and awareness. Conscience was reduced to a bundle of Kantian categorical imperatives coming from outside, from one's parents, family, and what is now even more threatening, from the state. On the other hand, it is becoming increasingly evident that the therapy process itself — no matter how it is brought about — is a process of rational self-awareness and personal responsibility. It is a movement from a negative irresponsibility for oneself to an acceptance of responsibility for one's actions toward self and others. We see this suggested in the following interview excerpt of a woman who has extricated herself from the miseries of a sexual infatuation:

> . . . but when you stop and think of what could have happened why you see things different. (Long Pause) . . . but I know even now, just by not seeing John, I'm better physically and spiritually too (Curran, 1952, p. 149).

It is evident here again in this excerpt from another therapist of a man now out of a series of peccadillo affairs:

> . . . I think, among other things that have transpired here, you have through your subtle process stimulated my conscience gland. (Laughs) Before I was a free agent. But now it is pleasant to think that before I wasn't immoral, but certainly amoral, and now I feel that I would like to be a moral person. There is over-all a sort of healthy resolve on my part. I think it's healthy to walk in the paths of righteousness without being dramatic about it, simply because I can find life more worth living (Snyder, 1957).

It was this type of awareness of the central source of responsibility that caused Rogers to say in his APA Presidential Address in 1947:

> If we take the remaining proposition that the self, under proper conditions, is capable of recognizing, to some extent, its own perceptual field, and of thus altering behavior, this too seems to raise disturbing questions . . . We discover within the person, under certain conditions, a capacity for the restructuring and the reorganization of self, and consequently the reorganization of behavior, which has profound social implications. We see these observations, and the theoretical formulations which they inspire as a fruitful new approach for study and research in various fields of psychology (Rogers, 1947).

Sin and guilt are, in the Judaeo-Christian tradition, also the result of conscience. We see this in David, in Paul, in Augustine. But it is an entirely different conception of conscience than the Kantian blind and often unreasonable categorical imperative.

> Conscience, says Aquinas, according to the very nature of the word, implies the relation of knowledge to something: for conscience may be resolved into *cum alio scientia,* i.e., knowledge applied to an individual case. But the application of knowledge to something, is done by some act. Wherefore from this explanation of the name it is clear that conscience is an act . . . (Aquinas, 1947).

A recent theologian explaining this has said:

> Conscience is the intellectual consciousness or reasoned awareness of right or wrong in a situation here and now to be judged . . . It is the same cold reason with which we work out a problem in mathematics, — only, to be entitled to the name conscience, it must be engaged upon issues of right and wrong, good and bad, and not upon mathematical quantities. The judgment of conscience is always reasoned judgment. (Glenn, 1936, p. 294).

One major goal of counseling psychotherapy is the movement of conscience toward a constructive and practical outcome.

Self Awareness—Before and After Therapy

Counseling can aid in this process because, as the person mirrors himself and slowly sees all the factors that enter into a given series of actions, he grows more able to develop the immediate means to a reasonable solution. This seems to be the basic difference before and after counseling. Before counseling the individual may and usually does consider himself guilty of an unreasonable series of actions. Sometimes this feeling of guilt is excessive. In this case he must, and often does, slowly correct this excessive self-blame as he comes to a more adequate understanding of himself, his past influences and what he has done. But counseling, as in the two excerpts cited, does not always do away with guilt. The person may still feel his acts are truly wrong but in the beginning, while he recognizes the wrongness of his actions, he is glued to the immediate needs which are desirable and attractive. He feels himself unable to do without the things which fulfill these needs. Through counseling, he is able to see that, while these immediate needs are pleasurable, they are ultimately unhappy and dissatisfying. Moreover, he can now perceive other factors which, in his focus on these immediate pleasures, he previously avoided considering. As he begins to act on these new insights, he finds that they bring him greater permanent happiness and self-approval. This in turn further stimulates him to follow his reasonable judgments.

Conscious Struggle for Responsibility

Unless a person makes a conscious effort to grasp all the integrated factors that enter into a situation, he may find himself led quickly by a particular emotion to seek an immediate good which is temporarily satisfying, but is at variance with the integration of the total good which he is seeking. He is responsible for having failed to make an integrated effort because he has the basic ability for such integration. It is not an adequate excuse for the person swept along by his emotions to say that he could not help it. In many instances he *could* have controlled these impulses. With the aid of a skilled counselor, he can objectify and see all the factors which enter into his practical choices. As long as he fails to do this, he may be quickly conditioned by the emotional tones which particular persons, places or things have for him. These emotions may be so strong that, unless an intense effort to prevent it is made, he will find himself swept along a path of conduct which is unreasonable and which in the long run solves nothing.

A person who seeks help is capable of broadening his perceptions by reasonable analysis so that he can combat this tendency to immediate reactions and precipitant judgments. He can slowly learn to take solutions which include much greater integration of the various factors which enter into his problem. We see this taking place as we compare the early interview excerpts with later ones in which these attitudes form themselves into integrated unified solutions. These, in turn, give a realistic and accurate evaluation of the complex aspects of the personal problems presented.

It is difficult to know where responsibility lies in cases of this sort. Objectively, we can consider any unreasonable act morally wrong. We cannot, however, always make the person performing that act completely responsible since, in particular instances his responsibility may be diminished either from lack of knowledge, which could be considered invincible (that is, which he had no opportunity or obligation to acquire) or by the degree to which his emotions made him incapable of acting reasonably at that time.

A person's conscience (as a function of his own reasoning) can witness and retain evidence of past unreasonable conduct as well as given approval or disapproval to present actions and serve as a guide to the future. In this sense, if we were to do away with conscience — that is, the person's capacity to make a reasonable judgment about his conduct — we would do away with one of the main forces for therapy.

THEOLOGICAL SIN AND GUILT

Theological sin, as distinct from sin and guilt generally considered, implies at least implicit acceptance of and relation to a Supreme Being. In this sense sin is not only against ourselves and/or our neighbor, but that same sin being against ourselves and/or neighbor is also against God.

But here too, sin and guilt cannot be separated from love. "God is love," says John the Evangelist in the New Testament, "and he who dwells in love, dwells in God and God dwells in him." Sin is therefore in some way an impediment to this love between God and man much like the insensitive, inconsiderate and selfish person withdraws and prevents the love of others from reaching him. Consequently the sinner by his sin, hurts essentially himself in his love relationship with God. A line in the Psalms says, "He who commits sin is the enemy of his own soul."

This idea that sin is ultimately against God, has profound implications for another important point Ellis raises — using sin as a reason for condemning others as worthless and inferior. Psychologically we know this is most often, if not always, a compensation for refusing to face one's own guilt and sense of sin which provides a vicarious satisfaction through trying to make someone else more sinful. This reveals the profound psychological sublety in Christ's warning, "Judge not, that you be not judged." This kind of condemnation of others is not only psychologically vicious and unsound but it is directly against the core concept of the Judaeo-Christian tradition. This tradition is one of sincere and realistic humility before God in the face of another's sin and the intense self-awareness that as has been said, speaking of a sin of another, "There, but for the Grace of God, go I."

REFERENCES

Aquinas, St. T. *Summa theologica*, Vol. 1, Q. 79, A. 13. Translated by Fathers of the English Dominican Province. New York: Benziger Brothers, 1947.

Curran, C. A. *Counseling in catholic life and education*. New York: Macmillan, 1952.

Glenn, P. J. *Psychology*. St. Louis: Herder Book Co., 1936.

Rank, O. *Truth and reality*. New York: Knopf, 1936.

Rogers, C. R. *The American psychologist*, 1947, 2, 9.

Snyder, W. U. *Casebook of non-directive counseling*. New York: Houghton Mifflin, 1947.

(16)

COUNSELING AS A RELATIONSHIP

C. H. Patterson
University of Illinois

In dealing with counseling the usual approach treats counseling as a process — as a series of stages or phases, not necessarily discrete but nevertheless discernible. We thus have the total process broken down into sub-

Reprinted by permission of the Author and the *Journal of Rehabilitation*, November-December 1959, 13 15.

Dr. Patterson's article reproduces a paper presented at the Sixth Annual Institute for Rehabilitation Personnel, Southern Illinois University, June 30, 1959.

processes: the intake process; the initial interview; the evaluation process, including interviews and testing; the problem exploration stage (including, in vocational counseling, occupational exploration); the problem solving stage, including the selection of a vocational objective; and the closing stage, which in vocational counseling includes placement.

On this view, the attention, the emphasis, of the counselor is focused upon *techniques*. Now while techniques are necessary, they are — or should be — secondary. They are not the essence of the counseling process, only means to the goal. Concern with techniques as such may be detrimental rather than helpful to good counseling. It tends to lead to a situation in which the counselor uses techniques as devices by which to manipulate or influence the client toward the acceptance of his, the counselor's, goals or objectives. This is the kind of thing represented by such phrases as counseling a client into, or out of, a vocational field, or counseling a client to accept this or that goal or objective, or toward this or that decision. To call such activity counseling is a misuse of the term, if not a desecration of the very concept. Counseling is not something you do to, or practice upon, a client. It is something you engage in *with* the client.

The word *with* suggests that, rather than being a matter of techniques, counseling is a *relationship*. This point of view has been discussed and developed by a number of writers, but mainly in the area of psychotherapy. I think it has value in all counseling areas.

IN AID OF GOOD RELATIONSHIPS

It is obvious that counseling is a *human* relationship. Since we are, of course, constantly engaged in relationships with other people, it might appear that there should be no difficulty in learning to be a counselor; we would simply apply what we know about human relationships in our work with our client. To some extent this is true. Counseling and psychotherapy are often made to appear to be more complicated, more mysterious, more esoteric, than is actually the case. The emphasis upon techniques, the attempt to classify kinds of clients and kinds of problems and to match these with specific techniques, contributes to this impression. To view counseling as basically akin to other human relationships is to remove this aura of mystery and magic. This might be threatening to some professional counselors and therapists, suggesting that learning counseling or even psychotherapy is not necessarily a long, complicated process.

Granted this is the case, we must beware of oversimplification. Counseling is based upon the principles of *good* human relations. While these principles are in general known, they are necessarily widely practiced outside of counseling and psychotherapy, nor do they necessarily come automatically and easily. It is also true that their application in counseling as compared with their application in other interpersonal or social relationships, involves somewhat different techniques, methods, and skills. Let us consider briefly what these principles of good human relations are, and how they may be manifested in the counseling relationship.

Good human relationships are those which are productive of or conducive to good mental and social-psychological health. Since the goal of counseling or psychotherapy is the attainment of good mental health, the basic principles of good human relations and counseling are clearly the same. One might say that the providing of good human relationships keeps people healthy, while in counseling and psychotherapy we are concerned with restoring people to good mental health or improving their mental health. What is good for one purpose is likewise useful in fulfilling the other.

What now are the requirements of good mental health which can be met as individual interacts with individual, whether in general human relationships or in specific situations such as teacher-student, employer-employee, or counselor-client relationships?

MARKS OF MENTAL HEALTH

The first and basic requirement of every individual if he is to be mentally healthy is that he have at least a modicum of self-esteem — that he accept himself, that he feel that at least in some respects he is a person of worth. The achievement and maintenance of this self-esteem is the basic drive and motivation of every person. To have it is to be, to the extent that it is present, mentally healthy. A social environment which facilities the development and maintenance of self-esteem is a healthy environment.

How does one go about providing such an environment? What can one do to promote self-esteem in other people? We have some evidence, both from research and from experience, regarding the conditions which promote or foster self-esteem or mental health.

It is difficult, if not impossible, to accept or respect oneself if one is not accepted by others. One of the first principles of human relations, therefore, is the acceptance of others. Acceptance involves recognition of another as an individual, a unique person, who is respected as a person and treated as worthy of respect. Acceptance includes the recognition of the right of another to be himself rather than conform to what you might want him to be. One accepts others by being interested in them as individuals, showing respect for their opinions or contributions or expressions of feelings, taking time to listen to what they have to say.

It is not always easy to accept others as they are, particularly when they differ greatly from ourselves. We tend either to ignore or reject those who are unusual, or attempt to change them. It is easy to be critical, derogatory in our remarks, belittling and condemning. Our own needs for self-esteem may interfere with our accepting and respecting others. We may want to feel superior to others in order to bolster ourselves. Our own unsatisfied need for self-esteem thus prevents us from esteeming others. Thus a vicious circle develops — a situation in which the mutual respect so necessary for good human relationships and good mental health is lacking. The circle must be broken. Those who have some security, some degree of self-esteem, must manifest respect for others who in turn may develop enough self-esteem to be able then to show respect for others, and so on. It is not always easy to listen to others — to really listen — instead of thinking of what we are going to say next. But listening to another is the simplest, most basic way of showing respect for him.

Acceptance and respect form the foundation for the second basic principle of good human relations. Acceptance leads to understanding. People want and need to be understood. They need to feel that others know and appreciate what they are, who they are, and why they are as they are and behave and think as they do. But understanding is more than "knowing what makes people tick." It entails something more than glib use of psychological terminology. Understanding of another is not obtained by standing on the outside and looking at him. It comes only from imaginatively getting on the inside and looking out, seeing things as he does. It is this kind of "feeling understood" that people want — release from the feeling that they are alone, isolated, so different that no one else sees things as they do.

A third factor in good human relationships is confidence and trust. One may not agree with another's decisions or acts, but one respects the other's rights to them — within, of course, the limits imposed by rights of other people. The recognition of freedom of thought and action means that the manipulation of others, either by subtle or by overt methods, for one's own goals, or even for the presumed good of those manipulated, is not consistent with good human relations.

Finally, good human relations are characterized by openness, integrity, and honesty. There is no place for deceit, trickery, or subterfuge. Such performance is inconsistent with respect, understanding, and recognition of the freedom of choice of others.

MUTUAL RECOGNITION OF WORTH

The existence of these conditions in human relationships appears to make possible the optimal development of the individual. They foster self-esteem, self-confidence, independence, responsible decisions and behavior. These are the characteristics of good mental health. Taken together, these conditions provide an optimum environment for the development of the individual. An important characteristic of this environment is the absence of threat. We are beginning to realize that only where threat is not present can the individual develop to his fullest potential. A threatened individual is anxious, tense, afraid, inhibited, withdrawn. Threat leads to a narrowing or restricting of perception, of thinking, of activity. Learning, or modification of behavior, does not occur. A person under threat is emotionally disturbed. Only in a nonthreatening environment — one that is accepting, understanding, trustworthy, dependable, consistent — can the individual be free to learn, to solve problems, to make adequate decisions and choices, to act intelligently, to express himself — in short, to be mentally healthy.

Now the counseling relationship is a good human relationship. It could not be otherwise. The goals of the individuals concerned are the same; the basic principles must also be the same. The counseling relationships is one in which the counselor accepts the client, respecting him as an individual of worth. The counselor endeavors to understand the client. The counselor recognizes the right of the client to make his own decisions, and determine his own actions. The counselor attempts to provide a nonthreatening atmosphere in which the client may explore his problem, look at things in a different light, and reach a more adequate solution.

Or does he? How many counselors actually are applying the principles of good human relations in their counseling? I have heard counselors say, "That may be all right in psychotherapy. But we can't be permissive and completely accepting. We can't allow the client to make his own decisions. We are responsible for what happens. We have to justify the expenditure of money on the client, and we must avoid wasting money on foolish decisions." But does this justify violation of the principles of good human relations, of good mental health? It should not. Any program which requires such violation should be examined and revised. No goal which is achieved at the expense of good mental health in the client can be justified. What does it profit a counselor, a client, or society, if the client gets a job but loses his independence, self-respect, or sense of personal adequacy in the process?

FORESTALLING DEFENSE REACTIONS

The counselor who cannot trust the client and his decisions is perhaps not able to make any better decisions himself. How many of the counselor's decisions are less foolish than those of some client? May it not be that the counselor's lack of confidence in the client is itself the cause of the client's insistence upon poor or inadequate choices?

We are all aware of the reaction of individuals to challenge, to criticism, to attempts to force changes upon them — the child who becomes more demanding the more his desires are thwarted; the girl who insists on marrying the clearly inferior boy to whom her parents violently object. Some would see such conduct as willfulness or unreasoning refusal to listen to reason. Actually, it is the universal defensive reaction to threat. So in counseling, the persistence of the client in clinging to an unsuitable choice may be a reaction to the threatening aspect of the relationship.

Some counselors are afraid to show interest in the client, acceptance of him, confidence in him, because they are afraid they will be trapped by the client, imposed upon, or taken advantage of. This attitude is not conducive to a good relationship. It indicates that the counselor feels threatened by the client.

Now it is true that the counselor in an agency that expends public money on a client has a responsibility. He must be convinced that the money is being well spent. And to do this he must evaluate the plans and program of services provided for the client. But in the counseling process itself, as we commonly think of it, it is the client who makes the decisions, even the final decision regarding his vocational objective. This has been stressed for a long time even by those who are non-client-centered to some extent, and make suggestions or list alternatives. (Such counselors commonly say, "Well, the client does have the final choice, makes the final decision.")

Thus we have a dilemma. How can we resolve this?

EVALUATION IS NOT COUNSELING

The resolution, in my mind at least, consists in the fact that the counselor *avoids making decisions during the counseling process.* The counselor's evaluation is not, on this view, a part of counseling. When he is evaluating he is not counseling. When he is evaluating, he is not doing psychotherapy. When he has to evaluate to make decisions, then he is not a counselor. What this means in practice is that the decisions should be limited to (a) the early stages of the counseling process (or prior interviews), when decisions have to be made regarding eligibility, feasibility, need for services, etc., and (b) the concluding stage, when the counselor, since he has to approve the decision of the client, must make his own decision whether he can accept that decision or not.

The evaluative attitude, then, is to the greatest extent possible kept out of the counseling process. Counseling continues on the basis of the best accepted counseling principles. If after the counseling is completed the counselor cannot accept or approve the decision or choice of the client, he simply tells the client so, giving his reasons. This can be a difficult situation to handle, since it can be threatening or coercive for the client. Actually, such outcomes are far fewer than those would expect who are unable to trust the client to make his own decisions.

Another way in which some counselors violate the principles of good relationships is in failing to be completely honest and sincere with the client. The counselor has certain objectives or goals for the client and is perhaps afraid that the client will not reach or accept them on his own. This "bag of tricks" concept of counseling is often held by nonprofessional people, by those who make referrals to counselors in schools or other agencies to have the client "straightened out." But good human relations are open, honest, and sincere; counseling must be the same.

WHAT COUNSELING REALLY IS

An important implication of counseling as a relationship has to do with what the counselor does or gives to the client. Rather than being concerned with giving or providing services, or even the giving of advice or information, the counselor should be concerned with his psychological contribution to the relationship: Instead of giving concrete, material, or tangible goods or services, the counselor gives himself. He gives his time, interest, attention, respect, understanding, all of which are intangible, yet are the essential elements of counseling as a relationship.

The counseling relationship then is a special application of the principles of good human relations. It is specialized in several respects. *First,* it is the conscious, ordered, purposeful application of the principles in a formal, planned situation in which one person, who is in need of special assistance, is helped by another person, who is presumably not urgently in need of help for himself. Its purpose is thus not simply the fostering or maintenance of personal adjustment or adequacy in the more or less average, adjusted, or adequate person, but the assistance of those who are in trouble, who are to some extent or in some respects inadequate, who have problems which they have been unable to resolve by themselves.

Second, the counseling relationship is closer, more intense, more concentrated, than the usual social relationship. The principles of human relations are applied in their purest form, without the formalities and banalities of ordinary social intercourse. The relationship is limited to the essentials, uncontaminated by social sparrings, which are essentially either protective defenses or reassurances. Almost all ordinary human relationships seem to have some element of threat in them, or are easily perceived as threatening by the individual who feels inadequate or needs help. The counseling relationship carefully avoids or eliminates every possible element of threat.

Third, the counseling relationship is on a deeper level than ordinary social relationships. This is possible because of the lack of threat, which enables the client to look at himself closely and deeply, to expose himself to the counselor, establishing a relationship which is unlike any other. The counselor must be especially qualified if he is to handle this intimate relationship adequately, in a way which is really helpful to the client. He must have sufficient self-esteem so that he is not threatened by the client.

GIVING OF SELF A PAYING INVESTMENT

Viewing counseling as a relationship leads us to consider it from a point of view which emphasizes new aspects. Our concern is not with techniques, with what we do, but with what we are; not with what we can give in the way of goods and services, but with how much we can give ourselves; not with tangible, concrete, limited outcomes, such as good vocational choices or other decisions, placement in employment, etc., but with whether the client has maintained or improved his self-esteem, his self-respect, his independence, his status as a human being. This is the goal of all counseling, whether educational, vocational, rehabilitation, marital, or therapeutic. Other objectives are minor, or important only as they contribute to the development of a self-respecting, responsible, independent human being. Such an outcome is not achieved by techniques or the giving of material things, but only as the result of a good human relationship, the giving of oneself in the service of others.

$$\boxed{17}$$

GUIDELINES FOR CAREER DEVELOPMENT

Lawrence P. Blum
University of Wisconsin—Milwaukee

MODERN GUIDANCE BEGAN AS VOCATIONAL GUIDANCE

Concern for vocational guidance, vocational adjustment, and career development has always been a major aspect of guidance services. The guidance movement had its roots in the vocational concerns of individuals. Frank Parsons, a public spirited and versatile social scientist and social worker, established the Vocation Bureau in Boston in 1908 as a part of the Civic Service House of that city. In this agency he established the spirit and pattern of vocational counseling with sufficient soundness to cause it to be influential

---

An original article for this book.

to the present time. His philosophy of guidance and methods for implementing vocational guidance are set forth in *Choosing a Vocation,* published in 1909, shortly after his death. He states the essentials of vocational guidance as follows: "There are three broad factors: (1) a clear understanding of yourself, your aptitudes, abilities, interests, ambitions, resources, limitations, and their causes; (2) a knowledge of the requirements and conditions of success, advantages and disadvantages, compensation, opportunities, and prospects in different lines of work; (3) true reasoning on the relations of these two groups of facts."[6] It is worthy of note that Parsons attempted the difficult task of individual assessment long before the creation of the array of instruments which the counselor now has at his disposal. It was also long before systematic procedures for analysis of the details of the world of work become available.

Further evidence of the vocational emphasis in early guidance activities is seen in the fact that the first professional organization of guidance workers, established in 1913, bore the name National Vocational Guidance Association. From 1933 to 1939, the National Occupational Conference, financed by the Carnegie Corporation, published *Occupations,* a journal dedicated to publicizing techniques and content relevant to vocational guidance. These and many other phases of the history of guidance provide sufficient documentation of the large place that vocational guidance has in the development of the guidance movement.

Guidance Now Is Vocational Plus Many Additional Areas

With the passage of time many additional responsibilities were crowded into the guidance field. To accommodate this broadened range of activity the National Vocational Guidance Association banded with other groups functioning in guidance to become the American Personnel and Guidance Association, and its publication, *Occupations,* for many years the key publication in the guidance field, became the *Personnel and Guidance Journal.*

The interests and duties of counselors have likewise broadened and, in the process vocational counseling and guidance have not received the attention they once had. This reduction of emphasis on vocational counseling is summarized by Wrenn in his review of the findings of Project TALENT, one phase of which surveyed the status of counseling in American secondary schools. Project TALENT was a project concerning Identification, Development, and Utilization of Human Talents, conducted by the American Institute for Research, under sponsorship of the U. S. Office of Education. In analysing the findings Wrenn notes that of counseling duties reported by counselors "counseling for college" and "counseling for high school" were cited with greatest frequency. Also frequently cited were "counseling for developing potential" and "counseling for inadequate achievement." All of these rank higher in frequency than did "counseling for occupations." As Wrenn states "The interpretation of what is meant by an item may vary, but the low ranking vocational counseling suggests a disturbing absence of what many assume to be a vital counseling area for adolescents." He goes on to state that "counseling for occupations" ranks much lower than other counseling emphases in the three- to four-year senior high school."[11]

**There Seems to be a Resurgence of Interest in
Vocational Guidance and Counseling**

Several factors account for the renewed interest which has become apparent in vocational guidance and counseling. One such factor has been the emergence of thoughtful theories concerning the process of decision making in vocational and career areas. Hoppock[2] reports and discusses no fewer than 17 of these and his list is being added to each year. The net result of such proliferation of theories is that all of them require testing in guidance practice before they can be fully accepted. They do, however, provide vocational counselors with hypothetical explanations about the way in which occupational plans are developed. Another factor responsible for renewed interest in vocational guidance involves concern over the influence of technological change upon the career possibilities of youth.

THE IMPACT OF AUTOMATION ON CAREER DEVELOPMENT

The increased mechanization and instrumentation of activities related to the production of goods has been variously regarded as a blessing or a Frankenstein. Those who regard it as a blessing point to the tremendous possibility of producing consumer and luxury goods in such quantity and so inexpensively that they can be available to all at low cost. The net result, they feel, is a heightened living standard and a better life for all. A recent report points out as an example that "automatic machines, linked by transfer equipment, move engine blocks through a complete manufacturing process, performing 530 precision cutting and dulling operations in 14 1/2 minutes as compared to 9 hours in a conventional plant."[7] "In petroleum and chemicals the story is almost ancient: as far back as 1949 catalytic cracking plants were turning out 41,000 barrels a day with instruments. . . . In a Texaco refinery the computer controls 26 flow rates, 72 temperatures, 3 pressure levels, and 3 gas combinations."[7]

> Another report concerns an automatic lathe "which gauges each part as it is produced and automatically resets the cutting tools to compensate for tool wear. In addition, when the cutting tools have been worn down to a certain predetermined limit, the machine automatically replaces them with sharp tools. The parts are automatically loaded into the machine and are automatically unloaded as they are finished. These lathes can be operated for five to eight hours without attention, except for an occasional check to make sure that parts are being delivered to the load mechanism."[4]

The fact that fewer people can produce vastly more goods is certain to affect the kinds of opportunities awaiting young people. The "viewers with alarm" feel that substantially increased unemployment will accompany technological change. Others take a more moderate view that unemployment need not necessarily follow, but that employment displacement is most likely.

Specific activities related to careers are to have at least the following effects:

1. There will be an higher premium on training and skill. The technical demands of the mechanical era are such that the training for them cannot be completed within a conventional period of schooling. Any young man or

woman who does not contemplate continuing his education or training beyond high school can be regarded as a dropout from educational experience and be subject to all the disadvantages of those who drop out before high school graduation. The handicap experienced by those who leave school prior to graduation is well documented, as Samler comments "The relationship between training, skill, and employment is only too clear. For 1963 three-quarters of male professionals worked an entire year at full-time jobs as did two-thirds of male white collar workers. However, this is true of only one-third of the laborers. In 1963 the average unemployment rate for the nation was 5.7. For the 14-19 age group it was 15.6. . . . Comparison of unemployment rates between high school graduates and dropouts reinforces the same unhappy point. The data reveal that only 8 per cent of the graduates, but 14 per cent of the dropouts were unemployed."[10] As Wolfbein states "whether it be the unskilled, or semi-skilled, the young school dropout or the older man who also has a high rate of long term unemployment, one of the great common denominators which ties them all together is lack of skill."[10]

2. Business, industry, and employers generally must assume greater responsibility for education and training.

The expectation that many candidates for careers on the automated scene will not have the requisite skill makes it imperative that employers pay more attention to the training and selective placement of these people. Much recent information regarding the ways and rates of learning among adults can be applied in business and industry. It is incumbent also upon school guidance personnel to establish such relationships and communication with employees that the employers have a clear picture of how their training and educational efforts can supplement those of the school.

3. School guidance people must continually reappraise their career information.

The changing employment picture has resulted in an accelerated rate of obsolescence of occupational information. It is probable that the total supply of occupational information in the files of school guidance personnel will be obsolete and nearly useless within five years. In some career areas items of information acquired as recently as one or two years ago have reduced utility. The rapid decline of assembly and production line opportunities, the replacement of middle-management executive personnel with computer apparatus for decision making, the increased demands for skilled workers are areas which are in a constant state of flux and about which school guidance personnel need constantly replenished information. Career information of the future must include more detailed attention to the psychosocial aspects of work. When individuals establish patterns of relationship to machines more than to people, there are implications for morale and the kinds of people most likely to be succesful employees.

THEORIES OF CAREER DEVELOPMENT HAVE INFLUENCED VOCATIONAL GUIDANCE

The reports of numerous theories of career development in recent years have been influential in focusing attention upon the role of the curriculum, teaching staff and guidance personnel in shaping career plans. One conclusion deriving from these theories is that the term "choice" regarding the selection of an occupation or career is a misnomer. This is true because there is, in reality, no point in time when an individual makes a "decision" to be this or that. A more accurate way of describing the selection and entering upon an occupation is as a "process" to which many forces have contributed. In a real sense a person "becomes" something vocationally rather than "decides" to be something.

After examining numerous reports of investigations of the influences on vocational development, Miller prepared the following summary of the most influential forces.

1. The most frequently given reason for choice is liking for or attraction to the occupation. This is true of both high school and college students.

2. The second most frequently given reason for choice is a belief in fitness or qualification for the occupation.

3. A considerable proportion of both high school and college students feel that they have been influenced in their occupational choices by parents.

4. Other persons significant in the student's life — teachers or professors, friends, and relatives other than parents — are regarded as being influential in choice, but their influence is reported somewhat less frequently than is the influence of parents.

5. Of the influences felt to be important by both high school and college students, the hope of financial reward — is yet to be among the four or five most frequently mentioned reasons.[5]

Among the earliest of the theories of vocational development was that of Ginzberg[1] which is summarized as follows:

"The basic elements in the theory which we developed were three: Occupational choice is a process; the process is largely irreversible; compromise is an essential aspect of every choice. Concerning the first element, it can be said that the process begins at the birth of the individfual and may remain open until death. We began the study of the process in individuals at about the age of eleven, which appeared to be the first time, that a young person recognizes that he will eventually have to do something about choosing his future work. We found that the process of occupational decision making could be analyzed in terms of three periods — fantasy choices (before 11); tentative choices (between 11 and 17); and realistic choices (between 17 and young adulthood when a person finally determines his choice). The child, in the fantasy period, believes that he can become whatever he wants to become. He makes an arbitrary translation of his impulses and needs into an occupational choice. During the tentative period, his translation is almost exclusively in terms of such subjective factors as his interests, capacities, and values. Adolescents consider their choices tentative, because they sense that they have not effectively incorporated the reality factors into their considerations. They are able to do this during the realistic period, when they seek to work out a compromise between their interests, capacities, and values, and the opportunities and limitations of the environment."[9]

The ideas embodied in Ginzberg's theories have become basic to career development thought since they were first presented. In some instances extensions and minor alterations of the basic concept have occurred. For example, Super and his students see career development as a process extending throughout the entire lifetime of the individual. He states, "Like other aspects of development, vocational development may be conceived of as beginning early in life, and as proceeding along a curve until late in life. Thus the four-year-old who plays carpenter and storekeeper is in a very early stage of vocational development, and the septuagenarian, who no longer teaches or does research but still attends scientific meetings or writes his professional autobiography, is in a very late stage of vocational development."

Just as general development can be broken down into major life stages placed sequentially on a continuum, each stage having characteristics which are peculiar to it and which justify singling it out, so the continuum of vocational development can be broken down into vocational life stages, each defined by its peculiar characteristics. We have seen that the major vocational life stages may be classified as the Exploratory, Establishment, Maintenance, and Decline stages. Most of these can in turn be divided into substages. The Exploratory Stage has Fantasy, Tentative, and Realistic (or Initial) Substages characterized by appropriate attitudes toward work and occupation; Establishment begins with Trial and progresses into a Stable Substage as the individual begins to make his place in the world of work; the Maintenance Stage is as a whole characterized by stability in the field in which establishment has taken place earlier in life; and the Decline Stage begins with a Substage of Deceleration and progresses to one of Retirement."[8] Super also refines the theory by his view that career development is a mode of implementing a self concept. Total personal development and career development are thus seen to accompany each other.

It can be seen that achievement of the three basic stages varies from individual to individual. However, the following characteristics seem to prevail:

a. The three stages are developmental and follow one another chronologically.
b. Considerable overlap occurs as the transition is made from one stage to another.
c. The number of occupations considered becomes progessively fewer during the tentative and realistic choice stages until one occupation is selected.

A theory which is not clearly consistent with the developmental stages concept of Ginzberg, but which has proved influential, is that of Hoppock. Hoppock feel that individual needs, and the way in which they are met, constitute the basis of career development. His theory consists of the following steps:

1. Occupations are chosen to meet needs.
2. The occupation that we choose is the one that we believe will best meet the needs that most concern us.
3. Needs may be intellectually perceived or they may be only vaguely felt as attractions which draw us in certain directions. In either case, they may influence choices.
4. Vocational development begins when we first become aware that an occupation can help to meet our needs.

5. Vocational development progress and occupational choice improves as we become better able to anticipate how well a prospective occupation will meet our needs. Our capacity to anticipate thus depends upon our knowledge of ourselves, our knowledge of occupations, and our ability to think clearly.

6. Information about ourselves affects occupational choice by helping us recognize what we want, and to anticipate whether or not we will be successful in collecting what the contemplated occupation offers to us.

7. Information about occupations affects occupational choice by helping us to discover the occupations that may meet our needs, and to anticipate how well satisfied we may hope to be in one occupation as compared with another.

8. Job satisfaction depends upon the extent to which the job that we hold meets the needs that we feel it should meet. The degree of satisfaction is determined by the ratio between what we have and what we want.

9. Satisfaction can result from a job which meets our needs today or from a job which promises to meet them in the future.

10. Occupational choice is always subject to change when we believe that a change will better our needs.[2]

The idea that vocational development follows a sequence beginning with indefinite, probably fantasy-based choices, continuing with a period of tentative choices, and terminating with reality-based decisions has implications for the kinds of vocational guidance and educational experience which is provided.

It can be noted immediately that the period of indefinite, fantasy-based vocational experience coincides with the elementary school years. The implication for teachers and elementary school guidance personnel are several:

1. The normal fantasy life of the young child provides opportunity to determine "how it feels" to play vocational roles. He can be a cowboy, locomotive engineer, spaceman, teacher, etc., with no risk and with no need for consideration of reality factors.

2. In the later elementary school years introduction can be had to occupations which are close to the experience of the group. For example, the occupations of the fathers and or mothers of the class members can be discussed and a bit of role playing of these careers can be engaged in.

3. Attention can be devoted to subject matter content of a vocational nature. Biographies, for example, can be read with a view to discovering how people earned their living and possibly the factors which caused them to enter upon those particular careers. In arithmetic and science an opportunity exists to discuss careers and even role play some of the activities related to those areas.

The school experience coinciding with the period of tentative choices includes the junior high school years. The goal of school experience in this period is to provide sufficient knowledge in vocational areas so that valid attitudes toward specific careers can be developed. This experience necessarily is vicarious in nature. It can consist of vocational reading, visits, interviews with professional people, tours of work settings, and career films. It makes little difference whether this experience is provided as part of a formal course in occupations or as an incidental part of other courses. The important factor is that opportunity be provided for discussion and evaluation which have been created. It is important also to remember that the attitudes which are being developed at this stage are strictly tentative and are not to be regarded as career decisions or binding vocational plans. It is true that some individuals make a vocational choice while still rather young, but the majority do not arrive at firm plans during the junior high school years. The tentative nature of plans at this age is reported by Super and Overstreet who state that "Preferences expressed at the ninth-grade level should not be viewed as definite vocational objectives. . . . The task of the vocational counselor in the ninth-grade is essentially a matter of furthering vocational development rather than of fostering specific vocational choices."[9]

At the level of the senior high school the narrowing of possibilities as a result of considering reality factors can take place. It is the responsibility of instruction and counseling at the senior high school level to facilitate this narrowing of the field. This will necessitate identifying students in terms of their immediate plans. These plans may include withdrawing from school prior to graduation, entering the world of work immediately upon graduation, or continuing education and training beyond the high school. Each of these groups will require guidance of a special type at the time when it will be most beneficial to the recipient. Since it is true that people are most motivated to learn content which is to be used in the immediate future, it is sensible to provide the specialized guidance immediately prior to his need for it. It thus is probable that concentrated occupational guidance should occur in the ninth or tenth grade for those pupils who tend to drop out of school at that time. This guidance should be directed at the identification and development of abilities and skills which will be immediately useful in the labor market. Much as dropping out of school is deplored, those who do should have minimum handicap on entering the job market.

Those pupils who plan to complete high school, but not continue their education or training, need a program of guidance and instruction similar to that for dropouts. These people also have a real need for immediately available skills which are usable by employers. Detailed consideration needs to be given to identification of abilities, interests, and needs of individuals and the reality factors which are going to be influential in narrowing the range of possibilities and ultimately in arriving at a suitable entry job in the world of work. It is probable that the school agency should be more directly involved in the placement function than it customarily has been. This involvement can mean more cooperative relationships with the state employment service, and it can also mean continued contact with the new employee as he goes through his first employment experience. At present it is relatively rare for a school to continue the availability of its guidance services for postgraduates. Since career adjustment for the high school graduate may mean trying several jobs, however, it is important that counseling be available so he can systematically evaluate his experience with each.

For the pupil who plans to continue education and training beyond high school, the urgency for decision is somewhat reduced and the period for exploration and tentative choices extended. In fact it may be desirable deliberately to avoid early decision in order to gain breadth and depth in high school education. Counseling and guidance for these people consists of helping them understand their abilities, interests, and needs and explore with them their in- and out-of-school experiences. The aim is to arrive at eventual long-range career objectives for which education and training beyond high school are necessary.

THE ROLE OF OCCUPATIONAL INFORMATION IN CAREER DEVELOPMENT

The maintenance of supplies of recent and accurate occupational information in usable form is indeed a responsible guidance function. As was mentioned earlier our technology, as far as vocation and careers are concerned, is changing so rapidly that keeping up to date on developments is a major challenge. Since many young people will secure their first jobs in their home communities, it is important for guidance people to be familiar with opportunities in their community. This means getting out of the school and getting acquainted with potential employers in offices, shops, and business places. It also involves careful noting of help wanted ads in the newspaper and keeping in close touch with public employment service personnel. These latter can be a source for the numerous government publications which cover the national scene as well.

A well-planned program of follow-up on recent graduates and those who leave can also be a worthwhile source of local occupational information. Present students are well informed on what became, vocationally, of people they knew from preceding classes.

Numerous sources of occupational information are available on the national level and some of this is quite worthwhile. As a rule, that which is compiled by a nationally known publisher and disseminator of occupational information is satisfactory. Information which is supplied free from trade associations, professional societies, or training institutions may be very attractively presented but may suffer from serious defect as bona fide occupational information. One defect involves its tendency to be "recruiting literature" with a selective presentation of the facts regarding the area it represents. Some information from such private sources may be useful, but all of it must be read by the counselor before it is accepted as part of his selection of occupational information.

Probably the most serious deficiency of occupational information is its rapid obsolescence. The speed of change in the work world necessitates the constant removal of outmoded information. Any item in the file which has copyright or acquisition date prior to the past three years in all probability contains enough obsolete information to warrant its replacement.

The question is sometimes raised to when occupational information should be introduced into the counseling process. No definite answer can be given, but it can be assumed that the introduction of factual information is premature if the counselee has matters of a more personal, intimate, or emotional nature on his mind. The vocational indecision problem and the request for information may be a facade or an opening for a relationship with the counselor as a prelude to discussion of other matters. Little is gained by exposing a person to occupational information when his mind and emotions are pre-occupied with other matters.

THE ROLE OF TESTING IN CAREER DEVELOPMENT

Tests have long been used as aids in the process of decision making in career areas. Ability and achievement tests are employed when predicting suitability for certain educational or vocational opportunities is desired. Interest measures have been used to evaluate motivation factors and personality measuring devices to determine the personal suitability or adaptability of a person. In vocational guidance, as in many other areas, administrators of tests should allow for the factors which have been demonstrated to reduce the tests' utility. These include inadequate reliability and validity for the purposes for which they are being used. This is not to say that tests have little value in vocational guidance — because they do have value — but rather to suggest that their main value is supplementary rather than primary in nature. As a rule the more one knows about a person, the more supplementary test results become. If an individual is known in a primary sense by means of interviews, work samples, observations, and similar devices less reliance is necessary on test results. On the other hand if little is known in a primary sense, extensive reliance upon test results is essential. It can thus be seen that tests do have a value in supplementing what is known about people.

SUMMARY

It is the writer's contention that the vocational phases of guidance deserve re-examination and re-emphasis. This is true because of the social, educational, and technical changes which are occurring in the world of careers. These changes are rapidly making current information and assumptions about occupations progressively more obsolete. Current theories of vocational development stress the vital role of appropriate educational experience at every level. They also underline the importance of vocational guidance and the appropriate role of testing.

BIBLIOGRAPHY

1. Ginzberg, E. "Toward a Theory of Occupational Choice," *Occupations*, Dec. 1951, 492.
2. Hoppock, Robert. *Occupational Information*, McGraw-Hill, New York, 1963, ch. 7.
3. *Manpower Report of the President and a Report on Manpower, Requirement, Resources, and Training by the United States Department of Labor*, March, 1964, Washington, D. C. G.P.O., Superintendent of Documents.
4. Michael, D. N. *Cybernation, The Silent Conquest*, Santa Barbara, Fund for the Republic, 1962.
5. Miller, C. *Foundations of Guidance*, Harper, New York, 1961, Pg. 251.
6. Parsons, Frank. *Choosing a Vocation*, Houghton Mifflin, Boston, 1909, Pg. 5.
7. Selegman, B. B. Man, Work and the Automated Feast, *Commentary*, 1962, 34, 9-19.
8. Super, D. E. *Psychology of Careers*, Harper, New York, 1957, Pg. 185.

9. Super, D. E., & P. L. Overstreet. *The Vocational Maturity of Ninth Grade Boys, Career Pattern Study Monograph* 2, Bureau of Publications, Teachers College, Columbia University, New York, 1960.
10. Wolfbein, S. "Automation and Skill," *Annals of the American Academy of Political and Social Science*, 1962, 340, 53-59.
11. Wrenn, Gilbert C. *The Counselor in a Changing World,* American Personnel and Guidance Association, Washington, D. C., 1962, Pg. 115.

(**18**)

ATTITUDES TOWARD WORK[1]

C. H. Patterson
University of Illinois

Work means many different things to different people. That work is an important part of life is obvious — it consumes almost one fourth of our adult lives, more than any other activity except sleep, if sleep may be called an activity. If we do not include sleep, work occupies about one third of the average person's activities. It is thus an interesting question why it is only within the last few years that the meaning of work has been investigated by psychology and sociology. Anne Roe, in her book on "The Psychology of Occupations," (2) states that "If one wishes to understand the total psychology of any person, it is at least as important to understand his occupational behavior as it is to understand his sexual behavior." Yet the amount of effort given to the study and understanding of the meaning of work to the individual is infinitesimal compared to the study of sexual behavior.

While the meaning of work varies with individuals, there are perhaps two major types of attitudes. The two attitudes are expressed by the title of a recent article: "Work: pleasure or penance?" (8). Work as penance for sin has been the prevailing attitude and is often referred to as the Protestant ethic of work. It is based on the Biblical story of the original sin and the expulsion of Adam and Eve from the workless life of the Garden of Eden. God said to Adam, "Cursed be the ground because of you; in toil shall you eat of it all the days of your life; in the sweat of your brow you shall eat bread" (Gen. 3:17-18). Work is thus a curse, a punishment for sin.

Now whether we accept the Biblical story as fact or allegory, it is a significant indication of an attitude toward work. Work is not pleasant, it is disliked, yet it is necessary for life in order to wrest subsistence from the environment. It is a necessary evil. Man works in order to live, to satisfy the basic needs for food, clothing and shelter. Freud viewed work as an inescapable and tragic necessity; man must be forced into the reality of work (11).

The second approach to work is a much more recent one. In this approach, work is not necessarily an unpleasant activity. Work is, or may be, a pleasure.

Reprinted by permission of the Author and *The Vocational Guidance Quarterly,* 1959, 7, 155-158.

[1]Chairman's introduction to panel discussion of "Work: Its Social and Psychological Meanings and Values," 63rd Annual Conference, Illinois Welfare Association, LaSalle Hotel, Chicago, Illinois, November 17, 1958.

We not only work to live, but we live to work. Work is the natural exercise of the body and mind. It satisfies the basic need for physical and mental activity. And in our society, work satisfies psychological needs of a varied nature — the need for security, for sociability, for status, for self esteem and the esteem of others, for creativity, among others.

Writers and poets have extolled the virtues and benefits of work. Gibran, in *The Prophet* (5), writes: "When you work, you are a flute through whose heart the whispering of the house turns to music. . . To love life through labor is to be intimate with life's inmost secret. . . Work is love made visible." And Carlyle (1), wrote: "Even in the meanest sort of labor, the whole soul of man is composed into a kind of real harmony the instant he sets himself to work. Older than all preached Gospels was this unpreached, inarticulate but ineradicable, forever enduring Gospel: work, and therein well being." Work is thus conducive to physical and mental health. Work is therpay physical and mental therapy. It is the natural exercise of the body and mind.

More than this, in our complex economic society, work is the basis for social status. We no longer say to the individual — at least openly — "if you don't work, you don't eat," but the nonworking, nonproductive individual is not usually a full member of society. Lack of work, or inability to work, therefore affects one's status, in the eyes of others and of oneself. It is demoralizing, leading to loss of self respect or self esteem, a frustrating of the desire for independence and self-sufficiency, the loss of a sense of usefulness, of confidence in oneself. The end result of this process may be the acceptance of a dependent role, and a clinging to it for fear of losing what security one has, since confidence is lacking in the ability to become independent. Once this state is reached, motivation may be lost, and we face one of the most difficult problems in social rehabilitation. We have as yet found no answer to this problem. Our best approach would appear to be one of attempting to prevent such a condition from developing.

There are two kinds of satisfaction to be derived from work — the intrinsic and the extrinsic. The intrinsic includes the enjoyment of work for itself, the extrinsic satisfaction is derived from what the results of the work bring, both in terms of economic returns and psychological and social returns. The history of industrialization has tended to reduce or eliminate the instrinsic satisfactions in work. The mechanization of jobs has eliminated the creativity from such work. The pride of craftsmanship is no longer possible when one turns out standardized products on a machine. Work becomes routine, monotonous. In addition, the routine of machine tending cuts down on the social interaction on the job. This, and the increasing size of industrial concerns lead to a more impersonal atmosphere on the job. The increasing simplification of work results in the breakdown of jobs into simple, repetitive activities. The minute nature of these activities, and the larger number of them required to produce a finished product, not only prevents the worker from experiencing the satisfaction of completing a product, but reduces the prestige of the job. He may be deprived of a sense of status, the use of skill (4). Moreover, he has nothing upon which to build prestige and status outside the job. No one can understand or appreciate what he does. He is just a "hand," assembly line worker, etc.

The study of 4,000 jobs by the U. S. Department of Labor (13) indicates that 75 per cent of the jobs require adjustment to a relatively small number of situations, involve set tolerances or limits, are repetitive, short cycle jobs performed under specific instructions, with measurable criteria of performance. There is little creativity, independence, responsibility, judgment, evaluation or personal interaction involved. Seventy-five per cent of the jobs are limited to things or objects, requiring routine, concrete, organized activity, requiring no significant interest in people or ideas, or social welfare, or scientific-technical interests. They are nonsocial, carried on in relation to processes, machines, and techniques.

Now while it has been stressed, and is no doubt still true to a large extent, in a broad sense, that one's work is the center of one's life, it appears that a change is occurring. Because of the factors just listed, the job or the work situation, is becoming less and less the focus of the worker's life. The lack of intrinsic satisfactions, and the reduction of social satisfactions on the job, seem to be leading to a divorce between the job and the rest of the worker's life. When he gets home from work, he changes his clothes, and with this change he enters a different world. As Ginsburg (6) notes, the worker no longer "seeks his narcissistic gratifications solely or even primarily in his job. In fact there is substantial evidence that for most industrial workers, work and the work setting are not central life interests." Dubin (3) also notes that "Work is no longer a central life interest for workers. These life interests have moved out into the community . . . the problem of creating an industrial civilization is essentially a problem of social intervention and creativity in the non-work aspects of life."

Menninger (9) noted a number of years ago that perhaps 75 per cent of the patients going to psychiatrists suffer from an incapacitating impairment of their satisfaction in their work or their ability to work, and that in many it was their chief complaint. Perhaps this is less a reflection on the inadequacies of the individual worker than upon our industrial society. Rather than being merely a symptom of personal maladjustment, the difficulty in adjustment to work may be of primary importance. The significance of work, or lack of work, in the development of emotional disturbance and for the recovery and adjustment of discharged mental hospital patients is just becoming recognized.

Nevertheless, a surprising proportion of workers are satisfied with their jobs, probably about 80 per cent (2, 10). But the proportion who are satisfied decreases from the professional to the laboring classes. The satisfactions derived from work also vary with the occupational group, with the white collar workers emphasizing intrinsic satisfactions while the blue collar workers mention extrinsic aspects. (7)

I have said enough, I think, to point out the complex nature of the problems involved in the psychology and sociology of work. It is, as I have suggested, only recently that attention has been given to this field. With the increasing mechanization of work, and the resulting smaller opportunity for the many to find satisfaction in work, the problem will increase in importance. Disagreeable, monotonous jobs cannot be entirely eliminated, even by automation. How can the worker be given some satisfaction in his work? Can so-called morale builders, such as profit sharing, low cost restaurants, recreational facilities, social organizations and activities provided or sponsored by industry offer sufficient satisfactions? Will shorter working hours offer a solution? Or will this just transfer the problem of satisfying needs for activity, creativity, recreation, etc., to the community at large? These are some of the unanswered problems which we must face in the near future.

REFERENCES

1. Carlyle, T. *Past and present.*
2. Centers, R. Motivational aspects of occupational stratification. *J. soc. Psychol.* 1948, *28*: 187-217.
3. Dubin, R. Industrial workers' worlds: a study of the "central life interests" of industrial workers. *Soc. Probl.* 1956, *3*: 131-142.
4. Eaton, W. H. Hypotheses relating to worker frustration. *J. soc. Psychol.*, 1952, *35*: 59-68.
5. Gibran, K. *The prophet.*
6. Ginsburg, S. W. Work and its satisfactions. *J. Hillside Hosp.*, 1956, *5*: 301-311.
7. Lyman, Elizabeth L. Occupational differences in the value attached to work, *Amer. J. Sociol.*, 1955 *61*: 138-144.
8. Maule, H. G. Work: pleasure or penance? *Occup. Psychol.*, 1956, *30*: 232-241.
9. Menninger, K. A. Work as a sublimation. *Bull. Menninger Clin.*, 1942, *6*: 170-182.
10. Morse, Nancy C., & Weiss, R. S. The function and meaning of work and the job. *Amer. sociol. Rev.*, 1955, *20*: 191-198.
11. Riesman, D. The themes of work and play in the structure of Freud's thought. *Psychiatry*, 1950, *8*: 1-16.
12. Roe, Anne. *The psychology of occupation.* New York: Wiley, 1956.
13. U. S. Department of Labor, Bureau of Employment Security. *Estimates of worker requirements for 4,000 jobs as defined in the Dictionary of Occupational Titles.* Washington, D. C., U. S. Government Printing Office, 1956.

(19)

SOME PHILOSOPHICAL PROBLEMS IN MENTAL DISORDER AND ITS TREATMENT[1]

O. Hobart Mowrer
University of Illinois

In this provocative article, the author discusses some of the scientific and philosophical implications of Freudian theory, and takes the position that certain aspects of the Freudian view must be revised if we are to have a valid conception of neurosis and reliable methods for its alleviation and prevention. Whereas the Freudian view considers neurosis a disease, the causative factors of which lie *outside* the individual, Dr. Mowrer contends that neurosis is a *way of life* which is largely determined by the individual himself. An individual's neurosis, one may say, is his "own idea."

The root cause of neurosis is the denial, repression and repudiation of guilt; and the aim of therapy, therefore, should be to help the patient allow

Reprinted by permission of the Author and the *Harvard Educational Review*, Vol. 23, No. 2, Spring 1953, 117-127.

[1]This article is based upon a lecture delivered in the Great Hall of the Cooper Union in New York on January 16, 1953, as part of a lecture series entitled "Our Search for Mental Health."

this repressed guilt to return to consciousness, thereby enabling him to reassume the responsibility he has been trying to avoid. The re-acknowledgment of guilt and self-criticism is essential if the neurotic is to achieve mental health.

In the final section of the paper, Dr. Mowrer presents a critique of Freud's views on religion and metaphysics.

Dr. Mowrer is Research Professor in Psychology at the University of Illinois. He is President-elect of the American Psychological Association, and is currently President of the Division of Clinical and Abnormal Psychology and the Division of Personality and Social Psychology of that organization.

Asked if psychoanalysis gives us any particular philosophy of life, Freud characteristically replied that the only philosophy to which psychoanalysis leads is that of science in general. And this he vigorously contrasted with the *Weltanschauung*, the "world view" or philosophy, of religion. The possession of the kind of *Weltanschauung* that religion provides is, said Freud, "one of the ideal wishes of mankind. When one believes in such a thing, one feels secure in life, one knows what one ought to strive after, and how one ought to organize one's emotions and interests to the best purpose" (1, p. 216).

But "if this is what is meant by *Weltanschauung*," Freud continued, "then the question is an easy one for psychoanalysis to answer. As a specialized science, a branch of psychology — 'depth-psychology' or psychology of the unconscious — [psychoanalysis] is quite unsuited to form a *Weltanschauung* of its own; it must accept that of science in general" (1, p. 217).

The sentences just quoted are from the last chapter, entitled "A Philosophy of Life," of Freud's book, *New Introductory Lectures on Psychoanalysis* (1). In this chapter Freud develops at length his conception of the scientific outlook for man, its limitations and its possibilities. "It asserts," he says, "that there is no other source of knowledge of the universe, but the intellectual manipulation of carefully verified observations, in fact, what is called research, and that no knowledge can be obtained from revelation, intuition or inspiration" (1, p. 217). And "intuition and inspiration," Freud tells us, "can safely be counted as illusions, as fulfilments of wishes, [having] a purely emotional basis" (1, p. 218).

It will be the first task of this paper to show that one of the principal reasons why Freudian psychoanalysis has had such a widespread appeal in our time is that it, itself, generates or implies a *Weltanschauung* with some of the very qualities that its founder regarded as so objectionable and so contrary to the procedures and values of science. Indeed, as will be indicated a little later, many of the things which Freud said about the religious orientation apply much more aptly and specifically to his own position — or at least what most people regard as his position — than to the one he was criticizing.

I. THE FREUDIAN CONCEPTION OF NEUROSIS

Freud's theory concerning the causation and treatment of those personality difficulties which we commonly call neurosis can be most quickly summarized by means of a simple diagram. This theory starts (Figure 1) with some "instinctual force" or drive, D_1, demanding gratification in the form of some action or response, R_1. However, the resulting behavior, particularly if it is motivated by sex or hostility, is likely to be socially disapproved and to bring down upon the individual (represented by the circle in the diagram) something called punishment. This is represented here as a second drive, D_2, which commonly takes the form of pain of some sort. And pain, as we well know, produces, among other effects, an emotional reaction of *fear*. This we have labeled, R_2.

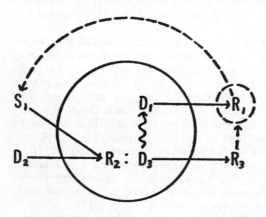

Figure 1

The Freudian conception of neurosis represented diagramatically.

What has been said thus far will have been easy enough to follow, but what comes next will require closer attention. It will be noted that there is a broken line extending from the forbidden behavior, R_1, over to something labeled S_1. S_1 is simply a designation for the incidental stimulation which accompanies the performance of R_1, the stimulation, the happenings, the sensations that make us aware that we are performing, have just performed, or are *about* to perform the response, R_1. If, now, R_1 is punished, if, that is to say, the occurrence of R_1 is followed by D_2, then we see that S_1 will be, as we say, "associated" with D_2, with the result that the fear reaction, R_2, that is produced by the punishment tends to get connected, by a form of learning which we call *conditioning*, to S_1. This means, quite simply, that when the individual later starts to gratify D_1 by making response R_1, he will, by virtue of the occurrence of S_1, be reminded of the punishment and will experience anticipatory fear. That is to say, the performance or contemplation of R_1 will arouse S_1, and S_1 will now produce the fear reaction R_2.

If the reader has followed the discussion thus far, he will readily see how it will continue, in terms of Freud's theory. The fear response R_2, aroused by the contemplated performance of the socially disapproved response, R_1, will create a third drive, D_3, and the individual will be prompted, if this fear drive is at all powerful, to do whatever he or she can to diminish it. The solution, at least in principle, is perfectly straightforward. Since R_1, through the mediation of S_1, is arousing the fear drive D_3, all the individual has to do is to make an incompatible response, R_3 — some response that will *stop*, or "inhibit," R_1. One might say that the fear drive, D_3, thus *blocks*, by a form of "feedback," the intended gratification of D_1.

But this is not quite the end of the story. Obviously when one experiences desire and fear simultaneously, there is conflict; and conflict, as we all well know, is painful. In most instances we manage sooner or later, to resolve conflicts realistically, integratively; but as Freud has repeatedly emphasized, for the child there is likely to be no integrative, no realistic solution to either his sexual or aggressive needs. And every expression of these impulses is regarded as "bad"; and all such behavior is so persistently and so severely punished that, finally, in many instances the individual resorts to a desperate expedient. The impulse or desire, D_1, proves to be so painfully irreconcilable with the fear drive, D_3 that the individual begins, according to Freud, to do a very remarkable thing: he begins to *repress* D_1 to refuse to access to consciousness, to deny its very existence, as indicated in the diagram by the wavy arrow. When thus finally excluded from consciousness, D_1 produces no temptation and no fear, and intrapsychic peace is once again restored. The conflict is ended, and the individual is enormously relieved.

Sometimes, says Freud, these repressive solutions to conflicts prove enduringly satisfactory; indeed, he even thought that civilization itself is, in part, built upon the capacity of human beings to disown and deny certain brutish impulses more or less permanently. In other instances, however, this strategy meets with very imperfect success. Some impulses — and here Freud pointed particularly to sex, though to some extent also to aggression — these impulses, though they lose the struggle for conscious acknowledgment and direct gratification, continue to assert themselves but now "unconsciously," "neurotically." With the return or, rather, threatened return of repressed impulses to awareness, old conflicts are partially reactivated and the individual experiences the peculiar form of dread or panic known as neurotic anxiety. The resulting actions which we call *symptoms* are, said Freud, a compromise formation which serves the double purpose of (a) controlling the neurotic anxiety, so that it is not so unbearable as it otherwise would be and at the same time (b) allowing the imprisoned, repudiated impulses which lie behind the anxiety to achieve at least a partial, surreptitious satisfaction.

II. THE PHILOSOPHY IMPLICIT IN FREUDIANISM

In the interest of brevity we have had to be highly synoptic here, but the foregoing is neither unfair nor inaccurate as a summary of the Freudian position. And this position, we must agree, is not an unreasonable one. It could be well that this is the way neurosis develops and manifests itself. But more to the point is the question: Is the position, or theory, the *true* one? Does it conform to the clinical facts? Growing evidence indicates that in one important respect it does not.

It will presently be indicated wherein the Freudian view has to be drastically revised if we are to have a really sound conception of neurosis and reliable procedures for its alleviation and prevention. For the moment, however, let us examine the Freudian view of neurosis in the context of Freud's remarks, quoted at the outset, concerning psychoanalysis and the philosophical views one espouses. Despite Freud's assertions to the contrary, there can be no doubt that psychoanalysis does generate some very speicific and — one may add — rather singular philosophical implications, implications which laymen have been quick to sense — and either eagerly embrace or emphatically reject!

Traditionally, it was the individual's "own fault" if he got something wrong with him mentally. He was, in some sense, "responsible." Perhaps the alleged causal sequence was a little obscure or hard to trace, but the disturbance was always, in principle, due to something which the individual had himself *done*. Neurosis was, in short, either a natural or supernatural retribution for misconduct.

How very different is the Freudian position. Immediately we note that in this frame of reference neurosis is a result of something that has been *done to* the individual. He has been punished so severely, we are told, for attempting to gratify natural, biologically given needs that he is thrown into conflicts that can be resolved only by repression — and this predisposes the individual to neurosis. Mental disease is thus not a disgrace, not a stigma, not something to feel guilty or ashamed of; it is something that "might happen to anybody."

What a relief it is to discover that it is one's parents, and behind them the irrationality of "society" 'itself, that have caused one's neurotic suffering! And how comforting to learn, if one is oneself a parent, that it is the very excess of moral zeal on the part of parents that causes neurosis and that one may, indeed *should*, be less concerned about the moral training of one's children and *more* interested in seeing that their instinctual outlets do not become obstructed!

Surely it is not hard to see how profound and how primordial an appeal this kind of theorizing or, may we say, philosophizing must have to many rebellious, immature persons and, in some degree, to all of us. Freud was himself very active in pointing out the ambivalence, or mixed feelings, which every human being has toward the regulations and restraints which are necessarily imposed by the conditions of social life. Yet psychoanalysis fans the hope that we can, and for our own psychological health *should*, take these restraints and regulations somewhat less seriously than we have traditionally thought we should.

In the same chapter from which the earlier quotations are taken one finds Freud making statements such as the following one:

> The same father (the parental function) who gave the child his life and preserved it from the dangers which that life involves, also taught it what it may or may not do, made it accept certain limitations of its instinctual wishes, and told it what consideration it would be expected to show towards its parents and brothers and sisters, if it wanted to be tolerated and liked as a member of the family circle, and later on of more extensive groups (1, p. 224).

This universal dependence upon the father, says Freud, has caused mankind to create the notion of a Heavenly Father and the attendant conceptions of salvation and damnation which are part and parcel of religious ideology. Then there follows this remarkable passage:

> . . . the ban which religion has imposed upon thought in the interests of its own preservation is by no means without danger both for the individual and for society. Analytic experience has taught us that such prohibi-

tions, even though they were originally confined to some particular field, have a tendency to spread, and then become the cause of severe inhibitions in people's lives. In women a process of this sort can be observed to follow from the prohibition against their occupying themselves, even in thought, with the sexual side of their nature. The biographies of almost all eminent people of past times show the disastrous results of the inhibition of thought by religion (1, p. 234).

Yet this is the author who in the same context condemns the religious *Weltanschauung* as based upon illusions, "as fulfilments of wishes," with a "purely emotional basis." In all soberness we must ask ourselves: Which is likely to have the more profound "emotional" appeal, a philosophy which calls for restraint and sacrifice, or one which ridicules and promises to deliver us from such limitations? If at this point one becomes confused by Freud's arguments, it is scarcely surprising. Traditionally religion, more than any other great social institution, has been concerned with ethics, with morality, with the planned, organized, integrated style of life, with, that is to say, the attainment of satisfactions and happiness through the strategy of postponement, saving, sacrifice, and labor. Yet we are now asked to believe that the motives for such a regulated, controlled existence are unrealistic, illusory, emotionally biased! Surely it is psychoanalysis that enflames and appeals to the more primitively emotional side of our natures; and contemporary clinical researches are showing that psychoanalysis also has more than its fair share of that which is unrealistic and illusory.

III. A MORE DEFENSIBLE VIEW OF NEUROSIS

Let us now sketch another way of looking at neurosis and the therapeutic challenge it offers to us. Here (see Figure 2) we start, as does Freud, with some drive or desire, D_1, instigating some form of gratification, R_1. Again, with Freud, we assume that this behavior elicits punishment, D_2, and that

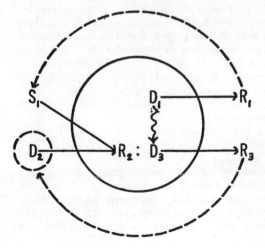

Figure 2

A modified conception of neurosis which eliminates the difficulties inherent in Freudian theory.

the fear $(R_2:D_3)$ produced by this punishment becomes connected, through conditioning, to the incidental stimulation, S_1, which R_1 produces.

But at this point our views diverge sharply from those of Freud. We assume that the individual headed for neurotic troubles is one who, when impulse and fear are in conflict, tries to resolve this conflict, not by controlling the impulse, but instead by *evasion and deception*. The fear we assume, results in behavior, R_3, which instead of blocking R_1 tries to prevent punishment, D_2 from occurring; and this strategy commonly involves secrecy and falsehood.

Some individuals have had so little moral training that, as long as they can avoid actual social chastisement, their actions, however deviant, bother them very little — and the deception involved in protecting these actions, even less. These are the characterless individuals known as psychopaths: the dead-beats, swindlers, confirmed liars and criminals. But for most persons who attempt to avoid punishment for disapproved action, the picture is very different. Even though they succeed in averting *external* punishment, their conscience *"hurts"* them — not only because of having engaged in behavior R_1, but also because of the duplicity. R_3, involved in concealing R_1.

Finally the fear, the guilt, the bad conscience which such an individual thus experiences will drive him to one of two things: he will either (a) confess and, as we say, "take his punishment,"or (b) begin to *repress* (see wavy line in Figure 2) these emotions. If a person can, by repression, keep his conscience from "bothering" him, he will have achieved a kind of peace and freedom; he can engage in forbidden behavior R_1 without the occurrence of the complex of fear and guilt here labeled $R_2:D_3$.

But repression, as we have already seen, is likely to be imperfect, with the result that the forces which are thus excluded from direct awareness eventually express themselves in a very troublesome way, that is to say, as neurotic anxiety, depression, and inferiority feeling. And these painful emotions cause the afflicted individual to try to reduce or avoid them by whatever means he can discover, thus giving rise to those forms of behavior which we know as neurotic symptoms.

In the beginning and in the end, our theory is thus very similar to that of Freud. We assume, with him, that neurosis originates in a conflict between biological impulses and social fears, between forces of the *id* and those of the *superego;* and we assume that in the person destined to be neurotic such a conflict is resolved by the process known as repression. We further assume with Freud that repression is likely to be only partially effective and that the repressed forces, in attempting to get back into consciousness, will periodically besiege the ego in such a way as to produce neurotic anxiety, panic, or depression, and that neurotic symptoms are the individual's efforts to control these disagreeable experiences.

But in one respect there is a basic disagreement with Freud. He held that in the conflict between desire and conscience it is always desire that suffers and falls under repression, and that the energies thus imprisoned make themselves felt as neurotic emotions, which lead to symptoms. But it now appears that it is conscience, not desire, which is repressed and imprisoned in neurosis, and neurotic emotions and symptoms represent an involuntary — and often very alarming — outcropping, not of "instincts" such as lust and hostility, but of one's own denied sense of shame and self-criticism. In numerous technical publications the author has elaborated upon this distinction and given both logical and empirical support for it (3, 4, 5, 6). This conception of neurosis has far less appeal to neurotics and other immature persons than does the strictly Freudian conception. And it is, rather obviously, related to the traditional religious view in such matters, which is epitomized by the familiar adage: Be good and you will be happy, i.e., normal, non-neurotic. In contrast, the Freudian position says, in essence: Be happy (have pleasure) and you will be good. However much this point of view appeals to neurotic individuals, we are still very far from having seen it clinically confirmed.

IV. MENTAL HEALTH AND THE CAPACITY TO BE GUILTY, RESPONSIBLE

There is, moreover, another problem which we must face in this connection. In addition to appealing to the undisciplined, the rebellious, instinctual side of human personality, Freud's theory is likely to receive quite a different type of support. Note how very "scientific" it sounds. It does not talk about individual choice or responsibility: it puts everything in a strictly cause-and-effect framework, and all of the "causes," very conveniently, are placed *outside* the individual himself.

By contrast, the view of neurosis which has just been sketched focuses the spotlight, in a quite uncomfortable but often highly productive way, directly upon the individual himself. Discerning critics of this position have been quick to cry: "But you seem to be saying that if a person becomes neurotic, it is his own fault. Surely you cannot mean this and at the same time claim to take a scientific view of human nature." How often we have been told in recent decades that all behavior is "caused" and that the individual is not responsible, is not to blame or in any way at fault if he develops a neurosis! It is not surprising, therefore, if our position is quickly challenged on this score.

In replay we may say two things. First, it must be admitted that, according to this view, the neurotic individual *is* responsible in the sense that his neurosis is, one may say, his "own idea." Who urged him to meet the threat of punishment for socially disapproved behavior by deception and evasion? Who told or required him to turn against his conscience and repress it when it bothered him in connection with his various misdeeds? The Freudian view makes neurosis an illness which is created by others. Is it not rather an *invention,* a creation of the individual himself? It has been impressed upon us all too often that neurosis is a disease. This is wholly misleading. Neurosis is a *way of life,* and to liken it to a disease, however comforting for the moment, can only lead us into frustration and despair in the long run.

We need not become involved here in the subtleties of free-will vs. determinism. There is an eminently satisfactory scientific solution to this problem, but we cannot pursue it at this time (2). All that needs saying here is that neurosis, as a way of behaving, as a life style, is probably just as much the choice of the individual himself, just as much determined by himself as is any other form of conduct. If a person is responsible for *any* action, then he is neither more nor less responsible for the steps that lead to neurosis.

But there is an important sense in which the neurotic is *not* responsible. He is not responsible precisely in the sense that he *ought* to be. He tries to have his cake and eat it too; he tries to engage in certain forbidden actions and at the same time avoid the normal consequences of such actions. Irresponsibility is thus perhaps the neurotic's greatest offense; and one of the main objectives of therapy is to get the patient, little by little, to reverse this trend and become increasingly willing to *be* responsible, to take rather than evade consequences, and in this way to be changed by reality instead of trying to live on in a false world of his own creation. Personal freedom and psychological health imply, not an absence of guilt, but a lively capacity for it; and it is the very fact that the neurotic is denying, repressing, repudiating his guilt that is the root cause of his difficulties. In therapy we feel a distinct advance has been made when the patient begins to reacknowledge his guilts and moral fears and self-criticisms, for then, and then only, is he in a position to take realistic measures, as opposed to neurotic ones, for coping with his problems.

What has just been said may, in its brevity, sound very arbitrary. One of the difficulties in clinical writing is that so little of the evidence on which one's inferences are based can be readily conveyed to others. But perhaps a fragment of clinical material will illustrate the kind of observation which constantly intrudes itself upon our attention. A colleague recently gave the author the following excerpt from the opening remarks of a young man who had just reached a turning point in his treatment. The patient began as follows:

> I've been in a mood all week, and I'm just beginning to come to my senses. (Pause.) Talking about that, I, my wife, when she was commenting upon how lousy I've been feeling — she was a little mad at me yesterday — she said, "That's all you're interested in. You're just plain narcissistic — just interested in yourself and your school and so forth." And that's been pretty true, I guess.
>
> In fact, when I first read a little bit of Mowrer, when I was reading about the neurotic, the neurotic not being so far from the psychopath as we think, uh, this was completely foreign to me. (A little laugh.) Since the psychopath is, is completely rejected by society inasmuch as he just destroys, and is anti-, or a-social, is just, most of his behavior is just motivated against society when he does behave, uh, I couldn't place myself in the same boat. But I think recently, oh several weeks ago, I started seeing some of the same — in the same direction, I should say. When you have neurotic problems, you have enough conscience to work on that and develop it, but there is a lot of the same things. That is what I just saw.
>
> And that — I don't know — I didn't like the way Dorothy (his wife) said it about me, but, uh, it contained a large element of truth.

In this context the patient did not specify some of the more serious forms which his immaturities and deviations had taken, but the passage quoted serves well enough to illustrate the principle that re-acknowledgment of guilt and self-criticism is an essential and significant step along the road which the neurotic has to follow if he is to recover, if he is to leave his fool's paradise and return to responsibility and mental and moral health.

It would be possible to give many other clinical excerpts indicating that the neurotic, far from having *too* much guilt, as the Freudian position implies, has *too little*, too little in the sense of not letting it enter consciousness and participate in the control of his decisions and actions. The rightful aim of therapy, of a rational, *effective* therapy is, therefore, to help the patient allow his repressed guilt to return to consciousness and thereby enable him to re-assume the responsibility — and realistic learning — he has been trying to avoid.

V. ETHICS AND METAPHYSICS NOT INSEPARABLY LINKED

Finally, let us return to some of the other philosophical issues raised at the outset of this paper. The chapter by Freud on "A Philosophy of Life" from which the earlier quotations were taken contains one or two additional points which we must examine. In this chapter Freud goes on to attack religion most vigorously. He says:

> The truth could have been seen at any time, but it was long before anyone dared to say it aloud: the assertions made by religion that it could give protection and happiness to men, if they would only fulfil certain ethical obligations, were unworthy of belief. It seems not to be true that there is a power in the universe, which watches over the well-being of every individual with parental care and brings all his concerns to a happy ending (1 p. 229).
>
> . . . in our view the truth of religion may be altogether disregarded (1, p. 229).
>
> No attempt to minimize the importance of science can alter the fact that it attempts to take into account our dependence on the real external world, while religion is illusion, and it derives its strength from the fact that it falls in with our instinctual desires (1, p. 239).

As already indicated, there is another way of viewing the situation. But it will be more persuasive, perhaps, if another presents the argument. Dr. Jacob H. Conn, Assistant Professor of Psychiatry at Johns Hopkins University, has recently written to the author as follows:

> You may be interested in George Bernard Shaw's opinion as expressed in the speech which Don Juan makes in *Man and Superman*. The Devil has referred to Man as being an "engine of destruction," as the inventor of the rack, stake, gallows . . . gun, poison gas, and the "isms" by which men are "persuaded to become the most destructive of all the destroyers." Don Juan replies: "You take Man at his own opinion . . . . He loves to think of himself as bold and bad. He is neither one nor the other; he is only a coward. Call him tyrant, murderer, pirate, bully; and he will adore you and swagger about with the consciousness of having the blood of the old sea kings in his veins . . . . But call him coward and he will go mad with rage; he will face death to outface that stinging truth. Man gives every reason for his conduct save one, every excuse for his crimes save one; that is his cowardice.

To this Dr. Conn adds the following terse comment: "I believe Shaw was a better *Menschen Kenner* [student of man] than Freud. . . . Man would rather admit incest and hostility than inadequacy." With this thought in mind, we may ask once again whether religion, with its ethical goals, is more or less irrational, emotional, "instinctual" in its appeal than is Freudian psychoanalysis!

But in questioning and opposing the Freudian position on this score, one is likely to be misunderstood. It is easy to assume that if one agrees with some of the moral and social teachings of religion one is committed to the supernatural trappings of religion as well. This is not in the least true. One can substitute the scientific world view for the speculative one of religion without having to infer that *everything* religion has stood for is bogus. The primary, the socially and historically most important concern of religion has been the *moral* concern, and metaphysics has been introduced simply as a means of trying to make moral principles more impressive and to insure obedience to them. While this tactic may have seemed justifiable in the past, it has historically backfired: Many modern men and women look with suspicion and contempt upon any enterprise that would enforce morality with a myth, that would try to teach honesty with a dishonesty, with what many regard as a cosmic lie.

This is the error, the immorality of which traditional religion today stands accused, and it is not yet certain how it will acquit itself. In the meantime, it remains for those persons devoted to the scientific *Weltanschauung*, with its emphasis upon empirical truth, to make sure that they do as good a job with the ethical and moral issue, as religion has done, with its metaphysics. And here, it seems, psychotherapists have a unique opportunity and obligation. In the intimacy and deep sincerity of the psychological consulting room, we have the immortal lessons of personal and interpersonal morality continually reimpressed upon us. And we must not be so energetic and overdetermined in our rejection of religious mythology that we become obdurate to the great ethical principles for which religion has also stood. These are man's psychological and social salvation, today as well as in the past.

In his calmer moments Freud acknowledged much of what we have here been saying. In fact, in the same chapter from which we have previously quoted, we find statements such as the following:

> It is true that from the applications of science, rules and recommendations for behavior may be deduced. In certain circumstances they may be the same as those which are laid down by religion . . . . (1, p. 219).
>
> The ethical commands, to which religion seeks to lend its weight, require some other foundations instead, for human society cannot do without them, and it is dangerous to link up obedience to them with religious belief (1, p. 230).

But Freud was not as explicit about all this as he might have been; and his teachings, transformed by his less prudent followers into what is popularly known as "Freudianism," have fostered the error — may we not say "illusion"? — of supposing that the *scientific* view of human nature and neurosis is one that repudiates ethics and ethical responsibility almost as completely as it does metaphysics. This is a confused point of view, and the issue involved is one that modern man, in his quest for a new, naturalistic view of himself and his universe, cannot afford to be confused about. I believe we may now be on our way to reducing and correcting the confusion which Freudianism, in both its popular and professional version, has unfortunately contributed in this connection, while at the same time preserving all therein that is technically sound and valid. The challenge of a new era of psychological understanding and achievement lies before us.

BIBLIOGRAPHY

1. Freud, Sigmund. *New Introductory Lectures on Psychoanalysis.* New York: W. W. Norton and Co., 1933.
2. Mowrer, O. Hobart. "Freedom and Responsibility — A Psychological Analysis." *J. of Legal Education,* (in press).
3. Mowrer, O. Hobart. "Learning Theory and the Neurotic Fallacy." *Amer. J. Orthopsychiatry,* 1952, 22, #4, 679-689.
4. Mowrer, O. Hobart. *Learning Theory and Personality Dynamics.* New York: Ronald Press Co., 1950.
5. Mowrer, O. Hobart. "Pain, Punishment, Guilt and Anxiety." In Hoch, Paul H. and Zubin, Joseph (Eds.) *Anxiety.* New York: Grune and Stratton, 1950. Pp 27-40.
6. Mowrer, O. Hobart. *Psychotherapy — Theory and Research.* New York: Ronald Press Co., 1953.

(20)

A CRITIQUE OF THE PHILOSOPHY OF MODERN GUIDANCE

James J. Cribbin

New York University

One of the most successful methods of stirring up low moans and muffled mutterings, particularly in a Catholic graduate school, is to embark upon a discussion of either "principles" or "philosophy." This is especially true of guidance courses in which the students are enrolled not to organize their ideas but to organize a program, not to take counsel within themselves as to the role of modern guidance in traditional education but to learn how to counsel others. Yet, the importance of both "principles" and "philosophy" is brought home in a striking manner when one reads:

At the beginning of this study we were primarily concerned with per-sonnel practices and techniques. We had no clearly defined principles by which to proceed nor did we, at that time, feel any need for them. We were interested chiefly in introducing better guidance practices and were scarcely aware of the fact that such practices must ultimately be based upon sound psychological theory.[1]

If this happened in the green wood of experienced and sophisticated educators, one wonders what marvels take place daily in the dry of the ordinary school program.

Reprinted by permission of the Author and *The Catholic Educational Review,* Vol. 53, No. 2, February 1955, 73-91.

[1]Sister Annette, "Psychological Principles," *Student Personnel Services in General Education,* edited by Paul J. Brouwer (Washington, D. C.: American Council on Education, 1949), p. 225. [Emphasis] added.

So far as guidance has reference to theoretical considerations, three procedural alternatives are open to every personnel worker. He may temporize, meeting each emergency and contingency on a catch-as-catch-can basis, a process which makes Jack an erratic if not dull counselor. On the other hand, like the educators referred to in the quotation above, he can cope with the complexities of guidance on a trial and error basis until he develops a "felt need" for some frame of reference which will afford him consistency in action. Or, finally, he can formulate a system of ideas and ideals to guide his efforts to assist students, conscious of the need to implement these ideas in a practical way yet convinced of the primacy of principles over procedures. If one may take for granted the superiority of this third approach, it should be evident that a critique of the philosophy of guidance may serve some useful, if perhaps minor, purpose. Moreover, it is equally clear that such an analysis should consider at least three factors: (1) the principles which are fundamental to the movement, (2) the nature of the guidance process, and (3) the objectives which it seeks to attain. It is the purpose of this paper, therefore, to examine modern guidance from these three points of view.[2]

THE TERM "PRINCIPLE" IN MODERN GUIDANCE

After examining more than forty-five definitions, descriptions and definitional distortions of the term *principle*, the writer abandoned hope of finding any univocal interpretation of the word. Most frequently it was either confused with, or employed as a synonym for, *assumption*. Less often it was used interchangeably with such concepts as: *major postulates, hypotheses, basic concepts, general statements, conclusions, aims, premises, propositions, basic connections, characteristics, accepted bases, generalizations* and so on.

1. Principle Identified With Assumption

The most common element of these wrestlings with the idea of a *principle* was to identify it with *assumption*. Thus, the first sentence in Little and Chapman's work reads, "Implicit in this book are certain fundamental assumptions."[3] Wrenn, in a similar vein, writes of the college personnel program. "This educational philosophy (the student personnel point of view) is based upon three assumptions."[4] Finally, Froehlich, who writes for the small secondary school, has as his first subheading of his initial chapter "*Basic Assumption of This Book.*"[5] The copyright dates of all three works are 1950 or later, but

---

[2]Certain limitations of this paper are obvious. It is concerned with ideas as presented in standard, general texts in guidance rather than with those which deal with a specific area of the personnel program, such as counseling. It is oriented about the secondary school, although much of what is presented applies equally well to the college level.

[3]Wilson Little and A. L. Chapman, *Development Guidance in Secondary School* (New York: McGraw-Hill Book Company, Inc., 1953), p. vii.

[4]C. Gilbert Wrenn, *Student Personnel Work in College* (New York: The Ronald Press Company, 1951), p. 4.

[5]Clifford P. Froehlich, *Guidance in Smaller Schools* (New York: McGraw-Hill Book Company, Inc., 1950), p. 7.

it would make little difference if one were to consult the first (1930) edition of Jones' standard work in which a similar identification is made.[6]

2. Principle Not Unrestricted

A second characteristic of guidance literature is a tendency to deny that a principle, once established, need be accepted. Smith maintains that ". . . even principles must not be accepted as inviolable."[7] Chisholm declares that ". . . . the following principles might be developed or accepted by the faculty."[8] Hamrin avers that ". . . it is not necessary for every teacher to believe each of these aspects of basic philosophy."[9] On the other hand, several authorities have approached the essential idea of a principle, even though they may have in other sections of their works contradicted themselves. For instance, Lefever, Turrell, and Weitzel insist that "the only way in which this ideal can be accomplished is to start with a body of principles upon which all reasonable people can agree."[10] But perhaps Erickson and Smith best illustrate the general tenor of intellectual vagueness when they hold that certain "basic assumptions" (sic) apply to all schools without regard to the factors which serve to condition the character of the techniques and practices employed.[11]

THREE REASONS FOR CONFUSION

1. Metaphysical Reason

The reasons for this situation are three in number, metaphysical, historical and logical. For the first, one must look to those who teach the teachers. Rather than dredge up worn out quotations from Dewey, it might be better to look to Childs, the disciple on whom perhaps more than on any other Dewey laid his experimentalist hands. In his most recent work, Childs makes the following points: (1) all principles may be revised or even discarded; (2) all "truths" are subject to correction; (3) all values have a natural basis and origin; (4) principles do not give security; (5) the criterion of truth is not first principles but consequences.[12] He then adds: "It (the experimental method) lodges the authority of a principle, a value, or a belief not in the nature of the originating source — be it supernatural revelation, hallowed institution, mystical experience, the so-called laws of mind, the intuitions of the heart, necessary axioms, or common sense — but rather in its actual working, that is, in its observable outcome or consequence."[13]

[6]Arthur J. Jones, *Principles of Guidance* (New York: McGraw-Hill Book Company, Inc., 1930), p. 33.

[7]Glenn E. Smith, *Principles and Practices of the Guidance Program* (New York: The Macmillan Company, 1951), p. 2.

[8]Leslie L. Chisholm, *Guiding Youth in the Secondary School* (New York: American Book Company, 1945), p. 70.

[9]Shirley A. Hamrin, *Guidance Talks to Teachers* (Bloomington, Illinois: McKnight and McKnight, 1947), p. 18.

[10]D. Welty Lefever, Archie M. Turrell, and Henry I. Weitzel, *Principles and Techniques of Guidance* (New York: The Ronald Press Company, 1941), pp. 30-31.

[11]Clifford E. Erickson and Glenn E. Smith, *Organization and Administration of Guidance Services* (New York: McGraw-Hill Company, Inc., 1947), p. vii.

[12]John L. Childs, *Education and Morals* (New York: Appleton-Century-Crofts, 1950), pp. 20, 30, 166, 174.

[13]*Ibid.*, p. 173.

2. Historical Reason

The second reason is largely historical in nature. Guidance has always been something of an educational tourniquet, seeking to staunch the loss of human potentialities for good caused by an educational system which at times cannot seem to make up its mind whether it is physician or butcher. Even as the charitable bystander has little time for pondering Harvey's theory as he seeks desperately to stop the blood gushing from the severed artery, so guidance workers have been so beset by the pressing need to minister to those requiring immediate attention that they have had little time for the reflective mediations so dear, in theory at least, to the heart of the metaphysician. On the other hand, it would be unfair to imply that personnel workers have been unaware of the need for serious consideration of the nature, scope, content, ends, and means of guidance. Young social movements develop through a process of idea conflict. Guidance is young and has had more than its share of discussion and debate.[14]

3. Logical Reason

The final reason for confusion with reference to the meaning of principle is logical, namely, a failure to distinguish clearly between such terms as *principle, policy, rule,* and *practice.* Strictly speaking, a principle refers to a universal judgment or truth which, because it takes into account only essential factors, applies to every person, problem, or situation. *Policy,* on the other hand, has reference to all cases within a particular class, taking into account the pattern of generalized circumstances which apply to a general class of person, problem, or situation. Thus, *policy* and *rule* refer to basically the same idea, the former being a general guide for action which allows for individual discretion within broad limits, while the latter is a mandatory prescription of procedure. *Practice,* of course, has to do with the "here and now," a procedure to meet the particular circumstances of a specific person, problem, or situation.[15] Thus, it is a *principle* that one can not teach without a clear understanding of the nature of the educand. It is the *policy* of schools to employ tests in an effort to gain a clearer understanding of the student. It is the *practice* in this school to administer this or that test. The principal may make it a *rule* that no test is to be administered after 2 P.M., or on the day preceding or following a holiday.

Although the distinctions made may appear to be "much ado about nothing," the fact remains that the guidance of youth is far too important a task to be founded on the mere "takings for granted" which are assump-

---

[14]Cf. Jane Warters, *High-School Personnel Work Today* (New York: McGraw-Hill Book Company, Inc., 1946), chap. ii. Critics of guidance have stressed the inability of authorities to formulate a definition of guidance which will be acceptable to all. Cf. Nelson L. Bossing, *Principles of Secondary Education* (New York: Prentice-Hall, Inc., 1949), pp. 405-13, especially footnote 20, p. 408. On the other hand, the needs to be met and the services to be rendered in the guidance program are quite clearly defined. Moreover, there is at least as much uniformity in content and emphasis in recent guidance texts as is to be found in similar works in the fields of educational psychology, personality, and many other disciplines.

[15]Mortimer J. Adler, "In Defense of the Philosophy of Education," *Philosophies of Education* (Forty-First Yearbook of the University of Chicago Press, 1942), pp. 224 ff.

tions, or on the temporary working bases of crystallized experience and custom. The guidance worker can not be ever mindful of these distinctions but their validity may well serve to help him discriminate between the essential and accidental aspects of the process.

FIFTEEN PRINCIPLES OF GUIDANCE

After examining some two hundred and more expositions of the principles of guidance and pupil personnel, as presented in texts and journal articles, the writer came to the weary conclusion that many authors seemed to be engaged in a merry game of saying the same thing according to the apostle, the while making sedulous use of their Roget's so as not to say it in the same way as the apostle. The following fifteen principles, however, were proposed by a majority of those who, because of their long-time association with and prominence in the field, qualify as genuine leaders in guidance and student personnel.[16]

1. Guidance is based on the recognition of the dignity and worth of the individual and on his right to personal assistance in time of need.

2. Guidance is student-centered, being concerned for the optimum development of the whole student and the fullest realization of his potentialities for individual and social ends.

3. Guidance, as a point of view, is as old as good education. It is modern with reference to (1) the areas of the student's life which are considered to be the responsibility of the school, (2) the services which it offers students, and (3) the techniques employed to attain its objectives.

4. Guidance is a continuous, sequential, educational process. Hence, it is an integral part of education and not a mere peripheral adjunct.

5. Guidance has a responsibility to society as well as to the individual.

6. Guidance must respect the right of every student to the help and services it offers.

7. Guidance is oriented about co-operation not compulsion. Hence, it is monitory in character with no place for coercion.

8. Guidance implies assistance given students in making wise choices, plans, interpretations, and adjustments in the critical situations of life.

9. Guidance demands a comprehensive study of the student in his cultural setting by the use of every scientific technique available. Student understanding must precede student assistance.

10. Guidance should be entrusted to those only who are naturally endowed for the task and have the necessary training and experience.

11. Guidance is the prerogative of no special clique of specialists. It requires the co-operation of all, each working within his own area of responsibility and at the level of his own competence.

12. The focus of guidance is on helping the student realize and actualize his best self rather than on solving isolated problems, be they those of the individual or the school.

13. Guidance is the mediating agency between the student and a mass system of education.

---

[16]Only those principles which might properly be termed "philosophical" have been considered here.

14. Guidance is the individualizing, the personalizing, and the socializing element in education.

15. The guidance program must be under constant, scientific evaluation in terms of its effectiveness.

An examination of these fifteen principles indicates that those listed in numbers 2, 3, 5, 7, 13, and 14 are only partially true. Guidance is not primarily student-centered (Principle 2) but God-centered, and so the eternal element in guidance can not be ignored, as it is in Principles 2 and 5. The first sentence in Principle 3 is true but the remainder is an accidental characteristic of American education. Much the same comment may be made with reference to Principles 13 and 14. Principle 7 introduces a dichotomy which does not always exist. With respect to Principle 10, the personnel worker must first have the right to guide and only then do his training and personality become important. It would appear that the remaining principles are valid and might well be mulled over by Catholic guidance personnel for the truth they contain.

TEN MAJOR CONCEPTS OF GUIDANCE

A survey of the literature, much of it largely historical in nature at this date, indicates no fewer than ten different concepts of guidance. Naturally, in such a discussion the ideas of different authorities can not be subsumed under mutually exclusive categories, since many have at one time or another touched upon all of these different approaches to guidance. However, as symphonies differ chiefly because of their central themes, so also authorities have tended to stress certain ideas while devoting only minor attention to others. It is this phenomenon which has constituted the basis for classification. No conscious effort, however, has been made to force conformity to a given category.

1. Guidance as a "Racket" or Meaningless Term

Surprisingly enough, although probably hordes of non-guidance personnel have at one time or other entertained the idea, this accusation was made by one of the most respected pioneers in the field, Anna Y. Reed. In 1938 she declared, "Guidance has become a meaningless term — a commercialized racket."[17] Insofar as this represented a petulant protest against shoddy training of personnel and shabby performance of guidance functions, it contained a germ of truth. However, if it purported to be anything else, in the absence of proof it may simply be denied. It is one thing to admit that guidance is subject to human foibles; it is quite another to stigmatize the sincere, if not always successful, efforts of personal workers as a racket.

Other authorities have become dissatisfied with the term because it lacks a hard core of meaning. Thus, Wrenn rejects it because it savors overmuch

---

[17]Anna Y. Reed, "Is Guidance A Racket?" *The National Education Association Proceedings,* LXXVI (June, 1938), 628.

of paternalistic advice-giving and because it has lost its usefulness through excessive use.[18] Moreover, Kitson considers it as a useless abstraction,[19] while Williamson and Darley jettison it because of its pollyanna connotation.[20] This position is much more tenable than the shrill accusation of Reed. "Guidance," like the Bible, has suffered overmuch from individual interpretation. The continued use of the term to mean, Alice-in-Wonderlandwise, precisely what the speaker wishes it to mean at the moment of speaking has at times created a situation in which some programs represent the nearest approximation of *nihil creatum ex nihilo* to be found in education today.

2. Guidance as Self-analysis and Self-direction

This approach of Parsons to the guidance process, oldest in point of time, had three essential elements (1) self-understanding on the part of the client, (2) knowledge of the requirements and conditions of success, and (3) true reasoning concerning the relationships between the two.[21] At times, unfortunately, some counselors have interpreted these ideas so mechanically that the student has felt as though he were being put through an electronic sorter. However, if the corrective perspective of the findings of cultural anthropology, sociology, psychoanalysis, and the various branches of psychology be utilized in considering the aspects of guidance, the basic validity of Parson's analysis remains.

3. Guidance as Restricted to Its Vocational Aspects

A much more formidable theory of guidance would restrict the use of the term to its vocational phase. Traditionally the strongest of the personnel organizations, the National Vocational Guidance Association, has been primarily concerned with problems of vocational guidance and occupational adjustment. Since its founding in 1913 it has grown until, as of 1952, it numbered some 6,460 members in 86 branches.[22] Despite this growth, however, a division of thought developed as to the wisdom of restricting the major emphasis to vocational problems.[23] One section favored the traditional position for the following reasons: (1) it represented the origin of organized guidance

---

[18]C. Gilbert Wrenn, "The Evaluation of Student Personnel Work: A Critique of the Guidance Movement," *School and Society*, LII (November 2, 1940), 409; "The Guidance Movement," *The Measurement of Student Adjustment and Achievement*, ed. by Wilma T. Donahue and others (Ann Arbor: University of Michigan Press, 1949), pp. 3-4.

[19]Harry D. Kitson, "Getting Rid of a Piece of Educational Rubbish," *Teachers College Record*, XXVI (October, 1934), 31.

[20]E. G. Williamson and J. G. Darley, *Student Personnel Work* (New York: McGraw-Hill Book Company, Inc., 1937), p. 28, footnote 1.

[21]Frank Parsons, *Choosing a Vocation* (Boston: Houghton-Mifflin Company, 1909), pp. 4-5.

[22]Willa Norris, "Highlights in the History of the National Vocational Guidance Association," *The Personnel and Guidance Journal*, XXXIII (December, 1054), 205-208.

[23]"A Symposium Regarding Change of Name and Statement of Purpose of the National Vocational Guidance Association," *Occupations*, XX (October, 1941), 27-44.

in the United States; (2) it had a clear meaning, aims, principles, and techniques which all could understand; (3) it had a record of achievement in developing standards for improving training procedures, for composing and evaluating vocational literature, for the evaluation of vocational counseling agencies and the practice of vocational guidance; (4) it was feared that the uncritical acceptance of other so-called kinds of guidance might undo much of the valuable work which had already been accomplished. The opposing group, however, felt that the organization should emphasize the broader functions of guidance. The upshot of this disagreement was that in 1951 the NVGA joined with other guidance and personnel groups to form the American Personnel and Guidance Association, the while retaining unaltered its own organization and pattern of functions.

However much one may sympathize with the efforts of those who seek to prevent guidance from becoming so overextended as to be ineffectively superficial and amorphous, the fact remains that this position tends to ignore three facts: (1) "guidance" though vague, has kept constantly before the personnel worker the truth that the whole child is affected by any problem and by its solution; (2) student problems ignore semantic distinctions; and (3) at least logically, this stand tends to confine one's study of the individual to a few seemingly pertinent disciplines instead of seeking to understand him by a multidisciplinary approach.

4. Guidance as Identical With Education

This interpretation of guidance has persistently been attributed to Brewer,[24] despite the objections of Super[25] and some others. Whatever may have been Brewer's precise position in this matter, certain it is that this position has been advanced by some leaders in the field. Thus, Hawkes stated ". . . that education is guidance and guidance is education";[26] while Keller maintained, "I have a notion that guidance . . . in all its implications is education,"[27] and Hildreth contended that no valid distinction was possible between education and guidance in purpose, methods, or results.[28]

It is true that the spirit of the so-called "new" philosophy of education, in which an individual has a right to his own individuality and to an education suited to his real needs, is also the spirit of guidance and pupil personnel. This, however, is a far cry from making the two simply convertible. Bluntly, guidance is but one ingredient in the educational cake; by no means can it be taken for the entire pedagogical pastry.

---

[24]John M. Brewer, *Education as Guidance* (New York: The Macmillan Company, 1932).

[25]Donald E. Super, *The Dynamics of Vocational Adjustment* (New York: Harper and Brothers, 1942), p. 5.

[26]Herbert E. Hawkes and Anna L. Rose Hawkes, *Through a Dean's Open Door* (New York: McGraw-Hill Book Company, Inc., 1945), p. 37.

[27]Franklin J. Keller, "Same Door Wherein I Went, A Confession of Faith in Guidance As Education," *Occupations*, XIII (May, 1935), 689.

[28]Gertrude H. Hildreth, "Guidance in the Lincoln School," *Teachers College Record*, XXXVII (February, 1936), 432.

5. Guidance as a Mediating Agency and as a Series of Supplementary Services

This concept was proposed by both Proctor[29] and Reed.[30] According to the latter — and, in view of her pioneering efforts in behalf of the movement, it would be grossly unfair to give the impression that her contributions were negligible — guidance is of two kinds: (1) inherent, or the kind of help every conscientious teacher seeks to give his students, and (2) purposeful, or organized guidance, which endeavors to facilitate the student's progress along the educational highway. This concept of guidance as a series of supplementary services is one of the strongest trends in modern guidance.

6. Guidance as Distribution and Adjustment

Although throughout the twelve-year period, 1925-1937, Proctor altered his emphasis in guidance from one of a co-ordinating agency to one chiefly oriented about the processes of distribution and adjustment,[31] this approach to guidance is generally associated with the names of Koos, Kefauver, and H. C. Hand.[32] According to these authorities, ". . . the concept of guidance has two main phases: (1) distributive and (2) adjustive." The former phase has to do with the distribution of students in the most effective manner possible to suitable educational and vocational opportunities, whereas the latter aspect seeks to help the individual to adjust to his educational and vocational situations.

7. Guidance as Assistance in Making Choices

Two authorities have stressed the element of choice in guidance perhaps more than any others. The major theme of all four editions of Jones' work in the field, covering a period of time from 1930 to 1951, has been this problem of choice-making.[33] In fact, for Jones the guidance situation exists only when the student needs help in making choices, interpretations, or adjustments. Myers, the other authority who has emphasized the element of choice, holds that a guidance situation is had only when two sets of differences are involved, namely, differences among individuals and differences among possible choices.[34] With this as his criterion, Myers excludes from

---

[29]William Martin Proctor, *Educational and Vocational Guidance* (Boston: Houghton-Mifflin Company, 1925), p. 13.

[30]Anna Y. Reed, "If Guidance Is Inherent in Education, Who Shall Guide?" *Association of American Colleges Bulletin*, XXI (March, 1935), 121. Reed has also published two outstanding works in the field: *Guidance and Personnel Services in Education* (Ithaca: Cornell University Press, 1944), and *Occupational Placement* (Ithaca: Cornell University Press, 1946).

[31]William M. Proctor, "The Task of Guidance in a Modern School," *California Journal of Secondary Education*, XII (March, 1937), 142.

[32]Leonard V. Koos, "The Interpretation of Guidance," *The Clearing House*, VIII (September, 1933), 8; Leonard V. Koos and Grayson N. Kefauver, *Guidance in Secondary Schools* (New York: The Macmillan Company, 1932), pp. 15-17, 439, 609; and "The Concept of Guidance," *The School Review*, XL (March, 1932), 204.

[33]Arthur J. Jones, *Principles of Guidance* (4th ed.; New York: McGraw-Hill Book Company, Inc., 1951), pp. 78-79, 95, etc.

[34]George E. Myers, *Principles and Techniques of Vocational Guidance* (New York: McGraw-Hill Book Company, Inc., 1941), pp. 15-16.

the purview of guidance all such concepts as "civic guidance," "social guidance," "health guidance," and most of the other "57 varieties" which used to wander in and out of the literature in the field. It is Myers' contention that, since all are expected to be as civic-minded, as socially-mature, and as healthy as possible, these are matters for instruction not guidance.[35] Thus, for Myers, the fundamental guidance areas are educational, vocational, recreational and community service. The difference, then between Jones and Myers lies principally in this, namely, that for the former a guidance situation exists whenever there is an element of choice regarding either means or ends, whereas for the latter there must be simultaneously multiple possibilities for choosing within the individual and multiplicity of choice possibilities in the environment.

8. Guidance as a Clincial Process

First introduced by Viteles, but developed chiefly by Paterson, Williamson, and their students at Minnesota, the clinical approach to guidance has been characterized by the following: (1) it represents a protest against shoddy methods which so frequently masquerade as guidance; (2) it seeks to develop techniques whereby a comprehensive analysis of the individual may be made; (3) it is considered a method by which educators' professed interest in individualizing education may be translated into practice; (4) it seeks to introduce order by subdivision of labor among instructional, advisory, administrative and clinical groups, all of whom work co-ordinately for the benefit of the student, each, however, retaining his own sphere of independent action; (5) it stresses the role of the professionally trained counselor, whose task it is to help students with their more difficult problems of adjustment;[36] (6) it follows an orderly — but not necessarily mechanical — procedure in terms of analysis, synthesis, diagnosis, prognosis, counseling, and follow-up.[37] Since its inception certain shifts in emphasis have taken place, due largely to the attacks of the Rogerians on directive methods of counseling. A second major change has been the recognition of the need for gearing guidance to the attainment of the objectives of a democratic society. Williamson states that he was made conscious of this need by his experiences in post-war Germany, which "awoke him from his clinic ivory-tower dogmatic slumber."[38]

---

[35]The reader may, in using Myers' criterion, wish to determine just what is involved in moral guidance, what in moral instruction, or whether any distinction should be made between them.

[36]The terms "clinical" and "clinician" should not be confused with "counseling psychologist" or "clinical psychologist," although one may very well be the other. The whole matter of terminology for the different levels of competence in counseling is something of a bête noire, ranging from teacher-counselor to part-time counselor to faculty adviser, to faculty counselor, to professional counselor, therapeutic counselor, clinical psychologist, counseling psychologist, and psychiatrist.

[37]Donald G. Paterson, "The Genesis of Modern Guidance," The Educational Record, XVI (January, 1938), 41; E. G. Williamson and J. G. Darley, op. cit., pp. 28, 37-39; E. G. Williamson and M. E. Hahn, Introduction to High School Counseling (New York: McGraw-Hill Book Company, Inc., 1940), pp. 18-19, 74-80; E. G. Williamson, How to Counsel Students (New York: McGraw-Hill Book Company, Inc., 1939), p. 57.

[38]E. G. Williamson, Counseling Adolescents (New York: McGraw-Hill Book Company, Inc., 1950), p. vii.

9. Guidance as an Eclectic System

In guidance, as in other fields, there have been more practitioners than theorists. Hence, the vast majority of leaders have been content to combine into a workable system those elements, from whatever source, which have proved their usefulness. Accordingly, it was not possible to subsume under any of the above categories such authors as Erickson, Hamrin, Traxler, Germane and Germane, Davis, Warters, Allen, Dunsmoor and Miller, Chisholm, and a host of others of equal stature.

One authority, Strang, deserves particular mention because her prolific and her lucidly clear pen has done much to clarify the nature and purposes of guidance. Among her contributions, although perhaps none of these are solely hers, might be numbered: (1) her insistence on the need for understanding the student in terms of his developmental history and in his cultural setting; (2) her stress on "wholeness" in guidance which has enabled her, better than most, to integrate it with the total school program; and (3) her organismic interpretation of guidance as basically a process of self-realization and self-actualization.

Furthermore, Strang's explanation of the relationships existing between such concepts as education, personnel work, and guidance, although not completely satisfactory, are surely the easiest to grasp. For Strang, the broadest term of all is education. A basic aspect of education is personnel work, which can be subdivided into the personnel point of view and the personnel services. The former of these is identical with the guidance point of view and the spirit of all true education, since it is naught but the personal interest of the educator in the welfare of his students. The latter has three distinct aspects: the *consultant*, which is concerned with the formulation of school policies which will create an environment that is conducive to the best development of the individual; the *administrative*, which seeks representation for the personnel point of view in the business routine of the school; and, *guidance*, the central service of personnel work. Guidance, dealing directly with students, helps them to profit optimally from their school experiences. As such, it includes two distinct processes: *appraisal*, which embraces all efforts to understand the student; *adjustment*, which seeks to make available to him those experiences, information, and counsel that the process of appraisal has indicated to be necessary or desirable.[39]

10. Student and Pupil Personnel Work

This brief overview of the major interpretations of guidance gives no hint of the incessant beating of the hammers and the constant ringing of the anvil that have taken place as concepts have been submitted to intellectual trial by fire of those most interested in the best growth of the guidance movement. Certain it is, however, that from this matrix of idea conflict and experience has come a better comprehension of the nature, scope, objectives, and methodology of the process.

At the college level, although here too there has at times been generated a maximum of heat with the usual minimum of light, there has ever been a

---

[39]Ruth Strang, *Pupil Personnel and Guidance* (New York: The Macmillan Company, 1940), p. 25.

clearer understanding of the nature of student personnel work (the term "guidance" is rarely if ever employed at this level of education) if for no other reason than the fact that an official publication of the American Council on Education has its specific definition.[40] As has already been stated, the student personnel point of view is an attitude of mind which seeks the well-rounded development of the whole student through the acquisition of a pattern of knowledge, skill, and attitudes consistent with his abilities, aptitudes, and interests. Implementing this philosophy of education in a practical manner are seventeen personnel services organized to meet some fifteen major student needs.[41]

At the secondary level, too, the passage of time has brought clarification of understanding, despite the fact that as late as 1951 the U. S. Commissioner of Education could say, "The lack of an adequate understanding of· what should constitute pupil personnel services . . . has been a matter of deep concern to me and my associates in the Office of Education."[42] In the first place, although the two terms, historically, have had different connotations, it is generally agreed that the terms "guidance services" and "pupil personnel services" refer to the same functions and so can be used interchangeably. Secondly, and far more significantly, there is a large measure of agreement as to just what constitutes the core of such services. At the Office of Education conference just referred to it was agreed that the basic services included the following: child accounting, orientation, individual analysis, health, information, counseling, clinical, placement and follow-up, and home-school-community. Interestingly enough four of the most recent works in the field, Froehlich (1950),[43] Smith (1951),[44] Hatch and Dressel (1953),[45] and Hamrin (1953),[46] are all organized in terms of some or all of these services.

What does all this mean for Catholic education? The first noteworthy fact is that, although Catholic educators have been interested in the problems of guidance since the turn of the century, they have not played a role in the evolution of pupil and student personnel work proportionate to their strength in American education.[47] In fact, it has only been in the relatively recent past, excluding such remarkable individual efforts as those of Sheehy and many others, that Catholic educators have given serious and energetic attention to guidance problems in a practical way. More important, however, is the fact that now that the essential personnel services have been defined with a moderate degree of exactness, thanks to our peers in public education,

---

[40]*The Student Personnel Point of View* (rev. ed.; Washington, D.C.: American Council on Education, 1949).

[41]*Ibid.*

[42]*Pupil Personnel Services in Elementary and Secondary Schools* (Washington, D.C.: Federal Security Agency, Office of Education, Circular No. 325, 1951).

[43]Froehlich, *op. cit.*

[44]Smith, *op. cit.*

[45]Raymond N. Hatch and Paul L. Dressel, *Guidance Services in the Secondary School* (Dubuque: Wm. C. Brown, 1953).

[46]S. A. Hamrin, *Initiating and Administering Guidance Services* (Bloomington, Ill.: McKnight and McKnight, 1953).

[47]The writer has just completed some minor research which indicates this. See also Sr. T. G. Murray, O.S.B., *Vocational Guidance in Catholic Secondary Schools* (Teachers College Contributions to Education, No. 754. New York: Teachers College, Columbia University, 1938), pp. 15-38.

it is needful that we do something complete and efficient in this area. Certainly, it is inexcusable either for the individual guidance worker to be unaware of these services, or for the individual institution, within the unalterable limitations of its resources, to fail to provide them for those students who stand in need of help. Thanks to our confreres in public education, we have a funded capital of experience and concepts which we can make our own, a gift for which we may well feel grateful.

AIMS AND OBJECTIVES OF GUIDANCE

After examining over 120 different expressions of ends in guidance, the writer concluded that the scholastic distinction between ultimate aims and proximate objectives was one which concerned few guidance authorities. For this reason, it seemed prudent to restrict the first part of this section to a discussion of those authors who employed such terms as the following to indicate that they were thinking in terms of ultimate aims: basic aim, major end-goal, central task, primary purpose, crux of the matter, desired end, consummation of guidance, primary objective, supreme end, primary aim, central goal, final purpose, chief aim, final aim, chief interest and ultimate goal.

1. Ultimate Aims

The most frequently expressed ultimate aim of guidance was found to be that of the "best development of the individual." Although it was expressed in a host of ways, it was perhaps most eloquently phrased in *The Student Personnel Point of View* in such terms as "well-rounded," "optimum," "full and balanced" and "broad gauged" development of the individual, physically, intellectually, socially, emotionally and spiritually.[48] The second major point of emphasis centered on the need for helping the student grow in self-guidance and individual maturity. Miller has perhaps expressed the consensus in this matter in declaring that the goal is ". . . to make students self-supporting, self-contained, self-directing and replete with inner resourcefulness."[49] The third category of final ends was oriented about the need for maximizing the students' satisfactions and their social productivity, as Mathewson would have it.[50] Finally, and all too rarely, there were found authors who, like Neuberg, made the distinction between the specific aims of individual and social efficiency and the ultimate aim of individual happiness,[51] or who,

---

[48]*Student Personnel Point of View, op. cit.*, pp. 1-4. The writer realizes that these divisions are hardly mutually exclusive. Thus, this work stresses greatly the need for individual maturity and social effectiveness and nods in the direction of value systems and a philosophy of life.

[49]J. Hillis Miller, "The Need for Personnel Services in a Smaller College," *Student Personnel Services in Colleges and Universities*, ed. by John Dale Russell (Chicago: The University of Chicago Press, 1941), p. 20.

[50]Robert Hendry Mathewson, *Guidance Policy and Practice* (New York: Harper and Brothers, 1949), p. 12.

[51]Maurice J. Neuberg, *Principles and Methods of Vocational Choice* (New York: Prentice-Hall, Inc., 1934), pp. 70-72, 80.

like Brewer, emphasized that ". . . the purpose of it all is simply that students may learn to live better lives. This is essentially the guidance aim."[52]

2. Proximate Objectives

The variety of ways in which the proximate objectives of guidance were expressed in the guidance field was a function of the rhetorical resources of the individual author. However, it was possible to classify the objectives proposed under twelve general classifications with a minimum amount of overlapping.

These objectives were the following: (1) to develop student initiative, responsibility, self-direction, and self-guidance; (2) to develop in the student the ability to choose his own goals wisely; (3) to know one's self, to know the school and to be known by the school; (4) to anticipate, avoid and prevent crises from arising in the lives of the student; (5) to help the student adjust satisfactorily to school and to life; (6) to help the student to recognize, understand, meet and solve his problems; (7) to assist the student in making wise choices, plans, and interpretations at critical points in his life; (8) to help the students acquire the insights and techniques necessary to enable him to solve his own future problems; (9) to assist teachers to teach more effectively; (10) to help administrators to administer more efficiently by making a maximum contribution to the total school program; (11) to develop citizens who will participate in and contribute to the democratic way of life; (12) miscellaneous objectives: included under this category were such ideas as assisting the home, helping the community, building ethical character, and fostering better human relations and international understanding.

SUMMARY AND CONCLUSIONS

This paper has sought to analyze the philosophy of guidance, as revealed in standard texts covering the field, from three points of view: (1) the principles basic to the movement; (2) the nature of the guidance process; (3) the aims and objectives of the process. With reference to the meaning of the term *principle*, no consistent interpretation was found, due largely to the naturalistic and experimentalist influences in American education. The majority of authorities employed the word as a synonym for assumption or else used it in the sense of crystallized custom to be employed as a basis for the mechanics of guidance. The chief defect of the guidance principles proposed, as might be expected, was the disregard for God's rights (and this should be distinguished from the rights of any sectarian religion) in the matter. Apart from this, the principles of guidance presented are not easily distinguishable from those of true education; as such they are worthy of the consideration of Catholic educators.

Regarding the nature of guidance, it was found that some ten different foci of emphasis were evident in the literature. What was more significant, however, is the fact that with time has come clarification of understanding with respect to the number, nature, and content of those services which are essential to a comprehensive guidance or pupil personnel program. Lastly, as

---

[52]Brewer, *op. cit.*, pp. vii-viii.

in the case of the principles, the chief difficulty with the statements of aims was the omission of God's rights. The proximate objectives, on the other hand, are cogent and valid. In fact, the school personnel worker might very quickly make a rough evaluation of the efficacy of his efforts by examining what he does in the light of these dozen objectives.

CHAPTER 2: QUESTIONS FOR DISCUSSION

1. Glanz presents characteristics of the "free and responsible person." In which aspect do you feel that individuals in our society are typically farthest removed from being "free and responsible"? What are the major reasons or causes for this?

2. Rockewll and Rothney discuss several social ideas important to leaders in the early days of the guidance movement. What do you feel are the leading social ideas of the writers in the field of guidance and counseling today?

3. Which of the "major models" or patterns listed by Glanz seems most prevalent in your state? What strengths does it have in terms of the present needs of your state? Could you offer reasons for moving toward another pattern or model?

4. Patterson's analysis of Rogers' ideas on self was written in 1961. Do you see any evidence of a further shift or emphasis in his more recent writings? What factors might have brought this about?

5. Selden states, "If the ideal-self is an outgrowth of identification with parents or other meaningful adults, . . . the delinquent has not achieved the level of identification of the non-delinquent." Would this seem to hold true for all social classes? Why? By what means might a counselor aid in bringing about "success experiences" for students who are already legally "delinquent"?

6. Curran raises some interesting points concerning the similarity of pain to sin and guilt. Are sin and guilt restricted to believers in God? Explain.

7. Patterson argues that a counselor should "avoid making decisions during the counseling process." What reasoning of your own or from the literature would tend to support the wisdom of such a statement? What might tend to weaken it?

8. Blum traces the history of some major problems and ideas in vocational counseling. What are the chief problems which face the "career counseling" or "vocational counseling" practitioners today? What sources of relief from these problems seems probable?

9. Work, as Patterson says, has long been almost a definition of what a man *is*. As the work period shortens, because of technological developments, what are some of the most promising replacements for helping man define what he *is*? What do we lose, as work diminishes?

10. Mowrer gives several ways in which people cope with fears. Review his list, then see if you might extend it. What *positive* effects can fear and fear reactions have? Give examples.

11. Read Cribbin's last paragraph again. What are "proximate" objectives in guidance? In what way might a religiously-oriented counselor approach an agnostic or atheistic client? What special problems, if any, may arise?

Chapter

The School Counselor Today

INTRODUCTION

This chapter might well be labeled a "directional" one rather than a strictly philosophical one. In it men who are either counselors themselves or who are now educating counselors in colleges and universities speak out concerning the vital daily concerns of the counseling field. They have carefully considered the major trends, concerns, dangers, viewpoints, and roles which the counselor must fulfill, and present guidelines stemming from these endeavors. Their analyses of the problems and challenges which face school counselors are addressed to live, pertinent issues growing out of both literature and experience. Without such a presentation, the book would be incomplete.

These writers would have all school counselors examine themselves, not only at the outset but continuously, asking, "Have I been prepared for the sort of problem before me?" "What sort of preparation would have aided me in this situation?" "What am I going to do about recurring problems and types of problems in my school?" "What is my relationship to the community? To the larger society? To parents?" "Am I genuinely making contact with the deepest hopes, fears, and aspirations of the students who bring personal problems to me, or am I merely touching their lives superficially, if at all? "What sort of strength is this particular child before me seeking?" "When should I refer him to someone else?" "What can I do to work toward more pertinent counselor education and standards?"

It is in educational institutions that the greatest amount of counseling and guidance takes place, at least *formalized* guidance. The issues, views, ethical-moral outlooks, and new directions discussed in the other chapters of this book therefore all come to a focus in the school and in the work of the school counselor. As I have stated on another occasion, when you close the door of the counseling office, it is then a universe-of-two; but we can learn much from those who have "traveled the road" before us.

THE ROLE OF THE SCHOOL COUNSELOR

Gail F. Farwell

University of Wisconsin, Madison

Counseling is the primary function of the school counselor. In this function of counseling, the school counselor works individually with each pupil trying to help the counselee gain a meaningful perspective of his strengths and weaknesses, a clear vision of his opportunity, and a knowledge of the existing or possible interferences in his maturing and adjusting throughout life. It is not the function of the counselor to "tell" the pupil. There are enough "significant others" in each person's life committed to telling. Kahlil Gibran (1:62) in The Prophet eloquently develops a philosophy for this counseling function:

> No man can reveal to you aught but that which already lies half asleep in the dawning of your knowledge.
> The *counselor* [mine] who walks in the shadow of the temple, among his followers, gives not of his wisdom but rather of his faith and his lovingness.
> If he is indeed wise he does not bid you enter the house of his wisdom, but rather leads you to the threshold of your own mind.

The school counselor committed to assisting each pupil in the struggle for self understanding has his role defined for him. This counselor must recognize his prime commitment, the attendant functions associated with this commitment, and lastly, must have the courage to stand up and be counted in support of this commitment. Too many so-called school counselors do not have professional preparation for the task and consequently do not recognize the uniqueness of professional counseling. Rather, these school counselors (?) reflect much more vividly their experiential background as former instructor, and end up doing many things akin to this activity.

The role of the school counselor can be identified as: (1) He is a school staff member committed to education and the educational process; (2) It is his function to study human lives and the contingent environment in which they live; (3) The school counselor should devote a two-thirds majority of his time to counseling with individuals; (4) He is a consultant to teachers, administrators, and parents.

Many implications attend this role for the school counselor. School administrators should demand professionally prepared counselors. They should not select chemistry teachers for counselors but chemistry teachers to instruct in chemistry. It has always been a wonderment why counselors aren't hired in terms of their knowledge about counseling and their commitment to counseling rather than those reasons which have persisted during the past decades. In 1961, antiquated notions about the proficiency of personnel prepared as experts in instruction for implementing counseling procedures should be dissipated. I will support wholeheartedly the necessary commitment of the school

Reprinted by permission of the Author and *Counselor Education and Supervision,* Vol. 1, No. 1, Fall, 1961, 40-43.

counselor to education and the purposes of the school. I will continually support the desirability of a minimal amount of teaching experience or associated experience to familiarize the school counselor with classroom realities, problems and setting. This enables the school counselor to be more accepted as a school staff member. However, those persons who demand year upon year of classroom experience are closing their eyes to the tunnel vision created. The person intensely committed to school counseling will learn more about the total curriculum, the total school situation, and a broader segment of the pupil enrollment from his vantage point of counselor than in the restricted environment of one subject matter area, in one classroom, for years ad infinitum.

With what instruments can the school counselor work? The first instrument at the disposal of the school counselor is his personality. In the instructional program at the University of Wisconsin a requirement of the course Counseling: Theory and Issues centers on a paper "My Counselor Person" which is an attempt to have potential counselors turn inward for self reflection and assessment. If you will, self-knowledge on the part of the school counselor is as important as the counselee's self-knowledge which the counselor attempts to promote. This paper is followed by interviews devoted to clarification, further expansion and self-growth — counseling if you will. Developmental counseling is a growth process — growth in self-understanding and enhancement of adjusting as a necessary construct of life. Counseling as growth is one segment of the helping relationship continuum. One end of this continuum involving a telling (advisor or instructional function) with progression to counseling (self-growth) to psychotherapy (cure and treatment). The basic instrument for implementation of the school counselor role is one's own person.

Second, many instruments developed on the measurement and human development scenes are necessary for implementation of counseling. Such items as statistical concepts, standardized tests, rating scales, anecdotes, autobiographies and others too numerous to mention in this discourse are essential for functioning in a school setting. Conceptual knowledge in career development, personality development, curriculum implementation, administrative protocol and the evolving societal scene are essential if self-growth in the shcool setting is to be enhanced and the base for effective adult adjusting is to be established. Research tools are an essential ingredient for the school counselor. The professional role of the school counselor demands that he be a good consumer of research studies in many fields of endeavor and that he, too, research his own activity. The best way to improvement and development of quality in school counseling is to expand the research horizons.

Where will the school counselor function? Naturally in the school and at all school levels. We have minimized the work of the school counselor, through default, in the elementary school. The trait-factor theorists in counseling took us off on a measurement binge; the Rogerians made us face up to the real importance of relationship in counseling, not that people of other points of view didn't ultimately content with relationships. With developmental counseling focused on growth and implemented in the school setting, the importance of each pupil developing a counseling relationship and being helped to know and understand the contribution a counselor can make should receive emphasis in the elementary school. If we would do this, junior and senior high school students wouldn't approach the counselor's office with trepidation and wonder "what have I done wrong now." The pupil would have an expectancy for the contribution the counselor can make. The school counselor that will give of himself to his relationships with each counselee is in a position to help each pupil understand more meaningfully the meaning of child study (pupil appraisal) and to promote optimal performance on the assessment and evaluative instruments employed. Maturity plays an important role in all of counseling but young counselees are as open to psychological love, acceptance and understanding as the octogenarian, maybe more so. Counseling and the attendant pupil appraisal activity is important when internal placement and interferences to learning are the focus of attention. The school counselor works here to assist in greater performance in subject matter learning. At the elementary level curricular choices for pupils are few and far between. They may have a role in planning implementation but society determines much of the experiential base to be provided. The school counselor at this level will spend considerable time in direct consultation with teachers and parents to assist them in decision making on behalf of the pupil.

As the pupil matures and moves into the junior and senior high school much more emphasis is placed on self-determination, decision and choice making, and self-understanding. Effective relationships established at the elementary level promote developmental counseling at this level in contrast to much of what goes on today — "closing the barn door after the horse has escaped."

The area of social adjustment has not received much mention. Surely we're concerned with this, so are most of society's institutions. We must remember that much of social adjustment in the school still centers in settings where subject matter of the curriculum takes front seat. I want the counselor to be sensitive to total development but the school counselor continues to exist as a professional worker in this institution if his services and skills contribute to the unique characteristics of that institution.

In summary, the role of the school counselor is envisaged as a catalyst to human growth and self-understanding. He should spend a 2/3 majority of his time in one to one counseling or consulting relationships. He is expert in his knowledge of counseling theory and procedures, career development, measure and the role of the school in developmental behavior of young people. He is an educator; he is also an applied psychologist. He is a counselor because he has preparation for the role and selects this role rather than being promoted to it as a reward for good instruction. Let us recognize the unique role of the counselor in the educational setting. Let us accept, select and prepare those who want to be counselors. Let us strengthen our profession by defining the school counselor's role so that confusion ceases to exist.

BIBLIOGRAPHY

1. Gibran, Kahlil. *The Prophet.* New York: Alfred A. Knopf, 1953.

SOME NOTES TOWARD A PHILOSOPHY
OF SCHOOL COUNSELING

Paul Nash

Boston University

The field of school counseling is growing at an unprecedentedly fast rate.
There is a danger that many practices will perpetuate themselves simply
because no one has the time to examine their worth, that theories will be
accepted without rigorous examination of their assumptions because we are
concentrating on satisfying urgent practical demands, that the necessity for
systematic clarification of key concepts will be overlooked in favor of more
immediately rewarding tasks. These dangers can be offset only by a philosophical inquiry into some of these fundamental assumptions and concepts.
This article represents an exploratory consideration of some of the terms
that might be included in such an inquiry. It is suggested that at the heart
of a philosophy of counseling lies the problem of human freedom. Seven
concepts are studied that are thought to have relevance to counseling, and to
freedom: prediction, testing, conformity, efficiency, authority, values, and
finitude.

School counseling is one of the fastest growing fields in education. The
number of people directly and tangentially involved in it is increasing enormously. There is important financial support for the movement. Under such
circumstances, certain dangers present themselves. It is particularly in a
rapidly expanding and "successful" field that basic questions may easily be
avoided. The very momentum of its growth and success may discourage
fundamental inquiry, render efforts at clarification apparently superfluous,
stifle awareness of the need for philosophical thinking.

If this is true, there would seem to be an especially pressing case for the
sustained development of a philosophical inquiry into some of the fundamental
assumptions and concepts of school counseling. The present paper is intended
as a brief, exploratory consideration of some of the terms that might be included in such an inquiry.

An initial assumption that will be made is that at the heart of a philosophy
of counseling will be found the problem of human freedom. Seven concepts
will be introduced that are thought to have relevance to counseling and to
freedom.

CONCEPT OF PREDICTION

Counseling is often concerned with predicting the student's future. It has
in this respect been much influenced by so-called scientific psychology —
positivism, behaviorism, and operationalism — which assumes that a person's
past state inexorably determines his present and future states, that this process

Reprinted by permission of the Author and *Personnel and Guidance Journal*,
Vol. XLIII, No. 3, November 1964, 243-248.

of determination, although complex, is lawful and analyzable, and that human behavior (like animal behavior) can be accurately predicted once we know all the variables involved.

I do not propose to add to the formidable body of criticism and refutation that has been made of this behavioristic type of thinking. Instead, I should like to ask one or two questions that I think are logically antecedent to the mechanical and technical problems of prediction.

Why do we *want* to predict a student's future? Why are we so concerned with knowing what the future holds? Often the honest answer to this question will be ambivalent. On the one hand, successful prediction is associated with control, and control can enhance freedom. Through scientific prediction, for example, we have gained technological control that has partially freed us from the limitations imposed by our natural environment. No one need apologize for such a concern with prediction.

But, mixed with such worthy and respectable motives, on the other hand, are often some that are less wholesome. Why do horoscope writers still make a good living in this country? Why are insurance offices the most luxurious palaces of our day? Part of the answer must lie in our insecurity and fear concerning the future. This can be associated with a certain lack of faith that prevents us from being comfortable in the presence of *any* area of life whose future remains unpredicted. One of the attitudes we might hope maturity would bring to us is that of finding in the experience of each passing moment the confidence to trust the future to be at least as beneficent as the present. With this kind of maturity, one can afford to let aspects of the future go uncontrolled and unpredicted.

Moreover, do we have the *right* to attempt to predict a student's future? If our prediction becomes known to the student, his parents, or his teachers, what effect might it have on his decisions? And are we prepared to accept the responsibility for these effects? The *accuracy* of the prediction does not matter at this point. The mere *existence* of a prediction is an important factor when choices have to be made. Specifically, we must ask whether the act of prediction enhances or restricts the student's freedom through the external influence it adds to those factors governing his choices.

Usually, the answer to this question will depend upon the way in which the prediction is communicated to him. If it is presented as one more piece of information to fit into the matrix out of which the student must eventually make an autonomous decision, then it will probably enhance his freedom, for we become more free as we perceive more alternatives and become better informed about the probable consequences of choosing among them. But if the prediction is presented as a piece of dogmatic soothsaying, with all the spurious but impressive authority of a mysterious, scientific calculation behind it, then the student's freedom must be considered restricted. The younger and less mature he is, the less possibility will he have of rising up through the weight of the prediction to make an autonomous decision. In the extreme case, where the docile student is crushed by the prestige and certainty of the prediction, his freedom is reduced virtually to zero, for he is persuaded that in fact all alternatives save the predicted one are closed to him.

It may be argued that predictions are made in accordance with the best "scientific" techniques available and that this in some way excuses their use. This brings us to the second concept.

CONCEPT OF TESTING

Testing is frequently a major part of the technique of prediction. Particularly important in this respect are so-called aptitude and personality tests. Here again we must ask whether such tests do not restrict the freedom of the one upon whom they are perpetrated, in part because of the assumptions underlying them. Most tests have been formulated as a result of research carried out under behavioristic or psychoanalytic assumptions. Both of these outlooks put stress upon man's environment and personal history as exclusive determinants of personality they tend to ignore the pull of the future and the influence of deeply held aspirations in personality formation. Such assumptions do not enhance or encourage the individual's efforts to free himself from deterministic forces and to make his personality in part a product of his own design.

We use the tests as a *means* but there is constant danger that it will also dictate our *ends*. We tend to allow the questions we ask to be determined by the nature and limitations of the testing instrument we use. Mechanical, "objectvie," closed-ended testing procedures are relatively easy to score, and give a simulacrum of exactitude and pseudo-scientific objectivity. Hence, they are tempting and often employed. But we should realize the strict limits to the kind of information we can discover by such means. Moreover, the use of such tests exerts a subtle influence on us in gradually persuading us that only those things are important that can be "objectively" tested. Ultimately it leads to the belief that only such things *exist*. With the advent of machine scoring, we are increasingly tempted to limit our inquiries about man to the areas that the machine can manipulate. Eventually, we come to make man over in the image of the machine.

We must ask, in addition, whether the use of tests and other pseudo-scientific techniques does not often represent an abdication of responsibility on the part of the counselor. If we are afraid to take the responsibility of making personal, autonomous decisions, what better way is there to dodge the responsibility than to slough it off onto an "objective" test, a "scientific" technique, or a mechanical procedure? The test becomes a supposedly safe alternative to risky, conscience-pricking judgments. Not only individual decision-making but even warm, human interest on the part of the counselor may be replaced by the arid austerity of the test.

CONCEPT OF CONFORMITY

Behavioristic psychology is frankly concerned with encouraging conformity — with "behavioral engineering" — in order to bring the student's behavior into line with behavior that is valued and approved of by the culture. Counselors who are not dazzled by the promises and threats of the behavioristic outlook should constantly be estimating the potential cost of encouraging conformity. When the counselor insists upon the student's accepting social responsibility, it may merely amount to an insistence upon a conformity to the current modes of our transient and restricted society. And this may constitute a reinforcement of problems of adumbrated by our mass media of communication — that is, of the advent of uniformity and the concomitant decline in originality and creativity.

Are we in danger of constantly punishing students in subtle ways for differing from hypothetical norms we set up? For example, in making criteria for the advisability of entering various professions, test makers often choose not ideals but the average of current practice. If you do not conform to this you are not considered suitable. In using these tests, counselors are in effect measuring an individual's suitability for a profession in terms of his relation to the attitudes, limitations, and prejudices of the average men who at present fill that profession.

One might mention at this point the possible dangers in the enterprise of investigating the role of the school counselor. Might not an acute consciousness of one's role as a counselor make him less effective? One cannot simultaneously concentrate on both conforming to a role and being oneself. It may be that by concentrating on our role we are less likely to achieve the unselfconscious spontaneity that is essential if we are to respond honestly to the student.

CONCEPT OF EFFICIENCY

We need to be aware that we live in a society where efficiency is worshipped. One of the dangers associated with the uncritical worship of any idol is that the nature of the idol does not receive serious examination. There is an assumption in America that education should try to help the individual to operate more efficiently. But what might this mean? Too often, efficiency is seen in terms of fitting round pegs into round holes. This is merely acceptance of a parochial concept of *short-term* efficiency. In the context of the lifetime of an individual, efficiency may involve letting him do what he most deeply *wants* to do, even if this leads to some temporary difficulties and frustrations. It may well be that *long-term* efficiency is best served by letting the individual find out by direct experience what are the implications and consequences of his desires and aspirations. Otherwise, we may achieve a measure of vocational fitness at the price of a deep undercurrent of unresolved desires, untried talents, and frustrated aspirations.

If we espouse this ideal of long-term efficiency, is there any way the counselor can help the student avoid some of the less pleasant short-term consequences? This brings us to our fifth concept.

CONCEPT OF AUTHORITY

What should be the counselor's role in making the student aware of authority? One of the paradoxes of freedom and authority is that knowledge of the limits of our freedom increases our freedom. Knowledge of the forces of authority acting upon us renders us more able to deal with those forces. We enhance our own freedom for example, as we become aware of the factors in our personal history that have affected our development, of the urges within us and the restrictions society places on those urges, of the limitations imposed on us by our membership of various groups — social, religious, racial, national, cultural, of the authority inherent in our various deficiencies and talents. He is more free who knows that his behavior is partly determined.

We can help students to gain the courage to act freely and autonomously by urging them to make their demands and aspirations personally relevant. We can encourage the dreams and ambitions of our students and yet still encourage them to study themselves and the relationship between their talents and their dreams. Where this relationship is realistic, the student is more likely to be successful in effecting change, in exerting leverage. This success can then encourage him to further aspiration and effort. But where the relationship is drastically unrealistic, it is hard for him to escape the disillusionment that follows failure to carry out grandiose schemes, or the resentment that ensues when one refuses to accept any limits on his freedom and has them forced upon him unwillingly and uncomprehendingly. He who insists that "where there's a will there's a way," who believes that will power is the only prerequisite for successful action, who refuses to accept the intractability of nature, will be broken by nature — perhaps broken into neurosis or psychosis.

But if the individual is partly influenced by authority, he is also partly free. No man is either wholly determined or wholly free. How to exercise this modest degree of freedom most effectively is the art of life. The alcoholic is one of the least free of men, for he cannot choose whether he will drink or not: his conduct is determined by the authority of his compulsion. Such compulsions demonstrate clearly the existence of determinism in human affairs. But groups like Alcoholics Anonymous demonstrate equally clearly the existence of freedom, because here we have men who were unfree but who, through personal effort and the help of a group, have regained their freedom, albeit a knife-edge freedom maintained over an abyss of reversion to compulsive authority.

The counselor must not shirk the responsibility of helping the student to come to a realization that life represents a constant conquest of freedom in the face of internal and external forces that always wait to reduce it. This eternal task is the penalty and predicament of being human. When the student is tempted to adopt deterministic explanations, to account for his defects and failures by factors in his personal history or circumstances that have had an inexorable causal effect, he must be encouraged to resist such temptations. To be sure, such resistance will be accompanied by anxiety and guilt, but these, too, are part of the payment for freedom. The free person is not free from anxiety and guilt, but is able to live with them without being destroyed by them. Anxiety is the vertigo of freedom — an inevitable consequence of gaining height. The person who cannot stand anxiety and removes it by placing it on another person, on a leader, or on an institution, buys peace of mind at the cost of his freedom. Anxiety can be productive if it is a manifestation of thought about an unresolved conflict: it may be resolved by bringing the person to a higher and more creative level of operation.

Guilt is a concomitant of freedom because the free person is responsible, and because no one ever completely lives up to his responsibilities. The responsible person sees a gap between what he judges to be his responsibilities and his performance. Guilt — which is formed by this gap — can be a healthy force if it is accepted as an inducement to personal excellence. It is precisely when guilt is *not* accepted, *not* faced, that it becomes neurotic and hence destructive of freedom.

CONCEPT OF VALUES

What role do values play in the counseling situation? Should the counselor impose his own values on the student? Should he conceal them from the student? Clearly, if we intend to help a person toward freedom, it is not wise to try to impose our own values on him. If he should resist them, there ensues a struggle between counselor and student that ruins the relationship. If he accepts them, he has merely assumed a conforming posture that has no relevance to his unique needs and development. No growth towards autonomy has occurred.

On the other hand, extravagant and complicated attempts on the part of the counselor to *conceal* his values from the student introduce an artificiality into the situation that is again harmful to the relationship. Where there is both a genuine concern for the student and a natural warmth and spontaneity on the part of the counselor, he need not feel that the student must be protected from all expressions of opinion and judgment. Values are implicit in the counseling situation and cannot be concealed by merely refraining from saying certain words. Every glance, gesture, physical movement, pause, change of pace, reveals them. Until we sink to the level of counseling by machine, we can rest happily within this human and humane framework.

We should recognize that concealing one's own values may be the most effective way to manipulate another person. This is not to suggest that most counselors consciously *wish* to manipulate their students, but the urge to manipulate may exist below the level of conscious deliberation. Moreover, we must be aware of the tendency to conceal our true values from *ourselves*. If we deceive ourselves into believing that we accept a student's actions when they are really deeply repugnant to us, we will usually find ourselves punishing the student in some way, perhaps subtly and indirectly. If we feel condemnatory of a student, it seems that either we must admit it (to him, or at least to ourselves) or we are compelled to make him pay some penalty for his supposed offense.

Of course, our value judgments should always be made in the light of the purpose of helping the student to form himself a set of values to live by. A distinction between self-revelation and indoctrination might be helpful here. In an attitude of self-revelation the counselor might (when appropriate) say, in effect, "This has been good for *me:* you must make what use you can of this fact in the light of your own unique situation." In an attitude of indoctrination he might try to convince the student that "This will be good for *you,* and you should follow it." While the latter approach is destructive of freedom, the former may provide the kind of psychological and moral support that nurtures freedom. Moreover, a sense of timing is important in this matter. It may not be appropriate to answer all requests for our opinion directly and immediately. There will be many occasions when it may be more appropriate to reply by asking the student, "What do *you* think?" But this temporary and *ad hoc* evasion is different from a permanent and doctrinaire conspiracy never to reveal what we believe.

There is considerable contemporary support for the view that a genuine acceptance of the student necessitates a non-judgmental attitude — what Carl Rogers calls unconditional positive regard — on the part of the counselor toward the student's behavior. This does not seem to me to be a logically necessary consequence. I may accept a person in a deep and genuine way and refrain from judging him in any ultimate sense, but at the same time, I may without inconsistency make moral evaluations of his specific acts, intentions, and attitudes.

We should further recognize that a nonjudgmental, wholly accepting attitude toward a student's behavior would also be taken by a counselor who was indifferent to the student, who had no interest in what became of him. Even if this is *not* true in a particular case, it may be inferred by the student to be true, thus preventing the relationship from becoming a fruitful one.

CONCEPT OF FINITUDE

A consideration of the concept of finitude concludes this inquiry. I can think of no attitude more appropriate for a school counselor than one marked by an awareness of the finitude of his own knowledge and insight. It is appropriate on the grounds of the vastness of our own ignorance in the face of the infinite mystery of personality. It is appropriate as representing the greatest safeguard the counselor can possess against the danger of abusing his position of privilege. If we strive to enhance human freedom it is essential to carry within us an awareness of our finite limitations as students of human behavior.

Personally, I would ally the concept of finitude essentially with a sense of humor. I cannot imagine any greater gift for the counselor nor can I imagine a greater disaster than for the counselor to be devoid of one. A sense of humor is the faculty of being able to perceive the absurdity of our human situation, the oddity of events, the comic that is the other side of the tragic in life. It enables us to live with grace and serenity. It prevents us from taking ourselves too seriously. It helps us to avoid an attitude of arrogance about our powers and responsibilities. It puts our work and aspirations into the perspective of a gentle and modest finitude. It enables us to combine a genuine commitment to our present direction with a true openness to future change. It represents a gateway to truth and hence to freedom.

COUNSELING FOR AUTHENTICITY

Sidney M. Jourard
University of Florida

The first thing a school counselor must decide is his purpose. The teachers are there to teach and the administrative officials are there to see that the school functions smoothly as a social system. If the counselor is not to teach nor to administer, what is he to do?

I believe the counselor's assignment is to foster and defend the mental health of the students in all ways that he can. Unless a counselor is clear

An original article for this book.

about his commission, he will slip into myriad other roles and duties, or drop into some rut of busywork such as routine psychometric testing, that leads nowhere and contributes nothing to the school setting except bulging filing cabinets.

I have said that a counselor's job is to be a force in the direction of greater mental health among the pupils. This raises a fundamental question: What is mental health, anyway? The answer to this question is of more than academic importance, because the work of the counselor is necessarily guided by his understanding of this condition.

A VIEW OF MENTAL HEALTH

Mental health is not so much a state or a condition as a way of living![1] It used to be thought that if a person had none of the symptoms of "mental illness," he was, by definition, "mentally healthy." Now we have learned a little more, and can offer a better understanding of the connection between the way a person lives his life and the effect that it has upon his physical health, his ability to play the roles in life that are legitimately expected of him, his personal growth, and his experience of existence as free or bound, zestful or boring, going forward or standing still.

Let me define mental health, not in terms of "signs" or "symptoms" but instead as *the outcome of a way of living*. A person is mentally healthy if his ways of behaving yield certain valued consequences. The consequences I have in mind include physical wellness, some measure of social acceptibility, a sense of meaning and progress in life, a feeling of being a distinct individual with intrinsic worth, some degree of creativity, and the ability to cope with challenges that society and life present to everyone.[2] These outcomes are by no means the only identifying features of mental health, but they will serve as a guiding orientation. Now the question that arises is, "How must a person *behave* in order to experience his world as one that it is feasible to live in, and worth living in, in ways that are acceptable to society? And what happens when a person does not live his life in these ways?"

EXPERIENCE AND BEHAVIOR

Let me first distinguish between *experience* and *behavior*. Everyone experiences the world in a way that is unique to him. My experience of the world is different from yours. Experience refers to our perceptions, feelings, meaning, fantasies, or more generally, to our *being in the world*.[3] This *being* changes continuously from instant to instant. What we refer to as our Self (actually, our idea of our self, or our self concept) is an inseparable part of our *being in the world*. Our concepts of things and of other people, and our perception of these phenomena are also part of our being in the world, as are our thinking, reasoning, remembering, and fantasy. We *exist* in the world; we *are* in the world. We experience the world. Nobody but me can ever have a direct glimpse of my being, that is, my experience. I am the only one to whom my experiencing happens. I cannot dictate my experience to msyelf. Experience *happens* to me. It goes on from birth to death, in waking and in sleep. It is private and personal, but I can disclose it to other people if I choose, just as they can choose to disclose their experience to me, thus enriching my experience in my world. But we are not the only entities under the sun that have a being. Animals, machines, trees, the sun and the moon, the ocean, germs — all these have a being too. These all "disclose," that is, show, their being continuously, to all and sundry, but we are not always interested in receiving their disclosures. Our phenomenal world, our world of personal experience is continuously receiving the disclosures of our own bodies, of the being of other people, and of things. If our experience is rich, full of meaning, satisfactions, and hope, if we let our world disclose itself to us, we function fully and grow. We stagnate when we shut off our disclosure to the world, and when we do not let ourselves receive the disclosure of the world. If our surrounding world, including the people in it, discloses a being to us that crushes or disconfirms our being, we shut it out to save ourselves. And if we do not want others to know our experience, we end our authentic disclosure to others. But we sicken if we have too long attempted to shut out the disclosure of the world to us and our disclosure to the world. Ultimately, our throttled experience finds a way to break through, even if it breaks us in doing so.

Now that I have discussed experience in relation to mental health, I will turn to behavior. Behavior is public; it can be seen. Behavior yields consequences in the world and in the person who behaves. Not all behavior is effective in attaining the goals for which it has been undertaken, and not all behavior is acceptable to society. People are obliged to learn ways of behaving that are deemed good, right, and proper within their society. If they will not behave in the required ways, they are punished. The patterned ways of behaving that all, to be acceptable, must learn, are called *roles*. One speaks of "the male role," "the role of the teacher," "the role of the student." Societies work, that is, function and fulfill aims only when the members do their parts, when they play their roles adequately. In a school the teachers' roles require them to present lessons to pupils. The pupils' roles entail obeying the rules of the school and mastering subject matter.

There is an aspect of behavior in roles that we must note at this point. Human beings can behave in ways that *disclose*[4] their experience, and they can also conceal their experience. We speak of a person as a phony, a liar, an actor, a pretender, a cheat, a counterfeit[5] if his words and actions do not reflect or disclose his experiencing at the time he is doing something or talking about himself. We also speak of people's "putting themselves in what they do" or "just going through the motions" as they do what they do. In the former instance, we speak of the person as enthusiastic, or involved. In the latter, we may call him dispirited, depressed, or demoralized. If a person discloses his experience in words, and intends to let another know his experience, we call him "sincere" or "authentic." If he *mis*represents himself, if his disclosures have been chosen for their "cosmetic value" or for their power to manipulate another's perception and idea of him, we call him a fake. We thus can look at behavior and speech from the standpoint of whether or not they reveal or conceal a person's experience.

The other viewpoint from which we wish to discuss behavior is that of the consequences which it yields in the world, to the world and to the behaving person. People choose their behavior to attain objectives that are important to them. If I want to be a success in my profession, there is a universe of actions that I must engage in to accomplish that end. If I wish to be well-liked and popular, there are still other actions I must undertake. If I wish to stay healthy and grow, there may be still other actions I must undertake and some kinds of behavior that I must eschew. Now, fortunately, we cannot have everything in life, much as we might like to. Every value carries a price tag. We must make choices among the many values that make life worth living, and hope that the goals we have chosen to pursue will be sufficiently satisfying that we will not mourn the other values which we have forsaken.[6] One of the values that all of us treasure, the more so when we have lost it or when it is under threat, is our health — our physical health and our mental health. When health is endangered or lost, all other values are jeopardized or lost. Now the question that we must address is, "How must a person behave in order to achieve and maintain, or regain, health?" My remarks are naturally most relevant to mental health, but they likely have some bearing as well on physical wellness.

Impasses

First I will introduce the concept of the *impasse*. Everyone encounters impasses in his existence. They are experienced as blind alleys, traps, intolerable situations, paralyses of action, "not knowing where to turn."[7] When impasses happen, the person suffers from depression, boredom, anxiety, or guilt. If he can find some way out of the bind in which he finds himself, he will get on with his existence, and indeed he will have grown as a consequence of having coped effectively with his problem. But if the impasse cannot be surmounted, time and life will seem to stand still, and he will see no future for himself beyond the unendurable present. Physical breakdown may then happen, or a refusal or inability to get on with his customary roles and activities. At this point, the person may be sent to or seek a physician or a psychotherapist in order to be "cured" so he can get back to the life he had been leading up to that point.

But here I must point out something that has frequently been overlooked. If a person sickens, and thus "checks out" of his usual round of activity, this fact itself is testimony that his way of living up to that point has not been adequate to maintain wellness. His ways of behaving may have been superb means of attaining popularity, or good grades, or the approval of authority figures, but the sickness testifies these good things have been gained at the cost of wellness. His way has led into a sickening impasse. The physician or therapist who would *heal* a person rather than merely relieve him of his symptoms must look beyond the symptoms to the way the person has been living and behaving and experiencing in the world. If the specialist falls victim to the *fallacy of symptoms,* he is in danger of ridding his client of these pains only to throw him back into the very way of existing that generated them. What is called for in any effort to help sufferers is healing, in the sense of helping the sick one to find a way of behaving in the world that will secure values without jeopardizing his wellness and integrity.

Now I would like to contrast the way of living that almost certainly leads to breakdown, or to drastically diminished existence, with the way of wellness.

Inauthenticity and Authenticity

An *inauthentic existence* leads inexorably to breakdown or diminished vitality and impoverished experience of life. What is an inauthentic existence?[8] This is a way of living one's life that is radically alienated, or separated, from one's *experience* of himself in the world. The inauthentic person is one who strives to conceal or misrepresent his experience because he finds it threatening to certain values. The values threatened by his experience include his concept of himself — the way he likes to think about himself — and also the image or concept of him that is presently held by other people. He lives in dread that he may present himself before others in ways that will jeopardize his career, his good name, the love and regard of friends and family, etc. He fears that if these other people find out what he genuinely thinks, feels, wants, believes, what he has secretly *done*, they will banish him from their lives. If this happens, if he loses his status, his job, the regard of others, he feels that his life will be over, worthless. Consequently, to avoid these dreaded outcomes, he carries on a life of concealment and "seeming." His behavior with others does not disclose his experience, his true feelings and needs. Rather, it has been chosen for its appearance.[9] He wants to *seem* to be someone whom he is not. His life is akin to that of a perpetual impersonator. He does not put "himself," that is, his being or his experience, into what he says and does. Consequently, the imaginary person whose part in life he is "playing" does not behave in ways that satisfy his authentic needs.[10]

If the inauthentic person has carried out his life of duplicity long enough, he will lose the capacity to identify his own spontaneous and authentic experiencing. Instead he will find his consciousness filled wih ideas, beliefs, attitudes, and feelings that he is "supposed" to experience. This experience does not have the "feel" of vital, vivid reality for him. If he is at all a sensitive person, he may experience himself as *lost*. Indeed, he has lost something — his sense of being. In his efforts to maintain the charade that his life has become, he has been obliged to *repress* his genuine experience of himself and the world. Eruptions of spontaneous experience would shatter the concept of himself he has so carefully constructed in his own mind and in the minds of others. Accordingly he ruthlessly roots these possibilities of experience out of his being. He has lost his soul.

When the inauthentic person is alone, he finds himself in bad company. He is in a state of emptiness, boredom, or anxiety. He cannot stand solitude. Contrariwise, he may find he *must* have people around him to distract him from introspection. He doesn't like to note his experience of himself because it is too ugly, disgusting, frightening, or unreal.

In authentic existence, the person acknowledges his experience for what it is. He does not strive to legislate what he will or won't think, what he will or won't feel, what he does or what he doesn't perceive. Rather, he lets his experience, his being, happen as it happens.[11] He lets himself *be*. He does not define himself in some fixed way, and then strive to delimit his experiencing to that range which fits the definition. He does not define the being of other people or things in a congealed way, blinding himself to all aspects of their being that do not fit his present concepts. Rather, he is capable of adopting the mode of *letting be*. He lets his experience be what it is, and he acknowledges this increasingly diversified experience. His ideas of self and world change to keep pace with the vicissitudes of his experience of self and world. Who is able to be thus open to experience? People who are *secure* and *confirmed* in their being and in their identities are able. People who have been lucky enough to have parents, friends, teachers, or just *one* significant person (it could be the school counselor) in their lives before whom they could drop all defense and pretense and "just be," having their disclosure of experience received in an honest way and confirmed are able. The confirmation that I am speaking of is not wishy-washy permissiveness or chronic agreement. Rather, it is an attitude on the part of the other person that this individual has the right to be the person he is. It is an acknowledgment that he feels what he feels, means what he says, whether or not one approves of his views.

The authentic person, secure in his being, is capable of knowing his own values and setting his own goals. He can experience his needs and behave in ways that will yield fulfillment. Moreover, since he is not defensive, he can stand on the "ground" of his own being and enter into dialogue with others. He invites them to disclose their experience honestly to him, and he responds in honesty by disclosing his experience.

Because he is capable of being open to himself, the authentic person is able to discern whether he agrees with the values and attitudes of others. The insecure person frequently finds himself assenting to others' proposals in his eagerness to please and to be liked; later he may find he has himself in an untenable and unlivable position. The secure person can say "No."

Because he acknowledges his experience no matter how pleasant or unpleasant, an authentic person is sensitive to his "all-is-not-well" signals. The inauthentic person is less so because he has alienated himself, distanced himself, from his authentic experiencing. "All-is-not-well" signals is a term I invented to describe the at first, low-intensity signs of malaise, anxiety, pain, boredom, depression that signal the fact that one is in an impasse — one's ways of behaving in the world are doing violence to one's integrity as a person. The secure, authentic person notes these signals *before* a stressing or unsatisfying way of behaving in the world has a chance to produce breakdown. When his work, his relationships with others, his relationship with himself have reached an impasse, he can introduce *changes* before he gets some physical ailment, or before he becomes vulnerable to a break-through of repressed experience that will precipitate a "nervous breakdown" or symptoms. He can disclose his dissatisfactions in a relationship with parents, friends, or others, thus providing an opportunity for adjustments to be made in those relationships, to get them back into a satisfying mode. He can change his work habits, or his play habits, to yield more satisfaction or success or leisure.

The inauthentic person handles impasses in a different way. He has closed himself off from much of his experience. It is as if he "strains" his experience through a filter, and screens off all experiencing that will not fit present concept of himself or his world. Consequently, the early warning signals of an impasse (that were received and acted upon by the more authentic person) persist unnoticed. The inauthentic person may have disturbing dreams or periods of depression or anxiety, but he passes them off, represses them, and *continues* with the way of life that has been generating "all-is-not-well" signals. The impasse persists unnoticed. He is thus actively but unwittingly behaving in a way that will lead to his eventual breakdown. The suffering that he *then* experiences cannot be ignored. He must pay attention because he cannot work, or interact with others, or believe things about himself as he had been doing. Something has to give, and it is his health and his capacity to cope.

From all that I've said, it is clear that mental health is best fostered by seeking to make it safe for a person to acknowledge his experience to himself and to other significant people who confirm him as the one he is. It is true that such freedom to disclose oneself is rare. Indeed, there are many settings where disclosure of self is downright dangerous. In authoritarian families or classrooms the ones in power may be uninterested in the children's experience. They want only *behavioral* compliance with their rules. They may punish children when they discover that the latter have been thinking thoughts or feeling feelings that are "not proper." They may invalidate the children's experience; if the children say, "We don't like our work," the adult may say, "Oh, of course you like it." In such settings, the ability to conceal and misrepresent experience can be a virtual lifesaver. One can "play the game" if it is worth it or if he cannot escape, but one can *know* that he is just playing the game and has experience that differs from what is publicly displayed in words and actions. As a counselor, sometimes I have found it necessary to help a troubled but basically secure person learn ways of faking or "going along" with the rules, because the punishment for disclosure of opposition would be disastrous.

COUNSELING FOR AUTHENTICITY

Everyone who values his well-being heeds access to some person of unimpeachable trustworthiness to whom he can confide his experience. But a receiving ear is not enough. A person in trouble needs some kind of response from his confidant, responding that will help him confirm and acknowledge his experience more fully and find his resources and courage for coping. Hopefully, the counselor will be such a confidant.

The Counseling Relationship commences with a seeker, estranged from his being, suffering pains brought on by a way of life that was obviously unfit for *him* to live, though others may have had a vested interest in his behaving as he has. Indeed, the seeker has had a vested interest in his past ways as well. He wants only to be rid of his "problems" so that he can get back to his old ways. It is for the counselor not to get "hung up" on the particular "symptoms" that the client brings to his attention, but to invite the client to reveal his past and present ways of being. The client, if he trusts the counselor, will permit him to come to know him. But as the client discloses his experience to his counselor, he will also reveal or "act out" his "way," his "way to illness" in the very relationship. To his "way" the counselor should be alert. It is from this way, to some as yet undiscovered but authentic way of being, that the counselor is seeking to invite the client. The aim of therapeutic counseling is not relief from symptoms alone; beyond that, it is to help the client find his being for himself — his identity.

It has been my experience that a client is most likely to find this way if the relationship with his counselor is one which *invites, challenges,* or *permits* the emergence of authentic being in him. I have come to the opinion that these terms, rather than technique or persuasion, best describe effective counseling. It is my task as a counselor to invite my client to take the risk of disclosing himself spontaneously, utterly, defenselessly; to run the risk of trusting me utterly. It is for me to be *worthy* of that trust. And it is my further job to respond honestly to his disclosures in the spirit of good will, that is, respond to him in any and every way that I have learned in the past, or can invent and improvise on the spot (within limits of safety and his and my integrity) that I believe has some *hope* of fostering growth in directions described. My effectiveness as a liberator from sick ways, and as inviter toward a healthier way is enhanced by my own degree of liberation. The more firmly I am committed to *my* way of wellness, the more secure I am in my being, the more conviction is carried by my invitation to the client to try finding *his* way. The more strongly I become committed to helping him find his way (this commitment to the other goes through a growth process, starting only as a formal, professional declaration of intent to be helpful, and staying at that point, diminishing, or growing to a more intense involvement and commitment), the more single-minded I become in my aim with that client, the more I create a situation in which his trust of me and gropings for his way will develop. It is as if my single-minded purposefulness creates a wake, one which carries him along, which invites him or tempts him out of his shell, naked, to take a plunge into his world which will "grow" him to the stature presently latent. I must be authentic and honest with him and with myself in this relationship. I must be honest about my degree of commitment, neither under- nor overstating it to him. He is, of course, keenly interested in the degree to which I can be trusted, and the degree to which I am interested in him and his quest for wellness, as opposed to my interest in staying on good terms with "the authorities," or in proving the superiority of my theories and techniques over those of my colleagues and competitors, etc. With commitment, freedom within myself to respond to my client in *many* ways (not just saying, "mm-hm," or "You feel· . . ." or "The reason you did that was . . ."), with courage on my part to remain authentic, but with some compassion, then with these things and some luck, I may well be able to let a relationship develop in which my client can abandon his safe but strangling way of the past and seek and find a way that he can tread with dignity and hope.

Annotated Bibliography

1. See Jourard, S.M., *Personal Adjustment. An Approach through the Study of Healthy Personality*. New York: Macmillan, 1964 (2nd ed.). This book aims at portraying the major aspects of healthy personality, and can serve as a useful source of "signs" of mental health and the conditions which foster it.
2. See Maslow, A. H., *Toward a Psychology of Being*. Princeton: Van Nostrand, 1962. This is one of the richest sources available of ideas on human potentialities for growth.
3. This view of experience is an aspect of the phenomenological-existential approach to the study of man. See Combs, A. & Snygg, D., *Individual Behavior*. New York: Harper, 1959 (2nd ed.) for one readable statement of this approach. See also May, R. (ed.) *Existential Psychology*. New York: Random House, 1961, for an overview of the contribution existential philosophers have made to American psychologists.

4. See Jourard, S. M., *The Transparent Self. Princeton*: Van Nostrand, 1964. In this little book, I discuss the implications of self-disclosure for mental health and counseling.
5. Read Goffman, E., *The Presentation of Self in Everyday Life*. New York: Doubleday, 1959, for an excellent account of the way people "act" their way through their lives. See also his book *Stigma. The Management of Spoiled Identity*. New York: Prentice-Hall, 1963, for an account of how people handle concealed or visible faults.
6. An important book which explores the importance of finding values in life is Frankl, V. E., *Man's Search for Meaning*. New York: Washington Square Press, 1963.
7. Ronald Laing, a British existential psychiatrist, has written several books of the greatest lucidity that illumine the way in which others entrap us in untenable situations. See Laing, R. D., *The Divided Self* (1960); *The Self and Others* (1961): London: Tavistock Institute. (*The Divided Self* will appear as a Penguin paperback in 1965.)
8. The books by Mowrer are pertinent here. See Mowrer, O. H., *The Crisis in Psychiatry and Religion* (1961), and *The New Group Therapy* (1964). Princeton: Van Nostrand.
9. See Buber, M., *I and Thou*. New York: Scribners, 1958, and *Between Man and Man*. Boston: Beacon Press, 1955, for accounts of the fundamental concept of *dialogue,* which is what counseling is when it is fulfilling its purpose.
10. The many books that resemble Dale Carnegie's *How To Win Friends and Influence People* actually seek to teach people how to *seem,* or play-act, in order to get a good name. In fairness to Carnegie, he enjoins "sincerity" upon those who would benefit from his advice — but how can one turn sincerity on and off?
11. See Rogers, C. R., *On Becoming a Person*. Boston: Houghton Mifflin, 1961, for a fine portrayal of the importance of openness for healthy personality.

The interested reader will find many references in the books cited if he wishes to broaden and deepen his grasp of healthy personality and the role which counseling can play in fostering it.

(24)

ELEMENTARY SCHOOL GUIDANCE

Richard P. Koeppe

Director of Pupil Services, Madison, Wisconsin, Public Schools

Guidance services at the elementary level are not to come; they are already here. Late in starting, the growth of elementary school guidance in the past decade has been rapid. Indications are that its growth in the years ahead will even be greater.

Guidance services in elementary schools are related to several significant movements of the twentieth century. These include mental health, improved methods of educational measurement, the development of mental health

An original article for this book.

centers, and the child-study movement with its emphasis on theories underlying human growth and development.

The general acceptance of a need for elementary school guidance services, indeed the actual pressure for such services, is coming from a society which is becoming increasingly concerned about the waste in human resources. Recent events have put the spotlight on national waste in manpower so evident in mounting figures of mental illness, dropouts, delinquency, and unemployment. These are evident at a time in the nation's history when such forces as constantly improved methods of mass communication and travel, greater concentration of population in urban areas, changes in governmental organizations, and increased application of automation all foretell an even more complex society of tomorrow.

The concept of what guidance services at the elementary level ought to be has been slowly emerging in recent years. One of the earliest positions was the *guidance is good teaching* concept. Related to the mental health approach, advocates of this position identified elementary guidance as a process inseparable from teaching. The classroom teacher was held totally responsible for providing the services. Efforts to meet the needs of children relied heavily on grouping procedures and curriculum revision with little or no use of special services to the individual. All too often, the self-contained classroom was believed to be synonymous with the self-sufficient classroom. It became obvious that this approach was not the complete answer.

A somewhat later position accepted elementary guidance as a specialized service for children with severe problems, but not essentially for every child. The services were aimed at those pupils whose conduct was considered symptomatic of underlying difficulty. Subsequently early identification of pupils who were likely to encounter future trouble became important as a means of *remedial and preventive guidance.*

Most recently, however, the position is being taken that guidance services at the elementary level are not limited to children with problems. In the process of studying children referred for special help, school personnel recognized these techniques as applicable and beneficial to all children.

This most recent position is usually referred to as *developmental guidance* and takes its foundation from the developmental stages of growth through which all humans go. Careful study of each child's developmental history and his present physical, mental, and emotional needs is paramount. Once a pattern of growth and special needs emerges from the study of an individual child, it is possible to understand, anticipate, and help guide his development to the fullest of his potentials.

Guidance services in the elementary school are emerging as a process concerned primarily with assisting the child as a learner. Essentially it is the process of helping each child understand and accept himself in relation to his own needs and to those of his environment. Early identification of each child's needs and interests, interpretation of these to parents and teachers, and counseling for every child seem to be the chief services for developing adequate developmental guidance programs.

A review of the recent literature describing elementary guidance programs already in existence indicates that all seem to have abandoned the position that the classroom teacher can do it alone — that good guidance is merely good teaching. All existing programs have supplemented the efforts of the classroom teacher with additional nonteaching staff. The majority of programs seem to be remedial-preventive in nature in that they are geared to help those pupils with severe problems.

Even so, few remedial-preventive programs are based on premises which are compatible with the general principles underlying the developmental concept. Most existing programs reflect an expedient approach. What seems to have happened is that in order to get elementary programs going, compromises had to be made. Such compromise, in order to begin programs, is understandable, but it is essential these existing programs be improved as well as many new ones begun.

Guidance must ultimately become an integral part of the school function at all levels and not essentially an extra service offered only to those in trouble nor left essentially to the conscientiousness of the individual classroom teacher. Good guidance, good instructional practices, and a good curriculum are seen as complementary in helping each child through the process of growth to adulthood.

OBJECTIVES

The objectives of guidance services at the elementary level will vary depending upon whether the orientation is *remedial-preventive* or *developmental*.

An example of objectives of a remedial-preventive program is to discover abilities, interests, strengths, and weaknesses of pupils as an aid to teachers in counseling and planning for the retarded, average and gifted children; to prevent minor maladjustment problems from becoming serious; and to locate and refer pupils who are developing serious maladjustment problems to the proper resources. (23) The strong emphasis is on helping the "some" who have or are developing problems.

Advocates of the developmental school of thought would argue that such an approach accentuates the negative and is not broad enough in scope. They would instead accentuate the positive and include all children, not just some.

The rationale and objectives of a developmentally oriented approach would go something like this. The function of guidance is to facilitate the basic function of the school, that of instruction. The objectives of guidance will be achieved only if the service provided by professional staff members is directed toward specific aspects of their relationship to the *child as a learner* in an educational setting.

Guidance must help the individual child to profit from his educational opportunities and to realize his maximum potential. The objectives of guidance are concerned essentially with the developmental needs of children. The program of guidance services, then, is an outgrowth of the individual needs of children as recognized by the school.

Guidance must facilitate better understanding of the individual child. The school needs to know his uniqueness not only in physical and mental growth but also in his self-concept of ability and the way he approaches learning. Such understanding should facilitate the school's efforts to provide experiences designed to support and enhance the child's progress toward becoming an adequate person. (48)

As it is now evolving in elementary schools, developmental guidance emphasizes many specific objectives. Two objectives, however, that appear repeatedly in virtually all the sources are (1) the need of all children to develop better understanding of themselves and (2) the need of all chldren to develop maturity in their relationship to others.

Importance of the Self

Everyone has some idea of himself in general terms. For the most part he behaves, makes decisions, and interacts with others in a manner consistent with the picture he has of himself. Within the context of self-theory, probably the most basic objective of every person is the development of a positive regard for self.

It is generally accepted that the self has to be achieved; that the self-concept is learned; that experiences which teach an individual he is a positive person will produce a positive self; that self is achieved through social contact; that the concept of self-ability, in relationship to others, rather than actual ability, determines learning behavior; and that progress toward psychological health is progress toward becoming a fully-functioning person. (1, 48) The elementary schools need to pay more attention to what youngsters say of themselves. The pupil who says of himself, "I'm dumb" or "I can't think so good" is far from being ready to benefit from the learning situation.

Importance of Interpersonal Relations

The casual treatment of interpersonal relations is in interesting contrast to that found in adult life. While it is true that employees occasionally will be discharged because of their inability to do the job, far greater numbers are released because they are not able to work well with others. In today's society it is becoming more and more necessary for a person to become a member of a team than be solely responsible for a particular job.

It is not difficult for educators to be aware of the contribution made to vocational success by academic learning. Reference to this relationship is often made by teachers in an attempt to motivate learning.

In comparison with academic skills, however, a little has been done in the elementary schools toward helping pupils develop adequate and realistic concepts of themselves and helping pupils develop good interpersonal relationships. These usually are handled very incidentally. (44)

What guidance programs at the elementary level propose to do is take these functions out of the realm of the incidental and place them in the realm of the planned, the purposeful. If a pupil cannot be comfortable with himself, it is difficult for him to be comfortable with others. When personal concerns reach a certain magnitude, they begin to interfere with learning.

It is the contention of the advocates of elementary guidance that American education can help each child develop to his fullest only if the child has positive regard for himself and is able to get along with others. These are in essence prerequisites for being fully ready to learn, for developing to the maximum of one's potential.

THE "GENERALISTS" IN THE GUIDANCE SERVICES AT THE ELEMENTARY LEVEL

Much clarification of the guidance functions in elementary education has already taken place, but much yet remains to be done. One of the most uncertain aspects of guidance services in the elementary schools is the staffing question — Who provides the services? What follows in this chapter will be a discussion of the various persons who are being suggested as professional staff for the elementary level.

The terms "generalists" and "specialists" as they are used in this chapter are somewhat analogous to their use in the medical profession. The term "generalist" will be used to discuss those professionals who are prepared to provide their services to *all* pupils. The term "specialist" will be used to discuss those professionals who are prepared to provide their services to only *some* pupils. Under the heading of "generalists" in guidance services at the elementary level, the role of the elementary classroom teacher, elementary principal, and elementary school counselor will be described.

The Elementary Classroom Teacher

Regardless of what orientation one has toward elementary guidance, it is acknowledged that the role of the classroom teacher is a key one. Even though team-teaching procedures are entering the elementary school and even though subjects such as music, art, and physical education are often taught by itinerant teachers, the fact remains that the elementary classroom teacher spends more time with a given pupil than does any other professional educator.

Although guidance and good teaching are not synonymous, there is a close relationship between them and each can do much to enhance the other. The classroom teacher has many opportunities to provide guidance services for her pupils. She is expected to be a participant in, not merely a recipient of, guidance services for her pupils. The fact that a need exists for assistance to the teacher in no way diminishes or indicates a lesser guidance role for her.

The published material on elementary guidance is virtually unanimous in accepting the preceding statements. Entire books (34, 35, 36, 37, 39, 40, 41, 42, 43, 44, 46, 47, 49, 53) are devoted primarily to defining the guidance services provided by the classroom teacher. In one way or another, all seem to say that these services are as follows: (1) Creating a suitable classroom environment, (2) Collecting information about pupils, (3) Modifying instructional techniques, (4) Providing occupational information and developing attitudes toward the world of work, and (5) Assisting in curriculum revision. (42)

Creating a Suitable Class Environment. The most suitable classroom environment is one in which pupils are able to think and learn in the most effective manner. The first requirement of a good learning situation is respect for the individual child. Where there is no respect, there is little constructive learning. Every attempt must be made to have every child valued for himself, not because he is the best reader or lives on the "right side of the tracks" but just because he *is*. From this atmosphere grows the prime requisite of guidance — self-respect — and respect for others.

Another requirement of a good learning environment is the application of sound principles of mental hygiene to learning activities in the classroom. A classroom environment which, for one reason or another, threatens the child is apt to reduce his ability to concentrate, perceive things correctly, and remember.

Building self-confidence and a feeling of security in pupils is another important requirement in developing a satisfactory classroom environment. Children are helped to develop self-confidence in the learning situation when they are given opportunities to succeed and discover their own abilities. Each individual pupil consciously or unconsciously evaluates himself according to his ability to perform in certain aspects of the school work. This ascribed status has an impact upon his striving to learn, to assume responsibilities, and to get along with his peers. In an environment of respect and security, he feels free to question, explore, and make mistakes, As a result, he is more able to develop insights, draw valid conclusions, and learn.

Collecting Information about Pupils. The classroom teacher in the elementary school is in an excellent position to gather information about pupils which is essential for an effective program of guidance services. Teachers who know about children are able to help them more. This information would include the pupil's early life experiences, his physical growth patterns, his home, his friends, his interests and his hobbies. The school should know how a pupil is accepted by children of his age group and how he feels about them. How the child sees the world and how he thinks the world sees him gives the teacher and other professionals clues to his feeling about himself. This is important because it influences his behavior and his belief in himself as a learner throughout his school life and beyond.

Teacher techniques for collecting information about pupils are numerous. Some of the more common techniques are parent-teacher conferences, observation in the classroom, the anecdotal record, the questionnaire, the autobiography, sociometric devices, and standardized aptitude and achievement tests. These techniques are an attempt to collect, analyze, and interpret information as objectively as possible.

Modifying Instructional Techniques. Whenever teachers individualize instruction in terms of children's needs, a most valuable guidance service is being performed. More and more teachers are becoming aware that for children to be successful with academic learning beginning experiences with reading must be successful, and that success is dependent upon certain developmental factors. Therefore, when extended readiness is provided and children are given more help and more time to develop readiness, *this is guidance* in the classroom. When an alert fifth grade boy or a group of children are given a special project in history for which they must use material and research above and beyond the textbook to locate needed information, *this is guidance* in the classroom. When a teacher is aware that a child has been under emotional stress and differentiates the instruction for the time being to help the child over the rough spot, *this is guidance* in the classroom.

The varities of instructional methods are unlimited. It is only the inexperienced teacher who uses the same technique over and over with every class and each activity in a class.

Providing Occupational Information and Developing Attitudes Toward the World of Work. Choosing a lifetime occupation generally is considered to be a process rather than an event. In this process, a person collects information about jobs and attitudes toward work, makes a tentative choice of a vocation, changes his mind, collects new information, and makes new tentative choices over a long period of time. The classroom teacher at the elementary level has many opportunities to help pupils obtain information about occupations and develop wholesome attitudes toward the world of work.

Teacher techniques for providing occupational information and developing attitudes are numerous. Some of the more common techniques are relating school subject matter to various types of occupations, providing books and other reading material which describe various types of work, taking field trips to observe people at work, inviting adults into the classroom to describe their jobs, pointing out the different kinds of rewards for working, displaying pictures and poster material illustrating various kinds of jobs, showing films and filmstrips that deal with vocations, and encouraging pupils to include topics dealing with the world of work in written assignments. (5, 12, 13, 18, 49).

The use of the foregoing techniques seems all the more important when it appears that most of the leading textbooks used by elementary school children present an unreal and distorted view of the actual living world of the pupil. The reading media is limited in scope of occupations covered and tends to give the greatest attention to professional and managerial positions. (2, 33)

Assisting in Curriculum Revision. One of the most accessible methods of meeting the needs of individual pupils is through the curricular offerings. Broad curriculums are especially important in a nation where elementary pupils come from widely varied socioeconomic backgrounds. They have a broad range of abilities and interests. As a result, the school must offer a comprehensive set of educational experiences in order to meet the needs of all children.

It is within the power of the classroom teacher to make minor revisions, from time to time, in the subject matter being offered. However, in order to provide a continuous and related set of experiences for the pupil throughout the entire period that he remains in school, major revisions in curriculum must be made periodically.

The classroom teacher can assist in curriculum revision by reporting her observations about the adequacy of the present curricular offerings in meeting the needs of pupils in her classes; seeking the opinions of her pupils regarding curriculum; following up her pupils to see how well they progress at succeeding grade levels; serving on committees revising certain phases of the curriculum; reporting her observations of changes within the community which suggest a revision of the curriculum; sharing with others the special learning experiences of pupils of high and low academic ability which she has tried and found successful, and reporting the reaction of parents to the school experiences of their children.

Full-fledged guidance programs, complete with all of the foregoing teacher services, are often seen by the teachers as more chores conceived by the administrators to laden the already overworked teacher. Teachers will do more if the doing fulfills their own motives, gives them additional satisfaction, increases their pride in accomplishment, and enhances their sense of professional performance.

In order to carry out their guidance services properly, elementary classroom teachers will need training. This should be incorporated in undergraduate work and graduate work as well as ongoing in-service programs provided within school systems.

The limits of the classroom teacher's service, however, like those for any other professional person, do exist. They lie in such things as the relatively large number of children she must handle at any one time, the limitations she is subject to during school hours, and the lack of training in the more technical aspects of guidance services. These notwithstanding, the classroom teacher still plays a key role in the guidance services at the elementary level.

The Elementary Principal

That the elementary classroom teacher has vital guidance services to perform is not disputed. It is equally obvious that the elementary principal is also in a crucial position. No program of guidance services can succeed unless the principal provides the necessary leadership or at least support. Without this ingredient, only a minimum amount of attention will be paid to guidance services.

The elementary principal is in the best position to view and interpret the over-all philosophy and operation of the school. In schools where no professionally trained, nonteaching, nonadministrative staff are available, the principal often carries the entire load. Children who cause disturbances in class are sent to him. He frequently has conferences with parents. The principal also provides important counseling to teachers who are having problems in the classroom. These problems are on occasion related to personal-social concerns of the teacher outside the school. Where there is help from professionally trained personnel such as a counselor or consultant, the role of the principal may be somewhat different.

Regardless of the professional staff available to provide services to an elementary guidance program, the elementary principal must provide leadership in many areas. He must help develop and interpret a sound guidance philosophy within his building. In order to create the type of atmosphere within the classroom suggested previously, such at atmosphere must permeate the entire building. He must seek financial support for the guidance services which will make available the necessary physical facilities, equipment, supplies, and staff time. The principal must plan and implement in-service programs for his staff which will enhance their ability to provide the guidance services. He is also responsible for seeing that the guidance services provided, as well as instructional methods and curriculum, are constantly evaluated. One of the key roles a principal can play in helping develop and maintain quality guidance services is in the hiring of teachers. Through proper interview techniques, he can select those teachers with the guidance point of view or those capable of developing it.

The elementary principal has major responsibilities for the quality of guidance services provided. Just as with the teacher the elementary principal will need graduate study and in-service work in this area.

The Elementary School Counselor

The title elementary school counselor is most ambiguous and ill-defined at the present time. Where implementation of elementary guidance programs is under way, a variety of titles have been given to the professionally trained, nonteaching, nonadministrative school personnel. In addition to elementary school counselor, some of these titles are supervisor of guidance, guidance teacher, youth counselor, welfare counselor, guidance worker and elementary consultant. This situation is compounded by the fact that the current literature itself is unclear. In one survey done among elementary principals, the counselor educators instructed the respondents to use the term elementary school counselor as synonymous with "a qualified school psychologist." (31) Barr (35) states that the training of the elementary school counselor should be similar in nature to that of the school psychologist or school social worker. It appears that accord on what the elementary school counselor is has not yet been established.

More and more writers, however, are suggesting that the title elementary school counselor be reserved for or applied to those professionally trained persons whose major responsibility is *counseling* and who will provide this service *to all* pupils. (15, 22, 29, 42, 48) This suggestion seems especially appropriate in view of the 1964 adoption of a similar general definition for the secondary school counselor by the American Personnel and Guidance Association and its divisions. It is upon the foregoing definition that the discussion of the elementary school counselor will be based in this chapter.

The elementary school counselor is viewed as a member of a school staff, assuming a sufficiently large enrollment. The White House Conference on Children and Youth in 1960 made a firm recommendation that the ratio of pupils to elementary school counselors be six hundred to one. As a member of a school staff, the counselor must function within the framework of the administrative and instructional policies of the school. He has joint responsibility to the elementary school principal and the central office administrator. His is a staff, not line, position. It is important that the elementary school counselor be seen this way by pupils, teachers, principals, and parents.

The guidance functions ascribed to the elementary school counselor by his advocates vary slightly, but all descriptions in one way or another include the following: (1) Counseling all pupils, (2) Consulting with parents, (3) Identifying individual differences among and within pupils, (4) Working with teachers and other staff members, and (5) Interpreting to staff and community the guidance program.

Counseling All Pupils. The major contribution of the elementary school counselor will be his counseling skill. Counseling as used here will be defined as the one-to-one, face-to-face relationship in which the pupil is helped to develop a realistic and adequate concept of himself and to relate this to his environment, especially the school and learning.

In addition to counseling, the counselor will work with groups of pupils at one time, most often in a regular classroom setting. He will lead discussions which will help children understand their own behavior, their peer relationships, and the world of work. He may through such group procedures provide orientation for pupils coming into and preparing to leave the school. The elementary school counselor will spend approximately one-third to one-half of his time in either counseling or group procedures with pupils. He will develop extended counseling contacts with a very small number of pupils. Those in need of extended counseling will be referred to specialists within the school system or within community agencies.

The elementary school counselor needs techniques appropriate to the developmental level of the child. Much of the communication may be nonverbal involving the use of role playing, toys, and open-ended stories.

Consulting with Parents. The elementary school counselor will hold conferences with the parents to provide them with information about their child. He will gather information from the parents relative to their expectations of their child and home factors which may be influencing the pupil's learning at school. The value of individual and group conferences with parents as a means of improving pupil achievement is just beginning to be understood.

Identifying Individual Differences among and within Pupils. Information about pupils will be gathered from a variety of sources including information from the teacher, the home, the counselor himself, and the school aptitude and achievement testing program. The counselor's responsibility will be to provide for the collection, organization, and interpretation of the information. Much of the current information being gathered, at cost in both time and money, is not being used or used to its fullest value. The elementary school counselor can provide help in the development and use of records. He can make sure that the appropriate information is made available to pupils, parents, teachers, principals and specialists.

Working with Teachers and Other Staff Members. Implied thus far is that in order to be fully effective the counselor must develop and maintain good working relationships with the classroom teacher. Teacher and counselor have significant roles which implement each other and sometimes even overlap in a desirable but not wasteful way. A considerable amount of a counselor's time will be spent discussing levels of readiness, motivating drives, intellectual aptitude, and levels of achievement of pupils with their teachers.

In cases where certain pupils are also receiving services from specialists such as a nurse, reading consultant, speech therapist, school psychologist, or nonschool agencies, the counselor will develop and maintain the necessary working relationships in order to bring to bear the full effect of all that is known about the pupil.

Interpreting to Staff and Community the Guidance Program. The elementary school counselor will assist the principal and teachers in implementing and maintaining the guidance program in the school. Orientation sessions may be held with teachers new to the staff. Parent-teacher organizations as well as those of the community at large may be used to interpret to the parents and public the rationale underlying the guidance services. The need for interpretation is a constantly on-going process.

Preparation of the Elementary School Counselor. The preparation of the elementary school counselor will not need to vary greatly from that now provided for the secondary school counselor. Instead of adolescent development, the counselor would concentrate on child development. Instead of taking his supervised practicum in the secondary school, it would be taken in the elementary school. The large common core of course work would remain the same. These typically include personality development, theories of counseling, curriculum trends and development, learning theory, statistics, measurement and evaluation, research, and school administration. One of the more promising programs based on the described role of the elementary school counselor seems to be at Ohio University, Athens, Ohio. (29) The majority of advocates for this role favor successful elementary classroom teaching as a prerequisite for entering the training program; however, some suggest alternative experiences as a substitute.

The role of elementary school counselor is based on an affirmative answer to the question, "do all pupils need counseling?" The assumption underlying this answer is that all children encounter problems in the *normal* process of growing up. It is interesting to note that the expectations of elementary principals (16, 20, 21) and teachers (9) are that counseling is a necessary service to be provided by a professional to elementary children. These expectations, however, are that counseling be provided to only *some* pupils, not *all*. Typically these include the child who is a severe discipline problem in class and/or an underachiever.

Advocates of guidance and counseling services for all believe that through counseling there will be direct benefits to the pupil. The pupil through counseling (1) will be provided information about himself and will be assisted in interpreting the information about himself and will be assisted in interpreting the information so as to come to see himself as more adequate in the learning situation; (2) will gain increased motivation for learning; (3) will begin to develop independence by gaining more control and greater self-direction in solving problems. (42, 48)

The advocates further believe that through consulting with parents, identifying individual differences among and within pupils, working with teachers and other staff members, and interpreting the guidance program to staff and community, the elementary school counselor can help maximize the learning opportunities for all children.

More and more then, the title elementary school counselor is coming to be used to describe a professional whose major responsibility is counseling individuals and who provides this service to all pupils. Those persons who are now working in elementary schools, however, apparently do not see themselves in this light or at least are not functioning in this manner. A survey (28) done among persons responding to the title elementary school counselor indicates that they spend little time in counseling individuals and considerable time in group work, in testing situations, and with parents and teachers on an individual basis. It appears these persons are not as much counselors as they are consultants; not as much generalists as specialists.

THE "SPECIALISTS" IN THE GUIDANCE SERVICES AT THE ELEMENTARY LEVEL

The term "specialist," as used here, will mean those professionals who are prepared to provide their services to only *some* pupils. Under this heading, the role of the elementary school consultant, the school psychologist, and other specialists will be described.

The Elementary School Consultant

Many people who have described the role of the elementary school counselor seldom list counseling pupils as one of his major responsibilities. It is the contention of this writer that what they really mean to describe is an elementary school consultant. What these writers generally describe are professionally-prepared persons whose major responsibility is *consultation*, not counseling, and whose consultations deal with only *some* pupils, not all. It is upon this general definition that the discussion of the elementary school consultant will be based in this chapter.

The elementary school consultant may or may not be a member of a school staff. More often than not, he appears to be a person working out of a central office and serving several schools. Usually one consultant per one thousand pupils is recommended. Since he more directly serves teachers than anyone else, perhaps a more logical ratio would be one based on one consultant per so many teachers.

The guidance functions ascribed to the elementary school consultant by his advocates (1, 8, 9, 19, 20, 23, 27, 31, 51) are numerous. They appear, however, to group themselves into the following: (1) Identifying and planning for pupils with learning difficulties (2) Consulting with teachers, (3) Consulting with principals, (4) Consulting with parents, and (5) Working with *some* pupils.

Identifying and Planning for Pupils with Learning Difficulty. The major contribution of the elementary school consultant is to assist, through consultation, teachers, principals, and parents in their work with the elementary children who have special needs which interfere with their learning. In order to fulfill this contribution, the elementary school consultant must possess skill in identifying and planning for pupils with learning difficulties. Typically these include the gifted, underachievers, delinquents, retarded, physically handicapped, and the emotionally handicapped. In keeping with the identification function, most writers advocate his being responsible for supervising the school's testing program and maintaining the confidential records of these pupils. Since reading is perhaps the basic skill an elementary pupil is expected to acquire, the ability to diagnose reading difficulties is often expected of the elementary school consultant. In order to recommend plans for helping pupils overcome certain learning difficulties, the consultant must be an expert in remedial techniques as well as placement procedures in various individualized programs such as enrichment, acceleration, and special classes.

In cases where children need intensive diagnosis, the consultant is expected to make referrals to other pupil service specialists and community agencies and interpret their findings and recommendations to teachers, principals, and parents. It is assumed by those who advocate the elementary school consultant that he will of necessity involve the teacher in identification of pupils with learning difficulties.

Consulting with Teachers. The elementary school consultant spends a considerable amount of his time interpreting pupil data to the classroom teacher. He discusses with her recommendations for helping an individual child with learning difficulties. He supplies special materials and suggests teaching techniques.

In addition to consultation on an individual basis, the consultant provides in-service education for teachers. In-service programs felt to be within the realm of competency of the consultant include administration and interpretation of tests, construction of classroom tests, units on vocations, maintenance and use of the cumulative folder, improved parent-teacher conferences, mental health, and group dynamics.

Consulting with Principals. The elementary school consultant is in a position to study factors that might lead to curriculum and teacher improvement.

The consultant can provide the principal with information that will help him identify pupils' needs which may not be served in the present program.

The consultant will also assist the principal by recommending and participating in the placement of pupils. These principal-consultant conferences can lead to more meaningful in-service programs and new opportunities for promoting public relations.

Consulting with Parents. The elementary school consulant works with the parents of pupils who have learning difficulties. The consultant can help parents understand the various aspects of their child's strengths and weaknesses. He may advise them concerning family relationships that have a bearing upon the behavior of the child or upon certain stages of his development. Through parent-consultant conferences, the consultant can interpret the school program to the parent and promote increased understanding of the child which would benefit both the school and home. On occasion, if the seriousness of the situation so indicates, the consultant may refer the parents to agencies outside the school for family consultation.

Working with Some Pupils. The elementary school consultant spends time working with some pupils. Most of this involves groups of pupils with only very limited time spent in counseling. Such group or individual contacts with pupils involves those having personal, social, educational problems often characterized by disruptive behavior in the classroom and/or underachievement. Topics dealt with may include personal appearance, grooming, manners, and personal hygiene as well as helping pupils understand their behavior and their relations to others. These contacts help the consultant further identify and plan for the pupils with learning difficulties.

Preparation of the Elementary School Consultant. The preparation of the elementary school consultant will need to vary substantially from that of the elementary or secondary school counselor. The functions of the elementary school consultant are closely related to *identification* and *remediation-prevention.* The professional knowledge and techniques involved in these functions are found in the field of elementary education, guidance, psychology, social work, and health. Although the elementary school consultant may take course work felt necessary for the elementary school counselor, he must concentrate more in specific areas. Emphasis is needed in such areas as education psychology, with strong background in learning principles that can be applied to the classroom situation. Courses in reading, particularly remedial reading, appear necessary for the consultant. He could also benefit from courses in the gifted, the mentally retarded, the physically handicapped, juvenile delinquency, and speech correction.

Surveys done among elementary principals (20, 19) and teachers (9) indicate that they envision as most needed a person similar to the elementary school consultant described. This would seem logical when one considers the pupils involved. The needs of the gifted, delinquent, underachiever, and handicapped and the problems they present the classroom teacher and principal are more obvious and pressing.

Most of the literature on elementary guidance describes a person like the elementary school consultant. His role is described in terms of remedial, preventive, and problem-solving activities. The consultant is looked upon as a "master teacher." He works primarily with and through teachers as well as principals and parents, serving as a resource person to them. He appears to be a consultant, co-ordinator, and an occasional counselor of *some* in that order.

The School Psychologist

Of all the specialists working in elementary schools today, the school psychologist is singled out for comment because his role and preparation most closely resemble that of the elementary school consultant. He too is concerned with identifying and planning for pupils with learning difficulties. He also frequently consults with teachers, principals, and parents. He too works directly with some pupils.

School psychology has been defined as "that branch of psychology which concerns itself with the personality of the pupil in interaction with the educational process." (52) The study of the interaction implied in this definition usually takes the form of individual testing which seems to be the primary responsibility of school psychologists and the activity which takes up the largest share of their time in all types of school systems.

The school psychologist analyzes the psychological aspects of the learning problem of referred children by administering individual tests of intelligence and personality in order to gather diagnostic information. Among the more commonly known tests are the Wechsler-Bellevue and Stanford-Binet Intelligence Tests and the Thematic Apperception Test and Rorschach Ink Blot Test, both personality evaluation devices. Other evaluative measures used by the school psychologist include classroom observation, interviews with school personnel, parents, and pupils regarding the problem, and reviewing earlier school history.

School psychologists should have a thorough background in child development, problems of learning, social and emotional problems, and the administration and interpretation of group and individual tests of intelligence and personality. The American Psychological Association recommends that this preparation should be at the doctorate level or the equivalent and should emphasize both clinical psychology and education. (38)

The difference in preparation between the elementary school consultant and school psychologist seems to be one of degree. The psychologist is prepared particularly in intensive individual diagnosis of mental and personality functioning whereas the preparation received by a consultant is broader and less intensive in some of its emphases. The psychologist's background calls for the doctorate or its equivalent while the consultant could perhaps be prepared in a one, but more likely two year Master's degree program.

In some states certification as school psychologist is granted at various recognized levels of competency. The elementary school consultant is perhaps at the lowest level of certification whereas the doctorate would place a psychologist at the top level.

There appears to be room for both the elementary school consultant and the school psychologist, even within the same school system. This is especially true when one considers the shortage of psychologists many of whom are employed by agencies other than schools. This condition is further influenced by salary factors when hiring a consultant with a Master's degree versus a psychologist with a doctorate or its equivalent.

Other Specialists

There already exists within the elementary programs of many of America's school systems a wide variety of other nonteaching, nonadministrative, professionally prepared personnel. These include the school social worker, nurse, attendance officer, speech therapist, and reading specialist.

Social Worker. The social worker is prepared in the casework technique to help children, especially those whose problems have an emotional base. The social worker has a major role in work with parents and community social agencies. Typically he serves as a liaison person between school, child, family, and community.

Nurse. The nurse serves as a resource person to the school in health matters. The nurse can instruct school personnel on methods of handling specific health problems relating to an individual child's condition. Nurses advise pupils on personal health problems. They meet with teachers individually and in groups to discuss current health problems including prevention and control of disease. Nurses are often familiar with conditions and attitudes in a home which may help or hinder the child in his school adjustment. This information also is shared with school personnel to assist the child.

Attendance Officer. The primary function of an attendance officer, as his title indicates, is to act as a referral person to investigate children who are not attending school. Reasons for children not attending school are varied and the attendance officer often provides services beyond mere enforcement of the attendance laws. He may find himself, in the case of indigent families, looking for food and clothing for the family. He may have to arrange for transportation or home instruction in the case of extended illness.

Speech Therapist. The speech therapist's major responsibility is to diagnose and treat children who have problems of voice, articulation, and stuttering. She spends most of her time working with individual children or groups of children in an attempt to help the children over-come their particular speech handicap. The speech therapist also works with the classroom teacher and parents in order to give continuity to the remediation.

Reading Specialists. These individuals, as their title indicates, specialize in reading. They serve as resource persons to the classroom teacher. Typically the reading specialist diagnoses the reading problems of pupils referred to her by the teacher, counselor, or other specialists. Following diagnosis the reading specialist may work directly with the pupil individually or in groups in an effort to help him overcome his difficulties. She may also make suggestions regarding techniques and materials to the teacher for use in the classroom.

Coordination of Functions. The fact that the above generalists and specialists already exist in various numbers and combinations in school districts throughout America indicates that the answer to the question of — "Who provides the services?" — is a complicated one and can perhaps be answered in several if not many ways. It seems certain that guidance programs at the elementary level will vary in terms of who provides what service.

School systems which now find themselves with only teachers and principals and who wish to develop additional guidance services in the elementary schools have a variety of ways to begin. Whom do they add to their staff, an elementary school counselor, an elementary school consultant, a school psychologist, or some other specialist?

School systems which now find themselves with not only teachers and principals, but perhaps several or all of the specialists already at work face a different task when they set out to improve and expand their guidance services in the elementary schools. If gaps exist in their present program is better staff utilization the answer, do they need more of the present specialists, or do they need other different professionals to add to their staff?

Each program of guidance services at the elementary level must also take into account such reality factors as the degree of competency of the classroom teachers, the availability of community resources, and the very real problem of finance, all of which vary from district to district. It is obvious that as the scope of elementary guidance programs develop toward the optimal, careful planning and co-ordination are needed. Consideration also needs to be given to not speaking in terms of guidance services but instead speaking and planning in terms of pupil personnel services or pupil services. The guidance connotation is perhaps too limited for those programs which include classroom teachers, principals, elementary school counselors, elementary school consultants, school psychologists, social workers, attendance officers, nurses, speech therapists, and reading specialists working together as a team to help children.

These factors notwithstanding, the years ahead will see further rapid growth of guidance services in the elementary school. This is perhaps only the beginning of an exciting era in American education.

SUMMARY

The growth of elementary school guidance in the past decade has been rapid. Indications are that its growth in the years ahead will be even greater. The forces behind such growth in services are varied but all seem to relate to the concern over wasted and unfulfilled human potentials.

Elementary guidance services are usually described from one of three positions. The first position states that good guidance is merely good teaching. This position is being advocated less and less as it is becoming apparent that this approach is not the complete answer. The second position stresses the need for specialized service for those children with severe and special problems. It is usually referred to as the remedial-preventive approach to guidance. The third, and most recently taken position, asks that elementary guidance programs not be limited to children with problems. Its rationale is taken from the developmental stages through which all humans go. Its advocates agree that the techniques used in working with children with problems are applicable and beneficial to all children. This position is usually referred to as the developmental approach to guidance.

The purpose of elementary guidance is to facilitate the basic function of the school, that of instruction and learning. Some persons believe this can best be accomplished when children are studied and those showing minor problems are worked with and the problems prevented from becoming serious. Still other persons believe when all children are helped to better understand and accept themselves as worthy and when all children learn to develop and maintain good interpersonal relationships with others will instruction and learning be optimal.

Who provides the guidance services which help achieve these objectives remains a crucial question to be answered. Everyone seems to agree that the classroom teacher has vital guidance services to perform. The building principal and central office administrators are in key positions of leadership.

Beyond the teacher and principal a variety of other professionals are suggested as providing necessary guidance services. One of these is the elementary school counselor who offers as his major contribution counseling skill. He is more and more coming to be viewed as a generalist like the classroom teacher and principal in that he is expected to provide this service to all pupils. Another of these is the elementary school consultant who offers as his major contribution assistance to teachers, principals, and parents. The ability to identify and plan for pupils with learning difficulties is a necessary skill of the elementary school consultant.

Similar to the consultant is the school psychologist. His specialty is intensive individual diagnosis of mental and personality functioning.

A variety of other specialists are also providing services in some of America's elementary schools. These include school social workers, nurse, attendance officer, speech threapist, and reading specialist.

Elementary guidance programs already in existence show considerable variation in terms of who is providing what service. It appears that programs will continue to develop differently in different places. As elementary guidance programs grow toward optimal scope, the need for careful planning and co-ordination of effort will become paramount. Indications are that the years ahead for elementary guidance will be exciting ones.

QUESTIONS FOR DISCUSSION

1. Are the guidance expectations placed on teachers realistic?
2. Should experience as a classroom teacher be required in order to be a counselor, consultant, or other specialist?
3. Does a pupil's attitude toward himself and others influence how he learns in the classroom?
4. Do all children need counseling?
5. Can we counsel with the elementary school child, especially the very young?
6. Are both the elementary school counselor and elementary school consultant capable of achieving similar goals — the counselor serving as an immediate instigator of pupil growth through direct counseling contact with pupils, the consultant working indirectly through teacher, principal, and parent?
7. Can a developmental guidance program be built at the elementary level without an emphasis on counseling and without an elementary school counselor as described in this chapter?
8. Is the overlap in preparation and function among counselors, consultants, psychologists, social workers, and others necessary and desirable?
9. Is there a need to unify the many specialists now available to work in elementary schools into a more general type of pupil service worker?
10. Who should be responsible for co-ordinating the efforts of the variety of professionally-trained, nonteaching, nonadministrative personnel now working in many of America's school districts?

GUIDANCE SERVICES AT THE ELEMENTARY LEVEL
AN ANNOTATED BIBLIOGRAPHY

Articles

1. Apostal, Robert A. "Objectives of Elementary Guidance." *The School Counselor,* Volume 10, October, 1962, pages 23-26.

Immediate and ultimate objectives of elementary guidance are suggested in this article. The writer sees these objectives best achieved through strong support of the classroom teacher by a consultant-type guidance worker.

2. Arbuckle, Dugald S. "Occupational Information in the Elementary School." *The Vocational Guidance Quarterly*, Volume 12, Winter, 1963-64, pages 77-84.

Dr. Arbuckle contends that presentation of much occupational information in the elementary school is unreal and distorted in the actual living world of the child. He contends that the only important use of occupational information and knowledge is the extent to which it actually helps a child become involved in the learning process leading to critical thinking, respect, and understanding.

3. Barbe, Walter B., and Chambers, Norman S. "Career Requirements of Gifted Elementary Children and Their Parents." *The Vocational Guidance Quarterly*, Volume 11, Winter, 1963, pages 137-140.

According to the authors, there is mounting evidence that with gifted children the selection of a career is of major concern to them much earlier than had previously been thought. Using 156 children in grades three through six, attending special classes for the gifted and their parents, comparisons were made between the ranking importance given to ten selected career choice requirements.

4. Gelenter, Selma. "How Elementary Counseling Helps." *The School Counselor*, Volume 7, May, 1960, pages 90-91.

The article gives a brief description of how an elementary child with problems was helped over a period of years by the cooperative efforts of a teacher and counselor.

5. Grell, Lewis A. "How Much Occupational Information in the Elementary School?" *The Vocational Guidance Quarterly*, Volume 9, August, 1960, pages 48-53.

This article, written by an elementary principal, takes the viewpoint that elementary school youngsters definitely can gain information and attitudes toward the world of work that will be useful at some future date. The elementary classroom teacher is seen as in the best position to carry out such a program interwoven with other aspects of the curriculum. Various methods of doing the interweaving are presented.

6. Harrison, Edna L. "The Counselor's Role in the Early Identification of Gifted Children." *The Personnel and Guidance Journal*, Volume 39, May, 1961, pages 735-738.

The article discusses the role of the counselor in identifying and properly placing the gifted kindergarten pupil. The counselor is seen as chairman of a team including the principal, teacher, parent, and on occasion other specialists such as the nurse.

7. Harrison, Edna L. "The Elementary School Counselor and the Gifted Underachiever." *The Personnel and Guidance Journal*, Volume 41, April, 1963, pages 716-719.

A detailed description of an elementary counselor's role in helping gifted underachievers. Special emphasis is given to ways in which the counselor can work with the classroom teacher.

8. Harrison, Edna L. "The Elementary School Counselor's Unique Position." *The School Counselor*, Volume 11, December, 1963, pages 107-109.

A warning is given that the idea that teachers are the key persons in elementary guidance has led many to presume a natural ability to counsel. Mrs. Harrison differentiates "conferring" from "counseling" and uses this as a basis for drawing the dividing line between the work of the teacher and that of the counselor.

9. Hart, Robert N. "Are Elementary Counselors Doing the Job?" *The School Counselor,* Volume 9, December, 1961, pages 70-72.

Dr. Hart, an elementary school principal, compiled a list of 41 duties performed by elementary counselors. He sent these to a group of classroom teachers in 38 school districts employing elementary counselors and to a group of 20 authorities in the filed of elementary school guidance, asking them to place the duties in order of importance. He found that teachers and authorities differed on what duties were deemed important.

10. Hill, George E. "Elementary School Guidance: Criteria for Approval by State Departments of Education." *Counselor Education and Supervision,* Volume 2, Spring, 1963, pages 137-143.

In this article, the author reports on his evaluation of published standards for guidance in the elementary schools furnished to him by fifteen state departments of education. He concludes that much clarification of the guidance function in elementary education remains to be done and that one of the most uncertain aspects of guidance services in the elementary schools is the staffing question — WHO provides the services?

11. Hill, George E., and Nitzschke, Dale F. "Preparation Programs in Elementary School Guidance." *The Personnel and Guidance Journal,* Volume 40, October, 1961, pages 155-159.

The authors report on the results of a questionnaire responded to by persons in charge of 154 preparation programs in elementary school guidance. They found preparation programs for guidance workers in elementary schools not well defined and that little differentiation was made between preparation for the elementary school and preparation for the secondary school. They called for a clarification of the elementary guidance function which takes into account the significant role of the teacher in a self-contained classroom and her relations to special service workers such as school psychologist, school social workers, and instructional supervisors.

12. Kaback, Goldie R. "Occupational Information in Elementary Education." *The Vocational Guidance Quarterly.* Volume 9, Autumn, 1960, pages 55-59.

Professor Kaback describes occupational information projects at the first through fourth grade level. The primary objectives of these projects are to develop respect for the worth and dignity of all types of labor and to provide a basis for later vocational choice and planning.

13. Kaye, Janet. "Four Graders Meet Up with Occupations." *The Vocational Guidance Quarterly,* Volume 8, Spring, 1960, pages 150-152.

Miss Kaye, a fourth grade teacher, describes a unit on occupations she developed and taught in Scarsdale, New York. The purpose of the unit was to have children learn more about occupations in general and the work of their fathers in particular. The unit was not purely on occupations but was integrated with several other areas of the curriculum which helped the children improve research skills, study skills, and interviewing skills.

14. Klein, Ruth A. "The School Nurse as a Guidance Functionary." *The Personnel and Guidance Journal,* Volume 38, December, 1959, pages 318-321.

This article reports on a survey done among school nurses in New Jersey. Professor Klein found high agreement among the nurses as to what should be and what should not be their duties. Nurses did see themselves as members of a team including teachers, parents, principal, counselors, psychologists, speech specialists, reading specialists, attendance officers, and occasionally even the janitor.

15. Koeppe, Richard P. "The Elementary School Counselor — What Is He?" *The School Counselor,* Volume 12, October, 1964, pages 11-13.

It is the suggestion of this article that the term "counselor" when used by a person on the elementary level be in keeping with its recognized use on the secondary level: namely, someone who provides his services to *all* pupils and whose major function it is to *counsel.*

16. Kokovich, Anthony, and Matthews, Gerald E. "An Elementary Principal Tries Group Guidance." *The School Counselor,* Volume 12, October, 1964, pages 6-10.

An elementary building principal describes his group guidance attempt with five boys selected from a group suggested by the teachers. Results were believed worthwhile enough so that the principal undertook further group procedures.

17. Lifton, Walter M. "Social Forces and Guidance in the Elementary Schools." *The Vocational Guidance Quarterly,* Volume 12, Winter, 1963-64, pages 89-92.

A summarization is made of some of the societal pressures existing today which are different in kind or degree from those experienced by the present adult population in their formative years. Where these pressures appear to be destructive, specific suggestions for alternate society, parent, teacher, and counselor behavior are suggested.

18. Lifton, Walter M. "Vocational Guidance in the Elementary School." *The Vocational Guidance Quarterly,* Volume 8, Winter, 1959-1960, pages 79-81.

This article discusses the role and use of vocational guidance in the elementary grades. The author asks that more research be done in this area. He also asks for the development of schools for vocational guidance material at the elementary level.

19. Mattick, William E., and Nickolas, N. A. "A Team Approach in Guidance." *The Personnel and Guidance Journal,* Volume 42, May, 1964, pages 922-924.

This article describes the attempts of the Bellevue Washington School District to evolve a true team approach at the elementary school level. The attempt seems to have overcome the problems of lack of communication among specialists involved in the study of the same child *and* the frequent failure of the recommendation of specialists to have an impact on the child in the classroom. The elementary guidance consultant is viewed as a specialist in remedial techniques.

20. McDougall, William P., and Reitan, Henry M. "The Elementary Counselor as Perceived by Elementary Principals." *The Personnel and Guidance Journal,* Volume 42, December, 1963, pages 348-354.

The article reports on the responses of 169 elementary school principals in Idaho, Oregon, and Washington regarding their perception of the training, background and functions of the elementary school counselor. The majority of responding principals favored the viewpoint that elementary guidance be concerned with specialized services to individual pupils rather than general curriculum guidance for all.

21. McGee, Robert T. "Guidance in the Elementary Schools." *The School Counselor,* Volume 7, December, 1959, pages 28-30.

An elementary school principal stresses the need for "preventive"guidance at the elementary level. He discusses the role of the classroom teacher and building principal.

22. Miller, Dorothy. "Developmental Guidance in the Elementary Schools." *The School Counselor,* Volume 9, March, 1962, pages 101-103.

    The writer is an elementary guidance consultant in the Clayton, Missouri, Public Schools. She describes the rationale for a developmental guidance program that is not limited to children with problems.

23. Miller, Oren W. "An Elementary Guidance Program." *The School Counselor,* Volume 8, October, 1960, pages 9-11.

    This article describes the Elementary Guidance Program as it is developing in St. Joseph, Missouri. It places emphasis on the role of the elementary consultant and school psychologist.

24. Meeks, Anna R. "Elementary School Counseling." *The School Counselor,* Volume 10, March, 1963, pages 108-111.

    Dr. Meeks presents a logical rationale for counseling in the elementary schools. She places strong emphasis on the needs of *all* youngsters not just *some.*

25. Meeks, Anna R. "Guidance in the Elementary School." *Journal of the N.E.A.,* Volume 51, March, 1962, pages 30-32.

    This article predicts continued rapid growth for elementary school guidance programs. Brief mention is made of the roles of teacher, principal, and counselor. These are supplemented by general case histories involving a sibling problem, underachievement, and a lack of readiness for reading.

26. Oldridge, Buff. "Two Roles for Elementary School Guidance Personnel." *The Personnel and Guidance Journal,* Volume 43, December, 1964, pages 367-370.

    The purpose of this study was to compare experimentally the perceived effectiveness of an elementary guidance staff functioning in a psychotherapeutic role to that of one with a broader guidance role. The guidance staff consisted of school psychologist and school psychometrist. The conclusion was that there is little evidence to support psychotherapy more effective than general guidance procedures.

27. Orgel, Rita G. "Contemporary Views of Elementary School Guidance." *The School Counselor,* Volume 8, October, 1960, pages 22-27.

    An elementary guidance specialist describes her duties and responsibilities in the Merrick Long Island, New York, elementary schools. She views herself as a consultant and a resource person doing (1) child study, (2) work with school personnel, (3) work with parents and community groups, and (4) research.

28. Perrone, Philip A., and Evans, David L. "The Elementary School Counselor? Coordinator? Or What?" *Counselor Education and Supervision,* Volume 4, Fall. 1964, pages 28-31.

    The article reports on the questionnaire results obtained from sixty-five persons serving as elementary school counselors. According to the findings, the elementary school counselors spend considerable time in group counseling, in group testing situations, and with parents and teachers on an individual basis. There seemed to be differences in the counselors' role in that some worked directly with pupils while others worked more with the parents and teachers of the pupils.

29. Raines, Bill. "An Approach to Practicum for the Elementary School Counselor." *The Personnel and Guidance Journal,* Volume 43, September, 1964, pages 57-59.

    This article contends that a supervised practicum must be a part of an elementary school counselor's preparation. The program described is the one at Ohio University and involves three major activities: (1) working as a counselor in an elementary school; (2) participation in a group counseling experience with other enrollees; and (3) having an individual conference each week with the counselor-educator. Rationale for the practicum is based on the premise that guidance programs in the elementary school should be primarily developmental rather than problem-centered.

30. Sherman, Robert. "The School Counselor: Generalist or Specialist." *Counselor Education and Supervision,* Volume 1, Summer, 1962, pages 203-211.

   This article presents a discussion of the school counselor as a generalist who serves all and as a specialist in counseling who serves . some. The advantages and disadvantages of each role are presented.

31. Shertzer, Bruce, and Lundy, Charles T. "Administrator Image of an Elementary School Counselor." *The School Counselor,* Volume 11, May, 1964, pages 211-214.

   This article reports the findings of a questionnaire responded to by 198 elementary school principals in Indiana. The researchers use the terms "qualified school psychologist" and "elementary school counselor" as synonymous. The administrator's image of an elementary school counselor suggested an individual who serves as coordinator, consultant, and counselor in that order.

32. Sukman, Charles A. "The Personnel Services Team." *The School Counselor,* Volume 10, March, 1963, pages 135-137.

   Sukman discussed the counselor as a member of a pupil personnel team. He describes the counselor's relationship to psychologist, special education teacher, home teacher, speech therapist, school nurse, and attendance officer.

33. Tennyson, W. Wesley, and Monnens, Lawrence P. "The World of Work Through the Elementary Readers." *The Vocational Guidance Quarterly,* Volume 12, Winter, 1963-64, pages 85-88.

   The purpose of this study was to determine how the world of work is presented to youngsters through their elementary reading texts. A descriptive analysis was made of the occupations mentioned in the leading reading texts used by elementary school children. The authors concluded that the view of the world of work presented through reading media during the first six years of elementary school is limited in scope and that professional and managerial occupations were given the greatest attention.

Books and Pamphlets

34. Arbuckle, Dugald S. *Guidance and Counseling in the Classroom.* Boston, Allyn and Bacon, 1957.

35. Barr, John A. *The Elementary School Teacher and Guidance.* New York: Holt-Dryden, 1958.

36. Bernard, Harold W., and Even, James C. *Guidance in Elementary Schools.* New York: Chartwell House, 1954.

37. Cottingham, Harold F. *Guidance in Elementary Schools, Principles and Practices.* Bloomington, Indiana: McKnight and McKnight, 1956.

38. Cutts, Norma E. *School Psychologists at Mid-Century.* Washington, D. C.: American Psychological Association, 1955.

39. Detjen, Ervin W., and Detjen, Mary Ford. *Elementary School Guidance.* New York: McGraw-Hill, 1952.

40. Driscoll, Gertrude P. *Child Guidance in the Classroom.* New York: Teachers College, Columbia University, 1955.

41. Garry, Ralph. *Guidance Techniques for Elementary Teachers*. Columbus, Ohio: Charles E. Merrill Books, 1963.
42. Hatch, Raymond N., Costar, James W. *Guidance Services in the Elementary Schools*. Dubuque, Iowa: William C. Brown, 1961.
43. Knapp, Robert H. *Guidance in the Elementary School*. Boston: Allyn and Bacon, Inc., 1959.
44. Kowitz, Gerald T., and Kowitz, Norma G. *Guidance in the Elementary Classroom*. New York: McGraw-Hill, 1959.
45. Lloyd-Jones, Esther, et. al. *Guidance in Elementary Education, A Case-Book*. New York: Bureau of Publications, Teachers College, Columbia University, 1958.
46. Los Angeles County Superintendent of Schools Office. *Guiding Today's Children: A Guidance Book for Teachers and Administrators of Elementary Schools*. Los Angeles: California Test Bureau, 1959.
47. Martinson, Ruth A., and Smallenburg, Harvey. *Guidance in Elementary Schools*. Englewood Cliffs, New Jersey: Prentice-Hall, 1958.
48. Meeks, Anna R. (Chairman). "Dimensions of Elementary School Guidance— (Tentative Draft)." Washington, D. C.: A.P.G.A., Dittoed Report, October, 1964.
49. Norris, Willa. *Occupational Information in the Elementary Schools*. Chicago: Science Research Associates, 1963.
50. Peters, Herman J., Riccio, Anthony C., and Quaranto, Joseph J. (ed.). *Guidance in Elementary Schools: A Book of Readings*. New York: MacMillan Co., 1963.
51. Smith, Hyrum M., and Eckerson, Louise O. *Guidance for Children in Elementary Schools*. U. S. Government Printing Office, 1963. OE Z5032.
52. White, Mary A., and Harris, Myron W. *The School Psychologist*. New York: Harper and Brothers, 1961.
53. Willey, Roy DeVerl. *Guidance in Elementary Education*. New York: Harper and Brothers, 1960.
54. Wrenn, C. Gilbert. *The Counselor on a Changing World*. Washington: American Personnel and Guidance Association, 1962.

$$25$$

COMMUNICATION AND JUNIOR HIGH SCHOOL COUNSELING

Richard W. Beck and Ray N. Wilson

Counselors, Columbus, Ohio, Public Schools

As early as Plato's time philosophers thought that methods should be devised by which every artisan could work at that for which he was naturally fitted. Many methods and devices have been used to this end, but it has remained for the twentieth century machine age to work out extrinsic formal services called "guidance and counseling."

We have all read of Dr. Frank Parsons, who coined the term "vocational guidance" and established the Vocational Bureau in 1908. He then was asked to outline a vocational guidance program to be used in the schools of Boston. From that date forward, some organized form of guidance has been in our school systems.

An original article for this book.

During the period of Dr. Parsons' work, the junior high school movement began. The junior high school had its beginning in Columbus, Ohio, in 1909, and Berkeley, California, in 1910. It has been stated that one of the felt needs leading to the junior high school movement was the gap that existed between the elementary school and the high school. The junior high school philosophy evidenced an underlying conviction that the students needed guidance in selecting from the progressively enlarged curriculum a program which was suited to their particular needs. As the junior high school developed it became obvious that electives should be related to career objectives; thus vocational and educational guidance became a necessary part of the new school. Advocates indicated that the school should guide the pupil in an exploration of the fields of human thought and action by equipping him with a knowledge of his capacities and interests.

The need for guidance in the junior high school is greater today than a generation ago because of the far-reaching social, industrial, and technological changes that have created new adjustment problems for adolescents. Guidance has become an integral part of the total educational process.

PURPOSES OF THE JUNIOR HIGH SCHOOL GUIDANCE PROGRAM

Effective guidance should be based upon a well-conceived plan with the counselor at the focal point. Counseling, testing, teacher conferences, case studies, parent conferences, and seeking with the administration and teachers the realization of the educational philosophy of the school should be part of this plan. The effective program must involve all of the staff, with the guidance counselor acting throughout as coordinator of the team effort.

What, then, could be considered the major areas of the junior high school guidance program? Three areas seem to encompass the total program: (a) educational guidance, (b) vocational guidance, and (c) personal-social guidance. In essence an effective guidance program is the total of all actions and interactions taken by the child and the school to promote better self-realization on the part of the child, develop his abilities and interests, and aid him make his own decisions so that a productive and fruitful life may be realized.

In order to obtain the three guidance aims, the counselor must be aware of the various roles that other faculty members have in the guidance program.

Role of the Principal

The principal is responsible for the total school program. Without his help, the guidance program loses much of its effectiveness. If he has no apprehension about delegating the responsibility of the total guidance program to well-trained counselors, the program should achieve the desired results. This necessitates a direct line of communication between the counselor and the principal. They must work as a team, inasmuch as both are concerned with the total education of the child. A guidance-minded principal will encourage constant evaluation and improvement of the total guidance program.

Role of the Classroom Teacher

The teacher, who has daily contact with students, is in the best position of any staff member to observe changing student behavior. It is the teacher who will make the majority of referrals to the guidance counselor. Close communication and understanding between the guidance personnel and the teaching staff is a basic requirement if an effective program is to be maintained. The guidance-minded teacher will encourage students to make full use of guidance facilities. Some teachers should serve on guidance committees and try to develop mental hygiene concepts in classroom activities.

Role of the Counselor

The primary function of the junior high school counselor is that of providing guidance services to the individual student. His success will depend largely on how well the school staff understands and accepts his function. Good communications within the school staff are essential. As has been stated, the guidance counselor's basic functions are in the field of education, vocation, and personal-social guidance. Under each heading appears a variety of items. Listed below, in no specific rank order, are some basic work areas for the counselor to consider.

1. Individual counseling
   a. educational
   b. vocational
   c. personal-social
2. Group counseling
3. Individual and group testing
4. Establishing grouping procedures
5. Homeroom guidance programs
6. Serving on the guidance committee
7. Presenting career materials
8. Referral source
9. Study habits
10. Counseling with teachers
11. Orientation day
12. Career day
13. Working with the parent-teachers association
14. In-service education
15. Placement procedures
16. Evaluation and follow-up studies
17. Plan and execute research
18. Parent conferences
19. Curriculum committees

Counselor Grade Assignment

The writers are aware of three basic plans of grade assignments used in the junior high schools at the present time. The first is in the assignment of a counselor to a specific class. The counselor works with a specific class as they progress through seventh, eighth, and ninth grades. In this manner the counselor becomes familiar with the majority of his students and their academic and personal problems. This counselor must, by necessity, be aware of the total development of junior high school students and understand the total curriculum. This plan might be labeled a continuous plan of counselor assignment.

A second plan that is in use might be labeled the grade level plan. Under this plan the counselor becomes a specialist at one grade level and would be concerned with the problems of students in that grade area. For example, a seventh grade counselor probably would work more with study habits than with vocational materials. The seventh grade counselor would be a coordinating figure between the junior high school and the elementary school program. Each year he would receive a new group of students and would be responsible for their orientation, counseling, testing, evaluation and any other items that might concern them.

A third plan, sometimes labeled the eclectic plan, would permit counseling with any student. The counselor using this plan must be well grounded in all phases of child development and the total educational structure of the school system. He must be prepared to do counseling, testing, vocational planning and answer any other problems that may arise in the school setting. This plan calls for the closest possible working relations among all counselors.

COMMUNICATION – THE KEY TO SUCCESS

"What do you do in your office? You have the easiest job in the school. Isn't every teacher a counselor? When I went to school we didn't have counselors. Why do we need them now? Why should we record test scores when you have all day in guidance?"

In beginning a guidance program, the counselor will no doubt hear remarks such as the ones stated. What will he say? Is there a good response? Do professional teachers really say these things? Are such remarks serious? Prospective counselors must be sure that students, staff, and the community understand the function of the guidance counselor as an integral part of our educational system. The writers have come to feel that communication is the key to a successful career in counseling. Without this key, regardless of the amount of his professional training, the guidance counselor will become ineffective in his school setting. A clear channel of communications is as important in the internal working of human relations among the staff and community as it is in the closely knit client-counselor setting.

A counselor should realize that those who are not aware of his function, his capabilities, and his training will see him only as another administrator. It is the counselor's obligation to his profession to communicate to all of those within his setting the ways in which he can serve, particularly in the areas of educational, vocational, emotional, or personal-social problems. Establishing this professional atmosphere requires that the counselor be communication conscious. The communication between faculty, community, and students is discussed in the following section.

Faculty Communications

To be an asset to the school the guidance counselor must have clients. Alone he cannot hope to reach students who have problems. It is imperative that the staff know him and understand his responsibilities. The guidance counselor can begin to accomplish this by making himself known to the total staff as soon as possible. The counselor might ditto a memorandum to all teachers indicating his objectives and requesting their assistance. Being realistic, the guidance counselor should know that not all of the staff will find time to read the notice. He should follow up with conversations in the lounge, at lunch time, or before school. The guidance counselor should try to answer questions presented to him in a straightforward manner.

Another path open to the guidance counselor is the use of the guidance committee. If he is fortunate enough to find a committee already formed, this may lead to a faster and better understanding with the staff. The committee should help outline what has been done in the past and help establish goals for the future. A guidance committee can be an asset to a sound program of guidance in the junior high school.

The guidance counselor may also further communications by developing a sense of humor. He must not be a know-it-all person although he may feel he is the best qualified person in child study in the school. He must listen and respect what other staff members say. The guidance counselor must earn the respect of the staff before he can function properly.

Some of the foregoing items might seem trivial, but junior high school staff relations are important. They will either enhance or detract from the counselor's capabilities and potential. Through the counselor's actions the guidance image of the school will largely be determined.

Community Relations

The guidance counselor should keep in mind that many citizens in the school community are not aware of his services. Some may realize that the school has a guidance counselor but may not be quite sure of his function. Educating the community as to his function should be a goal of the guidance counselor.

The Parent-Teachers Association can be a strong link with the community. The guidance counselor might contact the program chairman of the Parent-Teachers Association and ask for time to speak at one of their meetings. He should explain his function in laymen's terms. A question and answer period following the presentation may clarify many misconceptions. The guidance counselor should answer questions as directly as possible.

If the guidance counselor is working in a small community, he might contact the local newspaper staff and have them write a story on the function of a guidance counselor in the school. The same idea could be presented by an interview over the local radio station.

It is quite possible that for many parents the junior high school is the first contact with a guidance counselor. The counselor should take advantage of this initial contact to present a good image. Most parents realize that the junior high school period is a turning point in the lives of their children and that good guidance is needed. The counselor must let the parents knows what services are available to them and to their children.

Student Relations

A new counselor must meet and come to know the student body. In the course of the student-counselor conference, he should strive to find out the students' aspirations, desires, and problems. Junior high school students are neither small children nor adults. They no longer find themselves under the direction and care of one teacher the entire school day, nor are they given the individual attention they may have come to expect in the past. Junior high school students find these years to be a period of change — physical, emotional, and social. They are still dependent on their parents for many things, yet they feel they are old enough to make some decisions. Anxiety and frustration are a part of their everyday life. Often they try to release these tensions through school activities. The school must take this complex individual and try to transform him into a student who wants to learn. The guidance counselor's role becomes a vital one at this point. Teachers are involved in their presentation of facts and information, and too often they are faced with too many students, too many papers to grade, and too many outside activities. It is little wonder that many teachers lose track of the individual student and sometimes forget that not all students are interested. The guidance counselor must try to be a source that can be drawn upon by the student for the individual attention he needs.

Each child is different. Abilities vary from child to child. Interests also vary. The counselor knows that the cumulative records contain detailed information that might help the teacher better understand the students. The guidance counselor must try to bring this information to the teacher's attention. The counselor must try to be a bridge in the gap between the students and the teachers. This is not an easy task.

Students may, on occasion, picture the guidance counselor as an administrator. This is a view that should be dispelled quickly. The guidance counselor is not an administrator; he is a counselor.

The counselor must work with all students. He must try to convey to the teachers those impressions that will be helpful to them. Communication channels must be open at all times.

If the counselor fails to reach some student, he must remember that he is only human. His individual abilities are not perfect. He can only hope to shed some light on student problems and make the educational process a more pleasant and profitable experience.

CONCLUSION

The writers have tried to point out that communication is the key to effective guidance. The areas discussed have been found significant in the junior high school guidance program. The junior high school guidance counselor-candidate should give careful consideration to these areas before stepping into his first guidance position.

SELECTED BIBLIOGRAPHY

Barr, John, *The Elementary Teacher and Guidance.* New York: Henry Holt and Company, 1958.

Beck, Richard W., *A Study of Guidance Committees in the Junior High Schools in Columbus, Ohio.* Master's Thesis, Ohio State University, 1962.

Brown, J. E. and R. A. Dolen, "What Constitutes an Adequate Guidance and Counseling Program for the Junior High School?" Bulletin of the National Association of Secondary School Principals, Vol. 44, April, 1960. pp. 40-44.

Buxton, David R. and Herman J. Peters, *Basic Guidance Terminology*. Division of Guidance and Testing, State Department of Education, Columbus, Ohio. May, 1960.

Chauncey, H., "How Tests Help Us Identify the Academically Talented," Journal of the National Education Association. Vol. 47, April, 1958, pp. 230-231.

Coleman, W., "Assisting Teachers in Using Test Results," The Personnel and Guidance Journal, Vol. 36, Sept., 1957, pp. 38-40.

Conant, James B., *Recommendations for Education in the Junior High School Years*. Princeton: Educational Testing Service, 1960.

Cottingham, Harold F. and William E. Hopke, *Guidance in the Junior High School*. Bloomington, Ill., McKnight and McKnight Publishing Company, 1961.

Davis, Burton, *Guidance in the Junior High School*. Yokohama, Yamagata Press, 1936.

Davis, Calvin O., *Junior High School Education*. Yonkers, World Book Company, 1924.

Davis, Frank G. and B. Carnall Davis, *Guidance for Youth*, New York: Ginn and Company, 1928.

Detjen, Ervin and Mary E. Detjen, *Homeroom Guidance Programs for the Junior High School Years*. Boston: Houghton Mifflin Company, 1940.

French, Joseph L. and Hans H. J. Steffen, "Interests of Gifted Adolescents," The Personnel and Guidance Journal, Vol. 38, April, 1960, pp. 633-636.

Gesell, Arnold, Frances L. Ilg, and Louis B. Ames. *Youth — The Years from Ten to Sixteen*. New York: Harper and Brothers, 1956.

Gribbon, Warren D., "Evaluation of an Eighth Grade Group Guidance Program," The Personnel and Guidance Journal, Vol. 38, May, 1960, pp. 740-745.

Gruhn, William T. and Harl R. Douglass, *The Modern Junior High School*. Ronald Press Company, New York, 1956.

Guidance in the Curriculum, Washington, D. C.: Association for Supervision and Curriculum Development, 1955.

Guidance in Grades Seven, Eight, and Nine, State Department of Education, Division of Guidance and Testing, Columbus, Ohio, 1960.

Johnson, Mauritz, William E. Busacker, and Fred Bosman, Jr., *Junior High School Guidance*. New York: Harper, 1961.

Johnston, E. G., et al., *Role of the Teacher in Guidance*. Englewood Cliffs, New Jersey: Prentice-Hall, Inc., 1959.

Koos, Leonard V., *Junior High School Trends*. New York: Harper and Brothers, 1955.

McDaniel, Henry B., *Guidance in the Modern School*. New York: The Dryden Press, 1956.

McQueen, Mildred, ed., *Planning and Organizing the Case Conference*, Research Report. Chicago: Science Research Association.

Payne, Arthur E., *Organization of Vocational Guidance*. McGraw-Hill Company, 1925.

Peters, H. J. and G. F. Farwell, *Guidance: A Developmental Approach*. Chicago: Rand McNally and Company, 1959.

(26)

THE SECONDARY SCHOOL COUNSELOR AND HIS ROLE

Nick J. Topetzes

Associate Professor of Education, Marquette University

For many years the organizational structure of the secondary school was rather clearly defined and all persons involved in education were aware of their respective roles within this plan. The progress and increasing interest in the areas of counseling and guidance, with its major roles in the field of education, necessitated the introduction of trained personnel to carry out the various programs involved in the broadening scope of the total school program.

Like science, medicine, and educational methodology, guidance and counseling are undergoing vast and dramatic changes. The emerging counseling era has progressed unbelievably from "the babe in the woods stage" to a "giant" in the vastness and the complexity of its coverage in the area of social psychology; its theoretical aspects have promulgated new trends in the hallowed halls of counseling philosophy. In fact, these trends have changed almost drastically over a mere few years of the guidance movement. In this chapter, the writer would like to comment briefly on some of the more critical trends.

The contributions of the secondary school counselor to pupil, school, and society are dependent upon the existence of an environment consistent with his responsibilities. Such an environment includes both psychological and physical conditions of work. Desirable psychological and physical conditions of work can be developed and maintained only through the joint efforts of administrators and counselors. The school administrator assists the counselor to facilitate total counseling and guidance services within a school through his understanding support and leadership. The following are the major recommendations of the American School Counselor Association state of policy: [1]

1. The school counselor should be employed in a full-time counseling position. In order to better meet the needs of pupils, it is desirable to employ a counselor for a period extending beyond the regular school year.
2. The school counselor should devote no less than 50 per cent of his assigned time to counseling. The assigned pupil load should approximate 250 pupils to one full-time secondary school counselor.
3. The information provided as a result of the school counselor's counseling relationship with pupils and parents must be considered confidential. In matters of communication and others, the counselor should be guided by Ethical Standards of the American Personnel and Guidance Association.
4. The counselor should not function as an administrative assistant but should be freed from other duties such as substitute teaching, disciplinary action, and routine clerical tasks.
5. The counselor should have freedom of movement outside of his school building in order to carry out his professional responsibilities with feeder and receiving schools and other agencies.

An original article for this book.

6. The counseling center should provide counseling offices, a waiting room, storage space, and a conference room. Each counselor should have an individual office with visual and auditory privacy. The counselor's office should have appropriate furnishings to accommodate at least three persons other than the counselor, furnishings to meet the counselor's professional needs, a telephone, and adequate lighting, heating, and ventilation.
7. The school counselor should have adequate non-pupil paid clerical and secretarial assistance.
8. Provision should be made for coordination of all pupil personnel services by a local supervisor professionally trained and certified in guidance and counseling.

The fact that the school counselor has a major role in the total pattern of the school distinguishes him from college counselors, who rarely have duties other than counseling.

The secondary school is the counselor's professional community. He is employed to assist in the individual development of members of the high school not only directly (through interviews) but by helping the community (the whole school) create a development-nourishing climate. The counselor does this by (1) contributing to the improvement of the curriculum in general; (2) helping the school to find ways in the curriculum to account for pupil problems, particularly life-course decisions; and (3) helping the school to improve its appraisal program and to administer that program. [3]

The counselor serves individual teachers as a consultant in assessing the adequacy of development of individual pupils. This assessment covers the broad sweep of development, a pupil's year-by-year march toward satisfying individuality, and the strengths which need emphasis.

Secondary school counselors join the school system's administrative staff in planning and carrying out research about school characteristics. They present data to that staff concerning present and former students, with recommendations about the curriculum significance of the data.

Secondary school counselors frequently are involved with the school's staff in planning and carrying out research on pupil development problems and in planning the group activities of the curriculum for helping students work on their common educational, vocational, and personal problems. In secondary schools counselors will be consulted when the curriculum specialists are setting up the school's program of group activities which are concerned with student's decisions, their other problems, and the school's mental and emotional health education. In some schools counselors coordinate the school's nonacademic placement activities.

The secondary school counselor may participate in many activities with groups of pupils dealing with pupil problems, including regular meetings with groups which are considering certain problem areas. Some counselors meet with parent groups on matters relating to educational, vocational, personal-social, and health problems, including prognosis and decisions about education beyond high school and about military service.

Today the secondary school counselor will be among the school personnel who meet with community groups to report on the nature of pupil problems and to study with them activities which the community can carry out to meet such problems.

Secondary school counselors contribute their services in planning the procedures for acquiring and recording appraisal data, and in evaluating the assessment program. The counselors consult with persons on the school's staff describing the nature of the student population served by the school. Counselors provide teachers with data and materials which they may need in connection with pupil problems. The counselor counsels with individual students to help them with educational, vocational, or personal-social decisions and plans they must make, with their relationships with others, or with other topics of behavior effectiveness.

Secondary school counselors frequently have a major responsibility in the maintenance of the school's cumulative records system. In many schools, the counselor administers group testing programs. Occasionally the counselor has a special appraisal function such as the administration of an individual mental test, like the Stanford-Binet or Wechsler-Bellevue, to the student whose development is a concern to a teacher, or the making of a home visit. High school counselors also help teachers by giving them summarized appraisal data about grade or class groups so that the teachers can have quick reference data at hand.

Willis E. Dugan, in his article, "Guidance in the 1970's," in the March, 1963, issue of the *School Counselor*, states:

> The single most critical issue that faces the profession of the secondary school counselor in the next decade is the achievement of quality — quality in counselor preparation, standards in state certification and the guarantee of competence for school counselors on-the-job. A continuing and critical examination of where we stand and the issues that face our profession is positive evidence of our desire to aspire to excellence. We face a decade of great promise and rewarding effort in assisting school children and youth in the fulfillment of their highest potential. [6]

Sighting the immediate forthcoming changes within many states, one can hardly deny the continued change in professional status to be critical. Education has changed radically since the start of formal guidance about fifty years ago. New objectives, new types of schools, new curricula, and new teaching methods have emerged. The population boom has forced the schools to revamp their methods of presentation to emphasize the mass rather than the individual student. The close student-teacher relationship so fondly cherished in a bygone day has now been replaced by a somewhat impersonal form of education.

Forces outside the school, the changes in society and increased pressures of modern living have contributed to the frustration of pupils, parents, teachers, and administrators to the extent that counseling has been called upon to solve the remaining problems. The counseling profession is now faced with the responsibility of emotional stress caused by this new era in education.

Probably the most critical trend facing us today therefore is the ever growing need to equip the counselor to handle the societal expectations now being demanded of him — expectations which require him to be specifically trained to deal with complex social, intellectual, emotional, and philosophical problems of the "whole man" reflected in his client.

Modern counseling has just crossed the threshold of the greatest challenge of crucial trends in the history of guidance. The following is a brief outline of some of these areas:

1. The trend toward more research with greater depth in school guidance and counseling. This research will place the limelight on such objectives as:

   A. Increasing the accuracy of the individual's self-percepts.
   B. Increasing the accuracy of the individual's environmental perceptions.
   C. Integrating the individual's self-percepts with environmental realities and perceptions.
   D. Presenting relevant information about the individual.
   E. Improving the individual's ability to make and execute plans.
   F. Other areas relating to those mentioned, and important to the training of the counselor and his working with the student, might include:

      1. Improved self-concept.
      2. Decrease in droptout rates.
      3. Improved school achievement.
      4. Decrease in school problem behavior.
      5. More realistic educational planning.
      6. More realistic post-high school education.
      7. Greater satisfaction with post-high school progress five years and more after graduation.
      8. Decreased incidence of problem behavior (job mobility, antisocial actions) five years after graduation.

2. The trend toward recognizing, understanding, and acting upon the societal expectations of the counselor. Harold F. Cottingham, in his article from the *National Catholic Guidance Journal*, entitled, "Theory as an Emerging Dimension in the Guidance Movement," Fall, 1964, states: "One of the clearly observed phenomena of our time is the growing sensitivity of society generally to our human resources. Manpower supply, manpower development and utilization are, without doubt, urgent concerns of our nation — and in turn, these become major concerns of our schools and guidance departments." [4] Three generalizations are implied by this urgency: (1) A growing awareness and respect for *individuality*, (2) An increasing regard for the powerful force of *self-responsibility*, (3) An expectation that *full development of human resources* will be achieved in future guidance techniques.

3. The trend toward the behavior theory in guidance. Unquestionably, guidance is based on behavior theory, i.e., studies and philosophical presuppositions which help to identify and clarify man's place in his environment. This trend will reveal greater understanding of the whole man through three basic subcategories: philosophical, psychological, and sociocultural media. Through such media, the counselor will perceive greater depth regarding the philosophical and psychological phenomena of man. Through philosophical techniques of guidance, the counselor hopes, that the various theories of man's essence will be brought together to help him understand himself. Cottingham also says: "Guidance practitioners, like

people, can be grouped by the way they react to a question. There are those who do not hear the question but know the answer anyway; those who hear the question and have only one stock answer with which they reply to any question; those who hear the question but have no answer; and, hopefully, those who understand the question and have a thoughtful reply to it." The counselor hopes a clarification to the philosophical question of guidance will present its answer, with more counselors being concerned with the last of these groups. Perhaps this trend will present more objective integration of the varied philosophical schools of thought such as realism, scholasticism, idealism, pragmatism, experimentalism, and existentialism. Perhaps they can have a more meaningful and conclusive objective for the counselee.

4. The trend towards a deeper and more widely interpreted use of the psychometric theory. Brief references can be made at this point to a number of opinions expressed by individuals prominent in research or theory in the field of behavioral assessment and measurement. The underlying premise here is that since guidance and counseling deal with individuals whose needs and characteristics must be appraised as they are assisted, it is important to look at relevant theoretical bases for the assessment process. Cottingham feels that much will be said about an overview of the various theoretical assumptions on which the use of tests and more objective measurements are predicated.

5. The trend toward a greater recognition of the whole person through which close follow-up study will be made — from the elementary to college preparation. This plan will follow a student through his/her elementary, intermediate, and secondary school years in an endeavor to help him/her to help himself or herself to solve emotional, educational, vocational, social, and other problems.

6. The trend toward a greater use of group and multiple counseling, so as to allow for a more concentrated use of individual counseling for those who need it.

7. The trend toward greater specialization with regards to the counselor's recognizing talent, skill, and ability in each individual. Through such help, the counselor will be able to help the counselee develop complete awareness, of self, personal worth, and emotional stability. This in turn will help the individual achieve the self-concept earlier with greater confidence and accuracy in his own evaluation of himself.

8. The trend toward more detailed specialization in counseling and guidance. This trend, as mentioned earlier, will probably be one of the most pronounced areas in professional counseling. It will involve greater depth in the areas already worked, i.e., secondary education, but will also tap horizons now virtually untouched. This will include specialized areas of adolescent psychology, and especially advancement in elementary professional counseling — that is, separated from the classroom teacher theory, which is now the real only common form of elementary guidance. The specialized counseling will attempt to master methods of counseling to assist the counselee to achieve early self-discipline in social, intellectual, emotional, and aesthetic maturity.

EMERGING RESPONSIBILITIES

Rapid change in the modern world has markedly affected the counselor's responsibilities. The responsibilities of the school counselor for the decade of the sixties are emerging.

One of the emerging responsibilities of the school counselor is to ascertain his readiness for counseling duties and other closely allied duties such as the responsibilities for group counseling, the record program and the testing program.

Another responsibility for the secondary school counselor is to concern himself with the developmental progress of the adolescent who can profit from attending school in a suitable learning climate. Today this is sometimes difficult because the high school boy or girl frequently becomes confused and disheartened in the milieu of change within seemingly sure conditions of stability.

A major emerging responsibility of the secondary school counselor is to assist the counselees in the exploration of the self. In our present world of uncertainty there is need for each person to be fairly sure of his self-identity in the deepest psychological sense.

Decision-making is another major emerging responsibility for the counselor. The secondary school counselor is to assist the individual in decision-making rather than in a narrow commitment-of-lifelong choice.

Being aware of socioeconomic trends is another responsibility of the secondary school counselor. The counselor is to focus part of his career energies on interpreting such trends rather than exclusively on educational and occupational information. Today the accent is often too heavy on current educational-occupational opportunities. More emphasis should be placed on trends or expected changes.

Interpretative programming is a counselor's responsibility which is emerging with great force as one of his chief duties. Interpretive programming identifies the parents and involves them in the guidance process so that through participation and communication they might better understand the total guidance program. Since the counselee reflects his family and home background it is important the counselor learn more about the parents. Such knowledge will help the counselor to understand the pupils better and, in turn, the parents will learn about the ways and means of the guidance process.

A significant emerging responsibility is the need for the counselor in the secondary school to spend at least half of his time in the counseling interview situation. Today more and more counselor educators are accepting the fact that counseling is a consuming, full-time job.

Other salient responsibilities for the counselor are to understand well the nature of the learning process; to take an active part in helping in the design of the instructional program (this pertains especially to the placement of pupils to provide opportunities for maximum development); and to take a good look at the meaning of his work in terms of research results. There is real need for a variety of research approaches to assist the secondary school counselor in determining the affect and effect of guidance and counseling. [11]

The counselor with his colleagues needs time to formulate research problems that may grow out of the day-to-day work in guidance. First the counselor may wish to sample his pupil population and make a descriptive survey to answer questions such as the following about bright students:

1. Do they select courses and career goals in line with their potential and interests?
2. Do they have an accurate concept of self in relation to appraised abilities and interests?
3. Do they achieve at each level of education in line with their developing potentials and interests?

These representative questions may also be turned into experimental research problems by: (1) comparing the group before and after counseling with a like group not receiving counseling; (2) comparing the behavior of bright students in the area of career choice with that of pupils of average ability; (3) comparing achieving bright students on the foregoing questions with underachieving students of similar ability.

The guidance movement with focus on the counselor's job is on trial for its effectiveness. If ever the counselor needed research, now is the time.

Each counselor must be alert to the signal given by Cottle and Downie:

> Many counselors avoid research activities, perhaps being overcome with the awesome connotation of the term in this scientific age. Such fears are groundless, although research does take time. If any research is to get done, the counselor should see that a certain part of his time is budgeted for it, and he should be determined to see that time so allotted is actually spent in carrying on research. It is very easy to give up this time to other seemingly important activities. [5]

In summary, the secondary school counselor should apply himself in individual appraisal, consult and possibly counsel with parents and professional colleagues on behalf of pupil growth and decision making, implement research that contributes to assisting school learners in maximizing their potentials against the backdrop of the environment, and serve in the staff activities that are common to all school personnel.

There is a merging agreement and understanding of what should be included in an effective guidance and counseling program in the secondary schools. The early emphasis in guidance centered on a narrow concept of specialized services rendered by a few specialists for the so-called problem children. The results were measured by the number and frequency of tests administered, the number of vocatioinal counselors, the use made of occupational and educational information and the existence of a cumulative record of some type. Now a much more comprehensive program is envisioned.

The following basic concepts constitute minimum standards for an effective guidance and counseling program:

1. Individual counseling services must be provided for all pupils.
2. All professional staff members must participate in the program.
3. The services of many specialists are needed.

4. In order to utilize best the services of specialists their duties must be coordinated under a well-defined personnel program.
5. Pupils need assistance in all life adjustment areas, health, social, economic, leisure, civic, home and family, educational and vocational.
6. Cumulative records must not only be available for each pupil but that there must also be a well-defined plan to utilize the information in the records.
7. The school administrator must have a vital interest in and knowledge of what constitutes adequate pupil personnel services.
8. A continuous in-service training program for staff members responsible for pupil personnel services is essential.
9. Guidance tools such as tests, source materials in occupational and educational information must be re-evaluated periodically.
10. Constant evaluation is necessary to determine the effectiveness of and need for betterment of pupil personnel services and their relationship to improved instructional services.
11. The professional school counselor needs professional training and supervised practice in broad areas of life adjustment.
12. The functional relationships and responsibilities of teachers and specialists must be mutually understood. Close liaison relationships between all staff members must be maintained in order to assure maximum pupil adjustment.
13. In order to have an effective pupil-personnel program, it must be administered by a person with experience and professional training in school administration, community services, and guidance techniques. [9]

The secondary counselor today is identified with a guidance and counseling program which functions to assist all pupils in (1) appraising and understanding their abilities, aptitudes, interests and educational needs; (2) increasing their understanding of educational and occupational opportunities and requirements; (3) helping them make the best possible use of these opportunities through the formulation and achievement of realistic goals; (4) helping pupils maintain normal personal-social adjustments, and (5) providing information useful to school staff members, parents and community in planning and evaluating the school's total program, as the pupils attempt to make satisfactory adjustments for life as well as for a living.

The counselor implements his responsibilities for meeting these needs by employing his professional competencies primarily in counseling.

Counseling is concerned with promoting the pupil's self-understanding and self-acceptance, facilitating personal decision-making and planning, and the resolving of special problems.

Counseling is the process in which an experienced and trained person assists a second person: (1) to understand himself and his opportunities, (2) to make appropriate adjustments and decisions in light of this understanding, (3) to accept the responsibility for this choice, (4) to follow a course of action in harmony with his choice.

Counseling is carried on in a one-to-one social environment. It is not advice-giving. Counseling produces changes and not solutions. It is concerned primarily with attitudes, not actions. The secondary school counselor must help the counselee know how he feels about himself and various aspects of his environment. The counselor must help the counselee develop a desire for change. Actions will change as counseling progresses as a result of attitude changes. In most cases, counseling is more an emotional than intellectual process. For example, a shy or bashful girl seeks help through counseling. The high school counselor suggests extracurricular or social experiences. More important is the exploration of attitudes behind the shyness.

Counseling is a relationship between people. The relationship is developed between the counselor and the counselee based on an attitude of mutual respect and the acceptance of the counselee as a person; the counselee attains self-understanding, self-discipline, self-direction, and self-actualization in his total adjustment. "Counseling is a learning-oriented process in which the counselor, professionally competent in relevant psychological skills and knowledge, seeks to assist the client by methods appropriate to the latter's needs, and within the context of the total personnel program, to learn more about himself and to accept himself, to learn how to put such understanding into effect in relation to more clearly perceived, realistically defined goals, to the end that the client may become a happier and more productive member of society." [8]

Counseling is concerned with creative help. The high school counselor needs to help the counselee to attain a clearer sense of identity. Counseling is individualized and personalized.

Dugald S. Arbuckle in his book, *Guidance and Counseling in the Classroom*, states, "There would seem to be general agreement among all counselors that with regard to descriptions of counseling:

a. It may be in some respects a *process*, but it is also a *relationship* between two people, the counselor and the client.
b. It is a relationship that is established because the client feels a need, not because the counselor feels that the client has a need.
c. It is a relationship characterized by the warmth, the permissiveness, the acceptance, and the understanding of the counselor, so that the client feels that he is in a truly free atmosphere.
d. It is a relationship in which the counselor believes that he is involved with a fellow human whom he respects as an equal and with whom he will work so that this person may come to a greater understanding, and thus a greater acceptance of himself.
e. It is a process that is concerned with difficulties of an emotional, an attitudinal, and a feeling nature. Thus the procedures and techniques that may be acceptable and profitable to one who is more rational and under less emotional stress are of little value.
f. The difficulties or tensions must be such that improvement depends on a personal reorganization rather than a change of the environment." [2]
   Counseling is to reduce psychological discordance.

The counselor's task is to help the counselee to examine and analyze his own problem (educational, vocational, personal-social, emotional) so that he can gather, evaluate, and organize pertinent data in regard to the problem; think through possible solutions; and choose and try out solutions to see if they fit his needs. If the solution proves to be out of harmony with the appraisal data and evaluation facts and needs, it is expected that the counselee will modify his plan of solution. Counseling should help the counselee make his own decisions.

COUNSELING AND DISCIPLINE

One of the issues facing counselors today revolves around the question "Can counselors successfully act as disciplinarians?" There are mixed feelings concerning this problem. Assigning counselors to disciplinary roles is defended on the grounds that the counselor knows the student best, that the counselor is best trained to handle behavior problems, that one person can more effectively work with the student. This assumes that there is no difference between the student's relationship to counselors and his interaction with teachers or administrators; the unique nature of counseling is not recognized. When a counselor becomes another authority figure, he looses an effective tool. He gives up the opportunity of being a sounding board where a student's aggressive feelings could be released.

Discipline, as currently used, has essentially two dimensions. One is the traditional use which implies externally imposed authority and compulsion; the other is a concept that implies self-discipline and self-direction. Within the framework of the first definition, most observers would categorically separate the counseling and disciplinary function; within the frame of reference of the second, most counselors would accept counseling and discipline as being very closely related. It is necessary that one have a clear-cut understanding of the frame of reference of the individual who is using the term discipline.

Warters says that: "If discipline is interpreted as the fixing of blame and the giving of penalties, then very definitely the counselor should not play a role in discipline; for to do so would make it very difficult for him to maintain a satisfactory counseling relationship with the student. If, however, discipline is seen, as interpreted by Spencer — in the 1860's — as character education and the development of controls from within to replace controls by some outer authority, and if behavior problems are seen as symptoms of maladjustment with a need for assistance, rather than of moral depravity, and a need for retaliation or punishment, then the counselor should play a major role in discipline." [13]

The most important point here is that the individual secondary school counselor should formulate his own definition of discipline and have a clear-cut understanding of the frame of reference of others when considering the relationship between counseling and discipline.

Counseling long has been a self-initiated relationship at the adolescent age and a seemingly wanted one at the child level. It is centered not on the community, school, or group but upon the individual and his own unique problems — as though he were more important than everyone else in the home, school, and community. This centering of counseling upon the isolated individual pupil has been characterized recently as an instance of individual relativism as opposed to cultural relativism.

Discipline is a "public" matter in two respects: It is imposed conformity to other persons, and there is nothing private or confidential about it. One either conforms voluntarily publicly to group requirements or one is compelled to do so by social pressures, punishment, or some other means of regulation.

Counseling is highly personal and confidential. Except for certain persons who are motivated to be abnormal publicly, most persons desire to discuss their intimate adjustments with one counselor at a time. This is the reason that the highly prized confidentiality of counseling is a necessity – the pupil desires it, profits through it, and suffers relapses when it is not honored.

From the viewpoint of a counselor, the absence of privacy and confidentiality are among the four most devastating weaknesses in most programs of discipline. The ineffective use of punishment for rehabilitation is a third weakness, and the fourth is the inhuman, impersonal manner in which individuals often are handled and processed, sometimes even in education. In the public schools any misunderstanding of this relationship becomes extremely serious. It is intimately related to the level of understanding that teaching and administrative personnel have about the functions, goals, and objectives of the guidance program and the roles of guidance personnel. Too often the teacher and administrator perceive the counselor as a disciplinarian, and when their level of expectation with respect to the desirable change in the counselee is not immediately met, their conclusion then is often to assume that guidance and counseling are ineffective. In the past this has to often militated against guidance services. Unfortunately, even the secondary school counselor sometimes has an inadequate understanding of the relationship between the two, or he considers himself a disciplinarian in the "coercive-authoritarian" point of view. In such situations it would be safe to predict that the results of counseling and guidance would be limited indeed.

The necessity for an adequately defined relationship between counseling and discipline cannot be ignored. It is of great concern to public school educators and involves an extensive amount of re-education and in-service training on the part of guidance workers with individuals who will tend to be quite resistant to the ideas presented – i.e., the idea that counseling and discipline, as traditionally understood, are separate objects and separate concepts. The counselor who understands the concepts implied will reject the cloak of externally imposed disciplinary authority or will soon lose his effectiveness in the counseling situation.

In summary, disciplinary functions are often justified from the standpoint of administrative expediency, that is, the onerous job of discipline prejudices students against administrators so the counselors should share in it. By acting in the place of the principal or the vice-principal, the characteristic relationship of the counselor and counselee is sacrificed. Hence the counselor's effectiveness in working with the total student body is hampered.

Most disciplinary offenses are actually outgrowths of personality problems. The boisterous, noisy student is often revealing his own feelings of insecurity. While the counselor should not be expected to mete out punishment, he could be influential in preventing a repetition of this unacceptable behavior. Working with the discipline problem is difficult, and progress is slow. The hostility which the offender has built up against the school often reflects itself upon the counselor until rapport is established. The importance of effective counseling as a means of student control cannot be overestimated.

SUMMARY

The role of the school counselor is envisaged as that of a catalyst to human growth and self-understanding. He should spend two-thirds of his time in one-to-one counseling or consulting relationships. He is expert in his knowledge of counseling theory and procedures, career development, measurement, and the role of the school in developmental behavior of young people. He is an educator; he is also an applied psychologist. He is a counselor because he has preparation for the role and selects this role rather than being promoted to it as a reward for good instruction. Let us recognize the unique role of the counselor in the educational setting. Let us accept, select and prepare those who want to be counselors. Let us strengthen our profession by defining the school counselor's role so that confusion ceases to exist.

The secondary school counselor today needs professional preparation for the school counseling position. His primary function is identified with counseling, but he performs secondary functions which are required of many school staff members, regardless of title or primary function.

The emergence of the school counselor as an educator, contributing to the school enterprise in a unique way complementary to the functioning of administrators and teachers, is taking shape. There is some resistance to allowing school counselors a unique and rightful place in contributing to the development and education of children and youth. In these instances the counselor is not a counselor as such but is seen as an administrator, or a teacher or a clerk.

A more evident unique function for the school counselor is emerging. Although there are many gradations and deviations, counselors are achieving more time for the major function for which their preparation qualifies them, namely, that of being a counselor to boys and girls, their parents, and the other significant adults in their lives. In this counseling there is a greater acceptance of the fact that the counselor should not be seen in the image of the teacher as representing society and the "tried and true" of the cultural heritage. Rather, the counselor may be seen better as committed to the individual and his experience as he sees it. This does not mean that all is well. It does mean, however, that for the counselor of prime focus are the functions of (1) assistance to the individual in clarification of experience and confrontation of the continuity of experiences, as they might ultimately be reflected in adaptability, (2) choice and decision making, and (3) positive mental health. Personal growth and a person's educational development within the total scope of his development is characterized by ups and downs, and ultimately an integration.

There is emerging a more clearly identifiable role of the secondary school counselor; primarily, he should be counseling, and secondarily performing those functions that contribute most directly to meaningful counseling relationships. Interested readers are encouraged to investigate the recent statement of the American School Counselor Association on the functioning of the secondary school counselor and the American Personnel and Guidance Association's more general statement on the role and function of counselors.

The secondary school counselor is an educator with special professional training at the Master's Degree level and beyond. The school counselor is a generalist in a number of school functions and may be a specialist in at least one type of service. The high school counselor's skills should include not only those necessary for the individual counseling relationship but those essential to working effectively with groups. The counselor is concerned primarily with the normal growth needs of the high school students and more with personality development than with problem crises.

There are two special areas of competence associated with the role of the secondary school counselor: he is professionally trained in the art and science of counseling pupils and he is a guidance specialist professionally trained to meet the noncounseling guidance needs of pupils.

The school counselor's primary resource is his counseling skill, and this should not be an unused resource. The major portion of the counselor's day should be spent counseling pupils; he is not administrator, teacher, disciplinarian, welfare officer, clerk, or statistician.

The secondary school counselor is expected to be familiar enough with standardized tests of intelligence, achievement, aptitude, interest, and personality so that he can utilize test results in the process of counseling. He has direct responsibility for individual counseling of the students assigned to him; this responsibility is more directly related to educational and vocational than to personal-social counseling. The important thing is for the counselor to recognize his limitations in therapy and to establish methods of appropriate referral.

Often the secondary school counselor has responsibility for group methods in guidance. Finally, the counselor is expected to establish relationships with great numbers of students, so that counselees will come to identify him as a person to whom they can turn for counsel and assistance within the secondary school setting. After all, counseling may be thought of as the core of the helping process, essential for the proper administration of assistance to students as they attempt to solve their problems.

Counseling is an interpersonal relationship in which the counselor assists the client to adjust more effectively to himself and to his environment. Counseling, situations range from a few minute's help in finding the answers to simple, immediate questions to a series of more formal interviews dealing with complex educational, vocational, and personal problems of adjustment. The goal of counseling is to stimulate in the counselee the development of a more confident feeling of personal adjustment on the one hand, and an increase in his effectiveness in dealing with his environment on the other.

The counselor needs a well-defined point of view with respect to the nature of the counseling process if he is to be effective in any attempt to aid counselees to make appropriate choices, plans, and adjustments. The counselor needs also to understand the responsibilities and knowledge needed by the counselee in order to make counseling effective. The counselee must understand his role in the counseling relationship. He must accept major responsibility for making the counseling process achieve appropriate objectives through the attainment of a steadily increasing degree of self-directiveness. He must view counseling as a learning process through which the counselee enhances his own skills in problem solving.

REFERENCES

1. American School Counselor Association. STATEMENT OF POLICY FOR SECONDARY SCHOOL COUNSELORS. American Personnel and Guidance Association, 1964. 11 pp.
2. Arbuckle, Dugald S. *Guidance and Counseling in the Classroom.* Boston: Allyn and Bacon, 1957. pp. 63.
3. Byrne, Richard Hill. THE SCHOOL COUNSELOR. Boston: Houghton Mifflin, 1963. pp. 274-282, 256.

4. Cottingham, Harold F. "Theory as an Emerging Dimension in the Guidance Movement," *National Catholic Guidance Journal.* 9, No. 1 (Fall, 1964), 7.

5. Cottle, Wm. C. and Downie, N. M. *Procedures and Preparation for Counseling.* Englewood Cliffs, N. J.: Prentice-Hall, 1960.

6. Dugan, Willis E. "Guidance in the 1970's," *The School Counselor.* 10, No. 3 (March, 1963), 96.

7. Farwell, Gail F., *Counselor Education and Supervision,* Vol. I, No. 1, Fall, 1961. pp. 40-43.

8. Jones, Arthur J., *Principles of Guidance.* New York: McGraw-Hill Co., pp. 211.

9. Miller, Leonard M., *Growing Agreement in Basic Concepts.* Department of Health, Education and Welfare, June, 1962.

10. UNITED STATES DEPARTMENT OF LABOR, *Occupational Outlook Quarterly.* Bureau of Labor Statistics, Vol. 6, No. 3, September, 1962. pp. 3-6.

11. Peters, Herman J., *The School Counselor,* Vol. 9, No. 4, May, 1962. pp. 134-137.

12. Strowig, Wray, *School Counselor Certification,* Unpublished paper given at Counselor Educators Conference, University of Wisconsin, Madison, March 31, 1965. pp. 2-4.

13. Warters, Jane, *Group Guidance: Principles and Practices.* New York: McGraw-Hill Book Co., Inc. 1960. pp. 229.

(27)

COLLEGE AND UNIVERSITY COUNSELING

George D. Demos

Dean of Students, California State College at Long Beach

Bruce Grant

Counseling Psychologist, California State College at Long Beach

The graduate student who is preparing for a career in counseling probably has been alerted to the lamentable fact that the literature on counseling reveals a pacuity of data about college counseling. The foregoing statement also is applicable — though to a lesser degree — regarding elementary school counseling. Counselor education programs tend to focus their emphasis on the secondary school counselor.

It is hoped that in these pages the future counselor will acquire some insights about counseling in colleges and universities[1] which will prove helpful in assisting him in choosing the most appropriate educational level (i.e., elementary, secondary, or higher education) for his own counseling career. If he elects to become a college counselor, it is obvious that he should learn what is involved in this classification of counseling. If he chooses to be an elementary school or secondary school counselor, it is incumbent upon him to enrich his understanding of the other kinds of counselors and the nature of their work.

An original article for this book.

[1]College counseling as used herein refers to counseling in the two-year college, four-year college, university, and graduate school; for purposes of brevity, the term "college counseling" is used throughout the article.

INTERPRETATION OF COLLEGE COUNSELING

Even though there are many different definitions of counseling in the literature, most authorities agree that counseling is a one-to-one, face-to-face relationship between an individual who seeks help and another person who is professionally educated to give this help. The nature of the assistance needed can be classified into three major areas of guidance: educational, vocational, and personal-social.

The foregoing definition certainly is acceptable for college counseling, as it should be for *all* counseling relationships. In addition it is important to add that ". . . counseling consists of more than the face-to-face interview, the collection of information, and the summarization and interpretation of that information."[2] The professional counselor renders a service that is unique in education: He provides a learning situation in which the subject matter is the individual (the counselee) and his present and possible future environment. The concept of the subject matter of guidance services can be examined in *A Philosophy of Guidance Services.*[3] *It is easily transferable to the* meaning of counseling.

Counseling in its particular reference to colleges has been identified as ". . . the generic service of student personnel work,"[4] which is the term used in colleges to include a variety of nonacademic services focusing on the students. If "student personnel services" is replaced by "pupil personnel services," which is the term used in secondary schools to identify those activities designed to help students, it appears that there is no basic difference revealed between college and secondary school counseling.

To those of us who are actively engaged in college counseling (and who have been secondary and/or elementary school counselors), however, there is no doubt about there being some distinct differences in counseling at the various educational levels.

DIFFERENCES IN COLLEGE, SECONDARY, AND ELEMENTARY SCHOOL COUNSELING

The college counselor's[5] counselees are primarily undergraduate students; in addition he sees some prospective and graduate students plus a few parents, and (in some institutions) faculty and staff members. The high school counselor's counselees are students, students together with parents, and parents. The elementary school counselor works mainly with parents, teachers,

---

[2]Williamson, E. G. *Student Personnel Services in Colleges and Universities.* McGraw-Hill Book Company, Inc., New York, 1961, p. 186.

[3]Grant, Bruce and Oldenburg, Richard. *A Philosophy of Guidance Services.* Lucas Brothers Publishers, Columbia, Missouri, 1964, pp. 1-2.

[4]Williamson, E. G. *Student Personnel Services in Colleges and Universities.* McGraw-Hill Book Company, Inc., New York, 1961, p. 180.

[5]An increasing number of college institutions are referring to their doctoral trained counselors as counseling psychologists. This more prestigious title is used to differentiate the college counselor from the plethora of "counselors" within our society. See Thompson, A. and Super, D. *The Professional Preparation of Counseling Psychologists.* Bureau of Publications, Teachers College, Columbia University, New York, 1964.

and administrators in terms of helping pupils, seldom having counseling interviews with the youngsters themselves.

In college the problems of counselees are mainly vocational and personal-social; most educational counseling is handled by faculty advisors. This is duplicated in high schools except that there the counselors also handle the educational guidance. In the elementary school, counseling is almost exclusively personal-social, with little if any vocational and minimal educational counseling.

Even though most of the program planning and advising regarding the pros and cons of taking specific subjects is done by faculty advisers in the colleges, the professional counselor at this level engages in considerable educational counseling as it is integrated into vocational counseling. In a study designed to determine the kinds of problems counselees bring to college counseling centers, Callis[6] reported that more than one half of the problems are vocational and one quarter, educational, and that approximately the same findings held for high school counselees.

High school counselors supply teachers with considerable data on students and often confer with them regarding students with behavior difficulties; sometimes these counselors are even involved in disciplinary action against the same students they are trying to help. Elementary counselors follow the foregoing pattern rather closely except that they work more with the parents than the pupils and seldom are involved in any disciplinary action. College counselors give little information to professors regarding students, as they adhere quite closely to the confidentiality of the counseling interview.

In his position in the professional community of the college, the college counselor has more motivation, time, and encouragement to engage in those professional activities which help him to attain eminence in his specialization. While he is a practitioner, it is possible for him to be concurrently a researcher, creator, author, lecturer, and consultant. Not that all college counselors have or exploit some of these additional talents, but the point is that they function in an environment in which a diversity of professional development and fulfillment is easier to actualize and much more apt to occur than in the other educational levels. It is not uncommon to find college counselors, in addition to working in the counseling center, teaching a class in psychology, educational psychology or guidance, conducting research and/or consulting in a neighboring school district, business firm, or county office. The college counselor usually not only is in demand to engage in such myriad activities, but they also add to his professional respectability and image within the college community. In view of this diversity of opportunities, college counseling has attracted many able professionals who heretofore went solely into the teaching ranks.

One of the striking differences that each of the writers noted when he moved from secondary to college counseling is the reduction of clerical work to an absolute minimum. To the unsophisticated this may seem to be a trivial factor, but to the professional counselor who is suddenly released from the burden of clerical duties the change makes a significant impact in his attitude.

---

[6]Callis, R. *The Need for Differentiation of Counselor Behavior.* University of Nebraska Counseling and Guidance Institute, Lincoln, Nebraska, June 25, 1962.

There are many other so-called "little things" that the writers detected in moving into college counseling: no more disrupted counseling appointments as a harried principal turns to a counselor for a period, a morning, or even a day of substituting for an absent teacher; no more trying "to switch hats" in playing the dual role of disciplinarian and counselor; no more "policing" the grounds while students who need help wait in a crowded office; no more having to teach a class or two that regular teachers "shy away from" because of the calibre of the students assigned to these classes; no more hectic situations involving being called out of a class to handle "emergencies"; and no more having to stop frequently in corridors to receive verbal reports on misbehaving students.

There is little question that the elementary and secondary counselors are much more apt to function as practitioners (whenever nonguidance activities do not infringe upon their time) than college counselors who — like their academic brothers — are so often engaging in more and more research, creative activities, and consultive work.

The college counselor within his community of scholars is afforded unparalled opportunities for professional development in the association with top men in his and related fields. On a daily basis he has the possibilities for enrichment that often come to the elementary and secondary counselors only when they are able to attend counseling institutes, summer school, professional association meetings, etc. Consequently, it is inevitable that college counseling receives an almost continuous impetus for improvement. In addition, college counseling centers in many cases offer leadership in providing outstanding in-service training opportunities for their staffs. Through the means of hiring local consultants, primarily psychiatrists and/or psychologists, these centers staff cases, review and critique new developments and books, conduct sensitivity training seminars for the staff, invite guest lecturers, plan visitations, etc., all of which provide for a most instructive and stimulating environment. The University of Minnesota Counseling Center, under the direction of Dr. Ralph Berdie, has been a model for such invigorating in-service activities.

Questions that the graduate student who is attempting to make up his mind about what is the most appropriate educational level of counseling for him should be asking himself are:

1. Would my greatest sense of satisfaction and fulfillment come from being a practitioner or in being a practitioner who is simultaneously involved in research, writing, creativity, or consultive work?
2. Am I willing to pay the price of the additional education that is involved in college counseling?
3. Am I more a practitioner (doer) or a theorist (thinker), or am I both a practitioner and a theorist?
4. Do I prefer working at a high level of competency, utilizing the best in available knowledge and skills, or do I wish to seek and develop facts — to pioneer in the enhancement of the profession?

Another important point for the graduate student to keep firmly in mind is illustrated in the lamentably frequent occurrence of the outstanding teacher's moving into administration to become a mediocre principal. What about the effective secondary or elementary school counselor who moves into college counseling to discover that there is just enough difference in the new educational level to change what had been an "outstanding" counselor into a "mediocre" one?

One of the writers recalls the statement made by a sage counselor educator to a group of graduate students, most of whom had become enamored with college counseling, strongly favoring it over elementary or secondary: "College counseling isn't all it's 'cracked up' to be." Remember that an effecfective practitioner will not necessarily be successful in research or creative endeavors; also, achievement in these ancillary activities may be measured in terms of publications, so that the hoary warning, "publish or perish," may actualize itself to the detriment if not the jeopardy of one's counseling career.

The age group with which the elementary, secondary, and college counselors work should be a matter of significant concern to individuals preparing to become counselors. Just as some teachers who are most effective with a certain level of maturity prove to be less than competent when shifted to another level, so is this possible in counseling. There is quite a difference in attempting to help a fourteen-year-old boy resolve a personality clash with a teacher and assisting a twenty-year-old young man in dealing with his hostilities towards authority. In addition, the approaches to what superficially appears to be the same problem vary considerably in terms of the age group. For example, note the implications involved in helping the fourteen-year-old boy who is trying to choose a vocation in comparison with the twenty-year-old with the supposedly identical problem of trying to select an occupation; in the instance of the young boy, the factor of immaturity impinges upon whatever science is brought to bear upon the situation; with the twenty-year-old young man (granting normal maturation and assuming sufficient intelligence in view of the fact that the individual has survived two years in college), scientific career planning in depth is possible, with the prognosis of a successful culmination of a scientific career study.

FUNCTIONS OF COLLEGE COUNSELORS

What counselors do varies to some degree from school to school, regardless of educational level. To complicate the situation even further there are instances when even the title is meaningless. For example, some high school principals, school nurses in elementary schools, and faculty members in colleges do some limited but highly effective counseling at the same time in the same schools, there may be so-called counselors who are engaged in disciplining, typing and filing personnel reports, or collecting money on delinquent loan accounts.

Perhaps an operational description of one college counseling center presumed to be rather typical of most centers can help delineate the functions of college counselors. The following tables pertaining to the Counseling Center were taken from the *Annual Report — Student Personnel Services*[7] of the California State College at Long Beach. At that time one of the writers was director of the center and the other served as one of the counselors.

---

[7]*Annual Report — Student Personnel Services,* California State College at Long Beach, 1962-63, pp. 18-32.

Table I through Table VII indicate the wide variety of counseling cases, the large number of voluntary cases, the predominance of student clients, the length of interviews (average length considerably longer than secondary school — usually one client per hour scheduled), the variety of reasons clients request counseling, and the kind of referrals made, all of which should serve as interesting comparisons with the secondary and elementary counselors' functions.

TABLE I

Reason for Counseling (Stated by Client)

Coun-selor	Admin.	Career	Educa-tion	Finan-cial	Pers. (sur)	Pers. (dep)	Extra-Cur.	Hous-ing	Employ-ment	Total Inter.
1	254	89	29	4	88	60		1		525
2	114	113	440	5	109	12	1	2		796
3	52	409	227	3	39	2				732
4	62	33	335	743	58	5	7	2	3	1248
5	53	10	255	52	40	43	38	17	2	510
6	264	20	53	2	69	51	32			491
7	5	5	77		12	8		1		108
8	131	202	114		339	196				982
9	178	60	139	1	52	4	1			435
10						558				558
TOTAL	1113	941	1669	810	806	939	79	23	5	6385

TABLE II

Reason for Counseling
(By Counselor)

| Reason for Counseling | Counselor | | | | | | | | | | Total |
	1	2	3	4	5	6	7	8	9	10	
Test Interp.	105	31	8	5	1	17	11		34		212
Test Referral	1	5	54			3			15		78
Study Helps	31	155	3	7	43	10	4	35	143		431
Probation–Disqal.	34	36	7	32	7	2	4		15		137
Academic Advise.	81	32	1	5	151	17	21	101	4		413
Personal	117	179	91	130	119	273	9	688	112	558	2276
Financial	4	3	3	795	48			3			856
Declar. of Major	8	17	3	5	2	8			4		47
Change of Major	1	30	28	3	5	8	1		2		78
Career	30	26	166	23	8	9		50	12		324
Educational	82	40	162	147	40	44	7	1	93		616
Withdrawal	4	12	4	1		3		4	1		29
Fresh. Interview	19	200	202	93	3	62	49	100			728
Catalog Interp.	2	28		2	3	4					39
Extra–Curricular	4	1			38	31	2				76
Immigration Nat. Serv.	1	1			29						31
Foreign Government	1				13						14
TOTAL	525	796	732	1248	510	491	108	982	435	558	6385

TABLE III

Reason for Interview

Counselor	Voluntary	Referred	Requested	Required	Total
1	366	99	46	14	525
2	588	38	15	155	796
3	448	47	10	227	732
4	1029	22	38	159	1248
5	350	14	46	100	510
6	417		73	1	491
7	52	6	3	47	108
8	350	88	434	110	982
9	360	9	66		435
10		558			558
TOTAL	3960	881	731	813	6385

TABLE IV

Type of Client

Counselor	Student	Pros. Stu.	Former Stu.	Faculty	Staff	Parent	Other	Total
1	389	102	24		1	4	5	525
2	666	86	34	2	1	4	3	796
3	640	44	44				4	732
4	1142	61	25	1		1	18	1248
5	467	26	6	2			9	510
6	416	57	10	2	1	4	1	491
7	102	3	3					108
8	723	56	82			121		982
9	411	14	9				1	435
10	558							558
TOTAL	5514	449	237	7	3	134	41	6385

In addition to the tables, selected parts of the *Annual Report — Student Personnel Services*[8] may be of interest to the reader. These sections help to delineate the work of the college counselor.

1. *Group Work*

Considerable emphasis was placed on group counseling by several members of the Counseling staff. Experiments were conducted in attempting to handle some of the freshmen interviews through group sessions instead of the traditional individual interviews. Despite the fact that no carefully con-

---

[8]*Op. Cit.*, pp. 22-29.

TABLE V

Length of Interview

Counselor	0-9	10-19	20-29	30-39	40-49	50-59	60-69	70-90	Over 90	Total
1	15	28	79	216	39	26	119	3		525
2	28	108	68	150	305	110	15	9	3	796
3	91	144	121	174	103	37	43	17	2	732
4	69	620	214	187	67	52	17	15	7	1248
5	12	107	144	100	43	64	8	10	22	510
6	90	33	78	95	51	97	40	7		491
7		12	46	33	7	8	2			108
8		126	219			637				982
9	188	30	42	99	13	17	30	9	7	435
10							558			558
TOTAL	493	1208	1011	1054	628	1048	832	70	41	6385

TABLE VI

Type of Student

Counselor	Regular	Foreign	Veteran	Voc. Rehab.	Total
1	521	3		1	525
2	793	3			796
3	732				732
4	1123	119	2	4	1248
5	179	330	1		510
6	491				491
7	107	1			108
8	732		100	150	982
9	435				435
10	558				558
TOTAL	5671	456	103	155	6385

trolled research studies were conducted to indicate whether or not groups were as effective as individual interviews, several of the counselors and psychiatrists who conducted these sessions felt there were inherent values to groups which were not likely to accrue by the traditional individual interview; namely, there are individuals who respond better to peers than adult authority figures. It is well known in group dynamic literature that the influence of peers can be very great with some individuals. It also aids shy individuals to participate vicariously through other members of the group. Frequently, these individuals would feel too inhibited to bring out certain subjects in an individual interview but do profit from discussions and the interactions that occur when other members of the group feel free enough to discuss these problems or issues.

TABLE VII

Referral Made To

Referred to:	Counselor										Total
	1	2	3	4	5	6	7	8	9	10	
Psychiatric	18	11	1	2	3	7			5		47
Health Service	1	2	1						2		6
Counselor	2	10	3	2	1	2			2		22
Off Campus	80	37	13	2	3	10	1	2	8		156
Testing	19	50	5	6	5	8			18		111
Admin. Rec.	23	66	11	6	2	24	7		27		166
Placement	22	46	25	8	4	13			11		129
Faculty	16	68	27	5	8	12	1		25		162
Career File/Libr.	42	136	36	14	22	43	2		14		309
Stud. Affairs	3	64	67	2	7	6	1		4		154
TOTAL	226	490	189	47	55	125	12		116	0	1262

2. *Research*

A continued research emphasis was carried on during the year and several members of the Counseling Center Staff were conducting projects of various kinds which were of value both to the college as well as the general area of counseling psychology. Such projects as:

a. A comparative study of high potential students who are not achieving (underachievers — on probation) compared with students on the President's List (students achieving very successfully in college)
b. Continued emphasis on the college dropout and awareness of this loss in human resources
c. Critical problems faced by counselors
d. Problems of freshman orientation
e. Problems related to disabled students
f. Cognitive processes involved in achieving and nonachieving students
g. Problems of the college freshman relating to success in college
h. Problems of college students relating to successful career choice

3. *Communication*

Closer cooperation between Counseling and the Academic Divisions took place during the previous year. Indications of this closer relationship were indicated by the increase in the number of referrals made to the Counseling Center by faculty members and the fact that five divisions invited the Director to speak to their faculty regarding the role of the Counseling Center and ways and means of expediting the problems of their students. As a result of this increased interaction between administration and faculty, better relations and a closer understanding and empathy of mutual problems seemed to have developed.

4. *Professional Activities*

The Counseling Center Staff have also been involved in many professional organizations, have presented a multitude of reports at conventions, have taken part in symposia, have contributed scientific and scholarly articles to various professional journals, spoke before community organizations, participated in all-college committees, and sponsored college clubs and organizations. Certain members also taught classes and supervised field workers in both Education and Psychology.

5. *Freshman Interviews*

Between six and seven hundred freshman students reported to the Counseling Center for an interview during 1962-63. Most of these were held on an individual basis, although in some cases, the counselor saw two or three students together and one counselor saw freshman students in groups of six. In all cases, an endeavor was made to ascertain the student's present progress, study plan, time schedule, vocational goals, etc. The general education requirements were explained and clarification of catalog statements was given if desired. Prior to the interview an autobiography and ACT test scores were placed in each student's folder, thus furnishing background information. During the interview the student was given printed material concerning methods of study and the student was encouraged to return at a later date if he so desired.

6. *Undeclared Majors*

Advising of undeclared majors was done on a group basis during Freshman Orientation and during registration for both semesters. Several hundred students were seen in this manner each semester. A suggested list of courses for undeclared majors was prepared and distributed to the students for program planning. All undeclared majors thus contacted were urged to return to the Counseling Center for individual vocational/major planning sessions.

Since January, 1963, the Records Office has included the Counseling Center in its dissemination of information, classifying it as the advising center for all undeclared majors of undergraduate status.

7. *Study Skills Laboratory*

Small group sessions over a period of four to six weeks were led by counselors for students who indicated a desire to perfect their study skills. Following an individual diagnosis of study habits, the group discussed and tried out various methods of developing reading speed and comprehension, note-taking, listening, exam preparation, and planning of term papers. Some publicity concerning the Study Skills Laboratory was given by the student newspaper.

Basic study skills were discussed with Resident Hall Assistants in their orientation meetings prior to the opening of school. These students, in turn, passed along information and aids to the students in their dorms.

8. *Career Counseling*

The following excerpts from the Career Study Guide Manual should be helpful in defining what has been developed for career counselors.

> The Career Study Guide was designed for use by counselors who wish to help their counselees make a thorough and systematic investigation for the purpose of determining a wise career plan.
>
> This instrument is intended primarily for college counselors; however, it is applicable for counselors in private practice, social service agencies, industry,

adult education, and governmental employment services. In addition, high school counselors could use it with students of sufficient maturity.

Criteria are provided to assure that the counselor and counselee proceed in a systematized manner toward the attainment of an increased understanding of both the counselee and the world of work.

Utilization of the Career Study Guide requires the usage of two additional instruments: the Needs and Traits Rating Scales. Each of these tools represents a unique approach to the counselee's acquiring an understanding of himself. He determines his own needs and traits, and rates them according to their intensity. The rating process does not involve a comparison with others, but is introspective in nature.

9. Career Information File

The Career Information File includes three sections: (1) Vocations and Areas, (2) General Career Information, and (3) California Colleges.

File folders and catalogs are filed alphabetically in accordance with the Career Information Filing Plan, which is revised annually. An inventory is made annually, accounting for each file folder and catalog in the File; this is reported in An Inventory of the Career Information File. In addition, a running inventory is kept which reflects the changes made in the File between inventories and shows the number of items in each of the file folders.

At the time of the annual inventory obsolete items (over five years old) are removed from the File. During the year (free) items are received from extensive sources; each item is examined to determine its suitability for placement in the File. A total of 132 items at a cost of $35.97 were ordered for the File during the school year of 1962-63.

A record of the usage of the File is made and reported monthly and yearly in the Monthly Report on Usage of Career Information File and Annual Report on Usage of Career Information File.

Additional aids and data for the counelor and counelee in the utilization of the Career Study Guide are included with the Manual. They are as follows:

a. Criteria of Quality of Career Information
b. Criteria of Quality of the Organization of Career Publications
c. The Role of the Career in Living
d. Vocational Career, Company Career, and Industrial Career
e. Some Occupations for College Students to Consider in Career Planning
f. Some Career Possibilities for College Students to Consider in Career Planning
g. Classification of Industries
h Some Selected Sources of Information in Investigating Companies and Industries

10. Rehabilitation Services

Through the past six years, offices of the College have cooperated immeasurably in helping to conduct a registration in microcosm for the handicapped and disabled students on campus. The "rehab student registration" was just one of the student personnel services offered to students. Publicity about its scope and depth has been carefully confined even on campus, however, because students are conscious enough of their physical inadequacies without inviting invidious exposure. In philosophy, our rehabilitation counseling program has provided services that are essential for physical welfare on a voluntary basis. From this premise, the disabled students have been given complete freedom to work out their own histories within the College setting, and have been encouraged to achieve their own responsible independence.

Special Services were Continued or Established for Handicapped and Disabled Students

1. Special registrations were organized for the disabled students and coordinated with the Registrar, the Office of the Dean of Instruction, the Business Office, the Coordinator of Summer Sessions, the Office of Student Affairs, and Academic Departments.
2. Certain classes scheduled to meet in rooms on upper floors were relocated on ground floors to accommodate nonambulatory students, in arrangement with the Assistant to the Dean — Curriculum.
3. Student volunteers were organized to help push wheelchair students between classes and classroom buildings, in arrangement with the student veterans club on campus.
4. In some cases, car pools were arranged with the Office of Student Affairs to help transport disabled students to and from campus.
5. Special "readers" and tuotors were arranged for blind students and other handicapped students, in arrangement with the Placement Office and volunteer student organizations.
6. Cooperatively, the Physical Education Department organized and conducted a special class for disabled students in Adaptive Education, providing supervised recreation and physical improvement for volunteer handicapped students.
7. In cases where disabled students were required to achieve credit in certain courses required for graduation, courses where their physical disabilities obviated completing the course, arrangements were made with the Academic Department and the Registrar to substitute other required courses.
8. In cooperation with the Testing Office, special tests were individually administered to and interpreted with disabled students.
9. Through the Counseling Center, specialized counseling and counseling referrals were conducted with students who had difficulty in making campus and personal adjustments to their physical handicaps.
10. Administrative representation and student liaison were developed with the Los Angeles and Orange County and city offices of Vocational Rehabilitation, the veterans Administration, and selected community service organizations.
11. The Counseling Center gave careful support and assistance to the College Placement Office and certain Academic Departments in helping disabled students to locate jobs, and to adjust career plans and college plans accordingly.

The student rehabilitation services have been, and continue to be, the product of individuals, offices, departments, and agencies working cooperatively with handicapped and disabled students.

In addition to the foregoing the Counseling Center provided help in the following areas: foreign students, financial aids, loans, scholarships, and workshops. The Counseling Center is rapidly becoming what some call a "behavioral science center," and its services are being felt in virtually all walks of campus life.

In such a maze of processes being performed, it is helpful to turn to standards, i.e., *what should be. Improving Counseling — An Evaluative Instrument for Improving Counseling Centers*[9] provides criteria on the functions of counselors.

Under the general direction of the Director of Counseling, each counselor:

A. Does interviewing ....   _____
B. Writes interview records ....   _____
C. Conducts group counseling or guidance activities when appropriate ....   _____
D. Utilizes referral services and resource materials ....   _____
E. Participates in the evaluation of the Counseling Center ....   _____
F. Assists the Director of Counseling in the development of policies and procedures ....   _____
G. Participates in research, writing, service studies, or projects as assigned by the Director of Counseling ....   _____
H. Participates in in-service training activities ....   _____
I. Participates in community and professional activities ....   _____
J. Assists in controlling access to and use of counseling records and files in Counseling Center ....   _____
K. Works cooperatively with faculty, administration, and staff in interpreting and developing services of the Counseling Center   _____

For additional information on the standards for organization and functions of a counseling center, including staffing, contacts, and records and referrals the graduate student should refer to this section of the instrument.[10]

Certainly these criteria are applicable to each educational level and to nonschool agencies; however, the alert student should detect some standards which the college counseling service is more apt to be meeting today. At the same time, the graduate student should realize that when functions are placed within the frame of reference of "criteria" — what should be — there are no real differences in the functions of counselors at the various educational levels.

In the performance of these functions, however, by the very fact that he is in a college counseling center, more is *expected* of the college counselor. His superiors, colleagues, and the public expect him to be *the best.*

KINDS OF COLLEGE COUNSELING

The college community — particularly the four-year college and university — usually includes more specialized services (under the heading of student

[9]Grant, Bruce, Demos, George D., and Oldenburg, Richard. *Improving Counseling — An Evaluative Instrument for Improving Counseling Centers.* Lucas Brothers Publishers, Columbia, Missouri, 1965, pp. 7-8.
[10]*Op. Cit.,* pp. 11-13.

personnel services) than the high school or elementary school (under the heading of pupil personnel services). While there is a variance from college, in general, the following student personnel services are usually available:

1. Counseling center	6. Financial aid office
2. Testing service	7. Health service
3. Placement service	8. Records office
4. Admissions office	9. Foreign students office
5. Housing service	10. Student affairs office

Each of the preceding services attempts to offer some counseling. Those services other than the counseling center obviously restrict their counseling to the particular activities they perform. For example, the admissions office counsels prospective students in terms of matters pertaining to admission, referring the individual to the counseling center when other difficulties arise.

Another kind of counseling peculiar to the college community is the educational counseling done by the faculty. This probably in most instances should be labeled academic advisement, but for some faculty members and in some cases the process of educational counseling is not only performed — it is done in a highly competent manner.

Williamson[11] gives an interesting description of the varieties of college counseling, including the following categories.

1. Faculty advisers	7. Financial counseling
2. Psychological counseling	8. Religious or pastoral counseling
3. Mental hygiene	9. Marriage counseling
4. Residential counseling	10. Student organizations
5. Foreign student counseling	11. Extracurriculum experiences
6. Disciplinary counseling	counseling

It is apparent that colleges offer considerable opportunity for counseling by those individuals other than professionally educated counselors. In addition, there are multiple prospects for specialization and depth counseling, both in and out of the counseling center. For example, marriage counseling may become a specialty of one or more members of the professional counseling staff while it is concurrently being practiced by one or more members of the sociology department.

One of the significant trends in college counseling is the emergence to the forefront of two counseling specializations: (1) career counseling and (2) marriage counseling. Each offers tremendous professional opportunities to the young counselor who is willing to devote himself to the additional preparation necessary to qualify as an expert in these fields.

New and challenging innovations are being introduced into what has been traditionally referred to as vocational guidance. For example, the writers after several years of experimentation and practice in depth career counseling de-

---

[11]Williamson, E. G. *Student Personnel Services in Colleges and Universities.* McGraw-Hill Book Company, Inc., New York, 1961, pp. 188-205.

veloped the *California Career Study Guide*[12] and *Designing Your Career*,[13] to which the graduate student contemplating specializing in career counseling is referred for study and utilization. In addition *Vocational Guidance Readings*[14] includes information regarding other innovations in the field as well as presents a diversity of writings that are organized and integrated to serve students of vocational guidance.

PROBLEMS IN COLLEGE COUNSELING

One of the ways to gain insight into a complex operation is to identify and reflect upon its problems.

In the vast majority of colleges a handful of professional counselors are being engulfed by the massive enrollment explosion. It is not uncommon to have a half dozen or the equivalent full time counselors serving a student body of 10,000 and up — with emphasis on the *up*.

Of course, for years secondary counselors, together with counselor educators, have been fighting the battle of trying to get the ratio of students down to 300:1 or 250:1, etc. The college counselor regards these efforts with empathy and concern, but being human cannot but help being either amused or irked as he confronts his own situation. Simple arithmetic points up most forcibly that "counseling for all students" is not only unrealistic but improbable today, with a poor prognosis for the near future.

Even in the most enlightened and progressive college, which utilizes all of its talent in the student personnel services in an integrated effort with a "personnel-minded faculty," dedicated and concerned people are "going forward one step while sliding back two" as they are inundated with the flood of students.

There is a grave danger that in the attempt to serve additional students more and more group situations are going to be introduced to replace the counseling interview. This is a direct deterioration of one of the most basic philosophic justifications of counseling and student personnel services. "We like to think that we provide *personalization* as well as *individualization* in our relationships which provide services directly to an individual student."[15] This is in no way to imply that groups cannot be advantageous in some situations. There is no question in the finds of the writers that group counseling can and does add another dimension to some problems for some people. It needs to be emphasized, however, that groups are most effective when they *supplement* individual counseling rather than *supplant* it. It is the writers' fear that administration by expediency will attempt to cope with the rising college enrollments by curtailing some "ancillary" services by "putting more

[12]Grant, Bruce and Demos, George D. *California Career Study Guide*: *Manual, The Scientific Study of Careers, Self-Evaluation in Career Planning.* Western Psychological Services, Beverly Hills, California, 1964.

[13]Demos, George D. and Grant, Bruce. *Designing Your Career.* Lucas Brothers Publishers, Columbia, Missouri, 1965.

[14]Demos, George D. and Grant, Bruce. *Vocational Guidance Readings.* Charles C. Thomas Publisher, Springfield, Illinois, 1965.

[15]Williamson, E. G. *Student Personnel Services in Colleges and Universities.* McGraw-Hill Book Company, Inc., New York, 1961, p. 182.

chairs into the counselors' offices." This is an improper manner in which to form groups, and counselors should be unalterably opposed to such practices.

Rather startling, after what has just been pointed out, is the realization that even with these thousands of students, sometimes the counseling office "suffers" from *too few clients*. This results from the situation in which the counseling center dares not publicize its services too aggressively or carry out any campaign for increasing the number of students who seek out the service on their own. It is obvious that if such an "advertising" campaign were even mildly successful, too many students would appear all at once, and the "waiting list" problem would arise again. So, to prevent a deluge of clients who simply could not be served when they arrived, the counseling center often finds itself in the same predicament as the swimming pool contractor during the winter: "looking for business."

Having to minimize acquainting students with the counseling service produces a situation — especially in large colleges and those institutions suffering severe growing pains — in which many students actually complete four years of college without ever setting foot in the counseling center. Still another sad result of this matter is the increasing number of students who leave with their bachelor's degree without ever having known there is such a service as the counseling center.

Compared to the gravity and significance of the massive enrollment difficulties other problems may seem trivial, but they do exist and at times can seem to be even more annoying and frustrating in their impact on the professional lives of the counselors.

Parr[16] points out the problem of differing viewpoints on what clients should be served by the college counseling center: (1) attempting to serve all students the counseling office assumes need some guidance; (2) serving students who come for assistance by providing extensive personal counseling; and (3) serving the entire college family (students, faculty, and staff). A perusal of the philosophical implications and methodology involved herein is recommended.

The full time counselor or the part time counselor has been an unresolved controversy among directors of counseling and even among counselors themselves. It is recommended, however, that a coterie of full time counselors (one-half to three-fourths) maintain the counseling center, with the rest of the staff composed of part time faculty from the behavioral sciences. It is also desirable, if possible, to secure high level consultants from outside the college. This can improve relations among various academic departments on campus by bringing in a variety of competent professors with counseling competencies and also add vigor, depth, and breadth to the existing staff. These consultants and part time staff members can frequently be used for in-service training for the remaining staff as well.

In too many high schools counselors often find themselves having "to wear *three* hats": counselor, disciplinarian, and teacher; few of them relish this, though some enjoy teaching a class or two (but not the disciplining). Their college colleagues do not have to contend with the discipline function

[16]Parr, Henry J. "The Counseling Center: Its Psychology, Personnel, Publics and Promise." *The Journal of College Student Personnel*, June 1962, pp. 185-187, 194.

but often are required to play the dual role of counselor and teacher; some enjoy this; others do not.

Salaries for high school and elementary counselors have long been "a sore point" with them. The issue is whether or not they should receive additional money for being a counselor. Some high schools have actually approached this situation by paying a counselor more than he is eligible to receive in accordance with his placement on the salary schedule for teachers (which generally is based on the amount of education — degrees and/or units — and number of years of experience as a teacher).

In colleges the usual practice is for counselors to receive the same salary as they would as professors. In general a potential college counselor can determine his probable salary range in terms of the current prevalent range for college teachers at the particular college in which he is interested.

It is interesting to note the salaries for college counselors that were reported as *realistically adequate* by directors of counseling. ". . . six thousand ($6,000.00) to twelve thousand dollars ($12,000.00) with the modal salary falling at ten thousand ($10,000) and the mean salary being eight thousand six hundred forty-two dollars ($8,642.00)."[17] Unless positive action is taken to inflate the salaries of college counselors to a level that is reasonably competitive with the salary schedules of top level colleges, high schools in wealthy school districts, consultive fees, private agencies salaries, and the incomes of counselors in private practice, it is obvious that promising young counselors and graduate students considering becoming college counselors will quickly turn away from the consideration of employment in the majority of our colleges.

The time is *now* for the salaries of college counselors to range from $12,000.00 to $20,000.00, depending upon education, experience, and degree of competency.

PREPARATION FOR COLLEGE COUNSELING

The essential educational requirement for college teaching has long been the doctorate. So it is for college counseling. In the current decade which has produced the first critical shortage of college teachers as a residue of the college enrollment explosion, there is a concomitant dearth of professional counselors. Demand far exceeds supply to such an extent that some college counseling centers are forced to operate without the staff members possessing the doctorate; others find only the director having it; and still others present an amazing variety of academic backgrounds, with little or no professional education in counseling. This is particularly apparent at the junior college level where a heavy responsibility rests with the "counselors" for academic advising of students. Due to this fact, counselor positions are frequently filled with instructors from a wide variety of academic departments. Fortunately there appears to be a recent movement to hire more professionals in counseling at this level.

[17]Glazer, Stanford H. "College and University Counseling Centers Pragmatic Questions of Mutual Concern." *The Journal of College Student Personnel*, March 1964, pp. 168-169, 175.

A regrettable aspect of the education of the college counselor is that even the authorities in the field disagree on some points as to just what this preparation should be. Because of this situation each graduate student who elects to become a college counselor should examine carefully the various proposals, arguments, and philosophical differences as prescribed by different counselor educators.

Since the counselor — college, secondary, elementary, private, or agency — needs to understand individuals and environments, it is questionable to jump on any one band wagon to proclaim, "the counselor should be a psychologist (because he needs to know the individual)" or "he should be a social scientist (because he needs to know many environments)." Both of the foregoing are true, but in addition the counselor must be an educator, for the essence of all that he is trying to accomplish is integrated in the fulfillment of the concept of education. Yet who among the graduate students has sufficient time, money, or stamina to remain in school long enough to earn doctorates in psychology, sociology, economics, political science, and education?

It is apparent that there is a strong need for an interdisciplinary approach to the education of the college counselor. Until such a plan is satisfactorily evolved by some progressive university, perhaps a plan similar to the following might be pursued by those students fortunate enough to be made aware of its possibilities before they have already proceeded too far along on the route of preparation. For example, those graduate students (beyond the master's degree) who peruse the following will find it difficult to avoid an emerging irritation over what might easily have been changed in their preparational background had they but known in time.

At the undergraduate level as broad a program as possible in what is referred to as the liberal arts but what might be more correctly identified as liberal education (for it should also include the sciences — both natural and social) is recommended. In fact if it were possible to avoid a major in order to permit the acquiring of some depth along a broad range of subjects (going beyond the introductory or survey courses to take two or three additional subjects in the discipline), this would be preferable to having to accumulate some twenty-four to thirty-six units in a particular subject in order to satisfy the college's requirement of a subject major.

If there must be an undergraduate major, hopefully may it be natural sciences (rather than, for example, chemistry) social sciences (instead of, for example, anthropology) humanities (in place of, for example, philosophy); etc. Best of all would be simply the label *Liberal Education*, which would include some 130 units spread across the range of the humanities, natural sciences, social sciences, fine arts, and applied sciences.

At the master's degree level it is suggested that the program be in the social sciences: anthropology, political science, psychology, sociology, economics, history, and geography, coupled with a joint major in education: educational philosophy, educational psychology, educational sociology, and student personnel services. If a joint major is not possible, major in one and minor in the other. If individual subjects must be selected for specialization (or a major-minor sequence), psychology and education are preferable.

In the doctoral program the student must of necessity move into an intensive degree of specialization which will of course be dictated at that time by his particular needs, interests, aptitudes, personality traits, value system, goals, and health. It would seem logical, however, that this specialization should be in guidance and personnel, counseling and guidance, counseling, counseling psychology, or whatever the current terminology happens to be. But whatever this counselor preparation is called, it should include considerable depth in the following (which today are offered in some colleges in the education department while in other institutions almost identical courses are given in the psychology department[18]):

1. The individual
2. Present and possible environments of individuals — with strong emphasis on the world of work (supported by an enriched background in economics and sociology)
3. A variety of work experineces outside the college or public school communities
4. The methodology and skills involved in professional counseling
5. A diversified and intensive internship, carefully supervised and conducted in a manner paralleling the internship provided for the physician

THE HOPE FOR THE DEVELOPMENT OF COUNSELING

In the final analysis the proposition of counseling emerging into public acceptance as a profession worthy to take its place alongside of physician, dentist, lawyer, and the others rests on the accomplishments of the college counselors who (rightly or wrongly is beside the point) have been placed in a position of leadership in carrying the profession forward or letting it slip backward.

College counselors owe it to all counselors to continue the good fight of forcing educational standards upward; of moving promptly to censure counselors who attempt to counsel before they are adequately prepared. It is time to put a stop to the practice of a principal's going to one of his teachers to announce, "You get along well with students (or in some unbelievable cases, 'You don't get along well with students'), so I want you to be a counselor for a couple of periods this year. Then next summer you can go back to college to start taking courses that will equip you to become a qualified counselor."

College counselors should also look askance at anyone posing as a counselor educator who has never counseled. It is a travesty on our profession to have some professors teach something they themselves have never or have minimally experienced. The writers feel strongly that the instruction in counselor education courses would improve immeasurably if counselor educators would concurrently engage in counseling activities. The writers have made a policy of practicing their preachments in classes with very salutory effects.

College counselors should move rapidly to construct a set of ethical standards relating to the practice of professional counseling; they should then provide for means to enforce adherence to these criteria, acting as swiftly and surely as a medical board does in hearing the case of a physician accused of malpractice, neglect of patients, or incompetency.

---

[18]The writers have an esteemed colleague whose doctoral program consisted of identical courses offered in the education and psychology department; he was permitted to label each of these courses education or psychology, in accordance with his preference.

Strong screening programs should be established early in the preparational program of counselors to facilitate the "weeding out" of individuals who should not be permitted to become counselors. Personality deficiencies should "wash out" candidates even more quickly than insufficient scholastic aptitude. Other aptitudes should be determined such as creative, scientific, and social, and candidates for college counseling should be expected to be significantly above average in these as well as in scholastic aptitude.

Screening devices should easily sort out the individual who would be apt to use his counselees to nourish his own ego, to restructure his own personality, to resolve his own career problems, to reshape his own marriage, etc. Quick disposition should be made of the person who really has no intention of being a counselor but expects counseling to serve as a steppingstone to becoming a vice-principal, then a principal, etc.

When the college counselor begins his career in counseling, he should remember that he has an obligation to remain always a scholar — to study the research and developments in his own and related fields. There should be a few years of experience to enrich the doctorate then the college counselor should embark upon a lifetime journey of research and creativity in order that he can make his contribution to the enhancement of his profession. There are so many new and better ways of doing yet to be developed — many are still to be "imagined." The challenge is so great, with so many diversified opportunities in what is still an embryonic profession, that any young professional counselor today with the vision and courage to proceed will find the professional and personal rewards unlimited.

Suggested Additional Readings

Annual Report — Student Personnel Services. California State College at Long Beach, 1962-63.

Arbuckle, Dugald S. *Student Personnel Services in Higher Education.* McGraw-Hill Book Company, Inc., New York, 1953.

Brayfield, Arthur H. "Counseling Psychology." In *Annual Review of Psychology.* Annual Reviews, Inc., Palo Alto, California, 1963, pp. 319-350.

Callis, R. *The Need for Differentiation of Counselor Behavior.* University of Nebraska Counseling and Guidance Institute, Lincoln, Nebraska, June 25, 1962.

Canon, Harry J. "Student Counsel for a Counseling Center." *The Journal of College Student Personnel,* June, 1964, pp. 251-252.

Collins, Charles C. "Junior College Counseling: A Critical View." *Personnel and Guidance Journal,* February, 1965, pp. 546-550.

Demos, George D., and Grant, Bruce. *Designing Your Career.* Lucas Brothers Publishers, Columbia, Missouri, 1965.

Demos, George D., and Grant, Bruce. *Vocational Guidance Readings.* Charles C. Thomas Publisher, Springfield, Illinois, 1965.

Glazer, Stanford H. "College and University Counseling Centers Pragmatic Questions of Mutual Concern." *The Journal of College Student Personnel,* March, 1964, pp. 168-169, 175.

Grant, Bruce, and Demos, George D. *California Career Study Guide: Manual, The Scientific Study of Careers, Self-Evaluation in Career Planning.* Western Psychological Services, Beverly Hills, California, 1964.

Grant, Bruce, Demos, George D., and Oldenburg, Richard. *Improving Counseling — An Evaluative Instrument for Improving Counseling Centers.* Lucas Brothers Publishers, Columbia, Missouri, 1965.

Grant, Bruce, and Oldenburg, Richard. *A Philosophy of Guidance Services.* Lucas Brothers Publishers, Columbia, Missouri, 1964.

Hanfmann, Eugenia, Jones, Richard M., Baker, Elliot, and Kovar, Leo. *Psychological Counseling in a Small College*. Schenkman Publishing Company, Inc., Cambridge, Massachusetts, 1963.

McGowan, John F., and Schmidt, Lyle D. *Counseling: Readings in Theory and Practice*. Holt, Rinehart and Winston, Inc., New York, 1962.

Parr, Henry J. "The Counseling Center: Its Psychology, Personnel, Publics and Promise." *The Journal of College Student Personnel*, June, 1962, pp. 185-187, 194.

Stefflre, Buford. *Theories of Counseling*. McGraw-Hill Book Company, Inc., New York, 1965.

Thompson, Albert S. and Super, Donald E. *The Professional Preparation of Counseling Psychologists*. Bureau of Publications, Teachers College, Columbia University, New York, 1964.

Tyler, Leona, *The Work of the Counselor*. Appleton-Century-Crofts, Inc., New York, 1961.

Williams, J. E. "Changes in Self and other Perceptions following Brief Educational-Vocational Counseling." *Journal of Counseling Psychology*, 1962, pp. 18-28.

Williamson, E. G. *Student Personnel Services in Colleges and Universities*. McGraw-Hill Book Company, Inc., New York, 1961.

Wrenn, C. Gilbert. *The Counselor in a Changing World*. The Commission on Guidance in American Schools, American Personnel and Guidance Association, Washington, 1962.

(28)

COUNSELOR CERTIFICATION IN PERSPECTIVE[1]

R. Wray Strowig
University of Wisconsin, Madison

Certification is of vital concern to school counselors, their employers, and to counselor educators. The purpose of this inquiry is to move toward a better understanding of the functions, trends, and problems of school counselor certification. The subject of certification is most germane at this time in the history of guidance in the United States. Professionals and laymen are acutely aware of local, state, and national developments with respect to school pupil personnel programs, as well as the preparation of counselors and other pupil personnel specialists (Wrenn, 1962).

First of all, comment is in order about the procedure used in this inquiry, because it illustrates how the subject of certification has been neglected. The method that was used in developing this paper had to be analytical, based upon apparent historical trends and one's own judgment of their value. In surveying the literature, hardly any empirical research on certification was found. As Stefflre (1965) says about the counseling field as a whole, "Research has not helped us describe the function we are talking about, the specialist who is performing the function, or the purpose for which he was

An original article written for this book.

[1]Revision of a position paper on school counselor certification given at the first annual conference of Wisconsin counselor educators, supervisors, and directors of guidance, sponsored by the State Department of Public Instruction, Madison, Wisconsin, March 30-31, 1965.

hired." Examination of a dozen professional books revealed mainly repetitious generalizations about certification. Perusal of five issues of the *Review of Educational Research* (1951, 1954, 1957, 1960, 1963) failed to reveal any research studies of counselor certification that went beyond norminal descriptions of status. In fact, there were very few status studies. Moreover, examination of the contents, size, and heading in those *Review* summaries that were devoted to certification leads one to believe that far less attention has been paid to this subject lately than was the case a decade ago.

The dearth of good research on certification may be corrected soon. Much concern was generated in the profession by the ASCA and ACES studies of secondary school counselor role, function, and preparation. Many careful re-examinations of certification requirements will surely follow. Almost a decade ago, Barry and Wolf (1957) pointed out that, "Certification requirements as established in some states tend to emphasize the technical and to minimize experimentation." Perhaps, it is not too much to hope that certification requirements soon will be restructured to permit needed research to be done.

PROFESSIONAL FUNCTIONS OF CERTIFICATION

Opinions differ about the contribution of certification to professional growth. Wrenn (1962) said that requirements "are generally limited, unimaginative and untied to the past." Mathewson (1962) was more supportive of certification: "At the heart of Professional advance, lies the establishment and maintenance of state standards of certification, training, and practice." According to him, counselor certification and preparation have "unquestionably up-graded the whole perspective and practice in guidance," even though there are still weaknesses to both. McCulley (1961) wondered if the school counselor's duties are perceived to be different enough from other educators' to warrant certification.

One of the pro arguments is that students, administrators, and faculty are assured that the counselor who is selected has minimal preparation. Con arguments include: "(1) administrators are hampered in making appointments, (2) since applicants for counseling jobs must still be screened for personality factors, certification does not assure suitability, (3) 'all teachers are counselors' and therefore no special guidance training is needed" (Johnson, Stefflre, and Edelfelt, 1961).

Professional licensing (*sic*) is one mark of a profession. Sociologists offer a number of criteria or characteristics that mark a profession. Byrne (1963) modified Greenwood's "attributes of a profession" in the following questions, which are answered herein in terms of counselors:

"Is there a body of theoretical knowledge?" Yes, indeed, a tremendous body of facts, theories, and skills undergirds counseling. Unfortunately not all counselors are aware of much of this knowledge.

"Is there professional authority?" Yes, to some extent, as viewed by students and staff, counselors have limited authority.

"Has counseling community sanctions?" Legally, no. No privileged communication or expert witness sanctions are guaranteed. There is the limited sanction to practice the profession in schools, which is simply an extension of the teaching sanction. This lack is a basic defeat in counseling as a profession.

"Is there an ethical code?" Yes, but there is no requirement to subscribe to it. Society would expect an ethical code as an accompaniment to community sanctions.

"Is there a professional culture?" One is developing, primarily, however, in larger schools which employ more than one counselor. In one-counselor schools, counselors apparently identify more with teachers and administrative positions than other counselors do. (Wasson and Strowig, 1965)

"Do its practicioners have occupational autonomy?" Not completely, for counselors practice in schools, which exert much control over them, and they are certified by non-counselors. Moreover, they lack the sanctions necessary for autonomy.

In general, counseling possesses many of the attributes of a profession. It would be fair to conclude, however, that counseling is only an emerging profession. It has not flowered to full maturity yet, Certification has been both a help and a hindrance. The central fact that certification of counselors does exist is a great help to the profession. The problems of certification referred to below indicate some of the hindrances that certification provides to professionalism. Viewed strictly from the outlook for the counselor, himself, certification may be said to influence the field as follows. Certification tends to:

1. Ensure a more uniform minimum quality of some practitioners, while affecting part-time and minimally trained counselors very little.

2. Upgrade the profession, mostly in terms of preparation.

3. Partially control the content of counselor education programs.

4. Restrict the size and richness of the pool of talent from which counseling may draw by restricting who may practice the profession.

5. Legitimize counseling as a para-teaching function, rather than as an independent counseling function.

6. Accrue prestige within the counseling profession, a necessary element in developing a professional sub-culture.

7. Enhance the counselor's economic status and security.

APPARENT TRENDS IN CERTIFICATION

All in all, there have been many influences on school counselor certification. The national associations, such as APGA and its divisions as well as APA division 17, have had great influence on state certification, albeit of a rather indirect nature. The U. S. Office of Education, through the several vocational education acts and NDEA has a powerful impact on counselors, counselor education, and certification. One of the strongest mutually influential interactions has been between certification and counselor education. Each helps to determine the other, and both influence counselor roles. By far the most influential, however, in determining both content and implementation of counselor certification is a group that does not belong to the counseling profession, namely, local and state administrators and teachers. Emerging from this complex of forces and developments are certain trends in the certification of school counselors. Among these are the following:

1. Certification of counselors is an example of social change at an accelerated rate. The earliest professional counselor worked in the first decade

of this century, but it was nearly a quarter of a century later before the first counselor certification regulations were established — New York State, 1924 (Barry and Wolf, 1957). By 1951, roughly another quarter-century later, twenty-one states had counselor certification requirements (McDaniel, 1956). As of 1963, only half as much time had elapsed, but over twice as many states, forty-six, had such requirements (Camp, 1963). Only Alaska, Kansas, Michigan, and Washington had none, although each of them had special NDEA eligibility requirements involving certification. We have nearly reached the peak, then, as measured by states which have certification "on the books." Conclusions about uniformly general acceptance of the concept of certification should be made cautiously: (a) Requirements vary greatly from state to state. (b) In some states they are not enforced consistently. (c) Requirements in some states tend to emphasize certain roles, e.g., educational-vocational guidance, to the exclusion of others (Barry and Wolf, 1957).

2. Emphasis on vocational guidance, as opposed to other functions, is relatively less than formerly, although it is still strong. This trend may be reversed shortly when the impact of Federal legislation during the past two years is felt on the fields of vocational education and general economic opportunity for disadvantaged youth and adults.

3. As counseling has found more financial support, and as more counselor educators and counselors have acquired preparation in the behavioral sciences, there has been an increased stress on developing psycho-social understandings and personal counseling competencies, as compared to other guidance skills.

4. Teacher certification and experience regulations remain about the same. Miller (1965) reported that about three-fourths of the 46 states require teaching experience in varying amounts.

5. Multi-level certification is popular. One reason for this is that more schools can slip in under the tent of accreditation by means of an easy entry level of counselor certification. Another reason is that top levels of certification encourage professional growth. Keeping NDEA eligibility requirements separated from, rather than integrated with, regular accreditation plans has provided comparatively weak assistance to regular certification.

6. The tendency has been to name *credits* and *courses* in spelling out certification regulations, rather than functional behaviors or competencies. *Competencies* may become increasingly popular.

7. There is no evidence that professional associations of counselors wield more than recommending power over certification, although many state associations have influenced counselor certification by means of recommendations to the real certification authorities.

8. Unilateral certification regulations that derive from unilateral counselor education programs are not integrated with other pupil personnel specialties, such as social work, psychology, and nursing except, perhaps, at the remote level of teaching certificates and experience. California is an exception (Camp, 1963). Conversely, little attention is paid to "specialty" positions such as deans, elementary consultants, and directors of pupil personnel, who are within the guidance field. There is very little differentiation among specialties, either by function or setting.

9. Discrimination in certification requirements continues to exist according to how much assigned time counselors have for counseling and related guidance duties. Counselors working less than half-time are virtually ignored

in most certification requirements. Moreover, some states appear to be certifying counselors temporarily, even though they do not meet fully qualified standards. Is the presumption here that "provisional" couneslors can perform just as well as professional ones; that a "provisional" counselor cannot harm clients and other students?

10. Almost no attention is paid in certification regulations to professional codes of ethics or other personal (non-academic) qualities of counselors. Certification continues to be based almost solely on academic achievement, teaching, and other work experience.

PROBLEMS OF CERTIFICATION

From among the functions and trends in school counselor certification, there are some problems that need solving as certification continues to reflect and influence professional growth. The problems that follow are not altogether original; neither is the list exhaustive. Among the most important certification problems are the following:

To what extent should the profession determine its own standards and do its own regulating (Byrne, 1963)? Most other professions set their own standards for eligibility to practice. A profession may actually administer the licensing program, backed by legal sanctions in the several states. Counselor certification, however, is not ultimately determined by counselors, supervisors, and counselor educators. Rather, people who are typically from the ranks of school administrators and teachers, and who may be expected to make counselor certification fit the general patterns of teacher-administrator programs of certification, make final determination of regulations. In addition these people often administer the licensing program details. It is true that counseling groups are frequently consulted in planning certification requirements, but theirs is not the authority to make binding decisions. The lack of regulatory power and leadership applies even more to the failure of counseling groups to be involved in the operation of counselor certification regulations.

How can the effectiveness of each and every certification requirement be determined? Validation of regulations should be deliberately planned and continuous. There should be no "sacred cows." Highly academic abstract regulations are often justified on the basis of the most experienced, educated, consensual judgment available. It is better, however, to frame regulations in terms of performance of competency. Once each regulation is described in terms of competency, it is desirable to experiment continually with the various methods of regulating. To do this empirical validating requires an open mind as well as provisions for enough flexibility to do comparative studies of variations in certification standards. We know hardly anything about the effectiveness of certification requirements. Much work needs to be done.

How can certification requirements best avoid counselor role stereotyping, while at the same time ensuring competence and knowledge? This problem has many facets. One is that many staff members do professional counseling and guidance work, but their counseling and guidance behavior is not regulated by counselor certification. Titles proliferate, and we are still not clear on who is, or is not, covered by counselor certification. Among the confusing terms are these: deans of boys or girls, directors of guidance or pupil personnel, vocational, educational, or other counselors, guidance worker, guidance consultant, director of pupil research. Operational definitions are badly needed, as is agreement on commonalities.

Another form that this problem takes is in creating a narrow crooked tunnel through which would-be counselors must enter in order to work in schools. The tunnel is narrow in the sense that only people certified and/or experienced as teachers may enter, leaving out of consideration many people from backgrounds in other fields who may be well qualified to become counselors. The tunnel is crooked because one cannot take a direct academic route into counseling. No other profession outside of education requires that one become qualified as a professional in a different field before being able to practice in one's own. Teachers themselves are not required to become counselor's in order to understand and appreciate the work of counselors. What is so unique about formal schooling that counselors must become teachers before moving into their primary professional choice? Are not hospitals, courtrooms, and churches just as unique as schools? Do teachers really make better counselors than others?

Another aspect of role stereotyping has led to the development of separate curricula and certification requirements for counseling, social work, psychology, and nursing — all of which may be called specialized helping professions to the field of education. Granted that each has different historical origins, as well as certain unique contributions to make, it would, nevertheless, seems that foundational preparation and part of basic certification should be required of all in common. The remainder of preparation and certification should be specialized. The question of whether or not to create separate requirements for counselors according to level of setting — elementary, junior high, secondary, junior college — should be answered similarly.

How can counselor certification better ensure that there are plenty of counselors who are of a high enough quality in schools? Part of the trouble is that, until only recently, not enough professional recognition was accorded counselors. Largely, however, the difficulty is that deciding what are (1) adequate numbers of counselors and (2) standards of quality both involve making value judgments upon which it is almost impossible to get full agreement. One argument is that since something is better than nothing, we should get people into schools as counselors even if they are not well prepared. Once they get on the payroll, we can induce them to improve. The traditional argument of the older professions, however, has been to maintain high standards even though there may be too few professionals available to serve the public. There has always been a shortage of high quality counseling in schools, no matter how lenient the standards are. Besides, human beings are precious enough to require the best care. The experience of physicians is frequently cited as an example of the latter argument. Physicians are selective. Counselors, likewise, could be selective. They cannot argue, however, that quality is a matter of life and death. They can only say that the improvement of life is exceedingly important, and that properly certified counselors are more likely to improve the lives of children and youth.

Counseling is just beginning to acquire some professional authority and community sanctions. The proper policy would seem to be to stress quality more and more. Communities respect high quality. Moreover, such a policy supports the improvement of life, provided that the quantity of counselors does not diminish. The experience of other professions is that a raise in quality does not drive more people out of the profession than it attracts. Besides, the better qualified counselors are not the ones who will leave when standards are raised.

High certification standards should apply to all who are entitled to a counseling position, regardless of school size, exact title, or amount of time spent in counseling work (Byrne, 1963). It is possible and realistic, on the other hand, to differentiate among persons who perform different kinds of functions. It is also possible and realistic to set up levels of certification that encourage counselors to improve themselves beyond a minimally acceptable level.

To bring about improvements with all deliberate speed is important. Our communities are ready by and large, but improvement must be educative, not capricious or arbitrary. It is better, therefore, to invoke change gradually. Neither raising nor maintaining high quality certification standards will work without reasonable ways of enforcing them. The traditional mode of enforcement is to require a school to have certified counselors in order to be accredited or to receive state or federal funds. These status and financial incentives are sorely needed as support for counselor certification.

How can counselor certification protect and enhance the professional welfare of the individual counselor? The usual viewpoint about the professional person's welfare is that it influences the welfare of those whom he serves, i.e., what is good for the school counselor is good for his students — an example of a vague generality. More concretely, the counselor who moves from state to state will be helped if there are reciprocity agreements on certification between the states. The counselor will also be helped if the application-evaluation-certification process is efficient. Reciprocity between counselor education institutions and certification agencies should enhance efficiency. Another help to the counselor would be to guarantee him due process, i.e., provide the right and means of appeal from administrative decisions as to his certification. Among professionals, the primary source of appeal is to a board of one's peers. Finally, it will help the counselor and those he serves if certification provides ways of committing him to a professional code of ethics, as well as assuring one and all of his personal qualifications as a counselor. Like it or not, counseling is a rather personal affair which carries with it strong ethical overtones.

SELECTED RECOMMENDATIONS

No doubt current regulations on the certification of school counselors have been recommended by professional people who worked long and hard at their task. Needless to say, there have been company compromises. One of the most influential of these for many states was the idea that a modest beginning was more achievable than some ideal would be. Undoubtedly, this was true. On the other hand, it has become necessary almost at once to begin considering how the certification regulations should be upgraded. This task has been the continual concern of the state guidance supervisors and other professionals. For example, the Wisconsin Personnel and Guidance Association has an active statewide committee on revision of certification.

The recommendations that are offered below are based on current state regulations as viewed in the light of the foregoing analysis. Following the recommendations there is a concluding section on implementation. Neither list is exhaustive. Rather, those stipulations that appeared to be most vital at this time were selected for mention. This is as it should be, for a complete proposal for a revised code will be the work of many hearts and minds in each particular state.

Recommendation "A"

The certification of a counselor is not just a matter of being assured that he passed certain courses or even whole curricula. Certification by course and credit should be eschewed. Rather, the code should be geared to the man — what he is and does. More specifically, it is recommended that certification be based partially on skills and undertandings that grow out of predominantly graduate (professional) level preparation. The ASCA report (1964) lists these as "Professional Competencies." These competencies are minimal requirements for the certification level called Professional Counselor below. Lesser or greater levels of certification would involve modifications of the ASCA list.

Recommendation "B"

Professional Competencies are primarily a product of academic preparation, but Professional Responsibilities are acquired in field and laboratory settings. Both facets of professional development may be under the supervision of counselor education institution, and both are closely related (hopefully!). Responsibilities, however, are qualitatively different from Competencies as portrayed in the ASCA report (1964). Hence, it is recommended that state counselor certification requirements include recognition of the determination of Professional Responsibilities at the same level as Competencies described in the ASCA report cited in "A" above. Endorsement of the applicant for certification by laboratory and field supervisors should be mandatory.

Recommendation "C"

Counselors seeking certification should be required to swear or affirm their commitment to a professional code of ethics for school counselors. The code of APGA, or a state version thereof, may be appropriate, although a briefer, more general, Hippocratic-type statement is preferable. The writer is aware of the dangers of loyalty oaths, the reluctance of some people to swear to anything, and the futility of legislating beliefs. On the other hand, a profession is a voluntary association, not open to anyone without meeting prerequisites. Counselors must stand together on their commitments to their practice. There is presently little to compel them to do so. To affirm one's ethics may help to live up to them, and it may assist in building a professional culture.

Recommendation "D"

The applicant should be required to furnish evidence that character and personality are not inimical to the practice of counseling at the time of application. Usually, the evidence would be in the form of opinions from people who know the person and who know counseling well. This recommendation is stated negatively because there is little agreement on the positive attributes of successful counselors. It is geared to opinions of the applicant at the time of application because no one should be asked to evaluate another person for all time. This recommendation forces recognition of the importance of personality in counseling that goes beyond academic and practical preparation.

Recommendation "E"

It is necessary to provide for different levels of certification, both in order to recognize and upgrade professional advancement and to supervise the work of people who are doing related guidance tasks but who are not qualified counselors. Therefore, it is recommended that there be three levels of certification.

The main level may be called "Professional Counselor." It is this level that is the guideline for other recommendations in this paper. It may be the entry level of certification for many counselors, although there is a lower level of certification. The professional level, however, is the lowest one that uses the title, counselor. The Professional Counselor's academic preparation should be the equivalent of a master's degree in counseling, assuming that the Competencies referred to above are covered in the preparation program. (Let counselor educators worry about one vs. two-year master's degrees.)

It is further recommended that the lowest level of certification be called "Guidance Worker" or some similar title that does not include the term, counselor. Guidance Workers would be paraprofessionals in a sense, although they might or might not be teachers, e.g., housewives who had taken a short term intensive institute in guidance techniques. A school might employ such people temporarily, but after a period of, say, five years the school would be expected to employ a Professional Counselor. For the individual, however, this level of certification would be as permanent as any other (see below).

The third level of certification could be entitled "Specialist in ————," and would designate the competency and responsibility of a Professional Counselor who had secured advanced preparation and/or significant experience in an area of specialization. A master's degree in counseling, plus approximately one academic year of preparation in specialized competency areas would be minimal. Requirements for scholarly and practical advancement could vary in quantity and type according to the specialty. Among these specialties might be: advanced counseling, pupil personnel administration, research, psychometrics, admissions and placement, elementary school guidance consultant, vocational counseling. One person might specialize in several areas. Suitable certificates should be issued for each specialty, and schools should be induced to reward advancements tangibly.

Recommendation "F"

No certificate should be permanent. All three certificates should be renewable indefinitely, provided that evidence of professional growth is presented in the form of further studies and experience that is relevant to the certificate. Ordinary on-the-job experience, presumably, would not count, since that accumulates for everyone.

IMPLEMENTATION

It is important to consider carefully how changes can be made best. Many a good program has failed because it was not well executed. Here are a few suggestions. The last one is the most important, perhaps.

1. Allow a period of three to five years for transition from the present plan to a new one. School, counselors, and counselor education institutions should be well informed at an early date. There should be no grandfather clause that lasts beyond ten years after the new plan begins, although currently employed counselors should be given ample time to meet the new certification requirements.

2. Begin work on defining the scope of certification in terms of various job titles used in schools (see above). At the same time, commence explorations with fellow professions — social work, nursing, and school psychology — in search of common bases for preparation and certification.

3. Develop interstate reciprocity agreements, especially at the approximate level of Professional Counselor. In doing this, work with certification stipulations, not titles, and provide for meeting requirements by examination or other suitable means in emergencies.

4. Build into the certification code definite provisions for doing research studies to improve certification. This will involve granting authority to persons or groups to deviate from regulations for a stated time period in order to accomplish the research.

5. Get the colleges and universities that prepare most of the state's counselors to indicate in detail how they prepare people to meet particular standards. The certification agency and each institution should publicize this information. There is no intention here of forcing institutions to have identical programs of preparation. Institutions could continue, of course, to endorse an individual *en bloc* if he had successfully completed their entire program, and if that program met standards of certification in all of the competencies and responsibilities.

6. Put teeth into certification by recognizing the levels as special classes of membership in the professional association and by having the state apply the sanctions of school accreditation and financial aids to schools that employ certified guidance personnel.

7. The chief state school officer and the leaders of the state counselor associations should support the administration of counselor certification by the state as follows: Jointly appoint a Counselor Certification Board composed of school counselors, pupil personnel administrators, counselor educators, and state supervisors of guidance, the latter serving as executive secretaries to the Board. Terms of office for other Board members should be rotated at different times to provide continuity. The state association should help pay for necessary expenses. The Board would make policy and would execute certain tasks. Its functions would be to: (a) conduct a program of regular and systematic evaluation of counselor certification; (b) encourage and conduct research studies designed to test new ideas in certification; (c) keep counselors and the public informed about counselor certification; (d) receive communications from laymen and professionals about certification problems; (e) explore ways of cooperating with other professional groups; (f) determine acceptable kinds of "irregular" preparation and experience for certification,

e.g., conferences, workshops, contribution to a research project in counseling; (g) conduct hearings and written examinations of applicants for certification whose cases cannot be decided through routine procedures; (h) demonstrate the efficacy of cooperation between a professional group and state school authorities in ways that enhance the dignity, creativity, and growth of school counselors everywhere.

REFERENCES

(Page numbers are listed in the order of mention in text.)

American School Counselor Association. STATEMENT OF POLICY FOR SEC-ONDARY SCHOOL COUNSELORS. American Personnel and Guidance Association, 1964. 11 pp.

Barry, Ruth and Beverly Wolf. MODERN ISSUES IN GUIDANCE-PERSONNEL WORK. New York: Bureau of Publications, Teachers College, Columbia University, 1957. Pp. 94, 83, 134.

Byrne, Richard Hill. THE SCHOOL COUNSELOR. Boston: Houghton Mifflin, 1963. Pp. 274-282, 256.

Camp, Dolph. GUIDANCE WORKERS CERTIFICATION REQUIREMENTS. (rev.) Washington: U. S. Dept of Health, Education, and Welfare. 1963 (OE-25005A). 107 pp.

"Guidance and Counseling." REVIEW OF EDUCATIONAL RESEARCH. 21 (1951) 159-166.

"Guidance, Counseling and Pupil Personnel." REVIEW OF EDUCATIONAL RESEARCH. 24 (1954) 109-112.

"Guidance and Counseling." REVIEW OF EDUCATIONAL RESEARCH. 27 (1957) 174-185.

"Guidance and Counseling." REVIEW OF EDUCATIONAL RESEARCH. 30 (1960) 115-130.

"Guidance, Counseling, and Personnel Services." REVIEW OF EDUCATIONAL RESEARCH. 33 (1963) 171-178.

Johnson, Walter F., Buford Stefflre, and Roy A. Edelfelt. PUPIL PERSONNEL AND GUIDANCE SERVICES. New York: McGraw-Hill, 1961. Pp. 208.

McCully, C. Harold. "A Rationale for Counselor Certification," COUNSELOR EDUCATION AND SUPERVISION. 1 (1961) 3-9.

McDaniel, Henry B. GUIDANCE IN THE MODERN SCHOOL. New York: Dryden, 1956. Pp. 446.

Mathewson, Robert Hendry. GUIDANCE POLICY AND PRACTICE (3rd. ed.). New York: Harper and Row. 1962. Pp. 181, 95.

Miller, Carroll H. GUIDANCE SERVICES. New York: Harper and Row. 1965. Pp. 229.

Stefflre, Buford. (ed.) THEORIES OF COUNSELING. New York: McGraw-Hill, 1965. Pp. 269.

Wasson, Robert M. and R. Wray Strowig. "Professional Isolation and Counselor Role." PERSONNEL AND GUIDANCE JOURNAL. 43 (1965) 457-460.

Wrenn, C. Gilbert. COUNSELOR IN A CHANGING WORLD. Washington: American Personnel and Guidance Association, 1962. Pp. 176.

CHAPTER 3: QUESTIONS FOR DISCUSSION

1. Farwell raises the question of whether counselors must have had teaching experience. How do you feel about this matter? What are your reasons? Have you read any statements in the literature which tend to support your stand?
2. Nash presents a number of concepts which he deems as potentially dangerous in counseling today. Which of these do you feel poses the most serious danger?

3. For what reasons might a person keep leading an "inauthentic existence" as Jourard describes it?
4. Koeppe's discussion questions, near the end of the essay, present some vital questions in relation to the goals he sets up for elementary school counselors. Select one of these and discuss views about it you have read, heard, or wondered about.
5. Beck and Wilson list several ways that communication between the counselor and others can be improved. In what additional ways might this be done?
6. Topetzes makes the point that the counselor's chief expenditure of time and his main skill should be in *counseling*, an actual one-to-one relationship with students. What do you feel should occupy second place in his activities? What are some activities common to large numbers of counselors which should not be part of their assignment?
7. Demos and Grant present an array of expectations for the college counselor. What do you feel are the major unresolved problems in higher education which will affect the success of this field?
8. Strowig's recommendations on certification depart significantly from present practices in many states. Which of his recommendations do you feel would create the most serious problems in your state? Which do you feel might do the most to improve counselor preparation in your state? Give reasons for your answers.

Chapter

Ethical and Moral Outlooks

INTRODUCTION

Any time that one person enters deeply into the world of meanings of another, the question of values and value conflicts arises. The counseling relationship, and indeed the whole idea of guidance itself, brings into question the legitimacy of such relationships as well as how they might most effectively be carried out. The age-old philosophical question, "What is man's proper relationship to his fellow men?" now arises with new urgency. The writers who have contributed to this chapter offer clarifications, viewpoints, and experiences to the counselor-candidate and to others. Perhaps no area of counselor education is so vital as this. Ethical problems arise even at the outset: does the counselor feel he has a reasonable chance of possessing strengths necessary to aid the client?

Since the majority of those reading this book will likely be school counselors, two Codes of Ethics have been presented instead of the usual code for counselors. The second code is that of the National Education Association, intended for the teaching profession. It becomes necessary for the counselor, who often serves a dual role in schools (or at least functions in a school setting) to be cognizant of the principles by which both professions operate. He must examine them carefully for possible conflicts or needed clarifications. Further, he must ask himself whether the pooled professional judgments of his peers and predecessors are acceptable to him in his deepest life commitments. If they are not, then he is faced with vital decisions indeed. Is he then to believe the old quotation, "One man with courage is a majority" or is he to heed the words of Mowrer that if one is functioning in any given social system, he must either play by the rules of the system or withdraw honestly and openly from it? At various points the counselor will ponder this again and again, and will realize that no one else can make such judgments for any given case. In many ways counseling is a lonely task, one in which the existential statement comes home to the counselor with awe-inspiring heaviness: Man is alone with his fellows in a hostile world; he defines himself by his actions; he has no one to blame but himself, no one to turn to except his fellow men; whatever meaning is to be found, he himself must find. It is to the counselor as meaning-seeker that this chapter is addressed.

250

THE PLACE OF VALUES IN COUNSELING AND PSYCHOTHERAPY

C. H. Patterson

University of Illinois

The place of values in psychotherapy has been receiving increasing attention recently. The accepted point of view has been that the therapist's values should be kept out of the therapeutic relationship. Wilder, (in 7) commenting upon a paper by Ginsburg puts it as follows: "It has been taken for granted that the analyst must not try to impose his value systems on the patient," and he adds: "and I still think this to be true." In line with this "hands off" approach, therapists have been exhorted to become aware of their value systems, for the purpose of keeping their own values out of the therapy and to avoid deliberate or unconscious indoctrination of the client (7).

Perhaps few therapists feel that values should not be *dealt* with in psychotherapy. As Green (8) has pointed out, therapists *must* deal with values, since they are part of the personality of the patient, and the source of many of his problems. That some therapists still are uncomfortable in doing so seems to be indicated by Zilboorg's (35) defense of subjectivity.

Recently there has been developing the realization that the therapist's own values cannot be kept out of the therapeutic relationship.

HOW VALUES AFFECT COUNSELING AND PSYCHOTHERAPY

Besides the fact that many of the client's problems involve values and value conflicts, there are other ways in which values affect the therapeutic relationship.

Values and Counseling Ethics

Values and ethics are related; the ethics of individuals and groups reflect their values. In fact, ethics might be considered as an expression of a group's values, an attempt to represent or express them in a systematized form. This is no doubt why Sutich (28) became involved in values in his discussion of ethics. Bixler and Seeman (3) state that "ethics are principles of action based on a commonly accepted system of values," thus relating professional ethics to social values. The APA code of ethics (1, p. 49) states that a cardinal obligation of the psychologist "is to respect the integrity and protect the welfare of the person with whom he is working." This is clearly an expression of the value of the individual in our society, as is recognized in Principle 1.13: "The psychologist should express in his professional behavior a firm commitment to those values which lie at the foundation of a democratic society, such as freedom of speech, freedom of research, and respect for the integrity of the individual" (1, p. 10).

Reprinted by permission of the Author and the *Journal of Counseling Psychology,* Vol. 5, No. 3, 1958, 216-223.

Philosophy of Counseling

From ethics and values to philosophy is only a short step. A philosophy is an integration of values, usually resulting in statements of postulates and assumptions, or principles.

It is only natural, and to be expected, that philosophies of counseling and psychotherapy should reflect the philosophies of the societies in which these activities operate. The prevailing philosophy of our society is a democratic one. This is more than a political term, although Meehl and McClosky (15) would make it primarily such. Democratic principles and values have permeated our economic, social, educational and occupational institutions and relationships. And as Sutich (28) points out, "It is evident that modern therapeutic and analytical principles have their roots in democratic principles. And it is equally evident that most American psychologists are committed to the support of democratic principles throughout the entire range of human behavior."

What are the democratic principles which are accepted by counselors and psychotherapists? Bixler and Seeman (3), in their discussion of counseling ethics, present the postulates of Hand (10), which succinctly express these principles:

1. The belief that human life, happiness and well-being are to be valued above all else.

2. The assertion that man is master of his own destiny, with the right to control it in his own interests in his own way.

3. The determination that the dignity and worth of each person shall be respected at all times and under all conditions.

4. The assumption of the right of individual freedom; the recognition of the right of each person to think his own thoughts and speak his own mind.

The philosophy of the client-centered approach to counseling appears to many counselors to be an expression of this democratic philosophy in the counseling relationship. Rogers (21, p. 5), speaking of the development of client-centered therapy, writes that "some of its roots stretch out . . . into the educational and political philosophy which is at the heart of our American culture." Green (8) feels that client-centered therapy is supported by the "democratic-liberalistic idealogy."

The philosophy of client-centered counseling is expressed in the attitudes which the client-centered counselor holds and expresses toward his clients. These basic attitudes may be stated simply. The client-centered approach to counseling and psychotherapy is based on the following attitudes toward others, whether as clients or persons in other relationships with the counselor:

1. Each person is a person of worth in himself, and is therefore to be respected as such.

2. Each individual has the right to self-direction, to choose or select his own values and goals, to make his own decisions.

These, as simple as they seem, express the philosophy of client-centered counseling. They would probably not be disagreed with by most counselors today. Nevertheless, the extent to which these attitudes are implemented in counseling varies tremendously.

Goals of Counseling and Psychotherapy

Goals are influenced by our values, and therapeutic goals are no exception. The therapist has goals, either specific or general, and these are influenced by his values. Since no complete cure is possible, according to most therapists, what constitutes "tolerable conflict" is a matter of the therapist's values (6).

Concepts of mental health vary. Adjustment has often been conceived as the goal of counseling and psychotherapy. However, there has been increasing dissatisfaction with this concept. The question must be raised, "adjustment to what?" It is evident that adjustment to certain situations is undesirable — the conditions should be changed. And if everyone were adjusted, change and progress would cease. Therapeutic progress or even success can be achieved while the client remains unadjusted to his environment, or to some aspects of it. The concept of adjustment is static. It leads to a subjective interpretation, influenced by the bias of the evaluator, or to a mass, statistical interpretation leading to the definition of adjustment as non-disturbing behavior.

Integration is another concept applied to the goals of psychotherapy. This places the stress on the internal state of the client, rather than on his adjustment to a particular environment. Presumably an individual can be integrated as a person and at the same time be in conflict with his environment. But it has been pointed out that a paranoiac may be integrated but yet not be mentally healthy.

Realizing the inadequacy of adjustment and integration, alone or in combination, as criteria of mental health, Jahoda (12, 13) and Smith (26) have added to them a third, which they call "cognitive adequacy," or the perceptual adequacy for testing reality, thus proposing a triple criterion. Jahoda (12, p. 213) examined five criteria of mental health: absence of mental disorder of symptoms, normality of behavior, adjustment to the environment, unity of the personality, and the correct perception of reality. The first two were discarded, since symptoms are normal or abnormal depending on the cultural context, and it is difficult to define what is normal. Also, recognizing that adjustment may be "passive acceptance of social conditions to the detriment of . . . mental health," she proposes a criterion of active adjustment, or "mastery of the environment, involving a choice of what one adjusts to, and a deliberate modification of environmental conditions" (12, p. 216). Integration, or self-consistency, is not acceptable alone, since it doesn't imply freedom from conflicts with the environment. Correct perception of reality, both of the world and of oneself, while difficult to establish, since the majority judgment is not necessarily correct, is still useful as a criterion. No one criterion is adequate by itself.

While it is thus difficult to define mental health, counselors and psychotherapists have stated various goals of psychotherapy. Adjustment, integration, and an adequate perception of reality usually are included in these goals. One of the most extensive lists of the goals of therapy is that of Maslow (14, Chap. 12) in his study of the characteristics of normal, healthy, "self-actualizing people." This list includes most of the goals mentioned by other authors. Included is the goal of adequate interpersonal relations stressed by

Sullivan, who writes that "One achieves mental health to the extent that one becomes aware of one's interpersonal relations" (27, p. 102).

There has been concern on the part of some regarding such goals as independence, spontaneity, and self-actualization. These goals seem to emphasize the individual to the detriment of society, and to encourage antisocial or asocial behavior. Mowrer (16, 17) has criticized psychoanalysis for its emphasis on freeing the id from the rule of the superego, and suggests that psychotherapy should strengthen the superego. Actually, self-actualization depends on other people. The individual is dependent on the esteem and regard of others for his own self-esteem — for his mental health. He is thus dependent on satisfactory interpersonal relations. This means that mature, responsible behavior is essential. In the goals listed by Maslow there is this concept of responsibility, as well as independence. Mowrer (16, 17) also has emphasized responsibility. Shoben (25) has suggested the "development of responsible individuals capable of maintaining and advancing a democratic society" as the goal of student personnel work, involving the "dual commitment to the worth of the individual and the furtherance of democracy."

The goal of psychotherapy might well be thought of as the development of a responsible independence. Counseling and psychotherapy thus would attempt to facilitate the development of individual independence in a client who takes responsibility for himself, his behavior, his choices and decisions, and his values and goals. This would be consistent with the democratic concept of the freedom of the individual, and also with the concept of the responsibility which accompanies freedom. Such a goal is clearly an expression of the value of a democratic society.

There may seem to be the possibility of a conflict between the attitudes and goals of the counselor and the desires or wishes of the client. Should the counselor be committed, as Meehl and McClosky (15) state "to help the client achieve the client's end," whatever it is? Most counselors would say no. Almost every therapist, and not only the client-centered counselor, is prepared "to thwart the momentary motivations of his client, apparently in terms of long-time goals, which are assumed to be mutually acceptable" (15). The counselor's ethics, values, and philosophy determine his goals in counseling, and he should not be required to compromise these if he does not choose to do so. The client who does not wish to work under these conditions is not compelled to do so. He has the freedom to accept or reject any counselor and his services. To the charge that the counselor is putting himself in the position of thinking he knows best what the goals of counseling should be, the answer can only be one of "Guilty" — the counselor must be free to choose his own goals for the counseling process. Actually, counselors and therapists have always done so. Psychoanalysts have insisted on the goal of personality reorganization as opposed to symptom relief.

Therapeutic Methods

It should be obvious that if values influence, or even determine, the goals of therapy, they also influence methods and techniques, which are means toward the goals. The APA code of ethics recognizes that "the psychologist's ethical standards and his professional techniques are inseparable" (1, p. 37). Methods and techniques will not be dealt with here; it is sufficient to point out their relationship to therapeutic goals. Techniques are not chosen primarily on the pragmatic basis of whether they provide relief to the client, but in terms of their appropriateness to the ultimate goal of therapy. If this goal is client responsibility and independence, then it would appear to follow that all techniques should be consistent with this goal. The client learns responsibility by practicing it, and this should begin in psychotherapy, not at its conclusion.

Influence of the Counselor's Values on the Client

We indicated earlier that the generally accepted point of view has been that the counselor's values should be kept out of the counseling relationship. In addition to Wilder, others have stressed this avoidance of influencing the values of the client (5, 33). Therapists have been exhorted to become aware of their value systems, and those of the society and culture in which they work, to better avoid impressing them upon the patient. Some writers have insisted that the client's value system cannot be influenced by psychotherapy, or that only those values which are consistent with his existing value system will be accepted by him.

But it is possible for the therapist to avoid influencing his client? There is growing opinion, and some evidence, that he cannot. Ingham and Love (11, pp. 75-76) express this conviction. Wolberg (in 7), commenting on Ginsburg's paper, states that "No matter how passive the therapist may believe himself to be, and no matter how objective he remains in an attempt to permit the patient to develop his own sense of values, there is an inevitable incorporation within the patient of a new superego patterned after the character of the therapist as he is perceived by the patient. There is almost inevitably an acceptance by the patient of many of the values of the therapist as they are communicated in the interpretation or through direct suggestion, or as they are deduced by the patient from his association with the therapist." Parloff (19) states that "The disclosure of many of the therapist's values is inevitable," and "such disclosure and communication may occur without the therapist being aware of it." It might be expected that the therapist, by reason of his position and prestige, would become an example to the client, and that the client would tend to imitate him, consciously or unconsciously, in terms of his perception of the therapist. The APA statement quoted earlier continues by saying that "the attitudes, values, and ethical concepts of the psychologist are expressed in his clinical relationships and very directly influence the directions taken by his client" (1, p. 37).

There is some evidence that what these writers claim happens actually does. Rosenthal (23) studied 12 patients presenting a wide variety of diagnoses, and ranging in age from 18 to 46, who had from three weeks to one year of psychotherapy. It was found that, in general, patients' scores on a moral values test changed during therapy, with those patients rated as improved becoming more like their therapists; while those rated as unimproved tended to become less like their therapists.

In another study, Parloff and his associates (20) had observers list topics discussed during therapy by two schizophrenic patients. The patients and the therapist then ranked the topics from most to least important. While both patients differed from the therapist's values, as indicated by agreement in their rankings of topics, at the beginning of therapy, they came closer to the therapist's values as therapy progressed, though one patient came no closer after the first six weeks of treatment.

There is also some clinical evidence that the therapist influences the patient's values without consciously attempting it or being aware of it. Parloff (19) refers to the well-known fact that patients conform in their verbalizations to the terminology and theories of the therapist. If therapists value dreams, patients dream; if the therapists value sexual material, patients produce it, etc. "The literature is replete with examples of patients unwittingly adapting their productions and even use of symbols to the particular psychodynamic theories and preferences of their therapist" (19).

The mechanism of such influence is suggested by some interesting experiments of Greenspoon (9) and Verplanck (30, 31). In these studies it was found possible to control the subjects' verbal behavior by means of operant conditioning, without awareness on the part of the subjects. In the case of psychotherapy, it is easy to imagine the effect on the client of such responses of the therapist to the patient's verbalization as a trace of a smile or a pleased look, an incipient nod of the head, or other mannerisms indicating his attitude, favorable or unfavorable, toward the patient's productions. And all this may be unknown to the therapist and the patient. Parloff (19) presents some evidence that the therapist's responses may be classed by observers as "approving" or "disapproving," and that these responses were related to the therapist's ranking of the topics responded to in terms of their importance. This occurred without the therapist being aware of the differential nature of his responses as "approving" or "disapproving."

CONSCIOUS INFLUENCE OF THE CLIENT'S VALUES

As has been indicated above, it has been generally agreed that the therapist should not consciously attempt to manipulate the patient's values. Recently, however, there have been what Wilder (in 7) refers to as "rising voices to the effect that the analyst not only does but should transmit his own value system to the patient." Taylor (29), in a letter to the editor taking issue with the writer of an article making a plea for the abandonment of guidance in counseling, suggests that there are common, general patterns of human conduct which are ethically "good," and that counselors are justified in introducing them in guidance. Weisskopf-Joelson (34) proposes that the inculcation of a philosophy of life be considered as one of the objectives of psychotherapy.

Gardner Murphy (18) has recently asked: "Shall personnel and guidance work . . . attempt to impart a philosophy of life?" While admitting that "no one knows enough to construct an adequate philosophy of life," he suggests that "it is not true that the wise man's sharing of a philosophy of life is an arrogant imposition upon a defenseless client." He feels that the young need help and advice from those who have thought things through. But he warns counselors not to "attempt the arrogant and self-defeating task of guiding men and women without a rich, flexible, and ever-growing system of values of your own."

There is some slight evidence, in the studies of Rosenthal and Parloff (23, 19, 20) that those clients who improved, or improved most, tended to approach most closely to their therapists in values. This, if true and borne out by other studies, might appear to be an argument for direct intervention toward influencing the values and philosophies of clients. However, it must be remembered that this result occurred where no overt or direct attempt was made to influence the client. It might not hold where direct influence was attempted. Indeed, every counselor well knows the resistance that often develops where direct influence is attempted, and the resistance that often follows the attempt to fulfill a direct request of the client for advice or other help.

Granted that the counselor will influence the client, whether he desires or directly attempts to do so, is it therefore justifiable to attempt conscious, direct manipulation? The present writer believes not. There are a number of reasons for this.

First, while there are no doubt some generally, or even almost universally, accepted principles or ethical rules, these do not constitute a philosophy of life. One may even question how much agreement there is on ethical principles or rules of behavior. Each individual's philosophy is different, unique, and something which is probably not adequate for any other individual.

Second, it is too much to expect all counselors to have a fully developed, adequate philosophy of life ready to be impressed on the client. All counselors are not, to use Murphy's term, wise men.

Third, the counseling relationship is not, in the opinion of the writer, the appropriate place for instruction in ethics and a philosophy of life. The home, the church, and the school are more appropriate sources for such instruction.

Fourth, an individual does not develop a system or code of ethics, or a philosophy of life, from one source, or in a short interval of time. It is a product of a long period of time and many influences.

Fifth, it would appear to be best for each individual to develop his own unique philosophy, and not be deprived of the experience of doing so. Such a philosophy will probably be more meaningful and effective than one adopted from someone else, no matter how wise a man he be.

Sixth, we must still accept the right of the client to refuse to accept any system of ethics, or any philosophy of life.

Now this does not mean that the counselor refuses to discuss ethics, values, or philosophy. It does not mean that he is not concerned about the influence he has on the client in these areas. He recognizes this, and attempts to be a constructive influence. But he does this not by attempting to manipulate the client in the counseling process. He does it by being himself. As Murphy suggests (18), "A great deal of what you communicate to your client is not what you say but what you are." Further than this, the counselor on some occasions must express his own values. He may do so on the request of the client. But he carefully identifies these expressions as his own, perhaps only opinions, and avoids imposing them on the client, or implying that the client ought to feel the same way.

There may also be times when the counselor, whether on the request of the client or not, feels it necessary or desirable to inform the client of the attitudes, standards, or values of society, or the ordinary or generally accepted rules of ethics and morality.

The counselor should not strive to be an amoral, ethically neutral individual. Such a goal would be impossible of achievement — all of us have values, merely by being living human beings. Nor should the counselor attempt to pretend that he is amoral. It is unlikely that he could successfully give this impression to his clients, but it is also undesirable that the counselor attempt to appear to be other than he actually is. Further, the attempt to appear to be neutral as regards social and ethical standards may lead to the danger of appearing not only to accept the client's unethical or immoral behavior, but of approving or condoning it. Counselors are not indifferent to social and moral standards, and should not attempt to appear to be so.

Biestek (2) presents an excellent discussion of the behavior of the counselor in the area of ethics and standards. He points out that while the counselor may judge the attitudes, standards, or actions of the client in terms of his own or prevailing standards, he does not judge the client himself. He further states that "this judgment is preferably made non-verbally; the client usually is able to make such appraisals of himself in the security of an accepting relationship." He suggests that the counselor cannot be indifferent to social, legal, or moral wrong, and must favor the good: "In the non-judgmental attitude the (counselor) does not relinquish his own sense of values, his personal and social ethics. He cannot remain interiorly indifferent to standards contrary to his own if he is to maintain the integrity of his own personality. He must remain true to them. He does not become moralistic, but he has a right to his own sense of social, moral, and spiritual values, personally and professionally" (2).

Ingham and Love (11, p. 77) add a second reason for avoiding indoctrination of moral standards to the usual one. This reason is that the therapist might fail. "And trying to impress moral values in psychotherapy without success interferes with the freedom of the participants' communication and the strength of their relationship."

The point of view expressed above may appear to be a departure from the client-centered framework. Like many other therapists, the client-centered counselor has professed neutrality, and has in many cases at least felt that he has achieved this. But, actually, he has perhaps been no more successful than have other therapists. De Grazia (4. pp. 152-158) gives examples of the expression of counselor moral attitudes and values from published typescripts of client-centered interviews.

The proposal that the counselor not only should be aware of, and has a right to have, his own moral attitudes and values, but should sometimes express them in the counseling relationship, is consistent with recent developments in client-centered thinking. Stressing that the therapist should be himself in the relationship between himself and the client, Rogers (22) suggests that he should express his own feelings as he experiences them.

SUMMARY

The approach to values in counseling as outlined in this paper appears to have several advantages. By recognizing that the counselor's moral attitudes and values do enter into counseling, it prevents the counselor from erroneously believing that he is neutral. Freed from this belief, and the feeling that it is necessary or desirable to be neutral, the counselor is better able to recognize and accept his own values. He then can be aware of them in the counseling relationship, and, when he feels that the counseling relationship would be improved or furthered by his expressing his own attitudes and feelings, he can do so. That is, he can freely be himself, without guilt about doing so, or without feeling that he should not have any feelings. Finally, this approach contributes to the openness of the counseling relationship, without violating its client-centeredness. In fact, the relationship is probably more client-centered. That is, where the counselor's attitudes and feelings are unexpressed, even unrecognized by the counselor, they may, and apparently do, have a pressuring influence on the client. Where they are expressed by the counselor and labeled as representing his own values, feelings, attitudes or point of view, or identified as those of others, or society in general, there is less coerciveness about them. While there are some who would sanction the counselor acting as a representative of society in prescribing moral or ethical values or standards (4), the majority of therapies, including client-centered therapy, still insist that the client must freely accept or reject such values, and develop or construct his own ethical system or philosophy of life. Some apparently fear that the client when given such freedom will choose wrongly or adopt an unethical or immoral course of behavior. The client-centered counselor would respect the client's right to do so. He would not feel that the counseling relationship is the place to teach moral or ethical standards, or a philosophy of life. He is confident, as apparently some are not, that the client in the therapeutic relationship will be aware of and influenced by social realities. He will leave to the family, the church and the school, as institutions representing the moral and ethical standards of society, the teaching of such standards.

REFERENCES

1. American Psychological Association. *Ethical standards of psychologists*. Washington, Author: 1953.
2. Biestek, F. P. The non-judgmental attitude. *Soc. Casework*, 1953, *34*, 235-239.
3. Bixler, R. H., & Seeman, J. Suggestions for a code of ethics for consulting psychologists. *J. abnorm. soc. Psychol.*, 1946, *41*, 486-490.
4. De Grazia, S. *Errors of psychotherapy*. Garden City, New York: Doubleday, 1952.
5. Deutsch, F., & Murphy, W. F. *The clinical interview*. New York: International Universities Press, 1955.
6. Ginsburg, S. W. Values of the psychiatrist. *Amer. J. Orthopsychiat.*, 1950, *20*, 466-478.
7. Ginsburg, S. W., & Herma, J. L. Values and their relationship to psychiatric principles and practice. *Amer. J. Psychother.*, 1953, *7*, 546-573.
8. Green, A. W. Social values and psychotherapy. *J. Personality*, 1946, *14*, 199-228.
9. Greenspoon, J. The effect of two non-verbal stimuli on the frequency of two verbal response classes. *Amer. Psychologist*, 1954, *9*, 384. (Abstract)
10. Hand, H. C. America must have generally democratic high schools. In *General Education in the American High School*. Chicago: Scott Foresman, 1942. Chapter 1.

11. Ingham, H. V., & Love, Leonore R. *The process of psychotherapy.* New York: McGraw-Hill, 1954.
12. Jahoda, Marie. Toward a social psychology of mental health. In Senn, M. J. E. (Ed.), *Symposium on the healthy personality. Supplement II: Problems of infancy and childhood.* New York: Josiah Macy Foundation, 1950.
13. Jahoda, Marie. The meaning of psychological health. *Soc. Casework,* 1953, *34,* 349-354.
14. Maslow, A. H. *Motivation and personality.* New York: Harper, 1954.
15. Meehl, P. E., & McClosky, H. Ethical and political aspects of applied psychology. *J. abnorm. soc. Psychol.,* 1947, *42,* 91-98.
16. Mowrer, O. H. Motivation and neurosis. In Brown, J. S., *et al., Current theory and research in motivation.* Lincoln, Nebraska: Univ. of Nebraska Press, 1953.
17. Mowrer, O. H. Some philosophical problems in mental disorder and its treatment. *Harvard educ. Rev.,* 1953, *23,* 117-127.
18. Murphy, G. The cultural context of guidance. *Personnel guid. J.,* 1955, *34,* 4-9.
19. Parloff, M. B. Communication of values and therapeutic change. Paper read at symposium on "Evaluation of Process and Results of Therapies: I. General Problems of Methods and Theory." American Psychological Association, New York, N. Y., August 31, 1957.
20. Parloff, M. B., Iflund, B., & Goldstein, N. Communication of "therapy values" between therapist and schizophrenic patients. Paper read at American Psychiatric Association annual meeting, Chicago, Ill., May 13-17, 1957.
21. Rogers, C. R. *Client-centered therapy.* Boston: Houghton Mifflin, 1951.
22. Rogers, C. R. *A theory of therapy, personality, nad interpersonal relationships, as developed in the client-centered framework.* Chicago: Author, 1956. Mimeo.
23. Rosenthal, D. Changes in some moral values following psychotherapy. *J. consult. Psychol.,* 1955, *19,* 431-436.
24. Seeley, J. R. Guidance: A plea for abandonment. *Personnel guid. J.,* 1956, *34,* 528-535.
25. Shoben, E. J. New frontiers in theory. *Personnel guid. J.,* 1953, *32,* 80-83.
26. Smith, M. B. Optima of mental health; a general frame of reference. *Psychiatry,* 1950, *13,* 503-510.
27. Sullivan, H. S. *Conceptions of modern psychiatry.* Washington: William Alanson White Psychiatric Foundation, 1947.
28. Sutich, A. Toward a professional code of ethics for counseling psychologists. *J. abnorm. soc. Psychol.,* 1944, *39,* 329-350.
29. Taylor, Charlotte P. Social and moral aspects of counseling. (Letter to the Editor.) *Personnel guid. J.,* 1956, *35,* 180.
30. Verplanck, W. S. The control of the content of conversation: reinforcement of statements of opinion. *J. abnorm. soc. Psychol.,* 1955, *51,* 668-676.
31. Verplanck, W. S. The operant conditioning of human motor behavior. *Psychol. Bull.,* 1956, *53,* 70-83.
32. Walker, D. E., & Peiffer, H. C. The goals of counseling. *J. couns. Psychol.,* 1957, *4,* 204-209.
33. Weiss, F. Psychoanalysis and moral values. *Amer. J. Psychoanal.,* 1952, *12,* 39-49.
34. Weisskopf-Joelson, Edith. Some suggestions concerning Weltanschauung, and psychotherapy. *J. abnorm. soc. Psychol.,* 1953, *48,* 601-604.
35. Zilboorg, G. Clinical variants of moral values. *Amer .J. Psychiat.,* 1950, *106,* 744-747.

SCIENCE AND ETHICAL BEHAVIOR

Nicholas Hobbs
George Peabody College for Teachers

Some years ago I got interested in professional ethics while serving on the Committee on Ethical Standards for Psychologists. Although the objective of this committee was to develop some guidelines for professional conduct, the empirical operations involved in the process, focusing on behavior more than on abstract ethical principals, constantly invited thinking about the behavior of psychologists as a psychologist thinks about behavior. In other words, interest in ethics refused to stay put at the professional level; I kept wondering about the relationships between ethical behavior and behavior theory. I think it was Gordon Allport who suggested to the Institute of Humanistic Studies for Executives at the University of Pennsylvania that I might talk to its interesting group of young officers of the Bell Telephone Companies on the topic, "Psychology and Ethics." I am grateful to him for this recommendation because the subsequent invitation precipitated me into an inquiry that I have enjoyed very much. I think other psychologists might be interested in the outcome, for the issues involved seem timeless. I must admit being both surprised and a bit daunted to find that a number of eminent psychologists have written on ethical problems, among them Wundt, Galton, James, Münsterberg, McDougall, Dewey, Kohler, Hollingsworth, Gordon Allport, and R. B. Cattell. The paper growing out of three annual lectures at the institute has been written a dozen times, added to, cut, and rearranged. It seemingly will not get finished, yet I think the time has come to see if other psychologists will find the problem as engaging as I have. I should like to add that I feel more tentative about some of the ideas than the formal style of writing might suggest (in the last revision I recast the whole business in the third person to see if it would give me more distance and better perspective). The paper might be thought of as a highly tentative effort to identify some of the parameters of an important human problem by examining the point of intersection of the trajectories of professional and scientific psychology. I hope interested readers will share their thoughts with me, for I am thoroughly caught up in the problem and only hope to understand it well enough some day to be able to let it alone.

Some writers claim that science is ethically neutral (Lundberg, 1950), but ethics clearly cannot be neutral about science. Ethical thought cannot escape the insistent implications of scientific findings. Indeed traditional modes of thought about ethics have been shaken to their foundations, and there have emerged the polar reactions of (a) rejecting science in ethics altogether and of (b) turning to science to find an entirely new basis for ethical theory.

IMPACT OF SCIENCE

Three conceptions related to science have made trouble for traditional, revealed, or rationally self-evident ethical theories. One of these is the con-

Reprinted by permission of the Author and *The American Psychologist*, Vol. 14, 1959, 217-225.

cept of probability. Probability theory is a central tool of all contemporary science. Its use generates an habitual mode of thought leading to skepticism of any conceptual system based on absolutes, as many ethical systems are. For the scientist, imperatives give way to probabilities, and ethical relativism is the consequence. A second source of disturbance in ethical thought comes from the findings of cultural anthropologists. Behavior strictly tabooed in one culture may be encouraged in another with no apparent ill effects. Ethical systems appear then to be, at least partly, the expression of a particular culture and to have no necessary pervasive validity. John Locke pointed out that "self-evident" values are simply reflections of early childhood indoctrination, and psychoanalysis lends confirmation to his observation. In the words of one writer on psychoanalysis: "The moral faculty is often the unconscious residue of our nursemaid's admonitions" (Feuer, 1955). Finally with increasing knowledge, science has, paradoxically, become increasingly tentative about what is known. One criterion of a good theory is that it be precise enough to be disproven. Traditional ethical theories are not thought of as time limited, whereas scientific theories are regarded by scientists as expendable. A scientific theory is simply the best formulation of which scientists are capable at a given point in time, and constant revision of theories is the expected order of things. Conant (1952), for instance, has suggested that it would be more accurate to call scientific theories "policies" to denote their tentative working relationship to an ongoing process of inquiry. Though Dewey and others have incorporated the notion of constant reconstruction in ethical thought, it nonetheless would be quite disturbing to apply Conant's suggestion to the field of ethics and talk not of ethics but of "ethical policies." Like Alice reciting "Father William," the words do not seem to come out right at all.

One reaction to the disturbance caused by science is to exclude it entirely from ethical thinking. This position has been taken by both scientists and ethical theorists. Thus, Bertrand Russell (1935): "Science cannot decide questions of value, that is because they cannot be intellectually decided at all and lie outside the realm of truth and falsehood." It is said that science has to do with means but not with ends, that science can perhaps increase our understanding of human behavior but cannot help us judge whether a particular act is good or bad.

Another reaction to the disturbance caused by science is to recognize its potency in problem solving and to turn to it as a source of authority for ethical systems. New developments in science have repeatedly freshened ethical thought, as may be seen from several examples.

Evolution and Ethics

The scientific theory which has had the most profound influence on the construction of ethical theories is evolution. The discoveries of Darwin and Wallace were immediately perceived as offering a new foundation for ethics. Evolution with its biological and ecological emphasis appeared to offer sources of value rooted in the nature of man and independent of the influence of man-made cultures.

It is a point both of interest and of warning to note that one of the first efforts to derive an ethical system from Darwinian theory fell forthwith into the trap of cultural bias. Spencer found in evolution, by placing central emphasis on the idea of survival of the fittest, biological justification for *laissez-faire* capitalism! The economically strong survive and the economically weak perish, and this is not only good business but it is morally right, a manifestation of the natural order of things. "Nature red in tooth and claw" implied a positive good and sanctioned unregulated economic competition. The fact that England was then in a most favorable competitive position does not seem to have been weighed in the formulation, at least not consciously. As we move on to examine contemporary efforts to derive ethics from science, the example of Spencer should alert us to similar confusions of what science warrants believing and what man wants to believe.

The growing sophistication of ethical systems based on evolutionary concepts may be seen in two fascinating papers written 50 years apart and delivered from the same platform — one by Thomas Henry Huxley and the other by his grandson, Julian Huxley (1947). Although T. H. Huxley based his ideas on the science of his day, he still subscribed to intuition as the ultimate asserter of right and wrong. "Cosmic evolution may teach us how the good and the evil tendencies of many may have come about; but, in itself, it is incompetent to furnish any better reason why what we call good is preferable to what we call evil than we had before." T. H. Huxley concluded that man must reach beyond the implications of evolutionary theory of his times. The cosmic processes of struggle and survival at a physical level must be combated by dedication to a higher ethical sense.

Fifty years later Julian Huxley was able to interpret the implications of evolutionary theory in a different light and reach conclusions quite at variance with those of his grandfather. He identifies three emergent stages of evolution: the inorganic level, which encompasses the eons of interplay of vast physical forces which made possible the appearance of life; the level of life, where the main mechanism of change is "natural selection between competing variants"; and the level of social organization, which is mediated primarily by the acquisition and dissemination of knowledge serving the end of more and more effective oragnization. "There is one direction within the multifariousness of evolution which we can legitimately call progress. It consists in the capacity to attain a higher degree of organization, but without closing the door to further advance." Ethics is a consequence of social evolution and a main contributor to further social development. Relativity in ethics is still very much present, but the situation is not chaotic. "Ethics are relative to a process which is both meaningful and of indefinitely long duration — that of evolutionary progress.

At this point, Huxley takes a huge and unnerving leap; he cannot resist a grand extrapolation. He finds that emerging ethical theory demands a one-world government. "This is the major ethical problem of our time [1953] — to achieve global unity for man. . . . Present-day men and nations will be judged by history as moral or immoral according as to whether they have helped or hindered that unification." One is reminded of Spencer justifying *laissez-faire* capitalism. The possibility of world government is intriguing but seems more required by Huxley's personal convictions than by his evolutionary theory.

George Gaylord Simpson (1950), the eminent Curator of Fossil Mammals and Birds in the American Museum of National History, also finds in evolution the basis for a most admiral ethical theory. He argues that many people have simply tried to substitute evolution for God or for His revelation as authority for absolute ethical principles and thus avoid responsibility for decision making. Such an endeavor he thinks is doomed to failure: "There is no real evidence whatever that evolution has had a goal, and there is over-whelming evidence that it has not. . . . Evolution has no purpose; man must supply it for himself." He argues that there is nothing in organic evolution that can serve as a guide in the fashioning of ethical principles but that such principles must be derived from social evolution. "The old evolution was and is essentially amoral. The new evolution involves knowledge, including the knowledge of good and evil."

Thus Simpson finds ethically good those acts which tend to serve the process of social evolution, and ethically bad those acts which warp or thwart this process. What kinds of specific propositions are derived from this view-point? His first ethical principle is that the "promotion of knowledge is essen-tially good." This includes not only the development of new knowledge but also the dissemination of knowledge so that it "may then be turned by human choice and responsible action for either good or evil." Here is his stirring appeal:

> Human responsibility requires, in each individual as well as in society as a whole, that the search for knowledge be a search for truth, as unbiased as is possible to human beings; that probable truths as discovered be tested by every means that can be devised, that these truths be communicated in such a way as is most likely to ensure their right utilization and incorporation into the general body of human knowledge, and that those who should receive this knowledge seek it, share in its communication, and in their turn examine and test with as little prejudice as possible whatever is submitted as truth.

From the observation of an important evolutionary characteristic of man — that of high individualization — Simpson draws his second major ethical principle:

> It is good, right and moral to recognize the integrity and dignity of the individual and to promote the realization of fulfillment of individual capacities. It is bad, wrong, and immoral to fail in such recognition or to impede such fulfillment.

The psychologist will find both of these statements appealing; but their very appeal, both in their endorsement of the methods of science for the solutions of the problems of everyman and in their concern for the integrity of the individual, should make him wary of accepting the ideas as ethically required. The ideas are those of a good man who devotes his life to the pursuit of truth. They are an expression of the finest aspects of our scientific and humanitarian culture. But are they more securely bound to the nature of man and of society than are ethical principles with a higher intuitive component such as would be associated with a commitment to a life not of action but of contemplation, not of pursuit of knowledge but pursuit of inner peace? Helpful here as a check on personal dedications is F. S. C. Northrop's (1946) analysis of how prior assumptions shape our evaluations of the moral com-mitments of people of our own and other cultures.

The effort to build an ethical system on the foundation of evolutionary theory has not been too fruitful. The situation is well summarized by Dobzhansky (1955): "Evolutionary ethics have not been formulated yet, and one may reasonably doubt that they can be made scientifically convincing or esthetically satisfying."

Psychoanalysis and Ethics

Next to evolution in its impact on ethical theory is psychoanalysis, with results that are equally open to varied interpretations. Just as evolution shook traditional ethical systems and then provided a basis for new but narrowly conceived systems, so it is with psychoanalysis. For some, psychoanalytic thinking has led to "ethical nihilism," to a "sphincter ethics" no more valid than the toilet training prejudice of a particular culture. But a much more positive construction is possible as can be seen in the work of Erich Fromm (1947) and others. For the purposes of this paper, I would cite the positive interpretation of psychoanalysis provided by Lewis Samuel Feuer (1955). He argues that:

> Freud's methods are a tremendous contribution to ethics as an applied social science. He provided the techniques for determining the extent to which attitudes are imposed or are the expression of autonomous choice, for the decision, in other words, as to whether values are authentic or inauthentic, expressive or repressive.

Feuer argues that psychoanalysis has provided a tool which can be used to uncover deeper layers of experiencing, closer to the true nature of the individual, at which levels one can find ultimate criteria for values in the "underlying realities of human personality." For instance, the ascetic is shown on deeper analysis to long for comfort, the passive individual to long for self-assertion, the Nietzschean superman to long for simple affection and acceptance. Monolithic ultimate values, such as the will-to-power, are seen as desperate and ever-unsuccessful efforts at allaying neurotic anxiety. Authentic values, on the other hand, reflect the "primal drives of the organism."

Many ethical precepts, embodying such symbols as "good" and "duty," are loaded with anxious promptings from childhood learnings in which values of parents are taken over by the child in order to avoid the catastrophic withdrawal of parental affection and support; such secondhand values have never been tested by the child against his own experience. Through analysis, one gains insight into the operation of these hand-me-down values, and they lose their control over behavior, to be replaced by personally authenticated values. A similar concept, without direct concern for ethics, is developed by Rogers (1951, Proposition X, p. 498).

The rejection of anxiety as an appropriate source of motivation for human behavior is an appealing notion, but it generates about as many problems as it solves. The fact that neurotic behavior is whipped on by anxiety (as revealed for instance in studies which show that the extreme authoritarian has deep disturbance in many areas of functioning) does not permit the conclusion that normal behavior is anxiety-free behavior. On the other hand there must be many deeply anxious people who lead exemplary lives from an ethical point of view. We must also allow for the possibility that Kierkegaard is right when he maintains that to be fully human is to experience and courageously deal with anxiety. Furthermore, human motivation is more complex than Feuer seems to assume. Apply his system of analysis, for instance, to the behavior of the conscientious objectors who volunteered to participate in the Minnesota starvation studies undertaken to provide a basis for planning the rehabilitation of victims of Nazi concentration camps. Their phantasy life was filled with longing for food, while the continuation in the experiment, doubtlessly conditioned by early acquired concepts of duty, required a denial of this fundamental need. It would be hard indeed to say that their behavior was neurotic and unethical, regardless of the extent it denied the primal drives of the organism.

Perhaps a more basic objection to the position taken by Feuer and Rogers is the discontinuity of the person implied in establishing a "wisdom of the body" criterion for the healthiness of behavior — not to mention Feuer's assumption that what feels healthy will be ethical.

It would be unfair to question the validity of Feuer's psychoanalytic method as an instrument for validating ethics without describing at least briefly the positive ethical commitments which are suggested.

The recommendations for ethical conduct are admirable, even though not clearly required by the antecedent analysis. What emerges is a liberal utilitarianism, substituting "happiness" for "good" in Bentham's famous equation: "The greatest happiness for the greatest number." The picture is of an individual who has shaken the incubus of a punishing superego and substituted therefor an ego vastly strengthened by a personal experiencing of the organically good, a person who knows happiness for himself and can freely seek it for others, a person who is spontaneous and free, who can give and receive affection with joy. That this happy picture is tempered by the recognition that such a fortunate individual would still live in a far from perfect world only adds to the honesty of the argument.

Other contradictory formulations could be added to this list. Ashley Montagu (1955), for instance, says that man by nature is cooperative and that he must move ever toward more cooperative patterns of living. Not so, says R. B. Cattell (1948). Cooperation within limited groups is good, but intergroup competition is essential to the emergence of new and more adaptable forms of behavior. Thus Spencer, the Huxleys, Simpson, Feuer, Montagu, and Cattell offer their diverse and often contradictory interpretations of the scientific bases of ethical theory.

ETHICAL IMPLICATIONS OF PSYCHOLOGY

Simpson (1950) has made the pertinent observation that many people today turn to science for ethical revelations, science being the twentieth century Mt. Sinai from whose heights might be brought down a new moral decalogue. Such a set of commandments, carrying all the persuasion of scientific authority, would bring new certitude and confidence to an anxious world and would relieve the individual of some sense of responsibility for the consequences of his behavior. But such a dispensation cannot come from science; science can never provide us with ethical imperatives. This is not to say that science has nothing to offer to us in our efforts to improve our ethics, or, more pertinently, to improve our behavior. Let us then turn to a consideration of some of the ethical implications of science, and particularly of psychological science.

Freedom of Choice

To talk about psychology and ethics intelligibly one must first come to grips with an age-old and possibly insoluble problem: that of freedom of choice of the individual. It is a problem that psychologists would often prefer to ignore but cannot let alone. In 1880, William James (1954) wrote: "A common opinion prevails that the juice has ages ago been pressed out of the free-will controversy, and that no new champion can do more than warm up stale arguments which everyone has heard." James goes on to say, "This is a radical mistake," and one is inclined to agree with him today for the issue is quickened every time psychologists get close to contemporary man and his problems.

Experimental psychologists generally seem less bothered by the problem than personality theorists and clinicians, though hewing the deterministic line is not always easy. In his book on the logic of problem solving in psychology, Benton Underwood (1957) says simply and persuasively: "Determinism is a necessary assumption for the scientific enterprise." B. F. Skinner (1953) is equally explicit: "If we are to use methods of science in the field of human affairs, we must assume that behavior is lawful and determined." From this point on, as though to provide a firsthand illustration of the complexity of the problem, Skinner gives the impression that the one person who is exempt from this rule is the psychologist himself. "Who's conditioning whom?" is not just a good joke; it is an unanswered question as well. While Skinner is too knowledgeable to claim such exemption, he has a hard time keeping in mind, for example, that Frazier is anything but a free agent in planning for the well being of the good people of *Walden Two* (1948).

George Kelly and Gordon Allport, as personality theorists interested in moving psychology closer to man, cannot easily accept the axiom of determinism that seems so simple to the experimentalist. Common sense makes trouble.

Kelly's position (1955) is a puzzler. He maintains ingeniously that freedom and determinism are two sides of the same coin. The behavior of a person is strictly determined by the constructs he uses to define the choice-demanding situation. However, the person does not have to accept these constraints; he may simply redefine his constructs. When he moves from lower order to higher order constructs, man gains freedom. Once a person adopts a construct, his behavior in the domain of the construct is determined by the construct; however, he remains free to redefine his constructs. Kelly does not specify what determines the choice of a superordinate construct system. If Kelly means simply that the adoption of a superordinate construct system increases the person's response repertoire, his degrees of freedom, all would be well within Underwood's postulate of determinism as a necessary assumption of psychological science. But Kelly is talking about human freedom in the classical sense. Saint Ambrose was a fourth century advocate of constructive alternativism. He observed: "A wise man, though he be a slave, is at liberty." Boethius, Epictitus, Marcus Aurelius, and others have endorsed a similar "let's rise above it" attitude. Does Kelly's constructive alternativism offer more than this today? The answer is unclear. In any event, it would appear that Kelly works three concepts of freedom interchangeably: (a) the classical freedom-determinism type, from which he would like to extricate man, at least partially; (b) the degrees of freedom type, which refers simply to richness of response repertory; and (c) the semantic construct type, or the north-south argument, which maintains that the contruct determinism requires the existence of freedom. Kelly solves the dilemmas of type a freedom by type b and c arguments.

Allport (1955), on the other hand, chafes under the restraints of science without really abandoning them. He first observes:

> It is customary for the psychologist, as for other scientists, to proceed within the framework of strict determinism, and to build barriers between himself and common sense lest common sense infect psychology with its belief in freedom.

But the kinds of alternatives that Allport describes do not join the issue. He first argues that, from the point of view of the actor, choice is "a paramount fact." Underwood and Skinner would not be discomfited by this. He then makes three additional points bearing not upon "freedom of choice" but rather on "degree of freedom." Allport is not at all sure that he has settled the matter: "These considerations fall short of solving the problem of freedom. They urge us, however, to forego naive solutions."

Anatol Rapaport (1954) argues persuasively that, without freedom of choice, ethics is meaningless. If man is not free to choose between right and wrong, between the better and the worse part, what good is it even to talk about ethics at all? This requirement of free choice as a postulate puts the psychologist in a difficult spot, unless one is willing to accept his definition of choice. The act of choice is the primary datum for nearly all of psychlogical science, but the psychologist has his own definition of choice which can cause difficulty unless one understands what the psychologist is trying to do.

The psychologist is concerned with understanding and explaining behavior, mostly human behavior. One of the ways in which a psychologist tests the validity of his explanation is to make predictions derived from some explanatory system. If a particular prediction is confirmed, as through an experiment, his confidence in the system is increased. If the prediction is not confirmed, and if he is confident of the adequacy of his experiment, he must go back and rework his explanations. Psychologists, like other scientists, work to advance understandings by testing specific "if − then" equations and working the results into more general formulations. The ground rules of science say that these equations cannot contain variables which are nonrandom in their operation but which at the same time are considered to be unavailable for any possible quantitative assessment. This does not mean that science maintains that all phenomena can be measured, since technical limitations (including those subsumed under Heisenberg's principle of indeterminancy) obviously limit what can be achieved in the way of mensuration. On the other hand, no scientific equation can contain an "X" variable which turns out to be the influence of any demon, pixie, gremlin, fate, entelechy, god, or spontaneous individual will. Now there is nothing in science that can disprove the existence and effective operation of demons, pixies, gremlins, fates, entelechies, gods, or undetermined individual choices. It is just that science is not set up to deal with these kinds of problems. There is no way for the scientist ever to write an equation incorporating such variables. The famous equation $E = mc^2$ does not suggest that engineers should build into an atom bomb a little man to decide whether or not the bomb is to explode. The psychologist cannot write such an elegant equation as this one of the physicist, but he too must write his equations without benefit of little men. Insofar as psychological science is concerned the notion of free choice is a homunculus. Psychology cannot prove that the behavior of the individual is determined, but for purposes of inquiry he must assume so and be content to live with whatever limitation this assumption may (or may not) make on his activities as a scientist.

But, one may protest, has not physics, the most advanced of sciences, had to admit ultimate indeterminacy? What about Heisenberg's principle after all? Surely psychology does not pretend to be more rigorous than physics! No, not at all. Indeterminacy in physics means something quite different from the freedom of choice involved in human behavior. Heisenberg's principle says that in certain restricted areas of physics an event cannot be measured because the process of measurement alters the nature of the event. This is a phenomenon very familiar to the psychologist, in whose work this kind of indeterminacy operates with a vengeance. The psychologist cannot give a person an intelligence test without altering his intelligence. But the effect is trivial, and no great harm is done by ignoring it.

And one may argue further that modern atomic physics has become a statistical science, dealing in probabilities and not in absolute predictions. The pathway of a particular molecule cannot be predicted and is random. Actually this development in physics has been comforting to psychologists, who are accustomed to dealing in probabilities. But it should be noted that there is nothing in physics that implies that a molecule chooses by an act of will to go in any particular direction. There is nothing in the probabilities and indeterminacies of atomic physics to establish the freedom of man or the existence of paraphysical influence in human affairs, as some writers fervidly assert (see, for example, A. H. Compton (1957) in a recent issue of the *Atlantic Monthly*).

What we need to keep in mind is that science is one system which has been invented by man for the purpose of finding order in events which often appear to be more or less randomly organized with reference to his existence. Man has invented other construct systems to achieve the same grand purpose or to permit orderly transactions in some more limited sphere. Each of these construct systems may have its own unique validity. While it would be esthetically satisfying (and possibly, though not necessarily, more efficient) to have one overarching construct system, there is little to be gained from forcing consonance where little or none exists. The criterion for the validity of a construct system is not its consonance with another system but its utility in giving order and meaning to human experience. Within a scientific construct system, the assumption of determinism (plus randomness, perhaps) is required.

There are other construct systems where different assumptions rule. For example, the individual scientist, getting up in the morning, chooses to shave or not to shave; he construes the world with the assumption of almost complete freedom of choice. The legal system for construing the world assumes a middle position on determinism and individual freedom; the criminal behavior of the young person or of the psychotic is considered to be determined by circumstance, while the sane adult is construed as being responsible for his behavior. A religious system for construing the world obviously has to assume the effective functioning of some supra-individual influence. And a poetic system might make even other assumptions. It is when we attempt to shift from one construct system to another, without explicit recognition of what we are doing, that we get into trouble.

The Process of Choice. Earlier it was suggested that psychology might offer a description of choice with more limited meaning than the popular definition with its implication of freedom of will. Here is the way many psychologists would see the situation. An individual is confronted with a situation requiring one of a given number of possible responses. The individual brings to the situation as he perceives it a collection of hypotheses (behavior potentials, habits, personal constructs, as you like) about what he should do based on past experience, including experiences in simliar situations. Within the limitations of the situation (a man in jail cannot choose to take a stroll in the park), of time available, of the individual's repertory of more or less appropriate responses, and from his habits of problem solving, the individual scans the situation and tries out various responses symbolically until there emerges into prominence (or until time runs out) a response that fits into his expectancies of establishing a more satisfactory state of affairs. He makes the response, or better, the response is made which is most prominent at the time when the response is required. The psychologist's incredibly complex task is to build a regression equation that will permit him to predict the relative prominence of various potential responses at any particular time. If this description of choice is acceptable, the psychologist can get about his business. The problem will still give him plenty of trouble, but it will not defeat him by erecting insurmountable theoretical barriers.

There are inescapable facts, however, that make it difficult to accept the description of determined choice just offered: the introspective realness of the experience of choice itself and the insistence of feelings of responsibility for the consequences of one's own behavior. People, including psychologists, act in the assumption of freedom of choice, and no amount of talk about the ground rules of science is going to change much this primary assumption. That people are going to behave as though they have freedom of choice is an important datum that must be included in a scientific system which says they do not in fact have such freedom. There may be some comfort in face of this contradiction in noting that science not infrequently can get ahead with its business only when it does adopt a formulation at variance with daily experience.

The process of choice or of choosing is not complete with the occurrence of a particular determined event. The event itself becomes a part of the past experience of the individual, and it is also likely to alter future circumstances either for the individual himself or for others. Behavior is a product of interaction of the individual and his environment. Psychology is concerned with the nature of this interaction. Interactions that involve the welfare of individuals and of man may be described as ethical behavior, and psychology is not only interested in such interactions but has contributed significantly to their development. Thus the individual and his world are engaged in a process of continuous reconstruction of each other. Man remakes the world, and the world remakes man in an ongoing process.

The extent to which psychological science can contribute to this process of interaction valid observations about the nature of man, to this extent psychology can make a contribution to ethical behavior and then, secondarily, to ethical theory itself by supplying the philosopher with more data to work into his ethical systems.

But more pertinent, and intriguing, are the direct contributions that psychological science can make to the ethical behavior of the individual. Psychology makes its most distinctive contribution to ethical behavior by altering both the kind and the number of hypotheses that the individual brings to any given choice situation involving the welfare of others.

Psychology can (or better, will) alter the ultimately determined process of choice in a number of ways. Suppose for instance that psychology could demonstrate, what many have asserted, that the probability of a satisfactory choice occurring will be partly a function of the amount of time devoted to the symbolic manipulation of alternative courses of action. Common sense says that this is true, and the late Thomas Watson of IBM promoted the idea with his ubiquitous signs. But we really do not have much precise knowledge about what goes on when we think. If psychology can add to our understanding of the mechanisms of thought, it will make a contribution to ethical behavior.

Psychology may also increase the probability of the occurrence of ethically good responses by freeing a person to act on ethically good hypotheses that he already has but cannot use. This is what the psychologist attempts to do in psychotherapy. People may often not be able to use the knowledge they have about what is ethically good because of debilitating anxiety evoked by the anticipated consequences of efforts at constructive behavior. A common expression of this dilemma may be seen in the plight of the person who cannot risk loving for fear of getting hurt. There is the intriguing possibility that man may already know all that he needs to know to achieve fullest self-realization for himself and others. A simple factoring out of common elements in the major revealed or intuitive and rational developed ethical systems of the world might yield say 90% of the ethical ideas that are important to have. If this commonality be found, then all the energies that go into efforts at refinements of ethical theories on the basis of new knowledge might well go into investigations of why man cannot act on available hypotheses as to what is good. Such incapacities, of course, are a primary concern of research in clinical psychology.

Regardless of the adequacy (or inadequacy) of available hypotheses about human behavior, good or bad, psychology must and will go on testing old hypotheses and generating new ones to be tested. Such is the nature of psychological science. If psychology can make widely available to people the results of a number of verified "if – then" statements about the behavior of people in relationship one with the other, the required consequence will be an improvement in ethical choices, if the description of the process of choice, given earlier, is accurate. For good to ensue from an increase in knowledge requires the assumption that we live in an orderly universe of which individual expressions of choice are an integral part. To the extent that choices are in harmony with whatever universal order there is, to that extent they should be ethically good. The incompleteness of our knowledge of the universe and of man possibly accounts in part for the large number of disparate criteria that have been suggested as bases for ethical systems. Psychology has no such confident solutions to offer. It can only accept some responsibility for continuous enquiry into man's changing behavior in an evolving world.

So far it has been suggested that psychological knowledge should result in more ethical behavior: (a) by clarifying the process of decision making; (b) by divesting repressed responses already in the individual's repertory of their anxiety-producing potential, thus making them useful in problem solving; and (c) by adding to the response repertory of the individual a number of alternative ways of behaving. All of this appears to be to the good.

Control of Behavior

But if the psychologist at this point in the process of scanning the problem situation shifts construct systems and speculates on his personal responsibility as a scientist and a citizen, there emerges a much less sanguine view of the conequences of a constantly growing body of verified knowledge about human behavior.

As psychological knowledge grows, the possibility of more effective control over human behavior increases, with profound consequences for ethics. The very process of enquiry that promises to improve decision making also adds to the gravity of the decisions made.

Increasingly man will be able to employ the results of psychological science to manipulate his fellow man often without his victim knowing that he is being controlled.

Developing psychological knowledge presents the same conjunction of good and evil that we have all felt so keenly in the development of atomic energy. Atomic energy can ease man of drudgery and disease, and it can also annihilate him. Psychological knowledge can bring man increased certitude, dignity, and joy, and it can also enslave him. These antinomies are among the most exiciting and demanding developments of our time. They have within them the seeds of ultimate tragedy or triumph. The stakes seem to be getting even higher, and the rules of the game, embodied in ethics, ever more important.

REFERENCES

Allport, G. W. *Becoming*. New Haven: Yale Univ. Press, 1955.
Cattell, R. B. Ethics and social sciences. *Amer. Psychologist*, 1948, 3, 193-198.
Compton, A. H. Science and man's freedom. *Atlantic Monthly*, 1957, 200(4), 71-74.
Conant, J. B. *Modern science and modern man*. New York: Columbia Univer. Press, 1952.
Dobzhansky, Th. G. *Evolution, genetics, and man*. New York: Wiley, 1955.
Feuer, L. S. *Psychoanalyses and ethics*. Springfield, Ill.: Thomas, 1955.
Fromm, E. *Man for himself, an inquiry into the psychology of ethics*. New York: Rinehart, 1947.
Huxley, T. H., & Huxley, J. *Touchstone for ethics, 1893-1943*. New York: Harper, 1947.

James, W. *Essays in pragmatism.* New York: Hafner, 1954.
Kelly, G. A. *The psychology of personal constructs.* New York: Norton, 1955.
Lundberg, G. A. Can science validate ethics? *Bull. Amer. Assn. Univer. Professors,* 1950, *36,* 262-275.
Melden, A. I. *Ethical theories.* New York: Prentice-Hall, 1955.
Montagu, A. *The direction of human development.* New York: Harper, 1955.
Northrop, F. S. C. *The meeting of east and west.* New York: Macmillan, 1946.
Rapaport, A. *Operational philosophy.* New York: Harper, 1954.
Rogers, C. R. *Client-centered therapy.* New York: Houghton-Mifflin, 1951.
Russell, B. *Religion and science.* New York: Holt, 1935.
Simpson, G. G. *The meaning of evolution.* New Haven: Yale Univ. Press, 1950.
Skinner, B. F. *Walden two.* New York: Macmillan, 1948.
Skinner, B. F. *Science and human behavior.* New York: Macmillan, 1953.
Underwood, B. J. *Psychological research.* New York: Appleton-Century-Crofts, 1957.

(31)

SOME ETHICAL AND SCIENTIFIC VALUES IN THE COUNSELING PSYCHOTHERAPEUTIC PROCESS

Charles A. Curran

Loyola University, Chicago Illinois

The English essayist, G. K. Chesterton [1], once described a young man who left England on a journey of discovery. He was determined to discover by himself a perfect country and there settle and raise a family. He went from city to city, from civilization to civilization, from the most primitive to the most developed, in a difficult and thorough search. Finally, across a sea he came to an unknown shore and found there if not a perfect setting, one that was the most satisfying. And as he explored, in delight, his newly found land, he climbed a hill to look at a new landscape and there off in a distance, the gleaming towers of the cathedrals and buildings of London. He had found by long and arduous pursuit, what he had, in a way, always known and loved.

The counseling psychotherapeutic process is, as I have seen it, a search for values but not in the usual sense of this phrase. It is rather, an adventurous and thrilling personal pursuit, in an independent and sometimes seemingly dangerous way, of values which are uniquely new and personal for the client. As the therapeutic process moves forward, one of the most consistent things I have observed is the increasing anxiety of the client, particularly the younger client, to safeguard his newly acquired cache of self-determined values and to resist forcibly the counselor or anyone else trying to impose, even surreptitiously, values from the outside.

But the astonishing thing here is, as Chesterton's analogy suggests, that this intensely jealous and often fiercely independent pursuit does not necessarily produce social rebellion or philosophical and theological anarchy. Rather, the opposite seems most often to happen. When the client, with deep personal integrity and security, probes himself in the searching and sincere pro-

Reprinted by permission of the Author and the *Personnel and Guidance Journal,* September 1960, 15-20.

fundity of his relationship with the counselor, he retraces the basic steps by which civilization and society itself has, in some way, been formed. Or to put it another way, he surprisingly finds, in this absolutely personal pursuit, many of the basic values that are most fundamental to our whole Western Civilization and often shared in varying forms by all civilized societies if these societies are really understood. Here, it seems to me, with a strange twist and in a way G. Stanley Hall and others of his time would perhaps never have dreamed, we have "ontogeny recapitulates phylogeny."

In this paper, therefore, I would like to discuss (1) the client's personal pursuit of values in client-centered therapy particularly as I have observed it in clients, and some things this seems to imply, and (2) how this is related in some ways to the philosophical and theological value systems of Western Civilization.

A GREATER RATIONALITY

Rogers has recently said, describing his observations of this same therapeutic process, the following:

> I have little sympathy with the rather prevalent concept that man is basically irrational, and that his impulses, if not controlled, will lead to destruction of others and self. Man's behavior is exquisitely rational, moving with subtle and ordered complexity toward the goals his organism is endeavoring to achieve. The tragedy for most of us is that our defenses keep us from being aware of this rationality, so that consciously we are moving in one direction while organismically we are moving in another [5, p. 202].

A major factor in personal conflict and unhappiness, as Aristotle pointed out, is this fact: that a person can seek an apparent good which satisfies one or the other of his needs but which is actually contrary to the over-all reasonable good of his whole person. Problems arise apparently because an individual's craving for particular personal, emotional, or sensual satisfactions are leading him away from the reasonable goals which he ultimately seeks. A man is, therefore, capable of a most complex self-deception. He can allow himself to be misled by particular urges to objects and goals which he knows will not really satisfy him nor ultimately be good for him.

For a number of years now we have been doing research on this process of the shifting perception of motivating personal values in the client's counseling awareness. It invariably involves a shift in focus and an increasingly broader realization of all the factors involved in a situation or personal relationship. This in turn results in a changing perception of what is really good and thus his choices and actions change. We have discussed this research elsewhere [3] but to illustrate this, may we consider excerpts from a second interview and contrast it with the insight stage of the tenth interview with the same person [3].

These data were drawn from a series of interviews of a married woman in a serious infatuation with another man. In the second interview the only thing she considers beyond herself and John is one brief phrase: "I've got people that I don't want to hurt either." In the whole of the first and second interviews the above statement represents the only expression of consideration for any factors or persons except herself and John. However, if we contrast this limited viewpoint with the insight stage of the tenth interview, we have a striking change in perception. The superimposed image of John and herself has given away to quite a different picture of the whole situation.

> When John and I were together it just sorta pushed everything into the background . . . But you just can't turn aside and say, "Well, I'm going back to where I was" — even though I, if I really wanted to — I couldn't do that. It's hard to give up John after all the good times we've had and the things we've done, but when you stop and think what could have happened why you see things different. (Long pause) . . . but I know even now, just by not seeing John, I'm better physically and spiritually too . . . Yes, the way it was before I wasn't really happy, it was just a state of conflict and misery and fear of being found out and thinking of the kids and all — no, it really wasn't happy, even when it seemed most enjoyable . . . There's no happiness in it. You're always under a constant strain. (Pause) I'll lose a lot in a worldly way but I'll gain too. I would gain more than I would lose spiritually.

Observe here the perceptual language in the phrase, "When John and I were together it just sorta pushed everything into the background," suggesting the superimposed image of "John and I" blocked out the over-all awareness of her responsibilities to her husband, family, and God. The second phrase, "But when you stop and think what could have happened why you see things different," suggests that the thinking process of the counseling interviews also brought about a different self-perception. When we analyze what is the difference in these perceptions, it seems to be the removal of the superimposed, narrowed focus on "John and I" for the broad reality awareness of the responsibilities to husband, children, and God. Now, even though giving up John is a severe sacrifice when she focuses on the pleasure that John brought her, she sees herself to be better off physically and spiritually, when her perceptions are clearly on the total field of responsibilities, as distinct from John [3].

Stated in goal-directed language, this viewpoint would suggest that the superimposed image is itself an apparent good and that the self tends to move towards this apparent good until its perceptions are broadened and the reasoning and insightful process of the personality, in this case brought about through counseling, brings out from the background the real good, the total perceptual field. This puts into its proper perceptual organization the immediate good, which in this case, came from the relationship with John. When the immediate good is measured against the total perceptual field of all values involved, the self chooses and moves towards the relationship of husband, children, and God in the total perceptual field, as the real good, and rejects the apparent good which previously was a narrow focus on "John and I."

TOWARD INNER VALUES

We see too in these insight excerpts and this description of the therapy process, a goal directed and self-responsible morality. That is to say, we are not dealing here with some type of built-in Kantian "categorical imperative"

which can be variously explained by the effects of social mores or early conditioning and learning of cultural attitudes or the imposition of family attitude
or some other type of code. All these things may in fact be operating in the
client in the counseling relationship and probably are operating, but the peculiar quality that the therapeutic process seems to reveal is an inner capacity
where, by holding up inadequate and ultimately unsatisfactory goals, I can
stimulate myself to want these goals and to project on them much more
meaning than they really have. Evil, then comes in the degree to which I am
responsible for such self-deception and for the impulsive yielding to emotions
or basic drives which cause me to seek these disproportionate goals.

Obviously, there is a wide variety of degrees of responsibility in such
matters and while certain objective factors — such as legal or theological codes
may determine — doubtless enter here, there is at the same time almost always
a strong factor which only the person himself at the deepest level of his self-
understanding — best acquired through counseling — would only know and
be able to reveal.

We see in the therapy process therefore, an inner value system which is
yet objectively effective in producing a better operational fulfillment and
achievement. Operational reality, by implication, has apparently some kind of
reasonable substructure, granting all its apparent disorder, into which the
client's own reasonable process penetrates. The therapy process, as we see
it, ultimately facilitates not only a more reasonable integration and control of
the personality but also somehow a better, more adequate way of living. This
pursuit of a basic reasonableness in the midst of widespread disorder, which
the counseling therapy process implies, is what joins its implications to our
whole legal, social, philosophical, and theological tradition in one of its most
ancient Judaeo-Greek-Christian forms.

Let us pursue further what happens philosophically in the client's therapeutic process. It seems to me one way of illustrating what happens might
be symbolized by a triangle. The client begins at the point, with unique and
personal events, situations, feelings, and reactions that seem peculiarly to
happen only to him. Slowly he moves down to the discovery that others share
many of these things — that he is not as different or unique as he thought.
He begins to adapt himself to others and to learn from others but in a way
most interestingly personal and self-determined. In counseling, where the
counselor struggles to understand him and thus he is helped to understand
himself, he studies and investigates himself in an intense search which the
counselor's responses keep objective and in a sense impersonal.

THE DISCERNING LISTENER

In our focus on the release and emotional oneness and commitment of
the counseling relationship, we have perhaps somewhat overlooked the degree
of value that the counselor's accurate understanding and verbalization adds
to the client's clarification and objectification of himself. In a recent research
project we have been having clients comment on their reactions to the interview a few minutes after it is over. One of the most consistent comments is
the way the counselor's response helped them to understand what, in a complex and often emotionally involved way, they had just said. The following
illustrates this:

> I've never been listened to so well — no one before ever cared so much about what I was saying. I have confidence in speaking. Even if what I say is stupid or foolish, I am not made to feel stupid or foolish myself. I trust the counselor to hold what I say and not to let it slip or become blurred. In such a situation I can react to myself and my own thoughts and feelings much as I might react to those of someone else. There is an objectivity about the counselor's responses that is freeing.

Another person said:

> When I finished last time I thought I was too confused to say anything more. Then, as I heard your responses, I somehow understood what I had said and it seemed very easy to say something further. I didn't sound really as foolish or stupid as I thought. I began to become understandable to myself.

But this reasonable objectivity about oneself in counseling is the exact opposite of a cold analysis. On the contrary, it is only possible to a maximum degree in a profound relationship of mutually deep commitment. It is a commitment made possible by a love on the counselor's part which Greek and Medieval philosophers called *amor benevolentiae* — a love that concerns only the other and his good. This they contrasted with *amor concupiscentiae* where the person was seeking some self-determined return from the other. But in the commitment of mutual love of *amor benevolentiae*, the counselor is not only a catalytic agent of emotions, he is at the same time and even more essentially a warm, understanding, auxiliary reasoning power.

TOWARD ULTIMATE VALUES

Where does this mutual process of client reasonable self-search lead? It leads, it seems to me, down the triangle to issues and values that are increasingly more universal and more ultimate. It can lead — it does not always — to the most ultimate question of all, the meaning of life itself and to a struggle with all these final anxieties which in the traditional language of Western civilization one would have to call philosophically metaphysical and theological.

But even when the basic and most universal issues of life, symbolized by the broad base of the triangle, are not questioned by the client, they seem contained and implied in the values by which he questions and changes more immediate personal situations. Some years ago Rogers wrote, discussing a case, that insight tends to move through the "difficult and painful . . . not for its immediate but for its longtime satisfaction" [4, p. 210].

This awareness might be carried to ultimate conclusions. The analysis of the counseling process demonstrates that increased insight and a broader understanding of his personal values, aims, and purposes enable a person to direct himself towards and eventually to reach, more ultimate goals that are more permanently satisfying. But no transient, material thing can, upon analysis, produce the permanent security, peace, and lasting happiness that each one seeks. The fear of loss is the other side of every human possession and security. This kind of evaluation should logically lead a person to seek a final and ultimate Good, which will be a permanent source of happiness.

Each man seems therefore to be in a state of both being and becoming for which no transient goal or value — however immediately satisfying — can offer any final longtime fulfillment. We seem to have implied here a profound core existential anxiety in man — an essential dissatisfaction to which Augustine's famous remark was applied: "Oh God, Thou has made us for Thyself Alone and our hearts are ever restless until they rest in Thee." This being and becoming would be then, something both unique and yet shared by all mankind and, I believe, by God.

A TASK IN FREEDOM

But it is not only this pursuit of values that are ultimately the most universal and perduringly rewarding that relate the counseling psychotherapeutic process to the pursuit of values well-known in the tradition of Western Civilization. It is also in the more immediate values which the process of change in itself contains.

The counseling psychotherapeutic process at its best facilitates a person's own reasonableness, literally frees him to be more reasonable when he is enslaved by conflicting, emotional, instinctive, or somatic urges. This greater state of reasonableness not only enables him to study himself in an unthreatened and non-defensive way and to accept and use all he learns about himself, but it also makes him capable of a more adequate judgment of his own immediate or ultimate life goals and better means to them. Finally, this counseling psychotherapeutic process seems to do a third thing. It integrates the person's whole psychosomatic self so that he is now also able — often to his amazement — to do with surprising ease, what he now knows he should do and wants to do.

We have here an illustration in which a client discusses deep positive changes in himself:

> . . . and yet, frankly, it hasn't been at the expense of much consciousness on my part. Does this happen? I just don't know . . . I just don't want to be naive and say that this change has to be due to what we have done at this table. But I know that it is the *greatest* cause for the change. There may be other factors like my work, a change in Marie, and so on, that help to make me more agreeable, too. I'm not perfect or a new person but my temperament has been of fewer moods and less apartness. The changes have been obvious to Marie, too, and she tells me so . . .
>
> Yep, that's it. The same personality with greater control and more integrated function . . .
>
> And the role that you played did it.
>
> If you said to me to quit browbeating my wife, or to stop this, or to stop that, it would have been a useless attempt, I think that technique would have completely failed. Instead I've brought these things out time and again, time and again. The fruits of these discussions are that I'm better and that the cure has been effortless on my part. I'm not perfect or anything, but I've been so much better, and it's noticeable to others especially Marie [6, pp. 243-262].

This, perhaps surprisingly, is very similar to, if not the exact process that Aristotle and many of the ancients and medievalists considered the prudential process. Prudence was considered an incommunicable ability that could be acquired ultimately only by oneself. It could not as such, be taught. The first stage of this prudential process was the self-investigation and inquiry which was called counsel. But this is not seeking counsel from another, as it later implied, but rather taking counsel with oneself, sometimes with the help of another. From this concept apparently came our modern word, "counseling."

This first stage led then to the second prudential stage which involved a double judgment — the rejection of past reactions, operations, and plans and the development of new and more adequate personal solutions. The third prudential stage followed from this and was the self-command stage which brought order and integration into the emotions, impulses, and bodily functions so that a prudent man could carry out what he judged to be according to his own reasonableness.

VALUES REDISCOVERED

What I mean to say here in this discussion of the values of the therapeutic process as they relate to our civilization might be best illustrated by an incident reported in the Korean War. There was great difficulty in the soft mucky terrain and the huge modern tanks were bogging down in the mud. But in one section the soldiers found a path, overgrown with bushes and not used for many years apparently, which actually held up even the largest tanks and trucks and immeasurably facilitated their movements. When they investigated the history of this valuable passageway they learned it was at least a thousand years old, constructed by hand in some very ancient, now forgotten dynasty.

This exactly illustrates something of my astonishment in the dawning realization that many of the things this counseling process is revealing about human nature in a fresh and dramatic way, are yet not so completely new but that some of the ancient philosophical conceptions of Aristotle's Ethics and what used to be called the Cardinal Virtues can yet hold this powerful modern and new psychological movement. To be sure, much underbrush and debris have gathered here, that must be swept away. Much misunderstanding, confusion, and misinterpretation of ancient ethical and characterological terms like prudence, temperance, fortitude, and humility must be carefully clarified and adapted to all that we now profoundly know of the therapeutic process. But I am convinced that there is yet much that could be helpful to us, even now, like the ancient road in Korea. There is evidence, I believe, that would join these new psychotherapeutic discoveries to the ancient ethical tradition and value scheme of our Western Civilization, without in any sense warping the meaning and usefulness of either. But we must be willing to drop our own historical stereotypes and, perhaps, even ancient prejudices and seek to understand these conceptions with something of the freshness and clarity they really had for the men of much earlier times. By this I do not mean necessarily any return to some basic theological or philosophical unity, however desirable this may or may not be. I rather mean the common ethical concepts which in fact we all more or less accept by implicit observation in Western democratic society and which most of us want to preserve for ourselves and our children. But we accept these values too implicitly perhaps, and we are in danger of chopping at the roots of the tree or letting someone else chop at these roots and eventually jeopardize the tree, while we yet enjoy and treasure its fruits. We need to seek, perhaps, not only personal integration but to see that this can also be in some way an integration with the whole civilization that produced us. We need to know not only our relationship to our parents, family, and immediate environment but also to those older peoples whose thoughts and values have affected us with equal, if unknown, potency.

What then, finally, would be the personal values involved for us if we could do this — as the ancient Korean road proved so valuable to the movement of the modern tanks? Basically, I think it would do two things. It would free us from the more recent, probably Kantian, ethical concept that all personal values must be imposed from without which has come not to mean either by parents, society, or even more threatening and dangerous, by the state. It would restore again the possibility of starting out, like Chesterton's traveler, on a thrilling personal pursuit of oneself in a fierce and independent search for reasonable self-values and yet allow that one would ultimately come by this process, not to violent rebellion and anarchy, but to ancient and secure traditional values. These values have helped to carry through many centuries the burden of human hearts and, I think, can still help this burden.

Secondly, this would restore our own sense of belonging to the civilization that produced most of us and is basically responsible for our whole democratic tradition. It would make a place for education in values which in no way would impinge on a man's freedom to be unsparingly honest and sincere with himself and his own self-determined pursuit, through counseling psychotherapy, or by other educational and social means. This kind of personal pursuit the Greeks and Medievalists would have called, with a meaning strange to our modern ears, the seeking of humility. But by this word they would not have meant a fawning, inferior, "Uriah Heep" sort of thing, the "umble" man, but something very clean, dignified, and positive. This concept of humility has been defined as "the reasonable pursuit of one's own excellence." Such a definition, it seems to me, gives in one phrase about as good a statement as anything we have to delineate a core therapeutic concept and basic value scheme. This could be equally applicable to counseling, psychotherapy, education, and society itself without in any way doing violence to society and the rights of others and yet at the same time without distorting or warping the person's profound and deep need of personal integrity, responsibility, and basic independence.

REFERENCES

1. Chesterton, G. K. Orthodoxy. New York: Lane, 1918.
2. Curran, C. A. The counseling relationship and some religious factors. J. Counsel. Psychol., 1959, 6, No. 4, 266-270.
3. Curran, C. A. Some preliminary perception experiments related to insight in counseling therapy. In Bier, William (Ed.). Perception. New York: Fordham University, 1957.
4. Rogers, C. R. Counseling and psychotherapy. Boston: Houghton Mifflin, 1942.
5. Rogers, C. R. A note on "The Nature of Man." J. Counsel. Psychol., 1957, 4, No. 3, 202.
6. Snyder, W. U. Casebook of non-directive counseling. New York: Houghton Mifflin, 1947.

ETHICAL RESPONSIBILITIES OF THE COUNSELOR

JAMES F. ADAMS

Department of Psychology, Temple University

One of the marks of the professional status of counseling is an increasing concern with ethical problems. This old adage about an ounce of prevention being worth a pound of cure is particularly apropos in this area. Many of the ethical problems which arise in counseling could have been either avoided or settled with a minimum of concern if the counselor had considered them in advance or had been aware of his ethical responsibilities (12). Hence the need for some general guidelines and considerations.

COUNSELOR'S LEGAL STATUS

Wrenn (16) has pointed out that the counselor actually has more legal protection, in a broad sense, than he may realize. A counselor does not have to release confidential information, personnel or counseling records, upon the *request* of a police officer, an officer of the court, or any other court official. Quite the contrary, the counselor should probably not release such information, for the counselee would then have every right to bring legal action against him. An exception to this statement may be found in those states, e.g., California, where the counselor may legally release information to certain public agencies and is protected under the law in such release. However, in general, the only legal way in which a court can gain access to a counselor's records is by serving a warrant for release of the records. Further, if the counselor keeps personal records which are not a part of the official records of the institution which he serves, these records do not have to be released when the official records are taken into custody. They would need to be mentioned specifically in the original subpoena or subpoenaed separately.

Schmidt (11) discusses the problems of the counseling and clinical psychologist with respect to professional recognition, privileged communication, libel, slander, the right of privacy, malpractice, and criminal liability. Gradually psychologists are gaining certification in a number of states. This certification usually affords the psychologist the same rights for "privileged communication" as is given to ministers, lawyers, and physicians. Insofar as counselors meet the requirements for certification, they would of course have the same protection under the law. However, for those counselors who are not certified or do not reside in states which have certification, the problem remains.

The last comprehensive survey of the counselor's right to "privileged communication" was conducted by Smith (14). At that time Michigan was the only state in which the counselor was protected under the law. A California attorney general's opinion suggests that confidential communication,

Reprinted by permission of the Author and *The School Counselor*, May 1965, 197-205.

since it is information not required by law, *might be privileged*. While this is hardly a satisfactory state of affairs, it does suggest the possibility that in California, if the issue were to arise, counselors would have legal protection. Montana specifies privilege in civil proceedings only for any information obtained "in the study and observation of child mentality." Oklahoma makes it a misdemeanor for a teacher to reveal any information concerning a child, "except as may be required in the performance of his contractual duties." It would seem that Oklahoma counselors, if they are also considered teachers, should take a close look at their "contractual duties." Seven states empower the local board of education to rule on the disposition of information as long as there is no legislation to the contrary. Thirty seven states have no laws or rulings which are of any help to a counselor in the withholding of confidential information. Information on this problem was not available for Hawaii or Alaska.

Counselors should note that where they do not have privileged communication, they do not have an obligation to reveal confidential information unless they are under oath before a court of law. The mere request for the information on the part of an office or court official does not obligate a counselor to reveal the information. If under oath a counselor refused to reveal confidential information, he could be cited for contempt of court. It would behoove counselors to be very certain that they are justified in withholding such information. It is likely that if the counselor's case for the withholding of such information were very strong, his professional societies, such as the American Psychological Association or the American Personnel and Guidance Association, would come to his aid. However, the counselor should make his decision to withhold legally requested information on the basis of his own personal and professional ethics and should not count on receiving aid from an outside source. It will take a number of favorable court decisions to establish precedent, and it is the writer's opinion that tests of a counselor's right to privileged communication should very clearly concern a violation of counseling ethics since unfavorable decisions will not strengthen the counseling profession's position (4).

Another point to consider is the possession of "hearsay evidence" (16). When a counselor possesses information that a counselee has broken a law and this information has been gained in a counseling session, it is likely to be considered as "hearsay evidence." This type of evidence is not generally admissible in a court of law. Certainly an objection by an attorney as to the admissibility of the evidence would rule out the information in most cases. As much of what is gained in a counseling interview is "hearsay evidence," the possession of such information will not normally be a legal problem, although it may be an ethical problem for the counselor. Further, the possession of such information, while an ethical problem, is not a legal problem *until* the counselor is under oath. Many problems of this nature can be readily solved by encouraging the counselee to go to the proper authorities himself. The fact that a counselee reveals something of this nature to his counselor frequently indicates that he is asking for support and encouragement in making restitution.

In a juvenile court case, "hearsay evidence" may carry more weight. Attorneys are usually not present and the admissibility of evidence is left to the discretion of the judge. In an instance of this nature the counselor will have to decide for himself whether or not his testimony is a violation of counseling ethics and in the best interest of the counselee and society.

None of the foregoing should be interpreted to mean that the counselor will not cooperate with any agent of society. The intent of what has been said is only to point out that counselors may have more protection under the law than they realize and the counselor is not under an obligation to "reveal all" upon request but should use caution and discretion.

ETHICAL PRINCIPLES IN COUNSELING

Ethical standards which are of importance for counselors have been proposed from a number of sources and discussed in many more (7, 16, 5, 8, 14, 6, 1). Many of these standards are equally applicable to all of those who are in the helping professions. Some of the more pertinent of these standards will be discussed within this section.

Counselors in all areas of work should clearly recognize the limits of their competence and should not offer services which fail to meet the professional standards of recognized specialists in the fields in question. Furthermore, a counselor should not attempt to diagnose, treat, or advise a counselee with reference to problems which are not within the counseling domain. There are times when it is very difficult or impossible to obtain the aid which is necessary for the counselee. To be realistic, there are also situations which occur when there are mandatory professional referral sources available which, in the counselor's opinion, may do more harm than good, i.e., there are "professionals" in all fields who are incompetent in their profession but who are "available." There are then, two separate problems, the first one that of no available referral source. Tyler (15) states that there are some individuals whom the counselor, by virtue of his training, cannot help and that good intentions do not guarantee good results. While this is quite true, this writer cannot help but feel that the *skilled* counselor has the responsibility in this situation to act in a supportive role i.e., be aware that he is *not* conducting therapy but at the same time realizing that by being an empathic listener he may give the individual the time he needs to resolve his own problems. It would be quite easy to become diverted into a discussion of whether or not, in fact, this isn't therapy and, perhaps, the best type of therapy (10). In any case, the counselor will need to carefully weigh the pros and cons for continuing the relationship, and if there is any question of his being able to conduct the type of support necessary, he should follow Tyler's advice and terminate the relationship.

The second problem, i.e., referring, when in the counselor's opinion there is substantial evidence that a mandatory referral source is not a good one, is not an easy one to resolve. However, it occurs frequently enough that the issue is one which must be faced, although the writer does so with some trepidation. As an opinion which is neither supported nor negated from other sources, it would seem that the ethical thing to do would be to continue to refer individuals to this "professional" when absolutely necessary, even though in the counselor's opinion little of a beneficial nature for the counselee may be accomplished. At the same time, the counselor has a very real responsibility to sensitize his administrators and fellow counselors to the problem. Incompetency is much more difficult to document than unethical behavior; yet the counselor should do everything he can to remedy a situation of this type through documentation and through enlisting the aid of other professionals if possible.

A counselor should not normally accept a counselee who is receiving psychological assistance from another professional worker unless an agreement has been reached as to the respective areas of help being offered or unless the counselee's former professional relationship has been terminated. This principle has both ethical and practical implications. Counselors should work in cooperation with other agencies and professional workers far more than they do at the present time (9, 13). Without this cooperation there can be much duplication of effort as well as a loss of valuable information. If counselors wish to consider themselves as professional people, they will need to develop professional relationships.

The counselor should also insist on ethical standards with respect to his associates. As a general rule, the counselee's permission should be gained before communicating any information to another person or agency. A counselor in a school setting should assume, until proved wrong, that other school personnel are capable of maintaining confidences. He should be quite sure that they are aware of the need and the reasons for maintaining this confidence. It is the counselor's responsibility to help develop this awareness. Many problems in this area could have been avoided if counselors had assumed this responsibility, or educative function, prior to expecting its automatic occurrence. If the counselor finds that his professional colleagues are not able to act in a professional manner, he should withhold confidences even though their knowledge of the counselee's problem might benefit the counselee. Many times a counselor can sensitize teachers to the fact that a child has a problem without being specific about what has been told the counselor in confidence. The welfare of the counselee is a primary consideration, and considerable thought should be given to this before a confidence is revealed (without the counselee's permison) to teachers or other professional people.

The counselor should guard confidences which are extended to him in respect to a counselee. When informaion is gained from other professional workers or parents, it is not wise in most instances to inform the counselee that the information has been obtained. This is not to say that the counselee should be unaware of the fact that the counselor has contacted and is working with the pertinent outside agencies (although it is desirable to get the counselee's permission to make this contact); but rather that by telling the counselee of the information obtained, the counselor may be destroying another very essential relationship. As a rule, the only time a counselor should reveal a confidence received from another professional or, for that matter, a confidence received from counselee or his parents, is when it is quite clear that there is imminent danger to the counselee or to society. Of course, if permission is given to release the confidence, it ceases to be an ethical problem and becomes one of wisdom.

A counselor should present or report his findings with respect to a counselee accurately and simply to facilitate understanding. It should not be assumed that the referral source or the recipient of the report understands complicated psychological jargon unless this is known to be true. In many instances the counselor does not have the professional training to make a diagnostic judgment (e.g., schizophrenic behavior), and typing a counselee with such a term can have deleterious effects. If the counselor feels that the counselee has an emotional problem, he can state it just as simply as that, i.e., "I feel that the counselee has an emotional problem which needs attention." Psychological nomenclature which is misused, and even sometimes when correctly used, can be harmful. The rule is that any communication concerning a client should promote the welfare of the client. It should be insured that any recipient of a communication (or possible future recipient) concerning a counselee can understand and profit from that communication. With respect to this, the professional training and experience of the recipient, if known, should be considered.

The counselor should refuse to suggest or support unwarranted assumptions, invalid applications, or unjustified conclusions with respect to psychological instruments or techniques. This is frequently done with the individual intelligence test when questionable clinical conclusions are drawn from very meager evidence. Many counselors have had an introductory course in the use of projective techniques. While this experience is valuable in sensitizing the counselor to an area of personality evaluation, the use of these same tests for diagnosis, without much more extensive training, is most unethical and may be harmful to the counselee.

Occasionally a counselor is found who has been oversold on a personality theory. Psychoanalytic personality theory seems to produce this result quite frequently. It should be remembered that there is *no* personality theory to the present time which has been sufficiently validated to warrant unrestrained enthusiasm. In any case, diagnosis of this type is seldom a function of the school counselor, and it seems to this writer that many counselors verge on being unethical in their diagnoses which are based on personality theory and which are largely unsupported from objective evidence.

As a member of a helping profession a counselor should be willing to devote part of his services to work not included in his duties or for which he will receive little, if any, financial return. School counselors occasionally will have students come back to them after they have graduated from school. Within limits the school counselor and other counselors have a continuing responsibility for past counselees. The problem of performing counseling without financial remuneration when the counselee is unable to afford a fee is not as simple as it seems. In our society a premium is placed on that for which we pay financially. Frequently services which are offered for nothing are evaluated at the same level. Consequently the counselor should be very sure that the counselee cannot pay at least a token fee if this is the customary practice.

A cardinal obligation of the counselor is to respect the integrity and to protect the welfare of the counselee. A counselor's ultimate responsibility is to society, and his professional behavior should reflect his awareness of this. The welfare of the counseling profession and of the counselor are clearly subordinate to the welfare of society. In most instances the welfare of society can be best served by protecting the welfare of the counselee. Only when it is quite clear that either society or the counselee is in imminent danger should a counselor consider breaking a counseling confidence.

Bordin (3) notes four areas of counselor responsibility to be considered in ethical decisions: to society, to his sponsoring unit, to his client, and to his profession. Another source for ethical consideration is the counselor himself. Most certainly a counselor's values will enter into his ethical decisions. It is impossible to state precisely what personal ethical standards a counselor should hold, particularly in a constantly shifting environment and society. About all that can be said is that a counselor should be aware of his values and his reasons for holding them. A counselor should not insist that all individuals hold the same standards that he personally holds. This is not to imply that a counselor must compromise his personal standards, but it should be remembered that they are *personal* standards. A statement from Ethical Standards of Psychologists (5) is worthy of note as it applies equally well to counselors.

"Very often the resolution of ethical problems requires that the psychologist choose between two or more interests that are in conflict. Are the psychologist's obligations primarily to the social group, or to his individual client, or to his profession, or to himself? There is, of course, no simple answer to this question. Most situations where ethical decisions are necessary involve an implicit hierarchy of values, and this hierarchy has to be redefined for each situation. The equation of ethical responsibility is a complex one: weights for the variables must be computed anew as each new ethical problem is solved."

HOW DO COUNSELORS FEEL ABOUT ETHICAL PROBLEMS

A study by Smith (14) will be considered in some detail because of its pertinence to this topic and because of the large number of counselors found in the secondary schools. In this study professional members of the National Vocational Guidance Association submitted critical incidents in which ethical decisions were involved. From these incidents an ethical questionnaire was constructed. This, in turn, was sent to 1,225 professional members of NVGA. Six hundred questionnaires, or approximately 50 per cent, were returned. The questionnaire was scored to indicate the degree to which the respondents would favor revealing confidential information to some authorized agency or person. A near normal distribution of scores was found. A high score on the questionnaire indicated that the respondent favored revealing confidential information to an authorized agency or person; a low score indicated the converse. In other words, a high score indicated that the respondent's major loyalty was to society; a low score indicated that the respondent's major loyalty, or feeling of responsibility, was to the counselee. The group most closely associated with secondary school counseling showed the greatest preference for social obligation choices. Public school employees emphasized civic responsibility more than did any other occupational field. All educational counselors below the college level were significantly higher in social obligation choices than were college counselors. The greater the amount of public school teaching experience the respondent had, the greater was his degree of loyalty to society, and the lesser was his feeling of loyalty to the counselee.

One hopeful sign found was that the more graduate units in guidance, psychology, and related subjects, the greater was the loyalty of the respondent to the counselee. Respondents with the doctorate had the lowest mean scores on the questionnaire or were the highest counselee-centered group. Neither amount of counseling experience nor amount of time devoted to counseling proved to be a significant factor when comparing responses to the questionnaire.

A comparison of related items concerning access to cumulative records ranked administrators, other counselors, parents, teachers, social welfare agencies, law enforcement agencies, and employers — in decreasing order — for accessibility to records. Availability of records to the latter two groups was considered extremely debatable. Respondents tended to agree that personal problem information should not be available, but they tended to disagree as to whether administrators, other counselors, welfare agencies, or the counselee himself should have access to this information. Three fourths of the respondents agreed that when information was received directly from the counselee, the counselor had a responsibility to maintain the confidence.

Smith concludes that, with the exception of imminent harm to the counselee or others, respondents tended to place loyalty to the counselee above loyalty to society, although there was a tendency for public secondary school counselors not to share this direction of loyalty. Based upon the concurrence of at least 70 per cent of the respondents, Smith proposes that the following ethical standards be considered by counselors:

1. The counselee commands the primary loyalty of the counselor under ordinary conditions.
2. A counselor is justified in revealing confidential information to selected individuals when the counselee or others are in imminent physical danger.
3. A counselor should not voluntarily, nor upon request of the police, reveal counselee information of any offense short of guilt of a major crime.
4. A counselor should not voluntarily, nor upon request of administrators or parents, reveal any information about a counselee or former counselee received in confidence.
5. A counselor is not released from maintaining a confidence because others have the same knowledge.
6. A counselor is released from maintaining a confidence if he gains the counselee's consent to reveal such information.
7. When two counselees are seeking help on a mutual problem, a counselor should not reveal either counselee's confidence to the other.
8. When two counselors are working with the same counselee, it is ethical for them to share confidential information.
9. Confidential information may be revealed to another counselor if the counselee's anonymity is maintained.

Smith also proposes the following standards relating to the confidentiality of cumulative records:

1. Cumulative records should contain a counselee's transcript of grades, achievement test results, mental ability and other aptitude test results, interest inventories, personal problem information, and discipline records.
2. Teachers and other counselors who are directly concerned should have routine access to all cumulative record data except discipline and personal problem information.
3. All data concerning a Counselee except personal problem information should be available to school administrators.

4. Parents and social welfare agencies should have access to achievement test results, interest inventories, and transcripts of grades.
5. A counselee should have access to his own transcript of grades and all test data except mental ability test results.

It might be said, as a practical criticism of these cumulative record proposals, that most schools have extremely lax filing systems. It is possible for almost any determined person to obtain access to cumluative record files with little difficulty. Furthermore, withholding materials from the files before handing them to a responsible person seems a little like questioning a person's patriotism. A more practical proposal might be for the counselor to keep two sets of records. In one set of files would be kept materials on the student to which authorized personnel would have access. In the counselor's personal file would be kept the confidential materials on the counselee.

Lastly, Smith proposes several standards relating to other aspects of counseling:

1. A counselor should not intervene in a counselee's curriculum choice despite predictive evidence of academic or emotional outcomes.
2. A parent who has given information about a counselee's problem should be promised confidence.
3. A counselor's record of a counselee's psychotic behavior should be made available to other schools.
4. It is ethical for a counselor to gather information about a counselee from other schools without the counselee's consent.

It will be noted that almost all of Smith's proposals can be subsumed under the heading of counseling in a manner which will do the most to promote the counselee's welfare. It is also apparent from her study that there is a further need for school counselors to consider their ethical responsibilities with respect to their own school and their personal professional status. Lack of agreement of these counselors on many ethical problems highlights the need for continuing thought in this area. Perhaps the school counselor could sensitize his administrative and teaching colleagues by an open discussion of ethical problems and communicate his ethical responsibilities to those with whom he works.

CONCLUSION

Schwebel (12) believes that the causes of unethical behavior can be categorized into three areas: "The overpowering self-interest of the professional worker as expressed in personal profit, self-enhancement, and the maintenance of security and status poor judgment, due in part at least to inexperience in problem solving in counseling; ignorance of technical knowledge and of one's own values." It may be that not much can be done to help the counselor in the first of Schwebel's categories; however, by being familiar with the problems which are likely to arise in the ethical area and by being adequately trained in counseling, the counselor should have little excuse for violations of ethical principles because of the last two categories.

Many of the considerations which have been discussed here are common problems for counselors. The theme running through almost every ethical consideration is that the goals and purposes of society can be best served by keeping the welfare of the individual counselee as the paramount concern.

REFERENCES

1. Adams, J. F. *Problems in Counseling: A Case Study Approach.* New York: Macmillan Co., 1962.
2. American Personnel and Guidance Association. Ethical Standards. *Personnel guid. J.,* 1961, *40*, 206-209.
3. Bordin, E. S. *Psychological Counseling.* New York: Appleton-Century-Crofts, Inc., 1955.
4. Carter, T. M. Professional immunity for guidance counselors. *Personnel guid. J.,* 1954, *33*, 130-135.
5. Committee on Ethical Standards for Psychologists. *Ethical Standards of Psychologists.* Washington, D. C.: The American Psychological Association, 1953.
6. Committee on the Preparation of Ethical Standards. A proposed code of ethics for A.P.G.A. *Personnel guid. J.,* 1959, *38*, 168-170.
7. Gluck, S. et al. A proposed code of ethics for counselors. *Occupations,* 1952. *30*, 484-490.
8. Hahn, M. E. and MacLean, M. S. *Counseling Psychology.* New York: McGraw-Hill Book Co., 1955.
9. Mitchell, H. E. A brief history of an interdisciplinary relationship. *J. couns. Psychol.,* 1955, *2*, 201-204.
10. Rogers, C. R. The characteristics of a helping relationship. *Personnel guid J.,* 1958, *37*, 6-16.
11. Schmidt, L. D. Some legal considerations for counseling and clinical psychologists. *J. couns. Psychol.,* 1962, *9*, 35-44.
12. Schwebel, M. Why? unethical practice. *J. couns. Psychol.,* 1955, *2*, 122-128.
13. Shoben, E. J., Jr. Some thoughts on interprofessional relationships, *J. couns. Psychol.,* 1955, *2*, 196-201.
14. Smith, Carol E. *Development of Ethical Standards in the Secondary School Counseling Relationship for the Use of Counseling Information.* Unpublished Doctoral Dissertation, University of Southern California, 1956.
15. Tyler, Leona E. *The Work of the Counselor.* New York: Appleton-Century-Crofts, Inc., 1961.
16. Wrenn, C. G. The ethics of counseling. *Educ. psychol. Measmt.,* 1952, *12*, 161-177.

$$\boxed{33}$$

CONFIDENTIALITY, WHERE IS OUR FIRST OBLIGATION?

Robert F. Cox

Guidance Counselor, Susquehannock Jr.-Sr. High School, Glen Rock, Pennsylvania

One concern of many writers in the guidance field has been with the lack of writing on the subject of ethics in counseling. There is a general feeling

Reprinted by permission of the Author and *The School Counselor,* Vol. 12, No. 3, 153-161.

that our desire to emerge as a profession should be matched by a greater desire to identify ourselves as a group with a code of ethics. My concern in this paper is with the narrower area of confidentiality and I would like to further limit the content to certain aspects of confidentiality as they apply to the actual counseling relationship.

There is much to be said about the proper confidential use of test results, student records, and transcript materials. But the basic area in guidance is still the counselor's office and the area of basic interest still centers in the activities that take place in this office between the counselor and the counselee. It is here that the distinction is made between the professional counselor and the teacher who asks questions. It is here that the student decides for himself whether he can find someone who is here to accept him where he is and help him go where he wants to go, or whether he will find someone who is likely to look upon him as an object of curiosity and who will probably see to it that others share in approval or disapproval of what the student says. It is here he will decide whether this person he faces is here to help or to see to it that the school, which possibly may be the source of his troubles, is aware of his wrongdoing and that it has its will enforced. It is here he decides whether this is a fellow he can talk to. And if he decides this is not a fellow there is not much else in the guidance program, no matter how elaborate it may be, that justifies its existence.

Actually much of this student's decision has been made before he enters the office. He will have heard what happened to those who came to this office before him. He will have noticed whether the teachers by their words, their actions, or even by their looks have had access to information some of this student's friends have confided to the counselor. He will have noticed an administrative action which could only have originated in the guidance office. He will know of the pregnant girl who took her troubles to the counselor and found herself suddenly asked to leave school. He will know of the prank that was stopped before it happened and he will have some idea of the source of action that stopped it. He very often will have formed an idea of the reception the secret that so plagues him would receive if he were to share it with this man in the guidance office.

We say he has formed an opinion based on what he has seen and heard. He hasn't heard everything. He hasn't heard of all the times the counselor kept a secret. He doesn't know that this particular counselor subscribes to the practice of confidentiality as outlined by Bordin (2). "The counselor's decision will depend upon such a characteristic of the situation as whether the client came to him voluntarily or at the request of the administrator who expects that the counselor will make a report or recommendation to him," or "Where the information requested is of a general sort that might easily be obtained from many sources, and where the counselor feels he is in no position to press upon the administration the distinction between a counselor's responsibility to an administrator and his responsibility to a client, the counselor would probably accede to the administrator's request even when it comes without the client's knowledge." (p. 37) In short, he doesn't know that the counselor has decided in those cases the student has heard about that, in these cases, it wasn't worth fighting city hall. He doesn't know that this counselor figures he must weigh each confidence and decide which to pass on and which to retain.

But what if the counselor felt that the student should know this? What if he made it his policy to do as Wrenn said he would do in the creed he inserted in a speech to the NVGA in 1947? (9) "I will define my personal and ethical responsibility to my client as well as my legal and vocational responsibility to my organization and to society. I work for both the group to which I am responsible and for each individual that I serve as a client. This dual responsibility must be defined and understood by my employers and by myself." (p. 167) What if the student is made to realize that this counselor feels he must report some things, just as, as Thorne (8) points out, doctors must report tuberculosis, veneral disease, and gunshot wounds? Would our student go to the doctor with his VD until the consequences of not going were greater than those of going? What purpose does it serve, other than to clear the counselor's conscience, to serve notice that you must repeat some things you hear, but that you are unable to tell before you hear them which ones you will have to repeat?

Or what if our student finds himself facing the counselor who has rationalized his actions by telling himself that he is dealing with a minor and thus knows better than he what must be done with this information? Wrenn (9) believes that, "A child's trust in a counselor may be betrayed as well as an adult's," and that "A child is very much a person and the integrity of his personality must be protected. . . " (p. 172) I quote Wrenn here with what seems a rather obvious statement mainly because I am continually surprised by the number of counselors who seem to think that being a child is very different from being a person.

So far we have sent our student to: a counselor about whom he has heard tales of confidence violating, a counselor who makes it clear that he may have to violate confidence, and a counselor who considers him a child with little right of decision. Ethical considerations aside for the moment, how is our student likely to react to each of the three? There are, of course, all types of students and possibly all types of reactions. But is it not possible that, with the first type of counselor, no matter how justified the reasons for the broken confidences that the student has heard about, and no matter how much the counselor hastens to assure that, in this case, he will not repeat what he hears, our student will have no trust, and will relate nothing of his true feeling?

Is it not possible that, with the counselor who lays his cards on the table and admits he is going to be forced to repeat some of what he hears, the student will share what he knows to be harmless, but retain what he feels really threatens him? This, I would judge, is the most common reaction. It makes possible most of our present day vocational and educational counseling. It identifies the counselor as a likable, well meaning, and rather harmless fellow, but it does not provide the troubled student with the setting of strength and security wherein he can emotionally undress and change his psychological clothing.

Is it possible that, while there are a considerable number of youngsters, depending on age and home background, who desire to be considered children and who want to place themselves in the hands of an authority figure who will take complete charge of them and their problems, doing with both as they please, the majority of the students we work with will avoid any contact with this type of counselor?

Here I would like to propose a fourth counselor, a counselor who can say to his client that he has never repeated a confidence without the consent of the client, and that he never intends to. I believe that it is possible to be a counselor in a public school and operate without repeating confidences. I intend to discuss the arguments against such a program of operation in their proper places later in this paper, but, in this section of the paper, I will limit myself to the statement that I believe we not only can, but must be ready to make this assurance to our counselees. If we are content to restrict ourselves to vocational and educational counseling our present approach is enough to serve the purpose. But if we are going to attempt to promote ourselves to junior-grade psychotherapy, we can no longer operate as school employed investigators. We can't ask the student to tell us all and refuse to assure him that we are not going to use this information against him or to effect a change in his life that he does not want. We can't go in to the interview as agents and protectors of the school and ask the student to have faith in our good will as he attacks the school. We must be prepared to tell him that, as far as the world beyond the closed door is concerned, what he has said has not been said.

We must, at the same time, make this so definite and so clear that he will not be tempted to test us to his own detriment. To take the extreme, you want to make sure the fellow that threatens suicide is not going to be counting on you to thwart his attempt. You want to be sure that he understands that telling you about a future or past robbery does not relieve him of the responsibility of possessing the knowledge.

This, the fourth, counselor would be there for the sole purpose of counseling — of listening, of helping the student in his efforts to gather and organize a body of facts and ideas that will aid him in his attempt to solve, or at least deal with, his own problems. If this counselor is to be a manipulator, as most of us to some degree are, let him confine his manipulation to the counseling office, or to the outside only with the client's complete consent. To take the pregnant girl as an example: the counselor would first listen, and in listening try to guide the girl into her own working out of the problem. We will say here that it becomes apparent to the counselor that the girl really wants to go with the boy to face her parents, but that she is very much afraid. We will say also that the counselor, during the course of the session, comes to feel strongly that this would be the best thing to do. The counselor must first sit there patiently, maybe nudging a little in a subtle way here and there, while the girl tries to talk herself into the needed nerve. If the counselor sees this failing, he might start to manipulate within the counseling office by actively urging the girl to see the parents, or in suggesting that the girl invite the equally scared young man to come in with her to see the counselor. If the fear is still so great that action is impossible, the counselor may go so far in manipulating beyond the office door as to offer to go along with the pair if he feels this might accomplish the desired goal. But here he must stop. If the offer is rejected, he must realize that this is all he can do. He must realize that, no matter how tragic the outcome or how strong his feelings, if he manipulates without consent he is no longer a counselor. If he manipulates without consent the next pregnant girl will probably not give him a chance to offer to be of help.

This counselor can operate in this manner only if he subscribes to three basic principles: 1. That he, the counselor, will know in his mind how he will handle all confidential information before he asks the counselee to reveal that information. 2. That he will see to it by his actions and his words that client knows exactly how the counselor will deal with confidential information. And 3. That the counselor will under no circumstances depart from this policy, at whatever cost to himself or to his client.

THE COUNSELOR'S RESPONSIBILITY TO THE SCHOOL AND SOCIETY

The fourth counselor that I have been advocating rather clearly places his obligation to the client above his obligation to school or society. Although I am traveling quite a bit farther from an allegiance to society than they would condone, I find the ethical principles outlined by the American Psychological Association (1) establish a rather firm base on which to build. "The psychologist's ultimate allegiance is to society. . . In nearly all circumstances, the welfare of the public, of the profession and of the individual psychologist can best be served by placing highest value on the immediate responsibility of the psychologist. . . In service, the responsibility of most weight is the welfare of the client with whom the psychologist is working. (p. 2) When information received in confidence reveals clear and imminent danger that the client may do serious harm to himself or to others, intervention by the psychologist may be required. . . Otherwise, information obtained in professional work must be kept in confidence, recognizing that the clinical or consulting relationship can develop most fully only in an atmosphere of trust, and that the psychologist can serve society most effectively not by revealing confidences of antisocial events or intentions but by helping the individual realize himself as a socially competent and responsible person." (p. 5)

The "clear and imminent danger" part must be discussed before I can justify my stand, but the rest of the statement goes far in establishing that I am best serving society by serving the individual.

The American School Counselor Association isn't as definite about the subject. I did find a suggested code of ethics published in May of 1961 in which Mary Flanagan (3) suggests, "The counselor is primarily responsible to the counselee, then to the school, and ultimately to society and its institutions, unless there is a conflict with the legal statutes or accepted mores of the community, or when the status or reputation of the school or its students is in question. . ." (p. 139)

It seems to me that the poor counselor would be so busy worrying about the "accepted mores" and the "status or reputation of the school" that he may have trouble bringing himself to listen to anything more threatening than an observation on the weather. If we must put in all of these unlesses and or whens we might as well not try to set up a code.

Going back to our brothers, the psychologists, who are not as concerned with the accepted mores as more than an environment in which to view their client, we must take some notice of their concern for the fellow who may harm himself or others. What do we do with the information he gives us and will not let us give to anyone else? Schwebel (6) says we clear it with the administration and then go to the psychiatrist, physician or legal authority, but he acknowledges that the occasions when this is necessary are rare. Ohlsen (4) says that the counselor who breaks confidence to protect others should refer his counselee to another counselor because, "When he turns against the pupil to protect others, he destroys the counseling relationship." (p. 288) Patterson (5) says each counselor must decide for himself in each case. I can't find anyone who says that the counselor should keep it to himself.

But what if the counselor, as in one of our cases in class, is told by a girl that she is going to elope? We will say he feels this is wrong, but fails to talk the girl out of it. He calls the home and prevents the elopement. He feels he is justified because he has prevented her from doing harm to herself. But who asked him? The girl is carrying a problem around. She wants to think it through and has heard that the guidance office is a good place for this sort of activity. Unless this sort of thing happens often and she has heard that the counselor will take some action on what is said, she goes there looking for a place to talk and to think and maybe to even listen to what someone thinks of her elopement plans. She talks and listens to his arguments against her plan, and then she decided she will elope. She has asked for nothing more. She has brought a problem with her, examined it, gotten an opinion from the counselor and taken *her* problem on out of the office. What justification does the counselor have for listening? If she had chosen not to bring the problem to his office, he would never have heard about it. If she had not been led to believe that the counselor would not take any action she would probably not have brought the problem. So the problem is not his, but he makes it his. Now he assumes his God-playing role. He is so sure he is right he takes an action that can strongly alter the lives of at least two people, and he takes this action on the limited information he has heard in an interview. Are all elopements wrong? Is this one wrong for these two people? Are these parents right in this case? What is the right age to marry? What is the right age for these people to marry? Does he know enough to make a reasonable decision? Does he know enough to start fooling around with the lives of these two people uninvited?

He has called the parents, the elopement is off. The grateful parents tell their friends about the fine thing the counselor did. The friends discuss the affair over the supper table in front of the family. The family brings it back to school. Now who else is going to tell the counselor about their elopement plans, and who else is going to tell the counselor about the baby she is carrying? And how much help will this counselor be able to be to the others who might have been helped by the talking and the listening, but who now will not bring their problems to this adult who acts just like so many of the other adults and can be trusted no farther?

I see the counselor as one of a few with a very special job. There are many others in the school to enforce the school regulations. There are many others in society to enforce society's regulations and to see that right is done by society. Can we not afford a comparatively very small budgetary allotment for someone who will use a comparatively very small amount of school space to sit and concentrate his full allegiance on that most important institution, the individual?

While there is admittedly room for debate in the question of breaking confidence to prevent future harm, it seems only the more conservative educators still argue that the counselor must report harm that has been done. Most of our writers seem to feel pretty much as Ohlsen (4) does in the following passage: ". . . in his dealing with things which have already happened, which have no possibilities of dangerous future action . . . it is *not* the responsibility of the counselor to make sure that society's 'justice is done.' His first responsibility is to the person who seeks his help in achieving a better way of adjusting to life." (p. 289)

In summing up the section on responsibility to school and society with regard to confidentiality, we note the following points: 1. While saying that the psychologist's ultimate allegiance is to society, the APA states that society is best served by honoring the confidence of the individual. 2. That it is generally agreed that reporting of past antisocial action is not the counselor's responsibility. 3. While there is some justification for believing the counselor might break confidence to prevent future harm to self and others, there is caution against rushing to assume a God playing role and there is the strong possibility that great damage will be done to the counselor's future ability to be of help because potential counselees will fear similar confidence breaking.

THE COUNSELOR'S RELATIONS WITH THE SCHOOL STAFF

Our question here has been stated by Wrenn (10) "When fellow counselors, teachers, administrators inquire about a counselee, how does the counselor keep their good will while maintaining the integrity of his relationship with the student?" (p. 182)

We may first ask if we can ethically tell them anything. Mary Flanagan (3) in her suggested code of ethics says, "The counselor will not discuss case matters or information obtained from a counselee with anyone outside or within his profession except as it is necessary to the welfare of the counselee or the ultimate solution of his problem." (p. 139)

It is noted that she does not say anything about consent. Our psychologist brothers give a little more respect to the client in their statement of principles. (1) "The psychologist should give clinical information about a client only to professional persons whom the client might reasonably be expected to consider a party to the psychologist's efforts to help him, and the client's concurrence should be obtained before there is any communication exceeding these customary limits." (p. 6)

Patterson (5) acknowledges a fact that most counselors feel when he cautions that most teachers are not to be considered "professional persons" and warns against giving information to them without the consent of the counselee.

While the general findings of counselors with regard to policies of the school and to education in general should certainly be given to the staff and administrators in the hope of improving the school, there is no need to associate this information to any particular student or incident. If the administrator must take some action with regard to the client and asks the counselor for his opinion, it would seem to me that the counselor could give his opinion only if it were based totally on facts gained outside of the interview. If his opinion is based on information from the interview the counselor must obtain the consent of the counselee to venture the opinion. Any discussion with fellow counselors should have the counselee's consent.

By now the reader is probably saying that this is all very professional and fine sounding, but what about that "good will" that Wrenn mentioned? This counselor must work with these teachers, this principal and these counselors. They are often his friends. Can he get away with being this secretive? He often depends on these same teachers for background information, upon this principal for support with the school board and in school policy, and upon his fellow counselors for advice and support to the general guidance program. How does he live with these people?

It is very interesting to see the number of books and articles (2, 3, 6, 7, 9, 10) which contain the suggestion that the counselor first look to himself in dealing with this problem. Is he really interested in the welfare of his client as he is in his own welfare? Doesn't he know any better? Schwebel (7) devotes an entire article to this topic and ends up with a list of reasons why counselors so often do the wrong thing. "Practices that are contrary to the best interests of the client appear to stem from (a) the overpowering self-interest of the professional worker as expressed in personal profit, self-enhancement, and the maintenance of security and status. (b) Poor judgment, due in part at least to inexperience in problem solving in counseling. (c) Ignorance of technical knowledge and of one's own values." (p. 128)

The word "courage" comes up often. Sometimes it is courage of a special sort. Marshal Dillon, on the old radio version of "Gunsmoke" would open the program with, "It's a chancy job, and a little bit lonely." He, of course, was talking about his job as marshal, but he could just as easily be talking about the counselor's job. The counselor must be prepared to take chances in his protection of confidence. The student tells him he cheated on the last exam, the counselor keeps this information to himself, the student is later caught and announces that he had told the counselor all about it. The girl says she is going to run away, the counselor doesn't repeat the information, the girl runs away, and the counselor wonders what he should have done. It's a chancy job. And the counselor must have the courage to take some chances.

And it is a lonely job. How many people want to admit publicly that they ever had problems, much less point you out as the one who helped them solve these problems? Are the girls who invite you to their weddings the ones who knew you mainly as a nice person around school, or the ones who discussed their sexual problems with you? A good counselor is seldom a public hero. Might it then be natural that our counselor, after a rough day in the counseling office, wants to go to the faculty room and be accepted by his fellow faculty members. And is it not an easy way to draw attention to one's self by repeating something interesting you have just heard in the counseling office, while at the time rationalizing the repetition as a professional discussion with a fellow professional with the future good of the counselee as its aim?

As we must have the courage to take chances, we must also have the courage to be at least professionally lonely.

Often this matter of living with these co-workers successfully is one of gaining their respect for counseling as a profession. Wrenn (9) presents this argument rather concisely, "If people generally are to regard counseling with respect because counselors consider themselves to be professional men, then the members of this profession must have a clear understanding of its social purpose and obligation. So long as the counseling function is merely an arm or a projection of some institution there is little problem, for under these conditions it tacitly adopts the principles and procedures of its parent organization. If, however, counseling is to operate independently or is to have professional independence within an institution then its status as an independent profession demands a clear understanding of its ethical obligation." (p. 162-63) Thus, the counselor I have been advocating, who must have professional indepedence to operate as I have outlined, must identify himself as a professional, and make it clear to those around him that he is acting according to the principles of his profession, not by personal whim. The question of acceptance will then center on the professional and not on the counselor. Once the profession is accepted, the counselor's task is much easier, and his own acceptance becomes a matter of his own personality and not of his performance of his job.

In summing up the section on the counselor's relations with the school staff, we note the following points: 1. Although he may generalize the findings from a number of interviews in making suggestions with regard to school or educational policy, he may repeat actual contents of specific interviews only with the consent of the counselee. 2. The counselor must examine his own motives when tempted to reveal confidential material to a fellow worker and must have the courage to take chances in holding back information and the courage to experience the professional loneliness that often accompanies the keeping of confidence. 3. The counselor must identify himself as a professional, and make it clear that he is operating according to the principles of his profession.

SUMMARY

I have in this paper advocated a counselor that possibly doesn't exist in any school today. I know he doesn't exist in mine. But I believe that, if we are ever to do a really effective job of counseling and overcome some of the handicaps that have been set up for us and some of those that we have set up for ourselves, we must adopt and adapt the following points:

1. The counselor must know how he will handle all confidential interview information before the counselee enters his office, and he must be determined that under no circumstnces will he depart from that policy.

2. The counselor must see to it that by his actions and his words the client will know exactly how the counselor will deal with confidential information.

3. The counselor best serves society by honoring the confidence of the individual.

4. The counselor has no responsibility to report past anti-social action.

5. The counselor should make every effort to avoid the breaking of confidence to prevent the client's harming of self or others, knowing that by the breaking of such confidence he is jeopardizing his future effectiveness.

6. The counselor's responsibility to the school administration and staff should include only the reporting of generalized conclusions from numbers of interviews as they affect school and educational policy.

7. The counselor must examine his own motives for revealing confidential information, and must have the courage to take chances and risk professional loneliness.

8. The counselor must identify himself as a professional, and make it clear that he is operating according to the principles of his profession.

REFERENCES

1. American Psychological Association, *Ethical Standards of Psychologists, a Summary of Ethical Principles,* Washington, D. C., 1953.
2. Bordin, Edward S., *Psychological Counseling,* Appleton-Century-Crofts, Inc., New York, 1955.
3. Flanagan, Mary M. and McGrew, David R., A Suggested Code of Ethics for School Counselors, *The School Counselor,* Vol. 8, May, 1961, 136-141.
4. Ohlsen, Merle M., *Guidance, an Introduction,* Harcourt, Brace and Company, New York, 1955.
5. Patterson, C. H., *Counseling and Psychotherapy, Theory and Practice,* Harper & Brothers, New York, 1959.
6. Schwebel, Milton, Some Ethical Problems in Counseling, *The Personnel and Guidance Journal,* Vol. 33, Jan., 1955, 254-259.
7. Schwebel, Milton, Why Unethical Practices?, *Journal of Counseling Psychology,* Vol. 2, Summer, 1955, 122-128.
8. Thorne, F. C., *Principles of Personality Counseling,* Journal of Clinical Psychology, Brandon, Vermont, 1950.
9. Wrenn, C. Gilbert, The Ethics of Counseling, *Educational and Psychological Measurement,* Vol. 12, Summer, 1952, 161-177.
10. Wrenn, C. Gilbert, Status and Role of the School Counselor, *The Personnel and Guidance Journal,* Vol. 36, Nov., 1957, 175-183.

$$\boxed{34}$$

MORAL VALUES ACROSS CULTURES

M. Robert B. Klinger

Counselor, The International Center, University of Michigan, Ann Arbor

It is an axiom for many counselors that they need to know as much as possible about the counselees and their past and present environment to be effective in counseling. Some of the most perplexing problems brought to a counselor deal with a clash of moral values between the individual and a group. A counselor could aid his understanding and counseling effectiveness if he knew more about the moral codes of the clients with whom he is dealing. Mueller [2] postulated that "The first dimension to be explored by the counselor is the specific hierarchy of values and standards in the student population with which he deals." For the foreign student adviser this would include knowledge about the moral values arising out of the cultures from which the foreign students come.

Reprinted by permission of the Author and the *Personnel and Guidance Journal,* October 1962, 139-143.

The client may need counseling when:

1. society in general disapproves of the group norm, and the client has committed an "offense" by adhering to such a group norm;

2. the group to which the client feels he belongs disapproves of an individual's deviation from its norms — the client has committed an "offense" by violating a group norm;

3. the client needs education in the norms of his group;

4. the client is moving from one cultural group to another and therefore may be violating the norms of the group from which he is moving, may not know the norms of the group to which he is moving, and may be violating the norms of this new group.

The problems of foreign students will appear in any of the above classifications but may be further aggravated by differences in culture. The foreign student counselor will also find his work more complicated because he lacks knowledge of the norms of the other culture.

The study reported here is an attempt to distinguish between certain foreign student groups at the University of Michigan from American students as to expressed moral values and to determine preliminarily the structures and dimensions organizing the expressed values into larger entities.

THE INSTRUMENT, SUBJECTS, AND PROCEDURES

A questionnaire was developed based on the Scale of Student Behavior by Mueller [2] which used participal phrases describing "offenses" that students "committed" within the experience of Mueller as Dean of Women at the University of Indiana. Additional "offenses" were added from those that had been "committed" by foreign students at the University of Michigan over the past two decades as found in the files of the International Center.[1]

The first revised scale was used in a pilot study with 4 students from India. Through this experience, certain items were changed so the vocabulary would better fit a cross-cultural situation. Items were added that might be considered as "good" things to do by some groups and the scale was changed to cover both the positive and the negative values. The questionnaire in its final form had 130 items clustered a priori by groups ("driving violations," "premarital sex," "school rules," etc.) A table of random numbers was used to rearrange the items so as to avoid the a priori clustering.

The subjects for the analyses were all at the University of Michigan and included 70 United States Protestant high school graduates who were at the University for summer orientation prepararatory to enrollment in the fall semester, 50 United States Protestant graduate students, 50 Arab Moslems, 53 Chinese non-Christians, 86 Indian Hindus, 53 South American Roman Catholics from Columbia and Venezuela, and 63 Turkish Moslems. All sub-

---

[1]The question can be posed as to what is meant by a "moral value." For this study, and several similar ones, the "moral-immoral" dichotomy is taken to represent "good-bad," "praiseworthy-condemned," "legal-illegal," etc. The inclusion of certain items arose because in some cultures "offenses" appear that, to us, are not "bad" — "borrowing" in some cultures is almost as bad as "stealing," "speeding" is relative and can create felonious conditions, "not voting" is punished in some countries by law and by social pressure.

jects were males, the groups were each of the same religion, all subjects were of college age (18-28) and most were "middle class" for all groups.

Four methods of analysis were used: (1) a count of the number of items on which each group had low standard deviations as determined by the significance of the difference between standard deviations at the 0.01 level of significance; (2) a count of the number of items on which each group differed from each other group as determined by the significance of the difference between means at the 0.01 level of significance; (3) an analysis of the a priori clusters by comparing each foreign student group with the American graduate student group as to the significance of the difference between the means; and (4) an analysis of dimensions or structures by elementary linkage analysis.

The first method was used to distinguish for each group whether two sub-groups differed on "code-cohesiveness" which is defined as the amount of agreement on expressed moral values by a group. The second method was used to distinguish the relative severity (as to whether a given value statement is felt to be more "bad" or "good" thing to do) or leniency (as to whether a given value statement is felt to be less a "bad" or "good" thing to do) for each group in comparison with all other groups. The third method was used to determine those items and areas on which each foreign student group differed from the American Protestant graduate students.

The fourth method, elementary linkage analysis, deserves fuller description as it is a relatively new statistical tool. Correlations between each of the 130 items for each group were analyzed; typal structures were derived and typal relevancies were computed according to McQuitty's methods [1]. Basically, typal structures in the present study are clusters of items formed by linkage of each item with that item with which it has the highest correlation. The submatrices of related items are then analyzed for typal relevancies by extracting the first factor and calculating the derived loadings. Typal structures are similar to factors in factor analysis; and typal relevancies are similar to rotated factor loadings. The typal structures for each group were compared with those for each other group to determine whether any of them were similar to other structures. This was used as an approximation of a test of invariance of structures. For each group, therefore, there were described cross-group structures — those found in most or all other groups — and group structures — those not found in most or all other groups.

RESULTS[2]

In general, when standard deviations are analyzed, groups agree more on values when they are older, married, and further advanced in education. Foreign students agree more on values when they first come to the United States than after they have been here: the sojourn apparently leads to greater variation among them. Among all groups, political action in the form of voting is a good thing to do, and mobs or violence are generally bad. Telling a "white lie," borrowing when out of cash, and buying merchandise on credit are accepted but are neither good nor bad.

---

[2]There are close to 70 tables in the original study. All tables are omitted from this brief resume as even a selection of the tables would make this article too long.

On most moral judgments there is a range of responses on items that would cause agreement between some people from the extreme of any one group and some people in another group.

Certain structures (similar to factors as previously described) were found that appear to be similar across cultures leading to the conclusion that there are larger entities than individual values and larger entities than groups of values generally considered to be value-clusters. For all seven student groups premarital sexual behavior seems to be a similar structure, and for six of the groups obedience to rules and having obligations to others are similar structures overriding the included clusters.

The United States Graduate Protestants

When compared to the foreign students, the majority of the United States Graduate Protestants tend to be less severe in judging actions as bad or other actions as best. They differ most from the Indians and least from the Chinese. The majority tend to be less strict than all foreign groups on school and classroom rules, room cleanliness, and nakedness. They show racial bias in tending to consider it bad to marry a person from another race. Structure analysis grouped most items in five large structures: the cross-group structure of "premarital sexual behavior"; the similar structure for the United States Pre-Freshman Protestants of "good character"; the similar structure for the Indian Hindus of "self-improvement"; the similar structure for the Turkish Moslems of "group membership and leadership"; and a separate structure of "authority-based rules."

The Arab Moslems

The majority of the Arab Moslem group is the most severe of all in its judgment of what is very right or very wrong. The majority tends to consider it more wrong to disobey minor rules, to be naked, not to be clean in one's room, or to be prejudiced. Only on two items are they less strict than the United States Graduate Protestants: helping others even though inconvenient and marrying a person from another race.

Structure analysis grouped the items in 10 large structures: the cross-group structures of "obeying minor rules," "obligations to others," and "premarital sexual behavior"; and the separate structures of "carefulness and courtesy," "drinking prohibitions," "mannerly behavior," "personal constraint," "personal integrity," and "reputation."

The Chinese Non-Christians

The majority of the Chinese students tend to differ from the United States Graduate Protestants in expressing themselves as being more strict on school rules, cleanliness, vandalism, overriding ambition, and tardiness; they tend to be more lenient on religious items.

Seven large structures are found by structure analysis: the three cross-group structures of "obeying minor rules," "obligations to others," and "premarital sexual behavior"; three separate structures on "basic conventional principles," "modesty and sex," and "ungentlemanly behavior"; and one separate structure left unnamed because of the lack of sufficient data.

The Indian Hindus

The Indians are most different from other groups, as regards both means and standard deviations, which difference may lead to proportionately more misunderstandings.

The majority of the Indians tend to differ from the United States Graduate Protestants in expressing themselves as more strict on driving, family, job, and school rules, loyalty, cleanliness, nakedness, and tardiness they tend to be more lenient on religion and habit-forming drugs.

Structure analysis brought out six structures: the three general cross-group structures of "obeying minor rules," "obligations to others," and "premarital sexual behavior"; one in common with the United States Graduate Protestants: "self-improvement"; and two separate structures: "protecting one's reputation" and "trustworthiness."

The South American Roman Catholics

With the majority of the Turks, the majority of the South Americans are more lenient in general than are the other foreign student groups. They tend to express themselves as more strict on job rules. They tend to express themselves as less strict and consider having premarital sexual relations as good.

Five large and one included small structures are found by analysis: the three cross-group structures of "obeying minor rules," "obligations to others," and "premarital sexual behavior"; two separate structures: "religion and self-control" and "trustworthiness and restraint"; and one structure left unnamed for lack of data.

The Turkish Moslems (Engineers)

The majority of the Turks are, with the majority of the South Americans, one of the most lenient groups in their expressed values. They do not appear to have much in comomn as to the strictness or leniency with the other Moslem group, the Arabs, except for agreeing on modesty — that all forms of nakedness with either sex are bad.

The majority of Turks tend to express themselves as more strict than the United States Graduate Protestants on tardiness and nakedness. They tend to be somewhat less strict but still judge as bad the use of habit-forming drugs. They tend to be more lenient in considering premarital sexual behavior a good thing. They are also more lenient on religion.

Five large and one small included structures emerge from analysis: four cross-group structures, "obeying minor rules," two for "obligations to others," and the small structure on "premarital sexual behavior"; the structure similar to the United States Graduate Protestants on "group leadership and membership"; and a separate structure on "group behavior."

United States Pre-Freshman Protestants

The majority of United States Pre-Freshman Protestants, the youngest of all and presumably therefore least mature, are the most lenient of all. They tend to be more lenient than the foreign groups on nakedness, obeying job rules, slander, stealing, and vandalism. As with the graduates they are more strict than the foreign students on racial bias in considering it wrong to marry a person from another race.

Six large structures emerge from analysis: two cross-group structures on "obeying minor rules" and "premarital sexual behavior"; the structure similar to the other American group on "good character"; and three separate structures on "consideration for one's reputation," "group expectations," and "responsibilities."

IMPLICATIONS FOR THE COUNSELOR

There are several implications from this study for the counselor who deals with foreign students:

1. Despite certain cultural similarities, the differences among foreign students as individuals, even among those from the same country, may be considerable. It is, therefore, dangerous to say "foreign students" or even "Indian students," for example. The generalization "Indian student" may describe a better entity than "foreign student" but the range of difference is still great. Even with a fuller description, such as "Indian Hindu Brahmans, from Bombay, whose fathers are civil servants, who are studying civil engineering, and who are 23 years old, unmarried," there still will be a wide range of individual differences.

2. A violation or offense on some one rule, regulation, or other unit of moral values may not be an isolated violation but may be indicative of a more lenient standard on many other units of values, some not apparently related. Or, to go to the opposite extreme, a strict standard on some other unit of moral values may be indicative of a more strict standard on many other units.

3. There are certain behaviors that appear to be condemned by all groups, such as the use of habit-forming drugs or drunk driving. A foreign student probably would be fabricating if he said he committed such an offense because it is acceptable in his home country.

4. There are certain actions that appear to be extremely different for various cultures. For example, most Latin American Roman Catholics from Northern South America and most Turks tend to feel that premarital sexual activity is expected of them.

5. The local American citizens in the university community are likely to find most Indian Hindus "very different," Arab Moslems "too strict," Turks and Latins "too lenient in drinking and sexual behavior."

6. Perhaps an unexpressed reason for many older foreign students to be somewhat unhappy in a dormitory situation is the general practice of many residents going down the halls to the shower naked, or otherwise being "immodest."

7. Foreign students from some countries who swim may be hard put to find a pool on many campuses where they can really enjoy this sport because of the requirement of "no suits in the pool."

8. Restrictions on many campuses against drinking may be a source of friction for the administration in dealing with Latin Americans and Turks, and with some Chinese.

9. The faculty should be pleased at the attention most foreign students give to minor rules such as not cutting classes, being prepared, and not cheat-

ing. A foreign student caught violating these rules may be as severely condemned by his fellow countrymen as by the teacher or administrator. In fact, he may accept any punishment imposed if only the delinquency will be kept hidden from his group.

10. There are differences in dating behavior among the foreign students. The foreign male with few, if any, girls from his own country will expect dates. The differences may cause difficulties for the American girls unless orientation is given them. Many Indians may not date and some of those who do date may be "too different" for the American coed. The Arab may be "too strict" but could be expected to be "the gentleman." The Turk or Latin American may create difficulties in dating so that the girl will need to use all of her internal controls; but, if the man can find she is not available sexually, he would be likely to give her a good time. Dating the Chinese would be most like going with the majority of Americans. Again, in all groups, individual differences may far outweigh likenesses.

11. Proselytizing Protestant religious groups can expect to find themselves rebuffed by the majority of Arab Moslems, Indian Hindus, and possibly Turks. They might find themselves proselytized in return by some Latin American Roman Catholics who may try to gain converts even among "the home missionaries." Only with the Chinese can they expect to gain much acceptance and here the job would be to get them "to believe."

12. It is necessary to warn the counselor not to extend these findings to other groups — to Europeans or Africans, or other Asians, or other Latin Americans. There are dangers in extending these findings even to his own local students since they are based upon University of Michigan students. Much more study is needed and, even then, the individual is still unique and defies generalization.

REFERENCES

1. McQuitty, Louis L. Elementary linkage analysis for isolating orthogonal and oblique types and typal relevancies. *Educ. psychol. Measmt.*, 1957, 17.
2. Mueller, Kate Hevner. Theory for campus discipline. *Personnel guid. J.*, 1958, 36, 302-309.

(35)

METAPHYSICS, RELIGION, AND PSYCHOTHERAPY

Orville S. Walters[1,2]

University of Illinois

In the physical sciences, the swing from a thesis of prescientific speculation to the antithesis of a cocksure empiricism has been followed by a

Reprinted by permission of the Author and the *Journal of Counseling Psychology*, Vol. 5, No. 4, 1958, 243-252.

[1]Part of a symposium presented September 1, 1958 at the annual meeting of the American Psychological Association, Washington, D. C. In an earlier form this paper was presented at the 1957 Conference of Administrators of College and University Counseling Services, University of Illinois, November 5, 1957.

[2]The author is Director of Health Services at the University of Illinois. *Ed.*

wholesome heuristic humility in search of a synthesis. The resurgence of an attitude that is willing to acknowledge aspects of reality beyond the reach of science has been recognized both by its opponents and its advocates.

Hook (19), in describing this trend, comments: "In the schools, the churches, and in the literary arts the tom-tom of theology and the bagpipes of transcendental metaphysics are growing more insistent and shrill." He contends that "the refurbishing of theological and metaphysical dogmas about the infinite as necessary presuppositions of knowledge about the finite" indicates a latter-day "failure of nerve."

Flewelling (13), on the ther hand, declares that "the traditional abrogation of metaphysics by science has been brought to sudden pause." Citing the philosophical implications of relativity, indeterminacy and the new significance of the observer in physical phenomena, he concludes, "The positivistic philosophies, in faithful obedience to the dogmas of a discarded science, still 'hold the sack' waiting for the materialistic rabbit, while contemporary science approaches a new personalism."

METAPHYSICS AND THE SCIENCE OF MAN

The sciences of man have been slow in reflecting this change. The pendulum has swung from psychology's early identification with metaphysical philosophy to an extreme empiricism. As Borow (7) has expressed it, "When psychology joined the company of the experimental sciences, it embraced empiricism with a vengeance." There is increasing conviction that an ultimate synthesis will require recovery of some of the elements that were rejected by psychology in the process of achieving recognition as a science.

Psychology becomes most deeply involved in metaphysical issues when it turns to the treatment of personality ills. Contemporary psychotherapy is confronted by a question that has far-reaching theoretical and practical implications: What is to be the place of metaphysics in psychotherapy? At opposite poles are those who are trying to "exorcise the metaphysical gremlin," (7) and those who hold that "at the bottom of every neurosis there is a metaphysical problem" (2).

Some of psychology's reluctance to modify an empiricistic rigidity is traceable to the influence of Freud. In his lecture, "A Philosophy of Life," Freud (15, p .203) asserts the adequacy of science to achieve a full understanding of personality. While acknowledging that the world view of science is incomplete, he disdains and disparages the constructs of philosophy that would offer a more complete tentative picture of the universe. He denies any validity to philosophy and religion, and stakes out "the whole field of human activity" as the exclusive province of science.

Much of the psychotherapy now being taught and practiced has its roots in the Freudian system. Freud's personal philosophy has often been tacitly regarded as a part of psychoanalysis, although there is evidence that he himself acknowledged the separability of the two (26). Because they are frequently interwoven, Freud's reductive naturalism and the principles of psychoanalysis have had widespread influence upon American psychology and psychiatry.

Some of the present-day protests against this influence are voiced by Stern (41) and Maritain (22), who see Freud's reductionism currently producing a devaluation of man, contempt for the spirit and a loss of the meta-physical sense. Stern states that when divested of its Freudian positivism, psychoanalysis contains a movement toward personalism.

Freud's renunciation of metaphysics in favor of science has been continued and reinforced by some contemporary theoreticians. Feigl (12) lumps theology and metaphysics with magic, animism and mythology and describes them as "remnants of and regressions to . . . prescientific thought patterns." He con-demns the "something more" philosophy as a "seductive fallacy" and rejects the assertions of transcendent theology and metaphysics as "largely emotive."

PSYCHOTHERAPY AS APPLIED SCIENCE

The practice of psychotherapy plunges psychology into metaphysical issues. There is general agreement that science cannot determine values. The function of science is to observe, describe and classify what *is,* but not to decide what *ought to be.* Psychology, as long as it remains a pure science, does not make judgment of value. It is when turning to treat maladjustments of human personality that psychology moves away from the canons of scien-tific precision and ventures into the realm of values.

The transition from a pure to an applied science involves a value judgment of major consequence. Such a judgment presumes to differentiate between illness and health, and proposes to use scientific knowledge to displace the one the servant of the ethical judgments and, in some measure, the value system in favor of the other. In psychotherapy, psychology as a science thus becomes the servant of the ethical judgments and, in some measure, the value system of the therapist. As a healer, he seeks the recovery of his patient, sacrificing the neutrality and objectivity of the scientist for a stake in the outcome.

The application of psychological knowledge by one person to modify the attitudes and ideas of another involves the formation of further value judg-ments as to the need, the goal and the method of therapy. The counselor may be called upon, for example, to assist a person who is troubled by con-science. Is this illness or health? Is *any* trouble with conscience compatible with health? If so, how much? And if too much is present, how is the pres-sure of conscience to be abated? How much sensitivity of conscience should be left when the end-point of treatment has been reached?

In an effort to stay close to its scientific base, psychotherapy has concen-trated upon technics of uncovering the patient's conflicts, upon analysis of interviews and upon theories of personality organization. The patient, on the other hand, is struggling with metaphysical concerns: What is the good life? Where does it lead? How much freedom does man have? Are the claims of religion illusion or are they insight into transcendent reality? Before these questions science stands silent, claiming no competence in matters of ethical discrimination, moral responsibility, and ultimate destiny.

Not everyone is willing to concede this inherent limitation in the nature of science. There is confidence that science will ultimately be able to pro-vide a full explanation of the phenomena of the universe, including human behavior. This faith is responsible for most of the opposition toward permit-ting metaphysics to complement the incomplete world view that science now offers.

Freud proclaimed his loyalty to "the scientific *Weltanschauung*," not only staking out "the spirit and the mind" as proper objects of scientific investigation, but specifically rejecting religion and philosophy as collaborators in truth-finding. In this broad repudiation of philosophy, Freud was merely electing a different metaphysical viewpoint and enunciating an impassioned *credo* in the philosophy of scientism.

Feigl (12) similarly scorns "the sham completeness metaphysicians procure for their world pictures by verbal magic" and declares that it is a sign of maturity to be able to live with an unfinished world view. To proclaim such an affirmation of faith in the ultimate adequacy of science is to close the gaps in a science-centered *Weltanschauung* by philosophical scaffolding and to crystallize a unique value system. The unfinished world view is an abstraction. Commitment to something is necessary to existence. Even to repudiate metaphysics is to affirm a significant metaphysical position.

There are many who doubt that science will ever be able to offer a complete world view. Conant (10) expresses this viewpoint:

> As to the unifying, materialistic World Hypothesis, my doubt stems from its manifest inadequacy. As a conceptual scheme attempting to account for everything in the whole universe, it seems to me unsatisfactory because it is incomplete. It fails to provide for the altruistic and idealistic side of human nature.

Freud declared that since psychoanalysis is a part of science, it has no concern with judgments of value. It is no less valid to say that psychoanalysis, psychotherapy and counseling cannot be purely scientific, even though they are grounded in an empirical psychology, since they inescapably involve human values. The limitations of science are apparent wherever human autonomy becomes a variable in a problem.

Zilboorg (49) recognizes that the therapist cannot avoid encounter with philosophical, ethical and moral issues:

> Suffused with anxiety . . . man again is forced to contemplate what it is that he is, what it is that he wants, what it is that he ought to want, and what his place is in relation to his fellow man individually, to society, to himself as an autonomic person. These are ontological, metaphysical and fundamentally religious questions. A psychoanalyst, more than any other professional man, must cultivate a philosophy of values.

NEUROSIS AND WELTANSCHAUUNG

The scientific farmework in which any exploration of neurosis and anxiety begins is soon found to be inadequate to encompass all the phenomena, implicating as they do the values and the world view of the patient.

Masserman, who has produced what he calls "experimental neurosis" in animals, cautions against the drawing of sweeping identities between his experiments and "the almost incomparably more complex dynamics of clinical psychotherapy" (23, p. 458). In the treatment of neurosis, Masserman departs widely from the experimental approach to recommend that the therapist enter into the patient's "personal universe of desires, meaning, values and actions" (23, p. 488).

Rioch (34), in a review of "experimental neurosis" acknowledges that the degree of complexity, modifiability and variability of human behavior is of a different order of magnitude than that in lower forms and refers to Harry Stack Sullivan's contention that anxiety is limited to human beings.

Efforts to understand neurosis apart from an ontology of anxiety have been disappointing. Even after the creation and unrestricted manipulation of his metapsychological constructs, Freud (16, p. 92) concedes:

> We find ourselves abruptly confronted, once again by the oft-repeated riddle: What is the source of neurosis, what is its specific, underlying principle? After decades of analytic effort this problem rises up before us, as untouched as at the beginning.

Shoben (37) formulates a theory of neurosis based upon experimental findings and learning theory. His view of neurosis as a consequence of defective social learning fails to deal with the concept of conscience and superego, and identifies guilt with anxiety.

Mowrer (25, p. 483) draws upon both learning theory and Freudian concepts to elaborate his concept of neurosis, concluding that neurotic persons suffer because they have repudiated their own moral strivings. This makes the undoing of repressions preeminently a moral enterprise.

A similar view was advanced by Pfister (28):

> . . . The repressed conscience plays a still more troublesome role than the known conscience . . . There consequently remains nothing but to purify the known, and, very often, too, the unknown conscience. In every psychoanalytic transaction deserving of the name, it is of great importance to replace the ill-advised with a clear and noble-piercing voice of conscience.

Stekel (39), another of Freud's early pupils, described neurosis as "the disease of a bad conscience" and recognized that somatic complaints could have a similar origin:

> Important is the fact that the voice of conscience may find bodily expression, this being what we call somatization. . . . The psychotherapeutist, taking his patients by the hand, must help them to restore the ideals which, deliberately, or under compulsion, they have destroyed (40).

May, after a detailed examination of the various concepts of anxiety offered by Freud and by the deviant schools of psychoanalysis, formulates a broad definition of anxiety as "the apprehension cued off by a threat to some value which the individual holds essential to his existence as a personality" (24, p. 191). He concludes, "The system of value on the basis of which one confronts normal anxiety . . . broadly speaking . . . is the person's religious attitude toward life" (24, p. 230).

Winkler (44) argues the inadequacy of the leading psychological doctrines of man. Freud saw man as a natural organism, Adler viewed him as a social being and Jung emphasizes him as an individual. "In addition to this," Winkler continues, "he is also a person in the philosophic and theologic sense, and he relates as an individual to the transcendental reality. He can also fail in this regard, producing that which may be labelled 'existential neurosis.'"

Frankl (14) believes that every man has a will-to-meaning, the frustration of which produces existential neurosis. His logotherapy aims to revise the defective world view in terms of meaning and value. "Patients themselves bring us philosophical problems," Frankl writes. ". . . The proper diagnosis can be made only by someone who can see the spiritual side of man."

Progoff (30) traces the progressive emergence of this recognition through Freud, Adler, Jung and Rank. He writes,

> Their psychological investigations led them to a realization of the fundamentally spiritual nature of man. . . . They came in other words, to the metaphysical foundation of life that underlies psychology. . . . Psychological work fulfills itself only when it goes beyond psychology.

While psychological theory is moving to recognize the necessity of active encounter with the patient's value system, a parallel current is influencing the practice of psychotherapy. Pumpian-Mindlin (31) traces the ten-year evolution of practice in a mental hygiene clinic through various stages during which different emphases were found inadequate and dropped, one after another. The expression of hostility by the patient, the giving of love and affection by the therapist, the offering of psychodynamic interpretations and, finally, attempts at ego-integration, were all pronounced "not enough." In the continuing search for a more adequate approach, Pumpian-Mindlin concludes, "We must examine our culture and our values and those of our patients. We msut see how these affect the 'self,' the total person."

A similar awareness is apparent on a social scale. Schindler (36) holds that many personality disturbances are caused by "confusion on a spiritual level," growing out of cataclysmic events in the past few decades that have brought the fundamental questions of human existence to the psychiatrist's attention. May (24, p. 109), in applying Mowrer's concept of neurosis, observes: "The repression of guilt feelings, with its concomitant generation of neurotic anxiety . . . in some ways is pervasive of our culture as a whole." This view is supported by Riesman (33) who comments:

> Increasingly today, this new type of analytic work with people who are not obviously ill — whose "symptom" is their malaise, their whole way of life — people who are troubled about moral issues, or who ought to be troubled about them, forces analysts to become concerned with problems of casuistry, of values, as part of the very task of therapy.

Tillich (43) finds that the common denominator in all theories of anxiety is the awareness of conflict between structural elements of the personality. Only in the light of an ontological understanding of human nature, he believes, can a consistent and comprehensive theory of anxiety be formulated. In the interpretation of human existence, the psychotherapist can benefit by collaboration with the philosopher and the theologian. Tillich views existential anxiety as basic, growing out of the threefold ontological threat of death, meaninglessness and guilt. These belong to existence and cannot be eliminated. Existential anxiety is properly the object of priestly concern, while pathologic anxiety is the concern of the psychotherapist. The goal of both professions is to help the patient achieve full self-affirmation. They may collaborate fruitfully, but neither should try to replace the other.

FREUD, PSYCHOTHERAPY, AND RELIGION

Although he emphatically denies its validity, Freud (15, p. 206) acknowledges that religion possesses a philosophy of incomparable strength and consistency, that has successfully resisted severe criticism. Religion, he concedes, exerts power over the strongest human emotions. A religious view of the universe adds strength and stability to personality, Freud acknowledges, even while he is trying to refute religion's claim to truth by arguments from psychoanalysis.

Freud's attacks have undoubtedly contributed strongly to the reluctance of psychotherapy to appropriate and apply the insights of religion. This unwillingness to deal with religion is discussed by Gordon Allport (4). Noting that "psychologists write with the frankness of Freud or Kinsey on the sexual passions of mankind but blush and grow silent when the religious passions come into view," Allport argues that the phychologist has no right to retire from the field, since two-thirds of the adults in this country regard themselves as religious people and nine-tenths affirm belief in God. Seventy per cent of the 500 college students questioned by Allport felt that they needed some form of religious orientation or belief in order to achieve a mature philosophy of life. Seventy-five per cent of the women and 65 per cent of the men acknowledged praying, many every day.

In spite of Freud's professional atheism and his violently anti-religious writings, Zilboorg (50) believes that he had "unconscious, intense, positive religious leanings." There is a note of wistfulness in one of his letters to Oskar Pfister, a Swiss Protestant clergyman who was one of the earliest practitioners of psychoanalysis. In the letter, Freud complained about the kind of patients who came for analysis, describing them as "often very poor material." "You, on the other hand," he wrote, "have young people with recent conflicts who are attached to you personally, and who are in a suitable state for sublimation and indeed for its most convenient form — religious sublimation . . . You are in the fortunate position of leading them on to God and reconstructing the conditions of earlier times, fortunate at least in the one respect that religious piety stifles neurosis" (20).

Freud's observation that religion can give strength and stability to personality and can "stifle neurosis" is not bound to the hypothesis that he devised to explain the fact. By "genetic analysis" he arrived at the conclusion that "the religious *Weltenschauung* is determined by the situation that subsisted in our childhood" (15, p. 210). Religion provides ethical precepts and a sense of protection, Freud decided, by preserving childhood attitudes.

This explanation has two flaws: Freud's defective understanding of religion, and his neglect of one of the most significant aspects of personality, purposive striving.

Freud's anti-religious writings indicate a lack of any real acquaintance with religion. Immediately after the appearance of *The Future of an Illusion*, Pfister (29) replied with a paper giving effective answer to Freud's criticisms of religion. Dalbiez (11) has offered a comprehensive criticism of the logic and philosophy inherent in Freud's position. In biographies and critiques, friend and foe alike have referred to the evidence for unconscious bias in Freud's anti-religious pronouncements.

Allport (3, p. 92) warns against "the trivial view that holds adult religion to be merely a repetition of the experiences of the child," adding, "The most comprehensive units in personality are broad intentional dispositions, future-pointed." This aspect of universal human experience, largely unrecognized by an empiricism that sees man as a passive being responding only to forces outside himself, is illuminated by the insights of religion. "While religion certainly fortifies the individual against the inroads of anxiety, doubt and despair," Allport continues, "it also provides the forward intention that enables him at each stage of his becoming to relate himself meaningfully to the totality of Being."

The stability of personality and resistance to neurosis that Freud observed and acknowledged in religious people thus has an alternative explanation more inclusive than Freud's hypothesis, because it articulates with major aspects of personality that he failed to include. Poverty in representing the future, in Allport's opinion, is the chief shortcoming of American psychology. Leo Alexander (1) also comments, "The concepts of ego and superego must be widened to include the will and the purpose as the key to responsibility. There is undeniable historical and social evidence for the existence of will and purpose in human affairs." Limitations set by the canons of scientific method and by the philosophies derivative from science have prevented psychology from recognizing or adequately studying these facets of personality.

THE THERAPIST'S VALUE SYSTEM

Every psychotherapist is a philosopher of sorts. When the psychologist turns away from his measurements and statistics to deal with troubled individuals on a one-to-one basis, he leaves pure science behind. Becoming a participant in the healing process draws him inescapably into the realm of values. At this point, as Allport (5) has pointed out, "Whether he knows it or not, every psychologist gravitates toward an ontological position. Like a satellite he slips into the orbit of positivism, naturalism, idealism, personalism." Refusing, as Freud did, to acknowledge commitment to a basic philosophy, is to defend it less effectively than if it were consciously avowed.

Furthermore, the therapist's own value system is deeply involved in the process of psychotherapy. Developments in ego psychology have not abated metaphysical involvement. The therapeutic goal of psychoanalysis is described by Gill (18) in these terms:

> A progressive analysis from the surface to the depth; analysis of the defenses and the motives for defense; the development and analysis of the transference neurosis; a resolution of symptoms, and as complete a "structural" alternation of the neurotic aspects of the personality as possible.

The process is further elaborated with the statement, "The gross major decision is whether the defenses of the ego are to be strengthened or broken through as a preliminary toward a reintegration of the ego."

This view of psychotherapy makes it a prerogative of the therapist to decide what aspects of personality shall be dismantled, as well as the form and content of the restorative process. Here the personal philosophy of the psychotherapist may determine the pattern of reconstruction. Reorganization of his patient's personality cannot help but implicate the therapist's own value system.

Even apart from active intervention in the reintegrative process the therapist's value system exerts its influence. Wolff (46) in his survey found some therapists contending that treatment should consist of reshaping distorted value concepts, while others advocated exclusion of the therapist's values from psychotherapy as far as possible. Wolff (47) also reported that while only 6 per cent of 43 therapists regarded change of values as a goal of therapy, 48 per cent believed that therapy does in fact directly transmit or develop value concepts in the patient. An additional 24 per cent thought that values have an indirect effect in therapy.

Rosenthal (35) commented after his study upon the changing of moral values in psychotherapy:

> It may be that the therapist communicates his values to the patient in many unintended, subtle ways, even when trying to avoid doing so. The patient, who is often sensitized to the therapist's every word and inflection, may be able to receive these communications, and because of his trust, admiration and respect for the therapist, may permit himself to be influenced by them.

The world view of the counselor apparently exerts its influence in ways unrecognized by either the patient or the therapist himself — in the selection of subject matter for response or discussion, in nonverbal cues if not by verbal expression. This was true even of Freud in the analytic situation. The account of Wortis (48) describes frequent manifestations of his misanthropy and pessimism. If only in subtle, inadvertent expression, the therapist's value system appears to be a constant factor in the relationship.

The therapist usually conceives of himself and is often represented as the detached, dispassionate scientist. A more realistic view would see him as an involved participant with an interest in the outcome, following a sectarian psychotherapeutic doctrine or combination of doctrines, the selection and practice of which are tinctured by his own basic philosophy of life.

THE THERAPIST AND RELIGION

Recognition of the role of the therapist's philosophy of life raises questions fundamental to the success of therapy. Can a therapist that denies the importance of supra-empirical factors in neurosis achieve an empathic relationship with a patient who is burdened with a sense of sinfulness? To reassure such a patient that "this is not a moral problem but can be understood only with impersonal, objective, scientific attitudes" (42) may lead in a direction opposite to improvement and insight.

If metaphysical concerns are at the bottom of many neuroses, to avoid the discussion of religion in psychotherapy as Wolberg (45) recommends, may be to bypass the most significant area of conflict. Masserman (23, p. 494) advises assuring the patient that his philosophic or theological faith will not be challenged, confessing that "only in the early years of his inexperience and defensive dogmatism did he think it necessary to explore, let alone attack, the patient's religious beliefs or practices." This calculated inattention to an area of frequent personality conflict may easily overlook a greater difficulty for a lesser.

To ignore or minimize the field of metaphysical concern in favor of sexual conflict or any other predetermined framework may leave untouched the most important cause of difficulty. Reider (32), for example, tells how a patient called him ten months after treatment had ended to say, "I just wanted you to tell me that there is no such thing as hell where people go for their sins." He complied with a pontifical negative, giving no recognition that the patient's request expressed anxiety growing out of a metaphysical concern that had been presented at the beginning of treatment, and that had obviously remained unresolved.

The responsibility for determining what religious attitudes are healthy or neurotic is a crucial one, certain to be colored by the therapist's own basic orientation toward religion. This is well illustrated by Casey's (9) citation of an analyst whose own unconscious resistance to religious appeal led to his opposing any religious adjustment by his patient. In the presence of such an attitude, the question of Arnold (6) is pertinent, "whether the therapist can correctly evaluate the resistance of a patient with whose philosophy of life he cannot agree."

Many psychoanalysts believe that religious beliefs and practices have a sexual origin and represent infantile emotions. Others regard religious concepts as benign but delusional. Can a therapist with such views enter into the personal universe of a religious patient's meanings and values to establish emphathy on any other basis than as the discerning possessor of truth communicating with the naive victim of error?

The frequent concern of the religious-minded patient and his family over the therapist's attitude toward religion is not without relevance. The naturalistic orientation not only includes certain beliefs, but excludes others. In providing himself with one variety of philosophical stuffing "to stop up the gaps in the universe," (17) the naturalistic psychotherapist at the same time rejects those philosophies that are open-ended toward a reality beyond science. The patient's concern is whether such a counselor can be tolerant toward a world view that he regards as error, and can leave such faith undisturbed during treatment. How many therapists will recognize and acknowledge the error of attacking the patient's religious beliefs, as Knight (21) did in his analysis of a minister?

DOCTRINES OF MAN

The inability of science to provide a complete view of the universe is most apparent in its apprehension of the nature of human personality. There is no mature science of man; there are only doctrines of man. Science at its best provides a truncated view of man. Every doctrine of man includes a substantial body of theoretical assumptions. These doctrines vary from the biological emphasis of Freud with its destructive death instinct, through the deviant psychoanalytic schools that stress social and cultural factors, to those that postulate an inherent upward drive in man toward self-enhancement.

Somewhere between these extremes is the Jewish-Christian doctrine of man that recognizes both the potential for good and the tendency to evil in man's nature. In contrast to the relatively scant empirical data and unilateral focus characterizing most of the neonate doctrines of man, the insights provided by religion are supported by centuries of observation and experience, and deal with the full sweep of human existence.

The psychotherapist is not offered a choice between a scientific and an unscientific doctrine of man. Rather, the choice is among different views of man that are corollary to various philosophies. Most of today's psychotherapy is set in a context of naturalism or positivism. The empirical findings of scientific psychology are not bound inseparably to either of these basic faiths. Such a context is a psychology-plus-philosophy; there are other philosophies equally compatible with the science of man that may lead to a clearer understanding of the patient who is troubled by metaphysical concern. To quote Outler (27), for example:

> The Christian faith is at least an equal option for the thoughtful man. . . . It is at least as intelligible a faith, resting on at least as much experimental evidence and exhibiting a capacity to interpret the inescapable issues of human life in a fashion both more meaningful and truly profound. The truth claims of the Christian faith cannot be "proved". . . . But they can be tested by those who place themselves inside the circle of faith. . . . Moreover, the Christian faith can be an ample and hospitable context for the scientific enterprise, in all its proper dimensions and concerns.

The Thomistic affirmation is similar: "A truly comprehensible and tenable view of man is achievable within the Christian ideology" (8).

Among others, two factors have contributed to the growing congeniality between psychotherapy and religion. The first is an increasing insistence on the part of religionists that "psychiatry cannot adequately perceive the whole man without taking into account the contributions religion has made available for the search" (38). Coupled with some acceptance of this claim by psychotherapy is a measure of recognition that the synoptic view of man offered by religion is both comprehensive and penetrating, its validity being supported by an impressive empirical background and maturity. As a consequence, the offices of the minister are being more widely utilized to augment the skill of the psychotherapist in the recognition of metaphysical concern as contributory to neurosis, and in the resolution of that concern through the resources of religion.

REFERENCES

1. Alexander, L. Moralism and morality from the viewpoint of the psychiatrist. In I. Galdston (Ed.), *Ministry and medicine in human relations.* New York: International Universities Press, 1955. P. 97.
2. Allers, R. Psychiatry and the role of personal belief. In F. J. Braceland (Ed.), *Faith, reason and modern psychiatry.* New York: P. J. Kenedy & Sons, 1955.
3. Allport, G. *Becoming.* New Haven, Conn.: Yale Univer. Press, 1955.
4. Allport, G. *The individual and his religion.* New York: Macmillan, 1950.
5. Allport, G. The psychological nature of personality. *Personalist,* 1953, *34,* 347.
6. Arnold, M. B. The theory of psychotherapy. In M. B. Arnold & J. A. Gasson (Eds.), *The human person.* New York: Ronald Press, 1954. P. 529.
7. Borow, H. The logic of counseling research. *J. counsel. Psychol.,* 1956, *3,* 292.

8. Braceland, F. J. Clinical psychiatry — today and tomorrow. In *Faith, reason and modern psychiatry.* New York: P. J. Kenedy & Sons, 1955. P. 27.
9. Casey, R. P. Religion and psychoanalysis, *Psychiatry,* 1943, *6,* 291.
10. Conant, J. B. *Modern science and modern man.* New York: Doubleday Anchor, 1955.
11. Dalbiez, R. *Psychoanalytical method and the doctrine of Freud.* New York: Longmans Green, 1941.
12. Feigl, H. The scientific outlook: naturalism and humanism. In H. Feigl & M. Brodbeck (Eds.), *Readings in the philosophy of science.* New York: Appleton-Century-Crofts, 1953.
13. Flewelling, R. T. The metaphysical predicament of science. *Personalist,* 1953, *34,* 117.
14. Frankl, V. *The doctor and the soul.* New York: Knopf, 1955.
15. Freud, S. A philosophy of life. In *New introductory lectures on psycho-analysis.* London: Hogarth Press, 1933.
16. Freud, S. *The problem of anxiety.* New York: Norton, 1936.
17. Freud, S. Letter to Jung in Ernest Jones, *Sigmund Freud life and work vol. II.* London: Hogarth Press, 1955. P. 488.
18. Gill, M. M. Ego psychology and psychotherapy. In R. P. Knight (Ed.), *Psychoanalytic psychiatry and psychology.* New York: International Universities Press, 1954. P. 77.
19. Hook, S. The new failure of nerve. *Partisan Review,* 1943, *10,* 2.
20. Jones, E. *Sigmund Freud, life and work, vol. 2.* London: Hogarth Press, 1955. P. 489.
21. Knight, R. P. Practical and theoretical considerations in the analysis of a minister. *Psychoanal. Rev.,* 1937, *24,* 350.
22. Maritain, J. Freudianism and psychoanalysis — a thomist view. In Benjamin Nelson (Ed.), *Freud and the 20th century.* New York: Meridian Books, 1957.
23. Masserman, J. H. *The practice of dynamic psychiatry.* Philadelphia: Saunders, 1955.
24. May, R. *The meaning of anxiety.* New York: Ronald Press, 1950.
25. Mowrer, O. H. *Learning theory and personality dynamics.* New York: Ronald Press, 1950.
26. Ostow, M. Review of *The third revolution. Psychoanal. Quar.,* 1955, *24,* 448.
27. Outler, A. C. *Psychotherapy and the christian message.* New York: Harper, 1954. P. 255.
28. Pfister, O. What transformations does psychoanalysis require in ethics and moral education? *Psychiatric Quar.,* 1931, *5,* 407.
29. Pfister, O. Die illusion einer zukunft. *Imago,* 1928, *14,* 149.
30. Progoff, I. *The death and rebirth of psychology.* New York: Julian Press, 1956. P. 250.
31. Pumpian-Mindlin, E. Changing concepts of therapy in a veterans administration mental hygiene clinic. *Am. J. Psychiat.,* 1957, *113,* 1095.
32. Reider, N. Psychotherapy based on psychoanalytic principles. In J. L. McCary & D. E. Sheer (Eds.), *six approaches to psychotherapy.* New York: Dryden Press, 1955.
33. Riesman, D. *Individualism reconsidered.* New York: Doubleday, 1954.
34. Rioch, D. McK. Experimental aspects of anxiety. In J. H. Masserman & J. L. Moreno (Eds.), *Progress in psychotherapy, Vol. II Anxiety and therapy.* New York: Grune & Stratton, 1957.
35. Rosenthal, D. Changes in some moral values following psychotherapy. *J. consult. Psychol.,* 1955, *19,* 431.
36. Schindler, R. The development of psychotherapy in Austria since 1945. In F. Fromm-Reichmann & J. L. Moreno (Eds.), *Progress in psychotherapy 1956.* New York: Grune & Stratton, 1956. P. 267.

37. Shoben, E. J. Some observation on psychotherapy and the learning process. In O. H. Mowrer, *Psychotherapy theory and research.* New York: Ronald Press, 1953.
38. Steinbach, A. A. Can psychiatry and religion meet? In Simon Noveck (Ed.), *Judaism and psychiatry.* New York: Basic Books, 1956. P. 174.
39. Stekel, W. *Conditions of nervous anxiety and their treatment.* New York: Liveright, 1950. P. 22.
40. Stekel, W. *Technique of analytical psychotherapy.* New York: Norton, 1940.
41. Stern, K. *The third revolution.* New York: Harcourt Brace, 1954.
42. Thorne, F. Directive and eclectic personality counseling. In J. L. McCary & D. E. Sheer (Eds.), *Six approaches to psychotherapy,* New York: Dryden Press, 1955.
43. Tillich, P. *The courage to be.* New Haven, Conn.: Yale Univer. Press, 1952. P. 70.
44. Winkler, W. T. The present status of psychotherapy in Germany. In F. Fromm-Reichmann & J. L. Moreno (Eds.), *Progress in psychotherapy 1956.* New York: Grune & Stratton, 1956. P. 288.
45. Wolberg, L. R. *The technique of psychotherapy.* New York: Grune & Stratton, 1954. P. 333.
46. Wolff, W. *Contemporary psychotherapists examine themselves.* Springfield, Ill.: C. C. Thomas, 1956.
47. Wolff, W. Facts and value in psychotherapy, *Am. J. Psychotherapy,* 1954, 8, 466.
48. Wortis, J. *Fragments of an analysis with Freud.* New York: Simon & Schuster, 1954.
49. Zilboorg, G. Psychoanalytic borderlines. *Am. J. Psychiat.,* 1956, 112, 706.
50. Zilboorg, G. Some denials and affirmations of religious faith. In F. J. Braceland (Ed.), *Faith, reason and modern psychiatry.* New York: P. J. Kenedy & Sons, 1955. P. 99.

(36)

COUNSELING, CULTURE AND VALUE

Cornelius L. Golightly
Associate Professor of Philosophy, University of Wisconsin—Milwaukee

I

The rapid migration to urban centers of vast numbers of rural and semi-rural underprivileged people who experience difficulties in adjusting to urban life has created major social and educational problems for the larger society. Counseling is a valuable social instrument for dealing with these problems because it enlists the energies of the people from whom the problems emanate. Hopefully, not only can the problems be eliminated with the help of the underprivileged but these persons also may become positive assets to the society.

However, a practical difficulty intervenes. The theory and practice of counseling apparently were shaped by middle-class practitioners for middle-class clients. Unlike medicine and surgery which work equally well for rich

An original article for this book.

and poor, counseling has not worked as well for the poor as for the rich. For example, psychiatrists have been notably unsuccessful in the treatment of underprivileged individuals.[1] In order to meet this difficulty some writers like Frank Riessman[2] and Georgene Seward[3] have offered practical suggestions to teachers, social workers, psychologists, and psychiatrists on how best to counsel and deal with the lower classes. The difficulties of counseling the underprivileged and their *ad hoc* solutions raise the perennial question of the place of values in the social sciences. This paper examines the current problems of counseling the broad background of philosophical and methodological discussions of knowledge and valuation. A major presupposition is that the current counseling problems have implications for the older philosophical issues and that the insights of the latter may be useful in resolving present difficulties. The modest aim is that intellectual perspective may be reaffirmed in an area which under pressure for immediate results leans dangerously toward a narrow pragmatic professionalism.

Counseling is an activity in which a professional individual or social practitioner through face-to-face or personal contacts attempts to help individuals who are maladjusted, perplexed, failing or delinquent. Generally, the aim is to assist the individual to grow or achieve greater personality integration so that he can handle present and future problems more independently and responsibly in less confused and better organized ways.

In terms of a distinction which has been much debated since the time of Aristotle, counseling is a practical rather than a theoretical science. Aristotle used the distinction to draw a sharp line between the natural sciences which included both biology and psychology as well as physics and the sciences of ethics and politics. For Aristotle, the crucial differences lay in their purposes. The practical sciences, unlike the theoretical sciences, are for the sake of doing or making something, not for the sake of contemplating, defining, or knowing it. However, Aristotle also recognized differences as to the types of phenomena studied and the role of moral ends in the phenomena under observation. The subject matters of the practical sciences are not limited to things or natures, but involve the habits and skills of man as he seeks to achieve practical social and political ends. Man is a moral agent and however precise biological or psychological definitions may be, man's behavior varies according to environmental determination, educational background, and the influences of social and economic position. Aristotle's conclusion was that problems of political association cannot be separated from problems of morality. Accordingly, he did not develop separate sciences in the *Nicomachean Ethics* and the *Politics* but let them supplement each other by treating a common field according to different aspects. Furthermore, Aristotle repeatedly warned that because of differences in purposes, subject matters, and methods of accumulating and interpreting materials, the practical sciences are incapable of the exactness of the theoretical sciences.[4]

Perhaps a word of caution is necessary here about the Aristotelian distinction between theoretical and practical sciences. We have used it primarily as an heuristic device to place the problem of values in counseling in perspective. If the distinction is interpreted literally to mean the difference between pure and applied science, we should remember that these two terms do not necessarily draw a real distinction.[5] Pure or basic research, familiarly known as pure science, is usually conceived as the disinterested search for knowledge.

Knowledge consists of facts and interpretation and inference. The latter are formulated in probability laws that tell us what happens under what conditions. Facts are propositional statements about empirical observations. Both facts and the interpretation and inference which compose "theory" are subject to the verification procedures of the empirical methodology commonly called "the scientific method."

Applied science is somewhat ambiguous. Herbert Feigl has drawn attention to at least two distinct meanings of the term applied science. "It may refer to such *activities* as the constructing of buildings, the making of drugs, or the enacting of measures of social or political reform. It may also refer to the *cognitive* content of such disciplines as mechanical engineering, industrial chemistry, medicine, or social work. 'Applied science' interpreted in this second sense consists in a body of knowledge selected from pure science and focused for application in the first sense."[6]

In addition to Feigl's two distinctions we may add a third meaning of applied science, one which is frequently used in social science research. It is research undertaken specifically to guide practice, that is, research for application. Kurt Lewin coined the term "action-in-research" to denote the activity of applying research methodology to the diagnosis and solution of practical problems of taking action. Typically, it is research designed to help solve pressing practical problems. Such scientific activity is the focusing of pure science research on a limited area to insure the relevance of the cognitive products of the research for this selected problem at hand.

Now we can see that despite the frequent use of the terms basic or pure research and applied research or research for action, the terms do not draw a real distinction between the knowledge and methods of scientific research. The difference between the two seems to be not a question of subject matter or method but rather a question of motivation and intention on the part of the researcher. If the motivation is sheer intellectual curiosity and the intention is to advance the horizons of knowledge with fact and theory, then the research activity is considered basic or pure. If the motivation is pressure of a practical problem and the intention is to solve the problem then the research is called applied or action-research.

Now if motivation and intention are ignored and we look at the end products of the two research activities we find that they are the same. The end products of research, basic or applied, are collected facts and their explanation, which is theory. A fairly simple way of supporting the argument that pure science and applied science are not intrinsically different is to point out that their results overlap. The results of pure science may have fruitful application and the results of applied science may make important contributions to the wider horizons of scientific theory. Further, at any given moment of time, there may be no clear distinction between what is pure and what is applied.

Ronald Lippitt has compared the results of basic research and action-research as follows: "It is quite probable that the methodological sophistication . . . in these action-research projects, and the genotypic generalization range of the data, will be inferior to the work . . in more highly controlled experimental settings where our problem springs from previous theoretical development and represents a planned step in the stepwise development of a field of knowledge. On the other hand, there are certain areas of needed basic knowledge which are most accessible for clinical observation and systematic research if one gets immersed in this process of intense interaction between values, decision situations, and action."[7]

While the distinction between the practical and theoretical sciences poses a family of knotty problems as the history of the philosophy of science attests, our discussion of counseling will focus mainly upon the place of values in counseling. Generally, values may be examined in the social sciences under three headings: (a) as public objects of description and classification as they occur in studies of personality or culture (b) as hidden valuations, bias, or subjectivity as they are discussed in the literature called the "sociology of knowledge"; and (c) as deliberate intentional choices of means and ends, methods and goals.

Obviously, the last is of central importance in all counseling as a practical science. The first serves as a bridge between the facts and theory of the so-called pure behavioral sciences and the applied science of counseling. The important connection between the two, as Feigl has intimated, is that theoretic knowledge about values can be focused for application in the practical science of counseling. The second focuses upon a major source of weakness or error in counseling. All three of these topics have special significance for the current difficulties in counseling underprivileged or socially disadvantaged persons.

II.

Maladjustment, because of its negative and hence value connotations, is at best an unfortunate scientific concept. It is also ambiguous and imperfectly understood. We may delineate two logically distinct but perhaps factually overlapping types of maladjusted behavior. The first logically distinct type of maladjustment is behavior which is primarily a problem for society because it lacks social integration. For convenience let us use the familiar term of *social disorganization* for this type of maladjustment. The second logically distinct type is behavior which is primarily a problem for the individual himself because it lacks personality integration. For convenience, this type of maladjustment may be designated by this familiar term of *personality disorganization*.

As David Riesman has pointed out, behavior in any society, or class within the society, may be adjusted, anomic or autonomous. The adjusted respond in their character structure to the demands of their society. The anomic are the genuinely maladjusted, the rule-less or ungoverned who do not conform to the characterological pattern of the adjusted because they are socio-psychologically unfit. "The 'autonomous' are those who on the whole are capable of conforming to the behavioral norms of their society — a capacity the anomics usually lack — but are free to choose whether to conform or not."[8]

The nonconforming behavior of the autonomous individual sabotages society and thus is primarily a case of social disorganization. The nonconforming behavior of the anomic individual sabotages himself and perhaps society as well and thus is primarily a case of personality disorganization.

Now let us apply these distinctions to a counseling situation where the counselor is typically a middle-class professional reflecting the values of his middle-class culture and the client is typically deprived and segregated and reflects the values of his lower-class subculture. Negroes, Indians, Spanish-

Americans, Appalachian poor whites, migratory workers, slum-dwellers — the twenty per cent of our population who live on the outskirts of poverty — constitute a distinct subculture with values different from the prevailing values of the majority middle-class culture. Three-fourths of all Negroes, some fifteen million persons, and perhaps a tenth or more of all whites, an additional twenty million persons, constitute America's lower class. These are the people who are the perpetual concern of middle-class social workers, educators, legislators, and law-enforcement officials.

The most basic differences in middle-class and lower-class behavior are those between the habit formations of the lower class and the adjacent lower-middle class. "The patterns of behavior in these two groups, in either the white or the Negro population, are so widely different that it is common practice, even of sociologists, to speak of the lower class as 'unsocialized,' from their middle-class point of view. The social expectations and available goal responses of lower-class and lower-middle-class people are separated by a virtual chasm which is maintained by taboos on participation across class lives."[9]

The crucial value differences between the middle-class and the lower-class cultures are in their different habits of aggression, sexual behavior, education, recreation, and etiquette. Aggression and sexual behavior are the most important of these differences because from the middle-class point of view they involve first order moral values which are sanctioned by legal prescriptions and prohibitions. Education, recreation, and etiquette, while sanctioned by numerous cultural rewards and punishments, generally fall within the category of legal choice or permisison.

From the point of view of lower-class culture, extra-marital partnerships, sexual promiscuity and illegitimacy, fighting with fists and knives, and gambling are normal behavioral adjustments. However, depending on character or personality involvement, the individual may be described as adjusted, anomic or autonomous. From the point of view of middle-class culture, these habits of aggression and sexual behavior are never considered normal behavioral adjustments. Depending on character or personality involvement the individual may be either anomic or autonomous. He is never described as adjusted, however, because his behavior obviously is nonconforming.

If our exposition has been clear thus far, we can see in sharp outline the problems facing the middle-class counselor whose clients are from the deprived and segregated lower-class culture. Because of their recalcitrant, impulsive, physically aggressive and sexually promiscuous behavior which lacks social integration in the larger middle-class society, all lower-class clients from the point of view of the middle-class counselor are maladjusted or socially disorganized. In terms of personality integration or characterological response to the demands of the lower-class culture, however, the lower-class clients fall into three distinct groups: the adjusted, the anomic, and the autonomous. The adjusted, tautologically, are simply adjusted and hence are presumed to be free of hidden affect or feeling. The autonomous are nonconforming out of free choice and hence are presumed to have a measure of insight. The anomic individuals, because of their personality disorganization, are obviously ill. In terms of their relationship to the subculture, however, adjusted and autonomous cannot be maladjusted or socially disorganized. They are simply outside the conceptual framework within which the middle-class counselor is operating.

In a different sense, namely as an artifact of the ways psychiatrists respond to different classes, the anomic lower-class persons also probably fall outside the conceptual framework of the prevailing scientific discipline of counseling with its middle-class orientation. Initial treatment by a perceptive psychiatrist of their neuroses and psychoses may consist in attempting to bring them into adjustment with the norms of the lower-class culture. Since the anomic are demonstrably ill and especially if they are very ill, however, the counselor most often will recommend hospitalization. The expensive individual psychotherapy, which can be purchased privately or secured at clinics which provide largely for the middle class, is rarely available to the lower class. Thus the poor are usually sent to hospitals and, once there, receive the less humane treatment of electric shock or drugs.[10]

E. Franklin Frazier's studies of the folk culture of the simple Negro peasant of the rural south indicate that extra-marital sex relations and illegitimacy may be combined with well-adjusted, morally responsible behavior.

> "The attitudes of these women indicate that they regard sex relations as normal behavior during courtship which may or may not lead to marriage. When it results in the birth of a child, certain obligations are thereby imposed upon the mother. These obligations are the obligations which every mother should feel toward her offspring. The unmarried mother is as sensitive as the legally married mother to what is expected of the woman who is a mother. A certain distinction attaches to being fruitful. To say that a woman 'never did find anything,' meaning that she has never had a child, may imply disparagement as well as commiseration. Motherhood signifies maturity and the fulfilment of one's function as a woman. But marriage holds no such place in the esteem of many of these women. If they marry the father of their illegitimate offspring, it is not due to the fact that the woman regards it as an obligation on the part of the man . . . in many of these rural communities where relationships are sympathetic and informal and marriage and the family do not have an institutional character, the father of the girl's child is not guilty in the eyes either of her family or of the community of any offense against the integrity of her family . . illegitimate children have the same status as those born in wedlock."[11]

Some of the sex delinquency and illegitimacy of recent migrants represents the persistence in the urban environment of folkways that were relatively harmless in the rural community. In such cases where the behavior is simple and naive, individual character is uncorrupted and personality is well adjusted. The persons involved are problems for society but they are not problems for themselves. Inevitably, however, these simple folkways of the subculture conflict with the ideals and standards of the larger middle-class world. Further, the cohesiveness and sympathetic character of the simple community are lost. Then genuine social disorganization and personality deterioration set in. Ironically, social workers and other counselors often speed the process of making the individual a problem for himself without succeeding in changing his status as a problem for society.

Basically, as intimated earlier, the real problem lies outside the framework of counseling. Stated in its simplest terms, the real problem is the incorporation of the lower class into the middle class with the resultant elimination of the lower-class subculture with its behavior problems. The behavior of the lower-class adult, especially his freedom in sex and the expression of aggression, constitutes the cultural rewards, satisfaction and compensations of his lower-class status. Increased education, income, and respect are the cultural rewards, satisfactions and compensations of the middle-class. Upward mobility from the lower class into the middle class indicates that some adjusted and autonomous lower-class persons are *willing to trade* lower-class behavior for middle-class respectable behavior provided they receive in return the economic, educational, and status rewards of the middle class. But this is possible only when the opportunities are *genuine* and the larger society is politically and economically *open*. Always it is a risky business, for the individual may be suspended indefinitely between two worlds, the old and the hoped-for, and he may be literally a man without a culture.

III

Counseling as a practical science involves the making of decisions about values in a way that is never necessary in the theoretic sciences. Yet it is the theoretic sciences that provide the important knowledge about values which make wise decisions possible. The counselor probably will be predisposed to reject delinquency and illegitimacy under any circumstances. The same is true of other subcultural traits like intolerance, anti-intellectualism, illiberalism, prejudice, and aggression.[12] However, he can deal with them effectively only if he knows whether they are innocently based in a subculture or are the results of genuine social and personality disorganization. The crux of this is that despite being immersed in a process of intense interaction between values, decision situations, and actions, the counselor *qua* professional scientist should never confuse valuation and knowledge about values. Valuation occurs when knowledge about values is put to use but this is extraneous to the scientific activity of knowing, without prejudice or bias, what values are and how they operate in human behavior.

REFERENCES

1. A. B. Hollingshead and F. C. Redlich, *Social Class and Mental Illness*. New York: John Wiley and Sons, 1958.
2. Frank Riessman, *The Culturally Deprived Child*. New York: Harper and Row, 1962.
3. Georgene Seward, *Psychotherapy and Culture Conflict*. New York: The Ronald Press Company, 1956.
4. Richard McKeon, ed.: *The Basic Works of Aristotle*. New York: Random House, 1941. See especially McKeon's "Introduction: The Philosophy of Aristotle," p. XXVI.
5. *Cf.* Raymond L. Wilder, "The Nature of Modern Mathematics," *Michigan Alumnus Quarterly Review*, LXV (1959), pp. 302-312.
6. Herbert Feigl, "The Difference Between Knowledge and Valuation," *Journal of Social Issues* VI (1950), p. 40.
7. Ronald Lippit, "Action Research and the Values of the Social Scientist," *Journal of Social Issues*, VI (1950), pp. 54-55.
8. David Riesman, *et al.*, *The Lonely Crowd*, abridged edition. New York: Doubleday Anchor Books, 1955, p. 278.

9. A. Davis and J. Dollard, *Children of Bondage,* Washington, D. C.: American Council on Education, 1940, pp. 264-265.
10. Robert Coles, "Psychiatrists and the Poor," *Atlantic Monthly,* 214 (July, 1964) pp. 102-106.
11. E. Franklin Frazier, *The Negro Family in the United States,* Chicago: The University of Chicago Press, 1940, pp. 115-117.
12. See Frank Riessman, *op. cit.,* pp. 26-30, for a concise catalog of cultural traits of the underprivileged.

SCIENCE, SEX, AND VALUES

O. H. Mowrer

University of Illinois, Urbana

Recently, at a professional meeting, a psychiatrist asked me: "If a nineteen-year-old girl challenged you to show her why she should not engage in premarital intercourse, what would you say to her?"

My first comment would not be to nineteen-year-old girls but to psychiatrists and clinical psychologists. For several decades, the experts in this field have been, directly or indirectly, followers of Sigmund Freud, who held that the basic cause of "neurosis" is repressed sexuality, with a secondary emphasis on repressed hostility. And given this premise, it doesn't take much of a logician to infer that the way to be emotionally healthy is to *express* these "instincts" more freely. Now psychiatrists find they are being called upon to "treat," not neurosis, but promiscuity — and other "character disorders." Now the complaint is that our youth are not so "neurotic," perhaps, but demoralized, apathetic: "They just don't care" about others or their own ultimate best interests. Immediate pleasure is their idol, and the capacity to forego momentary satisfaction for subtler, long-term advantages is said to be "square." *This* is the voice of sociopathy!

Another psychiatrist also recently said to me: "Oh, for just a few *neurotic* patients! Everyone I seem to be seeing nowadays is a sociopath." Psychiatry, having sown the wind, should not be surprised to be reaping the whirlwind.

But instead of admitting that Freud's basic assumptions concerning the nature of personality disorder were deeply mistaken and that they have "sold" millions of dollars worth of idle, if not actively pernicious "therapy," psychiatrists and clinical psychologists are claiming that they have been misunderstood. Freud was really a great moralist, they tell us. The trouble is that the foolish, unintelligent public simply has failed to understand what he was really saying.

Just what did Freud say? Among other things he said: "We [analysts] are not reformers . . .; we are merely observers; but we cannot avoid observing with critical eyes, and we have found it impossible to give our support to conventional morality [which] demands more sacrifices than it is worth. We do not absolve our patients from listening to these criticisms

Reprinted by permission of the Author and the *Personnel and Guidance Journal,* April 1964, 746-752.

. . . and if after they have become independent by the effects of the treatment they choose some intermediate course . . . , our conscience is not burdened whatever the outcome" [4, p. 376-377].

Kitty Kallen, in an article entitled "My 'Lost' Years in Analysis," has reported that *her* analyst advised her (though married) to "act single" — this was to be her salvation and cure. Dr. Albert Ellis has written a book called *Sex Without Guilt*, which I understand has become a kind of handy pocket reference on many college campuses. Helen Gurley Brown has just published another best-seller entitled *Sex and the Single Girl*. And this morning, in reading for an article on group therapy which I am currently writing, I came across this passage in a ponderous technical volume: "The patient . . . fantasied disgracing [his wife] by making known their pre-marital intercourse. . . . With much hesitation he told the group about it and was dumbfounded that none of the members were critical of her. One even said he should be grateful to her for 'making a man of him.' . . . The doctor's failure to agree that the premarital act disgraced his wife was not effective. It took the reality of the group's approval of her to change his attitude [8, pp. 312-313].

So psychiatrists are now asking *others* what to do when young girls insist upon ignoring conventional sexual standards! Isn't this, in effect, precisely what they have been recommending as "therapeutic" for some time now?

Then there is the economic aspect of the situation. Moral subversion, particularly in the area of sex, has become big business. In the areas of art, literature, entertainment, and advertisement, there is constant intimation that those who observe the conventional restraints are something less than fully human. Censorship is manifestly "repressive"; and repression, as we all know, will make you sick — sick, sick, *sick*. Thus, according to what one writer has called "the new psychological liberty," you can not only "get well" but have fun in the process. And anyone who obstructs this pleasant path to healthy-mindedness is a crank and a kill-joy. Besides, you may be interfering with someone else's "business": that is, not just the personal privileges of others, but also their inalienable right to make an easy, albeit perverse, dollar.

The image-makers have made sex the epitome of all that is high and holy. On most college and university campuses, anyone today can buy magazines and paperbacks with pictures on or in them that you would not have found in the corncrib of a livery stable when I was a boy. Even as a university professor, I continually receive, as do others, advertising for "sexy" books and magazines. Two or three days ago, for example, the mail brought an announcement of a new book called *The Dictionary of Erotic Literature*, with a "Special Pre-Publication Offer for Teachers." And this morning I received an impressive blurb for Volume III of *The Encyclopedia of Erotic Literature* ("for only $19.50 plus packaging and freight charges"), which the publishers characterize as "a bold breakthrough in the annals of erotica."

At least by our silence, if nothing else, we adults seem to be giving sanction to this sort of thing. Is this progress — or perdition? We used to think some things were worthy of being called "vice." Now we have become so open-minded and "objective" that virtually nothing seems really vicious to us. So why should our youth not take pleasure when and where they find it and let the more remote consequences, for themselves and others, fall as they may? To counsel them otherwise is repressive, unscientific, and "square."

Where, in all this, does religion stand? First it must be observed that our churches have very largely "accommodated" themselves to what they take to be scientific and "modern" in this area. By and large, religion has become sophisticated and soft. Good theology, taking its cue from psychiatry and clinical psychology, is supposed to be *accepting* rather than in any way "judgmental." Hell has conveniently been liquidated, and that leaves only Heaven, where *everyone* is presumably "accepted." Preachers are told that if they say anything about "sin" it will only make people feel guilty; and everyone knows that guilt feelings are the specific foci of neurotic suffering. So, if you don't want to make people sick, don't talk to them about being either good *or* bad.

Or, suppose that a clergyman has the temerity to speak out in opposition to this philosophy — what can he say? There is a great deal that he *could* say, with excellent Biblical support; but he is likely to resort to metaphysical arguments which, for better or worse, many adults, not mention youth, no longer find very meaningful or convincing. "How do you *know* that . . .?" is likely to be the rejoinder. And the effort which the clergyman makes, in terms of "revelation," "faith," and "miracle," to substantiate his position is likely to leave his questioners quite unmoved.

To sum up, "science" seems to give no support for morality and virtue. In fact, Freudian psychoanalysis provides an excellent rationalization for just the reverse. The profit motive presently permits, and indeed protects, almost every conceivable form of moral subversion. And religion either goes along with all this or, when it protests, does so in a vernacular which, for many people today, is a "stumbling-block" rather than an aid to clarity and conviction.

In the following pages, I shall suggest the basis for a different approach which has, I believe, some promise of resolving our perplexities in this area, and of providing the basis for concerted practical action.

SOCIAL CYBERNETICS

A year or so ago I was speaking at an Eastern college and during a luncheon with several faculty members and administrative officers, the president said: "There is no doubt that the moral fiber of our society is disintegrating. The question is: What can we *do* about the situation. How can such a trend be *arrested and reversed?*

Perhaps an even more fundamental question is: How does such a trend *get started?* In our own particular situation, many forces undoubtedly have been at work: increasing industrialization and urbanization, with loss of primary-group contacts and controls; greater physical mobility, both locally (through the automobile) and nationally (through frequent change of residence); unsettled world conditions; unprincipled advertising, which encourages people to live beyond their means (and then to do questionable things to augment their income); etc.

But I would call attention to an even more ubiquitous consideration, namely the tendency of all societies periodically to question the very concept of morality. Morality, as rules and regulations, arises in the course of social history as the solution to serious human problems. And such regulations always entail restraints and sacrifices. Then, as generations pass, the old diffi-

culties tend to be forgotten and only the odious rules remain. Things are now
so much improved that "progress" seems like a wonderful thing, and people
begin to wonder if it wouldn't be possible to get rid of the rules, too!

In the name of science, Freud said: "Conventional morality demands more
sacrifices than it is worth." And much of the Western World has called him
Discoverer, Liberator, Genius, Messiah, and started applying his great "insights." Do we now *like* the discernible consequences?

The sociologist, Pitirim Sorokin, has posited a recurrent cyclic course for
all societies and civilizations: Idealism, sensuality, decay; idealism, etc. Because of the tendency just noted for ensuing generations to doubt and "reality-
test" the moral solutions which have been passed on to them, it seems unlikely
that this cyclic tendency will ever be completely eliminated. In fact, one might
plausibly argue that, within limits, this is a good thing. But there is a question as to how great the magnitude of any particular cycle or "phase" ought
to become before corrective forces are brought into play. Sometimes, as Toyn-
bee and others have pointed out, societies deteriorate to such an extent that
regeneration or recovery becomes impossible. Sometimes they "fall" — that
is, they are either pushed over by outside forces or simply collapse from lack
of inner vitality.

In response to the question raised by the college president, I think we can
now say that any system, be it mechanical, biological, personal, or social,
which is to "survive" must be *self-regulatory*. And one of the great principles
of self-regulation (recently termed "cybernetics" or "servo-theory") is that
the system has to know what it is doing as it does it, and then has to act
correctively on the basis of this information. In other words, such a system,
to be intelligent, stable, and adaptive, must have some means of getting
prompt and accurate informational *feedback*. And the more precise and immediate the feedback, the more stable the system is, provided it *also* has the
facilities, the motivation, and the power to behave adaptively in response to
this feedback. So we ask: In light of present evidence, what are the effects
of our current trend toward "more liberal"sexual standards and practices?

Serious as our present situation obviously is, there are some reassuring
circumstances: (1) we probably have a more explicit understanding than
ever before of the nature of society and its "dynamics"; (2) we have excellent
resources and devices for quickly gathering relevant information; and (3) we
have unprecedented facilities for putting such information back into the system where it was collected. Social scientists are becoming more and more
interested in what they call *action research*, in which a given institution,
community, or entire society is studied and then given the information thus
derived. In test cases, such a procedure has proven highly effective [5, 6].
We seem to be limited here mainly by the "paralysis of analysis" (*i.e.*, a certain perverse pessimism which holds man essentially helpless and determined
by factors beyond his control) and by the fact that our great mass media
tend to be clogged with entertainment and advertising.

Let me give two examples of the kind of information that is already available in the area of sexual morality and needs to be much more widely disseminated.

In the *American Sociological Review* for February, 1960, there is an
article on "Cultural Relativism and Premarital Sex Norms [2]." Here it is
shown that (1) "the more permissive the culture regarding sexual matters,

the greater will be the incidence of premarital pregnancy"; and that (2) "the divorce rate is significantly higher for premarital than postmarital pregnancy couples." The comparative data were derived from Copenhagen, Denmark (very permissive), Utah County, Utah (very strict), and Tippecanoe County, Indiana (intermediate). The illegitmacy rate for Copenhagen was found to be 11.2 per cent; for Tippecanoe County, 2.9 per cent; and for Utah County, 0.9 per cent. If we see nothing wrong with children being born out of wedlock, then these figures are not very significant. It is unfortunate that the general public cannot know the anguish of unwed mothers and their immediate families and close friends. Here, incidentally, is another kind of "feedback" that is very much needed. And the *Saturday Evening Post* recently ran an article presenting the plight of illegitimate babies themselves — we now have too many of them, more than are "needed" to meet adoption demands [10].

The *Sociological-Review* article goes on to show that a "forced marriage" is only half as likely to survive as are marriages which are fully voluntary. But what's wrong with divorce? For one thing, studies show that homes in which divorce has occurred produce a disproportionate share of delinquents and emotionally disturbed children [11, 12].

Perhaps the trouble is that we haven't yet gone all the way in liberalizing sexual standards. Perhaps, if we became completely and consistently "permissive" in this area, everything would be all right. Here, too, we have highly pertinent, though not widely publicized, data. With the success of the 1917 Russian Revolution, the Old Bolsheviks took the position that monogamy was just another vestige of the iniquitous capitalistic system and set out to liquidate it. Divorce, which previously had been difficult to obtain, became extremely easy — a postal card notifying the other partner that the relationship was ended would suffice. Incest, bigamy, and adultery were dropped as official crimes, and abortion was officially sanctioned. No distinction was made between the state of children born legitimately, nonregistered co-habitation was given the same legal status as registered co-habitation, parental authority over children was systematically weakened, and additional measures were taken to "uproot the traditional structure of the family."

What was the result? By 1935, roughly 18 years after the introduction of this regime, Soviet policy makers were taking a radically different position. N. S. Timasheff, in a book called *The Great Retreat*, says: "Dissolution of family ties, especially of the parent-child relations, threatened to produce a wholesale dissolution of community ties, with rapidly increasing juvenile delinquency as the main symptom. . . . Everywhere, wrote the papers, gangs invaded workingmen's dwellings, ransacked them, and destroyed or spoiled what they did not take away; if somebody dared to resist, he was mercilessly killed. . . . Sometimes the schools were beseiged by neglected children; other times gangs beat the teachers and attacked women, or regularly fought against one another. . . . Millions of girls saw their lives ruined by Don Juans in Communist garb, and millions of children had never known parental homes" [9, pp. 196-197].

By 1939 an official Soviet journal was saying: "Sound moral ideals must be inculcated into the mind of young persons. They must know that lack of care for their parents is found only among savages and that in every civilized society such conduct is considered dishonest and base" [9, p. 202]. Abortion had been made illegal, and marriage was again being stressed and idealized.

Here is an instance of "vicarious feedback," that is, a report of what happened in *another* contemporary society which also thought it could eliminate the restraints and sacrifices which sexual morality pre-supposes. Because centralized control is weaker in this country than it is in Communist Russia, we have moved into the cult of permissiveness, not by official fiat and policy, but by scarcely noticeable stages. But, by the same token, it may be more difficult for us to renounce and eliminate it. "Knowledge of results" is manifestly not enough. There must also be a clear intellectual appraisal of the facts and a mobilized public opinion.

Let us now turn our attention to the more conceptual or "ideological" aspects of this problem.

THE REALITY OF MORALITY

Nearly 20 years ago, I became convinced that the personal condition we misleadingly call "neurosis" is essentially what earlier generations knew, more accurately, as a state of "unredeemed sin" or "hardness of heart." Freud enticed the world into believing that persons so afflicted have been over-socialized and are thus the victims of their own excessive morality and virtue. Neurosis, he argued, represents an incapacitating "false guilt," which comes from mere temptation to do forbidden (but really quite admissible) things or from one's having done things which are actually not wrong but "natural" and innocent. As one long associated with psychoanalysis but ultimately disillusioned by it, I have come to believe that in so-called neurosis the guilt is not false but *real,* that is, guilt which arises from deeds committed but neither acknowledged nor atoned for, about which the individual's social reference group (*and* conscience) has a very legitimate right to be concerned.

Skepticism concerning psychoanalysis is today widespread and growing; people, generally, are prepared for and welcome questions concerning theoretical soundness and efficacy. But they are not prepared, it seems, to hear a professional psychologist take issue with psychoanalysis in quite the way I do. Reactions commonly assume two diametrically opposite forms. In college and university circles, I most often hear something like this: "But how *can* you take morality seriously? Today we *know* that ethical standards are relative to time and place, that they constantly change and fluctuate. So how can one trust *any* of them? Aren't they all just so much confused, and confusing, nonsense? How, without absolutes (which are ridiculous), can one say that anything is *either* good or bad? The moral question is really quite a hopeless one. And if that is so, hadn't you just as well do pretty much as you like — as long as you can get by with it?"

Then, in religious circles (*some* religious circles, I should say, since relativism has made deep inroads here too), I am likely to get this response: "As a scientist you seem to question the divine or supernatural sources of moral authority. If you do that, aren't you irrevocably committed to relativism? And we know what chaos *that* produces. Don't you *believe* that. . .?" And here I am likely to be quizzed on whatever "article of faith" the speaker happens to accept, in such a way as hopefully to strike terror into the heart of anyone who presumes to deviate therefrom.

It is, I believe, entirely possible to be a scientist without being a complete relativist — to take morality seriously without being an absolutist. What both the positions just delineated overlook is that all of us live and function in some sort of social group. And a group is not just a random aggregate of individuals. It is a *system*, an agreed-upon way of doing things, a way of solving certain problems which calls for short-term sacrifices for long-term satisfactions and gains. In other words, a social system is always, in this sense, a *moral system*. The details of different social systems naturally vary; and at this level of analysis, morality is, to be sure, relativistic, "pluralistic." But the fact of one's sociality, of one's "belonging" and being committed to some social system is undeniable, universal; and it is from this circumstance that we reach a kind of moral bedrock, or "absolute." If one is functioning in a given social system, then one is honor-bound to "play the game," as prescribed in the system. Or, if one *must* deviate from it, to do so openly, honorably, and take the stipulated consequences of such disobediance, or else leave the system.

In other words, the concept of loyalty and its obverse, disloyalty or cheating, are important dimensions of social life everywhere. The particular form and content of the behavior which is prescribed may vary enormously from group to group, or from time to time within the same group; but the obligation to "shoot square" with one's present reference group is universal, and imperious! And it is, I submit, either feigned ignorance or willful rejection of this principle that is the basic problem in every instance of neurosis and functional psychosis. Let me give a homely illustration.

This is the imaginary (but "true") story of a college girl whom we shall call Mennonite Mary. My office telephone rings, and the dean of women is saying that there is a young lady in her office she would like me to see. The girl is a junior, and during her first two years at the university had an excellent record. But now she is depressed and very tense, isn't sleeping properly, can't concentrate on her studies, has fallen behind in her classwork, and is thinking about dropping out of school, but insists she doesn't want to go home. The dean is afraid the girl may have to be hospitalized. Will I see her?

When the girl arrives, we chat informally for a few minutes and then I say: "Mary, you've been living with this problem for some time now. What do *you* think the difficulty is?"

"Well," she say, "it may sound silly to you, but I think its connected with the fact that I have been playing cards."

"You mean you've been gambling?"

"Oh no, not that!" she says. "I've just been playing a little birdge with the other girls at the dormitory where I live. I'm not very good at it, and don't do it often. But I think this is the basis of my problem."

At this point a Freudian counselor might easily conclude that here is a "classical" instance of a rigid, unrealistic conscience reflecting overly strict moral training. Everyone knows that playing bridge is not really a sin! What awful parents and what a ridiculous "superego" this girl must have! So the stage is set for a protracted campaign designed to "liberate" or "detach" this girl from her "hostile, rejecting" parents and to reduce, through the "transference relationship," the strength and severity of "the internalized voice of the community." Or, a religious counselor might attempt to assure Mary of God's loving forgiveness of her "sin" and send her on her way, perhaps temporarily relieved but not permanently so.

But we talk on, and presently I ask Mary where she lives. "Down near ————ville," she replies. And then I say: "You don't happen to come from the Mennonite community near there do you?" Mary confirms my conjecture.

Then I ask Mary if her parents know she has been playing cards. Immediately she blushes, squirms in her chair, tears come into her eyes, and she says: "That's the awful part of it. My parents trust me. They think I am living according to their standards. They send me money and are proud of me, up here at the university. But I am ashamed of my background and haven't wanted it known. So I sometimes play cards and *act* as if I were not a Mennonite."

Now we are getting somewhere. We have discovered that Mary's problem is not simply that of playing or not playing bridge. She is being dishonest, hypocritical, and disloyal to her family and old friends. "But what's wrong with that?" someone will ask. "Maybe Mary wants to *change* her religion and her friends. Isn't that her right?" Indeed it is. But it is *not* her right to continue to take money from her parents without telling them of her decision in this matter and giving them, too, an opportunity to decide whether they want to continue supporting her. Nor does it bode well for the future that Mary is misrepresenting herself to others. Mary is cheating, and she has too much character not to be bothered, deeply bothered, by this fact. Any system of "therapy" which tries to "shrink" her conscience and to deny her culpability in this situation is very far from being "scientific" (or, for that matter, genuinely religious), for it doesn't take all the facts into account and is correspondingly ineffective.

Recently I was at a meeting where there were both Protestant and Catholic theologians, and someone made the following suggestion: "We Christians are going to have to get together and *agree* on what is moral and what is not. At present we are offering the world a sort of ethical smorgasbord: you just shop around from one church to another until you find what *you like* in the way of morality and then you take that. We must get together and present a consistent position with respect to what is sin and what is not."

I don't at all agree with this. It is quite unrealistic even to suggest that, for example, Protestants are going to accept the Catholic position on birth control or that Catholics are going to accept Protestant disapproval of drinking and gambling. Here are "cultural alternatives," which constitute the essence of "religious pluralism." This type of "freedom of choice" is one of the great premises of a democratic society. But once one has made a choice and committed himself to a given moral order or system, then he is *not* free to cheat on that system, no matter what it is. If one is going to be a Catholic, or a Protestant, or whatever, then one ought to be a *good* one — or else openly work to change the system, or get out of it.

Our present difficulties in the realm of morality do not, in my judgment, come from lack of complete agreement as to what is or what is not a "sin." It's rather that we don't really believe and enforce what we are presumably already agreed on, namely the importance of being honest, responsible, "square" with respect to the commitments we have already made. No one can play "fast and loose" with the rules of his reference group without being in trouble with his conscience (if he has one) and fearful, "shy," and "insecure" with respect to the group itself.

Dr. Victor Frankl, in his recent tour of American university campuses, said: "Freud stressed the will to pleasure; Adler stressed the will to power. I believe our deepest need is greater *meaning* in our lives." And Professor Charles Osgood and his colleagues in the Institute of Communications Research at the University of Illinois have shown that the principal element in the meanings which words have for us is the *evaluative* one, that is, a connotation of goodness or badness. But we intellectuals, for some decades now, have been trying to tell ourselves, and others, that virtue and evil are myths. Is it any wonder that we are suffering from what Frankl calls an "existential vacuum," that is *meaninglessness?*

Baudelaire once observed that the devil's "cleverest wile is to convince us that he does not exist." If this is so, His Satanic Majesty must take deep satisfaction in his accomplishments as he surveys the contemporary scene!

REFERENCES

1. Brown, Helen G. *Sex and the single girl.* New York: Random House, 1962.
2. Christensen, H. T. Cultural relativism and premarital sex norms. *Amer. socio. Rev.,* 1960, 31-39.
3. Ellis, A. *Sex without guilt.* New York: Lyle Stuart, 1958.
4. Freud, S. *A general introduction to psychoanalysis.* New York: Liveright Publishing Corp., 1920.
5. Goodwin, L. Religion and the behavioral sciences. *Relig. Educ.,* 1960, July-August, 253-256.
6. Goodwin, L. The historical-philosophical basis for uniting social science with social problem solving. *Phil. Sci.,* 1962, *29,* 377-392.
7. Kallen, Kitty. My "lost" years in analysis. *The American Weekly,* March 6, 1960.
8. Powdermaker, Florence B., & Frank, J. D. *Group psychotherapy — studies in methodology of research and therapy.* Cambridge, Mass.: Harvard Univ. Press, 1953.
9. Timasheff, N. S. *The great retreat.* New York: E. P. Dutton & Co., 1946.
10. Trombley, W. Babies without homes. *Saturday Evening Post,* 1963, *236,* 15-20.
11. Wahl, C. W. Some antecedent factors in the family histories of 390 schizophrenics. *Amer. J. Psychiat.,* 1954, *110,* 668-676.
12. Wahl, C. W. Some antecedent factors in the family histories of 568 male schizophrenics of the United States Navy. *Amer. J. Psychiat.,* 1956, *113,* 201-210.

(38)

AN EXAMINATION OF CLIENT STRENGTH AND COUNSELOR RESPONSIBILITY

Joseph Samler[1]
Vocational Rehabilitation and Education Service, The Veterans Administration

A central motif runs through our present approaches in psychotherapy and counseling. The client has a history which makes his problems under-

---

Reprinted by permission of the Author and the *Journal of Counseling Psychology,* Vol. 9, No. 1, 1962, 5-11.

[1]This paper was presented in preliminary form at the NDEA Guidance Institute at the University of Florida, in November 1960. The writer is indebted to Louis S. Levine, Donald E. Super, and Leona Tyler, as well as to his long-suffering colleagues at work for reviewing the manuscript. This does not mean that the points made or progression in thinking necessarily is shared by the reviewers, but rather that their criticisms and evaluation were most useful to the writer.

standable, if not inevitable. He is not to be held responsible for past difficulties or present unhappy life patterns. It is as if he were acted upon rather
than acting, neutral and imprinted upon rather than an agent in his own
right.[2] There are other views but the extent of their influence seems a moot
question. Thorne's first edition was published in 1950. Rosen's particular
therapy in psychiatry is well known. Williamson's writings over the years have
emphasized client responsibility. In vocational counseling at least, Super
continuously has urged the need to work to and from existing client strengths
and assets. Yet with the possible exception of the effect on vocational and
rehabilitation counseling, it is questionable how much counseling practice has
been affected. It is not that client strength is lacking as a firm concept. Client
strength and responsibility for self is a central issue in Rogers' work, for instance, but it is a goal to be achieved as a result of counseling, not a resource
to be immediately utilized.

The literature reflects our enormous commitment to the client's history in
our attempt to understand him. Perhaps it is a price we have paid in order
to simplify what cannot be simplified; to seek lawful relationship with variables that can be identified, leaving out factors so variable, e.g., self-awareness,
that they would make our quest for science, or at any rate for a science as we
know it, quite impossible. To put it quite badly, the client in our counseling
approaches is never at fault. He is the present product of circumstance — a
possessive mother, a cold and distant father, lack of love in infancy, a hostile
environment, or other inimical circumstance. The world in which he lives is
one he was in effect forced to inhabit. His low self-esteem, his filled cup of
unhappiness, his distress and discomfort are, so to speak, supplied to him.
His guilt is pointless, and useful only for examination.

We seem to have neglected aspects of the human being that are central
to his humanity: his cognitive character, his essential autonomy, the possibility
within him for self-direction and determination of choices, the planful and
purposive aspects of his living, his symbolic activity, and his great capacity
for ideation. Our philosophies and our procedures seem based upon a view
of the human being as almost totally a feeling organism. We are all ready
to attest that behavior has both cognitive and affective components, but we
do not act that way in the consulting room.

There are probably many reasons for neglect of given cognitive resources
in the human personality. For example, the extant personality theories set
before us as models do not, generally, provide for man's strength, his self-
awareness, his ability to pull himself into the future, his self-determining
capacities. It seems no great exaggeration to posit a kind of combined model
in which the individual is moved by unconscious motives, deflected from
self-awareness by anxiety, and perceives anything but objectively. Not infrequently he is misled by our symbols of communication. His interests are
determined for him by early childhood experiences, and he is caught up in
the inevitability of response to cultural expectations he had no part in establishing. The import of the discussion thus far is that this is an insufficient
model and a misleading one.

The central point about presumed client passivity is reflected in current
literature. In addressing himself to this problem Shoben (1961) points out

---

[2]The emphasis on personal history in psychoanalysis is well known. It is apparent
that classical behaviorism also contributed to our present problem. In denying consciousness to the individual, a premium is put on his passivity.

that we have exchanged the devil of which the demented once was possessed for the modern devil of the disturbed's client's parents. The client himself remains a neutral and acted upon figure. He goes to the root of the problem in noting that the clear result of looking for lawful relationship between unhappy history and personality problems is to ignore the idea of individual responsibility.

In a framework much more threatening to the counselor committed to present counseling philosophy. Mowrer (1960) urges that: "The unassailable, brute fact is that personality disorder is the most pervasive and baffling problem of our time; and if it should turn out that persons so afflicted regularly display (or rather hide) a life of too little, rather than too much, moral restraint and self-discipline, the problem would take on an empirical urgency that would require no fine-spun argument."

We come to terms with the central problem in a thoughtful proposal presenting a new descriptive framework for categorizing individuals with respect to many behaviors and qualities. Levine and Kantor (1960) urge that:

> The impulse-ridden, id-driven image of man utilized by psychologists for some years has recently been challenged by personality theorists and clinicians. The validity of the old image has been questioned. Is man only a hapless and hopeless organism, a servant to his surroundings and a prisoner of his inhibited passions? From such questioning and from clinical observation and theory, a new image is gradually taking shape, one in which the developmental, integrative and ongoing aspects of life are alluded to by concepts such as Allport's 'becoming.' This new image includes the 'soft voice of intellect'; it includes man's productivity as well as his passion, his creativity as well as his conflicts, and his resourcefulness and resilience as well as his repressions and rigidities.

The emphasis on what at best can only be a corrective must not be mistaken as an invitation radically to change our orientation. It is not intended that counseling would offer only a prescription of limits and a set of demands on the individual. The problem of self-direction is in any case as old as is man's awareness of himself. It is as persistent as are his questions about the reasons for and purpose of his being, and quite likely will remain with us as a central problem. The emphasis on an available element of choice to each individual is offered as a corrective to the prevalent practice which views the person as being acted upon, with none or most limited volition, intent, and freedom of his own.

The idea that a degree of self-determination is available and should be called upon is central to what I am trying to say. The immediate problem which we will not resolve but must consider, deals inescapably with the problem of determinism. Unless there is at least hope of forcing this closed door we cannot refer to elements of responsibility for self in our perception of and expectations from the people who come to us for help.

THE PROBLEM (STILL) OF DETERMINISM

The philosophy of science, including the science of human behavior, hews to determinism as its basic principle. It is perfectly clear why this should be so. If given events are to be predicted and controlled, then the lawful relationships between effect and cause must at least be postulated and hopefully identified and found.

It is possible to take courage from a great and imaginative soul. Writing in 1884, the opening sentences of William James' "The Dilemma of Determinism" are:

> A common opinion prevails that the juice has ages ago been pressed out of the free-will controversy, and that no new champion can do more than warm up stale arguments which everyone has heard. This is a radical mistake. I know of no subject less worn out . . . (1948).

Hobbs in his consideration of this problem (1959), says he is inclined to agree with James because, Hobbs says, "The issue is quickened every time psychologists get close to contemporary man and his problems."

The issue has always been keen but it is persuasive to think that it is more troublesome now than it has been before. Not only are we in psychology becoming more self-conscious but there is currently a wave of worry in human behavior about values, ethics, sin, guilt, morality. Here we are up against it for it is clear that without choice between one course of action and another, without some measure of free will, there is no sense in talking about values and ethics. This of course only identifies a possible motivation for a belief in free will; it does not provide an answer.

If determinism is an inescapable fact in science, an equally hard nut to crack is the common conviction every day that man has a certain amount of freedom of choice in his behavior.

There is no way out of complexity here because we talk of human behavior. Perhaps the outline of a possible answer, not yet properly taken into account, is in James' definition of *in*determinism. "The parts," he felt, "have a certain amount of loose play with one another . . . . Of two alternative futures which we conceive, both may now be really possible; and the one becomes impossible only at the very moment when the other excludes it by becoming real itself." James' thinking in this remarkable essay is seemingly as pertinent now as it was three quarters of a century ago. His grand affirmation, basic to his thinking, is that man is a rational organism and that it is given him to work toward his conception of the "good." Determinism he says ". . . virtually defines the universe as a place in which what ought to be is impossible."

We have still to take into account an assumption which has built into it human intention and commitment to a given way, self-selected. To some it may seem presumptuous, but to others the only possible definition of our humanity. It is completely understandable that science as we know it has not as yet been able to come to grips with so subjective, so seemingly capricious a force. I believe that we must require that science suit itself to our needs, and our needs require as a first condition an affirmation of our rationality and ethical nature. Wheelis puts it into a nutshell when he says "we have gained determinism, but have lost determination."

The critical question is whether in the study of man we have carried over the postulates of a science that may not be applicable to organisms that have self-awareness and self-understanding. The "if-then" paradigm of classical science seems to fall quite short in considering the organized complexity of the human being. For here each part stands in interrelationship to the other.

We become greatly uncomfortable with personality theory based upon white rat experiments, for instance. The plain fact is that a rat is not a man. And it may be that our difficulty with learning theory, and the fact that none really is satisfactory, is that we cannot really account in present models for motivation, self-scrutiny, the nuances of need, and so on, especially in their complex interrelationships. It is not enough to call them "intervening variables." If this is true, our urgent requirement must be that a science be brought into being that will take the human condition into account.

BEHAVIOR AS A CRITERION

This is our assumption, then, that there is a measure of basic freedom of choice available to the individual, and that within limits he can move in given directions. The central point in this discussion is that the nurturing atmosphere of the consulting room, the incredible investment of one person in another, the almost total address to the client's emotional life, these are not the only necessary conditions of change. Indeed it is a startling truism that all therapies, deep, superficial, rationalized or not, honest or not, have their successes.

In therapy at least, we do not seem to capitalize on the individual's *present* strengths. In all counseling we have the theoretical signposts for working to existing strength and this seems to be the development of greatest promise for differentiating therapy from counseling and the clinical psychologist from his colleague in counseling. The contrast is the emphasis on pathology as against an emphasis on the individual's abilities. As counselors in rehabilitation probably know best, the orientation is vastly different and the results vary remarkably with the orientation.

It seems a safe statement that practice in vocational counseling relative to the basic orientation is quite varied. As against Super's differentiating and healthy emphasis is the continued force of analytically-oriented psychology with its interest in the profound search and major restructuring of personality.

Nevertheless there is greatest hope for productive change here. The necessary directions have been brought to attention by a number of counseling and vocational psychologists. Brayfield (1960) presented a map of the country to travel in a recent paper. Leona Tyler (1960) in her excellent treatment of minimum change therapy underscores the possible positive aspects of the personality defenses. In addressing themselves to the foundation task of a descriptive framework for behavior, Levine and Kantor (1960) urge that "some 'defensive' behavior enables the individual to attain psychological objectives other than those involved in guarding against overwhelming anxiety experiences." Actually, much of the short-term therapy may be considered as approaching a different orientation, provided it is not considered "second-best." The emphasis on ego-psychology is of course for consideration, although its analytic orientation relates it basically to personality restructuring.

In the paper already referred to, Levine and Kantor urge "effectiveness"[3] as the keystone of a new descriptive framework for behavior. The central

---

[3]Levine and Kantor state that: "The generic term of 'effectiveness' can be defined nominally as the fullest utilization of ability and the commitment of energy to goals valued by the individual and congruent with the social expectation for the roles he assumes. The utilization of his ability and energy is to be considered relative to the opportunities available to him as set by his imposed social position."

ideas in the present paper are congruent with Levine and Kantor's development. The point is that it is an aspect of the individual's strength to respond to the need put before him to behave, to perform, in other than destructive ways. The point is, further, that it is appropriate, at least in given types of problems, to require such change, and to put force and emphasis on such requirement.

This is in no way startling with certain types of cases, e.g., acting out, manipulative clients. The need for the imposition of limits is clearly set forth, for instance, by Murphy & Guze (1960). Ford, Robles & Harlow (1960) affirm the position that permitting or condoning diffuse and uncontrolled acting out of instinctual drives, whether libidinal or aggressive, is the antithesis of psychotherapy.

The question is whether the approach of the counselor in requiring certain behavior, e.g., setting limits, may not be extended. A few not too hypothetical case instances may be useful.

THE SPECIFIC INSTANCE IN CONTEXT

The requirement for particular behavior, the urgent proposal for change in behavior, cannot be made by an up-stage, moralistic counselor, separated from and emotionally distant from his client. A requirement made in this atmosphere carries its own negation. The communication must be embedded in the same kind of deep concern for the client that characterizes present relationship therapy. *It should in fact arise out of the concern.* The basic message is one of understanding of and feeling for the unhappy person but it is accompanied by the involvement of aspects of his being other than his defenses.

Here is a person suffering from a condition we might call deep prejudice. The reasons for his disability are available from the literature and may relate to his early childhood experience, great hostility in his makeup, rigidity, and so on. Let us assume that possibly he may want to change but finds himself helpless because the nucleus of his disability is in the basic structure of his personality. Given, say, three years of therapy it is not impossible to assume that something can be done with his problems. But for many reasons this may not be feasible, and yet we have one more recourse. We can say to such a person, "Look, however you feel is your business, and whether or not you change is your business, but *act* differently. You don't have to spit when you pass a Jew or a Scandinavian, or a Hottentot in the street." "Keep your feelings if you must but change your behavior!"

Let us consider the case of a person with a real full-blown "poor me" operation. When such a person has an itch it is the worst itch any one ever had, when there is any pain, the whole world knows about it, and so on. Confident of the unreality of such feelings we are justified in saying, "Look, be as terribly sorry for yourself as you please, drown in your own tears if you must, but keep it to yourself, don't keep pushing it on your family or your friends." Again a change of behavior is strongly urged, without, at the moment anyway, working for basic examination of personality needs and defenses.

A third illustration, but out of the consulting room, may also be familiar. Here is a worker in industry, government or the schools. He is unhappy for whatever reason and doing his work badly. The supervisor, let us assume a competent psychologist, has a choice of a sort. He can play a therapeutic role and help the worker achieve insight and understanding, hopefully leading to better work. It seems to me that this is not warranted, and that what should be required is the kind of work behavior which will help achieve necessary performance. The key question here is whether in going along with unsatisfactory work we are not in fact dealing quite disrespectfully with the worker.

It is to be hoped that the reinforcement of the results of acceptable behavior may in itself be curative. Thus the "poor me" boy cited before may find that behavioral control of his great sorrow results in enough comfort so that he will be moved to greater inhibition of his self-sorrow on his own.

But the necessary disclaimers are obviously in point: It is critically important that requirement for changed behavior which says in effect, "control yourself" can work only in particular situations and under given circumstances. It would be useless to instruct a paranoid person to stop being suspicious of all around him, and probably equally unproductive to say to the man desperately searching for a semblance of intimacy to stop seducing every woman he meets. Only the general proposal can be made here. We have still to find out, following accepted procedure, under what conditions and in what manner the requirement for change in behavior can work.

It should provide thoughtful material for us that life in fact sets constant limits to behavior and that learning takes place quite frequently in what seems like desirable directions. The need for establishing limits in helping children grow and adjust is nowhere questioned, quite the contrary. It is not so clearly seen that in our working world we are nearly all confronted with quite firm demands to which nearly all of us respond quite well.

Similarly, although it seems very odd to call it to attention, learning takes place as a result of cognition. We seem not to build on the examples before us of the salutary, quite didactic communication that suddenly gives insight. The counselor says "What I do not understand is why you are so intolerant of hypocrisy," or to the protesting mother: "The worst thing you can do to a child is to be indifferent to him."

We tend to identify the counseling session as a learning situation, but, granted the profound emotional involvement in many personality problems, we are not ready to carry over to counseling what we take for granted in other learning and teaching settings.

THE PROBLEM OF COUNSELOR RESPONSIBILITY

Implicit in the requirement for change in behavior, in setting limits, in urgent statement of counselor belief, in firm cognitive formulations, is the idea of counselor responsibility.

The dicta are well known: we cannot assume responsibility for the client; we are not and cannot be so knowledgeable; we simply cannot foretell the future well enough; our science at best deals in probabilities. The very issue urged in this paper argues against it because *self* determination cannot be someone else's.

I must dismiss out of hand the issue of respect for the client. The acknowledgment of his integrity is not in question. It is out of concern for him and in his own interest that we do what we do. Similarly the application of the concept of democracy must be viewed quite sceptically. As Meehl and McClosky (1947) have clearly demonstrated, the term is meaningful in politics but has no pertinence in helping people in trouble.

Perhaps as is not uncommon, the answer we get depends on the questions we ask. The question of acceptance of responsibility totally, must be answered in only one way; but a question whether in given instances and in particular circumstances it is improper for the counselor to accept responsibility is capable of different answers. Indeed it is already answered. In whole classes of conditions it is perfectly clear that responsibility is assumed by the worker. This is apparent in working with the suicidal, in dealing with the abnegation of responsibility of the schizophrenic, with the dangers offered by the paranoid, the hazards of the impulse ridden, or in dealing with the desperate retardate reflecting insistent parent need for considerable education.

The principle of nonacceptance of responsibility, therefore, is by no means absolute. It follows logically then that the problem is not one of taking over but rather of the specific and individual instance in which specified assumption of responsibility by the counselor is wararnted, its desirability in terms of the client's interest, and its feasibility. Presently no more than the theoretical point can be made; we lack the instances and examples to specify where and in what manner the counselor properly can play a role as here postulated. What cannot be dismissed, however, is the reiteration of concerned therapists and counselors that as the occasion warrants, dogma or not, they *do* step into such roles.

The instance of the brillant student who attended college only as a result of the table pounding, home visits, and urgent insistance of the counselor, is a typical enough case in point. Involvement of the police and the law on the counselor's initiative, positive environmental changes — these are all in the counselor's repertory. This is reality and we cannot ignore it.

The assumption of counselor responsibility even though safeguarded and made specific to the particular instance leads inevitably to the question of values. Or perhaps it is much more correct to say that counselor responsibility flows out of a particular view of the nature of values and of the counselor's role in the promulgation of given values. The problem is too complex to be treated in limited space. But it makes sense that thinking on the problem should start with what seems to be clear, that whether the counselor wills it or not, he affects in his client value derivation, commitment, and integration. There is reason to think that the professed neutrality of counselor and therapist is more a professional stance than it is reality. If these points are admitted, the problem seems to be either to work toward an impossible neutrality or to determine which values to support, under what conditions, and with how much force.

It ought not to be irreligious to propose that if value commitment and promulgation work in bringing about lasting client change in desirable directions then it provides its own justification. It is not inconceivable that there are means other than the acceptant, nurturing relationship in helping people to change.

CONCLUSION

A final and critical point remains to be made but it can be made best in the context of a quick recapitulation.

The counseling client is too often regarded as remarkably passive, neutral, acted upon, nonresponsible. Emphasis is placed upon his history or his situation as the unhappy factors leading to his ills. The discussion urged that in so regarding the client we have lost sight of his available strengths, his cognitive ability, planfulness, ideation, drive to autonomy and his freedom to an extent to choose, that is, his aspects of self-determination.

Inevitably we have had to consider the age-old question of determinism and free-will. The basic intention in that part of the discussion was to show that determinism does not so foreclose the argument as to make it idle to talk of a measure of self-determination.

With this hope in mind, the possibility was offered of working to the individual's strengths in terms of his cognition, the planful and purposive aspects of his being, and the possibility within him presently for self-direction. This is a broad highway, however, to the critical problem of the frank assumption of responsibility by the worker and in turn this led to involvement in values and to the proposal that the counselor accept responsibility for the promulgation of values with his clients.

An important point may now be made. It is clear that the higher the abstraction, the more universal is agreement and so everyone is against sin and for motherhood. The difficulty makes itself evident in the particular situation, but this is why a presumably skilled, experienced, and feeling person is on the other side of the desk. At the risk of sounding quite stuffy, it must be stated that the proposal made in these pages is not for the ill-trained but well meaning. It requires not an exercise in safety, and in using techniques that are difficult to abuse. It requires the utmost in understanding and the greatest possible concern for the client; relative ease in going beyond surface behavior; and a level of sophistication that can come only with arduous work and commitment to this most difficult task.

Received February 20, 1961.

REFERENCES

Brayfield, A. H. In symposium honoring Donald G. Paterson: Vocational counseling — past, present, and future. *American Psychological Association Convention*, 1960.

Ford, E. S. C., Robles, C., & Harlow, R. G. Psychotherapy with child psychotics. *Amer. J. Psychother.*, 1960, *14*, 705-718.

Hobbs, N. Science and ethical behavior. *Amer. Psychol.*, 1959, *14*, 217-225.

James, W. *Essay in pragmatism.* (Castell Alburay, Ed.). New York: Hafner, 1948.

Levine, L. S. & Kantor, R. E. Psychological effectiveness and imposed social position. *Personnel guid. J.*, 1962, *40*, 418-425.

Meehl, P. E., & McClosky, H. Ethical and political aspects of applied psychology. *J. abnorm. soc. Psychol.*, 1947, *42*, 91-98.

Mowrer, O. Some constructive features of the concept of sin. In symposium, The role of the concept of sin, in psychotherapy. *J. counsel. Psychol.*, 1960, *7*, 185-188.

Murphy, G. E., & Guze, S. B. Setting limits: the management of the manipulative patient. *Amer. J. Psychother.*, 1960, *14*, 30-47.

Shoben, E. J., Jr. Personal responsibility, determinism, and the burden of understanding. *Personnel guid. J.*, 1961, *39*, 342-348.

Tyler, Leona E. Minimum change therapy. *Personnel guid. J.*, 1960, *38* 475-479.

ETHICAL STANDARDS

American Personnel and Guidance Association

PREAMBLE

The American Personnel and Guidance Association is an educational, scientific, and professional organization dedicated to service to society. This service is committed to profound faith in the worth, dignity, and great potentiality of the individual human being.

The marks of a profession, and therefore of a professional organization, can be stated as follows:

1. Possession of a body of specialized knowledge, skills, and attitudes known and practiced by its members.

2. This body of specialized knowledge, skills, and attitudes is derived through scientific inquiry and scholarly learning.

3. This body of specialized knowledge, skills, and attitudes is acquired through professional preparation, preferably on the graduate level, in a college or university as well as through continuous in-service training and personal growth after completion of formal education.

4. This body of specialized knowledge, skills, and attitudes, is constantly tested and extended through research and scholarly inquiry.

5. A profession has a literature of its own, even though it may, and indeed must, draw portions of its contents from other areas of knowledge.

6. A profesion exalts service to the individual and society; above personal gain. It possesses a philosophy and a code of ethics.

7. A profession through the voluntary association of its members constantly examines and improves the quality of its professional preparation and services to the individual and society.

8. Membership in the professional organization and the practice of the profession must be limited to persons meeting stated standards of preparation and competencies.

9. The profession affords a life career and permanent membership as long as services meet professional standards.

10. The public recognizes, has confidence in, and is willing to compensate the members of the profession for their services.

The Association recognizes that the vocational roles and settings of its members are identified with a wide variety of academic disciplines and levels of academic preparation. This diversity reflects the pervasiveness of the Association's interest and influence. It also poses challenging complexities in efforts to conceptualize:

a. the characteristics of members;
b. desired or requisite preparation or practice; and
c. supporting social, legal and/or ethical controls.

The specification of ethical standards enables the Association to clarify to members, future members, and to those served by members the nature of ethical responsibilities held in common by its members.

The introduction of such standards will inevitably stimulate greater concern by members for practice and preparation for practice. It will also stimulate a general growth and identification with and appreciation for both the common and diverse characteristics of the definable roles within the world of work of Association members.

There are six major areas of professional activity which encompass the work of members of APGA. For each of these areas certain general principles are listed below to serve as guide lines for ethical practice. These are preceded by a general section which includes certain principles germain to the six areas and common to the entire work of the Association members.

Section A

GENERAL

1. The member exerts what influence he can to foster the development and improvement of the profession and continues his professional growth throughout his career.

2. The member has a responsibility to the institution within which he serves. His acceptance of employment by the institution implies that he is in substantial agreement with the general policies and principles of the institution. Therefore, his professional activities are also in accord with the objectives of the institution. Within the member's own work setting, if, despite his efforts, he cannot reach agreement as to acceptable ethical standards of conduct with his superiors, he should end his affiliation with them.

3. The member must expect ethical behavior among his professional associates in APGA at all times. He is obligated, in situations where he possesses information raising serious doubt as to the ethical behavior of other members, to attempt to rectify such conditions.

4. The member is obligated to concern himself with the degree to which the personnel functions of non-members with whose work he is acquainted represent competent and ethical performance. Where his information raises serious doubt as to the ethical behavior of such persons, it is his responsibility to attempt to rectify such conditions.

5. The member must not seek self-enhancement through expressing evaluations or comparisons damaging to other ethical professional workers.

6. The member should not claim or imply professional qualifications exceeding those possessed and is responsible for correcting any misrepresentations of his qualifications by others.

7. The member providing services for personal remuneration shall, in establishing fees for such services, take careful account of the charges made for comparable services by other professional persons.

8. The member who provides information to the public or to his subordinates, peers, or superiors has a clear responsibility to see that both the content and the manner of presentation are accurate and appropriate to the situation.

9. The member has an obligation to ensure that evaluative information about such persons as clients, students, and applicants shall be shared only with those persons who will use such information for professional purposes.

10. The member shall offer professional services only, through the context of a professional relationship. Thus testing, counseling, and other services are not to be provided through the mail by means of newspaper or magazine articles, radio or television programs, or public performances.

Section B

COUNSELING

This section refers to practices involving a counseling relationship with a counselee or client and is not intended to be applicable to practices involving administrative relationships with the persons being helped. A counseling relationship denotes that the person seeking help retain full freedom of choice and decision and that the helping person has no authority or responsibility to approve or disapprove of the choices or decisions of the counselee or client. "Counselee" or "client" is used here to indicate the person (or persons) for whom the member has assumed a professional responsibility. Typically the counselee or client is the individual with whom the member has direct and primary contact. However, at times, "client" may include another person(s) when the other person(s) exercise significant control and direction over the individual being helped in connection with the decisions and plans being considered in counseling.

1. The member's *primary* obligation is to respect the integrity and promote the welfare of the counselee or client with whom he is working.

2. The counseling relationship and information resulting therefrom must be kept confidential consistent with the obligations of the member as a professional person.

3. Records of the counseling relationship including interview notes, test data, correspondence, tape recordings, and other documents are to be considered professional information for use in counseling, research, and teaching of counselors but always with full protection of the identity of the client and with precaution so that no harm will come to him.

4. The counselee or client should be informed of the conditions under which he may receive counseling assistance at or before the time he enters the counseling relationship. This is particularly true in the event that there exist conditions of which the counselee or client would not likely be aware.

5. The member reserves the right to consult with any other professionally competent person about his counselee client. In choosing his professional consultant the member must avoid placing the consultant in a conflict of interest situation, *i.e.*, the consultant must be free of any other obligatory

relation to the member's client that would preclude the consultant being a proper party to the member's efforts to help the counselee or client.

6. The member shall decline to initiate or shall terminate a counseling relationship when he cannot be of professional assistance to the counselee or client either because of lack of competence or personal limitation. In such instances the member shall refer his counselee or client to an appropriate specialist. In the event the counselee or client declines the suggested referral, the member is not obligated to continue the counseling relationship.

7. When the member learns from counseling relationships of conditions which are likely to harm others over whom his institution or agency has responsibility, he is expected to report *the condition* to the appropriate responsible authority, but in such a manner as not to reveal the identity of his counselee or clients.

8. In the event that the counelee or client's condition is such as to require others to assume responsibility for him, or when there is clear and imminent danger to the counselee or client or to others, the member is expected to report this fact to an appropriate responsible authority, and/or take such other emergency measures as the situation demands.

9. Should the member be engaged in a work setting which calls for any variation from the above statements, the member is obligated to ascertain that such variations are justifiable under the conditions and that such variations are clearly specified and made known to all concerned with such counseling services.

Section C

TESTING

1. The primary purpose of psychological testing is to provide objective and comparative measures for use in self-evaluation or evaluation by others of general or specific attributes.

2. Generally, test results constitute only one of a variety of pertinent data for personnel and guidance decisions. It is the member's responsibility to provide adequate orientation or information to the examinee(s) so that the results of testing may be placed in proper perspective with other relevant factors.

3. When making any statements to the public about tests and testing care must be taken to give accurate information and to avoid any false claims or misconceptions.

4. Different tests demand different levels of competence for administration, scoring, and interpretation. It is therefore the responsibility of the member to recognize the limits of his competence and to perform only those functions which fall within his preparation and competence.

5. In selecting tests for use in a given situation or with a particular client the member must consider not only general but also specific validity, reliability, and appropriateness of the test(s).

6. Tests should be administered under the same conditions which were established in their standardization. Except for research purposes explicitly stated, any departures from these conditions, as well as unusual behavior or irregularities during the testing session which may affect the interpretation of the tests results, must be fully noted and reported. In this connection, un-

supervised test-taking or the use of tests through the mails are of questionable value.

7. The value of psychological tests depends in part on the novelty to persons taking them. Any prior information, coaching, or reproduction of test materials tends to invalidate test results. Therefore, test security is one of the professional obligations of the member.

8. The member has the responsibility to inform the examinee(s) as to the purpose of testing. The criteria of examinee's welfare and/or explicit prior understanding with him should determine who the recipients of the test results may be.

9. The member should guard against the appropriation, reproduction, or modifications of published tests or parts thereof without express permission and adequate recognition of the original author or publisher.

Regarding the preparation, publication, and distribution of tests reference should be made to:

"Tests and Diagnostic Techniques" — Report of the Joint Committee of the American Psychological Association, American Educational Research Association, and National Council of Measurements used in Education. Supplement to *Psychological Bulletin*, 1954, 2, 1-38.

Section D

RESEARCH AND PUBLICATION

1. In the performance of any research on human subjects, the member must avoid causing any injurious effects or after-effects of the experiment upon his subjects.

2. The member may withhold information or provide misinformation to subjects only when it is essential to the investigation and where he assumes responsibility for corrective action following the investigation.

3. In reporting research results, explicit mention must be made of all variables and conditions known to the investigator which might affect interpretation of the data.

4. The member is responsible for conducting and reporting his investigations so as to minimize the possibility that his findings will be misleadng.

5. The member has an obligation to make available original research data to qualified others who may wish to replicate or verify the study.

6. In reporting research results or in making original data available, due care must be taken to disguise the identity of the subjects, in the absence of specific permission from such subjects to do otherwise.

7. In conducting and reporting research, the member should be familiar with, and give recognition to, previous work on the topic.

8. The member has the obligation to give due credit to those who have contributed significantly to his research, in accordance with their contributions.

9. The member has the obligation to honor commitments made to subjects of research in return for their cooperation.

10. The member is expected to communicate to other members the results of any research he judges to be of professional or scientific value.

Section E

CONSULTING AND PRIVATE PRACTICE

Consulting refers to a voluntary relationship between a professional helper and help-needing social unit (industry, business, school, college, etc.) in which the consultant is attempting to give help to the client in the solving of some current or potential problem.[1]

1. The member acting as a consultant must have a high degree of self-awareness of his own values and needs in entering a helping relationship which involves change in a social unit.

2. There should be understanding and agreement between consultant and client as to directions or goals of the attempted change.

3. The consultant must be reasonably certain that he or his organization have the necessary skills and resources for giving the kind of help which is needed now or that may develop later.

4. The consulting relationship must be one in which client adaptability and growth toward self-direction are encouraged and cultivated. The consultant must consistently maintain his role as a consultant and not become a decision maker for the client.

5. The consultant in announcing his availability for service as a consultant follows professional rather than commercial standards in describing his services with accuracy, dignity, and caution.

6. For private practice in testing, counseling, or consulting the ethical principles stated in all previous sections of this document are pertinent. In addition, any individual, agency, or institution offering educational and vocational counseling to the public should meet the standards of the American Board on Professional Standards in Vocational Counseling, Inc.

Section F

PERSONNEL ADMINISTRATION

1. The member is responsible for establishing working agreements with supervisors and with subordinates especially regarding counseling or clinical relationships, confidentiality, distinction between public and private material, and a mutual respect for the positions of parties involved in such issues.

2. Such working agreements may vary from one institutional setting to another. What should be the case in each instance, however, is that agreements have been specified, made known to those concerned, and whenever possible the agreements reflect institutional policy rather than personal judgment.

3. The member's responsibility to his superiors requires that he keep them aware of conditions affecting the institution, particularly those which may be potentially disrupting or damaging to the institution.

4. The member has a responsibility to select competent persons for assigned responsibilities and to see that his personnel are used maximally for the skills and experience they possess.

---

[1]This definition is adapted from "Dimensions of the Consultant's Job" by Ronald Lippitt, *The Journal of Social Issues,* Vol. XV, No. 2, 1959.

5. The member has responsibility for constantly stimulating his staff for their and his own continued growth and improvement. He must see that staff members are adequately supervised as to the quality of their functioning and for purposes of professional development.

6. The member is responsible for seeing that his staff is informed of policies, goals, and programs toward which the department's operations are oriented.

Section G

PREPARATION FOR PERSONNEL WORK

1. The member in charge of training sets up a strong program of academic study and supervised practice in order to prepare the trainees for their future responsibilities.

2. The training program should aim to develop in the trainee not only skills and knowledge, but also self-understanding.

3. The member should be aware of any manifestations of personal limitations in a student trainee which may influence the latter's provision of competent services and has an obligation to offer assistance to the trainee in securing professional remedial help.

4. The training program should include preparation in research and stimulation for the future personnel worker to do research and add to the knowledge in his field.

5. The training program should make the trainee aware of the ethical responsibilities and standards of the profession he is entering.

6. The program of preparation should aim at inculcating among the trainees, who will later become the practitioners of our profession, the ideal of service to individual and society above personal gain.

(40)

THE CODE OF ETHICS OF THE EDUCATION PROFESSION

Adopted by the NEA Representative Assembly
Detroit, Michigan, July 1963

PREAMBLE

We, professional educators of the United States of America, affirm our belief in the worth and dignity of man. We recognize the supreme importance of the pursuit of truth, the encouragement of scholarship, and the promotion of democratic citizenship. We regard as essential to these goals the protection of freedom to learn and to teach and the guarantee of equal educational opportunity for all. We affirm and accept our responsibility to practice our profession according to the highest ethical standards.

Reprinted by permission of *The National Education Association*.

We acknowledge the magnitude of the profession we have chosen, and engage ourselves, individually and collectively, to judge our colleagues and to be judged by them in accordance with the applicable provisions of this code.

PRINCIPLE I

Commitment to the Student

We measure success by the progress of each student toward achievement of his maximum potential. We therefore work to stimulate the spirit of inquiry, the acquisition of knowledge and understanding, and the thoughtful formulation of worthy goals. We recognize the importance of cooperative relationships with other community institutions, especially the home.

In fulfilling our obligations to the student, we —

1. Deal justly and considerately with each student.
2. Encourage the student to study varying points of view and respect his right to form his own judgment.
3. Withhold confidential information about a student or his home unless we deem that its release serves professional purposes, benefits the student, or is required by law.
4. Make discreet use of available information about the student.
5. Conduct conferences with or concerning students in an appropriate place and manner.
6. Refrain from commenting unprofessionally about a student or his home.
7. Avoid exploiting our professional relationship with any student.
8. Tutor only in accordance with officially approved policies.
9. Inform appropriate individuals and agencies of the student's educational needs and assist in providing an understanding of his educational experiences.
10. Seek constantly to improve learning facilities and opportunities.

PRINCIPLE II

Commitment to the Community

We believe that patriotism in its highest form requires dedication to the principles of our democratic heritage. We share with all other citizens the responsibility for the development of sound public policy. As educators, we are particularly accountable for participating in the development of educational programs and policies and for interpreting them to the public.

In fulfilling our obligations to the community, we —

1. Share the responsibility for improving the educational opportunities for all.
2. Recognize that each educational institution may have a person authorized to interpret its official policies.

3. Acknowledge the right and responsibility of the public to participate in the formulation of educational policy.
4. Evaluate through appropriate professional procedures conditions within a district or institution of learning, make known serious deficiencies, and take any action deemed necessary and proper.
5. Use educational facilities for intended purposes consistent with applicable policy law, and regulation.
6. Assume full political and citizenship responsibilities, but refrain from exploiting the institutional privileges of our professional positions to promote political candidates or partisan activities.
7. Protect the educational program against undesirable infringement.

PRINCIPLE III

Commitment to the Profession

We believe that the quality of the services of the education profession directly influences the future of the nation and its citizens. We therefore exert every effort to raise educational standards, to improve our service, to promote a climate in which the exercise of professional judgment is encouraged, and to achieve conditions which attract persons worthy of the trust to careers in education. Aware of the value of united effort, we contribute actively to the support, planning, and programs of our professional organizations.

In fulfilling our obligations to the profession, we —

1. Recognize that a profession must accept responsibility for the conduct of its members and understand that our own conduct may be regarded as representative.
2. Participate and conduct ourselves in a responsible manner in the development and implementation of policies affecting education.
3. Cooperate in the selective recruitment of prospective teachers and in the orientation of student teachers, interns, and those colleagues new to their positions.
4. Accord just and equitable treatment to all members of the profession in the exercise of their professional rights and responsibilities, and support them when unjustly accused or mistreated.
5. Refrain from assigning professional duties to non-professional personnel when such assignment is not in the best interest of the student.
6. Provide, upon request, a statement of specific reason for administrative recommendations that lead to the denial of increments, significant changes in employment, or termination of employment.
7. Refrain from exerting undue influence based on the authority of our positions in the determination of professional decisions by colleagues.
8. Keep the trust under which confidential information is exchanged.
9. Make appropriate use of time granted for professional purposes.
10. Interpret and use the writings of others and the findings of educational research with intellectual honesty.
11. Maintain our integrity when dissenting by basing our public criticism of education on valid assumptions as established by careful evaluation of facts or hypotheses.

12. Represent honestly our professional qualifications and identify ourselves only with reputable educational institutions.
13. Respond accurately to requests for evaluations of colleagues seeking professional positions.
14. Provide applicants seeking information about a position with an honest description of the assignment, the conditions of work, and related matters.

PRINCIPLE IV

Commitment to Professional Employment Practices

We regard the employment agreement as a solemn pledge to be executed both in spirit and in fact in a manner consistent with the highest ideals of professional service. Sound professional personnel relationships with governing boards are built upon personal integrity, dignity, and mutual respect.

In fulfilling our obligations to professional employment practices, we —
1. Apply for or offer a position on the basis of professional and legal qualifications.
2. Apply for a specific position only when it is known to be vacant and refrain from such practices as underbidding or commenting adversely about other candidates.
3. Fill no vacancy except where the terms, conditions, policies, and practices permit the exercise of our professional judgment and skill, and where a climate conducive to professional service exists.
4. Adhere to the conditions of a contract or to the terms of an appointment until either has been terminated legally or by mutual consent.
5. Give prompt notice of any change in availability of service, in status of applications, or in change in position.
6. Conduct professional business through the recognized educational and professional channels.
7. Accept no gratuities or gifts of significance that might influence our professional duties.
8. Engage in no outside employment that will impair the effectiveness of our professional service and permit no commercial exploitation of our professional position.

CHAPTER 4: QUESTIONS FOR DISCUSSION

1. Read again the summary of Patterson's essay on values in counseling. What are his major points? If any of them disturb you, give your reasoning on them.
2. Hobbs raises the question of whether free choice (or free will) does in fact exist. Philosophers generally state that "Ought implies *can*" (i.e., it is meaningless to say that someone "ought" to do something which he is *unable* to do. If free will does not exist, what differences take place in law, human relationships, and guidance? Can you find some "middle ground" for the extreme positions on this matter?
3. Curran quotes the old philosophical principle that "ontogeny recapitulates phylogeny." What does this *mean*? What evidences do you see of this in counseling and guidance?

4. Adams quotes Smith's study of how information should be used in counseling. Do any of the findings trouble you? What alternative ways of viewing the use of such information do you feel might be better?

5. Cox offers guidelines for the school counselor in the last paragraph of his essay. Do any of these suggestions trouble you? For what reasons?

6. Klinger's article on moral values across cultures teaches far more than ways of viewing "foreigners" who come to our country. What other "movements from culture to culture" other than country-to-country need the careful attentions of counselors and teachers? Do you see parallels between this and Haberman's article in Chapter 1?

7. After reading Walters' article, consider the often-made statement that "A clergyman must stop being a clergyman before he can counsel anyone." Do you believe this? Discuss the statement for all of its possible meanings in counseling.

8. Golightly raises the question of middle-class counselors' attempting to function with underprivileged clients. What are the major social class differences, according to sociologists? If Golightly's analysis is valid, what measures must we take to improve services to the underprivileged client?

9. Mowrer states, "If one is functioning in a given social system, then one is honor-bound to 'play the game' as prescribed in the system. Or if one *must* deviate from it, to do so openly, honorably, and take the stipulated consequences . . . or else leave the system." What meanings might this have for a counselor in school situations?

10. Samler states that there are times when a counselor simply must step in and accept responsibility for the client. How might a counselor defend himself against critics in such cases? What sorts of instances might warrant such assumption of responsibility by the counselor? What are some of the problems arising from such actions?

11. Compare the APGA Ethical Standards with the NEA Code of Ethics. Since the counselor is generally regarded as a member of both the counseling and teaching professions, he might well examine both codes. Do you see any fundamental conflicts between the two codes? Are there points with which you cannot agree, or which need clarification?

12. Bring to the attention of the class a situation which is not covered or not clearly covered by the codes of ethics. Discuss possible approaches, and the problems involved in each of them. What "guiding principle" seems to emerge?

Chapter

5

New Directions

This group of essays may prove to be the most controversial of all the chapters in this book. The essays express viewpoints which in many ways do not coincide with the thinking of many thoughtful and well-established men in the fields of counseling, guidance, and therapy. They raise a host of questions about "usual" procedures, value orientations, emphases in research, and order-of-importance in helping relationships.

The counselor must ask himself, "How do these ideas square with what I have read about helping relationships, techniques, and viewpoints on objectives?" He must then ask himself, even if he rejects the major emphases proposed, "What can I learn from each of them?" From the standpoint of the philosopher, of course, his major question might well be, "**On what grounds** do I reject or accept their major premises and recommendations?"

Regretfully, not all "new directions" can be included in any single book, nor can any new current thought be elaborated in great detail. One of the most widely-discussed new viewpoints in counseling and therapy today is existentialism and counseling. The rapprochement between this brand of philosophy and counseling offers promising and exciting times ahead in the formulation of guidance theory and practice. Those interested in this way of viewing the human condition might survey several journals which have provided thought-provoking essays about existentialism and helping relationships in the past few years: APGA *Journal, Journal of Counseling Psychology, Journal of Humanistic Psychology, Review of Existential Psychology and Psychiatry, Existential Inquiries, The American Psychologist* and others. The works of Rollo May, Adrian Van Kaam, Abraham Maslow, Viktor Frankl, O. H. Mowrer, recent writings of Carl Rogers, and shorter works by Edward Dreyfus and others also bring into focus the major contentions of existential philosophy. In particular those who wish further reading might investigate Rollo May's *Existence*, Jean-Paul Sartre's *Existentialism*, and Carlton Beck's *Philosophical Foundations of Guidance*. Another book dealing with the particular relationship of existentialism to counseling is now in press by Beck. (*Guidance in a New Era*, Prentice-Hall, 1967).

351

The counselor should ask himself, "What can I learn from all of these writers about the human condition and human aspirations? What differences in emphases do they demand?"

THE LOGIC OF COUNSELING RESEARCH

Henry Borow

University of Minnesota

It took psychology a long time to divest itself of the intuitive and speculative trappings which marked its pre-twentieth century identification with metaphysical philosophy. When it finally joined the company of the experimental sciences it embraced empiricism with a vengeance. The discovery that man's behavior was not after all inscrutable, that it was orderly and potentially predictable within the sphere of natural law, produced the exhiliration of a heady wine. Radical behaviorism of the 1920's and its applied counterpart, trait-measurement psychology, made common cause in their zeal to (1) measure and (2) correlate anything which breathed and moved. This was a free-wheeling period in psychology's history, in America if not in Europe, during which the connections between controlled observation and behavior theory troubled few workers. For many psychologists, building a body of knowledge about man's behavior rested on the strategy of formulating an expanding list of response-response laws (e.g. correlations between two trait tests).

With scientific maturity has come a tempering sobriety. We are no longer so supremely confident about the explanatory powers of our instruments. Two insistent interdependent questions disturb us: (1) *What* is being measured? (2) What does it *signify*? In research in psychotherapy and counseling psychology these questions are caught up in the enigmatic criterion issue. Contemporary clinicians and counselors seem to sense that a descriptive language which includes only sense data (i.e. observation) terms is too impoverished to permit them to talk in a satisfactory way about their clients' behavior. They use hypothetical constructs freely in behavior description and explanation. Yet about this state of affairs many of them seem most unhappy and apologetic. Their statements leave the impression, and in this feeling I believe they are wrong, that they will not have exorcised the metaphysical gremlin until they recast all constructs in language referring to the observable. If they are merely insisting that we need to locate proper indicator variables for our hypothetical constructs for purposes of research, there is no quarrel. Such indicators are the empirical referents which we must use to formulate and test laws which we then hope to connect with theory. But I fear they propose ultimately to supplant the terms of theory by those of observation. Like the radical behaviorists (e.g. Skinner) they want to build a reduction language by translating the hypothetical terms of behavior science as purely operational

Reprinted by permission of the Author and the *Journal of Counseling Psychology,* Vol. 3, No. 4, 1956, 292-296.

terms. Operationism, they seem to be saying, will lead us out of our conceptual wilderness.

OPERATIONISM IN QUESTION

This is perhaps not the place for a critique of operationism. Since, however, the strategy of much current research design in counseling and psychotherapy is rooted in operationism, a few dissenting comments may not be inappropriate. In a private communication, Vernon Dolphin, a former Minnesota colleague, points to an abortive attempt to frame operational definitions in psychology which frequently occurs but is seldom challenged. Dolphin notes that it is dispositional terms (e.g. compliant, manic, anxious) for which operational definitions are commonly contrived. He contends, and I believe correctly, that dispositional terms are logically distinct from operational terms. Unlike the latter, they "carry implications of an indeterminate kind and number" and cannot be adequately defined by single, specific acts or discrete behavioral items. They cannot in consequence, Dolphin writes, be made over into operational terms. I would add that neither can clearly theoretical terms be operationally defined. Such constructs as the unconscious, guilt and over-compensation, like the term electro-magnetic action in physical science, are essentially non-instantial variables. They do not exist in the data language even though we may come to some agreement about their indicators in the world of observation. Operational terms tend to be descriptive in character; theoretical terms are explanatory. The two proceed from different logical bases and cannot be strictly equated. How, for example, is the lavish theoretical language of psychoanalysis to be cast in operational terms? Those readers who have inspected the valiant but unconvincing attempt by Albert Ellis (1) will doubt that this trick can be carried off. Even if it were possible to reduce terms of theory to the data language, one would still have to decide whether the result would be salvation or disaster.

Herbert Feigl and Michael Scriven of the Minnesota Center for Philosophy of Science at the University of Minnesota have noted the limitations of operationism in this connection. Scriven's (6) recent paper "A Study of Radical Behaviorism" is a detailed and systematic attack on Skinnerian psychology partly on the ground that it attempts to strip the science of behavior bare of theory and partly on the ground that it often makes use of theory while denying that it does. Ernest Nagel of Columbia University, in an invited address at the University of Minnesota, forcefully contended that theoretical (non-operational) terms are essential to science, that with the help of theory one can make a wider range of deductions than from laws alone. Proper statements of theory, Nagel believes, allow us to establish a better relationship between the other statements in science.

Where does all of this leave us in counseling psychology? Does it mean a return to untestable metaphysical speculation in talking about our procedures and our clients' behavior? I do not think so. The language of theoretical science and that of metaphysics are not equivalent and the use of one does not require that we lapse into the other. When we say there are hypothetical constructs (as well as operational terms) in the language of psychodynamics, we are admitting only that certain statements in our science which tend to be explanatory in character are not directly testable. It is no different in the other sciences. They have theories and they have laws. So does psychology. Laws, which have an observation base, can be confirmed or disconfirmed on the strength of the experimental evidence. Strictly speaking, theories are never confirmed in this manner. Because they cannot be put to test of direct observation, they must be accepted, modified, extended or rejected according to their ability to unify the known facts and laws of our science. A theory which logically connects a large number of laws, which helps us "explain" the laws and the causal relations between them, and from which the laws themselves may be deduced and accurate predictions made is a sound theory. It is this type of theory we seek for the counseling process. We shall never get it by precipitously rewriting all the statements of counselor and client behavior into alleged operational terms.

THE CHARACTER OF FUTURE RESEARCH

Three rather general proposals might be made regarding the direction research in counseling should take if it is to be fruitful.

(1) High priority should be given to research which tries to bring a semblance of order and standardization to the descriptive language of counseling phychology. It is saying nothing new to assert that terms in science must be used with precision and rigor. It may, however, surprise some counselors to learn how inconsistent and inefficient the terminological fabric of their field is. A few years ago Vernon Dolphin and I essayed an informal survey and analysis of the language of adjustment. We found for some common terms, e.g., adjustment, a variety of conflicting and disjointed definitions. Conversely, some concepts (e.g. sound mental health) were represented in the literature by a host of verbal labels. Some readers will recall the attempt of Rotter (4) to come to grips with the problem in his recently published book. Here Rotter confronts questions such as "The problem of labeling and categorizing," "The problem of an inadequate language of description," and "Criteria for an ideal language of description." In a yet unpublished symposium paper, "Toward a Concept of the Normal Personality," delivered before the 1956 Convention of the American College Personnel Association, E. J. Shoben of Columbia University attacked what he called the "lack of conceptual clarity concerning the nature of psychological normality." Shoben called into serious question the concepts of conformity and statistical normality as criteria by which the normal personality is identified. In an eloquent and thoughtful explication of the concept of integrative adjustment, he proposed four distinguishing characteristics of the person to whom the label is to be applied. These were self-control, acceptance of personal responsibility, social interest, and ideals. Shoben freely admitted that this was but a first approximation to the reformulation of the concept of integrative adjustment.

The four descriptive terms are, of course, themselves global in character and require delimitation and clarification. Even if they were to prove acceptable to the body of counselors, sets of factual referents would have to be evolved by which counseling researchers might make repeatable observations and classify their findings. Lest the reader be puzzled, there is no contradition between this last statement of mine and what I said earlier about the inordinate use of operational definitions. As I understand him, Shoben is using the term "integrative adjustment" as a summary descriptive term rather than as an explanatory one and as such it will require observation-based indicators to be useful. Incidentally, Shoben wisely notes that one cannot hope to avoid questions of ethical values in defining something which brushes the social code as broadly as does this one. He says, "At this point the behavioral sciences and ethics meet and merge — (it) seems unlikely that any conception of normality can be developed apart from some general considerations that are fundamentally moral." Meehl (2) has also raised the issue of psychotherapy's convergence on ethics. He writes, "A rigorous, sophisticated consideration of the ethics of therapeutic 'guidance' — by workers competent in axiology and casuistry is long overdue. Current thinking on this topic is almost wholly confined to cliches."

(2) More evidence, much more, is urgently needed on precisely what occurs during the counseling process. Except for the Rogerians and to a far lesser degree some schools of psychoanalysis, moment-to-moment factual reports of the counselor's and client's operations are absent from the experimental literature. To feed into a counseling outcomes experiment an assortment of unanalyzed "homogeneous" counselors loosely categorized as "eclectic," for example, is to obscure forever the specific inter-counselor behavior differences which contribute to variance in momentary and long-range client behavior. Tedious as it may be to compile and to analyze, we need to know what a large assortment of counselors do with a large assortment of persons who come for help. If this suggests to the reader that we invite the risk of forcing the description of counseling into an ideographic mold, it is a risk we shall have to take. Should the nature of counseling and its net effect turn out to be functions of the *particular* counselor, the *particular* client and the *particular* problem set, this is something we had better discover sooner than late.

The principal point then, I think, is that we need a much more nearly exhaustive report on what counseling is as actually practiced. The editor of this section of the *Journal*, Harold Pepinsky (3), comes close to expressing the same concern. He argues that the counselor must be explicit in telling what he does with a client. In enumerating two requirements of the counselor as a theory builder, Pepinsky says the counselor must specify "the kinds of responses he wants the client to make as an end-product of counseling and (he must specify) the decisions by which he makes it maximally likely that such client responses will occur." One certainly would not wish to quarrel with these laudable proposals with which Pepinsky exhorts counselors. I would, moreover, agree with him that counselors are not now doing these things. That they are not is attributable, I believe, to personal and situational conditions quite different from those which Pepinsky invokes as an explanation. That is another matter. My thesis here is that if we are to talk to one another univocally in this field we need desperately to know what counselors are now doing in counseling. This is a straightforward research problem in factual description. It is not an alternative to Pepinsky's proposals in which the counselor functions both as a practitioner and as a theorist testing his hypotheses. Both research emphases are needed. If they were adopted, we might get somewhere with counseling.

(3) My last proposal takes the form of an admonition. It is that research on the overall evaluation of outcomes is likely to furnish a spare yield until

more basic questions about personality formation, the nature of counseling and the counselor-client interaction are given better answers. Is Pepinsky (3) right when he asserts that it is premature to speak about a general theory of the counseling process? Is Meehl (2) right when he contends that "the state of theory (in psychotherapy) and its relation to technique is obviously chaotic whatever our pretentions?" The evidence is on their side. What we need then is analytic research that will feed back to theory and nourish it. I have been struck with how many attempts have been made to assess counseling "in the mass" and how little all of this has taught us. Where does it lead? Even when results have been positive (i.e. in the predicted direction), and the frequency of such occurrences has been depressingly small, the cause of scientific explanation has not been well served. The antecedent conditions of client "improvement" in such global attacks on counseling have not been convincingly teased out and too often the nature of the "improvement" itself has not been formally (logically) analyzed.

Of course, the most important question we ask about counseling in the long haul is "does it work?" Yet we are hardly in a position currently to make a rigorous formulation of the issue. Research attempts in this domain have often been immodest to the times and logically over-extended. Before we can get intelligible information on this jackpot question we will have to raise and frame answers to a number of others. I conceive of these prior questions as concerned with the clarification of terms and with the establishment of the lower-order causal connections of the therapeutic process. How are the descriptive terms in the language of mental health to be formulated? What counselor dispositions and behaviors and what assigned therapy tasks accompany what client movements in counseling? Which are the stable and non-subjective criterion variables which may best serve as unambiguous referents for the client constructs we wish to manipulate through the therapeutic strategy? The state of our knowledge about therapy and counseling being what it is, experimental attacks on the problem must continue to be pressed on many fronts. I do not wish to propose a moratorium on all research on counseling outcomes. My plea is rather for a redress of balance in our total research program.

REFERENCES

1. Ellis, Albert. An operational reformulation of some of the basic principles of psychoanalysis. In H. Feigl and M. Scriven (Eds.), *The foundations of science and the concepts of psychology and psychoanalysis*. Minneapolis: University of Minnesota Press, 1956. Pp. 131-154.
2. Meehl, Paul E. Psychotherapy. In Stone, C. P. (Ed.), *Annual Review of psychology, volume 6*. Stanford, California: Annual Reviews, Inc., 1955. Pp. 357-78.
3. Pepinsky, Harold B. Research notes from here and there. *J. counsel. Psychol.*, 1956, 3, 222-28.
4. Rotter, Julian B. *Social learning and clinical psychology*. New York: Prentice-Hall, 1954.
5. Schrier, Harvey. The significance of identification in therapy. *Amer. J. Orthopsychiat.*, 1953, 23, 585-604.
6. Scriven, Michael. A study of radical behaviorism. In H. Feigl and M. Scriven (Eds.), *The foundations of science and the concepts of psychology and psychoanalysis*. Minneapolis: University of Minnesota Press, 1956. Pp. 88-130.

42

PATTERN ANALYSIS IN COUNSELING

Edward W. Robinson

Western Illinois University

In the field of counseling, the problem of determining counseling effectiveness is ever present, and does not lend itself to an easy solution. Each counseling philosophy, or technique, that has been developed has ultimately to be rejected or accepted on the faith one has in the person proposing the system. The main reason faith is so essential is that a working definition of adjustment acceptable to all counselors has not yet been presented. One of the purposes of this paper is to attempt to present a definition of adjustment that can be measured and, to a degree at least, objectified.

It is generally true that a well-adjusted person can be recognized as different from the neurotic or psychotic individual, even by the intelligent but untrained observer. The generalization holds true, however, for only those subjects who occupy extreme positions on our scales of adjustment. Blum[1] found that grade school teachers could adequately separate those children who are having extreme emotional difficulties from those who are generally considered as normal. At least, in his study, the agreement in selecting cases of maladjustment was as high between teachers and clinically trained persons as it was between two clinically trained persons.

The school counselor, however, is much more concerned with those pupils who fall within the normal range and are not nearly so easy to detect, but show signs of moderate lack of adjustment. The ability to separate the extremely abnormal from the extremely normal thus is of little help to the counselor. As those that are abnormal will probably be recognized and referred to a specialist, they generally are little problem to the counselor after a referral has been made. The need for techniques of a more definitive nature would seem to be apparent. Another purpose of this paper is to attempt to provide one of these techniques.

It is interesting to note that in Blum's study[1] even the trained psychologists were in disagreement concerning whether some of the children should be classified as being poorly adjusted. Since the process used to separate the poorly adjusted children from the normal group was very subjective and dependent upon the training of the psychologist, the findings are not surprising. The primary difference between the teachers' evaluation and that of the psychologists was the level and degree of training, as both had learned to evaluate adjustment subjectively. Although the writer is willing to accept the clinical judgment of those psychologically trained, it must be remembered that there is a possibility where the disagreement exists that the teachers are more accurate than the psychologists.

It is obvious that if disagreement can occur among trained persons concerning the adjustment of extreme positions on the subjective adjustment scale,

An original article for this book.

the task of determining the effects of malfunction in those that are generally considered as normal would be much more difficult. The lack of success with problems of underachievement, school dropouts, delinquency and so on would tend to substantiate the degree of difficulty in determining and helping pupils with so-called normal problems.

In an attempt to attack this problem at its base, many definitions of normalcy and adjustment were examined. Three representative samples will be presented here. It is recognized that many variations of these three exist, but these variations cannot be covered in this paper.

The first definition to be presented is probably best represented by the writings of Horney,[2] in which the counselor is to aid the client into insight concerning his own personality structure. It would seem that anything the client finds as he spends long hours in this examination will aid him in self-acceptance, and adjustment becomes a matter of self acceptance. Whether the long hours are spent in the reflective, nondirective, client-centered counseling, or in psychiatrically centered therapy sessions is of little importance in relation to the concept of normalcy. If the counselor is to aid the client into personality insight, the client must completely understand himself in relation to a static personality structure. In other words, the acceptance of the personality as unchanging is inveterate. The process of becoming a person becomes one of using this personality structure in the particular culture and environment in which the person happens to be located. If the client learns to accept this static personality, and understand it, then he is considered to be normal in his time and place.

Since this definition of normalcy is so dependent upon the time and place the personality is located, it is impossible to establish any objective measurement of normalcy. There is no objective method of determining whether the client was normal when he came in for therapy or when he decides to quit therapy. Never will this individual be pronounced cured, since the cure depends upon the static personality in time and space. *Normalcy, then, is what the counselor sees and becomes a concept in the mind and emotions of the counselor.* No quarter is shown for the individual who happens to arrive at the office of a counselor who would himself not be accepted as normal by the rest of the population.

The second definition of normalcy to be explored was that which maintains normalcy is statistical. In this concept, the individual who conforms to the group in which he is functioning is considered to be normal in the particular trait being measured. The position is best represented by Hathaway and McKinley[3] and the Minnesota Multiphasic Personality Inventory. The many subdivisions of this particular inventory indicate the complexity of the personality of the individual. In each of these scales the individual is considered to be normal when he scores like the majority of other individuals taking the same test. This particular test finds wide usage in the clinical setting. Many serious objections have been raised to its use in the school setting however, as many of the items are not suitable for use in the public school. Other tests that have been constructed for use in schools have met with limited acceptance. One of the serious objections to these tests is that they tend to fix the blame for the condition of the individual rather than give insight into personality malfunctions. Thus the statistical definition used to determine normalcy has been questioned by many in the psychological field.

The serious objection to the use of intelligence testing which supposedly tends to eliminate creative persons is another example of the rejection of the statistical concept of normalcy. Since intelligence is considered as one of the functions of personality, the rejection of intelligence testing must be considered as indicative of the rejection of the statistical concept of normalcy. Here again the interpretation that is being placed on the measurement of intelligence is that any individual occupies a given position in relation to the standardizing population for that particular test. Terman[4] indicates the lack of validity in the scale being used for this measurement. The same lack of validity is noticed by Thurstone[5] in his writings concerning the development of the Test of Primary Mental Abilities.

There thus seems to be a philosophical split between the two groups that inhibits the establishment of an objective concept of normalcy. While one group insists it be clinical and subjective the other insists it be statistical and restrictive.

The position stated by Horney and that stated by the statisticians has one element in common, however, as both would insist that normalcy is concerned with a static position within the individual and his relationship with the standardizing population in time and space. While the first would be in terms of self-concept as it now exists, the second is concerned with a statistical average as it now exists. Either of these positions denies the growth concept in normalcy and, in the counseling process if not in theory, denies the possibility of growth for the personality of the individual and thus for society. The longer these definitions are used in counseling, the longer will be the delay in establishing a defensible base for counseling theory and counseling activity.

Appearing in the literature more recently is a concept of normalcy that would seem to be more in agreement with the idea that the human being is a constantly growing and developing organism. Overstreet[6] indicates that man is in the constant process of maturing and never reaches maturity, or a static condition. The same idea is discussed by Allport[7] as he speaks of the process of becoming, and by Rogers[8] in his latest book, *On Becoming a Person*. Maslow[9] has used this concept and has formulated from it a definition of normalcy. To him, normalcy is *functioning in accordance with design*.

The limitation in this concept to adjustment of a fundamental unit, MAN, instead of working with an everchanging relationship between MAN and his society and culture, simplifies the problems for the counselor and the client. Behind this concept lies the concern that MAN, functioning in accordance with his design, can adjust to any reasonable environment in which he finds himself. The placing of importance on MAN instead of his environment in the counseling interview will allow the diagnostician to be concerned with the malfunction *within* the individual, rather than having to adjust each relationship. This process is neither directive nor nondirective, but occupies a third orientation to man.

An example to illustrate the foregoing construct would seem to be in order. It can best be seen in the approach the medical profession takes to physical health. There are basically three approaches that medicine could take to this problem as it concerns physical health.

The first of these would be to rid the environment of all harmful bacteria in order that man would not be attacked by them. If this alternative were successful, man would be reduced to a state of vegetation if he survived at all. Since nature seems to perform in a cyclical pattern, the destruction of any part of the cycle is a dangerous practice. The dependence of higher forms of life on lower forms is self-evident.

The second alternative would be to "inoculate" man so that the harmful effects of the bacteria would be eliminated. This process is actually one of strengthening man, and is generally used wherever possible in medical science today. It is suggested that this same alternative be used in the psychological adjustment of man with adaptive modifications. An attempt will be made to show how this is possible.

The third alternative would be to consider the health of man in every given situation in which he may find himself, and be ever ready to make adjustments in either the environment or the individual as the need exists. This alternative would insist that each person has his own personal physician, or psychologist, with him at all times to make a constant check on him and on the environment. The medical profession has not followed the last idea except for treating very special citizens, but has leaned toward the strengthening of man so that he can withstand any reasonable environment. This strengthening of man, actually calling on the internal strengths that already exist within him, is inherent in the counseling based upon the definition of man functioning in accordance with his design.

Counselors and guidance personnel are today caught in the dilemma of which of these three choices to make. This is especially true wtih counselors in the educational setting. While some would like to construct the perfect curricula and emotional climate for their client, (the bacteria free environment) others would like to be continually available to adjust the individual to his environment, making changes either in their client or the environment as the counselor interprets the need. It is the thesis of this paper that the alternative of inoculation, or building resistance into the client, is neither manipulatory or evil and is worthy of trial. The problem is how this should be accomplished.

If this definition of normalcy and adjustment can be accepted, together with the concept of building strength into the client to fight his own psychological battles, then it will be possible for us to proceed with determining what man's design is and the process it goes through from birth to death concerning growth and development. It is to this definition of normalcy and adjustment that the fundamentals of Pattern Analysis are related. It should also be noted that this particular system of determining problems of the stoppage of psychological growth and development within the normal individual was taught to the writer by the hundreds of normal cases seen over a five year period in a college counseling setting. The theoretical position expressed here thus is an attempt to correlate the facts gleaned from these pupils into a meaningful framework. The framework was not built first and the facts forced to fit.

It was noted in counseling that when two values within the individual were in opposition to each other, and of approximate equal strength, the individual was incapable of using his intelligence and emotions to best advantage. The intelligence and emotions seemed to be inately there but no longer functional to the advantage of the client. It was also noted that on many occasions these problems were expressed in physiological symptoms such as headaches, high blood pressure, ulcers and so on. (These reports came from the medical department of the school.) Another symptom that was generally present was the retardation of thought processes, with a specific area of intellectual retardation in function. The symptoms for a specific intellectual retardation seemed always to come from the identical causal agency. These causal agents could be and were reduced to the lack of basic need fulfillment as it applied to a specific need. Thus *Pattern Analysis is the process of determining the specific need that is being frustrated within the individual by his reaction to a specific intellectual factor in relation to his specific reaction to other intellectual factors.*

Several generalizations which emerged from these observations (approximately 2,600 cases) are listed here.

1. It is actually possible to identify problem areas and to predict the symptomatic responses the individual client will present in the counseling interview through a Pattern Analysis of test scores as described in this paper.
2. The highest score an individual makes on a factored test of intelligence is representative of the intellectual ability of that individual.
3. All scores below this level (the level of the highest score) are indicative of the type of problem and the degree to which this individual is not functioning in accordance with his own design, and are therefore indicative of the area and degree of maladjustment.
4. The depression of any given test score is indicative of a specific basic need that has not been fulfilled for the individual. *All* individuals having the same problem seem to reject the same area of intelligence.
5. Human energy (motivation) used for growth in the person who is free to function in accordance with his design is turned inward when a problem of conflicting value judgments threatens the self.
6. Human energy is again available for growth (intellectual, physical, and emotional) when the individual self is no longer threatened.
7. Counseling need not provide any specific relationship for all individuals. The relationship established is one that is congruent with the desires of the counselor and the client.
8. The individual our society calls well adjusted is functionally capable of achieving anything he desires, in relation to his total ability level, and will score equally well on any factored subtests as proof of his ability and adjustment.

The particular tests that have been used in this type of Pattern Analysis are The Differential Aptitude Tests, Form A & B and The Sequential Test of Educational Progress, Reading Section, Form 1A. In addition to the tests used, high school and college marks were examined as they appear on the profiles in this paper. The tests were given to large groups of entering freshmen and the results were profiled for each student. Each Pattern found will be presented here and an analysis and explanation of it will be given.

It must be remembered that there are some individuals in our society who are well adjusted and some who will show more than one problem. In the latter, one problem is likely to be hidden until another problem is removed. When either problem is removed, the problem that could not be seen previously will become apparent. The problems will be presented here as if only one problem exists, as it is the writer's desire to keep this paper as simple as possible.

The first pattern to be presented will be the one most of our honor students scored. This pattern represents the person who has no problems with which he is incapable of dealing. At least, there seem to be no blocking problems in terms of school achievement. This pattern is as follows:

The individual who brings to college this balanced intelligence seems to have few emotional problems he cannot handle. It seems to make little difference whether his scores are at the 95th percentile or the 65th percentile; he will do outstanding work in his college program. This does not seem to apply, however, if he scores below the 50th percentile. The students who score above the 50th percentile are usually placed in the honors program, not on the basis of their test scores but on the basis of their excellent high school marks. Although they did not always earn top marks in the honors program, they proved themselves capable of doing work of a higher caliber.

If the contention in this paper is accurate, i.e., that emotional problems tend to rob one of his functional ability to concentrate, then one would expect these students to perform in an exceptional manner. These expectations were upheld in most cases, and in those cases where performance was not up to expectations, a retest using alternate forms of the same tests indicated one of the problems in this paper. It can only be assumed that the change in test scores and the lowered production after the individual entered college were indicative of the problems that had occurred after college entrance.

It might also be mentioned that where counseling was successful with the cases to be examined, a retest using alternate forms of the same test produced these patterns of test scores. The grades of the pupil would also rise to the higher level on the profile. As this will be explained further in the article, no more will be said about it at this point.

The next pattern to be presented is the most common of all, and the one that has been found easiest to remedy in the counseling interview. It is presented in profile form.

When the score for verbal reasoning and the score for reading comprehension are lower than the other scores made by an individual, there is evidence in the counseling interview (undirected), derived from the symptomatic responses of the client, that the client is feeling inadequate. These feelings are indicated as feelings of guilt. The symptoms expressed by the client will be:

1. A seeming dislike for self. This may take the form of self-punishment (verbal) or conceit used as a cover for these feelings.
2. A dislike for talking before audiences or meeting new people.
3. The client will report extreme tension during examinations.
4. Extreme tension is usually noted in the counseling interview.
5. The conversation of the client is concerned with personal values, i.e., right vs. wrong, mistakes vs. being correct, things one should do vs. things one should not do, and so on.
6. Socially acceptable deficiencies will be stated by the client concerning himself, with a stated desire for self-correction. He will indicate that

12th Grade Pupil Profile
Test Scores and School Marks

Identification No. _____ Pattern #1 Date _____ Sex __M__

Percentile	Chemistry Grade	English Grade	For. Lang. Grade	Phy. Sci Grade	Nat. Sci. Grade	Algebra Grade	Reading	Sentences M	Sentences F	Spelling M	Spelling F	Clerical M	Clerical F	Mechanical M	Mechanical F	Space M	Space F	Abstract M	Abstract F	Numerical M	Numerical F	Verbal M	Verbal F	Percentile
99							67	76	79	98	99	92	93	65	53	94	88	46	45	40	38	48	48	99
97							66	75	78	97	98	91	92	64	52	93	87	45	44	39	37	47	47	97
95							(65)	68	73	93	95	80	84	62	48	88	80	45	43	(37)	35	(45)	44	95
90	(A)	(A)	(A)	(A)	(A)	(A)	63	63	69	89	93	74	80	(59)	44	(84)	75	(44)	41	36	32	42	42	90
85							61	58	65	84	90	70	76	58	41	80	70	43	41	34	30	40	39	85
80							60	55	62	79	87	67	74	56	38	77	66	38	37	33	28	38	37	80
75	B	B	B	B	B	B	58	52	60	76	84	65	72	55	36	74	62	37	36	31	26	36	35	75
70							(57)	49	57	71	82	63	70	(53)	35	72	59	37	36	30	24	35	34	70
65							56	46	55	67	79	61	69	52	33	(69)	56	(30)	35	(28)	23	(33)	32	65
60							54	44	53	63	77	60	67	50	31	66	52	35	34	27	21	32	31	60
55	C	C	C	C	C	C	53	42	51	59	74	59	65	48	30	63	49	34	32	25	20	30	29	55
50							51	40	49	56	72	57	64	46	28	61	46	33	30	24	17	29	28	50
45							49	37	47	52	69	56	63	45	27	57	42	32	28	22	16	27	26	45
40							47	35	45	48	65	54	61	43	26	54	38	31	27	20	15	26	25	40
35							46	33	43	43	62	53	60	41	24	49	35	30	25	19	13	25	23	35
30							45	31	41	39	59	52	59	40	22	45	31	28	23	17	12	23	22	30
25	D	D	D	D	D	D	43	29	39	34	54	50	57	38	21	40	28	26	21	15	10	21	20	25
20							41	26	36	29	50	49	56	35	19	34	24	24	18	14	9	20	19	20
15							36	23	33	24	45	47	54	32	16	27	20	22	14	12	7	18	17	15
10	E	E	E	E	E	E	33	20	30	18	37	45	52	32	14	21	15	19	8	9	5	16	14	10
5							29	16	25	11	29	42	49	23	11	15	7	14	2	7	3	13	12	5
3							27	11	20	3	19	38	46	23	7	10	3	8	0	4	1	10	9	3
1							24	4	14	0	7	34	42	16	4	5		1		2		8	7	1

(handwritten annotation across chart: "either or")

363

12th Grade Pupil Profile
Test Scores and School Marks

Identification No. _____ Pattern #2 Date _____ Sex __M__

Percentile	Verbal M	Verbal F	Numerical M	Numerical F	Abstract M	Abstract F	Space M	Space F	Mechanical M	Mechanical F	Clerical M	Clerical F	Spelling M	Spelling F	Sentences M	Sentences F	Reading	Algebra	Nat. Sci.	Phy. Sci	For. Lang.	English	Chemistry	Percentile
99	48	48	40	38	46	45	94	88	65	53	92	93	98	99	76	79	67							99
97	47	47	39	37	(45)	44	93	87	64	52	91	92	97	98	75	78	66							97
95	45	44	37	35	44	43	(88)	80	62	48	80	84	93	95	68	73	65							95
90	42	42	36	32	43	41	84	75	59	44	74	80	89	93	63	69	63							90
85	40	40	34	30	41	40	80	70	58	41	70	76	84	90	58	65	61	A	A	A	A	A	A	85
80	38	37	33	28	39	38	77	66	56	38	67	74	79	87	55	62	60							80
75	36	35	31	26	38	37	74	62	55	36	65	72	76	84	52	60	58		B	(B)	B	B	(B)	75
70	35	34	30	24	37	36	72	59	53	35	63	70	71	82	49	57	57	B						70
65	33	32	28	23	36	35	69	56	52	33	61	69	67	79	46	55	56					(C)		65
60	32	31	27	21	35	34	66	52	52	31	60	67	63	74	44	53	54		(C)	C	(C)			60
55	30	29	25	20	34	32	63	49	49	30	59	65	59	72	42	51	53	C					C	55
50	29	28	(24)	19	33	31	61	46	(61)	28	57	64	56	69	40	49	51	◯						50
45	27	26	22	17	32	30	57	42	46	27	56	63	52	65	37	47	49							45
40	26	25	20	16	31	28	54	38	45	26	54	61	48	62	35	45	47							40
35	25	22	19	13	30	27	45	35	43	24	53	60	43	59	33	43	46							35
30	23	20	17	12	28	25	45	31	41	22	52	59	39	54	31	41	45							30
25	(21)	19	15	10	26	23	40	28	40	21	50	57	34	50	29	39	43							25
20	20	17	14	9	24	21	34	24	38	19	49	56	29	45	26	36	(41)	D	D	D	D	D	D	20
15	18	14	12	7	22	18	27	20	35	16	47	54	24	37	23	33	36							15
10	16	12	9	5	19	14	21	15	32	14	45	52	18	29	20	33	33	E	E	E	E	E	E	10
5	13	9	7	3	14	8	15	11	27	11	42	49	11	19	16	25	29							5
3	10	7	4	1	8	2	10	7	23	7	38	46	3	7	11	20	27							3
1	8		2		1	0	5	3	16	4	34	42	0		4	14	24							1

364

he will work harder for grades, that he will try harder to improve his deficiencies (as he sees them) with will power.

7. He will report problems in areas of school that require reading and writing. Learning to read is difficult for children who show this problem at a young age.

Whenever the individual finds himself trapped between two internal values, one representing his social-moral responsibility and the other representing his obligation to himself, the inevitable result will be feelings of inadequacy or guilt. Why this particular problem tends to lower verbal reasoning scores is at best a guess. The Grant Study[10] conducted at Harvard University provides further evidence that the findings presented in this paper are accurate. Since the material presented in the Grant Study is concerned with relationship between physical masculinity and verbal reasoning the findings will be of interest here.

> In the realm of formal intellectual functions, academic interest and career choice, it is found that individuals with weakness of the masculine component are in many ways unlike those with the strong masculine component. In the matter of verbal functions, insofar as these are covered by tests of the multiple choice type, the individuals with weakness in the masculine component tend to be somewhat higher than the strong masculine variety. In the Alpha Verbal Test, the mean difference is 8 points (critical ratio 3.94) in favor of the group with the weakness of the masculine component, and in the Scholastic Aptitude Test 29.60 points higher (critical ratio 5.50). [Underlining the writer's]

In other words, there is an inverse relation between a strong masculine component and verbal intelligence. To indicate that this relationship exists, however, does not indicate the cause and effect relationship that initiated it. There are at least two possibilities present. One would be to consider that the law of compensation is working, i.e., that the individual has been given the strong masculine component in lieu of verbal intelligence. It has been found by writers such as Terman,[11] however, that strengths tend to accompany each other rather than compensate for each other. The other possibility is that something happened to the individual to rob him of his verbal intelligence (as it is measured) and that it is in some way related to the masculinity component.

It is the thesis of this writer that one can expect the problem to appear *most* often in the individual who has a strong masculine component. In effect, there are two strengths within the individual that are in conflict with each other. One of these is the strong psychological pressure that accompanies a strong physiological drive, such as masculine sex. The other strength is a moral code (can be a social code) which tends to inhibit the use of the strong sex drive. The result of this condition, this conflict in inner values, will be reflected in the lower score on a test of verbal intelligence.

This interpretation of the Grant Study would, then, support the material from the study of Pattern Analysis. The inverse relationship would simply be indicative of the problem that is stated here. The lower verbal score would be expected where high masculinity or femininity exists. Where there is no release that is socially and morally approved for the sexual pressure that normally exists within the adult, the result will be internal tension the individual cannot tolerate for long periods of time. Eventually either the dam to the emotional feelings will break or he will develop feelings of inadequacy. Neither of these releases is conducive to the type of individual that society considers well adjusted.

It is proposed that the reading score is lowered because there is a lack of ability to concentrate on the printed page when an internal value struggle is in process. The reader can experience this struggle if he will attempt to read a page of unfamiliar material while holding his breath. The battle between the will power to hold one's breath and the basic need for air will turn the required energy needed for reading comprehension inward in an effort to solve the much more demanding problem. The frustrated need is the one that becomes all important during the time it is being frustrated.

Although this problem is apparent in about seventy-five per cent of our adolescent population, the counselor will need to be more analytical of his material before he can classify this as a problem of adolescence. Study beyond that completed at the college counseling center indicates that adolescent development is one cause of this problem. The generalization needs to be broadened to include all causes for feelings of inadequacy, as the problem can be found in beginning school children. If they cannot see themselves as meeting the standards they have accepted for themselves, these feelings will result and verbal reasoning will be retarded at any age.

For this reason, the counselor must be concerned with the chronological age of his client at the onset of the problem. A measurement taken of a post adolescent's intelligence will not always yield the information as to the time the problem started, and the counselor will need to check previous tests or the school marks to determine if and when the test scores and grades have fallen. If the grades have been low from the early school years, the probability is that it is not a problem of feelings of inadequacy caused by adolescent development in our society but has its cause in the total environmental structure in which the child was reared. Generally the problem in preadolescence is caused by overdemanding parents who unknowingly impose standards for excellence on their children that the latter are unable to accept. The children never seem able to live up to these standards no matter how hard they try. Many times the standards shift upwards as the child achieves and the demands are met. If tests are given at a post-adolescent age many of these feelings from childhood will still be present and will show up in the test results.

The child with the problem from preadolescence has learned to protect himself from his hostile world, and likely will not get to the college level. Because school is highly verbal and this is the area of intelligence he is repressing, he likely will leave school at the first opportunity. If he does succeed in staying at a school, or if later the problem is corrected (with our present knowledge it is almost impossible to correct) and he decides to return to school there is still a large educational deficit to remove. Without reading skills, which this person would have trouble learning, other learning would be difficult.

This youngster will later make up a part of that group that are unemployable. New skills will be difficult to learn, since the accepted avenues to learning have been closed by both his emotional condition and his lack of learning skill. In our society, if he is fortunate enough to have money he will spend many hours in the care of psychiatrists. If he does not have money, he will become in the eyes of society one of these unimportant individuals who lives from the dregs of his community.

More generally, however, the problem is one that finds its roots in the adolescent change for the individual. Children generally are taught in our society that there are certain rules and regulations concerning "good" behavior which they must follow or be "bad." These rules are relatively easy to follow when there is no internal psychological pressure to do otherwise, but are much harder to follow when internal sexual pressures develop along with a growing human body. Since the need that causes the most problems is the need that is being frustrated at any given time, it is evident that parents (who have found a socially acceptable method of fulfilling the sexual need) and young children (who have not been confronted with the internal sexual pressure) can live with the values imposed by society and look at themselves as being "good." These values thus are inflicted on children by their parents while they are small children. These values must be lived with when the child becomes an adolescent, and the problem generally does not manifest itself until the sexual pressure appears.

Activities of a sexual nature are not necessarily involved with this problem, nor will the encouragement to become involved actively remove it. The writer has counseled with persons who have been married for ten years and are still carrying this problem. Sexual activity in marriage has removed the tension from the problem which leaves no motivating force to solve it. Since the problem is concerned with the value structure within the client regarding his thoughts and feelings about his sexual being and his social-moral-sex values, activities of a sexual nature are important to the counselor only as they give indication of the client's feelings and thoughts. The physiological and psychological factors involved in the sexual maturation of the body are in opposition to the value judgments concerning the rightness or wrongness of being sexual. The adolescent thus must choose between being a moral individual or a sexual individual. In his eyes he cannot be both, and either way he chooses, he loses. If he chooses to be moral, he loses his ability to a degree to do verbal reasoning. If he chooses to be immoral, he finds living with the guilt feelings even more destructive to verbal reasoning.

It is interesting to note that "good" activities for this individual concerned with the social moral values will generally be rejected. This person does not visualize himself as being strong enough (having enough will power) to face the value structure of his society. Thus the individual suffering from feelings of inadequacy will be likely not to date, to drop out of church activities, to avoid social gatherings within the school like clubs and generally to avoid situations where he cannot trust himself to be "good." He looks at himself as being "bad" and is usually out to prove it to others.

The counselor who practices promoting an affair as a method of reducing sexual tension, whether this be a simple date or be as extensive as free love, simply does not understand the problem or the feelings of the client. As the physical sexual values are already in opposition to the moral value structure of the client, the strengthening of either set of values simply increases the problem area within the individual. The client will feel more worthless after such an affair because the feelings of guilt in relation to his own moral social values will be strengthened. The counselor who practices reinforcing the "goodness" of the moral value structure of the client will have an identical effect upon his client because he will reinforce the other value in the controversy.

Another approach that is used excessively to help the individual with this problem — physical exercise to tire out the body — is generally not conducive to the growth of good mental health because it avoids the problem and removes one of the symptoms in the same way marriage does. It is at best a very temporary measure; continued exercise promotes a stronger more efficient body which in turn produces more sexual sperm and more psychological pressure to use it. The temporary effects of this approach indicate that it is only forestalling the problem that must eventually be faced.

Girls are much less likely than boys to suffer educationally with this problem. The same test score relationships will be noticed, and most of the other symptoms expressed in this paper are present in the counseling interview; however, grades do not fall as often with girls as they do with boys. This fact may be one reason why girls rather than boys are much more likely to be found on high school and college honor roles. The difference in the effect of this condition on grades has led the writer to believe that although the same problem exists for girls and boys, it is not as persistent for girls because of the differences in physiological and psychological structure. While the boy must be concerned with the physio-psycho-sex problem every day, the girl will develop sexual tension for only a short period in each monthly cycle. In those instances where the girl is constantly under tension, however, grades will fall.

The tension not only is created less often in girls, and is thus less persistent, but also is relieved with more ease. The young lady is expected to give vent to her feelings through tears, while the young man is expected by home and society to be brave, or at least not to show his emotional feelings. As tears are an excellent tension reduction mechanism within the human body and are accepted for the young lady, she has a method of dispelling tensions which the boy does not possess.

Since the use of Pattern Analysis as a diagnostic approach does not determine the type of counseling that will follow, there will be no attempt to spell out the counseling techniques that have been found to be effective in these cases. As the concern here is for the diagnosis of the problem rather than the techniques different counselors may employ, let it suffice to say that when counseling has been effective the following changes will be noted in the client. The simple process of dispelling tension, or teaching the client to withdraw from the problem will not bring about these results:

1. All of the symptoms reported earlier disappear, i.e., the verbal reasoning score rises on subsequent testing, the reading score rises on subsequent testing, school marks improve to the level of the new score obtained for the individual, and so on.

2. The client can be seen to relax in the counseling interview, probably signified by a long free breath.

3. About twenty to thirty minutes after the counseling interview is over the counselee will report a feeling of euphoria that last for about one hour.

4. The emotional tone of the client then settles at a higher level than was noticed previously. This is a letting down from the euphoric stage.
5. The client reports to the counselor that he has solved the problem by himself and no longer needs the counselor. (The dependency relationship is rarely even established.)

The next pattern to be presented looks almost exactly opposite to the first. This pattern consists of the high verbal reasoning score in relation to the low abstract score. It is presented here in profile form.

When the abstract intelligence measures lower for the individual than any other form of intelligence, there is an indication in the counseling interview that the individual is not receiving the emotional feedback he needs from the mother figure. It is impossible that the amount of this mother love was high and has been withdrawn. It is also possible for the client to feel that this emotional feedback was never present. The mind of the client does not accept this condition consciously. It is better classified as a feeling, thus the symptoms are given as unrelated to the problem. One might ask, then, how the symptoms can be applied to the problem. The answer to this question lies in the similarity of symptoms between clients who present this particular profile and their constant striving to gain mother love, as indicated in the counseling interview.

The symptoms that will be presented to the counselor will be as follows:

1. Test scores will remain fairly constant from early chronological measurement.
2. The client will consistently blame an outside agency for his problems, i.e., such statements as "Teachers are unfair," or "Grading is unfair," or "I could have done better with more help, but no one would give it."
3. Failure, or lowering of grades, in areas that require abstract reasoning such as mathematics, chemistry, physics, logic, etc.
4. A lack of desire for achievement in these areas.
5. The client reports a broken home situation. This condition is not always a physical split in the home as the parents may be living physically together but emotionally separate.
6. The client reports being overprotected, and has not been allowed to give of himself to the home.

When mother love is withheld from any person a set of two events occurs. The degree to which they occur will be dependent upon two basic factors. The two events are (1) that the individual will cease to attempt to solve his problems, and (2) he will place all causal relationships outside himself. Certain circumstances will always be at the base of his problem, and these will be circumstances over which he has no control. Because he has no control, there is no solution to the problem for him, and thus no reason for attempting to solve the problem. The more abstract the problem becomes the more he will avoid its solution.

The degree to which this problem occurs will be dependent upon first, the amount of mother love required and second, upon the amount given and the interpretation of that love. Each person has a different requirement in

12th Grade Pupil Profile
Test Scores and School Marks

Identification No. _____ Pattern #3 Date _____ Sex _____ M

Percentile	Verbal M	Verbal F	Numerical M	Numerical F	Abstract M	Abstract F	Space M	Space F	Mechanical M	Mechanical F	Clerical M	Clerical F	Spelling M	Spelling F	Sentences M	Sentences F	Reading	Algebra	Nat. Sci.	Phy. Sci	For. Lang.	English	Chemistry	Percentile
99	48	48	40	38	46	45	94	88	65	53	92	93	98	99	76	79	67							99
97	(47)	47	39	37	45	44	93	87	64	52	91	92	97	98	75	78	66							97
95	45	44	(37)	35	44	43	(88)	(80)	(62)	48	80	84	93	95	68	73	65		(A)		(A)	(A)		95
90	42	42	36	32	43	41	84	75	59	44	74	80	89	93	63	69	(63)	A		A			A	90
85	40	39	33	30	41	40	80	70	58	41	70	76	84	90	63	65	61							85
80	38	37	33	28	39	38	77	66	56	38	67	74	79	87	58	62	60							80
75	36	35	31	26	38	37	74	62	55	36	65	72	76	84	55	60	58	B	B	B	B	B	B	75
70	35	34	30	24	37	36	72	59	53	35	63	70	71	82	52	57	57							70
65	33	32	28	23	36	35	69	56	52	33	61	69	67	79	49	55	56							65
60	32	31	27	22	35	34	66	52	50	31	60	67	63	74	46	53	54							60
55	30	29	25	20	34	32	63	49	49	30	59	65	59	72	44	51	53		C		C	C		55
50	29	28	24	19	33	31	61	46	48	28	57	64	56	69	42	49	51	(C)		(C)			(C)	50
45	27	26	22	17	32	30	57	42	46	27	56	63	52	65	40	47	49							45
40	26	25	20	16	31	28	54	38	45	26	54	61	48	62	37	45	47							40
35	25	23	19	15	30	25	49	35	43	24	53	60	43	59	35	43	46							35
30	23	22	17	13	28	23	45	31	41	22	52	59	39	54	33	41	45							30
25	21	20	15	12	(26)	21	40	28	40	21	50	57	34	50	31	39	43							25
20	20	19	14	10	(24)	18	34	24	38	19	49	56	29	45	29	36	41	D	D	D	D	D	D	20
15	18	17	12	9	22	14	27	20	35	16	47	54	24	37	26	30	36							15
10	16	14	9	7	19	8	21	15	27	14	45	52	18	29	23	25	33	E	E	E	E	E	E	10
5	13	12	7	5	14	2	15	11	23	11	42	49	11	19	20	20	29							5
3	10	9	4	3	8	0	10	7	16	7	38	46	3	7	16	14	27							3
1	8	7	2	1	1		5	3		4	34	42	0		4		24							1

370

any of the basic needs, and that for affection (mother love) is no exception. There seem to be some members of our society who wean themselves at a very young age, and do not require the amount of affection that is needed by others. Some seem never to get enough affection. The amount of affection needed thus seems to be on a sliding scale. The amount of affection given also is a variable in the relationship, and too much is just as unhealthy as not enough. Too much seems to create a need within the individual that cannot be satisfied.

If the amount of affection that is given is the amount that is needed, however, the outcome seems to be a healthy individual who is willing to solve, and capable of solving, problems of an abstract nature. Some psychologists have falsely assumed that this need is constant and equal in each of us, and further that an overwhelming amount of affection is the answer to all problems. One example of this statement is the indication that the counselor always should provide an acceptance relationship in the counseling interview. To state this in another way, the counselor always should provide affection for his client. The reaction of the client who has a relatively small need for affection is one of "smother love," and he will reject the counselor and the total counseling situation when affectionate response is not needed.

When the need for affection is high, however, as indicated by the low abstract intelligence score in relation to the other scores for the individual, the client becomes what counselors have learned to call the "passive resistant" client. He will keep coming back for counseling as long as the counselor will see him. In the counseling interview he will generally agree with the counselor in anything suggested. He will, however, rarely use the information gleaned from the counseling interview to restructure his life pattern in any way. In effect, the counselor becomes the dispenser of affection, and the client will come often to satisfy his need for mother love. The counselor replaces the mother in this instance, and the client enjoys fulfilling his need in the counseling office.

It has been the writer's experience that there is very little effective counseling with these individuals with the techniques now available. In one sense, they are especially welcome clients since they come regularly, are willing to pay for the counselor's time, and advertise the counselor to their friends as being a wonderful person. They also become very dependent upon the counselor, since he is meeting their particular need for affection.

One such person was counseled in a college counseling setting for a period of twenty months. Each known approach to counseling was used for a six-month period. The client was seen once a week. The young man was six foot five inches in height, weighed 245 pounds, was 20 years old, played football and was attending college while living at home. Hour after hour was spent in a nondirective manner while he recited over and over how much his mother needed him, and therefore he could not live away from home. (At this time moving away from home had not been suggested in the counseling interview.) The next six month period was spent using an eclectic approach to counseling and the same procedure occurred as far as the young man's conversation was concerned. The third six months was spent using the Pattern Analysis approach suggested in this text. This also did very little to change the young man's approach to the situation. At about the end of eighteen months it was suggested to the young man that it might be advisable for him to move into the dorm on campus. This suggestion was made by the mother, and he duti-fully moved on campus. A few weeks later, he returned to the counseling situation and indicated that he had been home every evening for dinner and that his weekends were also spent at home protecting mother.

Any approach used by this counselor seemed to do little to help this young man become more self-reliant. Many other cases that are indicative of this pattern could be mentioned with the identical outcome. This person simply does not want to solve his problems, and will resist any counselor who tries to help him.

If the individual who fits this pattern does leave home to attend college, he will be constantly looking towards home for reinforcement. Each weekend will be spent going home, during the week telephone calls home will be numerous, and there will be a constant worry expressed in the counseling interview how mother is getting along without him. If he fails school and must return home, he gives external evidence of being extremely unhappy, but will do little to get himself reinstated at college.

It has been noticed that there are several occurrences outside the counsel-ing interview that seem to satiate this need for mother love and, if the situation is "right" so these can take place, the individual will accept substitutes for this needed affection. One such occurrence is a dorm mother who takes the mother's place or a roommate who will provide the affection needed. Another occurrence that seems to help is for the person to fall in love with a member of the opposite sex who meets this need. As long as the need is met, the in-dividual can maintain psychological equilibrium. When the need is not met, or when the need is fulfilled to the degree that it becomes "smother love," the individual will reject the total situation. To the writer's knowledge, however, no system of counseling has yet been devised that will do more than stall this particular problem.

The next pattern to be presented will be that of the lowered score of Spatial Intelligence. An example is presented here.

When this pattern of scores occurs, the client is in the process of rejecting the father figure. A conscious admission of this may or may not be forth-coming, but the following symptoms generally are expressed:

1. The pattern of test scores is likely to change from earlier chronological measurement.
2. Statements in the counseling interview by the client will indicate "My father could do more for me than he is now doing," "My father is not working up to his capabilities . . . . for the purpose of spiting me," or "My father is capable of a much better position than he now occupies."
3. The client reports grade trouble in areas that require this particular ability such as art, music, drafting, and so on.
4. The client reports being on the verge of problems of delinquency. Many times he will be in trouble with the administrative school officials.
5. Authority cannot be tolerated without a constant challenge.

The clients who present this set of symptoms vary from those who adam-antly reject the father figure to those who disguise their feelings because of

12th Grade Pupil Profile
Test Scores and School Marks

Identification No. _____ Pattern #4 _____ Date _____ Sex __ F

Percentile	Verbal M	Verbal F	Numerical M	Numerical F	Abstract M	Abstract F	Space M	Space F	Mechanical M	Mechanical F	Clerical M	Clerical F	Spelling M	Spelling F	Sentences M	Sentences F	Reading	Algebra Grade	Nat. Sci. Grade	Phy. Sci Grade	For. Lang. Grade	English Grade	Chemistry Grade
99	48	48	40	38	46	45	94	88	65	53	92	93	98	99	76	79	67						
97	47	47	39	37	45	44	93	87	64	52	91	92	97	98	75	78	66						
95	45	44	37	35	44	43	88	80	62	48	80	84	93	95	68	73	65						
90	42	42	36	32	43	41	84	75	59	44	74	80	89	93	63	69	63	(A)*	(A)	(A)	(A)	A	A
85	40	39	34	30	41	40	80	70	58	41	70	76	84	90	58	65	61						
80	38	38	33	28	39	38	77	66	56	38	67	74	79	87	55	62	60					(B)	(B)
75	36	35	31	26	38	37	74	62	55	36	65	72	76	84	52	60	58	B	B	B	B		
70	35	34	30	24	37	36	72	59	53	35	63	70	71	82	49	57	57						
65	33	32	28	23	36	35	69	56	52	33	61	69	67	79	46	55	56						
60	32	31	27	21	35	34	68	52	50	31	60	67	63	77	44	53	54						
55	30	30	25	19	34	32	63	49	49	30	59	65	59	72	42	51	53						
50	29	28	24	17	33	31	61	46	48	29	57	64	56	69	40	49	51	C	C	C	C	C	C
45	27	26	22	16	32	30	57	42	46	28	56	63	52	65	37	47	49						
40	26	25	20	15	31	28	54	38	45	27	54	61	48	62	35	45	47						
35	25	23	19	13	30	27	49	35	43	26	53	60	43	59	33	43	46						
30	23	20	17	12	28	25	45	32	41	24	52	57	39	54	31	39	45						
25	21	20	15	10	26	23	40	28	40	22	50	56	34	50	29	36	43						
20	20	19	14	9	24	21	34	24	38	21	49	54	29	45	26	33	41	D	D	D	D	D	D
15	18	17	12	7	22	18	27	20	35	19	47	52	24	37	23	30	36						
10	16	14	9	5	19	14	21	15	32	16	45	49	18	29	20	25	33	E	E	E	E	E	E
5	13	12	7	3	14	8	15	11	27	14	42	46	11	19	16	20	29						
3	10	9	4	1	8	2	10	7	23	11	38	42	3	7	11	14	27						
1	8	7	2		1	0	5	3	16	7	34		0		4		24						

* Grades for problem areas not on Profile.

373

social and moral values concerning the honoring of the father. If the home has taught that the social position of the father is above reproach, then the symptoms will be hidden by the client. If the father's position in the home is one in which the client has the right to reject, however, the rejection will be very open. It should be indicated that in either case the rejection is present.

There seem to be several basic causes why this rejection occurs. Each that has been noticed will be discussed briefly here.

1. The child has attempted to get love from the father and has been unsuccessful. In these circumstances, the individual must either reject himself as being unworthy of this love or he must reject the father as being incapable of giving it. If the tendency within the individual is to feel inadequate, as based on Pattern 2, the client will reject himself as being unworthy. If, on the other hand, the tendency in the home is to tear down the father's position, the rejection will be towards the father rather than towards self. In some homes, father is actually at the bottom of the pecking order.

2. The client has gone through puberty with a lack of self-acceptance concerning his sex-social role, and since the father is the aggressive member of society in the social-sex role, the rejection of this role also insists on the rejection of the person who plays it. The father thus is rejected not as a person but as a symbol of a role that the client chooses not to adopt. In this instance the solution to the problem that has been found effective is to help the client understand himself and his social-sex role. If he can accept this role, the relationship with father improves without the counselor's ever being concerned about it. Most of the cases showing low spatial perception with which the counselor will come in contact will be of this nature.

   It also has been noticed that girls are likely to reject the father figure on the same basis, except they are on the defensive sexually. While the young man is likely to reject the aggressiveness of the role within himself, the young lady is likely to reject the aggression construed to be a part of the male role, thus the rejection of the father figure.

3. Many of these cases seem to have their origin in the war years, in which the father was absent for an extended period of time and a very close association was developed between the child and the mother figure. In these instances, when the father does return he is an intruder in the family constellation. The adjustment necessary for the father to be an accepted member of the family does not always take place. When it does not occur, there is a subconscious rejection of the father by the child. Since this rejection is at the felt level rather than the intellectual level, it must be dealt with in terms of feelings.

Since this pattern so often accompanies the first pattern that has been indicated, it should be mentioned that the combination of pattern one and three should be expected by the counselor. It is the combination of test scores that seems to be related to juvenile delinquency. This fact is supported by the numerous studies that indicate the importance of the father-son relationship in the delinquency picture. The contention here is that the father-son relationship is a by-product of the problem, however, and not the causative factor.

The next pattern to be discussed is best indicated by the following profile. It is the pattern of the extremely low numerical and mechanical scores in relation to other extremely high scores. Although there are times when the abstract or spatial score is lowered along with the numerical, these profiles have been presented. When either the abstract or spatial is seen in relation with the low numerical, the individual who is causing the problem is working with numerical quantity. At least he, or she, represents numerical quantity to the client.

This profile is indicative of one of the generalizations that has been found to exist in all cases. *The individual will unconsciously reject that area of endeavor that is representative to him of an individual whom he is rejecting.* Thus if the father represents numbers and mechanics to his child, the rejection of these areas will unconsciously take place and the individual will find adequate reason for not being able to compete in them. The following symptoms will be present in the counseling interview:

1. The client will possess an explosive personality structure.
2. Reported reactions on the part of the client are rather violent. An extremely aggressive client.
3. The client will express strong likes and dislikes.
4. Subjects in school that require these abilities will be strongly rejected by the client. (He will rarely make the connection of why he is having problems with this subject matter.) He will not want to take these subjects, and if he is forced to take them he will rebel against the assignments.
5. The degree to which the teacher of this subject matter is like the rejected parental figure is generally the degree to which the subject matter is rejected.

This pattern is mentioned because it represents a reversal of the other patterns in one important respect. Here the person is openly rejecting an individual, knows that he is rejecting him and unconsciously rejects the subject matter areas that are represented by him. In the other patterns, the person is consciously rejecting the subject matter and the intelligence tests that represent the individual and unconsciously rejecting the him or unconsciously feels rejected by him.

The presentation by this individual in the counseling interview often takes the counselor by surprise, since the client is so open in relation to the information for which the counselor usually has to wait. The counselor is likely to make the supposition that this is not the "real problem." The experience of the writer is that the presentation of the problem is accurate and honest, and that there generally is a very acceptable reason for the client's reaction.

In most of these cases the client actually has been harmed by the rejected person in such a manner that almost any socially oriented person would agree that the client is not showing paranoid tendencies but has a legitimate complaint. Examples of this type of client are seen in the father who actually

12th Grade Pupil Profile
Test Scores and School Marks

Identification No. _____ Pattern #5 Date _____ Sex _____ M

Percentile	Chemistry Grade	English Grade	For. Lang. Grade	Phy. Sci Grade	Nat. Sci. Grade	Algebra Grade	Reading	Sentences M	Sentences F	Spelling M	Spelling F	Clerical M	Clerical F	Mechanical M	Mechanical F	Space M	Space F	Abstract M	Abstract F	Numerical M	Numerical F	Verbal M	Verbal F	Percentile
99							67	76	79	98	99	92	93	65	53	94	88	46	45	40	38	48	48	99
97							66	75	78	97	98	91	92	64	52	93	87	45	44	39	37	47	47	97
95							65	68	73	93	95	80	84	62	48	88	80	44	43	37	35	45	44	95
90		A	A	A		A	63	63	69	89	93	74	80	59	44	84	75	43	41	36	32	42	42	90
85							61	58	65	84	90	70	76	58	41	80	70	41	40	34	30	40	39	85
80							60	55	62	79	87	67	74	56	38	77	66	39	38	33	28	38	37	80
75	B	B	B	B	B	B	58	52	60	76	84	65	72	55	36	74	62	38	37	31	26	36	35	75
70							57	49	57	71	82	63	70	53	35	72	59	37	36	30	24	35	34	70
65							56	46	55	67	79	61	69	52	33	69	56	36	35	28	23	33	32	65
60							54	44	53	63	77	60	67	50	31	66	52	35	34	27	21	32	31	60
55							53	42	51	59	74	59	65	49	30	63	49	34	32	25	19	30	29	55
50							51	40	49	56	72	57	64	48	28	61	46	33	31	24	17	29	28	50
45	C	C	C	C	C	C	49	37	47	52	69	56	63	46	27	57	42	32	30	22	16	27	26	45
40							47	35	45	48	65	54	61	45	26	54	38	31	28	20	15	26	25	40
35							46	33	43	43	62	53	60	43	24	49	35	30	27	19	13	25	23	35
30							45	31	41	39	59	52	59	41	22	45	31	28	25	17	12	23	22	30
25							43	29	39	34	54	50	57	40	21	40	28	26	23	15	10	21	20	25
20	D			D	D	D	41	26	36	29	50	49	56	38	19	34	24	24	21	13	9	20	19	20
15		D	D				36	23	33	24	45	47	54	35	16	27	20	22	18	11	7	18	17	15
10							33	20	30	18	37	45	52	32	14	21	15	19	14	9	5	16	14	10
5	E	E	E	E	E	E	29	16	25	11	29	42	49	23	11	15	11	14	8	7	3	13	12	5
3							27	11	20	3	19	38	46	20	7	10	7	8	2	4	1	10	9	3
1							24	4	14	0	7	34	42	16	4	5	3	1	0	2		8	7	1

beats the child without a show of mercy or the father who attempts, and sometimes completes, the rape of his daughter.

As these cases are rare in college circles, little time has been spent on them here. They do need to be mentioned, however, as they represent one of the patterns.

SUMMARY

A new and different use of measurement is being proposed in this paper. It is proposed that the individual who is well adjusted will be able to use his intellectual functions in any way that he so chooses. It is further suggested that differential aptitudes are nothing more than an expression on the part of the client of areas of emotional rejection, and if these areas of emotional rejection can be understood, the information will be meaningful to the counselor in his therapy. As these rejections will control to a large extent the type of work and learning that will be completed in the school setting, they must become the business of the school counselor.

It is a further concern of the writer that until the field of counseling and guidance has some objectively measurable goal for which it is striving, it will continue in its disorganized manner. Until all counselors are working toward the same end, there can be little evidence that will support or reject our systems of counseling that are proposed. Until there is some evidence to indicate our starting point, as well as our direction and goal, there will be no approach to counseling that is more than sophisticated witchcraft.

In this paper is a proposal for an objective measure for adjustment and some methods that have been found useful to the writer in determining adjustment, normalcy, and mal adjustment. The work in this area has only started and the writer is sure that others who make this type of examination will find some verity in the statements made here. The writer is also sure that some of the statements made in this paper will have to be modified as more information and knowledge are accrued.

Each time a statistical study is made concerning the effectiveness of counseling techniques, there seems to be little evidence indicating either that one system is better than any other or that any system is very effective. It is time for counselors to face this fact and to explore every possibility of establishing an effective system. The exploration that has been made here shows promise of helping the client grow into the kind of person who does not need a counselor. If we are to make improvements in our stagnate field, new techniques will have to be developed to solve those problems that are not now affected by the techniques that are being used. It is my hope that Pattern Analysis will act as a key to the much needed knowledge.

BIBLIOGRAPHY

1. Allport, Gordon W., *Becoming: Basic Considerations for Psychology of Personality,* New Haven, Yale University Press, 1955.
2. Blum, L. E., Raths, James, "Can Kindergraten Teachers be Trained to Identify Emotionally Handicapped Children," Feb., 1964, *Elementary School Journal.*
3. Hathaway, Starke R., and Monachesi, Elio D., *An Atlas of Juvenile M.M.P.I. Profiles,* Minneapolis, University of Minnesota Press, 1961.

4. Horney, Karen, *The Neurotic Personality of our Time,* W. W. Norton and Company, New York, 1937.
5. Maslow, Abraham H., *Toward a Psychology of Being,* Princeton, N. J., Van Nostrand, 1962.
6. Overstreet, H. A., *The Mature Mind,* New York, W. W. Nostrand and Co., 1949.
7. Rogers, C. R., *On Becoming A Person,* Houghton Mifflin Company, Boston, 1961.
8. Seltzer, Carl C., Edited by Kluckholm, Clyde, and Murray, Henry, *Personality in Nature, Society and Culture,* Chap. 6, The Relationship Between the Masculine Component and Personality, Alfred A. Knopf, New York, 1949.
9. Terman, Lewis M., and Merrill, Maud A., *Measuring Intelligence: A Guide to the Administration of the New Revised Stanford Binet Tests of Intelligence,* Boston, Houghton Mifflin Company, 1937.
10. Terman, Lewis M., and Oden, Melita H., *The Gifted Child Grows Up,* Stanford, California, Stanford University Press, 1947.
11. Thurstone, L. L., *Primary Mental Abilities,* Chicago, University of Chicago Press, 1938.

REALITY THERAPY AND COUNSELING

William Glasser, M.D.
Los Angeles, California

Reality Therapy is an effective method of psychiatric treatment for people psychological problems. Although to date its principal applications have been in the treatment of office patients, mental hospital patients, and adult and juvenile lawbreakers, it has been practiced with some success in California schools, especially in the Sacramento area. It has the advantage that it can be taught in a relatively short period of time to teachers, administrators, school nurses, guidance counselors, and psychologists, whether or not they have any previous training in psychology. All that will be possible in this brief account will be a general description of the theory and practice but a book[1] is now available for those who wish to pursue this subject further.

THE THEORY

In order to understand the underlying theory we must assume that everyone has two constant psychological needs. First there is the need to love and to be loved, second there is the need for achievement or self-worth, the feeling that you are worthwhile as a person both to yourself and to others. In each instance these are two-way needs. It is not enough only to feel worthwhile to oneself or to feel worthwhile to other people; both aspects of worth must be satisfied. Similarly, to fulfill the need for love we need not only love others but also to have others love us. In order to satisfy the need to love, therefore,

---

An original article for this book.
[1]*Reality Therapy — A New Approach to Psychiatry,* William Glasser, M.D.; Harper & Row; New York, 1965.

there must be at least one other person in this world we love and he or someone else must love us. Ordinarily, there are several people who love us and whom we love and, in the case of self-worth, the feeling that we are worthwhile to at least a few people, hopefully many.

With this in mind, what happens if we do not satisfactorily fulfill these two basic needs? Under these conditions we will suffer and our suffering will be manifested either directly, by causing others to suffer, or most often by a combination of these two common conditions. From a treatment standpoint, and Reality Therapy is treatment, it should be emphasized that the way we suffer when we are unable to fulfill our needs is relatively unimportant. In psychological or psychiatric terms, this suffering is manifested as the "symptoms from which "diagnosis" of the person who has the problem is derived. For example, a person who is unable to fulfill his needs might become psychotic, that is he might withdraw from the real world and try to establish a world of his own, hoping that in his self-created world he might better fulfill his needs. All psychoses, which includes schizophrenia, autism, dementia praecox, and other common, but meaningless, psychiatric terms, can be understood as the behavior and thought processes that reflect the suffering of a person unable to fulfill his needs. Why he becomes psychotic is yet unknown but it is a common and not illogical choice for people who are unable to fulfill their needs. In the elementary, junior and senior high schools and in college, we see many evidences of psychotic behavior but we must not be misled by the extremeness of this particular expression of the inability to fulfill one's needs. With this, as well as all other psychological problems, we must understand that psychosis was, or is, the best the person is able to do at the time, but that if we can help him to fulfill his needs, the psychotic behavior will disappear. Psychosis is only one of the many psychological results of inability to fulfill needs. Far more common than psychosis in the school situation are the acting out problems or character problems, exemplified by students who seem to have no regard for the rights and feelings of others or normal social values. They behave irrationally, erratically, and with hostility for seemingly unexplainable reasons. If we examine this behavior in terms of need fulfillment, however, we can discover that the purpose of their behavior is either to gain recognition or attention or is an angry reaction to their inability to gain recognition through socially acceptable pathways. Most often it is a combination of these conditions. Rather than withdraw into a psychosis, the child with character problems fights the world in an attempt to wrest his need fulfillment from it forcibly. The fact that his antisocial methods fail only causes him to increase his unsuccessful struggles; character and behavior problems therefore tend to intensify as the needs are more and more unsatisfied.

In addition to these two main psychiatric catagories or ways in which people suffer, there are many neurotics, people who, unable to fulfill their needs, develop extreme anxiety about this inability. In an effort to free themselves from the anxiety they develop neurotic patterns of behavior — phobias, hysteria, obsessions, compulsions, hypochondriaisis — all examples of major neuroses. The last major group of people who suffer because they cannot fulfill their needs are those who either become severly depressed or have psychosomatic problems such as stomach ulcers, asthma, migraine headaches, or eczema. Although these kinds of suffering are indirect and difficult to understand, the depressed and psychosomatic sufferer uses these expressions to get attention, recognition and care, as well as to express hostility to the world because he is unable to fulfill his needs. Why one person chooses depression and psychosomatic illness, another psychosis, a third a behavior disorder, and a fourth neurotic behavior is not well known at present and, from the standpoint of Reality Therapy, is unimportant. What is important is to under- stand that none of these people is able to fulfill his needs. The form of suf- fering they exhibit, whatever their symptom or diagnostic catagory, will dis- appear once we can help them fulfill their needs.

Reality Therapy is a psychiatric treatment which attempts to solve this basic lack for those who are unsuccessful in fulfilling their needs, but it has been derived from careful observation of people who are essentially successful in fulfilling their needs. From this observation one important element has been found which is essential to need fulfillment — people. In order to fulfill our needs we always need someone whom we feel cares about us and thinks we are worthwhile. It is through this person and persons that we gain human involvement, closeness, psychological warmth and emotional ties which are necessary to fulfilling our needs. We assume, therefore, and this may seem to be a drastic assumption to some, that when the person is unable to fulfill his needs, when he is suffering in his own particular way, he does not have any- one close enough to him or involved enough with him emotionally so that he can fulfill his needs. Unless we, whatever our capacity may be, school teacher or psychiatrist, can provide this person, there will be no therapy.

It therefore follows that people who are unable to fulfill their needs and suffer psychologically are isolated, alienated, or separated from people at the time we become aware of their suffering. Further, we may assume that in the majority of cases this isolation from people has been going on for a long time. We will find in using Reality Therapy that intensive review of this misery, commonly referred to as the case history, is unnecessary. No matter how long the isolation has been, what is important to us as therapists is that the individual is isolated now. To help him fulfill his needs we must get enough peronally involved with him to break down his isolation. Whether the therapist is a psychiatrist, psychologist, social worker, school teacher, school psychologist, or administrator, he therefore must, fundamental to Reality Therapy as soon as possible get humanly involved with this suffering person. As limited as the therapist's time may be, he must develop a warm emotional involvement through which the person who is suffering can begin to feel "here is someone who cares enough about me so that I can begin to work toward the fulfillment of my needs, first through him and then through others."

Axiomatic to this process is the concept that the behavior which the suf- fering person exhibits is always unrealistic. He never engages reality in an adequate way but always distorts it, runs from it, escapes from a portion of it, or suffers at the hands of reality in a way which is always unrealistic. The job of the therapist therefore is not only to get involved with the person but to get involved with him in a way that he is able to present reality to the patient; only if the patient can learn to fulfill his needs within the bounds of reality will he successfully surmount his suffering. What we do is called Reality Therapy because the therapist's primary task, together with his in- volvement, is to be completely honest in every aspect of his relationship to the patient. Only through behaving within realistic social standards can the patient learn to fulfill his needs, and only after he fulfills his needs will he be able to be relieved of his suffering.

This brief discussion of the theory outlines the therapist's approach which we call Reality Therapy. Theory, however, is worthless unless it can be applied in a reproducible way to various problems. So far this theory has been used successfully in the treatment of adolescent delinquents in institutions, psychotic persons in mental hospitals, patients who come to a psychiatrist in private practice, and children in school situations by teachers, administrators, school nurses, and psychologists. As this theory becomes more well known it will be applicable to other problems, but its application has been successful enough so there is reason to believe it can be applied more widely in schools as one way to cope with the increasing number of school children who present serious problems.

Before explaining the specific application of this theory, I must emphasize that no theory will solve many specific and serious school problems. Children will continue to behave in ways which will baffle the best psychologists and psychiatrists and defy the most intensive work by classroom teachers and administrators. What needs to be established first, and has proven successful in institutions for delinquents and mental patients is a set of principles for working with pupils, principles which if applied through a school system will substantially reduce the number of children who manifest serious psychological problems. The writer therefore emphasizes Reality Therapy as a total approach to the whole school system as much or more than as a specific approach for problem children. If this is utilized, fewer requests will be made of the guidance counselor for individual help, freeing him to assist the classroom teacher in working out solutions for those children who require a more specific application of Reality Therapy to help them to fulfill their needs.

THE APPLICATION OF REALITY THERAPY — THE PROCESS

First and most important the teacher must attempt to get involved with his pupils so that they feel he genuinely cares about them. So that the child understands that his teacher cares, his principal cares, his nurse cares and others in the school really care about him, these people must be personal in their approach to him. This means that in their everyday dealings with children the personal "I" must be substituted for the impersonal "we," "they," "the school," or "It is good for you." As much as possible these impersonal phrases, should be eliminated from the school vocabulary. The teacher's approach should be, "I am interested in you," "I want to teach you," "I want to explain to you what you are doing," "I want to point out to you the things that you might do that are better," "I would like you to behave better for me," "I would like you to do your homework for me," "It is important to me that you are here everyday." These phrases emphasize the personal; they lead to involvement with the child not only as a teacher but as a person who cares about him, who teaches him important things which he needs to know. With this personal approach there is the obvious danger that the teacher, who becomes personally involved as the writer has advocated here, can also be hurt much more than the teacher who remains objective and from the child's point of view, detached. Objectivity, a poor approach to any child. is useless with problem children. They have had too much objectivity. They need personal interest, an immediate involvement with someone so that they can begin to fulfill their needs. Without this, they are helpless to change their behavior.

Although subjectivity is essential in the process of relating to the child, the teacher must take an objective and realistic approach to the child's behavior. Without neglecting his personal interest in the child, the teacher must stress that he cares about what the child does, his school work and his conduct. The behavior of the child must be emphasized more than the child's feelings; the completion of homework, for example, is more important than the fact the child may be upset. Reality Therapy emphasizes behavior and de-emphasizes the feelings or emotions that accompany deviant behavior. Teachers should learn that they can do nothing directly to make a child happy unless they condone bad behavior which is unrealistic — short-lived at best. If the teacher believes that the child behaves badly because he is emotionally disturbed, and that first he must work with the child's feelings, he will fail. Instead he must show little interest in the child's emotional upset and guide his counseling toward behavior by saying, "What is important to me is what you do; if you feel badly, I can't help you but I do know that if you do better you will feel better." This statement, stressing the personal interest of the teacher and the reality of the child's behavior, is the backbone of Reality Therapy. We believe very firmly that bad behavior leads to bad feelings, and that bad feelings can best be corrected by better behavior. We have been unable to correct bad behavior by changing bad feelings into good feelings because we have never been able to do this, even though it is a part of the psychiatry we learned. It just can't be done. Even if it could be done or if, as some may assume, this were a "chicken-and-egg" situation, we have been unable to help children unless the behavioral approach is used.

A further factor in the application of Reality Therapy (in practice these are all interwoven) is the necessity to accept the child as he is now, regardless of his past. In contrast to the teaching of most courses in guidance and counseling, as well as what is ordinarily taught in psychology and psychiatry, we believe that the patient's history, what has happened to him prior to our seeing him, is unimportant for therapy. The statement that our job is to help him, not to understand why he became the way he is, is not facetious. Why he becomes the way he is is important to sociologists and research psychologists who wish to change social patterns, but to help individuals fulfill their needs, the less we know about their history the better. If we can accept that he is doing the best he can do, regardless of how badly he is behaving, then we must accept him as he is. Reality Therapy therefore accepts the child as he is with the understanding that we believe that he can do better. Our emphasis is on what he is doing, on his behavior, and that better behavior will lead to better feelings and further better behavior.

Further, our acceptance of him does not mean we accept any excuse for present bad behavior. The child must understand that no one in the school, above all his teacher, will excuse him for doing something that is wrong. There must be no excuses for the child who disrupts the class, who doesn't do his homework, who doesn't come to school on time, who cuts school classes — any of the common behavior problems. With this approach consistently applied the child will learn that he can do better, that we are interested enough in him personally not to excuse or condone behavior which does not lead to need fulfillment. We never encourage him to look for the reason that he behaves the way he does. We are uninterested in discussing why he has not done his homework, why he disrupts the other children, why he fights, steals, lies, cheats or cuts school. On the other hand, we are extremely interested that we know and he knows what he is doing that is unsatisfactory. All of our discussions with him, brief as they may be, must point out to him what he is doing and ask, "How can this help you?" and "Do you feel that what you are doing is right?" Our job is not to look for excuses but to point out the reality of his behavior and further (this is essential to Reality Therapy) ask him to make a value judgment of his behavior in terms of right or wrong or good and bad.

In our work with patients, school children included, we emphasize the careful to derive the definition of right and wrong from the basic needs. By importance of right and wrong. In order to avoid confusion, however, we are this we mean that any behavior which leads to the fulfillment of the two basic needs, love and self-worth, is right, good, moral, or correct behavior. Any behavior which does not lead to the fulfillment of these basic needs — which necessarily must lead to separation from people, to lack of self-worth or self-demeaning behavior — we classify under the category of wrong behavior. The child must be helped to make this judgment himself (and we find he almost always can), to understand that when he does something right it benefits him because he fulfills his needs and he feels better. As we work with him, therefore, the child quickly discovers that we genuinely care about him and that our care is strong enough that we will not accept excuses for bad behavior. We care because we emphasize what he is doing now, that there are better courses open to him, that the behavior which is disrupting the class is irresponsible, unrealistic and, above all, that it is wrong. Further, he learns that we want to help him find better ways than he has been able to up to now.

Therefore, the last and the most important part of Reality Therapy is to make a plan through which the child can improve his behavior. This plan may take only a few seconds to evoke or it may take up to an hour (more than that is very unusual). The plan must always lead to behavior which will allow the pupil to get some recognition, to gain some satisfaction and to move toward a position where he is able to give and receive more love than before. A hypothetical plan for an elementary school child who is disrupting the class with bad behavior is to talk with him briefly, say that his behavior is not good and that he could do better, and then ask him to do something through which he gains an added sense of self-worth. For instance, he could become a playground monitor, take care of the classroom animals, wash off the blackboards or do any one of innumerable jobs around the school. More than this, to fulfill his need for love he might be asked to help direct other children to do these jobs. A simple plan carried out consistently over a period of time always succeeds in alleviating the less serious behavior disturbances. A more complex plan is necessary for more serious problems, but it usually can be worked out. The plan demonstrates that the teacher cares about him, doesn't accept the bad behavior, but is willing to help him toward doing something definite which will lead in the direction of the fulfillment of his needs.

For each child who fails to adjust, the teacher or the teacher and the administrator together must make some plan and then adhere rigidly to it. The plan always involves the nonacceptance of excuses and much positive reinforcement for what the person can do which is good. As emphasized in the beginning of this section, planning for children who are in serious difficulty in school is always difficult, and the best plan may not work as well once the child is in serious trouble as it might have earlier. We therefore feel it is important to apply these principles to the class situation from kindergarten to prevent serious problems later. Few plans are complex but putting them into action requires strength and a working knowledge of these principles. One public school, the Pershing Elementary School of the San Juan Unified District of suburban Sacramento, has attempted to utilize these concepts as part of a total school program. The following excerpt is contributed by Richard Hawes, Psychologist for the District.

Donald O'Donnell, Principal of the Pershing Elementary School and I were first introduced to Reality Theory during the early part of the 1963-64 school year. After consulting the school staff, we decided to try to apply the concepts to the Pershing Elementary School, and I also attempted to use these ideas in secondary school counseling. We wondered if the first phase of this therapeutic process, establishing personal relationships, would be possible in a classroom with thirty-five or more pupils and if the achievement of the first phase would actually minimize irresponsible behavior. We wondered whether we could develop specific techniques from these general principles which could be effectively applied in the typical school environment. We hoped to affect the classroom environment so that the pupils' ego development would be enhanced without distracting from the academic responsibilities of the school.

At this time (early 1965) the entire Pershing Staff is engaged in an experimental effort to improve their understanding of the concepts and to develop specific techniques within the classroom. Aside from encouraging an exciting experimental mood throughout the school, and of course, helping individual pupils, the most significant observation so far is the confidence and strength the individual teachers seem to be gaining as their ability to handle classroom behavior problems (which heretofore seemed impossible with the pupil's only hope lying in that elusive phantom — "outside professional help") improves.

Reality Therapy seems to offer a set of psychological concepts relatively conducive to application in the typical school situation by psychologically untrained people. It offers a way to operate with behavior problems immediately in the classroom or school situation. The process of establishing a personal relationship, not allowing irresponsible behavior, and learning new ways to operate or behave is designed to strengthen the function of the ego. As this process is applied by the teacher, it not only affects the pupil but also seems to strengthen the teacher's ego functioning significantly. Herein lies some of its greatest strength and potential. One of the Pershing teachers explained it this way when asked to comment on Reality Therapy: "It is hard to pin down isolated cases because the methods really changed my entire attitude and approach to discipline. It's impossible to isolate one event because one leads to another."

The first case concerns a ten-year-old fifth grade pupil who was originally referred to me as a candidate for the special education program for mentally retarded pupils because of consistently poor grades and his lack of production and participation in school. Surprisingly, individual testing showed that this healthy, well-built boy not only had bright-normal intelligence but had mastered the basic academic skills (reading, arithmetic, writing, etc.). His referral to the school psychologist was due to his attitude toward class assignments and almost total lack of achievement. He always seemed to find something else to do instead of the assigned class activity. The teacher's problem was to somehow get this reluctant pupil to experience that feeling of worthwhileness that comes with responsible achievement. This is how she did it: One day during class, Joe (as we will call him) was sitting sprawled at his desk tossing a paper clip into the air when he was supposed to be writing ten spelling words for his homework assignment. Mrs. B. approached Joe at his desk, placed her hand on his shoulder (the personal touch), and gently but with just the right amount of curiosity asked, "What are you doing?" Joe's reaction, and one we've experienced many times with this particular classroom technique, was bewilderment, mainly because teachers frequently say, "Stop doing that," or "Get going on your assignment," or "You'd better go to the principal, young man."[2] He did not know how to respond or what to say. At this time Mrs. B. encouraged him by saying something like: "Joe, tell me what you're doing? Describe it. Tell me and show me what you're doing — put it into words." To this Joe remarked, as he demonstrated tossing the paper clip, "Well, I'm throwing up the paper clip." To which Mrs. B. responded with an enthusiastic smile, "That's right, you are." Joe smiled spontaneously, and at this moment is demonstrated a very solid interpresonal experience which took no more time to transpire than some of the more typical procedures and remarks mentioned above which tend to discourage positive personal relationships and rob the pupil of the opportunity to accept and demonstrate individual responsibility.

At this point Mrs. B. simply asked: "Does that help you do the homework assignment?" Which was followed by Joe's equally simple response, "No." With that, Mrs. B. smiled knowingly at Joe, turned, and went on to another classroom activity leaving Joe with the decision to continue his paper clip tossing or to copy the list of ten words for his homework assignment. In Joe's case, as in many others where we have tried this particular technique, the results were encouraging. As the personal relationship between Joe and Mrs. B. became stronger through similar experiences, his irresponsible behavior began to disappear.

Throughout this episode, Joe was treated with dignity and respect as any person should be. The teacher felt he was worthwhile, and she expressed it by her actions. This not only fulfilled part of one of her basic psychological needs but also helped Joe fill his. A curious thing about this whole process is when one becomes more personally involved and consciously tries to make another feel worthwhile, it's very difficult not to feel more fulfilled yourself. This led another teacher to exclaim, as he became more involved in trying to apply these concepts to the classroom situation, "I don't know if these things I'm trying are doing the kids any good . . . (paues) . . . Yes! I know it's helping them, but man, is it helping me!" This statement reflects the significant insight we have discovered through the application of reality concepts: One important way to help another is to help yourself in terms of ego fulfillment. Feeling worthwhile as a result of engaging in activities which encourage the development of one's own ego

---

[2]These responses by the teacher suggest that she has decided to exercise responsibility over the pupil rather than having the pupil accept and demonstrate responsibility for himself. The statements also do not encourage a positive personal relationship.

in turn puts you in a better position to help another less fortunate with a significantly weaker ego.

Another illustration comes from a high school in the San Juan District and deals with the typical situation of an extremely angry teacher who has had considerable trouble with the student he sent to the administrator. Jane, the student, has had a long-term problem of disrupting classes — usually talking — and not producing in class commensurate with her ability. Her parents are quite upset because she has received several failing notices, and they are pressing her to do better. She is not too happy with school and threatens to drop out when she gets old enough.

Instead of holding a counseling or lecture session to point out why the pupil shouldn't behave as she has (she has been told this a hundred times), Mr. T., the dean, asks, "What happened?" To which Jane replies vaguely, "Oh we just don't get along well." "I know that," Mr. T. says, "but what I want you to tell me now is exactly what happened this period. I want you to tell me what you did, and what you said, and what he did and said." Again, Jane answered vaguely, "Well, I made a little noise and he blew his top. . ." At this point, Mr. T. interrupted, "Hold it, Jane, that's not what I want. I want you to tell me exactly what you did and said, and exactly what Mr. R. (the teacher) did and said."

"Oh, you mean exactly?" Jane queried.

"Yes, exactly," was the reply from Mr. T.

Jane began, "Well, Mary and I were talking in class, making plans for a date when he (Mr. R.) yelled clear across the room to shut up." "What were his words, Jane?" Mr. T. interrupted. To which Jane, mimicking Mr. R., replied: "All right you two, knock it off and get busy."

"What did you say?" asked Mr. T.

"O.K., already," Jane said with a rather sarcastic inflection and loud voice.

"And what did he say to that?"

"He said, 'all right, young lady, that's it for you. We're going to the dean!' "

At this point, Mr. T. (the dean) asks in a low-keyed and nonjudgmental way: "How do you feel it worked out?" (The manner in which this is said is critical. It must be said in a nonjudgmental or nonpunitive way. The main. point is that you want the pupil to think critically about what happened.) To which Jane hesitates, then rather indignantly said, "O.K!" Mr. T. re-responds, "O.K. Have a seat in the outer office and I'll see you a little later." (It is important at this point that the dean does not argue with the pupil. This approach would tend to defeat the build-up of a personal relationship. Isolating Jane at this time gives her a chance to work it over in her own mind without outside interference. The previous short discussion should encourage her to think about the recent class episode.)

At the end of the period she is sent to her next class with the comment, "I enjoyed talking with you, Jane, and I want to talk with you again. I'll call you in a couple of days." In the meantime, the dean meets with the teacher in order to give him a chance to express himself about the pupil which, hopefully, will somewhat relieve the teacher's anxiety. The dean then calls Jane to his office and encourages discussion about anything except the situation which just occurred. The sole purpose is to establish a solid personal relationship and not to focus on the irresponsible act. This is sometimes very difficult for school people to do, especially administrators, counselors and teachers, who feel they need to express their power rather than allow the student to express his feelings. The assumption is, if we are able to successfully develop a personal relationship, the irresponsible behavior which caused the classroom disturbances will tend to disappear. (Assuming, of course, that the pupil has been the irresponsible one and not the teacher.) The sessions are kept brief (between 5 and 15 minutes) because time is a factor in our district when a counselor, for example, is responsible for 500 or more pupils. It is becoming our opinion that if one has an hour to spend with one pupil during one month in order to establish a personal relationship, it is usually better to spend it in six 10-minute or four 15-minute sessions over a period of time rather than one 1-hour session once a month.

We're particularly encouraged at Pershing School, where Daniel O'Donnell and his staff are attempting to learn and apply reality concepts throughout the school's entire environment. We're learning that it is not easy to do this, and that one successful application of the reality procedure does not necessarily guarantee general responsible behavior thereafter by a pupil. However, we are beginning to realize that each situation where these concepts are applied encourages later positive behavior better than the more traditional ways of handling these problems. Mr. O'Donnell put it well when he said, ". . . The process of establishing a personal relationship tends to eliminate the irresponsible behavior and, in the interim, seems to reinforce the teacher's ability to deal with the specific situation and help set the tone for the entire class. Our experiences to date show that teachers can deal effectively with individual pupils with these concepts if the teachers can withstand temporary setbacks of individual unresponsible behavior."

It remains a question of taking the time and effort to think of new techniques and the strength to put them into practice, even though immediate results are at times discouraging. We welcome inquiries from interested school personnel and would be glad to share our experiences as we learn more about this approach to working with people.

(For further explanation of applied Reality Therapy, see "Reality Therapy: A Realistic Approach to the Young Offender" in *Crime and Delinquency*, April, 1964.)

MINIMUM CHANGE THERAPY

Leona E. Tyler

Professor of Psychology, University of Oregon, Eugene

I have some misgivings about the problem we are considering today. Any attempt we make to limit the duration of counseling, though we may think of it as a purely quantitative change, may turn out to have large qualitative effects. One of our ground rules, so basic that we seldom even state it explicitly, is that a person is *worth* whatever amount of time and trouble it takes to help him. We do not measure concern and kindness in hours or dollars. It would be as though a mother should say to herself: "Let's see. I can afford

Reprinted by permission of the Author and the *Personnel and Guidance Journal*, February 1960, 475-479.

This article was delivered at a symposium on Considerations in Controlling the Duration of Counseling Contacts held by the American Psychological Association in Washington, D. C., August 30, 1958.

to devote 10 years of my life primarily to the nurture of these children. That means that the total amount of time that each of them can claim is 10,000 hours." Instead of thinking in this fashion, a mother naturally assumes that she must give whatever the task demands, without rationing it. An increasing mass of evidence is showing that the optimal growth of a human being requires just this kind of unlimited commitment on somebody's part. Under favorable circumstances, a person has had enormous amounts of love and care devoted to him by the time he reaches maturity.

The experience of having someone really care about him is such an indispensable part of what counseling means for a client that we must be especially careful never to jeopardize it. It is for this reason that I am inclined to doubt the wisdom of setting arbitrary time limits. If what the client understands by the arrangements we make is: "You are worth spending 10 hours on, but no more," an experience he might otherwise have had simply will not occur. It has always seemed to me that there is a big difference psychologically, between limits that are inevitable and obviously necessary, such as those resulting from the end of a school term or the illness of the therapist and those that are arbitrary or unexplained.

However, after all this has been said, the fact remains that to prolong counseling contacts unnecessarily does not do a client any good and may even hamper his further development. And our own full schedules make it imperative that we try to avoid this type of error. Thus we do need to give some thought to the matter of how this can best be done.

CHANGE OR UTILIZATION

My own approach to this and other counseling problems has been to attempt to clarify the nature of the task itself. Elsewhere during the last year I have tried to distinguish between two kinds of helping process. Therapy generally has as its goal personality *change;* counseling attempts to bring about the best possible *utilization* of what the person already has. It is a distinction similar to the one Tolman years ago introduced into learning theory, the difference between learning and performance.

The only trouble with simple, clear-cut classifications like this is that they don't seem to fit a lot of the tasks and situations with which we are confronted. Certainly most of the work we do in facilitating occupational choices and educational decisions can be classified as *utilization* rather than as *change*. But what of the client with major or minor personality problems? Is the treatment we offer in such cases therapy or counseling? Is it perhaps really therapy, but called counseling in order to make it more palatable to him or to the community? It would not be so important what label we used, except that the ambiguity spreads out over our own thinking about what we call therapeutic counseling. And because we are not at all sure what we are trying to accomplish, we never know just when we are through.

What I have been questioning in my own mind more and more is the assumption that therapy should attempt to bring about as much personality change as possible. Could it be largely because of the enormous prestige psychoanalysis has acquired that we tend to assume that personality rerorganization is the goal toward which we should strive? Is it really true that the therapy that produces the most changes is the best therapy? Would it not be possible to make the opposite assumption and deliberately set as our goal "minimum-change" therapy? This would be a kind of undertaking that would fit in well with the rest of the activities that go on under the name of counseling. We would try in each case to help the person discover some unblocked path in which he could move forward, develop his unique personality, and thus transcend rather than delve into the anxieties and conflicts in which he is now enmeshed.

I picture this process in terms of a change of *direction* rather than in terms of distances or amounts. The difficulties a client is experiencing can be thought of as indications that he is headed in a direction that is wrong for him or that he has at some former time made a wrong turn into a blind alley. All of this may have occurred without conscious awareness, of course, Counseling can create a situation in which a person may become aware of the directional shifts that are possible for him and in which he can be sure someone will see him through what may be a difficult "rotation of his axis." In pursuing the implications of this geometric analogy a little further I calculated that a directional shift of only 10 degrees makes a difference of 170 miles in where one comes out if his journey is 1,000 miles long — enough to make a considerable difference in terrain and landscape. Similarly, a relatively minor shift in the psychological direction in which a person is moving may well change his life considerably over a long period of years.

This is what I mean by *minimum-change* therapy. It has made it possible for me to see how in principle therapeutic counseling could be shortened considerably without making it any less valuable. It involves no great change in the procedures we use, but some aspects of the complex counseling situation need to be emphasized or even modified to some extent.

Emphasis on Strength

In the first place, it implies that more emphasis than one ordinarily finds be placed on *positive* diagnosis. By and large, our diagnostic thinking rests on concepts taken over from psychopathology. We try to ascertain where a person's weak spots are. Many psychologists, especially in recent years, have criticized this approach and advocated the diagnosis of strengths. In minimum-change therapy we pay no attention to personality weaknesses that are adequately controlled or neutralized. We all have areas like this. It is only the difficulties that are actually blocking the person's forward movement that we must attempt to deal with. And as suggested in the previous section, it is quite possible that these may be by-passed rather than attacked. A person who knows his real strengths and is clear about his basic values may be able to turn away from anxieties about aspects of his life that would be very difficult to change.

Though there is a widespread current interest in ego processes and positive personality traits, we do not as yet have tests we can count on for this sort of diagnostic task. We are more likely to become aware of a person's strengths by observing things he does than by asking him questions. Some of this meaningful behavior occurs in the interview situation itself. For example, when Mary Hart flashes a sudden smile as she is struck with the amusing aspects of a particularly humiliating social experience she is recounting, we know that she possesses an asset that may be of considerable use to her. Call it a defense if you will, but in social situations and in personal emotional adaptation to the vicissitudes of life her ability to laugh at her own predicament will be a valuable asset. Other assets frequently showing up even in interviews where hostility, doubt, guilt, and anxiety are the main themes include moral principles of which the person is absolutely certain, demonstrated courage in the face of adversities, loyalty to those he loves. Whether or not it is advisable for the counselor to reflect or interpret such expressions at the time they occur is another question. But he can make a mental note of them.

We are more likely to become aware of a client's personality assets if we have some knowledge of his life outside the counseling room. In small or moderate-sized colleges, the counselor is likely to encounter his clients here or there — on the street, in the student union, at concerts, plays, or games. The growing practice of placing psychologists on the wards in mental hospitals serves the same purpose of permitting the kind of observation that positive diagnosis is based on. Conversations with a client's family or friends is another resource, but I am strongly of the opinion that it should not be used without the person's knowledge or permission. It is the characteristics he *knows* you have had a chance to observe — the things you can talk over together — that are grist for counseling's mill. In the last analysis, it is the client himself who must make the positive diagnosis we have been talking about if it is to be effective in his life.

Counseling Structure

A second point of emphasis in minimum-change therapy is the way in which the situation is structured for the client. We must take into account *his* expectations and goals as well as our own. To a person profoundly dissatisfied with the way his life has been going, the only thing that really looks good is change — complete change. What he may have read about psychotherapy in popular magazines or seen in movies leads him to expect or at least hope that some fundamental change will occur. True, the experience of countless therapists has shown that such a person will hang on to his unconscious defenses and fight every sort of change at every step of the way. But if anyone *tells* him at the beginning that small shifts of direction rather than larger changes in total pattern are to be expected he is likely to reject the whole undertaking. He thinks he wants to be made over.

It is in this connection that some explicit verbal distinction between counseling and therapy may be useful. Instead of trying to fight the person's wishful dreams about miraculous effects of therapy, I can simply explain that I am a counselor rather than a psychoanalyst and that my job is to help a person find out what his personality is like and decide how he can use the assets he has and get rid of the obstacles that are blocking his progress. If he accepts the situation on these terms, therapeutic counseling can proceed within the framework of the very broad general question "What kind of person are you?" Anything the person wishes to bring up can be considered but we have not committed ourselves to an analysis of all his problems and innumerable childhood experiences out of which they may have arisen.

Necessary Support

A third essential feature of minimum-change therapy is the use of the counseling relationship to reduce the client's anxiety enough to allow him freedom to consider new possibilities. This, of course, is nothing new or at all peculiar to therapy of this type. It seems to be the one common denominator linking together all sorts of diverse procedures. I suppose many workers in the psychotherapeutic vineyard would classify the approach I have been presenting as just another variety of *supportive* therapy. I would have no quarrel at all with that idea were it not that we are so prone to discredit support and to think of it as a suuperficial palliative measure to be used when more powerful methods are impractical. The idea of support should not be devalued in this way. Obviously by support I do not mean inspirational pep talks, shallow reassurance, or the encouragement of dependence. What I do mean is the act of lending one's own strength to the client for the period during which he needs it, so that he can be certain that his world is not going to fall apart if he moves. I have an idea that this is by far the most important thing we do for our clients, whatever our special theoretical predilections are. It is the crucial factor that enables his own development processes to operate.

I suspect that it would be possible in many cases to furnish this firm support much more economically than we now do if we are willing to use it without working for insight or drastic re-structuring of self-concepts. Once a client has established a new direction for himself, it may well be that regularly scheduled interview hours a month apart may be enough to maintain his courage and confidence. It is the quality of the relationship rather than the amount of time spent in the counselor's presence that constitutes support.

The Closing Phase

This brings us to the last point I wish to make about minimum-change therapy. Its intensive phase is brought to a close as soon as a clear direction has been established in the client's life, even though there are many emotional complexes still unexplored, many interpersonal problems still unsolved. Here again, as in the preliminary diagnosis, evidence from outside the interview room can be combined with what comes up during therapy sessions in judging whether a change of direction has been stabilized. A client may mention casually, without apparently attaching any importance to the remark, something that marks such a significant movement. Mr. Elridge, for example, may speak of having had a long talk with his wife the night before, an action unprecedented in his previous experience. Gwen Riley, who has always been an anxious, perfectionistic procrastinator, may say that she has handed in, on time, an assigned paper for a course she is taking. Or the counselor may note the change in the incidental observation we discussed earlier. When he sees Bill Laraway having a coke with a girl, he knows that Bill has taken the first step toward overcoming the paralyzing shyness of which he has been complaining. A newspaper item stating that Mr. Bellingham has given a talk before the Active Club indicates to the counselor that this client's inferiority feelings are being surmounted. I know that, taken alone, such examples sound trivial. But remember, it is these ten-degree or even five-degree changes in direction that we are trying to facilitate. A small change in the direction of closer emotional ties with one's family or greater willingness to assume responsibility is the kind of shift that has a profound effect on later development. When it is clear that this shift has occurred it is time to think about the termination of formal therapy interviews.

One way of characterizing this kind of therapeutic counseling is to say that its basic premises come from the psychology of development and individual differences rather than from the psychology of adjustment. Its most fundamental assumption is that there are many different ways of living an individual life richly and well, and that it is natural for a person to continue to develop throughout his life in his own unique way. We work with nature instead of fighting or ignoring it.

I have often been struck by the fact that almost any personality trait one can think of may be either an asset or a liability, depending on how it is used. Touchy oversensitiveness to slights and insults is not really basically different from tact and social awareness. Aggression can lead to high achievement as well as murderous rage. Timidity and reasonable caution, compulsiveness and constructive orderliness are opposite sides of the same coins. Instead of bewailing our heredity and the mistakes that were made in bringing us up, perhaps we can learn to turn what we have to good account.

I have been thinking a good deal about the way in which therapeutic counseling of this sort might be evaluated. It is an intriguing thought that the very failure to obtain clear evidence for personality change as a result of therapy may be construed as success rather than failure if we reverse our basic assumption — namely, that maximum change is what we are after. It may even be that Eysenck is right and that no kind of therapy produces change that is greater than that which time and the processes of nature would ultimately have brought about by themselves. The therapist may make a contribution only to the extent that he facilitates or speeds up this natural process. The kind of evaluation I should like to see would be designed to show whether our therapeutic efforts do in fact accomplish this facilitation, so that individuals find their way with less suffering and wasted time with therapy than without. And if so, we need to know what aspects of the help we give contribute most toward this end.

To come back at the end to the topic of this symposium, the point I have been trying to make is that we can best control the duration of counseling contacts by adopting consistently an attitude of respect for what each individual client now is and lending him support and understanding while he comes to terms with this unique self of his. Whether it takes him two hours or two hundred, if he succeeds the effort will have been very much worth while.

45

ZEN BUDDHISM, GENERAL PSYCHOLOGY, AND COUNSELING PSYCHOLOGY

Emanuel M. Berger
University of Minnesota

American psychologists have recently begun to show an interest in Zen Buddhism. A check of the *Psychological Abstracts* between 1938 and 1958 shows only one reference to Zen (Benoit, 1955) whereas there are four such references in 1959. In 1958 and 1959 there were articles concerning Zen by a number of American writers in *Psychologia*, a Japanese-edited journal of psychology. Two of these articles were by American psychologists (Van Dusen, 1958; Bruner, 1959). To the knowledge of the writer, the only piece on Zen to appear in any journal that is widely read by American psychologists has been a brief editorial (Thorne, 1969).

Writers associated with psychoanalytic or neo-analytic thought, and generally European in background, have shown a special interest in Zen (Horney, 1945; Jung, 1949). More recently, Erich Fromm contributed a paper on Zen and psychoanalysis to a book (Fromm, Suzuki, DeMartino, 1960).

Zen is a form of Buddhism that began in India, was introduced into China around the first century A.D., and was transmitted to Japan by the twelfth century. Zen thought is a blend of Indian Buddhism, Chinese Taoism, and Japanese Zen Buddhism. The recent development of Zen Buddhism has been greatest in Japan where Zen has influenced many aspects of the life of the people — painting, ceramics, architecture, gardening, archery, swordsmanship, and the language and thought of the people. A recently revised book (Suzuki, 1959) describes ways in which Zen has influenced Japanese culture.

Zen seeks to attain a new way of perceiving the world, of intuitively and directly experiencing reality. The achievement of this viewpoint is called *satori*, meaning enlightenment. *Satori* is a state which is apparently very difficult to attain — and about which there is still disagreement as to what the state is or how one attains it. It is characterized however, by a clear awareness of and openness to reality.

This paper describes those Zen concepts which seem most relevant to general psychology and to counseling psychology. Thus it will focus on such concepts rather than any special concern with *satori* or a general exposition of Zen Buddhism. For the reader who wishes a more comprehensive account of the history and concepts of Zen, several works are suggested: (Humphreys, 1949; Suzuki, 1934, 1949; Watts, 1957).

OBSTACLES TO FULLER AWARENESS OF EXPERIENCE

In Zen, anything that interferes with the freedom of the individual experience is abhorred. Dualistic reasoning, subject-object duality, and attach-

Reprinted by permission of the Author and the *Journal of Counseling Psychology*, Vol. 9, No. 2, 1962, 122-127.

ment to form are all considered to hinder a free experiencing of reality by their contrasting effects on awareness and openness to experience.

Dualistic Thought

Following Suzuki (1934) duality of reasoning takes the traditional Aristotelian form of: A = A; anything is either A or non-A; something cannot be both A and non-A; and it is this duality that Zen denies. For example, what we call a "stick" need not be experienced exclusively as the name we give it but may be in our experience a huge diversity of things all "non-stick," depending on the many ways we may use it or relate to it or perceive it in relation to something else. Potentially, the "stick" may even be something for which we have no name.

The non-duality point of view objects to the tendency to confuse our abstractions of the world with reality — to ignore the potential of objects, nature, or people for being something other than our abstractions of them as represented in the words or concepts we use to describe them.

It may be seen here that Zen anticipated semantics in what it has to say about non-duality. The pioneer work on semantics as such (Korzybski, 1941) is a refutation of Aristotelian modes of thought and suggests ways of avoiding the confusion of abstraction with reality.

Subject-Object Relations

A more particular duality that Zen opposes is that of subject-object, or self-external world. In a recent elaboration on this topic (Fromm, 1960), the duality of subject and object is considered to be based on the development of language and the concept of the self. Gradually the child becomes aware of himself as "I" and the rest of the world as anything other than himself. He is the subject, everything else is object. Language is used to refer to everything outside himself, and thereby objectifies everything that is "not-self" by giving it names and classifications. Zen says that this duality is not real, that both the self and non-self are part of the totality of the individual's experience. The self is not an entity separate from our experiencing, but a part of that experiencing.

Where the subject-object dichotomy is not assumed in our way of thinking, instead of thinking about the object in words or concepts, there is a mutual relation between subject and object. The subject "creates" the object in the sense that he experiences it in his own individual way, apart from names and conceptions about it, just as may poets and artists allow their imaginations to "create" something new and different in their response to ordinary objects. The object "creates" the subject in the sense that the subject is open to experiencing the object, to being affected by it. It is a two-way, mutual relationship, rather than a one-way one.

Thus Zen anticipated the modern concern of existentialism (May, 1960) with the subject-object split. The "split" refers to the barrier to experiencing the other person as a human being when the scientist-subject relates to man as an object to be studied and abstracted about, rather than related to and experienced as a total human being.

Attachment to Form

The teachings of Huang-Po, a ninth century Zen master (Blofeld, 1958) emphasize the necessity of ridding ourselves of attachment to form. Huang-Po also warns against conceptual thought, ideas of good and evil, or following various practices in order to attain enlightenment. Any "form" which limits and obstructs experience by saying what is good and bad, or what we should practice or what reality is in words or concepts, may also be considered as a kind of dualistic thought. All such "forms" leave out the possibility of reality and experience being something different in addition to what they represent, "non-A as well as A." In the words of Huang-Po, "Mind is like the void, in that it is without bounds or obstructions." "Mind" in Huang-Po's usage, means one's original nature or true self, as it is before experience has been limited or obstructed by the various kinds of dualistic thought.

NO-THOUGHT

The Zen answer to the forms of dualistic thought which are seen as obstacles to fuller awareness of reality, is called "no-thought." No-thought is a process in which we allow the mind to function on its own, free of thought about the environment, free of any object of consciousness, free of ideas of good and bad, free of established forms and practices. Thus, "no-thought" would short-cut the intermediate effect of such thoughts on behavior. Behavior would follow more directly from a spontaneous functioning of the organism. An assumption here is that our "original nature," the mind thus freed, is capable of marvelous functions.

For a fuller exposition of how "no-thought" avoids dualistic thought, the reader is referred to Suzuki (1949[b]) and Watts (1957).

In the major modern interpretation of "no-thought" Suzuki quotes Hui-Neng, an eighth century Zen master: "The main point is not to think of things good and bad and thereby be restricted, but to let the mind move on as it is in itself and perform its inexhaustible functions." Te-Shan, another somewhat later Zen master, is quoted in the same work: "See to it that you have nothing disquieting in your mind and be unconscious about your affairs. Then there will be emptiness which functions mysteriously, vacuity which works wonders." "Emptiness" here refers to the absence of the restrictions imposed on one's experience by the various forms of dualistic thought.

Variations on "No-thought"

Two writers on Zen Buddhism, Watts and Suzuki, have developed interpretations of "no thought" which as far as the writer can determine, do not completely and directly follow from records of what Zen masters have said. Nevertheless these interpretations seem to have a high potential value for psychology and therefore to deserve to be considered on their own.

Watts. In this interpretation (Watts, 1957), "no-thought" refers to "action on any level, physical or psychic, without trying at the same moment to observe and check the action from outside one's self."

This means going ahead without stopping, without blocking — but rather trusting the mind to act on its own. An important assumption here is that the human organism is capable of very complex activity on its own, spontaneously, and that we should trust it.

Watts says further that Zen is not against thought, but rather against thinking about one's thinking at the same time one is trying to think, in order to evaluate, criticize, and control one's thinking from outside oneself, so that we may be more perfect in some way. A Zen quotation says the same thing about the functioning of the mind in a more poetic manner:

"Like a sword that cut, but cannot cut itself
Like an eye that sees, but cannot see itself."

Suzuki. In a recent lecture, Suzuki (1960) speaks of becoming "conscious of the unconscious," and says that a special training is required on the part of the consciousness. The unconscious of a mature man, in his definition, incorporates all the conscious experiences he has gone through since infancy and these constitute his whole being. Thus training in basic techniques of a skill such as swordsmanship becomes part of the unconscious. Action left to the unconscious is "no-thought" in the realm of physical skill. Elaborating on this, Suzuki says: "When the swordsman stands against his opponent, he is not to think of his opponent or of himself, nor of his enemy's sword movements. He just stands there with his sword which forgetful of all technique, is ready only to follow the dictates of the unconscious."

THE PSYCHOLOGICAL RELEVANCE OF ZEN

Creativity

A recent publication of the Carnegie Corporation (1961) summarizes some results of studies on creativity directed by Donald W. MacKinnon at the Institute for Personality Assessment (IPAR). One general finding is that "creative people are more open to experience within and without." This corresponds to a major objective of Zen, freeing the individual from those obstacles which hinder a fuller awareness of the self and the world.

The Zen concept of non-duality points up the possibility of reality being something other than the words and concepts we use to describe it — and the Zen idea of "no-thought" emphasizes trusting our minds to work on their own, intuitively. These concepts parallel IPAR findings that "highly creative people in all fields are overwhelmingly intuitive." "Intuitive" means in their definition an "indirect perception of the deeper meanings and possibilities inherent in things" and involves focusing habitually on possibilities. Also the creative person is found to be nonconformist in ideas and this corresponds to Zen's admonishment not to be attached to form, but to trust one's own experience and intuition.

"No-thought" as interpreted by Watts means allowing the mind to operate on its own without attempting at the same time to observe, check and control our thinking in order to achieve some intended effect. Another way of looking at this is to say that the mind can operate in thinking, but it cannot operate effectively if at the same time it tries to make itself its own object, to be controlled and made to get certain results. If creativity in research is spontaneous, comes of itself, it then follows that creativity cannot be the result of will and intention. This corresponds well with reports of scientists who emphasize the intuitive nature of creative insights. The insight "came" to them and at a time when they were not struggling for it intentionally.

This interpretation of "no-thought" agrees with some findings of Morris I. Stein (1961) in his studies of research chemists. The creative chemist is more likely to "play" with things and ideas; to allow all kinds of ideas and feelings to enter his mind. Also, he is not so likely to try to force or pull out a solution as opposed to less creative workers who seem to try to achieve quickly and to achieve a synthesis earlier.

Physical Skill

The interpretation of "no-thought" by Suzuki is relevant for all kinds of physical skills. This means that having been trained in basic techniques, the swordsman, archer, or athlete then allows his organism to respond to whatever occurs in the contest, without thought of technique, without intellection.

Thus the batter in baseball responds intuitively with a swing for a home run or slices to an opposite field as the conditions permit, instead of intending to "murder the ball" no matter what the pitcher throws. The essence of this idea is that the performer acts with a minimum of self-consciousness, trusting his accumulation of technique and experience to guide his actions.

ZEN AND COUNSELING PSYCHOLOGY

Counseling Relationship and Technique

What has been said generally about non-duality, the subject-object relation and "no-thought" may all be applied specifically to the counseling relationship.

Then the concept of non-duality implies that we do not mistake descriptions, diagnoses, or test results, or any other abstractions about him, for the total reality of the counselee as a person. We are then open to his possibility for being in a vast variety of ways that are other than the abstractions we use to describe or think about him. The concept of ambivalence exemplifies the possibility of a counselee being both "A and non-A" at the same time, both loving and hating a particular person. What has been said about the application of the subject-object relation, implies for counseling a mutual, person-to-person, relationship in which roles are forgotten, in which each responds to and influences the other. Opposed would be a relationship in which the counselor is largely the subject — studying, analyzing, diagnosing, intellectualizing about the counselee as object. To the extent that the counselor is detached and analytical of the counselee, he is also not able to be open to experiencing and responding to the counselee as a person.

The foregoing considerations seem quite similar to existentialist views concerning relationship (May 1959) and what Rogers (1955) has said concerning treating the client as object.

The application of "no-thought" to the counseling relationship would mean that the counselor allows his total organism to act on its own, to experience and respond and to act without any attempt to achieve any special effect, without standing outside the relation and viewing either the client or self or the relationship objectively for the purpose of analyzing, manipulating, or evaluating what is being done. This corresponds to what Rogers (1955) has been saying about "trusting one's organism" in the therapeutic relation: "I let myself go into the immediacy of the relationship where it is my total organism which takes over and is sensitive to the relationship, not simply my consciousness."

Another way of looking at the application of "no-thought" to the counseling relationship might be to describe it as a continuum of "no-technique." To the extent that one applies technique to the relationship he must objectify it and intellectualize about it in order to apply principle to it, and in so doing departs from "no-thought" and "trusting one's organism" in the relationship, and then probably loses the person-to-person quality of the relationship. Interpretations to the counselee may necessarily require viewing him objectively. In another sense, they may have a "no-thought" character in that they arise in the counselor, "come" to him with little or no intellectualization or thought about principle, but rather from an accumulation of insights about people which may function as a "trained unconscious."

For the purpose of a maximally open person-to-person experience, we might want to "live" the relationship maximally by way of "no-technique" most of the counseling hour, and reserve intellectualizing about it for another time. It may be that for various reasons, we could never expect to lose ourselves completely in a "no-technique" relation. There would be other questions as to the effectiveness of maximum "no-technique" alone or whether some combination of "no-technique" with technique and interpretation might not be more effective under certain conditions.

Of course any self-conscious attempt to apply "no-technique" would probably be self-defeating, since the very naturalness and spontaneity of "no-technique" could be destroyed by intention and self-consciousness. "No-technique" is essentially experiential and nonself-conscious.

It might be appropirate here to say that recent personal experience in counseling gives a hint of a certain mutual transcendence of self when the relationship is nonintellectual and intuitive. Then it seems as if each stimulates the other so that each intuitively discovers and expresses insights that had occurred to neither person previously.

Counseling Training

It may be fairly common in the experience of those who have supervised practicum training to find beginning counselors frequently having difficulty in being natural and relaxed in the counseling relationship. They are not open to and responsive to the counselee as a person. They are preoccupied with intellectual considerations as to how they should operate as a counselor — what the book says — or what some respected "expert" says.

When the counselor comes to trust himself to respond appropriately to the counselee, without feeling that he must depend on "principles" and other external factors, without an intervening intellectual process but intuitively, then he will be able to operate without self-consciousness, spontaneously, naturally, with increased openness to the whole experience.

This is not to imply that spontaneity and naturalness are sufficient for counselor effectiveness. This is where Suzuki's version of "no-thought" as the "trained unconscious" comes in. It implies that a counselor should be well trained in counseling, research, and psychological principles but that at some point thereafter he must begin to trust himself to some extent to operate without conscious thought of these things, on the assumption that such accumulated knowledge has become part of his "trained unconscious."

Counseling Problems

Watt's (1958) discussion of *kuan* and the sexual relation suggests a hypothesis concerning problems of sexual adjustment. *Kuan* means "wordless contemplation" an open, receptive, nonstraining attitude. It also implies trusting the sexual organs to respond appropriately. It corresponds to "no-thought" in representing the absence of any attempt of the mind to split itself, as when it attempts both to act and evaluate its actions simultaneously. This would be "grasping" at experience, attempting to take hold of an experience that can only arise spontaneously and therefore cannot be willed, cannot be grasped by intention to do so.

It seems likely that many problems of sexual adjustment are of this very sort. One or both partners, lacking confidence in his own or his partner's sexual capacity, or for other reasons, grasp at sexual satisfaction and thus loses mutual satisfaction. The satisfaction of the grasping person is minimal compared to what is potential in a mutually satisfying relationship.

The writer has had some limited experience in the application of "no-thought" to counseling problems. In one case, the client was a graduate student who had failed Ph.D. orals twice, blocking, thinking but saying little. Interviews suggested that he was searching for a more complete and accurate formulation before saying anything, rather than simply allowing his thoughts to flow and saying what he thought even though incomplete and imperfect. It would be easy to oversimplify the case since there were other factors in it. However, he did pass his next attempt at the orals following counseling and a marked change in his behavior was reported by his advisor.

Another client blocked in writing themes. She reported considerable improvement after it was suggested that she elaborate on her thoughts at one time and attempt to get better organization and continuity at another, rather than trying to do both at the same time as she had been doing.

The concept of "no-thought" would be relevant to any problem in which there was a strong element of self-consciousness as opposed to spontaneity and trusting oneself to operate effectively without the necessity of attempting a strict control over what one does. It may be that certain problems of extreme self-consciousness have such long-developed affective components that the application of "no-thought" alone could not be expected to achieve any substantial improvements. We probably need to learn under what conditions the application of the "no-thought" concepts can be helpful in various problems in which self-consciousness is an important factor.

Received December 15, 1961.

REFERENCES

Benoit, H. *The supreme doctrine.* Long: Routledge & Kegan Paul, 1955.
Blofeld, J. *The Zen teaching of Huang-Po.* New York: Grove, 1958.
Bruner, J. B. The art of ambiguity — A conversation with Zen master Hisamatsu. *Psychologia*, 1959, *2*, 101-105.
Carnegie Corporation of New York Quarterly. July, 1961, *10*, No. 3.
Fromm, E., Suzuki, D. T., & DeMartino, R. *Zen Buddhism and psychoanalysis.* New York: Harper, 1960.
Humphreys, C. *Zen Buddhism.* London: William Heineman, 1949.

Korzybski, A. *Science and sanity*. Lancaster & New York: The International Non-Aristotelian Library Publishing Co., 1941.

May, R., Angel, E., & Ellenberger, H. F. (Eds.) *Existence*. New York: Basic Books, 1958.

Rogers, C. R. Persons or science? — a philosophical question. *Amer. Psychologist*, 1955, *10*, 267, 278.

Suzuki, D. T. *An Introduction to Zen Buddhism*. Kyoto: Eastern Buddhist Society, 1934.

Suzuki, D. T. *Essays in Zen Buddhism*. London: Rider. 1949. (a)

Suzuki, D. T. *The Zen doctrine of no-mind*. London: Rider, 1949. (b)

Suzuki, D. T. *Zen and Japanese Culture*. New York: Pantheon, 1959.

Thorne, F. C. Zen Buddhism and clinical psychology. *J. clin Psychol.*, 1960, *16*, 452-453.

Van Dusen, W. Zen and western psychotherapy. *Psychologia*, 1958, *1*.

Watts, A. W. *The way of Zen*. New York: Pantheon, 1957.

Watts, A. W. *Nature, man and woman*. New York: Pantheon, 1958.

COUNSELING FROM THE VIEWPOINT OF EXISTENTIAL PSYCHOLOGY

Adrian van Kaam

Duquesne University

Counseling is essentially a process of making-free, a humanizing of the person who has lost his freedom in sectors of his existence where he can no longer transcend his life situation by freely giving meaning to it. He behaves there more or less as a lower form of being, as a dehumanized, determined existence. It is the aim of counseling to assist the person in regaining his freedom in these areas by creating insight into the meanings he attributes to these situations, by starting the extinction of the responses which the counselee — after gaining insight — no longer likes to retain, and by the conditioning of other responses corresponding to his new free evaluation of reality. In order to make the counselee free we have to make the counseling session an existential situation where he can be present with his whole being spontaneously and pre-reflexively.

We know the person from his phenomenal universe, not from his isolated and interior world. Therefore from the very beginning the attention of the client is oriented towards himself as moving in a vivid universe of events and encounters. He moves in the present, in the "here and now" of his actual world as a human existence — as "consciousness that is involved." The counselee is not encouraged to escape his present by a flight into a past, where there are no decisions to make and where there is no necessity to shape freely a world of "here and now," where existence seems determined and explained by inescapable needs. Instead of forcing the client to revise the fixed history of his past, the counselor invites him to face his situation today, not to excuse himself but to return to his world in a new mode of being, to accept its challenges.

Reprinted by permission of the Author and the *Harvard Educational Review*, Vol. 32, No. 4, Fall 1962.

The aim of existential counseling is to make the client feel at home in his real world by reshaping his phenomenal world, to make his real situation bearable by making it bearable phenomenologically. The counselee reconditions his behavior in his real world by reconditioning his behavior in his phenomenal universe.

The counselee who transcends his barriers and who learns to conquer the regions at the other side will know how to move with a new freedom in his world of everyday reality. Only he can cope with anxiety who calls the real world his dwelling place, the whole world from high to low and from right to left, not only the bright side of the world but its shady side as well; the mature persons says yes to the whole universe.

THE EMBODIMENT OF OBJECTIVES IN ATTITUDES AND BEHAVIOR

The counselor translates these objectives of existential counseling into attitudes which he in turn embodies in word, posture, facial expression and movement.

The attitudes of the counselor are determined not only by his purpose but also by the situation of his client. He must clarify the existence or modes of standing-out of the counselee who exists in a personal world, which has to be explored and expressed by means of the therapeutic relationship. In order thus to understand the attitudes in which we must embody our objectives we should first of all gain an insight into the existential world and into the kind of relationship which can induce the counselee to explore and express the realms of his existence. The insight gained in these considerations will enable us to describe some desirable attitudes which may embody the objectives so that they are communicated to the counselee within this relationship.

THE EXISTENTIAL WORLD OF THE CLIENT

The main characteristic of the human existent is that he exists, literally stands out in a world of meaning. Subject and world, self and world are correlatives. When we know the world in which a person lives we know *him;* the counselee is best understood from his personally lived and experienced universe. His feelings, desires, hopes and ideas are embedded in a world of meaning, and consequently every experience explored by him has somewhere a place in this system of meanings. This structure as a differentiated whole explains partly the meaning of every single experience which belongs to it. Each single experience in turn colors all meanings which make up the world of the counselee as a whole. When he is able gradually to express the main lines of his existential world, the counselee will be able to understand the precise meaning of his problem within this system.

RELATIONSHIP AND EXPRESSION OF EXISTENTIAL WORLD

Relationship is the principal means for bringing to expression the world of meaning in which the client lives. The quality of the relationship determines to what degree the personal existential world will find genuine expression. The first task of the counselor is, therefore, to establish a relationship which leads to optimal communication. People learn to hide the personal world in which they live in order to protect themselves from being misunderstood, humiliated, condemned or abused. To reveal my personal world is in a sense to surrender my very being, to expose my sensitivity, my project of life, and to unveil my vulnerability when certain meanings which I cherish are at odds with the values appreciated by my environment. This fear of disapproval limits the free admission not only of base inclinations but also of sublime aspirations. It is difficult for many to verbalize their finer sentiments. They fear that the communication of refined feeling would sound ridiculous in the world of functional meaning which they share with contemporary man. This repression of the personal world under the pressure of the shared social world may be so effective that the client himself is not aware of the deepest meanings which constitute his personal existence. The counselor may make himself mistakenly the ally of this social worrld by lightly joking about noble sentiments in order to give the client the reassurance that counselors are regular fellows like the rest of the population. If he does so he can be sure that the personal world of experience of the counselee will remain a closed book. Some counselors may cherish the illusion that such "open-mindedness" may break barriers forgetting that an exclusive open-mindedness for the cultural-social scene may mean a closed-mindedness for the personal world of the individual in its unique, most revealing features.

THE IMPOSITION OF ONE'S OWN EXISTENCE

Every one of us has his own project of existence which implies among other things the style in which we embody our strivings in daily behavior. Such a style of existence has been formed in the light of individual experiences of the attitudes of the surrounding culture in which we are inserted by birth and education. This cultural component of our style of behavior and perception is mediated by the image of "ideal" behavior as held by the people of our home, neighborhood and society. This ideal style of life permeates our human relationships, being particularly pervasive in the meetings between us as counselors and the counselee who presents himself to us with his problems. The secret influence of this personal and cultural norm may be harmful. Existence as embodiment in space and time necessitates that we be present to others in some style of life. However, our personal embodiment of existence is not the only possible or desirable one for everybody else. The unconscious identification of our personal way of life with "the" way may limit our therapeutic relevance to that part of the population which is spontaneously in touch with our style of being while it averts others.

Therefore, the counselor should grow daily in the awareness of his prereflexive attitudes. Of course he cannot do away with a personal style of existence; as a human being he must embody his mode of being in concrete behavior, which is always limited in space and time and therefore necessarily onesided. But he can increasingly free himself from the identification of existence as such with his personal-cultural style of being. This inner freedom will enable him to sense the unique potentialities in those counselees who differ from him in expression and perception. When the counselor is deeply aware that his own modes are incidental and transient, he will distinguish what is essential from that which is accidental. This self-awareness will enable him to transcend the temporal to become aware of his cultural and subcultural stereotypes, of his antipathies and sympathies his emotional blocks will become manifest to him in this maturity. He may discover, for instance, that he *a priori* does not like people with esthetic inclinations because the good farmers at home confused artistry with frivolity. Or he may realize that he one-sidedly prefers "regular guys" because as a high school or college student he disliked some pale companions who were delighted more by books than by baseball. Another may find that he is unconsciously enamored with scholarly types because he is fed up with his more pragmatic colleagues who make great fun of him. Or a counselor may discover during this process of growing up that he unconsciously favors a certain compulsiveness because he has identified the compulsive mode of being with sound strictness and consequently distrusts spontaneity in himself and others.

The counselee in turn may be tempted to identify the counselor with his parents, teachers, administrators, supervisors or school friends. These identifications may harm the effectiveness of counseling, for such daily relationships usually imply some withholding of one's personal world in order to function smoothly within the frame of daily life. The counselor is usually an unknown alien for the candidate. He seems different from the people in authority whom he meets in school, family and society. His function is vague and unusual; he comes from a strange faraway world. This relative strangeness can be an advantage. If the counselor were identified with the authorities in the environment of the candidate, the client's daily mode of existence towards those people would be immediately adopted towards him. The interview would then structure itself in terms of this mode of existence; the formal, casual, dependent or superficially friendly features which characterize daily interactions would determine this new relationship and keep it on a level which may generate pleasantries, polite caution or formal respect but no experience in depth.

When the client, however, cannot experience the counselor as he does his daily associates, then no stereotyped mode of existence toward him is available. Moreover, the candidate faces this ambiguous situation alone and not in the company of his friends or classmates. Therefore he cannot fall back on a mode of existence which he could share with others towards this new person; he has to handle this interaction all by himself. Such a situation is conducive to responses which will reveal his unique way of being in the world and which are less contaminated by socially shared modes of existence.

On the other hand, if the ambiguity is too much to bear it will evoke too much anxiety in the client and paralyze communication. The effective counselor, therefore, should not make himself known too much by being too friendly and jovial and by removing all social distance. For in that case he and the client will act out superficial social roles which usually prevent communication on a deeper and more personal level. Neither should he be so distant, alien and withdrawn that his counselee freezes in anxiety. The counselor should not maneuver himself into a situation in which he will be forced to do most of the talking; yet he must avoid sitting there like a sphinx which would prevent the possibility of spontaneous communication. This attitude of professional composure and serenity may be inspired by an unauthentic, false image of the "wise," "mature" man without emotion, which is a neurotic imitation of real wisdom and maturity.

Ideally the counselor should be experienced by the counselee as a deeply interest, wise friend whose only interest is to help me in finding myself in relation to my possible project of existence. However, the counselor may have his own unconscious needs which may make it difficult for him to establish such an interested and at the same time detached relationship. Therefore he should explore his motivations after every session. Does he need to sound like an oracle, is he in love with his sonorous voice or clever verbalizations, does he feel that he "knows" people already through and through, is he authoritarian, domineering, does he need to be popular, to be liked or exalted as a "nice chap" by his counselee, is he afraid of depth in himself and others, does he repress his own feelings and paralyze his spontaneity, is he afraid to verbalize or to hear the verbalization of certain experiences? This list could be expanded indefinitely. It is only after a period of growth and experience that a counselor is able to approximate the ideal attitude which makes the relationship itself his most efficient instrument. A mature and experienced counselor is indeed a precious gift for a community.

THE STRUCTURE OF THE RELATIONSHIP

The relationship itself which should be established by the counselor — from the first moment of the initial meeting — differs from the structure of other relationships. First it is different because of its objectives, which we have discussed earlier, and second, it is different from other relationships because of the specific attitudes of the counselor.

The attitudes of the counselor aim at the expression of the personal existential world of the counselee. At the base of these attitudes is a genuine unconditional acceptance of the client regardless of what world of meaning he will reveal. Any trace of explicit or implicit disapproval diminishes the ability of the counselee to unveil his personal existence. On the other hand, the expression of this personal world can also be arrested by too great a personal involvement of the counselor in one or another aspect mentioned by the client. Such emotional concentration on one aspect prevents the narration of other dimensions of the world of meaning which may be just as important for full understanding. The counselor must encourage the client by his patient and accepting attitude to express spontaneously all vague and confused feelings, attitudes and motives which he may have in regard to his project of existence.

The counselor should be emotionally involved to the extent necessary to keep the client interested and alive in the exploration of his world. But this interest should be tempered with a distance which enables him to accept all aspects of existence expressed by the counselee without reacting to them favorably or unfavorably. Either reaction may encourage a positive or negative concentration on some particular aspect of the counselee's world at the expense of the revelation of other ones. The counselor must be a participant in the existential world of the client while being at the same time its respectful observer.

ATTITUDES OF THE COUNSELOR IN THIS
EXISTENTIAL RELATIONSHIP

The description of the counseling relationship implies the desirability of certain attitudes.

Creativity

The counselor should be creative. His counseling should not be a rigid application of rules which he has learned from books or formed for himself on the basis of experience with former clients. On the contrary, he should be convinced that every world of meaning is unique. Everything that the counselor says and does should be the creative outgrowth of his participation in this individual existence. This presupposes that the counselor is a mature person free from threat and therefore free from rigidity. Rigid behavior is a defense against the possible challenge of an unexpected world, a world which is communicated to us and which may expose us to our own repressed regions of being. The counselor who is not at home in his own existential world is unable to risk the full revelation of another world of meaning. There are two main forms of rigidity; one leading to a stiff formal attitude in order to escape communication in depth, the other leading to a compulsively "jolly good fellow" attitude which may be an even more effective defense against a truly existential encounter. Both defenses may be based on some neurotic insecurity in the counselor. Sometimes we find a curious combination of both defenses in the same insecure, anxious person; in the fulfillment of functional and administrative obligations he may be formal and rigid, while in his personal relations compulsively joking, gay, and funny. The mature person can be serious, gay, or detached according to the challenge of the situation. He adopts none of these attitudes compulsively; his behavior is not identical in different situations. Existential creativity implies flexibility of attitude, feeling, and behavior in authentic response to the real situation.

Acceptance

Another fundamental attitude in this relationship is acceptance, an attitude which generates in the counselee an experience of really feeling understood in his own existential world. The counselee feels that he really shares this personal world with the counselor, and this feeling enables him to explore this world further and to communicate the outcome of this exploration with less embarrassment. When the candidate perceives that the counselor co-experiences what things mean to him and still accepts him, he gradually feels a safe experiential communion with the counselor and with the world which the counselor represents.

That the counselor co-experiences what people and things mean to the client does not imply that he agrees with this meaning or that he approves of it. Acceptance of a person does not imply personal agreement with his thought or feeling as such. The co-experience and acceptance of the counselor implies only a non-judgmental attitude. His whole attitude communicates to the person: I do not judge at this moment whether or not your feelings and attitudes prove that you are personally guilty for maintaining them; I leave that to your own conscience for this moment. My special function here is not to judge how far you personally are responsible for those attitudes and feelings but to understand what region of your existence they reveal. Basically I respect and like you because deep down your nature is a gift of being; this gift is fundamentally good, and therefore, lovable no matter how it may be overgrown and veiled by attitudes, feelings, and opinions with which I could not agree personally.

The attitude acceptance is so fundamental for effective counseling and at the same time so different from our usual mode of encounter that it may be fruitful to go somewhat deeper into this matter. The views, feelings, and behavior of the counselee can be accepted under various aspects. For example, the counselor might consider expressed views, feelings, and behavior as isolated abstract norms of human conduct, in which case he can accept or reject them as such. When a client mentions, for instance, that he thinks that certain races should be exterminated, the counselor cannot accept this personally as a highly commendable norm for human existence. Or, he might consider those views, feelings, and behavior under the aspect of their usefulness for the counselee himself. For instance, the counselor may personally dislike poetry and would not accept and cultivate this interest in his own life; he may sense, however, that the poetical mode of existence may be very important for this specific person and he may accept it under this aspect. At the same time, he would reject under this aspect a suicidal interest of the counselee. However, he does not openly express the acceptance or rejection of those judgments as isolated judgments. For, regardless of his acceptance or rejection of those particular views, feelings, or behavior as isolated absolute expressions, the counselor always accepts and respects the client himself as a worthwhile human person dynamically present in those communications. For the same attitudes are not only categories of socially or personally acceptable or rejectable behavior but are also manifestations of a fellow human being. They manifest that the client is not an animal or an inanimate being; their specific content reveals that this human being has adopted certain modes of existence in the world.

The counselor *as counselor* experiences primarily in all these views, feelings, and behavior a wrestling, suffering, sometimes victorious, sometimes defeated human being who tries desperately to find his existential position within this world. It is in this last way that the understanding counselor experiences and accepts the views, feelings, and behavior of the client, namely, under the aspect of their being manifestations of the coping human person, desperately looking for a meaningful project of existence. He shows, therefore, deep genuine interest in those communications. It is this acceptance which opens up the client who becomes actively involved in the process of self discovery and its expression when he senses that the counselor really cares about what he thinks and feels; a climate is created in which the flow of communication is not halted by the anxious expectation of disapproval, rejection, criticism or other negative responses which the counselee expects on the basis of his past experience in family, school or society. Acceptance lessens considerably defensiveness and therewith the compulsion to rationalize, deny, or distort existential attitudes and inclinations in order to prevent disapproval.

If the counselor himself has deeply buried in himself some aspects of his personal existence he should become aware of it. The same anxiety which made him bury the awareness of regions of his own existence may close him when he senses the slightest indication of the same threatening reality in another. The implicit communication of this anxiety will prevent the free exploration of this specific area of existence. This danger points to the necessity for the counselor to evaluate himself continuously and thoroughly. Every session with a candidate should be a source of self reflection. What did I say? How did I respond? What did I feel? How did this communication affect me?

Was I uneasy, excited, threatened, at ease, uncomfortable? Why was I so? The personal existence of the counselor is his main tool. In order to keep it refined and sensitive he should work through his inhibitions, anxieties, and insecurities with a therapist whom he trusts. He should keep refining this instrument that he himself is. For, no amount of literature, study, or oratory can replace the impact of his very being upon the relationship with the counselee.

Gentleness

The counselor should maintain mildness in his approach. We do not mean anything sentimental, effeminate, or soft. Gentleness reveals itself in sensitive, considerate, and tolerant modes of existence. The counslor should be able to manifest this amenity spontaneously; it will be difficult for the counselee to express himself fully if this atmopshere of gentle consideration is absent. For some counselors it may seem nearly repulsive to be gentle. Sometimes a male counselor in a high school may believe that he should ideally give the boy he is counseling the impression that he himself is just another boy, one who is bigger, taller, heavier, and more muscular, yet a boy, an enlarged version of an adolescent who speaks and acts big, very big. This attitude was perhaps deeply rewarded by his friends in college or high school who looked up towards him as the real tough guy. For some it may take time to realize that the same behavior will be ineffective in their new adult role when they like to go beyond the peripheral and reach the core of human existence. Others may not have worked through their anxious concern about being a real man and the unconscious occupation with their manliness may paralyze their gentility. Others again have not worked through the loneliness of existence and remain unconsciously in search of a tenderness which fulfills sentimental needs. Their gentility lacks spine and strength; it has a sticky, slimy quality which repels certain people. Some counselors may develop unauthentic friendliness which does not originate in the depth of existence but is calculated and carefully added to behavior in those situations in which the good counselor should be pleasant. It is practiced as a tour de force, a feat of strength, a stunt of psychology. Such a forced gentility remains superficial and will not open up the deeper layers of existence.

Sincerity

Finally the attitude of the counselor should be straightforward, honest, and sincere. The counselor should be aware that he has been compelled in daily life to develop a social facade in order to protect himself against obliteration by the demands of the crowd. He cannot get involved in everyone's problems. He has had to develop a smooth, easy way of dealing with large numbers of people who accost the counselor with their questions, neuroses and venerations. Moreover, the population at large demands from him that he be "nice" regardless of his mood, his toothache or the troubles with his principal. The effective functioning and the serenity of the school community to which he belongs requires a smooth interaction between faculty and counselor which implies certain social niceties. How tempting it is to fall back on these habits when meeting the counselee. However, such habits, no matter how useful in the community at large, if introduced into the counseling session will prevent effectively that deeper communication which is the aim of this encounter.

EXISTENTIAL COUNSELING AND THEORIES OF PSYCHOLOGY

We described the openness of the existential counselor, and considered attitudes of his that foster optimal communication with the counselee. The final question to be dealt with is that of the relationship between existential counseling and theories of psychology. Does the openness of the existential counselor imply that psychological theory is superfluous; if not, what is its role?

The Avoidance of a Premature Use of Theoretical Concepts

Existential counseling fosters a self-understanding in the counselee, which is free from subjectivistic influences; it attempts to uncover the real structures and meanings of experience; it means a purification of the naive knowledge of self by a search for real self-experience beyond the subjectivistic explanations of everyday life. If the counselor, however, brings uncritically theoretical categories to naively experienced behavior he may be caught in another sophisticated form of subjectivism, which might distort the given phenomena. He may unwittingly substitute for the experience of daily life an artificially made up "scientific experience." He immediately "perceives," for example, in the counselee inferiority feelings, projections, archetypes, repressions, reinforcements, resistances, Oedipus-complexes, transferences, sublimations and the like. This artificial scientific *experience* is the abortive result of two sources: one is the naive experience of everyday life, the other the immediate interpretation of this naive natural experience by established scientific theories. Such an interpretation — when prematurely indulged in — prevents a respectful attention for the inner structure and meaning of experience itself in this unique situation. Consequently, established intersubjectivistic theoretical influences are substituted for or added to the subjectivistic distortions which are already present in the naive experience itself. This impoverished, made-over experience is then considerd as *the* full real experience, substituting for the experience in everyday life. This scientific experience is called fact and this fact is then hailed as the first primary original experience of the counselee. Out of the collection or enumeration of these facts one should come by induction to the establishment of laws which should govern the activities of counselors and clients alike. This process leads to a system of counseling autonomous and closed in itself, an empty game with splendid ideas irrelevant to real experience of people in vital situations, a mythology of behavior which claims to explain everything while it explains nothing.

Obviously much harm can be done by a counselor when his perception is distorted by the premature introduction of theoretical explanations. The existential counselor will penetrate first into behavior as it manifests itself and only then ponder how existing scientific theories may illuminate this behavior without distortion, or how scientific theories should be corrected, expanded, or renewed in order to keep in touch with behavior as given in reality today. Theories of personality and psychotherapy should supplement rather than supplant existential understanding. The existential counselor should draw on the rich fund of insight called science of psychology which is a collection of intellectual contributions by numerous enlightened theorists of behavior. But, his prudent selection from this treasure-trove of theoretical explanations should be illumined by real behavior as it manifests itself in his clients. His primary commitment is to existence, not to a theory about existence, even an existential theory. His existential openness for the communications of his counselee will enable him not only to spot the relevant theoretical explanation but also to adapt it to the concrete situation or even to improve it on the basis of his observation. In the last case he may possibly enrich the treasury of psychology so that others after him may have more knowledge available. It should be his wish, however, that his successors will neither abuse his ideas for the distortion of data or substitute his observation for their own existential perception. It should be his hope that they may be more sensitive to behavior than to his explanations about behavior, that their ears may not be deafened by the noise of theories, and that their eyes may not be blinded by expositions in journals, books, and papers, even if they happen to be his own.

Language Habit

Language habit in this context refers to the embodiment in our language of psychological theories. The language may be scientific or pre-scientific; likewise psychological theories embedded in the language may be scientific and pre-scientific. English, for instance, is a pre-scientific language; the psychoanalytic idiom is a scientific language. Language is not the experience itself of the counselee but an expression of this experience. Many words may communicate more than the pure experience of the client. They express, for example, also the pre-scientific view of his experience, which he has received from his culture in the package of his language. In that case the language habit implies not only the expression of experience but also the pre-scientific view which created this biased and selective expression. By the same token it conceals other real aspects of experience which fall outside the scope of the pre-scientific theory, which dominates the mood of his civilization, and therewith the cast of its language.

An example of the influence of theory on language is the term "experience." The German word for experience is "Erlebnis"; the Dutch word is "beleving." The German "Erlebnis" is derived from "erleben" which literally means "to live an event," for, "erleben" connotes "leben" which means "to live." "Experience" denotes thus in both languages the actuality of a lively presence of the subject to a reality here and now. The term experience in the English language, however, has lost this meaning under the impact of empiricism. "Experience" instead of indicating an awareness in the present points to an awareness in the past. Consequently, this language habit may obscure or falsify the perception of the counselor and of the client. They may — misled by the language — overlook or misinterpret behavior which embodies an actual "lived" presence of the subject to reality without reflection. An open perception, however, that momentarily suspends the language habit may rediscover this reality of behavior which was lost in the language. The rediscovery of such a reality may force the counselor or counselee to enrich the language with a new expression which covers the forgotten phenomenon. They may speak, for instance, of "lived" experience, or "lived" awareness. Language is thus the treasure-trove of accumulated theories, insights and observations uncovered by a people in the current of its history; the fascinating history of a-standing-out-together in certain ways toward reality. This shared ex-sistence towards reality reveals itself in peculiar ways to the cultural co-existents. The resulting insights are conserved in the constituted language of a people. This constituted language should be a help, not a hindrance, towards further discovery of reality; it should not suppress but support living language, not fossilize but foster vision, not limit but expand perception.

Constituted *scientific* language presents a similar problem. Psychoanalytic, behavioristic, or organismic terminology should not paralyze but nurture the openness of observation, should not limit but expand perception and vision. The counselor might profit fully from the treasure of scientific language if he frees himself temporarily from its influence on perception. For perception unadulterated by theoretical tenets prepares him for a new appreciation of what other theorists have seen before him. Yet, his previous open perception of "behavior-as-it-is" liberates him from the limitations inherent in the position of every theorist.

The existential openness with its attitudes of suspension and vigilance is fundamental in the counselor who should encounter people beyond theory and classification. Only afterwards may he see in what sense and to what degree he may characterize their behavior by constructs *about* behavior. Theoretical psychology becomes then a light that enlightens, not a veil that dims, the perception of the counselor.

SELECTED REFERENCES

1. Buytendijk, F. J. J. "The Phenomenological Approach to the Problem of Feelings and Emotions." In M. L. Reymert (ed.), *Feelings and Emotions, Mooseheart Symposium.* New York: McGraw-Hill, 1950. Pp. 127-141.
2. Dondeyne, A. *Contemporary European Thought and Christian Faith.* Pittsburgh: Duquesne University Press, 1958.
3. ———. *Geloof en Wereld.* Antwerpen: Patmos, 1961.
4. Frankl, V. E. *From Death-Camp to Existentialism: a Psychiatrist's Path to a New Therapy.* Boston: Beacon Press, 1959.
5. Kwant, R. C. *Encounter.* Pittsburgh: Duquesne University Press, 1960.
6. Lopez, Ibor, Juan. "The Existential Crisis." In J. Braceland (ed.), *Faith, Reason and Modern Psychiatry.* New York: P. J. Kenedy and Sons, 1955.
7. Luijpen, W. *Existential Phenomenology.* Pittsburgh: Duquesne University Press, 1960.
8. May, R. *Freedom and Responsibility Re-examined:* Unpublished paper read at the 1962 meeting of the American College Personnel Assosciation, Chicago, April 18, 1962.
9. ———. "The Meaning of the Oedipus Myth," *Review of Existential Psychology and Psychiatry,* I, 1 (1961), pp. 44-52.
10. Perquin, N. *Paedagogiek,* Roermond-Maaseik: J. J. Romen & Zonen, 1952.
11. Rogers, Carl R. "The Loneliness of Contemporary Man," *Review of Existential Psychology and Psychiatry,* I, 1 (1961), pp. 94-101.
12. ———. *On Becoming a Person.* Boston: Houghton Mifflin Company, 1961.
13. Van Kaam, A. "The Nurse in the Patient's World," *The American Journal of Nursing,* LIX (1959), pp. 1708-1710.
14. ———. "Freud and Anthropological Psychology," *The Justice* (Brandeis University), May, 1959.
15. ———. *The Third Force in European Psychology.* Greenville, Delaware: Psychosynthesis Research Foundation, 1960.
16. ———, "Assumptions in Psychology," *Journal of Individual Psychology,* XIV, 1 (1958), pp. 22-28.

17. ———. "Phenomenal Analysis: Exemplified by a Study of the Experience of 'Really Feeling Understood'," *Journal of Individual Psychology,* XV, 1 (1959), pp. 66-72.

18. ———. "The Impact of Existential Phenomenology on the Psychological Literature of Western Europe," *Review of Existential Psychology and Psychiatry,* I, 1 (1961), pp. 63-92.

19. ———. "Clinical Implications of Heidegger's Concepts of Will, Decision and Responsibility," *Review of Existential Psychology and Psychiatry,* 1, 2 (1961), pp. 205-216.

20. ———. "Psychology and Psychopathology of the Religious Mode of Existence." To be published in 1963 by Temple University Press, Philadelphia, Pa., in the book *Psychopathology: a Collection of Essays on Psychopathology by Various Experts of American Universities.*

21. ———. "Humanistic Psychology and Culture," *Journal of Humanistic Psychology,* I, 1 (1961), pp. 94-110.

22. ———. "The Fantasy of Romantic Love." In *Modern Myths and Popular Fancies.* A series of lectures given at the community college, sponsored by the Duquesne University Alumni Association, Oct. 6 to Oct. 27, 1960. Pittsburgh: Duquesne University Press, 1961.

23. ———. "Will and Religion," *Academy Newsletter of Religion and Mental Health,* Summer, 1962.

$$47$$

EXISTENTIAL ANALYTIC PSYCHOTHERAPY

Wilson Van Dusen

Mendocino State Hospital, Talmadge, California

Existential analysis is an example of a theoretical advancement which has far outstripped the development of actual techniques adapted to the new theory. There is no accepted technique of psychotherapy in existential analysis.[1] The technique varies with the analyst. What remains the same is the general program as to how the patient should be regarded and understood. All such analysts will begin with an attempt to understand the phenomenological world of the other person. Beyond that there are wide differences in practice. In part these differences are fruitful since they represent a continued exploration unhampered by a dogma of technique.

Two points will be made here. The first is that there is such an organic unity between the phenomenological approach and existential theory that the theory can and will be derived here from the basic phenomenological frame of reference. The second point is that there is a psychotherapeutic approach which most closely fits the theory. In fact a close adherence to the theory demands a particular approach. The approach has been called gestalt therapy, and considerable credit for it is due to Dr. Frederick S. Perls.[2, 3] So, in addition to redriving existential analytic theory from its phenomenological foundations, we will show a psychotherapeutic approach which fits this theory.

Reprinted by permission of the Author and *The American Journal of Psychoanalysis,* Vol. XX, No. 1, 1960, 35-40.

The door into existential analysis is through phenomenology and in this case the structure of the door implies much of the house. In the phenomenological approach to another person, one attempts to understand his mode of being-in-the-world. There are a number of immediate and important implications. One is not coming to his world with objective yardsticks or categories. One cannot translate his world into oral, and genital, id, ego or superego terms unless the patient spontaneously sees these as real characteristics of his world. There is no objective, outside-of-him system into which one can fit his world. One must be ready to discover worlds radically different from one's own. The patient's world may be a hole-like one out of which one crawls laboriously to look momentarily at daylight. His may be the seething restless world of the hipster,[4] where one swings from orgasm to orgasm in an attempt to break out of all boundaries. In every classificatory system our worlds differ relatively little, but in a phenomenological approach one encounters strange and radically different worlds. In therapy my own criterion as to whether I have understood the world of the other is whether or not he can recognize his world in my description.

The other day I examined a chronic schizophrenic patient of a colleague in an effort to get him more information about the patient. He told the patient I felt he was psychotic and the patient became angry and launched into a disturbed denial. Actually, I agree with the patient. He is not psychotic (the external-objective classification of him). Rather, he lived on the surface in his eyes and his tongue because his brain and heart were paralyzed. Of course, the patient is technically psychotic, but in a phenomenological approach I don't wish to be technical. I told the patient that I really saw him as living in his eyes with a paralyzed brain, and he accepted this. Someone understood him. He felt my colleague so misunderstood him as to be psychotic himself.

This is the effect of the phenomenological approach. Insofar as one can describe the world of the other person as he finds it, the other person feels understood. Then one can work with him in full communication and interchange. From the paralyzed brain and heart we go to other aspects of his world. He feels safe. He is understood. Any sort of judgment or technical approach to his world leaves him with the justified feeling that the therapist is bending him to the therapist's own ends. One discovers the being-in-the-world of the other, with even the terms and all the subtle qualities of the world of the other. This does not imply I am in his world. At the end of the hour he goes back to his hospital ward or his home and I return to my other professional duties. He knows I do. He knows mine is a different world. But as he leaves the door he feels someone is beginning to understand how he feels. I don't need to pretend to be in his world. When he says he is being poisoned I can quite seriously accept that he feels poisoned and even explore the qualities and circumstances of this poisoning without pretending I feel that material poison is being slipped into his food. Usually he doesn't mean poison *qua* poison. Even if he does, our exploring his poisoned world should open up other and more psychic aspects of poisoning.

So far we have said that the door into existential analysis is through an attempt to understand (not judge or value) the being-in-the-world of the other. This understanding is in his terms, with his qualities. It is the opposite of any sort of objective or technical approach to him, such as a diagnosis implies, for instance. He feels understood and not apprehended and bent by the other person. In this one need not pretend to have a world exactly like his. One remains an individual with a different world. He doesn't feel he is with an expert with mysterious powers. He is with another person who is attempting laboriously and slowly to understand him. Nor is he with the lover who cries when he cries. The transference is less than in classical analysis. As one meets and learns to describe the patient as he is here, one is also uncovering transference reactions. They too are described as part of his present being-in-the-world. They are discovered as they form and described so that they won't have a hidden effect on the relationship. If you wish, one could say there is a continuous analysis of transference. This phenomenological entering into the being-in-the-world of the other is the foundation of existential analysis. It is so fundamental that the therapist who learns how to do this alone is very likely to discover spontaneously for himself all the other aspects of existential analysis.

There are a number of collateral discoveries once one has entered the phenomenological door. Most of science is an attempt to find static law. One finds the world of the other is fluid and changing. The schizophrenic living in his eyes will be found to have a far richer and complex world than appears at first sight. Also it changes as we come to understand it. In one schizophrenic we are exploring a gesture as simple as rubbing his nose. It was at first a filling up of the hole of nothingness.[5] As we looked further it took on many and varied meanings. Not only is the therapist learning, but the patient is recalling in a gesture aspects of himself he had lost. We explore his style of movement, the changing emotional qualities in his voice and his experiences here. Whereas he may have appeared simple to himself, he grows more complex, varied, and subtle in this exploration. A simple symptom takes on layers of emotional and interpersonal meaning. As we explore, his awareness expands. He is not the same person from moment to moment. Nothing has been done to him. He hasn't been interpreted. He has simply participated in a discovery of himself here.

Another implication is that one will not want to discard any part of his being-in-the-world. One will not look exclusively at the outer world as he sees it, or at the internal. Both are his world. He may live more in one or another sphere (the introvert-extrovert dichotomy). If the solidity and resistance of material things engages him then we will look at this. If a fantasy plagues him, then it is an important part of his world.

Dreams can be used as an important part of this discovery. Boss[6] makes the important point that dreams are not, strictly speaking, symbolic. They speak in a purely existential language. They tell what is currently critical in one's life by describing it in terms of dramatic events. Dr. Perls goes after the meaning of dreams by having the patient play-act all aspects of the dream until the patient is caught up in the events and thereby finds their meaning.

Also, one will not grasp the patient soley by his words (a tendency in many overly logical therapists). Features of his world are his bodily sensations, his use of his musculature, his gestures, his choice and use of clothes, and even the inflections of voice underlying the words. Such a small matter as where he puts his gaze is quite important. Does he communicate eye-to-eye with the therapist or is he talking to a potted plant in the corner? No part of his world is so small as to be meaningless. This approach to patients implies a much richer and more subtle understanding than the simple grabbing another by his words. I would hope to be able to fully understand another person without having heard a single word of his. It would please me immensely to be able to imitate his movements and the sound of his uniqueness.

In the exploration of the world of another person one tends to center on the critical. In the past, experimental psychologists centered on unimportant aspects of the worlds of others. Look, for instance, on the vast number of studies of the two-point sensory threshold and similar works. They did this to grasp what could be translated into the modes of exact science. Because the psychotherapist is not attempting to catch what is measurable by science, he can afford to look at the critical. There is a most simple reason why the existential analyst centers on the critical. The patient insists on it. The patient's life and destiny are at stake. He cannot help but present the critical, even though what he presents may look very peripheral to the therapist. The term existential has come to be nearly equivalent to the term critical. How does one find the critical? By exploring all the aspects of the being-in-the-world of the other.

The space-time aspects of the world of the other person are found to be important. In classical Freudian psychoanalysis, the analyst shifts the patient back into an exploration of the patient's history. In exploring the being-in-the-world of the other, one explores the world here, now. Only insofar as past or future are tangled in the world here-now do these become of consequence. After all, his world is here-now. It's not back in toilet training in childhood or forward in after-life. He sits here before me and demonstrates his world. The centering in the here-now is a modern tendency coming into most therapies. Practically speaking, it causes an intensification and speeding up of therapy. There isn't the long escape into what mamma, papa, or sister did. "We are here. What are you doing now?" One need not wander for years examining aspects of the person projected in remote historical events. The person is here. We can study what he does here. In the hereness he shows how he chooses space, time, and the qualities of his world. One patient occasionally rubbed his hand across the bridge of his nose. It was perhaps two weeks before we began to understand this. The meaning was something like this. "I become anxious under your close regard (or anyone else's). In the anxiety, time and space suddenly develop a frightening hole. In the hole is nothing. I can't even remember. Nothingness. By touching my nose I am physically active and fill up the hole. Also I touch physical reality (my body) and come back to reality that way. Incidentally, my hand covers my eyes for a moment and your (analyst's) gaze is shut off for a moment." Here we begin to discover his problem in a palpable way. It is with us here. It is not in the historical past. It is so palpable we can study it together now.

With the basic phenomenological approach I believe many others will discover that to some extent all study of past or future is a subtle abrogation of present responsibility. One cannot exclusively steer the patient into the present, either. If the past or future intrudes into the session it says something about how the patient is present. In the existential-analytic approach one doesn't steer the patient into past, present, or future. One discovers where the patient is now in his present being-in-the-world. It is a simple discovery in this approach that all psychopathology involves some degree of escape from the here and now into the spatially or temporally there, into otherness. The well-integrated person looks at the therapist, eye-to-eye, with security and composure, and chooses his being-in-the-world now. He is content to be here.

In his approach one will undo projections as fast as they form. The patient may ask, with some feeling, "Do you think therapy should go on indefinitely?" The patient is bothered and is projecting responsibility onto the analyst. The analyst can help bring the projection back to the patient by simply asking: "Would you make that into a statement?" The patient says, "You feel therapy should be interminable." There is a little more emotion in the voice and actions. Can the patient say it again clearer and more forcefully? "You feel therapy should go on forever!" After a moment the analyst can ask how the patient feels now. What was projected into the other is then discovered as arising from one's own emotions. Usually the patient reacts after such an exchange as though he had been restored to power. The projection was not interpreted as a defect in the patient. The affect underlying it was recovered and the patient was restored to power.

There is no unconscious in this approach.[7] Nothing is totally outside the realm of his present being-in-the-world when that world is examined in considerable respect. One finds himself dealing with varying degrees of awareness from what is easily verbalized to not quite understood gestures to vague feelings that are not at first verbalized. Nothing is totally outside of his present being here (hence the term "dasein-being here-analysis"). There are a great many ways of exploring the present. While the patient talks, something of an emotion may show in the eyes, or voice, or a gesture appears. When the emotion is strong enough to grip the person, then a simple noting of its presence by the analyst may help bring it to the fore. With a little help its expression becomes clearer. Something has been discovered in the testing ground of the present relationship. He finds and determines himself, rather than finds himself interpreted by another person. Well-handled, one can tell from moment to moment whether gains are being made because the pathology and the choices around it are here.

In this I am dealing with findings from the phenomenological approach which others may not have experienced yet. I am so secure in these findings, though, that I would be inclined to say that anyone who has learned to understand the being-in-the-world of others and is involved in their care in psychotherapy will of himself enter into existential analysis. At this point I would like to clarify what differentiates between the phenomenological entrance and the inside of the house of existential analysis. In a few words, the entrance is phenomenological, the inside of the house is ontological, the essential nature of man.[8] This was touched upon when we examined the critical and found it in the here and now. In the other (there, in time and space) it is hidden. One can enter on the ontological, the critical, and the here and now by exploring the patient's choosing.

All the productions of the patient (words, actions, dreams, etc.) are, so to speak, puppets. By examining his choosing here and now with me, I deal directly with the puppeteer. This is the existential engagement. He is caught. All avenues of escape are sealed. As he grows in awarenss of the size and qualities of his world, his area of choice expands. In the beginning of therapy it appears he had no choice. He was caught as an actor in a repetitive, unpleasant drama. As awareness of his world expands he comes to deal with the playwriter — his forgotten choices. The drama changes. It appears more and more that he writes the drama. Therapy ends without any massive transference, because the therapist was no all-wise magician. He only permitted the patient to discover and choose himself.

In case it is not clear that this is relatively different from most other forms of psychotherapy, the difference will be underlined. Here there is no need to explore, or even to know, a patient's history. One could fully explore what is wrong here and what is chosen here without a history. In this approach there is no unconscious. His world is here. There are varying degrees of awareness in that world. There is no resistance or defense. This may be difficult to see, but both resistance and defense imply one is outside the world of the other and makes an outsider's judgment of their world. There is no denial. To say the patient is denying is to say that the analyst has a conception of the world of the patient that does not match with the patient's world. The patient doesn't deny. He states what he knows of himself at the moment. In this form of therapy both transferences should never become intense and burdensome. If you want, it is because this therapy is almost a constant analysis of transference, though even the term "analysis" is out of place here. One doesn't come to analyze (take apart) the world of the other. One comes to understand it. These few examples of differences from ordinary psychotherapy should suggest that this form of existential analytic therapy is relatively new. It has historical roots in the work of Adler, Rank, gestalt therapy, and the work of Freud, but in itself it is a major shift in what is seen in psychotherapy.

SUMMARY

Existential analysis is not yet identified with a particular therapeutic approach. By beginning with a phenomenological foundation one can rederive the structure of existential analysis, and by so doing one discovers a technique that is particularly close to the theory of existential analysis. From phenomenology one learns to enter the present being-in-the-world of the patient without overlooking any of the qualities of that world. By centering in the present world one discovers the critical and the role of the patient's choosing. By this the patient feels understood and not interpreted, and discovers that he changes as the horizon of his present experiences expands. Starting from a phenomenological foundation one rediscovers existential analysis and discovers that this analysis is a significant departure from classical therapies in several respects.

REFERENCES

1. May, R. *et al.*: Existence, A New Dimension in Psychiatry and Psychology, New York, Basic Books, 1958, 77.
2. Perls, F. S.: Ego, Hunger and Aggression, London, Allen & Unwin, 1957.
3. Perls, L.: Two Instances of Gestalt Therapy, Case Reports in Clinical Psychology, 3: 139-146, 1956.
4. Mailer, N.: "The White Negro," In, The Beat Generation and the Angry Young Men, G. Feldman and M. Gartenberg (Eds.), New York, Citadel Press, 1958, 342-363.
5. Van Dusen, W.: Wu Wei, No-Mind and the Fertile Void in Psychotherapy. Psychologia, 1: 253-256, 1958.
6. Boss, M.: The Analysis of Dreams, London, Rider, 1957.

7. Van Dusen, W.: The Theory and Practice of Existential Analysis, American Journal of Psychotherapy, 11: 310-322, 1957.
8. Van Dusen, W.: The Ontology of Adlerian Psychodynamics, Journal of Individual Psychology, 15: 143-156, 1959.

$$\boxed{48}$$

AN EXISTENTIAL APPROACH TO COUNSELING

Edward A. Dreyfus
University of California, Los Angeles

There are many approaches to counseling and psychotherapy[1] which legitimately may be termed existential, e.g., Boss (1963), Binswanger (1963), May (1958), to name a few. Each of these approaches, including the present one, has as its prime focus the nature of man's existence and how he experiences the world. The existential approach is not a system of techniques, but rather an underlying attitude which transcends all techniques.

It has been my experience that many students of counseling enter the counseling situation with the erroneous notion that if they know a series of techniques which have been employed by experienced counselors then they too are counselors. It is as though these novitiate counselors reason: "Dr. Jones is a counselor. He uses a particular technique. I use that technique. Therefore, I am a counselor." It is obvious that this is not a valid argument. These students fail to realize that Dr. Jones has spent many hours with clients developing his particular technique. More importantly, these techniques are firmly rooted in a theory of man and a philosophy of counseling. It is my belief that a counselor, armed with a myriad of techniques but with no theory of man or philosophy of counseling, would be like a surgeon entering the operating room with all of the standard techniques but with no understanding of anatomy or physiology.

Technique emerges from theory. Techniques alone are of little value without a more basic understanding of the subject with which one is working. Thus the counselor's approach during the therapy hour must be governed by his underlying philosophy of counseling. The philosophy of counseling, in turn, emerges from and in many ways is symbiotic with the theory of man. The way in which a person perceives man's existence will govern his philosophy of counseling. One cannot adopt a technique which is alien to his underlying philosophy and expect to be an effective counselor.

The existential counselor is concerned with an approach to counseling. He allows whatever technique that emerges during the counseling session to occur. These techniques will then be an expression of the philosophy. It may happen that the techniques which emerge will be phenotypically similar or identical to techniques which emerge from different philosophies. Such is the case with some of the psychoanalytic techniques. Boss (1963), for example,

---

An original article for this book.
[1]These terms are considered to be synonomous and will be used interchangeably as will counselor and therapist, patient and client.

contends that the psychoanalytic *techniques* (e.g., free association and dream interpretation) are acceptable, but psychoanalytic *theory* is not. Benda (1960) extends this notion by saying that there are no essential differences in the techniques of the existential therapist and the psychoanalytic therapist, but the underlying attitude and framework in which interpretation of the material thereby obtained is different. In counseling, technique in and of itself does little regarding change within the client. It is only what one does with and how one views the material evoked via the technique that allows change to occur. Thus I would maintain that when the existential counselor employs the technique of dream interpretation or free association (see Boss, 1958) it is quite different than when the psychoanalyst uses it.

To be concerned with technique and its development is the antithesis to what the existential approach stands for. The existential point of view maintains that man is not a machine to be operated upon in order to gain a particular effect. Technique implies manipulation; one manipulates objects, not people.

Existential counseling, then, is not a system of techniques but an underlying attitude toward counseling. It is concerned with the uniqueness of man. More specifically, it is concerned with the uniqueness of that particular man seated before the counselor during the therapeutic hour. It is concerned with the client as he presents himself in his particular world — in the world of the here and now.

The method employed by the existentially oriented counselor is called the phenomenological method. That is to say, the counselor is concerned with the immediate, existing world of the client at the moment. He is concerned with the raw data offered by the client. Hence the approach is ahistorical in the sense that the counselor does not attempt to actively delve into the client's past. The past is important only insofar as the client introduces it into the present. One of the main tenets of existentialism is that man is free; he is free to choose his way of being. Likewise he is free to explore with the counselor those areas of his existence that he, the client, feels important. This is quite in contrast to those schools of thought in which the client discusses those areas which the therapist judges to be important. The point of departure during the counseling hour is the conflict which brought the client to the counselor, not that which led up to the conflict.

The existentially oriented counselors, of course, are not the only group of therapists who use the phenomenological method. Carl Rogers (1951), among others, has been using this method in his nondirective counseling for years. In many respects, especially within recent years, his approach is very much akin to the existential position.[2] However, in his early works Rogers placed a great deal of emphasis on technique, particularly the technique of reflection. It seems that while Rogers has always been a proponent of the phenomenological method, it is only within recent years that he has adopted the existential position.

The existential position, as already mentioned, argues that counseling is a real life process and as such allows whatever "technique" that emerges during the counseling process to occur. The counselor does not passively

---

[2]A comparison of the two approaches has been made more explicit elsewhere (Dreyfus, 1962).

reflect the feeling tone and words of the client, but rather is actively involved in the world-experiences of the client. Benda (1960) characterizes the process as being similar to the obstetrician who gently guides the newborn baby from the womb, though it is the patient who is doing most of the work. As such there is active participation of the therapist in the emerging of the client into the world.

As I have indicated earlier, the existential counselor will even utilize the techniques of the psychoanalytically oriented therapist. Rogers, on the other hand, excludes such techniques. By doing so it would seem that he is not allowing the client to express himself and his experiences in all of the possible ways open to him. Hence the client is not entirely free during the therapeutic hour. We must admit that lying down on a couch, dreaming, and free associating are human modes of experiencing; not permitting them to occur binds freedom.

Now that I have stated an existential position regarding psychotherapeutic techniques, I would like to present a theory of man, draw from it a philosophy of counseling, and subsequently attempt to delineate some ground rules governing the counselor's role in the counseling process. It should be understood that this is only one of the many approaches which could be classified as existential in orientation.

A THEORY OF MAN

Man is born into an unknown world. From the moment of his birth he is continuously experiencing his world. He does not know what lies ahead, nor does he know what his potential for being in this world is. Despite this uncertainty, in the face of it, or even because of it, man moves forward. Hence, by virtue of the uncertainty of his existence, man is born anxious. It is this existential anxiety — the anxiety of being — that makes man a dynamic, emergent being. To explore the unknown is part of man's ontological make-up.

Man is a feeling, thinking, acting being. He feels a world, thinks about a world, and acts in a world. His actions are based on how he feels and thinks and are therefore outer representations of his inner world. Furthermore, man is basically authentic. That is to say, he is honest with himself and with the world. His actions are held to be genuine manifestations of how he experiences the world. It is through these four attributes — feeling, thinking, acting, and authenticity — that man explores his world and emerges a unique being. It is through these modes that man actualizes his potential.

Affect

When the infant is born he experiences the world solely through his senses and his body in general. He reacts to the world with his entire body. All he is aware of is that which he feels. He feels, he responds. He is happy, sad, hungry, content. Whatever the feeling, his response to the world is immediate. There is no past nor future only the moment exists. The infant does not think about being hungry, he simply experiences hunger and reacts. One can say that the infant's world is composed solely of feeling — he is all effect. He expresses his feelings through action; it is through action that he makes his

presence in the world known. As the child grows older, another process comes
to bear on his actions. The process of cognition intervenes between feeling
and action. He becomes capable of thinking about his feelings.

Cognition

Thinking allows one the opportunity to reflect upon his world and upon
his feelings. One becomes alert to his environment and capable of choosing
between alternative actions. One can choose to express affect or to inhibit it.
One can choose to act or not to act. With cognition, choice or intentionality
emerges as part of man's existence. Intentionality is ontologically given. Before cognition affect determined action. With intentionality man's fate and
actions are determined by man. He can now reflect on his past and determine
his future rather than live only in the immediate.

Man is essentially a conscious being, forever making choices regarding his
own existence. There is no single choice which is predetermined, over which
man has no control. When he perceives a limited array of choices of the
many possibilities, it is because he chooses to limit the choices.

Action

In order for men to emerge into the world extending himself beyond his
physical confines, he must act. His actions are determined by how he thinks
and feels about his world. He can choose to act on his feelings without thinking, or he can choose to disregard his feelings and act solely on the basis
of his thoughts. For the most part, however, man acts with respect to both
modes. Furthermore, it seems that the more one thinks the less one feels, and
hence the less one acts. It is the balance of these modes which will, in part,
determine the unique being-in-the-world of the person.

With the development of cognition, and hence with control of action and
freedom of choice, man emerges as a responsible being. While man has freedom of choice and action, he is also responsible for his actions. At birth, without cognition, the child is not responsible. The potential for being responsible,
however, is ontologically given. When man chooses a course of action he has
made a commitment — he is responsible. He stands alone as he determines
his own existence.

Authenticity

Man responds to the world in a way which reflects his feelings and
thoughts. There is little doubt that the child, as an infant, is genuinely hungry
or uncomfortable when he cries. When man behaves in a way which runs
counter to his feelings or thoughts he is being dishonest or inauthentic. While
man is a social being, he need not be governed by the crowd. He can stand
alone. He can look the other in the eye without trepidation. He can look
himself in the eye when he is authentic. He can accept responsibility without
shifting blame. Such authenticity is ontologically given.

It is only through the "socialization" process or "dehumanization" process
that man becomes inauthentic. It is through such a process that the existential
honesty is lost. To be sure, not being honest is a choice and one must accept
the responsibility. But since it is alien to man's essential way of being, he

experiences guilt. Likewise, one is inauthentic when he chooses to not-act, or when he fails to move in the face of anxiety, and thus he experiences guilt. This is existential guilt, or the guilt of not-being.

In summarizing this point of view, man is seen as born anxious in an unknown world. He moves into the world in the face of this existential anxiety. Each time he moves into the unknown he experiences anxiety. As he moves he is constantly emerging into a unique being. At first he reacts to the world in terms of his feelings. With the development of cognition he becomes conscious of his feelings and is capable of choosing a course of action. He is free to choose among many action- possibilities as his consciousness expands. While he has freedom of choice, he is also responsible for these choices. He is responsible for his behavior and hence his own existence. The combined interplay of affect and cognition will, in part, determine his uniqueness. When he commits himself to a choice, man stands alone, singularly responsible for the choice. He moves into the unknown continuously making choices. Failure to move, acting contrary to his feelings or thoughts, precluding choice, all leave man experiencing guilt for being inauthentic. When man realizes that he is being inauthentic, when he has so limited his choices, when he feels uncomfortable enough to the extent that he is unable to realize his potential, he seeks help.

A PHILOSOPHY OF COUNSELING

In developing a philosophy of counseling once one has some theory of man, two important questions must be answered. First, why does a person seek counseling? Second, what is counseling?

I began to answer the first question in the first part of this paper. A person seeks help because he feels uncomfortable; he feels unable to solve his problems alone. It is assumed that when a person enters the counselor's office his world-view — his perception of himself and himself-in-the-world — is somewhat clouded. He has difficulty seeing the action-possibilities open to him. He experiences disabling anxiety as opposed to existential anxiety. He feels inauthentic, not being able to realize his potentialities.

Most problems which bring a person to seek help concern one or a combination of the modes we have discussed, namely affect, cognition, action, and authenticity. He has difficulty experiencing, expressing, recognizing, or coping with affect. He may be depressed, angry, fearful, etc., but cannot deal with the feeling effectively. He may have difficulty in the cognitive sphere, such as not being able to concentrate, make decisions, or feeling so much that he cannot think. He may have difficulty acting upon his choices, or he may see only limited possibilities or none at all, or he may think so much that he cannot feel. A major source of difficulty centers about authenticity. The person has difficulty with intrapersonal and/or interpersonal relations. He cannot face himself or others; he feels inauthentic and guilt — he feels not himself.

At this point one may ask the question: How does a person come to be in need of counseling? The answer to this question will vary with the individual and can be understood only in terms of the person's unique being-in-the-world. It may be that he was taught to view the world as a place where the expression of affect is forbidden. In lieu of this, it may have been that his integrity was violated to the point where he could not exercise his freedom of choice or responsibility was usurped. Perhaps external control was placed upon him so that action was limited. Whatever the circumstances, however, the main concern is with the client's present world-view, clouded or distorted though it may be. How he came to be what he is will be elucidated in the light of the understanding which occurs during the counseling process.

Now let us turn to the second question; what is counseling? First and foremost, counseling is a process. It is not a series of techniques. Being a process, it flows, it develops, and like man, it is dynamic. Counseling entails a relationship between two or more people — a collaborative effort — the purpose of which is to illuminate a world which is, for some reason, clouded. Through this collaborative effort it is presumed that an elucidation of the client's world will occur and the understanding gleaned through such an elucidation will permit the client to perceive increased action-possibilities.

It should be clear that from this point of view, one does not *do* counseling; one lives it during the interpersonal encounter. One does not make change; change happens when the client feels that he is understood. In essence, counseling occurs when at least two people are engaged in a mutual relationship, each making an effort to understand the world of at least one of these persons who is finding it difficult to realize his potential. It is assumed that through such understanding an expanding of consciousness will occur, allowing for an increase in the possibilities for effective action.

To many counselors this approach may appear somewhat mystical. Many of these counselors have long believed that without a set of techniques they would not be counselors. Perhaps such an aura of mysticism stems from a reluctance on these counselors' part to engage in a truly interpersonal encounter. Thus their techniques serve to maintain some degree of distance from their clients.

In the proposed philosophy of counseling there is no correct method or technique. There is no expert in the sense of the counselor's knowing what to do in order to alleviate the client's problem. Both the counselor and the client are engaged in a human task, and to be human[3] does not require a technique. More will be said about the counselor's rôle in this approach in the next section of this paper.

In the form of counseling advocated here, one must believe that the goal of each person is to realize, to the best of his ability, his human potential. One must believe that solutions to problems in living lie within the individual, but for some reason or reasons the solutions cannot be recognized or acted upon. No counselor can know his client better than he knows himself. Counseling can be only as effective as the client wants it to be.

It may sound as though counseling must always involve very complex problems and must always be quite intense. This is not so. The approach, however, remains the same regardless of the complexity of the problem. For example, if a client comes into the counselor's office with a question regarding the courses that the client should take during the following semester, it would

---

[3]A discussion of what it means to be human can be found in a paper by Dreyfus and Mackler (1964).

be a violation of the client's integrity for the counselor simply to give him an answer (if such an answer could be offered). One must assume that the client has given the problem considerable thought even before thinking about asking for help. Often the client knows beforehand what he wants to do and is seeking confirmation. If the client is to actualize his potential, he has to assume responsibility for his actions. Thus if the counselor supplies an answer he is assuming responsibility for the client. To be sure, there are times when a simple answer will suffice. Too many counselors all too often feel, however, that when a client enters the office the counselor must *do* something. In many cases he should listen. Hearing is not necessarily listening. While a client may present what appears to be a simple problem, as in the example of the student trying to plan a program, it may well turn out to be an acceptable way of seeking help. The counselor must listen to what the client is trying to say and help him elucidate his world. Before the counselor can offer assistance he must first understand the client's immediate, existing world as the client experiences it at the moment.

This point of view assumes that each person is unique. The counselor operating from the existential viewpoint recognizes that the only similarity between one client and another is that they both enter the counseling situation with a somewhat clouded world-view. From there on the similarity ceases. The client is viewed as a figure standing out from the ground of other people, animals, and things. The goal of counseling is the illumination of this world and the elucidation of this client's existential uniqueness.

AN APPROACH TO COUNSELING

I have stated earlier that the existential approach is a way of looking at and understanding the world of the client as he sits before the counselor. I have also said the counseling involves a relationship between two or more people. Thus far I have dealt with only the client's world. Now I would like to focus on the counselor.[4] It is hoped that such a discussion will serve as a guide for counselors who may make the point of view put forth in the preceding pages compatible with their own theory of man and philosophy of counseling. The discussion will center about two concepts: encounter and confrontation. One might consider these concepts as the basic "tools" of the existential counselor.

Encounter

The encounter refers to the genuinely personal interaction between counselor and client; it is a truly human experience. In order for the counselor to feel comfortable with the feelings of his client, he must feel comfortable with his own feelings. He must recognize that there is no essential difference between himself and the client. He must be willing to engage in a relationship where his feelings may be exposed. The counselor is quite different than the physical scientist insofar as his role is concerned. The physical scientist works *on* his subject matter; the counselor works *with* his client. The counselor's

---

[4]A further discussion of the counselor's role within the existential approach can be found elsewhere (Dreyfus, 1964).

function is not to change the client but to allow change to occur. He cannot view the client as an object to be explored, manipulated, or exploited. The counselor's role as a conselor must be transcended by his role as a human being. He must respond to the client with the essence of his own humanness. While the counselor may be hoping that the existential authenticity of the client will emerge during the encounter, he too must be authentic.

During the encounter the counselor and the client are free to express their feelings. In such an atmosphere of freedom each is open to the other. Openness permits understanding and a growing awareness of self. The counselor must allow the client's world to unfold. Probing into the past is unnecessary and offers little to the client when his problems are in the here and now. Only as the past emerges into the moment will its exploration be of value. The client will allow his world to unfold to the extent that he feels understood. The counselor must feel and demonstrate a genuine respect for the client as a human being. Such respect requires that the counselor not force the client to reveal part of his world which he is not ready to reveal. To force such a revelation would be to violate the client's integrity. The client is not to be exposed because the counselor wants a specific piece of information. Counseling is for the client.

The counselor gleans a picture of the client's world as it is illuminated in the mutual sharing between counselor and client during the encounter. The counselor is being permitted by the client to share in the client's world. He is therefore obligated to share that which he sees with the client. Moreno (1960) has said of the encounter: "A meeting of two: eye to eye, face to face. And when you are near I will tear your eyes out and place them instead of mine, and you will tear my eyes out and place them instead of yours, then I will look at you with your eyes and you will look at me with mine" (p. 144). Such openness and mutuality as exists between counselor and client is the encounter.

While each relationship need not be a very intense one, it can be an existential one. It is existential in that two beings are meeting for the purpose, expressed or implied, of gaining a greater awareness of the existence of the other. The relationship is a human one where the other is free to explore and the two explore together. In the light of the existential encounter the client is free to explore his attitudes, his feelings, his thoughts, his actions, and his authenticity. The counselor is always with him during the exploration. The humanness of the encounter allows the client to become aware of his own humanness and the uniqueness of his own existence.

Confrontation

"Every confrontation is an encounter, but not every encounter is a confrontation. The encounter may not involve a dispute or controversy whereas the confrontation always contains some conflict" (Moustakas, 1962, p. 281). As used in this context, conflict refers to the client's being faced with a choice regarding his own existence. The counselor confronts the client with an aspect of the client's world and the client must choose how he will respond to it, what he will do about it, or whether he accepts or rejects the implications of the confrontation.

In counseling, as opposed to the courtroom situation where confrontation implies an "I caught you" attitude, confrontation implies a direct meeting of the counselor and the client on the issue of the client's existence. The counselor's concern for the integrity of the client which underlies the encounter is always present during the confrontation. The client is faced with a decision and is respected regardless of the choice he makes; integrity is not at stake, the issue is. The mutual respect is maintained.

The therapist actively engages in the confrontation and remains with the client throughout; he does not attempt to expose the client. During the confrontation the counselor and client may argue violently, but the argument is with regard to the issue and not with regard to the personal worth of the other as a person. The resolution of the conflict often brings the two people even closer. The client struggled and the counselor stayed with him during the struggle. In many respects the confrontation deepens the encounter; the counselor must be himself as a human being, fully committed to the client.

I am reminded of a movie in which the main character, a Negro war hero, had suffered hysterical paralysis of his legs as a result of a traumatic incident during battle. While in the hospital he met a white psychiatrist with whom he related in a meaningful encounter. The relationship continued for some time, but the soldier was still unable to walk. Then at one point during the therapy the psychiatrist stated in a very harsh tone "You are nothing but a lazy nigger!" The soldier's eyes met the therapist's in a blaze of fury. The soldier cursed his psychiatrist-friend, and as he crossed the room to attack the therapist for his cruel words he realized that he had walked — he cried.

The confrontation is quite well illustrated in this example. Two men had met in a meaningful encounter. They had displayed mutual respect and admiration. Meeting in the confrontation each pitted his own existence against the other. It was obvious the therapist had maintained his respect for the soldier as he remained with the patient during his struggle with the implied conflict. The anger of the therapist was not directed toward the patient as a person, but rather toward the issue of walking and the patient's giving up. The anger showed the therapist's human concern — that he really *cared* for the patient. The therapist stood fully committed to the soldier, exposing his humanness. At first the soldier thought he was being betrayed by his therapist and had to choose whether he was going to react and how. It wasn't until after the confrontation and after he had made a choice that he understood the confrontation.

Lest the foregoing example be construed as implying that existential counseling is applicable only to more severe forms of emotional disturbance, I should like to make some final comments regarding this approach and the kinds of problems faced when working within a school guidance setting.

Existentialism is concerned with the human condition. As such it is concerned with all forms of human experiencing. It is concerned with the bizarre as well as the normal. Its focus is on the unique experience of the client and how he perceives his world. Whether the problem presented by the client appears to the counselor as minor or major is of little import so long as the client feels it is important. The concern of the counselor is for the immediate existing person seated before him.

A student enters the guidance bureau and states that he is uncertain as to what course of study he should pursue. For him this problem is just as important as the problem of being dropped out of school is for another student, or the problem of being chased by the FBI is for the paranoid schizophrenic. Our imaginary student states that he would like to take some tests in order to learn for what field he is best suited. The counselor has a choice to make: namely, should he assign interest tests to the student or should he explore the uncertainty with the client, and then decide whether to assign tests. The existentially oriented counselor chooses the latter course. His position is that psychometric testing should be used to expand the psychological world of the client by opening more possibilities for action which may remain undisclosed. Psychometric testing is for the client *not* for the counselor. The client stated that he was uncertain as to a course of study which implies that he has some ideas or even that he knows what course he wants but desires confirmation of his choice. Perhaps it is making decisions in general which is difficult or making a commitment which is a problem. The counselor must be open to the client's world and allow it to unfold before he issues tests. To be sure it is often easier to assign tests, interpret the results, and give advice; however, the easy way may not be the best way. The counselor should be willing to engage in a human encounter with his client and be with the client as he, the client, elucidates his world. It is only against the background of the client's unique existence that psychometric tests can be of real value to him.

One does not have to spend many hours with each client before he makes the decision regarding the tests or pondering an answer to a student's question. Rather he should spend just enough time to be relatively certain that both he and the client understand the question. An encounter need not be more than a few moments. With some persons the encounter comes in a flash at the moment of meeting; with other persons it may take considerably longer. The need for confrontation may never arise.

The counselor should be prepared not only to hear what the client says but to listen to him saying it. He should recognize the world of the client for what it is at the moment without trying to classify, categorize, or in any other way violate the uniqueness of the client. He must be ready to engage the client, no matter how briefly, and stay with the client in whatever path he chooses to take along the road to self-actualization.

SUMMARY

Counseling is more than a series of techniques. It requires that a person develop a theory of man — a way of looking at and understanding the nature of man. From this theory one can develop a philosophy of counseling. This philosophy sets the stage for the interaction which will take place during the counseling session. It defines the roles of both the client and counselor. The techniques emerge from the philosophy. In this context some remarks regarding technique in existential counseling, psychoanalysis, and nondirective counseling were made.

I was concerned with developing an existential approach to counseling. The approach centers about the uniqueness of man and the nature of his being-in-the-world. It is concerned with the client as he presents himself in the here and now. In essence, the existential approach is an attitude toward man. It views man as responsible, free to choose his way of being, and as a constantly emerging being. Man is born into an unknown world and thus he is anxious. He moves in the face of this existential anxiety. Failure to move leaves him experiencing guilt — the guilt of not-being.

Within this framework four attributes of being human were discussed: affect, cognition, action, and authenticity. The additional concepts of freedom, choice, and responsibility were also discussed. Through these aspects of man's existence a theory of man and a philosophy of counseling were developed which led to an approach to counseling. Two important aspects of counseling emerged: the encounter and confrontation. The former refers to the inter-human relationship between counselor and client and the latter to the facing of an issue. Each confrontation is an encounter, but each encounter need not be a confrontation.

Finally some remarks regarding counseling in the schools were offered.

REFERENCES

Benda, C. E. The existential approach in psychiatry. *Journal of Existential Psychiatry*, 1960, 1, 24-40.

Binswanger, L. *Being-in-the-World* (Jacob Needleman, Translator), New York: Basic Books, 1963.

Boss, M. *Analysis of Dreams*, New York: Philosophical Library, 1958.

―――. *Psychoanalysis and Daseinanalysis*, New York: Basic Books, 1963.

Dreyfus, E. A. Counseling and existentialism. *Journal of Counseling Psychology*, 1962, 9, 128-132.

―――. The counselor and existentialism. *Personnel and Guidance Journal*, 1964, 43, 114-117.

Dreyfus, E. A. and Mackler, B. On being human. *Journal of Existentialism*, 1964, 5, 67-76.

May, R. et al. *Existence: A New Dimension in Psychology and Psychiatry*, New York: Basic Books, 1958.

Moreno, J. L. Concept of the encounter. *Journal of Existential Psychiatry*, 1960, 1, 144-154.

Moustakas, C. E. Confrontation and encounter. *Journal of Existential Psychiatry*, 1962, 2, 263-290.

Rogers, C. R. *Client-Centered Therapy*, Boston: Houghton-Mifflin, 1951.

$$\boxed{49}$$

DISABILITY, REHABILITATION, AND EXISTENTIALISM

Harry Easton

Harry Easton, formerly with the Jewish Employment and Vocational Service, St. Louis Missouri, is presently employed by the Bureau of Child Study, Chicago, Illinois

Stanley Krippner

Director of Research, Department of Psychiatry, Maimonides Hospital of Brooklyn, Brooklyn, New York

Existential thought can be applied to many of the problems faced by rehabilitation psychologists working with disabled patients. The existentially oriented psychologist would encourage his patient to reject societal interpretations of his disability. This psychologist would not hesitate to involve himself personally in the patient's struggle for self-direction, fostering an "I-Thou"

Reprinted by permisison of the Authors and the *Personnel and Guidance Journal*, November 1964, 230-234.

relationship with the patient. This psychologist also would encourage the patient to transcend his personal suffering and to find meaning in his anxiety and anguish. The rehabilitation program is seen as being most effective when the emphasis is placed upon the patient's "existence" rather than his "essence." Examples are given for each of these basic principles.

Many psychologists working with disabled patients in rehabilitation centers are aware of the patient who is unable to carry himself beyond hospitalization into gainful and meaningful activity. The patient performs satisfactorily within the rehabilitation workshop setting, is ostensibly oriented to reality, and possesses at least average potential for competitive employment. However, he is apathetic toward life in the outside world and is completely unable to take steps toward a vocational choice. He will often be described as "insecure," "unmotivated," "lacking in self-confidence," or "regressive." These superficial terms, however, do not delineate his basic problem, the inability to find meaning in one's existence.

This patient is suffering from one form of a condition which affects many individuals both in and out of hospitals and workshops, a condition which Rollo May (1958) calls "a repression of the ontological concern." Existentialist writers feel that without this concern, life is an insignificant void; without meaningful activities and goals, man ceases to exist in the fullest sense of the word.

Viktor Frankl (1963) points out that a loss of the will to meaning can result not only in a loss of the sense of being but an eventual death to the organism itself. It is precisely this aspect of the human condition that the authors feel must form the groundwork of a psychology of rehabilitation. It is the purpose of this paper, therefore, to explore the basic concepts of such existential writers as May and Frankl and to determine the relation of these concepts to the rehabilitative process.

AN ATTITUDE, NOT A CREED

Because existentialism is neither a creed nor a dogma, a great deal of diversity may be found among existential writers. Van Dusen (1962) notes that this diversity reflects a certain "livingness" that only a flexible body of ideas can entertain. Existentialism is more of an attitude than a creed, an attitude which one can apply to the widest possible range of human experiences. May (1958, pp. 11-13) describes the existential approach in its historical setting:

> Existentialism, in short, is the endeavor to understand man by cutting below the cleavage between subject and object which has bedeviled Western thought and science since shortly after the Renaissance . . . . Traditionally, in Western thought "existence" has been set over against "essence." Essence refers to the greenness of this stick of wood, let us say, and its density, weight, and other characteristics which give it substance. By and large, Western thought since the Renaissance has been concerned with essences . . . . The search for essences may indeed produce highly significant universal laws in science or brilliant abstract conceptualizations in logic or philosophy. But it can only do it by abstraction. The *existence* of the given individual thing has to be left out of the picture . . . . And the crucial question which confronts us in

psychology and other aspects of the science of man is precisely this chasm between what is *abstractly true* and what is *existentially real* for the given living person.

May (1958, pp. 37-38) concludes that the fundamental contribution of existential thought to psychology is its understanding of man as being. Our grasping of the being of another person occurs on quite a different level from our knowledge of specific things about him. We might know that our patient has a diabetic condition, a hearing loss, and an IQ of 89 on the Stanford-Binet. Yet, these are all facts *about* the patient. If we treat him merely on the basis of these abstractions, we overlook his reality, his being, and his uniqueness.

Existential writers attempt to understand man as a functioning individual, not as a statistical norm. One can compute age norms for death of the population at large but this has little meaning for the individual. As a result, Barnes (1962) refers to existentialism as the enemy of any philosophy that sees man in abstract and mechanistic terms, whether that philosophy be behavioristic, biochemical, or Marxist. Existentialists see man as more than a bundle of instinctual drives, more than a series of energy complexes.

Because existentialism depicts man in non-mechanistic terms, stress is placed upon his development. What one is today is not what he will be tomorrow. German existentialists use the term "Dasein," which means to stand out, to emerge, to become. Sartre (1957, p. 17) insists that man's existence precedes his essence; man exists before his purpose is achieved. However, this fact places man in continuous conflict. He faces anxiety and anguish because he is forever free to make choices. With each choice he stakes his future. As he is never sure of the correctness of his choice, man is in a perpetual situation of crisis.

In assuming what Green (1948) calls this "dreadful freedom," man defines himself. Upon man's freedom hinges his identity; man is the sum of his choices. If man chooses not to choose, he fails to recognize his freedom and negates his identity.

ESCAPE FROM FREEDOM

The problem of man's existential freedom becomes intensified when the organism is disabled by illness or by injury. In such situations it often seems easier to reject one's freedom. The patient thus escapes the anxiety and pain that are involved in making decisions but only at the expense of a loss of personal identity.

In rehabilitation centers, one often hears the phrase, "He has made a satisfactory adjustment to his disability." If this means that the individual has accepted his limitations, and society's interpretation of those limitations, the adjustment may be extremely detrimental. If the patient looks upon himself as inferior and inadequate, he may never unleash the potential that exists despite his limitations. Beethoven composed his Ninth Symphony despite his deafness. Theodore and Franklin Roosevelt entered the political arena despite their physical limitations. Sarah Bernhardt and Lionel Barrymore gave some of their finest performances from wheelchairs; James Thurber and Aldous

Huxley wrote some of their most brilliant passages while nearly blind. Churchill suffered from a speech handicap, yet he became a great orator; Edison was hard-of-hearing, yet he invented the phonograph. Charles Steinmetz and Toulouse-Lautrec were cripples and Helen Keller was multiple handicapped from infancy.

In assuming that a disability means an end to purposive activity, the patient is taking an "essential" rather than an "existential" position. The existential psychologist would see the disabled person as facing limitations which, in many cases, are forged by society. If the disabled person can break through the social limitations of his handicap, he may see possibilities for creative accomplishments. Fink, Fantz, and Zinker (1962) note that "we rarely encounter disabled individuals who develop their creative capacities to the fullest . . . ." It is the responsibility of the psychologist, therefore, to assist patients in asserting their personal freedom.

MOTIVATION AND EXISTENTIALISM

Another stock phrase often heard in rehabilitation centers is, "We must motivate the patient." Many psychologists explain the success or failure of rehabilitation in terms of an external force which is relatively impersonal and which can manipulate individuals toward self-sufficiency. Such a view of the handicapped person is mechanistic in nature and regards man as an object of a more powerful force. Existentialists, on the other hand, view man as a thinking, willing being. Motivation is basically internal and must spring from the organism if personal commitment and individual choice are to ensue.

It is true that motivation is of extreme importance; Block (1955) states that "Motivation is the *sine qua non* of rehabilitation." However, motivation is not to be viewed as something to be applied by an external agent; it is more than a mere stimulus-response reaction. As the existentialists have indicated, this brings about the subject-object split in which the patient becomes a mere object and the goals of freedom and identity become lost.

The rehabilitation psychologist, however, must sometimes initially use the power of his own personality to force the patient into decision making. In some cases where individual identity has been lost, the rehabilitative structure can make the patient aware that personal choice and commitment are the only realistic avenues open to him.

DISTANCE FROM THE CLIENT

A third non-existential term which is often heard in rehabilitation centers pertains to "psychological distance." Rehabilitation psychologists are urged to keep "distant" from their patients as emotional ties are "unprofessional." Existential psychlogists, however, would have no hesitation in committing themselves to a patient's welfare and in emotionally involving themselves with the patient's struggles. Carl Rogers (1951, p. 101) writes:

> . . . in every respect in which we make an object of the person — whether by diagnosing him, analyzing him, or perceiving him impersonally as a case history — we stand in the way of our therapeutic goal . . . . We are deeply

helpful only when we relate as persons, when we risk ourselves as persons in the relationship, when we experience the other as a person in his own right. Only then is there a meeting of a depth which dissolves the pain of aloneness in both client and therapist.

Furthermore, the concept of "distance" often leads the staff of a rehabilitation center to ignore basic needs of the patients. Fink, Fantz, and Zinker (1962, p. 7) note that in the rehabilitation of the disabled, the hygiene needs of patients are more often met than are their personal growth needs. Perhaps the reluctance to make a personal as well as a professional commitment to the patient's welfare leads to the recognition of only the most obvious and least subtle of the patients' needs. Fink, Fantz, and Zinker (1962, p. 7) state:

> It is crucial to provide the setting which will call forth growth behavior and not foster hygiene-seeking as an end in itself. The recognition of a hierarchy of human needs can provide the framework for clarifying the questions of patient motivation and can help us to specify the conditions which will lead to maximum growth and success of those we rehabilitate.

Another aspect of distance, which often leads to depersonalization, is one which is often created by the rehabilitation process itself. Block (1955, p. 99) has stated that "the complexity of this process, its lack of clearcut operational principles, and . . . obscurity of its goals constitute sources of bewilderment and vexation to the patient . . . ." Such feelings contribute to the patient's estrangement and prevent him from becoming an active part of the rehabilitation process. If the rehabilitation process is to be successful, the patient must become existentially involved in the treatment. Because rehabilitation is multidisciplinarian in nature, all members of the rehabilitation team must make an effort to motivate the patient to take an active part in his own development. They can best do this by creating an "I-Thou" relationship in which the patient is viewed as a fellow human being, rather than to create an "I-It" relationship in which the patient is a mere object to be classified and manipulated.

MEANING OF PAIN

One cliché which many patients hear all too often is that "You must put up with the pain." Disease and injury involve major or minor pain of both the mental and the physical variety. Instead of seeing pain as something to "stand," "bear," or "put up with," the existential psychologist recognizes in it a chance to aid the patient's search for identity. Frankl (1961, p. 5) charts a course for the rehabilitation psychologist when he writes, "Man is ready and willing to shoulder any suffering as soon and as long as he can see a meaning in it."

An individual in a chronic state of "non-being" would be especially threatened by pain which would seem to represent all of the inimical external forces which control him. A patient with strong personal identity, however, would be able to consider his condition and understand the forces behind his suffering. Once again, mental and physical anguish present not only pain but opportunity. The urgency with which John Foster Dulles worked towards strengthening European defenses was brought about by the knowledge that he was dying from cancer. Also suffering from cancer, U. S. Grant wrote a monumental biography which might never have been attempted had he not wanted to leave his family well provided for upon his death.

Mental anguish, anxiety, and guilt are regarded as inevitable by existentialists who see them as the price we pay for being human. We suffer as a result of realistic encounters with our responsibilities, our limitations, and the knowledge of our eventual termination. The goal of the existential psychologist, therefore, would not be to lessen the patient's realistic (as opposed to his neurotic) suffering but to help him find the meaning behind his torments.

In bearing both physical and mental anguish, self-identity is of prime importance. Identity is more than identification with parental figures and peers, although "being-with-others" plays an important part in personality development. The disabled patient must eventually find strength within himself and will himself to be what he desires to be. If he depends upon external forces for his happiness, he will become the "other-directed" man who has exchanged personal freedom for outside support and manipulation. Wheelis (1958, p. 205) has charted the course for attaining identity when he states, "Man can not recapture an identity out of the past. . . . Identity is not therefore to be found, it is to be created and achieved."

The problem of finding meaning in pain, therefore, is a process of moving forward, or as many existentialists describe it, a process of "transcendence." In the same way, one can turn his limitations into possibilities not by looking back to the past at what one was formerly able to do, but by looking to the present and future, to what one wills himself to do.

In retrospect, exisential thought can be of direct application to many of the problems faced by rehabilitation psychologists and their disabled patients. Existentialism encourages the patient to grow beyond mere adjustment, to reject societal interpretations of his disability, and to continue the creative life. Secondly, existentialism emphasizes the internal aspects of patient motivation. A third application encourages seeing the patient as a human being rather than as an object; in so doing, the psychologist and other members of the rehabilitation staff can involve themselves in the patient's struggle for personal growth and self-direction. Finally, existentialism sees a new dimension to pain and anguish, much of which is an inevitable concomitant of the human predicament. If there is meaning to suffering, there is also an opportunity for the patient to transcend that suffering and live every moment of his existence to the fullest extent. The rehabilitation program, therefore, is seen as being effective only when it encourages the growth of internal motivation, self-identity, and the fulfilling of one's potentialities for personal growth.

REFERENCES

Barnes, Hazel. Motivation and freedom. *Rehabilit. counsel. Bull.*, 1962, 5, 171-183.
Block, W. E. Operational principles for counseling the disabled. *J. counsel. Psychol.*, 1955, 2, 256-263.
Fink, S. L., Fantz, R., & Zinker, J. The growth beyond adjustment: another look at motivation. Cleveland: Highland View Hospital, 1962 (mimeographed).
Frankl, V. Logotherapy and the challenge of suffering. *Rev. existential psychol. psychiat.*, 1961, *1*, 3-7.
Frankl, V. *Man's search for meaning.* New York: Washington Square Press, 1963.

Green, Marjory. *Dreadful freedom: a critique of existentialism.* Chicago: Univ. Chicago Press, 1948.

May, R. The origins and significance of the existential movement in psychology. In May, R., Angel, E., & Ellenberger, H. F. (eds.), *Existence: a new dimension in psychiatry and psychology.* New York: Basic Books, 1958. Pp. 3-36.

Rogers, C. R. *Client-centered therapy.* Boston: Houghton Mifflin, 1951.

Sartre, J. *Existentialism and human emotions.* New York: Philosophical Library, 1957.

Van Dusen, W. The theory and practice of existential analysis. In Ruitenbeek, H. M. (ed.), *Psychoanalysis and existential philosophy.* New York: E. P. Dutton, 1962. Pp. 24-39.

Wheelis, A. *The quest for identity.* New York: W. W. Norton, 1958.

<hr>

(50)

EXISTENTIALISM IN COUNSELING: THE HUMANIST VIEW

Dugald S. Arbuckle
Professor of Education, Boston University, Boston, Massachusetts

Certain philosophical issues which appear to be of paramount importance to the counselor are discussed. Particular attention is paid to the humanism of existentialism and client-centered counseling as compared with the determinism of the behavioral sciences. Phenomenology is considered to be potentially either existential or deterministic. Other aspects of existentialism and determinism that are closely examined are reality, freedom, religion, and values. Both reality and values are viewed in a phenomenal sense, and as a part of the perceptual field of the individual; they are thus relative and dependent on each individual's particular perception. Freedom of the individual is considered to be the basic thread which permeates all views of existentialism. Some doubt is expressed as to the future of the freedom of man if man must see himself as a determined person living in a determined world. The relationship between existentialism and psychotherapy is examined.

There is general agreement today, in the field of counseling and psychotherapy, that the counselor, in his relationship with a client, is sharing of his self in a personal and human relationship with a fellow human. If we accept this general premise, then it would seem more logical, in any discussion of counseling, to move away from the more technique-oriented arguments about directive or non-directive, client-centered, or counselor-centered, diagnostic or acceptant. These, after all, are primarily symptomatic indications of one's basic philosophical concepts regarding man. The purpose of this paper is to examine certain of these concepts, with particular attention to humanism of existentialism, the empiricism of determinism and phenomenology, and the relationship that each of these bears to the others.

<hr>

Reprinted by permission of the Author and the *Personnel and Guidance Journal,* February 1965, 558-567.

This paper was part of a symposium, "Existentialism: What it Means to Counseling," held at the American Personnel and Guidance Association Convention, San Francisco, March 25, 1964.

DETERMINISM AND EXISTENTIALISM

Determinism and empiricism are close companions, and Skinner, as one of the most prominent determinists of the day, feels that if we are to use the methods of science in human affairs, then we must assume that behavior is lawful and determined. He feels that in the long run man is determined by the state, and that the only scientific logical conclusion that one can come to is that man's behavior is a product of his environment (Skinner, 1948, p. 273). The determinist's version of a counselor's function is given by Michael and Meyerson (1962): "The phenomena with which counselors deal, then is behavior, and the independent variable which controls behavior must be the environment."

Hobbs (1959) is another who accepts a psychological version of man's limited, and determined, "choice," and while he appears to be somewhat uneasy about this concept, he clearly feels that within a scientific construct system, the assumption of determinism is required.

Freud would certainly appear to have been deterministic, at least from the point of view of his scientific theories about man and his behavior, in which man appeared to be pretty much a victim of forces beyond his control, forces which he spent his life striving to suppress and direct. On the other hand, one has only to read Freud to sense the humaneness of the man above and beyond his theories, a feeling which is borne out by Binswanger, a contemporary of Freud.

Some writers have adopted an in-between attitude on determinism. Samler (1962), for example, wonders whether in the study of man we may have carried over the postulates of science that may not be applicable to organisms that have self-awareness and self-understanding, and he feels that there is a measure of basic freedom of choice available to the individual, and that within limits he can move in a given direction.

Combs and Snygg (1959, p. 17) would also appear to be deterministic in their phenomenological approach to human behavior, although their means of determinism would not be the same as those of empiricist Skinner or therapist Freud. They see lawfulness and determinism in our behavior at any moment of behaving. However, while phenomenologists Combs and Snygg would apparently feel that what one does, and what one sees, and what one chooses, and where one goes — in fact, all human behavior — is determined by the phenomenal or perceptual field, they do not see man as a hapless and hopeless organism, a creature who is the victim of his surroundings. They see man as part controlled by and in part controlling of his destiny (Combs & Snygg, 1959, p. 310). In this regard they agree with Shoben, who is critical of what he feels to be an oversimplification of determinism into a fatalism of events, and a neglect of the self-determining quality of human character (Shoben, 1953).

Sharply different in its concept of man is a humanistic existentialism, although existentialism by no means see eye to eye on all matters. Certainly the differences among such figures as Heidegger, and Kierkegaard, and Sartre, and Jaspers are quite apparent. Nevertheless, the existentialist is anti-deterministic in that he sees the person transcending both himself and his culture. Existentialism centers on the existing person, and it places priority on the existing man (existence) rather than on truth and laws and principles (essence). It sees a man as *being*. It also sees man with decision and will and choice, and there is the element of freedom and choice even in the seeing and the exploring, and the challenging, if necessary, of the determined world around him (May, 1961a; May 1961b).

For Sartre, one of the European stalwarts of existentialism, man is free, man *is* freedom, and if we accept the concept that existence does precede essence, then there can be no determinism. Man can be what he will (Sartre, 1947). Jaspers, too, would tend to see the true authentic "transcendental" self as being the source of meaning in life. This self is free, and it makes choice possible, and this self is not subject to study (Titus, 1959, p. 301).

Thus this self, this person-in-being as seen by the existentialist, is one who is not subject to empirical prediction and control. Ostow (1958) expresses this anti-deterministic concept when he indicates that the failure of religion, if failure it is, to obtain complete control over human behavior is because of the ultimate independence of the human spirit and the essential autonomy of the instinctual apparatus. Frankl (1958), too, feels that a real human person is not subject to rigid prediction, and that existence can neither be reduced to a system or deduced from it.

Thus, it would appear that one cannot be both deterministic and existential, but at the same time neither can be considered as absolute terms. Skinner might be considered to represent the extreme at the deterministic end of a continuum, where man would appear to be little more than a hapless thing, to be measured and manipulated and controlled for the furtherance of some unknown ends of some faceless "group," and Sartre might represent the other end of the continuum which would see man as supreme, answerable only to himself, responsible for his own actions. He may live in a world in which things and events have not been "determined" by him, but the human self is the determiner of the manner and mode and way in which he will grow and live and die in this somewhat "determined" outside. Enculturation is *not* the automatic fate of the true, of the existential, of the authentic person. He transcends both himself and his culture, and as Maslow (1961, p. 55) puts it, he becomes ". . . a little more a member of his species and a little less a member of his local group." Man is the maker and the master of his culture. The culture is his; he is not the culture's, but the attempt to suppress the existential self, while bound to fail, has a long history. Michael and Meyerson (1962) give a frighteningly accurate picture of the modern scientific version of suppression as they calmly accept the concept that the function of the "guidance" person is to influence and induce people to behave the way society thinks they should behave, and his major problem is to discover ways of getting people to behave the way we think they should behave. There is, apparently, little or no difference between the school counselor and the Chinese brainwasher!

This is the view of the behaviorist, the positivist, the determinist. Whatever the name might be, it would seem to spell autocracy, and whether it be the autocracy of the church, or of the state, or of science, the end result is the supression of the individual, the degradation of man.

Any "government" which is "of the people" obviously cannot consider democracy to be the suppression of the rights of the minority by the majority. This is nothing more than a slightly broader version of autocracy, in which more than one half of the people suppress the less than one half. If freedom is to go with democracy then we must think of the existing living human being, rather than the "law." When we accept as immutable and fixed a "law," democratic or not, which in effect says to a human, "You cannot be what you are — you cannot *be*," then we have indeed become encrusted and encultured. We then become the ones who are no longer free, we are the serfs and the slaves, and what may happen, as what has happened, is that the man we suppress or jail or torture or kill — he is the man who is free. The man lives within the laws of his culture, if he lives in a relatively "free" culture, but he is not bound by them. They do not control him, but, rather, his self transcends them.

PHENOMENOLOGY, DETERMINISM, AND EXISTENTIALISM

We have noted that the phenomenological approach and existentialism have often been apparently linked in the literature, but it is important to note that the existentialist self and the phenomenal field are not one and the same. The phenomenological approach seeks to understand the behavior of the individual from his *own* point of view. It attempts to observe people, not as they seem to outsiders, but as they seem to themselves (Combs & Snygg, 1959, p. 11). One can be phenomenological in his approach and still be deterministic, whereas one cannot be deterministic and existential. There would seem, however, to be little difference between the concept of the phenomenal self and that of the existential self, since both operate within the perceptual field. Combs (1959, p. 146) indicates his own feeling of the primacy of the *self* over the *field*, which is, of course, the opposite of the deterministic point of view, when he says, ". . . the perceptual field is usually organized with reference to the behaver's own phenomenal self," and ". . . the phenomenal self is both product of the individual's experience and product of whatever new experiences he is capable of." The degree of determinism, however, depends on the primacy of the field over the self. If one feels that one's actions are determined by the phenomenal field, then, of course, he has no choice, and he can hardly be held "responsible" for his actions. Combs would seem to at least be somewhat acceptant of this deterministic concept when he describes the term "conflict" as a term of external description. It is an outsider's description of what he observes and the behaver himself does not experience conflict (Combs & Snygg, p. 185).

May (1961a, p. 26) apparently feels no necessity of a phenomenological concept also being deterministic, and thinks of phenomenology, the first stage in the existential psychotherapeutic movement, as being the endeavor to take the phenomena as given. Nor does Rogers (1951, p. 532), who sees a goal of human development as being a basic congruence between the phenomenal field of experience and the conceptual structure of the self.

Again, however, it is important to note that unconditional acceptance is not *dependent* on the identity of the value system of the self with the value system of some other "well-adjusted" members of the human race. This *may* or *may* not happen, but it is the self, the transcendent self, the self-in-being, that is the determiner of the congruence.

Thus we might even say that it may be that an acceptance of the phenomenological field theory of human behavior might make it easier to see determinism as the fate of mankind, yet, on the other hand, the existentialist accepts the phenomenological concept without in any manner feeling that this means the dominance of the field in which the self operates over the self. In fact, one could hardly hold to an existential concept without being acceptant of the basic phenomenological approach to reality and to the self.

REALITY AND FREEDOM

The phenomenologist, the existentialist, and the client-centered counselor see reality in much the same way. When May (1961a, pp. 17-18) says "There is no such thing as truth or reality for a living human being except as he particulates in it, is conscious of it, has some relationship to it," and "The more absolutely and completely you formulate the forces and drives, the more you are talking about abstractions, and not the existing, living human being," he is expressing the phenomenological concept that reality lies in the individual's experience of the event, rather than in the isolated event. One might also say that there is, "really," no "event" without the human individual. Hatreds and bogey men and chairs exist only as they appear to the individual as they become a part of his experiencing, his living. Thus, we may say, with the determinist, that there *is* a world of reality, but it cannot be "reality" apart from the people who are the basic part of it. This is a problem faced by all student counselors, and many of even the more sophisticated and experienced counselors and therapists still appear to feel strongly that "reality," for them, must somehow, be reality for their client. Rather than accepting him, and thus his reality, and living through it and experiencing it with him, they sit on the outside, subtly or directly imposing their concepts upon him. They thus impede and make more difficult his growth toward greater freedom and self-actualization. It is difficult to modify or change one's reality if one is never allowed to deeply experience just what that reality might be.

Actually this ability to live another's reality with him might be considered as a description of empathy. This also means that the counselor is one who can live certainly in a world of uncertainty, one who accepts the probability in living with security. All too frequently in counseling, it really is "cases" that we are discussing, and with which we are working, whether we are in a staff conference "case" discussion, or involved in an actual counseling session. We operate with events, and problems, and questions and supposed meanings, and the real-life, experiencing person, either represented (and nothing more) on a piece of paper, or the flesh-and-blood person in front of us, is ignored and unseen, and we give him little help in the struggle to see who he is, because it is not "him" with whom we are relating.

In a different way, Barry and Wolf (1962, pp. 90-91) said much the same thing when they described realism as essentially a mask for the value judgments about the practicality and practicability of an idea, a feeling, a plan. It is a judgment dependent upon time and the point of view of the person making it.

Alas, how many thousands of students throughout the United States, have sat, today, in hundreds of schools, listening to their "counselor" as he said, among other things, ". . . Now Joe, let's be realistic about this, and. . ." The counselor is indeed making a value judgment, and even worse, in the name of an absolute reality (his), he is imposing this reality upon his unfortunate victim.

The existential concept of reality is closely related to freedom, which is the core of existential thought. This may be expressed as Sartre's consciousness as freedom, Jasper's existence as freedom, Kierkegaard's self as freedom, or Tillich's concept of man as freedom. To this unsophisticated individual they are all saying the same thing in somewhat complicated philosophical language —that I am free, that where I go and what I do depends on me, not on the forces outside of me, or even on the forces which I may have internalized as a part of me. I, and I alone, always have the ultimate choice, and this choice I am free to make. The very fact that one is alive means that he has the potential to be free, but one is never free to live, of course, until he is free to die.

Effectively expressing this point of view is Rogers (unpublished) when he talks of freedom as essentially an inner thing, something which exists in the living person, quite aside from any of the outward choice of alternatives which we so often think of as constituting freedom. So, too, Frankl, (1955, p. 65) and Buber (1937, p. 53), and May (1961a, p. 41) all stress the *inner* concept of freedom, and with it one can determine the ultimate direction, and make, when necessary, his final choice.

This movement toward freedom is also the core of the therapeutic process, and as one moves toward freedom — and responsibility — he becomes more aware of the deterministic forces pressing in on him (Michael & Meyerson, 1962). While determinism may be a fact of the physical world, it is man who completes that world, and it is man who makes of the world whatever reality he may wish it to become. Thus the growth that occurs in counseling might be considered to be the process, the experience, the learning to be free.

Freedom may not be the opposite of determinism, but one does not find the concept of freedom in a deterministic society. The existentialist would feel that the individual may live in a physical world which is, in a sense, determined, but the human individual, the existential self, the spirit of man, is not bound by any set of determined chains. Man basically *is* free, and any man can come to learn and to grow and to become the free person he is. This is the purpose of counseling — to help the individual to loosen himself from his deterministic shackles, and to come to realize and to see what he has always had — choice and freedom.

Being free is difficult, and one cannot be free without continually running the risk of losing one's person. The struggle to be free, too, is often much more intense and complicated, at the inner self-level, than is the struggle against overt and obvious forces of oppression. If education results in real understanding, then it can widen one's horizon of freedom, and the counselor must be concerned about the extent to which the educational experience helps to free each child.

RELIGION, VALUES, AND EXISTENTIALISM

The existentialist camp is dotted with religious figures such as Jaspers, Tillich, Marcel, Maritain, Kierkegaard, Buber, and May who outnumber the atheistic speakers such as Sartre and Heidegger. While theistic and atheistic existentialists would not agree on the question of the existence of a God, of some supreme all-knowing Being, some supernatural Deity, they would agree that man must live alone, that his living-now is all he can know, that man *is* only what he does and what he lives. Sartre would add that existence must precede essence. Neither would they see any ordered plan into which man must fit, and in his way the religious existentialists would likely differ from most of their more-dogma- and less-philosophy oriented colleagues. The religious existentialist would likely feel that there *is* meaning, but the decisions and the choices as to where to go and what to do to find that meaning must be the lonely choice of man, and his choice may be wrong. The atheistic existentialist would likely feel that there is no "meaning" that one seeks, but rather man evolves his own "meanings" as he moves and lives. Man *is,* and he creates his meanings. He does not seek *the* meaning.

Thus both would probably agree that determinism may be a part of the world in which man exists, but determinism does not apply to man. In this regard the theistic existentialist would probably not be very acceptable to most theologians who tend to see the world as a pre-determined place, operating on some Grand Plan under some Divine Order, in which man only exists, but does not actually live, since his life is determined and he thus cannot be free. To many theologians, possibly to most, God is some outer external force which controls and directs man to do its bidding. This is why it may be easier for many of them, for many "religious" individuals, to see God in a magnificent church, or in some symbol of power and might, rather than in some ordinary, insignificant man, even though surprisingly enough, the man that most "Christians" would say they try to emulate was a very ordinary, simple, loving, compassionate individual!

Religion is generally deterministic, and it sees man not only as living in a deterministic world, but very much a determined part of this deterministic world. If one holds the view that life is ultimately determined by Divine Will, then he is expressing a deterministic point of view. Both the non-religious and the theistic existentialist would feel that man is not *one* important determinant, but that man *is* the creator. He does not live in a "created" world; he creates it as he lives. This is the only world he can know.

The existentialist does not see a value as something which is apart from a person. Values are human products, and they exist only in a human community. Usually, a "value" implies a judgment, but the same act may have as many different values placed upon it as there are people who are involved in it. A generally accepted cultural concept is that certain "values" are better than others, and an equally acceptable concept is that values can, and should, be taught. The questionable assumption here is that the teacher somehow is the possessor of a value which is not possessed by the learner, and that it is the function of the teacher to teach this better value (his), to the learner, who either does not have this value, or has a "wrong" one. This concept detaches the value from the person, so that, just as one can be taught how to drive, one can be "taught" morality, virtue, and courage. This concept also makes possible the widely accepted tenet in counseling that "I like him but I don't like what he is doing." It obviously implies that the counselor should, and must, have as part of his value system a feeling of the rightness of his ways *for others,* an obligation to impose this rightness on others, and an assumption that this rightness can be imposed (taught) to others. While these assumptions are questionable from an existential point of view, they are, nevertheless, widely held.

Mueller (1958), for example, has indicated her feeling that not only can one teach ethics, but that the "counselor" must teach ethics as he "counsels." There would appear here, again, to be the concept of a detachment of a human act from a person, the idea that values are some form of appendices that one "learns" by being taught. There is an absence of the feeling that values, being a part of the person, can only come through an experiencing and a living and a human relationship. Close human contact with a patient and compassionate person may help another person to free himself so that he, too, may move in the direction of patience and compassion. He may thus "learn," from a counselor, from a teacher, from a friend, but he has not been taught. History would surely bear witness to the futility of the attempt of one person to "teach" another his value system.

Williamson (1958) also expresses a deterministic feeling of human limitations when he appears to view the counselor as one whose outside-of-me values control him, rather than one whose inner self is expressed in terms of his values. This concept also implies a striving by the counselor to achieve for the client something, some answer, some right path or goal which is external to the client, and possibly to the counselor. This is almost like the counselor who cheats on his income tax returns striving to convince the client who has been cheating on exams that the virtue of "no cheating" is something which he really should practice. Actually, this "virtue" is real for neither client nor counselor, and it is unlikely that any change is going to take place in either one. On the other hand, we might hypothesize that if the counselor is a "non-cheating" sort of fellow, in his living-being, regardless of any words, then he will see no point in trying to press this on to the client, who, in turn, might possibly internalize, or at least let stir around inside him the idea that this might be something worth incorporating so that it becomes a part of his being. People who believe, feel no particular pressure to convince others that they should believe the same way too. It is likely that the evangelist is actually very concerned about who he is and where he is going, and this is why he continually tries to convince others that they should follow him. He neither respects nor trusts the other fellow to find his right way, and, if his "religion" includes compassion and gentleness and love toward his fellows, he spends his time preaching it rather than practicing it.

The concept that one can separate a person from his values is a very common one in counseling. It is almost as if one can view a human act and the person who commits it as two separate entities. One might feel that the act of robbery, the taking away from one person of his belongings so that I can further my own interests, is questionable. But when a counselor is relating with another fellow human who has committed the act of robbery, he cannot now divorce the person from the act. Part of the person is the fact that he has committed a robbery, and since we accept the client as he is, the un-related fact of robbery, or what the counselor may think about it, has no relationship to the therapeutic interaction whatsoever. It is the person, all of him, with whom we are concerned, and the various bits and pieces, by themselves, mean nothing. The existential counselor, however, would not view acts at any time as being detached from humans, so that a question such as "Well, do you mean that you don't think that robbery is bad?" really isn't a question because robbery, per se, *really* doesn't mean anything. It is only when it becomes a part of an individual human's behavior that it means something, and the counselor, being concerned with the person, is not particularly aware of the "goods" or "bads" of the individual's actions.

This is likely why, too, practically every act that is labeled "bad" by someone, is labeled "good" by someone else. Robin Hood's thieving was considered wonderful by those who were the recipients of his loot, but not by those from whom he stole. Americans think affectionately of the "robber barons" who were the ancestors of some of our most illustrious current figures, political and otherwise!

Shoben (1953) expresses the "doing something to somebody" attitude when he comments that the field is committed to the development of responsible individuals capable of maintaining and advancing a democratic society. The existentialist would be more concerned with helping the individual to come to be able to release and use the potential that he has, and he would have little concern about whither the "inner man" would go. He would help the person to grow to freedom, and while a product might be a "democratic society," this would be somewhat meaningless, since in today's world we have earnest people who are sure they have "democratic societies" in such countries as China, Jugoslavia, Ghana, and Russia. Shoben, of course, means *his* concept of a democratic society, and while doubtless many of us would share this concept very closely with him, can we not, at least in a counseling relationship, operate on the assumption that the client who has learned to be free will help to develop a society in which all may live their life to the utmost, with respect for the rights and the integrity of their fellows, since they respect the rights and the integrity of their self.

While we could agree that the counselor might as well admit that he has his own values, but that there is no reason that these will be most meaningful for the client (May, 1962), it is important to distinguish between those values which are a part of the make-up of the inner self of the counselor, and are shown in his patience, his compassion, and his acceptance of the client, and values of judgment and evaluation. The counselor who feels that "robbery," *per se,* is "bad," is not actually too far removed from the counselor who feels that the client who has robbed is "bad," who in turn is not too far removed from the individual who feels that the person who has robbed is bad, and should therefore be punished. While such individuals may be being existential in the sense that they are saying "You, and you alone must be responsible for your deeds," they are not existential in the sense that they are not getting close to, or being understanding of, the existential self. They may be observing it, but they are not living with it.

Curran (1960) expresses more of a trust in the person-in-being when he indicates that we should seek a personal integration which is also an integration with the whole civilization which has produced us. This might then free us from the concept that all personal values must be imposed from without and restore again the possibility of starting out on a personal pursuit of oneself in a search for reasonable self-values.

This might represent a somewhat theistic existential point of view, in that while Curran trusts the individual to determine for himself how he will move and when and where he will move, he believes that there are, somehow, already established answers and values which the individual will come to find.

The individual does not develop and create his own answers, but he moves toward pre-established answers. In this case, in Curran's mind, these are likely established by some Deity or God. Curran also indicates the interesting concept that somehow the ancient values are more secure, and, we can assume, somehow better, than more recent values. Were the ancient and traditional values of the Romans more secure, and better, than some of the values that were being advanced by a heretic named Christ? Were the ancient and traditional values of the Greeks more secure than those of the heretic Socrates? The non-theistic existentialist would likely feel, with Curran, that the individual must find his own way, and, with Curran, he would have faith that the individual could find his own way, but he would differ with Curran in that he would have no pre-conceived concept of where the individual might end, or what his values might become. They might be like those of yesterday, or they might be like those of tomorrow, but man lives his life, and he creates his values. He never goes back, to what once was, although he may become like what once was.

In a sense, Curran would seem to have his "man" attempting to discover pre-existent truths and values, to somehow become congruent with what already is, and in this sense, of course, he is expressing the view of determinism. For him, what is, was, but for the existentialist, what is, is. Life is today, now, not yesterday, and we move away from yesterday, not toward it even though we may yearn for this return to the womb.

One cannot discuss values and freedom and living, without also taking into consideration that closely allied experience that eventually comes to all — death. The free man of the existentialist, the human who is never merely a victim of a predetermined culture, the person-in-being who is the maker of his values, this man, being free to live, is also free to die, and it would seem that no person can really be free to live if he is afraid to die. Feifel (1961, p. 71) expresses this feeling when he comments that we "are not altogether free in any deed as long as we are commanded by an inescapable will to live." Sartre (1947, p. 545) relates freedom with death when he says "The very act of freedom is therefore the assumption and creation of finitudes: If I make myself, I make myself finite and hence my life is unique."

It is ironic, and sad, that one of the basic feelings that many individuals learn from their "religion" is fear, and particularly fear of death. Feifel (1961, p. 68), for example, found, in a study of his patients, that the religious person, as compared with the non-religious person, was personally more afraid of death. There must be untold millions of Christians who spend much of their life trying to guarantee their entry into Heaven, but since they feel that they are not the ones who control their destiny, they are never quite sure whether their Deity is approving or disapproving. They thus seek as much as they can in the way of assurances that there is a Heaven, and that they, and a few of their chosen fellows, will be the ones who will be there. The old and hoary joke about each group in Heaven having to live their segregated lives behind walls for fear that they might discover there are other peoples in Heaven too, is not a joke to many. Equally shocking to some white, male Christians is the story of the angel, who, on being asked to describe God, said, "She is a Negro." Many "devout" Christians cannot accept doubt and uncertainty as part of their religion. They must know, particularly about the rewards and punishments of the hereafter, and this might logically tend to make them somewhat self-centered in their actions toward others. The one who does not know about the future, and will, with certainty, face this uncertainty, even to the point of dying to defend a fellow human, is indeed showing a far higher level of altruism and compassion.

The existential man would live his life of freedom and responsibility, and would not have to "know" about what happens after death. If his reason conflicted with some religious fairy stories, he would not be too disturbed, since his life is now, and he would live this the best he could. The rest he could accept, without fear, as the unknown. For him, the person is as he is, satisfaction must come from within, man is able to be free, man is able to choose, and so, to himself, become tolerable to behold. Whether he is tolerable to others is of secondary importance. He must first be tolerable to himself, and it would surely seem that most people who are intolerable of their self, are the ones who find others intolerable. One person becomes a heretic to another person because that person has not yet learned the life of the free man, and is thus afraid.

EXISTENTIALISM AND PSYCHOTHERAPY

It is unfortunate, but probably unavoidable that psychotherapy has come to have certain tags and handles, and these carry with them the obvious implication of a "method" of psychotherapy. It is probably just as safe to assume that Rogers was not thinking of a method of counseling when he used the term "non-directive" and later, "client-centered," as it is to assume that there is really only one Rogerian, namely Carl Rogers, as there was only one Freudian, Sigmund Freud. What is too often missed is that "client-centered" means literally, not just figuratively, what it says: it refers to a human relationship which is centered on one of the two people involved, the client. And the client-centered concept of man, and of the counseling relationship, is very much an existential point of view. This, it might be pointed out, is not the traditional doctor-patient relationship of medicine, nor is it the somewhat similar doctor-patient relationship as it is carried over into much of the traditional pre-Rogers psychotherapy. In much of this, as in much of counseling today, at best only lip-service is paid to the concept that the client must be the central figure, and the deciding agent as far as any choice or decision is concerned.

It would seem that at least the client-centered counselor and the existential therapist are talking pretty much the same language when they discuss man, the person-in-being, and the counseling relationship, the process of becoming. It should be noted too, that existentialism is primarily a product of European philosophers, rather than psychotherapists. The earlier existentialists, Kierkegaard (some would add Marx and Nietzsche), Sartre, Heidegger, Marcel, Jaspers, Maritain and Buber were, and are, tremendous beings, and while they lived fully, and wrote extensively about man, they wrote from a philosophical and theistic or atheistic point of view. It may be, in a living and experiencing way, they knew more about man than they knew man. Their modern American counterpart might be Tillich, while May would appear to be an American therapist who has an existential approach to man. This might be one reason while the older non-therapist existentialist had a somewhat more pessimistic and deterministic viewpoint of man, and the more optimistic point of view of client-centered therapist Rogers would appear to be shared more by therapist May than by theologian Tillich. Again, we note here that religion, at least in a formal and doctrinaire sense, would appear to be more a part of the make-up of Tillich, somewhat less of May, and still less of Rogers. On the other hand, Rogers, at least in the sense of his deep respect for the integrity of others, and his sense of responsibility that he shares living with others, is surely a deeply "religious" person.

Thus it would seem that client-centered therapy, as it views man, and the human counseling relationship of man with man, is very much existential. It is not as pessimistic as existential philosophy would appear at times to be. It is phenomenological in the sense of the phenomenological world of the individual as being the world of reality for the individual, but it is not phenomenological in a deterministic sense.

REFERENCES

Barry, Ruth, & Wolf, Beverly. *An epitaph for vocational guidance*. New York: Teachers College, Columbia University, 1962.

Buber, M. *I and thou*. Translated by R. G. Smith. Edinburgh: T. Clark, 1937.

Combs, Arthur W., & Snygg, Donald. *Individual behavior*. New York: Harper, 1959.

Curran, Charles A. Some ethical and scientific values in the counseling therapeutic process. *Personnel guid. J.*, 1960, *39*, 15-20.

Feifel, Herman. In May, Rollo, *Existential psychology*. New York: Random House, 1961.

Frankl, V. E. On logotherapy and existential analysis. *Amer. J. Psychoanal.*, 1958, *18* (1), 28-37.

Frankl, V. E. *From death camp to existentialism*. (Translated by I. Lasch) Boston: Beacon Press, 1955.

Hobbs, Nicholas. Science and ethical behavior. *Amer. Psychologist*, 1959, *14*, 217-225.

Maslow, A. H. In May, Rollo, *Existential psychology*. New York: Random House, 1961.

May, Rollo. *Existential psychology*. New York: Random House, 1961a.

May, Rollo. *Existence*. New York: Basic Books, 1961b.

May, Rollo. Freedom and responsibility re-examined. Unpublished paper given at Chicago, 1962 APGA Convention.

Michael, Jack, & Meyerson, Lee. A behavioral approach to counseling and guidance. *Harvard Educ. Rev.*, 1962, *32*, 383-402.

Mueller, Kate H. Theory for campus decline. *Personnel guid. J.*, 1958, *36*, 302-309.

Ostow, Mortimer. The nature of religious controls. *Amer. Psychologist*, 1958, *13*, 571-74.

Rogers, Carl R. *Client-centered psychotherapy*. Boston: Houghton-Mifflin, 1951.

Rogers, Carl R. Learning to be free, an unpublished paper.

Samler, Joseph. An examination of client strength nad counselor responsibility. *J. counsel. Psychol.* 1962, *9*, 5-11.

Sartre, Jean-Paul. *Existentialism*. (Translated by B. Freeman) New York: Philosophical library, 1947.

Shoben, E. J. New frontiers in theory. *Personnel guid. J.*, 1953, *32*, 80-83.

Skinner, B. F. *Walden two*. New York: Macmillan, 1948.

Titus, Harold H. *Living issues in philosophy*. New York: American Book Co., 1959.

Williamson, Edmund G. Value orientation in counseling. *Personnel guid. J.*, 1958, *36*, 520-528.

EXISTENTIALISM IN COUNSELING: THE RELIGIOUS VIEW

Richard P. Vaughan

University of San Francisco, San Francisco, California

The purpose of this article is to throw some light upon the contribution existential thought has to make to counseling and religious experience. The existential approach aims at grasping the total phenomenological world of the client, including the world of religious experience. Key concepts in the client's religious world are freedom, personal encounter with God, and the discovery of meaning in life. One of the goals of counseling is to promote that freedom which will permit the client on his own to participate in a true encounter with God and his fellow man and discover for himself a meaning of life.

Existentialism as a philosophical movement embraces a wide variety of positions. This divergence poses a special problem for those who hope to arrive at a more effective approach to counseling through the medium of existentialism. They can either espouse one position and seek a modification of their counseling procedure through the tenets of this position or they can attempt to find common denominators running through the various existential positions. I prefer to follow the latter course. Two common denominators proposed by Benda (1962) are subjectivity and a phenomenological approach. By subjectivity is meant that approach which is opposed to the objectivity of the natural sciences. It is "a recognition of the fact that human knowledge depends on the organization of man's mind and the world in which man lives is not recognizable as any objective reality existing independently of man." The second denominator, namely, a phenomenological approach to behavior, is related to the first. Phenomenology as a theoretical point of view advocates the study of direct experience taken at its face value. It asserts that behavior is determined by experience rather than by external, objective reality.

In addition to these two denominators of all existential positions, there are two other concepts that at least play a dominant role in many positions. These concepts are "freedom" and "the establishment of meaning for one's existence." Here freedom is taken to mean freedom so as to be able to make a choice. It signifies that distinctly human quality which allows an individual to make decisions and assume responsibility. Paul Tillich says that man becomes human only at the moment of decision (May, 1961). The last concept, namely the establishment of meaning for one's existence, can be looked at from two points of view: one can either make meaning for his existence or he can seek meaning for existence. In this presentation, we shall make use of the latter view, namely man strives to discover meaning.

Reprinted by permission of the Author and the *Personnel and Guidance Journal,* February 1965, 553-557.

This paper was part of a symposium, "Existentialism: What it Means to Counseling," held at the American Personnel and Guidance Association Convention, San Francisco, March 25, 1964.

It is the purpose of this paper to throw some light upon the contribution existential thought has to make to counseling and religious experience. When the existentialist faces such religious problems as God's existence, the immortality of the soul and belief (if he does so at all), he faces them as an existentialist. He is not concerned with theological proofs built upon revelation or with objective proofs for the existence of God and the immortality of the soul. He is concerned with man's religious experience. His approach to religion is phenomenological. This can be exemplified by the thought of Gabriel Marcel (1951), who maintains that any attempt to demonstrate God's objectivity is self-defeating because it transforms God into an object, a someone about whom I can talk as if he were not present. Marcel then goes on to expound a new "ontological argument" built upon personal experience, the notion of presence, and the I-thou relationship (Gallagher, 1962). Man's concept of God — and as a matter of fact, his whole religious belief — is a personal experience. It can not be dissected or treated as an alien or non-essential aspect of his life. The problems of religion are part and parcel of man's experience as man. They are not mere whims that come to the fore because of a passing religious revival (May, 1961). One of the main contributions of existential thought to counseling inasmuch as it effects religious development is this phenomenological approach to religion. It is a departure from the view that religious belief is a defensive maneuver, and to be treated as such, or that it is something alien to the counseling situation.

TECHNIQUE FOLLOWS UNDERSTANDING

The application of existential thought does not constitute a new school of counseling theory. Rather it introduces a distinctive approach, which can stand side by side with many of the traditional counseling theories. In a few words, this approach can be stated as follows: "Understanding first and technique second" or "Technique follows understanding" (May, 1958). The existential approach calls for a pervading attitude or mental set which concerns itself with an effort to understand the individual and his experience. Techniques, whether they be directive or non-directive, are subordinate to this primary goal. The counselor who makes use of this approach attempts to enter, insofar as this is possible, the personal world of the counselee. He does not reduce the counselee to an object to be analyzed according to theoretical constructs nor does he dissect manifestations of behavior into opposing psychodynamic mechanisms whose harmonious balance must be restored. He likewise opposes the positivistic-rationalistic distinction between willing, thinking, desiring, and feeling. His is a phenomenological approach through which he attempts to enter into the experimental world of the counselee, as the counselee sees it, and then endeavors to foster in the counselee a fuller appreciation of the reality that makes up this world.

Among the specific aims of the existential approach to counseling there are three that are particularly pertinent to our present discussion: (1) fostering freedom within the counselee; (2) improving his encounter with others; (3) discovering meaning for his existence. All three have a direct bearing on religious experience.

In existential experience man opens his whole being to be invaded and dominated by reality (Van Croonenburg, 1961). He takes reality into his being and makes it his own. The healthy individual is open to reality. He is able to discover and appreciate the meaning of reality. The neurotic, on the other hand, is closed to much of reality. He lives in a constricted world. Constriction has been imposed upon him by the mechanism of selective perception. As a result, he is no longer free to participate to the extent that is potentially his as a human being. A whole segment of reality becomes threatening. To protect himself, he resorts to withdrawal or compulsive reactions. He limits his experiential world to that part of reality that is safe. Freedom can only be restored by opening up his perceptual field, and thus permitting the individual to participate more fully in reality. To become a healthy person, he must be able to take a personal stand toward reality. He must be able to uncover personal meaning in reality (Van Kaam, 1961).

BEYOND RESTRICTIONS

The meaning of reality is, to a degree, the result of cultural and environmental background. What we hold as praiseworthy or blameworthy depends upon the views of parents and other important people in our lives. These views, in turn, reflect the cultural values of the civilization in which we live. We unconsciously assume the meaning that these various forces have placed upon certain actions. This restriction of meaning is a necessary part of society. The healthy individual accepts them and goes beyond them, finding personal meaning in the world of reality. The neurotic is more apt to be limited to the culturally and environmentally imposed meanings. His anxieties and fears deprive him of the freedom to discover meaning. He thinks and acts as he imagines others want him to think and act. Before he can discover freedom, he must discover himself as a being-in-the-world.

Religious experience is a part of the counselee's reality. The loss of freedom curtails or distorts this experience, just as it curtails or distorts any other experience. What one believes and values is dependent on openness to reality. When a large part of reality is closed to the individual, he is thrown back upon cultural and environmental forces. In this case, belief is not the product of personal conviction but rather the result of past experiences. If religious experience is to become a personal experience, then the individual must achieve a certain degree of freedom or openness to reality. One of the aims of the existential approach to counseling is precisely the fostering of this openness to reality — and this includes openness to religious reality. A natural consequence of this process would be fuller religious experience. It might be noted, however, that it is not the task of the counselor to "give" religious experience but rather to set the stage so that the counselee can on his own more fully experience the world of religious belief. This can be accomplished by lessening defensive reactions which result in selective perception, thus allowing greater participation in reality. The individual who is open to religious reality is able to make a free decision as to what he believes or does not believe. His belief is not the product of neurotic influences.

To further openness to the reality of religious belief, the counselor must understand the religious world of the counselee — restricted as it may be.

In other words, the counselor must enter into the religious world of the counselee, since this world is a part of the counselee's total experience. If he is to be effective as a counselor, he cannot dissect total experience, casting aside religious experience as one part of the counselee's world that is not the proper area of counseling.

ONTOLOGICAL COMMUNION

"Encounter" is a word that is sometimes used in existential thought to describe a special relationship that can exist between two individuals. Here again freedom and openness must be present if the individual is to realize this communion, which is somewhat vaguely expressed as one existence communicating with another. Marcel speaks of this relationship as an "ontological communion." In an effort to convey the full meaning of this experience, he offers the following example: "How often do I hear the tale of misfortunes and ills of others with whom I ought to sympathize, and yet inwardly I feel nothing? I cannot respond; they are just not there for me. But let me open a letter from a friend a thousand miles away telling me that he has been struck by a terrible disease, and at once I am with him, I suffer with him, we are together without qualifications" (Gallagher, 1962, p. 24). In the encounter, the other individual no longer remains a "he" but becomes a "thou." He becomes a special being in my eyes. In as far as I can, I enter into his world of reality. I participate with him in this world. He no longer remains someone "out there" who serves my purpose. Our friendship enjoys much more than subject-object relationship; we experience a certain undefinable togetherness.

The concept of encounter has special significance to the counselor. It means that the counselor should be much more than an investigator of psychodynamic and sociological influences. He should primarily concern himself not with problems and solution but with communion. He should strive to enter the world of the counselee and to participate in this world, so as to effect an encounter with the counselee. If he is successful in his endeavor, it is hoped that the counselee will be able to open himself to similar encounters with others in the future.

The encounter likewise has profound religious significance. To some degree, a man's relationship with God depends upon his relationship with his fellow man. If he is unable to communicate with others on anything but a subject-object level, he is apt likewise to find that his communication with God is on the same level. If he is unable to experience an encounter with others, it is hardly likely that he will experience an encounter with God. God becomes an object, but not an experience. Religious belief, if it remains, becomes something he ought to have because others expect it of him or because he expects it of himself. It is not personally meaningful. The individual who has experienced an encounter in the therapeutic relationship of counseling is, therefore, better disposed to seek a similar encounter with God.

ULTIMATE QUESTIONS

A final contribution of existentialism is the treatment of life's meaning. Most previous counseling theory either presupposed the meaning of life, such as one sees in the hedonism of the psychoanalytic theory or it simply skirts the problem, as exemplified by the Rogerian approach. For the existential counselor, the meaning of existence is a vexing personal problem. It is a problem which each individual must face and solve. A failure to do so creates what Frankl calls "the Existential vacuum," namely the total loss of the ultimate meaning to one's existence that makes life worth living, and as a result, produces "a new class of neurosis" (Frankl, 1962).

To seek the meaning of one's existence is characteristic of man alone. We cannot imagine the ant or the bee, in spite of its complex social system, posing this question to itself. This questioning presupposes consciousness which is a distinctly human experience. It is for man to question the purpose of his life. Although the various existential schools may differ widely as to what is the meaning of one's existence, they all agree that the question is an important one. They agree that it is a question that must be faced by each individual. It is the posing of this question that constitutes one of the major contributions of existential thought to counseling theory. If the counselee has faith in divine Providence, he has an answer to the meaning of his existence. Through the medium of counseling, he can make this realization more secure. If he does not have faith, the counseling session then becomes the place where he must seek to discover what is the meaning of his existence. He must face such questions as "What is the meaning of death — an inseparable part of existence?" "What is the meaning of suffering?" and "What is the purpose of life?" The answers to these questions have a direct bearing on his existential world. It is the function of the counselor to pose such questions, but the answers must come from the counselee if they are to become personally meaningful to him. Not infrequently, the answers to these questions may lead to religious convictions.

Contemporary existential thought, therefore, has a contribution to make to the counseling situation, which, in turn, can further religious experience. It offers a unique approach that attempts to enter into the counselee's world of reality and create an openness which will allow him to understand and fully participate in this reality. Furthermore, this approach disposes the counselee to seek the meaning of his existence. All these aims directly influence the counselee's world of religious experience, which is an integral part of his total experience.

References

Benda, Clemens E. The significance of existential thought for psychiatry and psychotherapy. Rev. existential Psychol. & Psychiat., 1962, 2, 121-123.

Frankl, Viktor E. Psychiatry and man's quest for meaning. J. Relig. & Hlth., 1962, 1, 93-103.

Gallagher, Kenneth T. The philosophy of Gabriel Marcel. New York: Fordham Univ., 1962.

Marcel, Gabriel. Being and having. Translated by Katherine Farrer. Boston: Beacon Press, 1951.

May, Rollo. Existence: a new dimension in psychiatry and psychology. New York: Basic Books, 1958.

May, Rollo. Existential psychiatry: an evaluation. J. Relig. & Hlth., 1961, 1, 38.

Van Croonenburg, E. Existential experience, heart of existentialism. Rev. Existential Psychol. & Psychiat., 1961, 1, 105.

Van Kaam, Adrian. Clinical implications of Heidegger's concepts of will, decision and responsibility. Rev. existential Psychol. & Psychiat., 1961, 1, 205-216.

(52)

EXISTENTIALISM IN COUNSELING: THE SCIENTIFIC VIEW

Ted Landsman

School of Education, University of Florida, Gainesville

The behavioral scientist can readily agree that existentialism is a powerful and meaningful movement for the counseling profession. However, to achieve its fullest usefulness it must grow to meet the scrutiny characteristic of the behavioral scientists' methods. Its weakness from this point of view includes the reluctance to formulate public definitions of its most prized concepts and its rejection of rigor in methodology. The possibilities of a scientific existentialism which by no means destroys the magnificence of its concepts are demonstrated in a number of available experiments. Counseling as a helping profession cannot responsibly accept existentialism wholly as it comes from contemporary philosophy but must extrapolate and develop it into an adequate science of man.

Professions have histories, none that I know of totally noble. Some, such as ministry and medicine, perhaps generally have often soared through proud ages of principled practices yet were still saddened by certain seasons of profane cruelty. In these many histories of many helping professions from philosophy to prostitution, science and deep human feeling have sometimes shared and often alternated as the figures to prophesy the choices. The stormiest eras have been steered over courses captained not by both but by only one, either heartless science or uncontrollable human feeling.

And now in our generation a great tide of human feeling emphasis, the tide of existentialism, seems about to seize the course of counseling, and we must ask if it is a favorable tide. Should we ride its powerful currents or struggle back to the secure grounds of what we once were? Where will this tide take us?

I find existentialism a powerful force. Nourished in the agony and despair of a defeated people, emerging into an uncertain light through the rescue of friends, searching with similar extremism for the immensities of positive human experience, peak, oceanic experiences. Expecting to die, the French existentialist made the most of death, relishing despair and anguish. Finding instead life, he made the most of it and now seeks to give new meaning to life. A scientist could not help but shrink from a force so powerfully uncontrolled, feeling filled, emotion laden, intruding itself upon the orderly, disciplined world of facts and ideas. A behavioral scientist however cannot afford to shrink from or ignore such a force. His overriding obligation is to assure that this strength be governed with the wisdom of tested knowledge. The untamed stallion is fearful, snorting and beautiful as the essence of all that is animal. Existentialism is a yet more fearful, more lovely for it is an

Reprinted by permission of the Author and the *Personnel and Guidance Journal*, February 1965, Vol. XL, 568-573.

This paper was part of a symposium, "Existentialism: What it Means to Counseling," held at the American Personnel and Guidance Association Convention, San Francisco, March 25, 1964.

untamed human essence. I do not doubt that all of us do love things which are wild and free, yet now I must perform a profane task and subdue existentialism to the chains of behavioral science.

BASIC DEMANDS OF SCIENCE

An Empirical Basis

Not more than a few years ago, existentialism would have difficulty meeting even the broadest definition of a science. In recent years a few experimental studies founded on an existentialistic theory system have made their appearance particularly in the new *Journal of Humanistic Psychology*. Science asks an empirical basis for hypothesis and experiment. Have the existentialists derived from observation of the natural event? Many of them have Sartre's (1953), Camus' (1954) and DeBeauvoir's (1953) writings betray an observation and even participation in the categories of existence which can scarcely be denied. Their writings as essays in another sense implicitly refer to real, observed events. Two of the most committed existentialist psychologists, May (1950) and Maslow (1962) are both intimately tied to counseling as a function of theory and also are to my mind free of criticism that their creations are fine spun or fanciful. May's sensitive perturbations are derived from many clinical hours in shared agony and reflected joy. Maslow's preliminary research is of real people and real events, hypothesized into general principles or laws. Not all the existentialists would be so virtuous by our standards and although it may be heresy to say so it seems that the most venerable existentialist Soren Kierkegaard (1957) is far more abstract than empirical in his writings. However, the existentialist of this generation has fashioned for himself an uncomfortable image as one who is too preoccupied with real, intense human existence to as to be too psychological to be a philosopher. That self same involvement prohibits objectivity in observation and therefore he is too philosophical to be a psychologist. The transition is made on the continent by people such as Merleau-Ponty (1956), and here by Maslow (1962a) and May (1950). This transition is almost directly to counseling and clinical work without having passed through the merciless sieve of experimental psychology or behavioral science.

Public Definition

A second rather fundamental demand of science is for public definition. It surely does not seem much to ask, that terms and concepts be somehow communicated so as to have a rather common meaning to most reasonable scientists. But, both old and new, the existentialists resist this simple entrance requirement. When existentialists define a term such as "dread," it is not merely my complaint that they are not operational; they are simply incomprehensible. When they are comprehensible, the meanings given by even two friendly existentialists may be quite disparate. Other than through the literature my first direct contact with this exasperating law of existentialism occurred four years ago. At a meeting of the American Ontoanalytic Society I presented this complaint; another speaker made an impassioned plea (they speak no other way) to retain vagueness and avoid definition of terms. She was roundly applauded. You can see I retain my wounds to this day.

Had I read the following passage by Kierkegaard (1957) I might have been spared that defeat: ". . . when it is a question of existential concepts it always is a sign of surer tact to obstain from definitions, because one does not like to construe in the form of a definition which so easily makes something else and something different out of a thought which essentially must be understood in a different fashion and which one has understood differently and loved in an entirely different way."

The existentialist's revulsion for definition must be more sympathetically understood even if it cannot entirely be accepted. The scientist asks for words and at best operations in definition so that elegant exactness might be available to two unfriendly scientists who wish to quarrel about meanings. The existentialists such as Kierkegaard have announced fears that definition changes meaning. And I must confess that operational definitions do exactly this under many circumstances. The existentialist also in many differing contexts shows less faith in words and more in relationships of people than do scientists. "We are," he doggedly insists, "in revolt against the whole very verbal world of academics we are dealing with concepts which cannot be communicated in words alone. They are communicable however, publicly by the whole range of expression available to man." That is, there is no actual denial of public communication, essential to behavioral science, in existentialism. Rather there is often a desperate attempt to seek communication. There is however, often the appearance that communication must come not by verbal communication alone but by experience shared. This is reminiscent of Zen Buddhism which is not unrelated to existentialism. Nothing in science precludes such a procedure. In a sense operationism coming full circle asks the same. But, the burden of proof, of demonstration must rest upon the presenter of the hypothesis, idea or concept. And I fear the existentialists do not entirely accept this responsibility.

Some of the concepts which cry out for clarification include:
Being, becoming, non-being and nothingness, being-in-the-world, being there
Anguish, agony, anxiety and angst
Loneliness and encounter
Despair and dread
Commitment
Being-able-to-be, being-allowed-to-be, having-to-be-in-this-world (Hora, 1962)

Of all these terms, only one appears in Verplanck's *Glossary of Some Terms Used in the Objective Science of Behavior* (1957). That one is "anxiety" and it is defined as "a secondary drive whose establishing operation is the development of a discriminated avoidance conditioned response." How would Kierkegaard feel about that? This is cited not to further berate the existentialist but rather to point out that there is a plague upon both houses, each apparently having cursed the other.

Methodology

A third general criterion which behavioral science would square with existentialism centers about rigor of methodology. It would be unfair and futile to hold existentialistic philosophy to this requirement. Methodology has meant something quite different to philosophers over the centuries. The epoche or transcendental reduction of Husserl (1952) is usually described as the method of phenomenology. It involves the naive description of phenomena. At best it could be thought of as a pre-method in the behavioral sciences. But after over half a decade of the availability of such a concept, I see little adaptation of it to a method of science. Perhaps, however, the reflection of feeling so familiar now as a technique in counseling is such an epoche — an immediate unquestioning observation of another's expression.

However, already the younger phenomenological or existential psychologists have sought without embarrassment to create novel, rigorous experiments in the context of existentialistic theories. A leader in this direction is perhaps Jourard (1963) who has already presented a broad range of research on the self-disclosures. A most hopeful forerunner of things to come is represented in studies such as by Blazer (1963). Blazer demonstrated a correlation of 0.86 between maturity and enjoyment of sensory deprivation on the part of 100 subjects. The methodology is quite undistinguished and follows a simple pattern. However, in a single study we find an existentialist concept, "transcendence of environment," operationally defined and studied as "sensory deprivation." This is certainly a far cry from Kierkegaard and from the viewpoint of behavioral science is supremely praiseworthy.

A similar term is *transcendent behavior* — in itself combining two words each of which would ordinarily not wish to be seen with the other in public literature. It can be clearly defined as a task performed by an individual in such a manner as to be superior to or to transcend his own usual or modal performance. Gayle Privette (1964) at the University of Florida collected reports of transcendent behavior and of modal behavior and reduced the material to a series of items. Subjecting these tender concepts to the rudeness of a multiple-factor analysis program in a 709 computer, she found three factors which seemed characteristic of transcendent behavior and not a part of modal behavior. These were (1) *clarity of focus upon self, the environment and the transaction*, (2) *intense commitment* and strangely enough, (3) *an absence of needs of other people*. Emerging here are three concepts often considered central in existential and phenomenological theory. A similar multiple factor analysis design by Winston Puttick (1964) applied to the problem of fully functioning persons indicates a factor called *childlike gaiety* as associated with such persons. Again, while the designs are not new, the concepts used and the rigorous approach to sensitive, existential concepts represent to me a high point in the application of behavioral science to existentialism.

Several years ago, it was my lament (Landsman, 1961) that we needed more rigorous methodology. Now, I feel comfortable in saying we are able to stand with the experimentalist, when we so need, to use conventionally controlled designs in the exploration of well-defined concepts of concern to counselors. One would have to confess that there are but few of these studies in the literature. Their reality is demonstrated, however, to my satisfaction. The problem newly defined is to refine methodology, create new designs and new statistical tools, such as new programs for the computers, so as to not only increase rigor but also so as to increase the precision with which we are to deal with the category of the individual, the deeply, human characteristics that are our concern in counseling rather than those that are particularly measurable. We are looking for the worth of man, not the measure of man. I see the intimations of improvement not in imitation of the methodology of the contemporary behavioral scientist but rather in the innovative creation of designs and tools more applicable to the depth orientation of the existentialist.

Theory

There are those among the behavioral scientists who require elegant theory and there are those such as Skinner (1957) who are respectable though entirely innocent of theory. Neither of these camps, however, would tolerate theory that is imprecise, vague, with hypotheses phrased in entirely untestable terms, fashioned apparently only in "sessions of sweet, silent thought." Here I cannot entirely defend my friends against their critics. Much, perhaps most, of our conceptual presentations are couched in enthusiastic but scientifically unendurable terms. But I venture that such unorganized, early thoughts such as presented by Maslow (1962b) are not to be dismissed. At the very least they are propaedeutic or pre-science and at best they represent a stage in hypothesis formulation perhaps unnecessary to animal psychologists but essential to an experimental existential psychology. The existentialist may well formulate his hypotheses while in isolation, which Miss Privette's evidence indicates contributes to insight and creativity. These pre-scientific formulations are truly individual insights. No one denies they still have to be translated into public insights, reformulated and researched. Thus Blazer (1963) selected one of Maslow's pre-scientific ideas, "transcendence of environment," more rigorously defined the term, formulated a design and then went on to an effective test of the hypothesis.

IMPLICATIONS FOR COUNSELING

But what does this have to say for counseling? The implication of existentialism is that it will be the key to the deepest understanding of the category of the individual. We anticipate that as the vague but penetratingly insightful philosophy becomes theory and science, it will lead to new approaches in counseling and in personality dynamics. Perhaps its greatest promise is the increasing emphasis upon the self of the counselor and his enrichment in training rather than upon the mechanics of his technique. Even when existentialists disagree as to whether or not essence is essential to the existence of an existential theory or regardless of the degrees of vagueness or clarity, all such positions eventually lead to an emphasis upon the self. Thus existentialists must summon hypotheses concerning the development of the counselor's self. This needs to include his enrichment, his manifestation of this enrichment in the helping relationship (that is, what he does in counseling) and also must deal with factors or elements in the counselor's self which engender fulfillment in his client.

The obligation of this philosophy to facilitate our understanding or the client is perhaps illustrated by the existentialist's preoccupation with the farthest reaches or both ends of the continuum of feeling — fullest joy to abysmal despair. Knowing about these reaches cannot help but advance counseling as science and skill. Finally issues such as choice and responsibility in the transaction, relationship, I-Thou experience, encounter or dyad are the fittest subjects for existentialism transcended into behavioral science.

If, however, these three subjects, counselor, client and their transaction, Should the present trend to subject such ideas to rigorous creative test continue, and I suspect it will, then the next generation should bring about some fascinating innovations in our mutually shared profession.

There are two other pecular forces loose in the current *Zeitgeist* which ought to be noted. First, it is difficult to determine which came first upon the other, counseling or existentialism, and which is influencing which. Rather it appears to be truly an interaction which will enrich both over the generations. That a philosophy itself over a hundred years old and imported only 20 years after its rebirth in post-war France should with such penetrating relevance torment a profession itself barely half a century old and, at this time in counseling history, is at best peculiar. Psychoanalysis and its attendant theory grew up together; existentialism and counseling meet as adults still a generation apart.

The second peculiarity is the turning of the behavioral scientist to existentialistic-like concepts. Harry Harlow's (1958) the "Nature of Love" is such a phenomenon. The peculiarity here is that when the experimentalists turns to existential subjects, he seems to pick up the existentialist's worst habits and become just as fuzzy as the rest of us. He is however, fascinating in his writing though unstatistical. Should this trend continue, the professional literature in the behavioral sciences might not only have relevance to humans but also be quite readable.

In summary then, the *weakest* link in the chain attaching existentialism to counseling practice is the denial of definition. In so doing, this inspiring effort to achieve the extremes of human experience, leaves the counselor in confusion concerning the transition to technique. The most *important* weakness however, is in the rejection of rigor in methodology. Its *best but unknown* future will achieve the reality of the present only through innovative methodology. Its *magnificence* lies in its courageous affirmation of an image of man which is just a little lower than the angels.

The tide existentialism is a favorable tide. It can lead to undiscovered richness in the single individual. But it is not the kind of tide upon which a counselor can drift. Even, if as a philosophy, existentialism goes in many, powerful, uncontrolled directions, counseling as an affected profession must in higher responsibility control its own use of this force. This control will come only through the persistent examination of this force in the clear light of the relevant sciences.

REFERENCES

Blazer, J. A. An experimental evaluation of transcendence of environment. *J. Humanistic Psychol.*, 1963, *3*, 49-53.

Camus, A. *The rebel.* New York: Knopf, 1954.

DeBeauvoir, Simone. *The second sex.* New York: Knopf, 1953.

Harlow, H. The nature of love. *Amer. Psychologist,* 1958, *12*, 673-685.

Husserl, E. *Ideas: general introduction to pure phenomenology.* London: Allen and Urwin, 1952.

Hora, T. Psychotherapy, existence and religion. In Ruitenbeek, H. R. (Ed.) *Psychoanalysis and existential philosophy.* New York: E. P. Dutton, 1962.

Jourard, S. J. *The transparent self.* Princeton, N. J.: Van Nostrand, 1963.

Kierkegaard, S. *The concept of dread.* Princeton, N. J.: Princeton Univ. Press, 1957.

Landsman, T. Discussion of the paper by Patterson, Kilpatrick, Luchins and Jessor. *J. Indiv. Psychol.,* 1961, *17,* 39-42.

Maslow, A. H. Notes on being-psychology. *J. Humanistic Psychol.,* 1962, *2,* 47-71. (a)

Maslow, A. H. *Toward a psychology of being.* Princeton, N. J.: Van Nostrand, 1962 (b).

May, R. *The meaning of anxiety.* New York: Norton, 1950.

Merleau-Ponty, M. What is phenomenology. *Cross Currents,* 1956, *6,* 59-70.

Privette, Gayle. *Factors associated with functioning which transcends modal behavior.* Doctoral Dissertation, Univ. Florida, 1964.

Puttick, W. H. *A factor analytic study of positive modes of experiencing and behaving in a teacher college population.* Doctoral Dissertation, Univ. Florida, 1964.

Sartre, J. *Existential psychoanalysis.* New York: Philosophical Library, 1953.

Skinner, B. F. *Verbal behavior.* New York: Appleton, 1957.

Verplanck, W. S. *Glossary of some terms used in the objective science of behavior.* Supplement to *Psychology Rev., 64,* November, 1957.

CHAPTER 5: QUESTIONS FOR DISCUSSION

1. Borrow recommends a "redress of balance" in counseling research. The article was first published in 1956. Do you see any encouraging "redress in balance" in the types of research and theoretical writings in the literature?

2. Robinson's Pattern Analysis approach to counseling runs counter to many long-held beliefs about human development and emotional difficulties. What are some of these differences? What support for his views, or statements running counter to them, have appeared in recent literature?

3. Glasser places great emphasis on "good and bad" behavior, "right" and "wrong" actions. Read his essay carefully to be sure you understand how he is using these terms. Then, what long-held beliefs does Reality Therapy seem to violate or play down?

4. In what ways are Tyler's ideas on minimum change• therapy different from common ideas and practices in school counseling? What recent developments have tended to support her position, as indicated by the literature?

5. Berger presents interesting differences in outlook between Eastern and Western cultures. What connections do you see between his observations on counseling and the existential movement in psychology and psychotherapy?

6. Many counselor educators view Van Kaam's existential outlook in counseling as a welcome corrective to recent "objective" ways of viewing people. What do you find appealing in his outlook? What criticisms might be made of the views?

7. Van Dusen has addressed himself to psychoanalysis, but has given interesting insights into perceptions of clients. What can the school counselor learn from his essay which may be helpful in working with the so-called "normal range" of clients with whom he has most of his contacts?

8. How do the views of Dreyfus differ from older positions and beliefs in counseling? Dreyfus uses the example of a baby's reacting honestly and authentically as a whole organism in expressing feelings. What factors tend to move man away from such "authentic" ways of responding as he grows into adulthood? In what instances do we see "authentic" behavior among adults?

9. Easton and Krippner state that "motivation is internal." What views in recent literature support this?
10. What similarities and differences do you see between the Rogerian counseling concepts and the main concepts of existentialism?
11. What major differences do you see between religious and nonreligious existentialism?
12. What criticism might most scientists give of existentialism today?

SUMMING UP

The philosophical aspects of guidance, counseling, and therapy have been the "dark area" of helping relationships. This book has brought together major articles which have dealt thoughtfully with these aspects of guidance and counseling. The new articles written especially for this book in order to fill gaps in the literature, the previously-published articles synthesizing important trends and viewpoints, and other articles have been addressed here toward providing guidelines for the new generation of counselors. We know in advance that much of our thinking will become dated and will be discarded in favor of the "new voices" even now taking their places in the field. But it is the task of every profession to pass on the best of past and present thinking to the novice, that he might examine it, think about it, and build on it.

It is my firm belief that the task of the philosopher is not merely to write for other philosophers: that is too safe, too remote from life as it is lived. It is, rather, his task to involve his best efforts in any area of education, of helping relationships, or other areas vital to human welfare whenever he is conversant with the literature and the issues. The rapprochment between philosophy and counseling cannot do other than benefit both. Since most philosophers are not conversant with the issues and literature of counseling, it falls to the counselors themselves to serve as their own "physicians," so to speak, until and if aid is forthcoming from the philosopher. Indeed, the leaders in the field of counseling have done an admirable job of pinning down the basic issues and addressing themselves to their resolution, consonant with present goals. It is now the task of the "new wave" to pursue an ever more intense study of philosophy and counseling, and to communicate the need for such examination to their own students. We can never know in advance who, sitting quietly perhaps, in our classes may be able to tie the loose end, turn the proper phrase, raise the synthesizing question, or bring forth, haltingly, a needed concept. They must raise questions frequently, and eyebrows occasionally, with their thinking.

Some of the articles in this book have indeed raised questions *and* eyebrows, but this is necessary before eventual refinements of new views can filter into the field. The philosopher William James once said, "A difference, to *be* a difference, must *make* a difference." This seems a sensible attitude to take in evaluating our literature, especially the theoretical-philosophical aspects of it. We must ask ourselves, "If we accept the views put forth by this writer, what seems indefensible or undesirable in present practice? What must be approached differently? How can we implement the change? How can we defend it, if it be a sweeping change involving many people? What are the alternatives? How can we best evaluate the changes we make in terms of chosen goals?"

We have tinkered with the machinery of helping relationships for a long time. Perhaps the time has come for a new design, based on what most of us have seen as design-weakness in older models. We do not wish to discard everything about the whole mechanism, but rather to help it fulfill better its intended purposes. We must also periodically examine those purposes, as our society changes. All of us who have participated in the present book hope that we have made a step in some of these directions.